T0265338

## Multibiometrics for Human Identification

In today's security-conscious society, real-world applications for authentication or identification require a highly accurate system for recognizing individual humans. The required level of performance cannot be achieved through the use of a single biometric such as face, fingerprint, ear, iris, palm, gait, or speech. Fusing multiple biometrics enables the indexing of large databases, more robust performance, and enhanced coverage of populations. Multiple biometrics are also naturally more robust against attacks than single biometrics.

This book addresses a broad spectrum of research issues on multibiometrics for human identification, ranging from sensing modes and modalities to fusion of biometric samples and combination of algorithms. It covers publicly available multibiometrics databases, theoretical and empirical studies on sensor fusion techniques in the context of biometrics authentication, identification, and performance evaluation and prediction.

DR. BIR BHANU is the Distinguished Professor of Electrical Engineering and serves as the Director of the Interdisciplinary Center for Research in Intelligent Systems and the Visualization and Intelligent Systems Laboratory at the University of California, Riverside (UCR). He is a coauthor of seven authored books and three edited books, has 12 patents, and has authored more than 350 reviewed technical publications, including more than 100 journal papers.

DR. VENU GOVINDARAJU is a UB Distinguished Professor of Computer Science and Engineering at the University at Buffalo (SUNY Buffalo) and the founder of the Center for Unified Biometrics and Sensors (CUBS). He has coauthored more than 300 reviewed technical papers, four U.S. patents, and two books.

# Multibiometrics for Human Identification

Edited by

BIR BHANU
*University of California at Riverside*

VENU GOVINDARAJU
*University at Buffalo*

**CAMBRIDGE**
**UNIVERSITY PRESS**

University Printing House, Cambridge CB2 8BS, United Kingdom

One Liberty Plaza, 20th Floor, New York, NY 10006, USA

477 Williamstown Road, Port Melbourne, VIC 3207, Australia

314-321, 3rd Floor, Plot 3, Splendor Forum, Jasola District Centre, New Delhi - 110025, India

103 Penang Road, #05-06/07, Visioncrest Commercial, Singapore 238467

Cambridge University Press is part of the University of Cambridge.

It furthers the University's mission by disseminating knowledge in the pursuit of education, learning and research at the highest international levels of excellence.

www.cambridge.org
Information on this title: www.cambridge.org/9780521115964



First published 2011

*A catalogue record for this publication is available from the British Library*

*Library of Congress Cataloging in Publication data*
Multibiometrics for human identification / [edited by] Bir Bhanu, Venu Govindaraju.
p. cm.
Includes bibliographical references.
ISBN 978-0-521-11596-4 (hardback)
1. Biometric identification. I. Bhanu, Bir. II. Govindaraju, Venugopal.
TK7882.B56.M86 2011
006.4–dc22 2011002441

ISBN 978-0-521-11596-4 Hardback

# Contents

*List of Contributors* *page* vii
*Preface* xiii

**Introduction** **1**

PART I: MULTIMODAL AND MULTISENSOR BIOMETRIC SYSTEMS

1 **Multimodal Ear and Face Modeling and Recognition** **9**
*Steven Cadavid, Mohammad H. Mahoor, and Mohamed Abdel-Mottaleb*

2 **Audiovisual Speech Synchrony Detection by a Family of Bimodal Linear Prediction Models** **31**
*Kshitiz Kumar, Gerasimos Potamianos, Jiri Navratil, Etienne Marcheret, and Vit Libal*

3 **Multispectral Contact-Free Palmprint Recognition** **51**
*Ying Hao, Zhenan Sun, and Tieniu Tan*

4 **Face Recognition under the Skin** **74**
*Pradeep Buddharaju and Ioannis Pavlidis*

PART II: FUSION METHODS IN MULTIBIOMETRIC SYSTEMS

5 **Biometric Authentication: A Copula-Based Approach** **95**
*Satish G. Iyengar, Pramod K. Varshney, and Thyagaraju Damarla*

6 **An Investigation into Feature-Level Fusion of Face and Fingerprint Biometrics** 120
*Ajita Rattani and Massimo Tistarelli*

7 **Adaptive Multibiometric Systems** 143
*Luca Didaci, Gian Luca Marcialis, and Fabio Roli*

PART III: HYBRID BIOMETRIC SYSTEMS

8 **Multiple Projector Camera System for Three-Dimensional Gait Recognition** 173
*Koichiro Yamauchi, Bir Bhanu, and Hideo Saito*

9 **Gait Recognition Using Motion Physics in a Neuromorphic Computing Framework** 206
*Ricky J. Sethi, Amit K. Roy-Chowdhury, and Ashok Veeraraghavan*

10 **Face Tracking and Recognition in a Camera Network** 235
*Ming Du, Aswin C. Sankaranarayanan, and Rama Chellappa*

11 **Bidirectional Relighting for 3D-Aided 2D Face Recognition** 258
*G. Toderici, G. Passalis, T. Theoharis, and I. A. Kakadiaris*

PART IV: DATABASES AND SECURITY

12 **Acquisition and Analysis of a Dataset Comprising Gait, Ear, and Semantic Data** 277
*Sina Samangooei, John D. Bustard, Richard D. Seely, Mark S. Nixon, and John N. Carter*

13 **Dynamic Security Management in Multibiometrics** 302
*Ajay Kumar*

PART V: PERFORMANCE OF MULTIBIOMETRIC SYSTEMS

14 **Prediction for Fusion of Biometrics Systems** 323
*Rong Wang and Bir Bhanu*

15 **Predicting Performance in Large-Scale Identification Systems by Score Resampling** 363
*Sergey Tulyakov and Venu Govindaraju*

*Color plates follow page 170*

# List of Contributors

**Mohamed Abdel-Mottaleb**
University of Miami
Department of Electrical and Computer Engineering
1251 Memorial Drive
Coral Gables, FL 33146
Email: mottaleb@miami.edu

**Bir Bhanu**
Distinguished Professor of EECS & Director, Center for Research in Intelligent Systems
University of California at Riverside
Riverside, CA 92521
Email: bhanu@cris.ucr.edu

**Pradeep Buddharaju**
University of Houston
Department of Computer Science
4800 Calhoun Road
501 Phillip G. Hoffman
Houston, TX 77204-3010
Email: braju@cs.uh.edu

**John D. Bustard**
School of Electronics and Computer Science
University of Southampton
Southampton, SO17 1BJ
United Kingdom
Email: jdb07r@ecs.soton.ac.uk

**Steven Cadavid**
University of Miami
Department of Electrical and Computer Engineering
1251 Memorial Drive
Coral Gables, FL 33146
Email: scadavid@gmail.com

**John N. Carter**
School of Electronics and Computer Science
University of Southampton
Southampton, SO17 1BJ
United Kingdom
Email: jnc@ecs.soton.ac.uk

**Rama Chellappa**
Center for Automation Research and Department of Electrical and Computer Engineering
University of Maryland
College Park, MD 20742
Email: rama@cfar.umd.edu

**Thyagaraju Damarla, Ph.D.**
US Army Research Laboratory
Networked Sensing & Fusion Branch
2800 Powder Mill Road
Adelphi, MD 20783
Email: rdamarla@arl.army.mil

**Luca Didaci**
University of Cagliari
Department of Phylosofical and Pedagogical Sciences
Via Is Mirrionis, 1
09123 Cagliari
Italy
Email: luca.didaci@diee.unica.it

**Ming Du**
Center for Automation Research and Department of Electrical and Computer Engineering
University of Maryland
College Park, MD 20742
Email: mingdu@umd.edu

**Venu Govindaraju**
UB Distinguished Professor and Director
Center for Unified Biometrics and Sensors
UB Commons
Suite 202
Amherst, NY 14228
Email: venu@cubs.buffalo.edu

**Ying Hao**
National Laboratory of Pattern Recognition
Institue of Automation
Chinese Academy of Science
52 Sanlihe Road
Beijing, China
Email: yhao77@gmail.com

**Satish G. Iyengar**
Graduate Research Assistant
Department of Electrical Engineering and Computer Science
3-127 Center for Science and Technology
Syracuse University
Syracuse, NY 13244
Email: siyengar@syr.edu

**I. A. Kakadiaris**
Computational Biomedicine Laboratory
Department of Computer Science
University of Houston
Houston, TX 77204
Email: ikakadia@central.uh.edu

**Dr. Ajay Kumar**
Department of Computing
The Hong Kong Polytechnic University
Hung Hom
Kowloon, Hong Kong
Email: ajaykr@ieee.org

**Kshitiz Kumar**
Carnegie Mellon University
5000 Forbes Avenue
Pittsburgh, PA 15213
Email: kshitizk@ece.cmu.edu

**Vit Libal**
Honeywell Prague Laboratory
V Parku 2326/18
14800 Prague
Czech Republic
Email: Vit.Libal@Honeywell.com

**Mohammad H. Mahoor**
University of Denver
Department of Electrical and Computer Engineering
2390 S. York Street
Denver, CO 80208
Email: mmahoor@du.edu

**Etienne Marcheret**
IBM TJ Watson Research Center
Route 134 Office #22-104
Yorktown Heights, NY 10598
Email: etiennem@us.ibm.com

**Gian Luca Marcialis**
University of Cagliari
Department of Electrical and Electronic Engineering
Piazza d'Armi
09123 Cagliari
Italy
Email: marcialis@diee.unica.it

**Jiri Navratil**
IBM TJ Watson Research Center
Route 134
Yorktown Heights, NY 10598
Email: jiri@us.ibm.com

**Prof. Mark S. Nixon**
School of Electronics and Computer Science
University of Southampton
Southampton, SO17 1BJ
United Kingdom
Email: msn@ecs.soton.ac.uk

**G. Passalis**
Computational Biomedicine Laboratory
Department of Computer Science
University of Houston
Houston, TX 77204
and Computer Graphics Laboratory
Department of Informatics and Telecommunications
University of Athens
Athens, Greece
Email: passalis@di.uoa.gr

**Ioannis Pavlidis**
Computational Psychology Lab
University of Houston
Department of Computer Science
4800 Calhoun Road
501 Phillip G. Hoffman
Houston, TX 77204-3010
Email: ipavlidis@uh.edu

**Gerasimos Potamianos**
Institute of Informatics and Telecommunications
National Center for Scientific Research (NCSR)
"Demokritos," Neapoleos, & P. Grigoriou Streets
Aghia Paraskevi
GR 15310 Athens, Greece
Email: gpotam@ieee.org

**Ajita Rattani**
Computer Vision Laboratory
Faculty of Architecture of Alghero
Department of Architecture and Planning (DAP)
University of Sassari
Palazzo del Pou Salit
Piazza Duomo 6
07041 Alghero (SS)
Italy
Email: ajita.rattani@diee.unica.it

**Fabio Roli**
University of Cagliari
Department of Electrical and Electronic Engineering
Piazza d'Armi 09123 Cagliari
Italy
Email: roli@diee.unica.it

**Amit K. Roy-Chowdhury**
Department of Electrical Engineering
University of California, Riverside
Riverside, CA 92521
Email: amitrc@ee.ucr.edu

**Hideo Saito**
Keio University
Yokohama 223-8522
Japan
Email: saito@hvrl.ics.keio.ac.jp

**Dr. Sina Samangooei**
School of Electronics and Computer Science
University of Southampton
Southampton, SO17 1BJ
United Kingdom
Email: ss06r@ecs.soton.ac.uk

**Aswin C. Sankaranarayanan**
ECE Department
Rice University
6100 Main Street, MS 380
Houston, TX 77005
Email: aswch@umiacs.umd.edu

**Richard D. Seely**
University of Southampton
Highfield Southampton
Hampshire, SO17 1BJ
United Kingdom
Email: rds06r@ecs.soton.ac.uk

**Ricky J. Sethi**
4732 Boelter Hall
UCLA Computer Science
University of California, Los Angeles
Los Angeles, CA 90095-1596
Email: rickys@sethi.org

**Zhenan Sun**
National Laboratory of Pattern Recognition
Institue of Automation
Chinese Academy of Science
52 Sanlihe Road
Beijing, China
Email: znsun@ nlpr.ia.ac.cn

**Tieniu Tan**
National Laboratory of Pattern Recognition
Institute of Automation
Chinese Academy of Science
52 Sanlihe Road
Beijing, China
Email: tnt@nlpr.ia.ac.cn

**T. Theoharis**
Computational Biomedicine Laboratory
Department of Computer Science
University of Houston
Houston, TX 77204
and Computer Graphics Laboratory
Department of Informatics and Telecommunications
University of Athens
Athens, Greece
Email: theotheo@di.uoa.gr

**Prof. Massimo Tistarelli**
Università di Sassari
Computer Vision Laboratory
Facoltà di Architettura di Alghero
Piazza Duomo 6
07041 Alghero (SS)
Italia
Email: mtista@gmail.com

**G. Toderici**
Computational Biomedicine Laboratory
Department of Computer Science
University of Houston
Houston, TX 77204
Email: george.toderici@gmail.com

**Sergey Tulyakov**
Research Scientist
Center for Unified Biometrics and Sensors
UB Commons, Suite 202
Amherst, NY 14228
Email: tulyakov@cedar.buffalo.edu

**Pramod K. Varshney**
Distinguished Professor
Electrical Engineering & Computer Science
Director of CASE: Center for Advanced Systems and Engineering
Syracuse University
Syracuse, NY 13244
Email: varshney@syr.edu

**Ashok Veeraraghavan**
Research Scientist
Mitsubishi Electric Research Laboratories
Cambridge, MA 02139
Email: veerarag@merl.com

**Rong Wang**
Program Manager
Pandigital Inc.
6375 Clark Avenue, Suite 100
Dublin, CA, 94568
Email: rwang@ee.ucr.edu

**Koichiro Yamauchi**
Keio University
Yokohama, 223-8522
Japan
Email: yamauchi@hvrl.ics.keio.ac.jp

# Preface

In today's security-conscious society, biometrics-based authentication and identification have become the focus of many important applications because it is believed that biometrics can provide accurate and reliable identification. Biometrics research and technology continue to mature rapidly, given pressing industrial and government needs and the strong support of industrial and government funding.

However, many of the applications warrant higher accuracy performance, which is not feasible with a single biometric today. It is widely believed that fusing multiple biometrics can also enable indexing of large databases and enhance coverage of the part of the population that is not able to provide any single biometric. Multiple biometrics is naturally more robust against spoof attacks as well, because hackers have to contend with more than one biometric.

This book addresses a broad spectrum of research issues ranging from different sensing modes and modalities to fusion of biometrics samples and combination of algorithms. It also covers theoretical and large-scale empirical studies on sensor fusion techniques in the context of biometrics authentication, identification, and performance evaluation/prediction.

As the number of biometrics architectures and sensors increases, the need to disseminate research results increases as well. Since 2006 we have organized a series of high-quality Annual Biometrics Workshops under the auspices of the IEEE Computer Society Conference on Computer Vision and Pattern Recognition. This series has emerged as the premier forum for showcasing cutting-edge research from academia, industry, and government laboratories.

The topics of interest at the workshop have largely centered around the theme of multibiometrics. They include sensing intensity, depth, thermal, pressure, time-series, and exotic; face, finger, ear, eye, iris, retina, vein pattern, palm, gait, foot, and speech; biometric templates, feature extraction, and selection; matching techniques and performance baselines; evolution of standards, competitions, and organized challenge problems; score-level, decision-level, and feature-level integration; architectures for evidence integration; fusion-based identification techniques; normalization techniques involved in fusion techniques; machine learning techniques in biometrics fusion; public databases and score files in multibiometrics; application-dependent personalization of multibiometrics systems; theoretical studies in showing models for integration; performance modeling, prediction, and evaluation of multibiometrics systems; and security improvement assessment for multibiometrics systems.

This book is based on a selection of topics and authors from the proceedings of the workshop series and runs the entire gamut of multibiometrics topics, including multimodal, multisensory levels of fusion, multiple algorithms, and multiple data acquisition instances. It addresses novel sensing devices for novel multibiometric modalities, security assessment of multibiometrics systems and their dynamic management, theoretically sound and novel approaches for fusion, publicly available multibiometrics databases, and issues related to performance modeling, prediction, and validation of multibiometrics systems.

The primary intended audience for this book is the research community in academia and industrial research labs. The secondary audience is graduate students working on master's theses and doctoral dissertations. This book will also serve as a useful reference for an advanced biometrics course that considers pattern recognition, computer vision, and machine learning as prerequisites.

The authors would like to acknowledge the support of the chapter contributors for timely submissions of their high-quality research work, the reviewers for important suggestions, Heather Bergman at Cambridge University Press for valuable guidance during the conceptualization of this book, Jhon Gonzalez and Suresh Kumar at the University of California at Riverside, and Achint O'Thomas at the University at Buffalo, State University of New York, for helping with the organization of files and setting up the Web interface for chapter submission and the review process.

Riverside, California
March 31, 2010

Bir Bhanu
Venu Govindaraju

# Introduction

Biometric systems are increasingly being used in many applications that require positive identification of individuals for access authorization. Traditional biometric systems rely on a single-biometric, single-sensor paradigm for authentication or identification. For high-security and real-world requirements, this paradigm is inadequate when it comes to reliably providing a high level of accuracy performance. Multibiometrics, the technique of using multiple biometric modalities and sensors, promises to rise to the challenge of making biometric authentication truly robust and reliable. Moreover, using multiple biometrics enhances the coverage of the section of the population that is not able to provide any single biometrics. Multiple biometrics is naturally more robust against spoof attacks as well, since hackers have to contend with more than one biometrics. Further, fusing multibiometrics enables indexing of large databases for identification of individuals.

Compared with other books on the same topic, the key features of this book are the following:

1. It includes the entire gamut of multibiometrics topics, including multimodal, multisensory levels of fusion, multiple algorithms, and multiple data acquisition instances.
2. It includes chapters on the latest sensing devices for novel multibiometrics modalities, security assessment of multibiometrics systems and their dynamic management, and theoretically sound and novel approaches for fusion.
3. It provides information on publicly available multibiometrics databases and addresses research issues related to performance modeling, prediction, and validation of multibiometrics systems.

The various issues related to multibiometrics systems can be placed into the following five categories:

1. *Multimodal and multisensory biometric systems:* Examples of multimodal systems are face and gait, face and voice, face and ear, fingerprint and face, face and lip movements, pulse and heart rate, etc. Examples of multisensory systems include systems based on color video, infrared video, multispectral imagery, range, and acoustics.
2. *Fusion methods in multibiometric systems:* Fusion in multibiometrics systems occurs at pixel, feature, decision, rank and match score levels. It includes fusions of soft (gender, age, ethnicity, height, weight, etc.) and hard (face, fingerprint, ear, etc.) biometrics as well as the integration of contextual information with soft biometrics. It also includes multiple algorithms based on multiple methods for feature extraction, feature selection, and matching.
3. *Hybrid biometric systems:* These systems may include multiple samples and multiple instances of a biometric modality. Examples of such systems are face recognition with changing pose in video, multiple instances of fingerprints, multiview gait, and various other combinations of biometrics systems.
4. *Database and security of multibiometric systems:* Multimodal databases are required to develop and validate robust fusion algorithms. The security of such biometric systems is also important to guard them from hackers and protect the privacy of individuals.
5. *Performance of multibiometric systems:* Methods are needed for performance evaluation and prediction on large populations to establish a scientific foundation of multibiometric systems.

This edited book consists of 15 chapters distributed among the five categories described above. Four chapters discuss systems that combine multiple biometric modalities and/or multiple biometric sensors to build composite authentication systems. Three chapters focus on the strategies involved in fusing features and scores when using multiple modalities or sensors. Four chapters deal with hybrid systems that attempt to tap novel uses of current technologies for biometric authentication. Two chapters cover datasets and security concepts for biometrics. The final two chapters investigate aspects of measuring performance of systems used for biometric authentication.

The following section elaborates on the chapters falling into each of the five categories.

## Part I: Multimodal and Multisensor Biometric Systems

Awareness in the biometrics community is growing regarding the benefits of using multiple modalities and sensors for authentication. Chapter 1 on multimodal modeling using face and ear biometrics for recognition uses a combination of two-dimensional (2D) face recognition and three-dimensional (3D) ear recognition. Models for the ear and face are extracted and enrolled in a database. Match scores for the two modalities are fused, and the system achieves a 100 percent rank-one identification rate. Chapter 2 on audiovisual speech synchrony detection tackles the problem of detecting synchrony between audio and video segments. The inadequacies of existing synchrony detection methods are highlighted, and a new approach that uses a time-evolution model is presented. The technique performs much better than the baseline set of existing techniques. Chapter 3 on multispectral contact-free palmprint recognition presents techniques that perform image acquisition, preprocessing, and image fusion for palmprint recognition using a contact-free multispectral sensor. Results are presented for performance on pixel- and score-level fusion that show that contact-free palmprint recognition can deliver high performance. Chapter 4 on beneath-the-skin face recognition presents novel feature extraction and matching techniques for thermal infrared imagery of the face. As opposed to traditional face recognition that captures a picture of the exterior of the face, thermal infrared imaging captures subsurface facial features that can be used for robust matching.

## Part II: Fusion Methods in Multibiometric Systems

With multiple modalities and sensors comes the challenge of reliably combining the scores that are output by the various components. Chapter 5 considers the issues involved in fusing information from several biometric sources (including multiple modalities, multiple features, and multiple matchers) and presents a copula-based approach to fusion. A detailed primer on the statistical theory of copulas is also presented, and tests are conducted on the NIST datasets. Chapter 6 presents a feature-level fusion of face and fingerprint biometrics. The framework presented is based on a robust set of features extracted from a scale-space filtering of the raw face and fingerprint images. Results are presented on both synthetic and real datasets. Chapter 7 on adaptive biometric systems discusses the issue of the evolution of biometric templates over time and presents a template update model.

## Part III: Hybrid Biometric Systems

Part III includes four chapters. Chapter 8 on a multiple projector-camera system for 3D gait recognition presents a system that can capture 3D human body measurements and applies these data to gait recognition. It utilizes 12 fast 3D cameras that can capture 1 million 3D points in 1 to 2 seconds. Chapter 9 on gait recognition presents a computational framework that integrates the physics of motion with the neurobiological basis for human perception. Results are reported on the USF gait dataset. Chapter 10 on face tracking and recognition in a camera network presents a technique that extracts rotation-invariant features from multiple calibrated-camera views of a face. The features are computed using spherical harmonics of a texture map, and they show good class-separation properties. Chapter 11 on a bidirectional relighting algorithm for 3D-aided 2D face recognition uses 3D data to perform robust 2D face recognition under severely degraded image acquisition conditions. A new 3D face dataset was collected for the purpose of testing the technique, which has been made available by the authors.

## Part IV: Databases and Security

Chapter 12 describes the process of constructing a large multimodal dataset comprising of gait, ear, and semantic data. Semantic biometrics relies on descriptions provided manually using visual cues to define a biometric template for an individual. An analysis of the data collected is also presented. Chapter 13 presents dynamic multibiometrics security and the need for high-security application multibiometric systems that adaptively adjust to varying security requirements. A new score-level approach to ensure multibiometrics security is also presented.

## Part V: Performance of Multibiometric Systems

To be useful in real-world scenarios, biometric systems need to operate under very high performance requirements. Chapter 14 presents two theoretical approaches to predict the performance of biometric fusion systems. These approaches allow for the selection of optimal combination of biometrics. Prediction tests are conducted on the publicly available XM2VTS and other multibiometrics databases. Finally, chapter 15 explores the problem of predicting (closed set) identification performance of biometric matchers in large-scale systems. Two major causes of prediction errors are identified. A novel score-resampling method that overcomes the binomial approximation effect is presented, and the score-mixing effect is reduced by using score selection based on identification trial statistics. Results showing the accuracy of the techniques are shown for the NIST biometric score dataset.

In summary, this edited book on *Multibiometrics for Human Identification* addresses a broad spectrum of research issues ranging from different sensing modes and modalities to fusion of biometrics samples and combination of algorithms. It covers publicly available multibiometrics databases and theoretical and empirical studies on sensor fusion techniques in the context of biometrics authentication, identification, and performance evaluation and prediction.

# PART I

## Multimodal and Multisensor Biometric Systems

# 1

# Multimodal Ear and Face Modeling and Recognition

Steven Cadavid, Mohammad H. Mahoor, and Mohamed Abdel-Mottaleb

## 1.1 Introduction

Biometric systems deployed in current real-world applications are primarily unimodal – they depend on the evidence of a single biometric marker for personal identity authentication (e.g., ear or face). Unimodal biometrics are limited, because no single biometric is generally considered both sufficiently accurate and robust to hindrances caused by external factors (Ross and Jain 2004).

Some of the problems that these systems regularly contend with are the following: (1) Noise in the acquired data due to alterations in the biometric marker (e.g., surgically modified ear) or improperly maintained sensors. (2) Intraclass variations that may occur when a user interacts with the sensor (e.g., varying head pose) or with physiological transformations that take place with aging. (3) Interclass similarities, arising when a biometric database comprises a large number of users, which results in an overlap in the feature space of multiple users, requires an increased complexity to discriminate between the users. (4) Nonuniversality – the biometric system may not be able to acquire meaningful biometric data from a subset of users. For instance, in face biometrics, a face image may be blurred because of abrupt head movement or partially occluded because of off-axis pose. (5) Certain biometric markers are susceptible to spoof attacks – situations in which a user successfully masquerades as another by falsifying their biometric data.

Several of the limitations imposed by unimodal biometric systems can be overcome by incorporating multiple biometric markers for performing authentication. Such systems, known as multimodal biometric systems, are expected to be more reliable because of the presence of multiple (fairly) independent pieces of evidence (Kuncheva et al. 2000). These systems are capable of addressing the aforementioned shortcomings inherent to unimodal biometrics. For instance, the likelihood of acquiring viable biometric data increases with the number of sensed biometric markers. They also deter spoofing because it would be difficult for an impostor to spoof multiple biometric markers of a genuine user concurrently. However, the incorporation of multiple biometric markers can also lead to additional complexity in the design of a biometric system. For instance, a technique known as data fusion must be employed to integrate multiple pieces of evidence to infer identity. In this chapter, we present a method that fuses the three-dimensional (3D) ear and two-dimensional (2D) face modalities at the match score level. Fusion at this level has the advantage of utilizing as much information as possible from each biometric modality (Snelick et al. 2005).

Several motivations can be given for a multimodal ear and face biometric. First, the ear and face data can be captured using conventional cameras. Second, the data collection for face and ear is nonintrusive (i.e., requires no cooperation from the user). Third, the ear and face are in physical proximity, and when acquiring data of the ear (face), the face (ear) is frequently encountered as well. Often, in an image or video captured of a user's head, these two biometric markers are jointly present and are both available to a biometric system. Thus, a multimodal face and ear biometric system is more feasible than, say, a multimodal face and fingerprint biometric system.

For more than three decades, researchers have worked in the area of face recognition (Jain et al. 2007). Despite the efforts made in 2D and 3D face recognition, it is not yet ready for real-world applications as a unimodal biometric, system. Yet the face possesses several qualities that make it a preferred biometric, including being nonintrusive and containing salient features (e.g., eye and mouth corners).

The ear, conversely, is a relatively new area of biometric research. A few studies have been conducted using 2D data (image intensity) (Burge and Burger 1998, 2000; Chang et al. 2003; Abdel-Mottaleb and Zhou 2006; Yan and Bowyer 2007) and 3D shape data (Abdel-Mottaleb and Zhou 2006; Cadavid and Abdel-Mottaleb 2008). Initial case studies have suggested that the ear has sufficient unique features to allow a positive and passive identification of a subject (Ianarelli 1989). Furthermore, the ear is known to maintain a consistent structure throughout a subject's lifetime. Medical literature has shown proportional ear growth after the first four months of birth (Ianarelli 1989). Ears may be more reliable than faces, which research has shown are prone to erroneous identification because of the ability of a subject to change their facial expression or otherwise manipulate their visage. However, some drawbacks are inherent to ear biometrics. One such drawback, which poses difficulty to the feature extraction process, is occlusion due to hair or jewelery (e.g., earrings or the arm of a pair of eyeglasses).

Based on the above discussion, we present a multimodal ear and face biometric system. For the ear recognition component, first, a set of frames is extracted from a video clip. The ear region contained within each frame is localized and segmented. The 3D structure of each segmented ear region is then derived using a linearized Shape from Shading (SFS) technique (Tsai and Shah 1994), and each resulting model is globally aligned. The 3D model that exhibits the greatest overall similarity to the other models in the set is determined to be the most stable model in the set. This 3D model is stored in the database and utilized for 3D ear recognition.

For the face recognition component, we are inspired by our previous work in 2D face recognition using the Gabor filter component of our attributed relational graph method (Mahoor and Abdel-Mottaleb 2008; Mahoor et al. 2008). We utilize a set of Gabor filters to extract a suite of features from 2D frontal facial images. These features, termed attributes, are extracted at the location of facial landmarks, which have been extracted using the Active Shape Model (ASM) (Mahoor and Abdel-Mottaleb 2006). The attributes of probe images and gallery images are employed to compare facial images in the attribute space.

In this chapter, we present a method for fusing the ear and face biometrics at the match score level. At this level, we have the flexibility to fuse the match scores from various modalities upon their availability. First, the match scores of each modality are calculated. Second, the scores are normalized and subsequently combined using a weighted sum technique. The final decision for recognition of a probe face is made on the fused match score.

The remainder of this chapter is organized as follows: Section 1.2 discusses previous work in 3D ear recognition, 2D face recognition, and multimodal ear and face recognition. Section 1.3 presents our approach for 3D ear modeling and recognition from video sequences. Section 1.4 outlines our method for 2D face recognition using Gabor filters. Section 1.5 describes the technique for data fusion at the match score level. Section 1.6 shows the experimental results using the West Virginia University database to validate our algorithm and test the identification and verification performances. Last, conclusions and future work are given in Section 1.7. As a reference, a summary of the acronyms used in this chapter is provided in Table 1.2.

## 1.2 Related Work

In this section, we will briefly outline some of the prominent works in 3D ear recognition, 2D face recognition, and multimodal ear and face recognition. It is worth noting that a direct comparison between the performances of different systems is difficult and at times can be misleading because datasets may be of varying sizes, the image resolution and the amount of occlusion contained within the region-of-interest (ROI) may be different, and some may use a multi-image gallery for a subject whereas others use a single-image gallery.

### 1.2.1 3D Ear Recognition

Three-dimensional ear biometrics is a relatively new area of research. A few studies have been conducted, and most of the related work has been based on ear models acquired using 3D range scanners. To the best of our knowledge, we are the first to develop a 3D ear recognition system that obtains 3D ear structure from an uncalibrated video sequence. In this section, we will review the literature on 3D ear reconstruction from multiple views and 3D ear recognition.

Liu et al. (2006) describe a 3D ear reconstruction technique using multiple views. This method uses the fundamental matrix and motion estimation techniques to derive the 3D shape of the ear. The greatest difficulty with this approach is obtaining a set of reliable feature point correspondences because of the lack of texture on the ear surface. They first use the Harris corner criteria to detect salient features in each image and apply correlation matching. Then they use Random Sample Consensus (RANSAC) (Fischler and Bolles 1981) to eliminate outliers from the set of detected features. The authors report that automatically extracting feature points in this way yields poor results. Therefore, a semiautomatic approach is used that allows the user to manually relocate feature points that are poorly matched.

Bhanu and Chen (2003) present an ear recognition system using a local surface patch (LSP) representation and the Iterative Closest Point (ICP) algorithm. They used 3D ear range images obtained from the University of California at Riverside (UCR) dataset as well as the Notre Dame collection. The UCR collection comprises 155 subjects with 902 images, and the Notre Dame collection comprises 302 subjects. They report a rank-one recognition rate of 100%. Bhanu and Chen (2005, 2008) also developed an algorithm for ear matching by using a two-step ICP approach. The first step includes detecting and aligning the helixes of both the gallery and probe ear models. Second, a series of affine transformations are applied to the probe model to optimally align the two models. The root-mean-square distance (RMSD) is used to measure the accuracy of the alignment. The identity of the gallery model that has the smallest RMSD value to the probe model is declared the identity of the probe model. They report that out of a database of 30 subjects, 28 were correctly recognized. Bhanu and Chen (2004) also propose a method for detecting an ear region from a 3D range image. Their algorithm is based on a two-step system including model template building and on-line detection. The model template is obtained by averaging the histograms of multiple ear samples. The on-line detection process consists of four steps: step edge detection and thresholding, image dilation, connected-component labeling, and template matching. The authors reported a 91.5% correct detection with a 2.52% false positive rate.

Yan and Bowyer (2007) present an investigation of ear biometrics on a database containing 300 subjects. They experimented with several different approaches including the "Eigen-Ear" with 2D intensity images, principal component analysis (PCA) on 3D range images, Hausdorff matching of edge images from range images, and ICP matching of the 3D data. Experimental results for the different approaches included 63.8% rank-one recognition for the "Eigen-Ear," 55.3% for the 3D range image PCA, 67.5% for the Hausdorff matching, and 98.7% for the ICP matching.

### 1.2.2 2D Face Recognition

Many algorithms for face recognition have been proposed during the last three decades. The literature on face recognition is vast and diverse. Zhao et al. (2003) present a literature survey of 2D face recognition in which the algorithms for 2D face recognition are divided into three categories. This is a clear, high-level categorization based on a guideline suggested by the psychological study of how humans use holistic and local features:

1. *Holistic matching methods*: These methods use the entire face region as the raw input to a recognition system. One of the most widely used representations of the face region is based on the Eigen-Faces approach proposed in Turk and Pentland (1991), which is based on PCA.
2. *Feature-based (structural) matching methods*: Typically, in these methods, local features such as the eyes, nose, and mouth are first extracted, and their locations and local statistics (geometric and/or appearance) are fed into a structural classifier.
3. *Hybrid methods*: Just as the human perception system uses both local features and the entire face region to recognize a face, a machine recognition system should use both. One can argue that these methods could potentially offer the best of the two types of methods.

We refer readers to Zhao et al. (2003) for a complete survey of the state of the art in the area of 2D face recognition.

### 1.2.3 Multimodal Ear and Face Recognition

Yuan et al. (2007) propose a Full-Space Linear Discriminant Analysis (FSLDA) algorithm and apply it to the ear images of the University of Science and Technology Beijing ear database and the face images of the Olivetti Research Laboratory face database. Their database composes four images for each of 75 subjects, in which three of the ear and face images for each subject make up the gallery set, and the remaining image makes up the probe set. An image-level fusion scheme is adopted for the multimodal recognition. The authors report a rank-one recognition rate as high as 98.7%.

Chang et al. (2003) utilize the Eigen-Face and Eigen-Ear representations for 2D ear and 2D face biometrics, separately. Then they combine the results of face recognition and ear recognition to improve the overall recognition rate.

Theoharis et al. (2008) present a method that combines 3D ear and 3D face data into a multimodal biometric system. The raw 3D data of each modality is registered to its respective annotation model using an ICP and energy minimization framework. The annotated model is then fitted to the data and subsequently converted to a so-called geometry image. A wavelet transform is then applied to the geometry image (and derived normal image), and the wavelet coefficients are stored as the feature representation. The wavelet coefficients are fused at the feature level to infer identity.

Pan et al. (2008) present a feature fusion algorithm of the ear and face based on kernel Fisher discriminant analysis. With the algorithm, the fusion discriminant vectors of ear and profile face are established, and nonlinear feature fusion projection could be implemented. Their experimental results on a database of 79 subjects show that the method is efficient for feature-level fusion, and the ear- and face-based multimodal recognition performs better than ear or profile face unimodal biometric recognition.

Xu and Mu (2007) have proposed a multimodal recognition technology based on 2D ear and profile facial images. An ear classifier and a profile face classifier based on Fisher's Linear Discriminant Analysis (FLDA) are developed. Then the decisions made by the two classifiers (ear and profile face) are combined using different combination methods, such as product, sum, and median rules, and a modified voting rule.

## 1.3 3D Ear Modeling and Recognition Using Shape from Shading

We utilize our recent work (Cadavid and Abdel-Mottaleb 2008) for 3D ear modeling and recognition, which is briefly reviewed in this section. We obtain an independent 3D reconstruction of the ear from each frame in a sequence

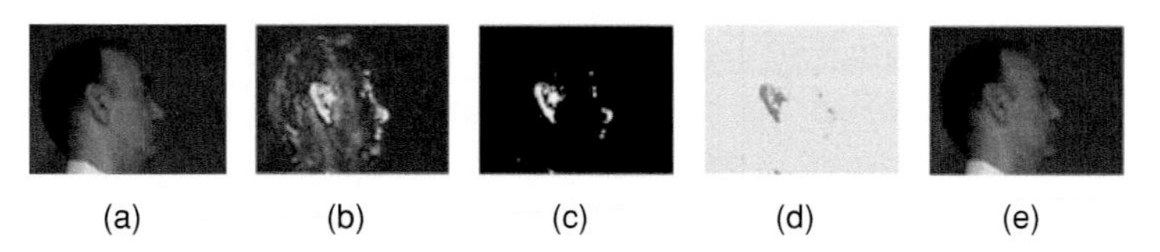


Figure 1.1. Ear segmentation. (a) Original image, (b) filtering using mathematical morphology, (c) binary thresholding using $K$-means clustering, (d) connected components labeling, and (e) detected ear region.

of frames. A Shape from Shading (SFS) algorithm, proposed in Tsai and Shah (1994), is used to obtain the 3D shape of the object from each video frame. The ill-posed nature of the SFS algorithm is apparent even between the 3D shapes derived from a pair of image frames with high redundancy, such as in neighboring video frames. These shape variations can be caused by various factors, including compression artifacts and changes in illumination. Our objective is to determine which of the independent 3D reconstructions is most reliable and exhibits the greatest fidelity.

Before acquiring the 3D structure for each frame in the set, a series of preprocessing steps are performed. First, the ear region is segmented from each video frame with a spatial resolution of $640 \times 480$ pixels. The segmentation algorithm, presented in Said et al. (2008), initially applies the opening top hat morphological operation to the raw profile facial image. The opening top hat transformation effectively enhances the ear region by suppressing dark and smooth regions such as the surrounding hair (i.e., dark) and cheek (i.e., smooth) regions. $K$-means clustering ($K = 2$) is then employed to separate the pixels contained within the filtered image as either low or high intensity, resulting in a binary image. Candidate ear regions in the binary image are identified using connected components labeling. Detected regions with size below a fixed threshold are discarded. The geometric properties, including the position and dimension, of the remaining candidate ear regions are analyzed to determine the true ear region. Last, the convex hull of the detected ear region is computed, resulting in the segmented ear. Figure 1.1 illustrates each step of the ear segmentation algorithm.

To reduce the blocky artifacts present in the video frames, which are primarily caused by compression, a median filter (of size $7 \times 7$) is applied to each video frame. By reducing the amount of noise in the video frames, the 3D reconstruction of the object will result in a significantly smoother surface.

### 1.3.1 Linear Shape from Shading

Shape from Shading aims to derive a 3D scene description from a single monocular image. The recovered shape can be expressed in several ways, including surface normals $\mathbf{N} = (x, y, z)^T$ and depth $Z(x, y)$. The surface normal is a unit vector perpendicular to the tangent plane at a point on the surface. Depth can be considered to be the relative distance from the camera to the imaged surface, or the relative height of the surface from the $xy$-plane.

SFS techniques can generally be categorized into three classes: (1) methods of resolution of partial differential equations (PDEs), (2) methods using minimization, and (3) methods approximating the image irradiance equation, also known as linear methods. PDE methods set out to directly solve the exact SFS PDEs (Prados and Faugeras 2003). In the minimization methods, shape is recovered by minimizing a cost function involving certain constraints such as smoothness. Linear methods are simple but provide only approximate shape estimates. PDE and minimization methods are significantly more computationally complex than linear methods but generally provide more accurate results.

In a biometric setting, for obvious reasons, it is crucial to acquire a representation of the biometric marker as quickly as possible. For this reason, we have selected the computationally efficient, linear SFS method to derive a 3D structure of the ear. Among the linear SFS methods, the one proven most successful is the Tsai and Shah Tsai and Shah (1994) method.

Here we assume that the ear surface exhibits Lambertian reflectance. A Lambertian surface is defined as a surface in which light falling on it is scattered such that the apparent brightness of the surface to an observer is the same regardless of the observer's angle of view. The brightness of a point $(x, y)$ on a Lambertian surface is related to the gradients $p$ and $q$ by the following image irradiance equation:

$$I\,(x, y) = aR\,[p(x, y), q(x, y)]\,, \tag{1.1}$$

where $R$ is a reflectance map that is dependent on the position of the light source, $p$ and $q$ are partial derivatives of the surface in the $x$- and $y$-directions, and $a$ is a constant that depends on the albedo of the surface. The albedo of a surface is defined as the fraction of incident light that is reflected off the surface. An object that reflects most of its incoming light appears bright and has a high albedo, whereas a surface that absorbs most of its incoming light appears dark and has a low albedo. For a Lambertian surface, the reflectance map can be expressed as

$$R\,(p, q) = \frac{-\,(p_s p + q_s q + 1)}{\sqrt{p_s^2 + q_s^2 + 1}\sqrt{p^2 + q^2 + 1}}, \tag{1.2}$$

where the incident light direction is $[\,p_s\;\; q_s\;\; 1\,]$.

Tsai and Shah's method (1994) sets out to linearize the reflectance map by approximating $p(x, y)$ and $q(x, y)$ directly in terms of the depth, $Z$, using finite differences:

$$\begin{cases} p\,(x, y) = \frac{Z(x,y)-Z(x-1,y)}{\delta} \\ q\,(x, y) = \frac{Z(x,y)-Z(x,y-1)}{\delta}, \end{cases} \tag{1.3}$$

where $\delta$ is typically set to 1.

Using the discrete approximations of $p$ and $q$, the reflectance equation can be rewritten as

$$\begin{aligned} 0 &= f\,(I(x, y), Z(x, y), Z(x-1, y), Z(x, y-1)) \\ &= I(x, y) - R\,(Z(x, y) - Z(x-1, y), Z(x, y) - Z(x, y-1)). \end{aligned} \tag{1.4}$$

In Eq. (1.4), for a pixel position $(x, y)$, the Taylor series expansion up to the first-order terms of function $f$ about a given depth map $Z^{n-1}$ can be expressed as

$$\begin{aligned} 0 &= f\,(I(x, y), Z(x, y), Z(x-1, y), Z(x, y-1)) = F \\ &\approx F + \left(Z\,(x, y) - \overset{n-1}{Z}\,(x, y)\right) \tfrac{\partial}{\partial Z(x,y)} F \\ &\quad + \left(Z\,(x-1, y) - \overset{n-1}{Z}\,(x-1, y)\right) \tfrac{\partial}{\partial Z(x-1,y)} F \\ &\quad + \left(Z\,(x, y-1) - \overset{n-1}{Z}\,(x, y-1)\right) \tfrac{\partial}{\partial Z(x,y-1)} F. \end{aligned} \tag{1.5}$$

For an $M \times N$ image, there will be an $MN$ number of such equations, forming a linear system. This system can easily be solved by using the Jacobi iterative scheme, simplifying Eq. (1.5) into the following equation:

$$\begin{aligned} 0 = f\,(Z\,(x, y)) &\approx f\left(\overset{n-1}{Z}\,(x, y)\right) + \left(Z\,(x, y) - \overset{n-1}{Z}\,(x, y)\right) \\ &\quad \times \tfrac{d}{dZ(x,y)} f\left(\overset{n-1}{Z}\,(x, y)\right). \end{aligned} \tag{1.6}$$

Then, for $Z\,(x, y) = \overset{n}{Z}\,(x, y)$, the depth map for the $n$th iteration can be solved for directly:

$$\overset{n}{Z}\,(x, y) = \overset{n-1}{Z}\,(x, y) + \frac{-f\left(\overset{n-1}{Z}\,(x, y)\right)}{\tfrac{d}{dZ(x,y)} f\left(\overset{n-1}{Z}\,(x, y)\right)}. \tag{1.7}$$

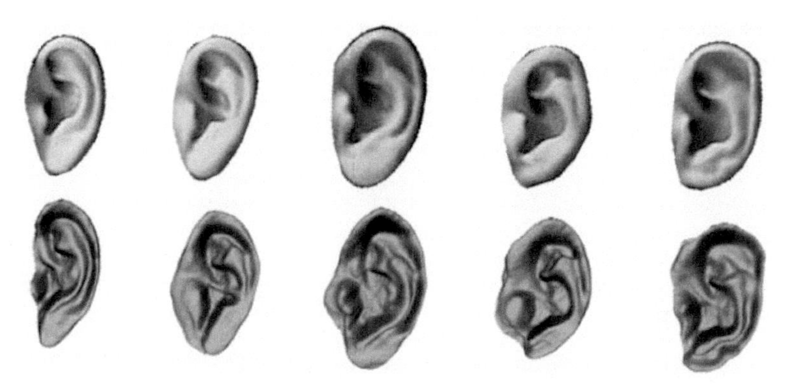

Figure 1.2. Sample ear images (row 1) and their corresponding 3D reconstructions (row 2) taken from the database.

Note that for the initial iteration the depth map, $Z^{0}(x, y)$, should be initialized with zeros.

Figure 1.2 illustrates a set of sample ear images and their corresponding 3D reconstructions using SFS.

### 1.3.2 Similarity Accumulator

After obtaining the 3D reconstruction of each video frame within the set, the resulting 3D models are globally aligned using the ICP algorithm. The global alignment process is illustrated in Figure 1.3. The 3D models independently derived from a set of image frames generally share surface regions that consist

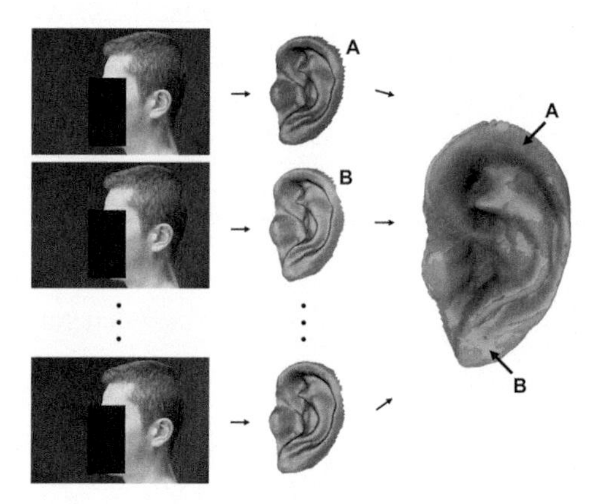


Figure 1.3. The 3D ear models obtained from the video frame set are globally aligned using ICP.

of the same shape. However, the shape differs in other surface regions. We devised a method for determining which 3D model shares the greatest shape similarity with respect to the rest of the 3D models reconstructed for each subject.

Suppose the model set, $M$, consists of $n$ models given by $M = \{m_i\}_{i=1}^{n}$. A reference model, $m_r$, is first selected from the model set, and all other models are globally aligned to it. Initially, $m_r$ is set equal to $m_1$. The similarity between a reference model $m_r$ and $m_i$, $\{i = 1, 2, \ldots, n; i \neq r\}$ is computed using a similarity cost function. The cost function, given by

$$S = -\alpha Dis - \beta Norm - \gamma Cur, \tag{1.8}$$

is made up of three weighted terms that consider the Euclidean distance between surface points, the difference in angle between normals (*Norm*), and the difference between curvature shape index (*Cur*) (Mao et al. 2006). The weighting coefficients ($\alpha$, $\beta$, and $\gamma$) sum to one. The optimal set of weights, determined empirically, are $\alpha = 0.11$, $\beta = 0.55$, and $\gamma = 0.34$. The *Norm* and *Cur* terms in Eq. (1.8) are further defined as

$$Norm = \frac{\cos^{-1}(normal1 \bullet normal2)}{\pi}, \tag{1.9}$$

$$Cur = \left| \frac{1}{\pi} \left\{ \operatorname{atan}\left( \frac{k_r^1 + k_r^2}{k_r^1 - k_r^2} \right) - \operatorname{atan}\left( \frac{k_i^1 + k_i^2}{k_i^1 - k_i^2} \right) \right\} \right|. \tag{1.10}$$

The *Dis* term is defined as the Euclidean distance between a vertex on $m_r$ and a tentative similar vertex on $m_i$. The *Norm* term computes the angle between normal1 (normal of a vertex on $m_r$) and normal2 (normal of a corresponding vertex on $m_i$). The $Cur$ term is a quantitative measure of the shape of a surface at a vertex, and $k_r^j$, $k_i^j$, $j = 1, 2$ are the maximum and minimum principal curvatures of the vertices on $m_r$ and $m_i$, respectively.

The similarity between the surface point in $m_r$ and every surface point in $m_i$ contained within a search window is computed (illustrated in Figure 1.4). The surface point on $m_i$ that shares the greatest similarity value with the surface point on $m_r$ is determined to be its most similar point. This process is then repeated for all surface points contained in $m_r$. The similarity values are stored in a matrix. Surface regions that share similar shape and position will result in higher similarity values than surface regions that differ. The resulting similarity matrices are summed to form the so-called Similarity Accumulator (SA), which indicates the fidelity of the reference model's shape. An illustration of this process is provided in Figure 1.5.

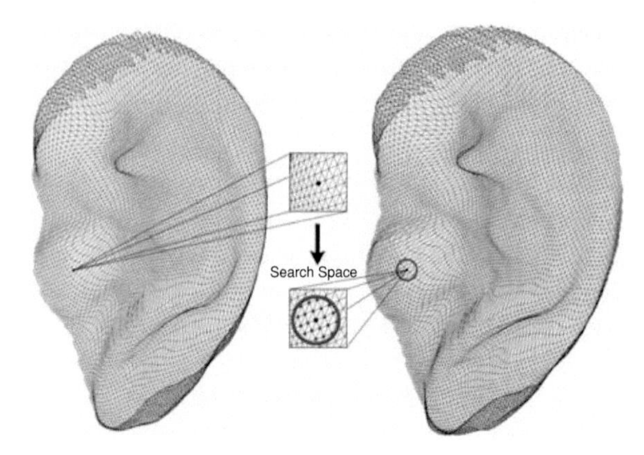


Figure 1.4. The similarity between a surface point in $m_r$ and surface points on $m_i$ contained within a search window is computed.

### 1.3.3 3D Model Selection

Once an SA has been computed for the initial reference model (e.g., $m_1$), then the second model, $m_2$, is designated as being the reference model. This process is repeated until all $n$ models have an SA associated with them.

The most stable 3D reconstruction is determined to be the 3D model that exhibits the greatest cumulative similarity. The mean value of each SA is

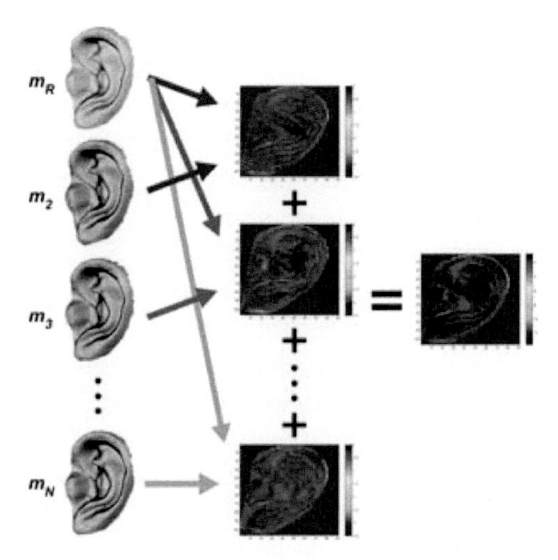


Figure 1.5. Similarity Accumulator.

computed using the equation

$$Mean(m_R) = \frac{\sum_{x=1}^{cols} \sum_{y=1}^{rows} SA(x, y)}{n}, \tag{1.11}$$

where $n$ denotes the number of pixels that are contained within the valid ear region. Then the 3D model that results in the greatest mean similarity, given by

$$\arg\max_{m_R \in [m_1, m_2, \ldots, m_n]} \quad Mean(m_R), \tag{1.12}$$

is declared the most stable model in the set.

### 1.3.4 Recognition Process

The process described in the previous section enables us to acquire the most stable 3D ear model for each subject in a gallery and probe set, respectively. To identify the gallery model that most closely corresponds to a probe model (subject recognition), a shape-matching technique is employed. A probe model, $X$, is globally aligned to a gallery model, $X'$, using ICP. Then the RMSD between the two models, given by

$$D_e = \sqrt{\frac{1}{N} \sum_{i=1}^{N} \left(x_i - x_i'\right)^2}, \tag{1.13}$$

is computed, where $\{x_i\}_{i=1}^N \in X$, $\{x_i'\}_{i=1}^N \in X'$, and $x_i'$ is the nearest neighbor of $x_i$ on $X'$. To minimize the effects of noise and partial information (due to occlusion) in the 3D models, only a certain percentage of surface points contribute to Eq. (1.13). The distances between the point set $X$ and their nearest neighbors in the point set of the gallery model are sorted in ascending order, and only the top 90% are considered. This process of aligning the probe model to a gallery model and computing the distance is then repeated for all other 3D models enrolled in the gallery. The identity of the gallery model that shares the smallest distance in Eq. (1.13) with the probe model is declared the identity of the probe model.

## 1.4 2D Face Recognition Using Gabor Features

For 2D face modeling and recognition, we are inspired by our previous work in which facial images were represented by a set of features extracted using

Gabor filters (Gaussian-modulated complex exponentials) (Mahoor and Abdel-Mottaleb 2008). Unlike the ear recognition component of this work, we model the face in the 2D domain instead of 3D because the database used to validate our approach has an exceptionally large number of subjects containing facial hair and/or eyeglasses (39.1% of the gallery), rendering the 3D reconstruction of the face surfaces difficult.

Gabor filters, which represent a popular choice for obtaining localized frequency information, are defined as follows:

$$W(x, y, \theta, \lambda, \phi, \sigma, \gamma) = \exp\left(-\frac{\acute{x}^2 + \gamma^2 \acute{y}^2}{2\sigma^2}\right) \cdot \exp\left[j\left(\frac{2\pi \acute{x}}{\lambda} + \phi\right)\right],$$
$$\acute{x} = x\cos\theta + y\sin\theta \quad \text{and} \quad \acute{y} = -x\sin\theta + y\cos\theta, \qquad (1.14)$$

where $\theta$ specifies the orientation of the wavelet, $\lambda$ is the wavelength of the sine wave, $\sigma$ is the radius of the Gaussian, $\phi$ is the phase of the sine wave, and $\gamma$ specifies the aspect ratio of the Gaussian. The kernels of the Gabor filters are selected at eight orientations ($\theta \in \{0, \pi/8, 2\pi/8, 3\pi/8, 4\pi/8, 5\pi/8, 6\pi/8, 7\pi/8\}$) and five wavelengths ($\lambda \in \{1, \sqrt{2}, 2, 2\sqrt{2}, 4\}$). To prevent the filters from having a DC response, we normalize the local intensity of the image such that the DC response becomes zero.

In this work, we calculate the response of a set of Gabor filters (eight orientations and five wavelengths) applied to the facial image intensity variations; these features are called attributes and are used to model the local structure of the facial image around a number of facial landmark points. We initially extract 75 landmark points using the improved ASM technique presented in Mahoor and Abdel-Mottaleb (2006). We then use a standard template comprising 111 vertices to include more landmark points at certain positions of the face, such as the cheek and the points on the ridge of the nose. Extracting these points using the ASM technique is difficult because of the lack of texture in these regions. Figure 1.6 shows a sample face in the gallery along with the points for extracting the Gabor features.

Before extracting the attributes, the raw 2D facial images are processed to normalize the image variations due to the effect of lighting and head pose. For lighting normalization, first the contrast of the images is normalized using histogram equalization. Then the intensity values of each image are normalized to have zero mean and unit variance. For pose and scale normalization, eye coordinates are used to align the faces such that the coordinates of the two centers of the eyes in each individual image are registered to the fixed locations with coordinate values (35, 40) and (95, 40) for the right eye and the left eye, respectively. The coordinates of the centers of the eyes are obtained automatically by

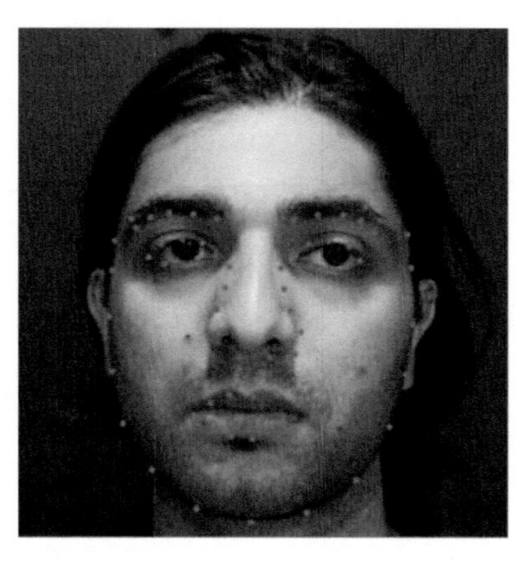

Figure 1.6. Extracted landmark points; 75 landmark points are extracted by the ASM method.

averaging values of the points surrounding each eye (the surrounding points of each eye are provided by ASM). This alignment is achieved by applying a 2D transformation (i.e., scale, translation, and rotation), in which the parameters of the transformation are estimated by Procrustes analysis.

For face matching and recognition, the distance between two given facial images is defined as the distance between their attributes:

$$D_f = \frac{\sum_{j=1}^{N} a_j \acute{a}_j}{\sqrt{\sum_{j=1}^{N} a_j^2 \sum_{j=1}^{N} \acute{a}_j^2}}, \tag{1.15}$$

where $a_j$ is the magnitude of the set of complex coefficients of the Gabor attributes, obtained at the $j$th landmark point. The identity of the gallery image that shares the smallest distance in Eq. (1.15) with the probe image is declared the identity of the probe model.

## 1.5 Data Fusion

We combine the ear and face modalities at the match score level, where we have the flexibility of fusing the match scores from various modalities on their availability. We use the weighted sum technique to fuse the results at the match score level. This approach is in the category of transform-based techniques (i.e., based on the classification presented in Ross et al. 2006). In practical multibiometric systems, a common fusion method is to directly combine the match scores provided by different matchers without converting them into a posteriori probabilities. However, the combination of the match scores is meaningful only when the scores of the individual matchers are comparable. This requires a change of the location and scale parameters of the match score distributions at the outputs of the individual matchers. Hence, the *Tanh-estimators* score normalization (Ross et al. 2006), which is an efficient and robust technique, is used to transform the match scores obtained from the different matchers into a common domain. It is defined as

$$s_j^n = \frac{1}{2}\left\{\tanh\left(0.01\left(\frac{s_j - \mu_{GH}}{\sigma_{GH}}\right)\right) + 1\right\}, \tag{1.16}$$

where $s_j$ and $s_j^n$ are the scores before normalization and after normalization, respectively, and $\mu_{GH}$ and $\sigma_{GH}$ are the mean and standard deviation estimates, respectively, of the genuine score distribution as given by Hampel estimators (Hampel et al. 1986). Hampel estimators are based on the following influence ($\psi$)-function:

$$\psi(u) = \begin{cases} u & 0 \leq |u| < a, \\ a \cdot \text{sign}(u) & a \leq |u| < b, \\ a \cdot \text{sign}(u) \cdot (\frac{c-|u|}{c-b}) & b \leq |u| < c, \\ 0 & |u| \geq c, \end{cases} \tag{1.17}$$

where $\text{sign}(u) = +1$ if $u \geq 0$, otherwise $\text{sign}(u) = -1$. The Hampel influence function reduces the influence of the scores at the tails of the distribution (identified by $a, b,$ and $c$) during the estimation of the location and scale parameters.

One of the well-known fusion techniques used in biometrics is the weighted sum technique:

$$S_f = \sum_{j=1}^{R} w_j \cdot s_j^n, \tag{1.18}$$

where $s_j^n$ and $w_j$ are the normalized match score and weight of the $j$th modality, respectively, with the condition $\sum_{j=1}^{R} w_j = 1$. In our case, the weights $w_i,\ i = 1, 2$ are associated with the ear and face, respectively.

The weights can be assigned to each matcher by exhaustive search or based on their individual performance (Ross et al. 2006). In this work, we empirically choose the weights for each matcher such that the maximum recognition rate is achieved.

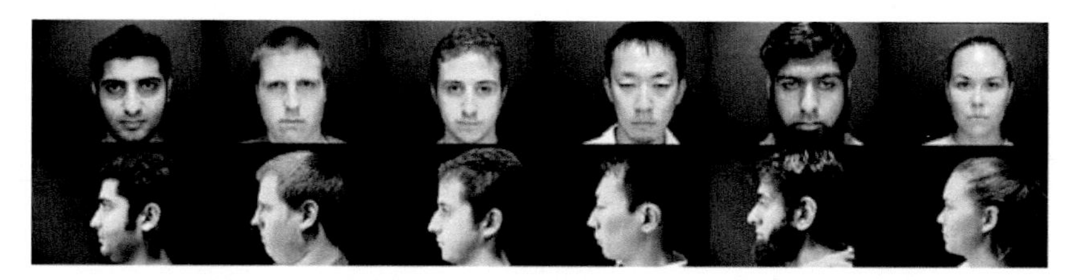

Figure 1.7. Sample face (row 1) and ear (row 2) image pairs taken from the database.

## 1.6 Experiments and Results

We used a dataset of 462 video clips, collected by West Virginia University, where in each clip the camera moves in a circular motion around the subjects' faces. The video clips and images of 402 unique subjects were used as the gallery, and 60 video clips are used as probes. The video clips were captured in an indoor environment with controlled lighting conditions. The camera captured a full profile of each subject's face starting with the left ear and ending on the right ear by moving around the face while the subject sat still in a chair. The video clips have a frame resolution of $640 \times 480$ pixels. A frontal facial image from each video clip was extracted and used for 2D face recognition. There are 135 gallery video clips that contain occlusions around the ear region. These occlusions occur in 42 clips where the subjects are wearing earrings, 38 clips where the upper half of the ear is covered by hair, and 55 clips where the subjects are wearing eyeglasses. There are 23 frontal images with facial expressions and 102 with facial hair. Figure 1.7 shows a set of sample face and ear image pairs taken from the database.

We tested the performance of our approach for ear recognition and face recognition separately and then fused the ear and face match scores using the weighted sum technique. The results of our experiments are reported in terms of the Cumulative Match Characteristic (CMC) for identification (Figure 1.8). The results of rank-one identification for the 2D face recognition, 3D ear recognition, and the fusion are 81.67%, 95%, and 100%, respectively. As the figure shows, by fusing the face and ear biometric, the performance of the system is increased to 100%.

Figure 1.9 illustrates the results of the verification experiments. The results are presented as Receiver Operating Characteristic (ROC) curves for the two individual modalities along with the fusion of the two modalities. As the ROC curve demonstrates, the ear and face modalities have a verification rate of 95% and 75% at 0.01 False Acceptance Rate (FAR), respectively. The verification rate of the system after fusion is boosted to 100%. The Equal Error Rate (EER) of the multimodal system is also 0.01%.

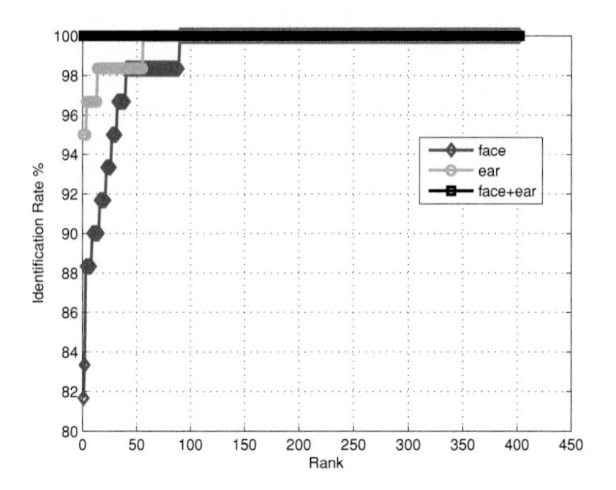


Figure 1.8. Cumulative Match Characteristic curves of the 2D ear recognition, 3D face recognition, and the fusion of the two modalities.

To justify the use of the 3D domain to model the ear in this work, we compare its performance to the well-known 2D representation known as Eigen-Ear presented in Chang et al. (2003). The rank-one recognition rate achieved using this method was 70%. Clearly, the Eigen-Ear representation is outperformed by our 3D representation, which yielded a rank-one identification rate of 95%.

We have also investigated the use of other techniques for data fusion (Max-Score, Min-Score, and Product-of-Score) and compared their results with the weighted sum technique. Table 1.1 compares the rank-one identification rate,

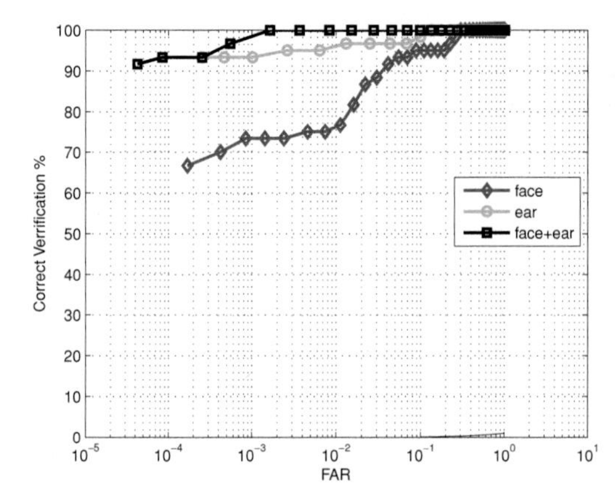


Figure 1.9. Receiver Operating Characteristic curves for the 2D ear recognition, 3D face recognition, and fusion of the two modalities.

Table 1.1. *Different Techniques Used to Fuse Normalized Match Scores of 3D Ear and 2D Face Modalities*

| Fusion Technique | Rank-One Identification (%) | EER (%) | Correct Verification (%) at 0.01 FAR |
|---|---|---|---|
| Max-Score | 95.0 | 3.5 | 96.4 |
| Min-Score | 81.7 | 6.5 | 76.2 |
| Product-of-Score | 98.3 | 1.4 | 98.3 |
| **Weighted Sum** | **100** | **.01** | **100** |

EER, and the correct verification rate at 0.01% FAR of the other techniques for fusion.[1] As this table illustrates, the weighted sum technique outperforms the other techniques for data fusion.

## 1.7 Conclusions and Future Work

We have presented an approach for multimodal face and ear recognition. The 3D ear structure is reconstructed from a single image using SFS. These 3D ear models were subsequently enrolled in a database and employed for biometric recognition. For face recognition, Gabor filters were utilized to extract a set of features for representing the 2D frontal facial images of the subjects. The extracted Gabor features were then used to calculate the similarity between facial images. This resulted in a match score for each modality that represents the similarity between a probe image and a gallery image. The match scores obtained from the two modalities (ear and face) were fused at the match score level using the weighted sum technique.

Our experiments on a database of 402 subjects show significant improvement in identification and verification rates (the result after fusion is 100%). The significant improvement in performance when combining modalities is primarily due to an increased robustness to occlusion. The database contains a large number of subjects possessing facial hair and/or eyeglasses (39.1% of the gallery). The registration accuracy of the ASM in the face recognition component degrades in the presence of occlusion because of the increased likelihood of mesh nodes getting stuck at local minima during the optimization. The performance shortcomings of the ear recognition component, on the other hand, were primarily due to a few images in which the ear region was only

[1] The *Tanh-estimators* score normalization method was used for all of the fusion techniques.

partially segmented. Eight subjects contained within the probe set possessed occlusions in the ear region. The segmentation was successful for seven, or 87.5%, of those subjects. In the entire probe set, 88.33% of the video clips were successfully segmented. Combining modalities improves the robustness to occlusion because of the increased likelihood of acquiring viable biometric data from at least one modality.

Future work will include the employment of 3D face recognition in combination with 3D ear recognition. The use of the 3D modality for both biometric markers will lead to an increase in the robustness for both illumination and pose variations. In addition, we will extend this technique to recognize faces using profile images.

## Appendix

### Table 1.2 Terms and Acronyms

Table 1.2. *List of Acronyms Used in This Chapter*

| Term | Acronym |
|---|---|
| Two-Dimensional | 2D |
| Three-Dimensional | 3D |
| Active Shape Model | ASM |
| Cumulative Match Characteristic | CMC |
| Curvature term in Eq. (1.8) | *Cur* |
| Distance term in Eq. (1.8) | *Dis* |
| Equal Error Rate | EER |
| False Acceptance Rate | FAR |
| Fisher's Linear Discriminant Analysis | FLDA |
| Full-Space Linear Discriminant Analysis | FSLDA |
| Iterative Closest Point | ICP |
| Local Surface Patch | LSP |
| Surface normal term in Eq. (1.8) | *Norm* |
| Partial Differential Equation | PDE |
| Principal Components Analysis | PCA |
| Random Sample Consensus | RANSAC |
| Receiver Operated Characteristic | ROC |
| Region of Interest | ROI |
| Root-Mean-Square Distance | RMSD |
| Shape from Shading | SFS |
| Similarity Accumulator | SA |
| University of California at Riverside | UCR |

## References

Abdel-Mottaleb, M., and J. Zhou. 2006. A System for Ear Biometrics from Face Profile Images. In *International Journal on Graphics, Vision and Image Processing*, 29–34.

Bhanu, B., and H. Chen. 2003. Human Ear Recognition in 3D. In *Workshop on Multimodal User Authentication*, 91–98.

Bhanu, B., and H. Chen. 2004. Human Ear Detection from Side Face Range Images. In *International Conference on Pattern Recognition*, 574–577.

Bhanu, B., and H. Chen. 2005. Contour Matching for 3D Ear Recognition. In *Seventh IEEE Workshops on Application of Computer Vision*, 123–128.

Bhanu, B., and H. Chen. 2008. *Human Ear Recognition by Computer (Advances in Pattern Recognition)*. Springer.

Burge, M., and W. Burger. 1998. Ear Biometrics. In *BIOMETRICS: Personal Identification in a Networked Society*, 273–286. Kluwer Academic.

Burge, M., and Burger, W. 2000. Ear Biometrics in Computer Vision. In *Proceedings of the International Conference on Pattern Recognition*, vol. 2, 822–826.

Cadavid, S., and M. Abdel-Mottaleb. 2008. 3D Ear Modeling and Recognition from Video Sequences Using Shape from Shading. *IEEE Transactions on Information Forensics and Security*, **3**(4), 709–718.

Chang, K., K. W. Bowyer, S. Sarkar, and B. Victor. 2003. Comparison and Combination of Ear and Face Images in Appearance-Based Biometrics. *IEEE Transactions on Pattern Analysis and Machine Intelligence*, **25**(9), 1160–1165.

Fischler, M. A., and R. C. Bolles. 1981. Random Sample Consensus: A Paradigm for Model Fitting with Applications to Image Analysis and Automated Cartography. *Communications of the ACM*, **24**(6), 381–395.

Hampel, F. R., P. J. Rousseeuw, E. M. Ronchetti, and W. A. Stahel. 1986. *Robust Statistics: The Approach Based on Influence Functions*. John Wiley and Sons.

Ianarelli, A. 1989. *Ear Identification*. Paramount Publishing Company.

Jain, A. K., P. J. Flynn, and A. Ross. 2007. *Handbook of Biometrics*. Springer.

Kuncheva, L. I., C. J. Whitaker, C. A. Shipp, and R. P. W. Duin. 2000. Is Independence Good for Combining Classifiers? *International Conference on Pattern Recognition*, **2**, 168–171.

Liu, H., J. Yan, and D. J. Zhang. 2006. 3D Ear Reconstruction Attempts: Using Multiview. *Lecture Notes in Control and Information Sciences*, January, 578–583.

Mahoor, M. H., and M. Abdel-Mottaleb. 2006. Facial Features Extraction in Color Images Using Enhanced Active Shape Model. In *Proceedings of the International Conference on Automatic Face and Gesture Recognition*, 144–148.

Mahoor, M. H., and M. Abdel-Mottaleb. 2008. A Multimodal Approach for Face Modeling and Recognition. *IEEE Transactions on Information Forensics and Security*, **3**(3), 431–440.

Mahoor, M. H., A. Ansari, and M. Abdel-Mottaleb. 2008. Multi-modal (2-D and 3-D) Face Modeling and Recognition Using Attributed Relational Graph. In *Proceedings of the International Conference on Image Processing*, 2760–2763.

Mao, Z., X. Ju, J. P. Siebert, W. P. Cockshott, and A. Ayoub. 2006. Constructing Dense Correspondences for the Analysis of 3D Facial Morphology. *Pattern Recognition Letters*, **27**(6), 597–608.

Pan, X., Y. Cao, X. Xu, Y. Lu, and Y. Zhao. 2008. Ear and Face Based Multimodal Recognition Based on KFDA. *International Conference on Audio, Language and Image Processing*, July, 965–969.

Prados, E., and O. Faugeras. 2003. "Perspective Shape from Shading" and Viscosity Solutions. In *Proceedings of the International Conference on Computer Vision*, 826–831.

Ross, A., and A. K. Jain. 2004. Multimodal Biometrics: An Overview. In *Proceedings of the European Signal Processing Conference*, 1221–1224.

Ross, A. A., K. Nandakumar, and A. K. Jain. 2006. *Handbook of Multibiometrics (International Series on Biometrics)*. Springer.

Said, E. H., A. Abaza, and H. Ammar. 2008. Ear Segmentation in Color Facial Images Using Mathematical Morphology. *Biometrics Symposium*, September, 29–34.

Snelick, R., U. Uludag, A. Mink, M. Indovina, and A. Jain. 2005. Large Scale Evaluation of Multimodal Biometric Authentication Using State-of-the-Art Systems. *IEEE Transactions on Pattern Analysis and Machine Intelligence*, **27**, 450–455.

Theoharis, T., G. Passalis, G. Toderici, and I. A. Kakadiaris. 2008. Unified 3D Face and Ear Recognition Using Wavelets on Geometry Images. *Pattern Recognition Letters*, **41**(3), 796–804.

Tsai, P., and M. Shah. 1994. Shape from Shading Using Linear Approximation. *Image and Vision Computing*, **12**(8), 487–498.

Turk, M., and A. Pentland. 1991. Eigenfaces for Recognition. *Journal of Cognitive Neuroscience*, **3**(1), 71–86.

Xu, X., and Z. Mu. 2007. Multimodal Recognition Based on Fusion of Ear and Profile Face. In *Proceedings of the International Conference on Image and Graphics*, 598–603.

Yan, P., and K. W. Bowyer. 2007. Biometric Recognition Using 3d Ear Shape. *IEEE Transactions on Pattern Analysis and Machine Intelligence*, **29**(8), 1297–1308.

Yuan, L., Z. Mu, and X. Xu. 2007. Multimodal Recognition Based on Face and Ear. In *Proceedings of the International Conference on Wavelet Analysis and Pattern Recognition*, 1203–1207.

Zhao, W., R. Chellappa, P. J. Phillips, and A. Rosenfeld. 2003. Face Recognition: A Literature Survey. *ACM Computing Surveys*, **35**(4), 399–458.

# 2

# Audiovisual Speech Synchrony Detection by a Family of Bimodal Linear Prediction Models

Kshitiz Kumar, Gerasimos Potamianos, Jiri Navratil, Etienne Marcheret, and Vit Libal

## 2.1 Introduction

Detecting whether the video of a speaking person in frontal head pose corresponds to the accompanying audio track is of interest in numerous multimodal biometrics-related applications. In many practical occasions, the audio and visual modalities may not be in sync; for example, we may observe static faces in images, the camera may be focusing on a nonspeaker, or a subject may be speaking in a foreign language with audio being translated to another language. Spoofing attacks in audiovisual biometric systems also often involve audio and visual data streams that are not in sync. Audiovisual (AV) synchrony indicates consistency between the audio and visual streams and thus the reliability for the segments to belong to the same individual. Such segments could then serve as building blocks for generating bimodal fingerprints of the different individuals present in the AV data, which can be important for security, authentication, and biometric purposes. AV segmentation can also be important for speaker turn detection, as well as automatic indexing and retrieval of different occurrences of a speaker.

The problem of *AV synchrony detection* has already been considered in the literature. We refer to Bredin and Chollet (2007) for a comprehensive review on this topic, where the authors present a detailed discussion on different aspects of AV synchrony detection, including feature processing, dimensionality reduction, and correspondence detection measures. In that paper, AV synchrony detection is applied to the problem of identity verification, but the authors also mention additional applications in sound source localization, AV sequence indexing, film postproduction, and speech separation.

In particular, the application of AV synchrony detection to the problem of sound source localization has raised significant interest in the literature. There the goal is to identify "who is speaking when" in an AV sequence encompassing multiple speakers. An initial approach to this problem by Hershey and Movellan (1999) employed mutual information (MI) (Cover and Thomas 1991) between image pixel values and average acoustic energy for source localization. Pixels with high MI localized the active speaking region. For calculating MI values, the authors assumed the underlying probability distributions to be Gaussian. Extending this work, Nock et al. (2002, 2003), as well as (Butz and Thiran 2002), also employed MI for AV synchrony detection but under a multivariate Gaussian density assumption. In other work, Slaney and Covell (2000) studied AV synchrony under a correlation criterion. Furthermore, Cutler and Davis (2000) and Barker and Berthommier (1999) proposed to apply Canonical Correlation Analysis on AV data to linearly project the data onto a space to maximize AV correlation. Fisher and Darrell (2004) formulated AV synchrony under the hypothesis testing (HT) criterion and related it to MI methods. Recently, Gurban and Thiran (2006) used likelihood scores for AV synchrony detection. AV synchrony has also been applied for "liveness" detection of AV data in Chetty and Wagner (2004) as well as Eveno and Besacier (2005).

Most of the past work on AV synchrony detection has been based on variants of MI- or HT-based methods (Bredin and Chollet 2007). In the former, AV segments bearing high MI values indicate that observing one of audio or visual features provides some prediction about the other, hence the AV streams can be considered in sync, or else not. In the latter, AV synchrony is quantified in terms of likelihood scores of features. One of the key assumptions in the conventional approaches including MI and HT is the statistical independence of AV feature frames. These approaches thus extract little information from the generation or evolution perspective of AV features, disregarding the fact that neighboring AV feature frames are strongly correlated.

In this chapter, we specifically propose a time-evolution model for AV features and derive an analytical method to capture the notion of synchrony between them. We also provide generalizations of our model for robustness to misalignments between the audio and visual streams. Throughout the chapter, we provide useful insights for the parameters in our model. This work summarizes and extends our previous work in (Kumar et al. 2009a, b).

The rest of this chapter is organized as follows: We review the mutual information-based approach for AV synchrony detection in Section 2.2 and the hypothesis testing one in Section 2.3. We present our proposed time-evolution model in Section 2.4 and its generalizations in Section 2.5. The usage of canonical correlation analysis is highlighted in Section 2.6. We then detail our experimental setup and results in Sections 2.7 and 2.8, respectively. We present discussion and future work in Section 2.9, with Section 2.10 concluding the chapter.

## 2.2 The Mutual Information–Based Approach

The problem of AV synchrony detection has primarily been approached using the *mutual information* (MI) criterion (Hershey and Movellan 1999; Nock et al. 2003; Bredin and Chollet 2007). Under this criterion, MI is evaluated between sets of audio and visual features, with high MI values implying AV synchrony. The MI criterion is mathematically defined as

$$I(A;V) = \mathbb{E}\log\frac{p(a,v)}{p(a)p(v)}, \tag{2.1}$$

where $I(A;V)$ denotes the MI between the audio (A) and visual (V) features, $p(a)$, $p(v)$, and $p(a,v)$ indicate the probability distribution functions (pdfs) of audio, visual, and joint audiovisual feature vectors, respectively, and $\mathbb{E}$ denotes expectation.

To compute (2.1), we adopt a parametric approach, assume an underlying density function for the probability distributions in (2.1), and estimate the parameters of that density function. A convenient choice for such a pdf is a single Gaussian distribution. For example, Hershey and Movellan (1999), as well as Nock et al. (2003), make such a density assumption for the task of speaker localization, under which the MI score becomes

$$I(A;V) = \frac{1}{2}\log\frac{|\Sigma_A||\Sigma_V|}{|\Sigma_{AV}|}, \tag{2.2}$$

where $\Sigma_A$, $\Sigma_V$, and $\Sigma_{AV}$ are the covariance matrices of audio, visual, and joint audiovisual feature vectors, respectively, and $|\bullet|$ denotes matrix determinant.

It is instructive to derive a simplification of (2.2) under the assumption that audio and visual feature vectors have identical dimensionalities, that is, $m_A = m_V$, all features are individually Gaussian distributed, and that the following hold:

1. $\Sigma_A$ is diagonal, implying audio features are mutually independent
2. $\Sigma_V$ is diagonal, implying visual features are mutually independent
3. Each audio feature is independent of all but one visual features (and vice versa for the visual features).

Under the above assumptions, we can simplify (2.2) to

$$I(A;V) = -\frac{1}{2}\log\prod_{i=1}^{m_A}\left(1-r_i^2\right) = -\frac{1}{2}\sum_{i=1}^{m_A}\log\left(1-r_i^2\right), \tag{2.3}$$

where $r_i$ denotes the Pearson correlation coefficient between the $i$th audio feature and its corresponding correlated visual feature. Equation (2.3) shows that the only statistics required for evaluating MI between audio and visual features are the correlation coefficients. The purpose of the above simplification is twofold: first, to demonstrate that the MI score under the assumptions in (2.2) is simply a function of the correlation coefficients, and, second, to relate the MI approach with the method that we develop in this work (see discussion in Section 2.9).

Most of the previous studies on synchrony detection employing the MI criterion evaluate MI scores under the Gaussian distribution assumption. An immediate extension is to consider *Gaussian mixture models* (GMMs) instead. Evaluating MI under such an assumption becomes mathematically intractable, though, forcing one to resort to approximations. We considered several such approximations, as proposed by Hershey and Olsen (2007), but the actual improvements over conventional MI were almost none, indicating that the approximations were not suitable for the task. We thus maintain the single Gaussian pdf assumption in our current work.

## 2.3 The Hypothesis Testing–Based Approach

*Hypothesis testing* (HT) is a statistical approach for deciding between two competing hypotheses. It assumes a finite number of underlying classes and models the features corresponding to these classes in terms of a parametric pdf, for example, a GMM. A classification decision is then made about a test feature on the basis of its log-likelihood score against the models. In its application to AV synchrony detection, we are interested in two classes, namely,

$$\begin{aligned} &\mathcal{H}_1 - \text{AV features are in sync,} \\ &\mathcal{H}_0 - \text{AV features are not in sync.} \end{aligned} \tag{2.4}$$

Following training of these two classes (e.g., using GMMs), at test time we evaluate the log-likelihood ratio (LLR) for the test data against the two class models. To proceed with our derivations, let us denote audio, visual, and AV feature vectors at time instant $n$ by $a_n$, $v_n$, and $z_n$, respectively, where $z_n = [\, a_n^T, v_n^T \,]^T$. Let also $Z$ denote a sequence of $N$ consecutive features $z_n$. A normalized LLR can then be computed on sequence $Z$ as in (2.5) and compared against an appropriate threshold $\lambda$ to provide a hypothesis for the underlying class as $\mathcal{H}_1$ or $\mathcal{H}_0$:

$$LLR = \frac{1}{N} \log \frac{p(Z;\mathcal{H}_1)}{p(Z;\mathcal{H}_0)} \gtrless \lambda. \tag{2.5}$$

Assuming that frames $z_i$ are independent, LLR simplifies to

$$LLR = \frac{1}{N} \sum_i \log \frac{p(z_i;\mathcal{H}_1)}{p(z_i;\mathcal{H}_0)} \approx \mathbb{E} \log \frac{p(z;\mathcal{H}_1)}{p(z;\mathcal{H}_0)} \,. \tag{2.6}$$

It is interesting to note that one could rewrite (2.6) as

$$LLR \approx \mathbb{E}\log\frac{p(z;\mathcal{H}_1)}{p(a)p(v)} - \mathbb{E}\log\frac{p(z;\mathcal{H}_0)}{p(a)p(v)}. \tag{2.7}$$

By comparing (2.7) and (2.1), it becomes clear that the normalized LLR can be interpreted as a "two-sided" MI, where an MI-like score is conditionally evaluated for the two classes, the difference of which becomes the HT score. In general, of course, one expects that HT will outperform the MI approach, as presented in the previous section, because of the training phase employed and the use of GMMs versus single Gaussian densities in MI. However, both HT and MI treat AV features as statistically independent. This shortcoming is addressed by our proposed modeling approach presented in the next section. There we specifically study linear dependence among the features evolving across time to analytically parametrize the notion of AV synchrony.

## 2.4 Time Evolution–Based Bimodal Linear Prediction

In this section we develop our algorithm for AV synchrony detection, based on what we term *bimodal linear prediction coefficients* (BLPC). In particular, we propose a time-evolution model for AV features that captures the presence of correlation at small time lags across feature frames and is capable of quantifying in its parameters the correlation variation between synchronous and asynchronous AV features.

The proposed model captures linear dependence among AV features as

$$a_n \approx \hat{a}_n = \sum_{i=1}^{N_a} \alpha[i]\, a_{n-i} + \sum_{j=0}^{N_v} \beta[j]\, v_{n-j}, \tag{2.8}$$

where, as in the previous section, $a_n$ and $v_n$ denote audio and visual features at discrete time instant $n$, respectively. For now, we assume that AV features consist of a single audio and a single visual element and jointly refer to them as an AV feature pair. We later extend our model for multidimensional audio and visual features in Section 2.6. In model (2.8), we assume that the current audio feature, $a_n$, can be linearly explained or predicted using past $N_a$ audio features, as well as the present visual feature $v_n$ and past $N_v$ visual features. The parameters involved in our model are vectors $\alpha$ and $\beta$ of lengths $N_a$ and $N_v + 1$, respectively. Next, we note that we expect parameters $\beta$ to assume values far from zero, when AV features are in sync. This holds because in our model we approximate synchrony with correlation. Thus, synchronous visual features will be correlated with audio ones and can linearly explain some of them. Similarly, we claim that parameters $\beta$ will ideally equal 0 for asynchronous AV features. This is further demonstrated in Figure 2.1, where we consider a particular AV

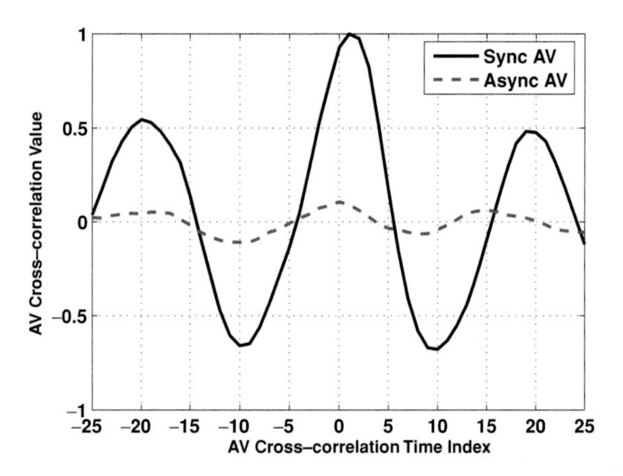


Figure 2.1. Cross-correlation of a specific audiovisual feature pair (acoustic feature MFCC-C0 and geometric visual feature of lower lip height; see Section 2.7), computed for the cases of synchronous and asynchronous audiovisual data streams. Features are normalized to yield maximum cross-correlation at unity.

feature pair and plot its cross-correlation sequence for both synchronous and asynchronous AV streams. The plots suggest that AV features in sync exhibit high cross-correlation within small time lags, whereas AV features out of sync exhibit negligible cross-correlation for all time lags.

In (2.8) we provided a time-evolution model of AV features, with parameters $\alpha$ and $\beta$ encoding information useful for AV synchrony detection. Our next task is to estimate these parameters from observed AV features. For this purpose, we formulate a minimum square error estimation problem and seek to minimize

$$\mathbb{E}\,[\,a_n - \hat{a}_n\,]^2. \tag{2.9}$$

To minimize (2.9), we differentiate it with respect to $\alpha$ and $\beta$, and we obtain the desired parameters by setting the differentials to zero. To proceed, we define:

$$\begin{aligned}
\Phi_{aa}^{N_a} &= \begin{bmatrix} \phi_{aa}[0] & \dots & \phi_{aa}[N_a-1] \\ \vdots & \ddots & \vdots \\ \phi_{aa}[N_a-1] & \dots & \phi_{aa}[0] \end{bmatrix}, \\
\Phi_{vv}^{N_v+1} & \overset{v \leftarrow a}{\underset{N_v+1 \leftarrow N_a}{\Longleftarrow}} \Phi_{aa}^{N_a}, \\
\Phi_{av} &= \begin{bmatrix} \phi_{av}[1] & \dots & \phi_{av}[1-N_v] \\ \vdots & \ddots & \vdots \\ \phi_{av}[N_a] & \dots & \phi_{av}[N_a-N_v] \end{bmatrix}, \\
P_{aa} &= [\,\phi_{aa}[1], \dots, \phi_{aa}[N_a]\,]^T, \\
P_{av} &= [\,\phi_{av}[0], \dots, \phi_{av}[-N_v]\,]^T,
\end{aligned} \tag{2.10}$$

where $\Phi_{aa}^{N_a}$ is a $N_a \times N_a$ Toeplitz matrix consisting of autocorrelation values of audio features at different time lags, matrix $\Phi_{vv}^{N_v+1}$ is obtained in parallel to $\Phi_{aa}^{N_a}$ but for visual features, and matrix $\Phi_{av}$ consists of cross-correlation coefficients between AV features at different time lags. Finally, vectors $P_{aa}$ and $P_{av}$ consist of autocorrelation coefficients of audio features and cross-correlation coefficients of AV features, respectively.

Using the definitions in (2.10), the final solution for the parameters can be compactly written as

$$\begin{bmatrix} \alpha_\rho \\ \beta_\rho \end{bmatrix} = \begin{bmatrix} \Phi_{aa}^{N_a} & \rho.\Phi_{av} \\ \rho.\Phi_{av}^T & \Phi_{vv}^{N_v+1} \end{bmatrix}^{-1} \begin{bmatrix} P_{aa} \\ \rho.P_{av} \end{bmatrix}, \tag{2.11}$$

where for convenience and later use we parametrize the solution by a variable $\rho$. For asynchronous AV features, we can safely assume that

$$\phi_{av}[n] = 0, \quad \forall\, n\,, \tag{2.12}$$

namely, that the cross-correlation coefficients for AV features are identically 0 for all possible time lags, and hence that

$$\Phi_{av} = \mathbf{0} \quad \text{and} \quad P_{av} = \mathbf{0}. \tag{2.13}$$

This is equivalent to setting $\rho = 0$ in (2.11) when obtaining parameters $\{\alpha_0, \beta_0\}$ for asynchronous AV features. On the other hand, for synchronous features, no such assumption holds, hence the solution in (2.9) results in parameters $\{\alpha_1, \beta_1\}$ ($\rho = 1$).

Next, in (2.14), we define a measure of closeness for the two types of prediction coefficients, with and without the asynchrony assumption of (2.13), as

$$D = \left\| \begin{bmatrix} \alpha_0 \\ \beta_0 \end{bmatrix} - \begin{bmatrix} \alpha_1 \\ \beta_1 \end{bmatrix} \right\|, \tag{2.14}$$

where $\|\bullet\|$ denotes the L2 norm. One can expect that $D$ will remain small for asynchronous AV features and large for synchronous ones, thus providing a measure of AV synchrony. Similarly to (2.14), we can derive two additional figures of merit, individually for $\alpha$ and $\beta$, namely,

$$D_\alpha = \|\alpha_0 - \alpha_1\| \quad \text{and} \quad D_\beta = \|\beta_0 - \beta_1\|\,. \tag{2.15}$$

Figure of merit $D_\alpha$ quantifies the distance between coefficients $\alpha_1$ and $\alpha_0$. One could view $\alpha_0$ as corresponding to the well-studied LPC-type coefficients for audio (Rabiner and Juang 1993), while $\alpha_1$ corresponds to LPC coefficients, when some of audio features can be linearly explained by visual ones in (2.8).

Thus, $D_\alpha$ captures the resulting change in LPC coefficients. We can also provide a similar interpretation for $D_\beta$, as an indication of the change in parameters $\beta$, when visual features can explain audio ones in (2.8).

It is worth mentioning that, in parallel to (2.8), one could also try to predict visual features from past AV features as

$$v_n \approx \hat{v}_n = \sum_{j=1}^{N_v} \beta[j]\, v_{n-j} + \sum_{i=0}^{N_a} \alpha[i]\, a_{n-i}. \tag{2.16}$$

It is instructive to explore the similarities and dissimilarities in (2.8) and (2.16). Relevant experiments are reported in Section 2.8.

In summary, in this section, we detailed a time-evolution–based approach to estimate bimodal linear prediction coefficients for an AV feature pair consisting of a single audio and a single visual element. Next, we provide the following extensions: First, in Section 2.5, we generalize causal model (2.8) to two noncausal ones. Then, in Section 2.6, we extend the approach to multidimensional AV features by employing canonical correlation analysis.

## 2.5 Generalized Bimodal Linear Prediction

In this section, we extend BLPC model (2.8) to include noncausal information, namely from future AV observations. The extension is motivated from empirical knowledge that audio features remain correlated with such future AV information. Model (2.8) is therefore generalized to the following two *noncausal* models:

$$\hat{a}_n = \sum_{i=1}^{N_a} \alpha[i]\, a_{n-i} + \sum_{j=-N_v}^{N_v} \beta[j]\, v_{n-j}, \tag{2.17}$$

$$\hat{a}_n = \sum_{\substack{i=-N_a \\ i\neq 0}}^{N_a} \alpha[i]\, a_{n-i} + \sum_{j=-N_v}^{N_v} \beta[j]\, v_{n-j}, \tag{2.18}$$

where (2.17) adds dependence on future visual observations, with model (2.18) further introducing dependence on future audio features. For simplicity, henceforth we will refer to models (2.8), (2.17), and (2.18) as BLPC-1, BLPC-2, and BLPC-3, respectively. The models predicting visual features in (2.16) could also be generalized similarly to (2.17) and (2.18).

The proposed model generalizations over BLPC-1 not only allow a richer AV feature representation, but also prove especially useful for AV synchrony detection in the presence of small misalignments between the audio and visual streams. Such misalignments are often caused by intensive audiovisual data acquisition and can be successfully captured by the noncausality introduced in the generalized BLPC models, as demonstrated in our experiments.

Generalized BLPC model parameters can be obtained similarly to the BLPC-1 parameters in (2.11). For this purpose, we define

$$\Phi_{av} = \begin{bmatrix} \phi_{av}[-N_a + N_v] & \dots & \phi_{av}[-N_a - N_v] \\ \vdots & \ddots & \vdots \\ \phi_{av}[N_a + N_v] & \dots & \phi_{av}[N_a - N_v] \end{bmatrix},$$
$$P_{aa} = [\,\phi_{aa}[N_a], \dots, \phi_{aa}[0], \dots, \phi_{aa}[N_a]\,]^T,$$
$$P_{av} = [\,\phi_{av}[N_v], \dots, \phi_{av}[0], \dots, \phi_{av}[-N_v]\,]^T. \tag{2.19}$$

Using (2.19) it can be shown that model parameters in (2.17) can be obtained by

$$\begin{bmatrix} \alpha_\rho \\ \beta_\rho \end{bmatrix} = \begin{bmatrix} \Phi_{aa}^{N_a} & \rho\,.\,I\;\Phi_{av} \\ \rho\,.\Phi_{av}^T\;I^T & \Phi_{vv}^{2N_v+1} \end{bmatrix}^{-1} \begin{bmatrix} I\;P_{aa} \\ \rho.P_{av} \end{bmatrix}, \tag{2.20}$$

where $\Phi_{aa}^{2N_a+1}$ and $\Phi_{vv}^{2N_v+1}$ are defined similarly to $\Phi_{aa}^{N_a}$ and $\Phi_{vv}^{N_v+1}$ in (2.11). In addition, $I$ denotes a row-eliminating matrix of size $N_a \times (2N_a + 1)$ that eliminates the first $N_a + 1$ rows of its operand. Similarly, it can also be shown that the parameters of model (2.18) are given by

$$\begin{bmatrix} \alpha_\rho \\ \beta_\rho \end{bmatrix} = \begin{bmatrix} J\;\Phi_{aa}^{2N_a+1}\,J^T & \rho\,.\,J\;\Phi_{av} \\ \rho\,.\,\Phi_{av}^T\;J^T & \Phi_{vv}^{2N_v+1} \end{bmatrix}^{-1} \begin{bmatrix} J\;P_{aa} \\ \rho.P_{av} \end{bmatrix}, \tag{2.21}$$

where $J$ is a row-eliminating matrix of size $(2N_a) \times (2N_a + 1)$, which eliminates the $(N_a + 1)$th row on its operand. Thus, operation $J\;\Phi_{aa}^{2N_a+1}$ results in the removal of the middle row in $\Phi_{aa}^{2N_a+1}$, and $J\;\Phi_{aa}^{2N_a+1}\,J^T$ eliminates both the middle row and middle column in $\Phi_{aa}^{2N_a+1}$.

As in (2.11), the solution in (2.20) and (2.21) is parametrized by $\rho$. For asynchronous features, we obtain parameters $\{\alpha_0, \beta_0\}$ by setting $\rho = 0$ in (2.20) and (2.21). For synchronous features, we obtain parameters $\{\alpha_1, \beta_1\}$ ($\rho = 1$). Following parameter estimation, a measure of AV synchrony can be defined as in (2.15).

So far, all BLPC models in Sections 2.4 and 2.5 have been presented for scalar audio and visual features. In practice, one expects to obtain multidimensional feature vectors of different dimensionalities from the audio and visual streams. To extend our proposed method to such cases, we need to design a feature transformation to establish only a few appropriate AV feature pairs to be modeled by (2.8). This is discussed in the next section.

## 2.6 Audiovisual Feature Pair Selection

As already mentioned, our models in (2.8), (2.16), (2.17), and (2.18) consider scalar audio and visual features. To cover multidimensional features, one would have to investigate all possible audio and visual feature pairs, exponentially increasing the number of models. To avoid this, we seek an appropriate feature transformation and in particular a projection for feature dimensionality reduction, such that the resulting audio and visual features can be collected into distinct AV pairs, with their scalar components correlated within, but uncorrelated across, pairs. It will then suffice only to consider a small number of time-evolution models of the resulting distinct AV feature pairs.

For this purpose, we employ *canonical correlation analysis* (CCA). We briefly overview the formulation, referring to (Hardoon et al. 2003) for details. The objective is to derive projection vectors $\{P, Q\}$ to transform features in $a$ and $v$ to respectively $a'$ and $v'$, namely,

$$a' = P^T a\,, \quad v' = Q^T v, \tag{2.22}$$

such as to maximize the correlation between $\{a', v'\}$. As a result of CCA, the following hold:

$$\mathbb{E}[\,a'\,a'^T\,] = \mathrm{I}, \quad \mathbb{E}[\,v'\,v'^T\,] = \mathrm{I}, \quad \mathbb{E}[\,a'\,v'^T\,] = \mathcal{D}, \tag{2.23}$$

where $\mathcal{D}$ denotes a diagonal matrix. Thus, we note that the projected audio features are correlated with only one of the projected visual features. Further, projected audio and visual features are, respectively, uncorrelated with other projected audio and visual features.

In our proposed approach, we apply CCA on the audio and visual feature vectors, and we collect the resulting correlated audio and visual scalar features into distinct AV feature pairs. We then employ any of the proposed BLPC models to describe each such pair. We subsequently compute any of the distances in (2.14) or (2.15) and add them over all pairs to obtain an overall distance to evaluate AV synchrony.

It is worth noting that this is not the first work in which CCA has found use with respect to the problem of AV synchrony detection. (Slaney and Covell 2000), as well as (Bredin and Chollet 2007), have applied CCA to the problem. It is also interesting to note that CCA objectives in (2.23) match the simplifying assumptions for the MI score in (2.3). This will later serve to compare the MI and BLPC approaches (see Section 2.9).

## 2.7 Experimental Setup

We now proceed to our experiments on AV synchrony using the methods presented so far. We perform experiments on an appropriate AV speech database, part of the "CMU Audio-Visual Profile Frontal Corpus" (AVPF), detailed in Kumar et al. (2007). In summary, the data were recorded in an anechoic room with a "head and shoulders" camera view of the speaker and contain isolated word utterances. In the experiments in this chapter, we use only the frontal part of this corpus, consisting of just over one hour of data. To facilitate our investigation, we further split the data into chunks of four seconds each, and obtained asynchronous segments by randomly mixing different four-second chunks of the audio and video streams. The total duration of the resulting asynchronous database was about eight hours. The original four-second chunks constitute the synchronous part of our data. Note that none of the BLPC approaches require training, with the exception of their CCA stage. Projection vectors for the latter are estimated from a held-out synchronous data segment of five minutes in duration.

In our experiments, we employ two AV systems that differ only in their visual feature extraction component: The first, referred to as "System-1," uses three-dimensional lip geometric (shape-based) features, consisting of the upper and lower lip heights and the lip width, as also depicted in Figure 2.2(d). The second one, referred to as "System-2," employs appearance-based visual features, namely, 40-dimensional *discrete cosine transform* (DCT) features of the mouth region image.

In both systems, certain preprocessing steps are required to track the mouth region of interest, as also depicted in Figure 2.2. For this purpose, we use color thresholding followed by a series of morphological operations for detecting lips in the face image. A binary image is first constructed around the mouth region by blue-channel thresholding of the original color one. The resulting image will in general have many connected components (see also Figure 2.2[b]), out of which we identify the one that appears closest to a typical lip region, using constraints based on mouth orientation, area, and distance from face edges. Correctly identifying such a region is especially important in the first image frame of a video sequence, because in subsequent frames we need search only over a small neighborhood around the corresponding region in previous frames. The selected lip region (see also Figure 2.2[c]) is filled in via morphological

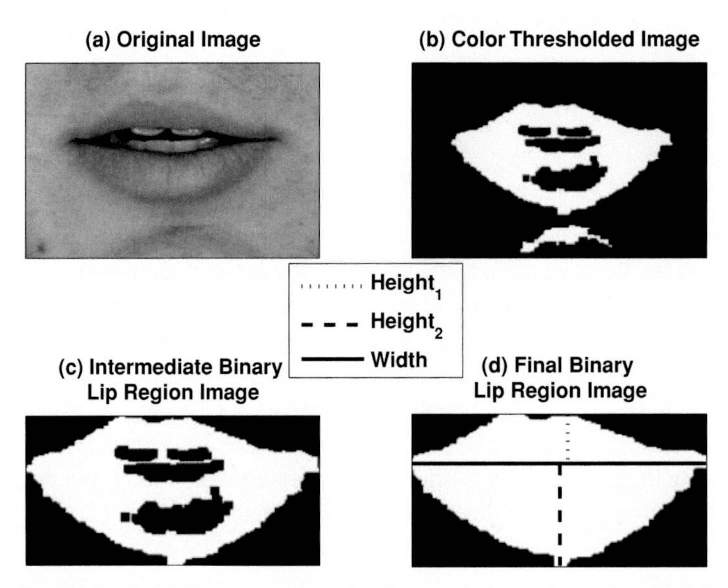


Figure 2.2. Visual feature extraction in "System-1" for an image frame of the AVPF corpus; see also Kumar et al. (2007).

operations to result in the final binary one (as in Figure 2.2[d]), from which we obtain lip width and two lip heights as shape-based visual features. Such features are depicted superimposed in the final lip region image in Figure 2.2(d). As shown there, the lip width is the horizontal length of the lip region, the upper lip height is defined as the shortest distance between the tip of upper lip and the line joining the lip corner points, and the lower lip height is similarly defined for the lower lip. For DCT feature extraction, the 40 top-energy coefficients are first obtained from the normalized gray scale values of the mouth region of interest – determined as above, but without binarization, and after its resizing to $100 \times 200$ pixels. More details on the visual feature extraction process can be found in Kumar et al. (2007).

For audio in both systems, we employ conventional 13-dimensional MFCC features.[1] These are extracted at a rate of 100 Hz, in contrast with visual features that are obtained at the video frame rate of 30 Hz. Thus, and to simplify AV synchrony experiments, the latter are upsampled to 100 Hz. Furthermore, to improve robustness, we apply mean and variance normalization to all features.

Following feature extraction, for the BLPC methods we need to apply CCA, projecting the audio and visual features to a lower-dimensional space. Because

[1] The Sphinx open source speech recognition engines software was used for this purpose (available online at http://cmusphinx.sourceforge.net/html/cmusphinx.php).

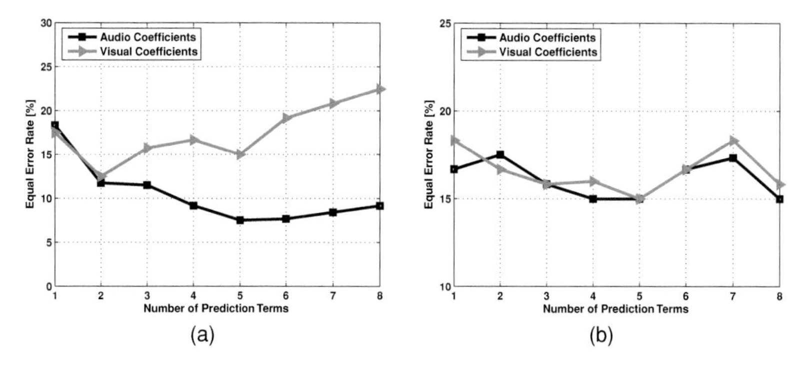


Figure 2.3. EER of BLPC-1 based AV synchrony detection, using geometric visual features ("System 1"), depicted for various numbers of prediction coefficients and for the two figures of merit of (2.15), namely, $D_\alpha$ ("Audio Coefficients") and $D_\beta$ ("Visual Coefficients"). Results employing two different modeling approaches are shown: (a) modeling *audio* features by means of (2.8); (b) modeling *visual* features by (2.16). The plots are drawn on different scales.

the maximum number of projections in CCA is limited to the minimum of the original feature vector dimensionalities, we project audio and visual features each to three-dimensional spaces in "System-1" and 13-dimensional ones in "System-2." To reduce the number of computations and facilitate GMM training, projected features are also used in the HT technique. On the other hand, for the MI approach, the original unprojected features are employed.

## 2.8 Experimental Results

In this section, we present AV synchrony detection results using the experimental setup of Section 2.7. In particular, we first study the effects of various choices in the BLPC-1 approach, to obtain a good AV synchrony detection system configuration. In particular, we consider both modeling approaches (2.8) and (2.16), while varying the number of prediction coefficients, in conjunction with the use of both AV synchrony figures of merit of (2.15). Furthermore, we perform these experiments for both types of visual features considered in this chapter, that is, geometric and appearance based. Following these experiments, we proceed to compare the best BLPC-1 model results to the baseline MI and HT approaches. Finally, we report experiments investigating possible benefits of the BLPC-2 and BLPC-3 models to robustness against AV stream misalignments.

In the experiments, results are typically depicted in terms of *equal error rate* (EER) (as in Figs. 2.3, 2.4, and 2.6), or in terms of *detection error tradeoff*

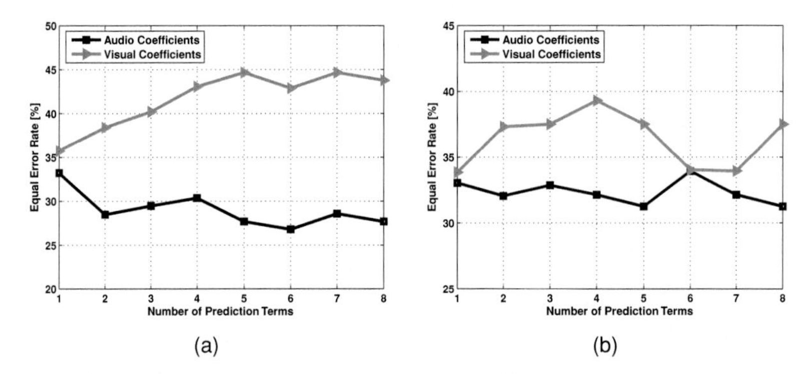


Figure 2.4. Similar to Figure 2.3, but when using appearance-based visual features ("System 2"). EER of BLPC-1-based AV synchrony detection when (a) modeling *audio* features by (2.8), (b) modeling *visual* features by (2.16).

(DET) curves (as in Figure 2.5). It should also be noted that, when reporting BLPC results, we assume $N_a = N_v$ in all models. Furthermore, in our BLPC experiments, we observed that although $\Phi_{av}$ terms are small for asynchronous data chunks, they are not identically zero. Consequently, we experimented with replacing $\rho \, . \, \Phi_{av}$ by $\Phi_{av}$ in (2.11), when estimating parameters $\{\alpha_0, \beta_0\}$. This resulted in better AV synchrony detection results. We therefore consistently employed this modification in all our BLPC experiments.

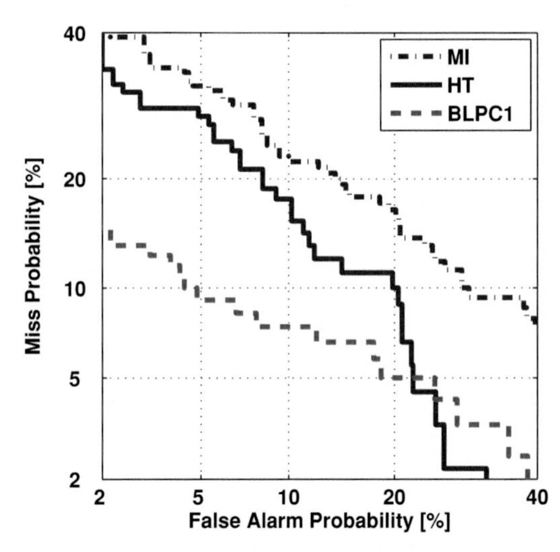


Figure 2.5. AV synchrony DET curves based on mutual information (MI), hypothesis testing (HT), and the best BLPC-1 variant.

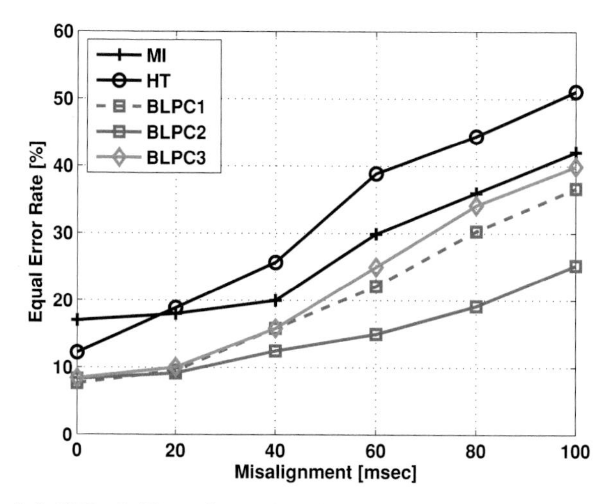


Figure 2.6. EER of AV synchrony detection based on MI, HT, and three BLPC models proposed in this work, when applied to AV data with various degrees of misalignment between their two streams.

### 2.8.1 "System-1" Results of BLPC-1

We first consider the time-evolution model in (2.8) for "System-1" (i.e., with geometric–based visual features), presenting results for the two individual figures of merit in (2.15) and for various numbers of prediction coefficients. As depicted in Figure 2.3(a), the figure of merit based on audio coefficients in (2.15), $D_\alpha$, performs much better than the one based on visual coefficients, $D_\beta$, hence indicating that even though under AV synchrony visual features partially explain audio features, the resulting coefficients $\beta$ do not change as much as coefficients $\alpha$ do, compared with the values they assume for asynchronous AV streams. Note that we also performed an experiment (not reported here), where we linearly combined the two individual figures of merit and obtained improvements over the use of $D_\alpha$ alone. These improvements, however, were very small (less than 0.5% absolute), indicating that the audio–based coefficients remain sufficient for AV synchrony detection.

We also note that the best performance is obtained when $N_a = N_v = 5 \sim 6$. This is not surprising, because we do expect that there should exist a middle range for the $N_a$ parameter, where the algorithm performs the best: Smaller values of $N_a$ do not quite capture the autocorrelation existing in the audio features at different time lags, whereas larger values of $N_a$ far exceed the range of time lags, where audio features bear significant autocorrelation to be useful to the BLPC model.

Next, we employ model (2.16) for "System-1," depicting results in Figure 2.3(b). One can observe that for most values of $N_a$, figure of merit $D_\alpha$ outperforms $D_\beta$. More importantly, though, the best results trail significantly the ones obtained by model (2.8).

The superiority of model (2.8) to (2.16), as well as figure of merit $D_\alpha$ to $D_\beta$, can be partially attributed to the fact that the audio feature extraction system is generally much more reliable than visual feature extraction, which suffers from localization errors in mouth region segmentation and tracking. Audio features generally suffer if recording conditions are not clean, but because the AVPF database was collected in an anechoic room under clean acoustic conditions, this is not the case in our experiments. Hence, in general, audio features will have less intrinsic variability than visual features, resulting in better performance.

### 2.8.2 "System-2" Results of BLPC-1

We next report similar experiments to the previous section, but employing "System-2" instead of "System-1," namely, using image appearance visual features based on DCT coefficients. By comparing Figs. 2.3 and 2.4, it appears that similar conclusions can be drawn: that BLPC model (2.8) is superior to (2.16), figure of merit $D_\alpha$ outperforms than $D_\beta$, and the optimal values of $N_a$, $N_v$ are 5 or 6.

In addition, it is clear that the results based on "System-1" are superior to "System 2" ones. It seems that three-dimensional visual geometric features of lip heights and lip width carry more distinct information about synchrony to audio than the 40-dimensional DCT coefficients. Therefore, in the following experiments, we consistently employ "System-1." Furthermore, when considering BLPC based AV synchrony detection, the audio feature time-evolution model is employed, accompanied by the figure of merit based on audio coefficients.

### 2.8.3 Proposed BLPC-1 versus Baseline Approaches

Next, we plot the DET curve in Figure 2.5 for the three broad methods discussed in this chapter, namely, the baseline MI and HT ones and the proposed BLPC-1, using "System 1." As a result of the earlier experiments, for BLPC-1, we employ time evolution model (2.8) and figure of merit $D_\alpha$. For MI, we use a single Gaussian density assumption for the features, whereas for HT, we train a two-class GMM with 512 mixtures per class. It is clear from Figure 2.5 that HT performs significantly better than MI, and that in almost all DET curve regions, the BLPC-1 approach is by far the best. In particular, BLPC-1 provides a 54% relative reduction in EER over the MI approach (from 17% of the latter to 7.67% EER of BLPC-1) and 37% over the HT approach (which yields a 12.22% EER).

### 2.8.4 AV Synchrony Detection for Misaligned AV Streams

Here we are particularly interested in the robustness of the proposed BLPC models to small misalignments of otherwise synchronous audio and visual streams, possibly because of capturing delays caused by intensive data rates. For this purpose, we introduce an artificial relative delay in the AV streams and use such data for testing AV synchrony detection techniques. Results are reported in Figure 2.6 in terms of EER. Note that we consider both positive and negative delays and average the results. We clearly observe that BLPC methods not only provide better EERs, but also remain more robust to AV stream misalignment than the MI and HT baselines. Interestingly, HT performs better than MI in the absence of misalignment, but its performance degrades rapidly when misalignment is introduced. Finally, among the two generalized BLPC models, BLPC-2 proves superior, indicating that including future audio information does not contribute to robustness on top of the already incorporated future visual information.

## 2.9 Discussion

In this section, we discuss and relate the methods presented in our work. First, the key difference between our method and MI or HT is that these methods extract little information from the time-evolution perspective in the features, which suggests that features in a small time window should bear high correlation among themselves. In these methods, the features are assumed to be independent, but in our approach we specifically capture the correlation across features for different time lags in parameters $\alpha$ and $\beta$.

Further, as shown in (2.3), the simplified MI criterion for AV features under the single Gaussian density assumption is effectively a function of only the cross-correlation at the 0th lag between audio and visual features. With an objective to compare MI with BLPC, we can show that for the BLPC model in (2.8), with $N_a = N_v = 0$, $\beta$ becomes the cross-correlation at 0th lag between the AV features. Thus, in this specific selection of $N_a$ and $N_v$, our measure in (2.14) and MI measure in (2.2) are both functions of cross-correlation alone. But nonzero values for $N_a$ and $N_v$ essentially allow BLPC to base synchrony decisions on cross-correlation at lags other than just the 0th one, thus in a way generalizing the MI criterion. Overall, MI approaches gather autocorrelation and cross-correlation statistics at just the 0th lag between the features, but our approach gathers these statistics at additional time lags, in an attempt to explain the time evolution model in (2.8) and capture the notion of synchrony between AV features.

Finally, we would like to comment on the best absolute value of EER, around 8%, in Figure 2.5. This appears to be high, and a question arises about the best possible attainable EER. Parameters such as length of AV segment and audiovisual feature types directly affect the best attainable EER. Longer AV segments will obviously result in smaller variance and larger confidence in synchrony detection, thus smaller EERs. Next, features which naturally exhibit better correlation between audio and visual streams will result in better fitting BLPC models. Further, the amount of intrinsic correlation between the audio and visual signals will directly affect EER. We know that phonemes such as /pa/ and /ba/ have distinct sounds but similar mouth motion, thus there is an intrinsic limit to the performance in AV synchrony, resulting in higher EERs. With respect to the above observation, one should expect that the autocorrelation and cross-correlations among AV features differ among various phonetic classes and contexts. Currently, the time-evolution model in (2.8) considers speech information in a context-independent fashion, which could be further generalized to include some context dependencies in speech. We intend to address that in our future work.

## 2.10 Conclusions

In conclusion, in this chapter, we have focused on the problem of reliable synchrony detection of audiovisual speech data, namely, determining whether a video segment containing a speaker in frontal head pose and its accompanying acoustic signal correspond to each other. We initially presented the mutual information and hypothesis testing approaches for this problem as baselines, highlighting that both ignore correlation of neighboring audiovisual features. To address this shortcoming, we specifically proposed a time-evolution model for audio visual features in the form of linear prediction. We highlighted that the model parameters capture the notion of audiovisual synchrony, and we derived a measure for synchrony detection based on these parameters. We then generalized our approach to improve robustness to small AV stream misalignments. We also proposed the use of canonical correlation analysis, as a means to extend our approach to multidimensional audiovisual features. Throughout this chapter, we provided useful analysis and discussion on our model and the parameters involved, also relating our approach to the mutual information criterion and indicating that our method extends it. We applied our proposed method on an appropriate audiovisual database considering two visual feature extraction approaches and obtained significant improvements over the baseline methods.

## References

Barker, J. P., and F. Berthommier. 1999. Evidence of correlation between acoustic and visual features of speech. Pages 199–202 of *Proceedings of the International Congress of Phonetic Sciences (ICPhS)*.

Bredin, H., and G. Chollet. 2007. Audiovisual speech synchrony measure: application to biometrics. *EURASIP Journal on Advances in Signal Processing*.

Butz, T., and J.-P. Thiran. 2002. Feature space mutual information in speech-video sequences. Pages 361–364 of *Proceedings of the IEEE International Conference on Multimedia and Expo (ICME)*, vol. 2.

Chetty, G., and M. Wagner. 2004. Liveness verification in audio-video speaker authentication. Pages 358–363 of *Proceedings of the 10th Australian International Conference on Speech Science and Technology (SST)*.

Cover, T. M., and J. A. Thomas. 1991. *Elements of Information Theory*. Wiley-Interscience.

Cutler, R., and L. Davis. 2000. Look who's talking: speaker detection using video and audio correlation. Pages 1589–1592 of *Proceedings of the IEEE International Conference on Multimedia and Expo (ICME)*, vol. 3.

Eveno, N., and L. Besacier. 2005. A speaker independent "liveness" test for audio-visual biometrics. Pages 3081–3084 of *Proceedings of the 9th European Conference on Speech Communication and Technology (Interspeech – EuroSpeech)*.

Fisher, J. W., and T. Darrell. 2004. Speaker association with signal-level audiovisual fusion. *IEEE Transactions on Multimedia*, **6**, 406–413.

Gurban, M., and J.-P. Thiran. 2006. Multimodal speaker localization in a probabilistic framework. Pages 4–8 of *Proceedings of the 14th European Signal Processing Conference (Eusipco)*.

Hardoon, D. R., S. Szedmak, and J. Shawe-Taylor. 2003. *Canonical Correlation Analysis – An Overview with Application to Learning Methods*. Department of Computer Science, Royal Holloway, University of London. Technical Report CSD-TR-03-02.

Hershey, J., and J. Movellan. 1999. Audio vision: using audio-visual synchrony to locate sounds. Pages 813–819 of *Advances in Neural Information Processing Systems*, vol. 12. MIT Press.

Hershey, J., and P. Olsen. 2007. Approximating the Kullback Leibler divergence between Gaussian mixture models. Pages 317–320 of *Proceedings of the IEEE Conference on Acoustics, Speech, and Signal Processing*, vol. 4.

Kumar, K., T. Chen, and R. M. Stern. 2007. Profile view lip reading. Pages 429–432 of *Proceedings of the IEEE Conference on Acoustics, Speech, and Signal Processing*, vol. 4.

Kumar, K., J. Navratil, E. Marcheret, V. Libal, G. Ramaswamy, and G. Potamianos. 2009a. Audio-visual speech synchronization detection using a bimodal linear prediction model. In *Proceedings of the 3rd IEEE Computer Vision and Pattern Recognition Biometrics Workshop*.

Kumar, K., J. Navratil, E. Marcheret, V. Libal, and G. Potamianos. 2009b. Robust audio-visual speech synchrony detection by generalized bimodal linear prediction. Pages 2251–2254 of *Proceedings of the 10th International Conference of the Speech Communication Association (Interspeech)*.

Nock, H. J., G. Iyengar, and C. Neti. 2002. Assessing face and speech consistency for monologue detection in video. Pages 303–306 of *Proceedings of the 10th ACM International Conference on Multimedia*.

Nock, H. J., G. Iyengar, and C. Neti. 2003. Speaker localisation using audio-visual synchrony: an empirical study. Pages 488–499 of *Proceedings of the ACM International Conference on Image and Video Retrieval (CIVR)*, vol. LNCS 2728.

Rabiner, L., and B.-H. Juang. 1993. *Fundamentals of Speech Recognition*. Prentice-Hall.

Slaney, M., and M. Covell. 2000. FaceSync: a linear operator for measuring synchronization of video facial images and audio tracks. Pages 814–820 of *Advances in Neural Information Processing Systems*, vol. 13. MIT Press.

# 3

# Multispectral Contact-Free Palmprint Recognition[†]

Ying Hao, Zhenan Sun, and Tieniu Tan

## 3.1 Introduction

In everyday life, human beings use hand to perceive and reconstruct surrounding environments. Therefore, its prevalence in the field of biometrics is not surprising. Along with the maturity of fingerprint and hand geometry recognition, palmprint and palm/palm-dorsa vein recognition have become new members in the hand-based biometric family. Although increasingly higher recognition rates are reported in the literature, the acquisition of a hand image usually relies on contact devices with pegs, which brings hygiene concerns and reluctance to use (Kong 2009; Morales 2008; Michael 2008). Recently a growing trend toward relieving users from a contact device has emerged, and the idea of peg-free, or further contact-free, palm biometrics has been proposed. However, accuracy of hand-based biometric systems degrades along with the removal of the peg and contact plane (Han 2007a, b; Doublet 2007; Michael 2008). The underlying reason lies in the fact that the hand is essentially a three-dimensional (3D) object with a large number of degrees of freedom. For this reason, naturally stretched-out hands of different subjects may appear substantially different on an image plane. Scale changes, in-depth rotation, and nonlinear skin deformation originating from pose changes are the most commonly encountered image variations in a touch-free environment (Morales 2008; Michael 2008).

"Palmprint" usually refers to a print made by an impression of the ridges in the skin of a palm or a digital image of a palm captured at resolutions of less than 100 dpi (Kong 2009). In this sense, a palmprint reflects the irregularity of the palm skin surface and texture. If we take a closer look at the human

[†] **Acknowledgments.** This work is funded by research grants from the National Hi-Tech Research and Development Program of China (Grant No. 2006AA01Z193, 2007AA01Z162), the National Basic Research Program of China (Grant No. 2004CB318100), the National Natural Science Foundation of China (Grant No. 60736018, 60723005, 60702024), and NLPR 2008NLPRZY-2.

skin, it is composed of many components, including veins, capillaries, hairs, and fibers, forming a multilayered structure. At the outermost layer, numerous fine furrows, hair, and pores are scattered over the surface of skin, while veins, capillaries, and nerves form a vast network inside. According to the optical study conducted by Igarashi et al. (2005), incident light reaches deeper into the skin when wavelength becomes longer, and light from 600 to 1000 nm typically penetrates the skin to about 1–3 millimeters, revealing the internal structures of human skin. The uniqueness of human skin, including its micro-, meso-, and macrostructures, is a product of random factors during embryonic development. Enlightened by Igarashi's work, we extend the concept of palmprint recognition from the superficial surface of the hand to skin components deep inside. To do so, multispectral imaging technology is adopted to reveal the visual contents of palm at different depths of the hand skin.

In the field of hand vein image acquisition and recognition, Wang and Leedham (2006) demonstrated in their pioneering work that no observable meaningful information of vein pattern can be obtained by passively imaging the infrared radiation emitted by palm-side skin. Recently, Wang et al. (2007) proposed using palmprint and palm vein images with fusion applied at the pixel level. They designed a dedicated device that is capable of simultaneous palmprint and palm vein image acquisition. The two images are then fused by a new edge-preserving and contrast-enhancing wavelet fusion method, and the fused image outperforms both individual modalities in biometric identification tasks.

Combining multiple imaging modalities is becoming an area of growing interest, particularly in the field of face recognition. Kong et al. (2007) proposed a software-based registration and fusion method to integrate visible and thermal infrared images for face recognition. By eyeglass removal in thermal image – and wavelet-based image fusion, they improved the recognition accuracy under a wide range of illumination changes. Singh et al. (2008) performed image fusion by using $2\nu$-granular SVM to learn both local and global properties of the multispectral face images at different granularity levels and resolutions. The success of both works is based on carefully designed multispectral imaging methods and image fusion schemes.

In the case that more than two wavelengths are involved, the redundancy and complementarity of different wavelengths should be analyzed to make full use of multispectral information for the purpose of recognition. The flowchart of multispectral palm recognition system is shown in Figure 3.1. A sequence of multispectral hand images is first obtained by illuminating the hand with multiple narrow-band active lights. Afterward, preprocessing is conducted independently on each image to achieve coarse localization of the region of

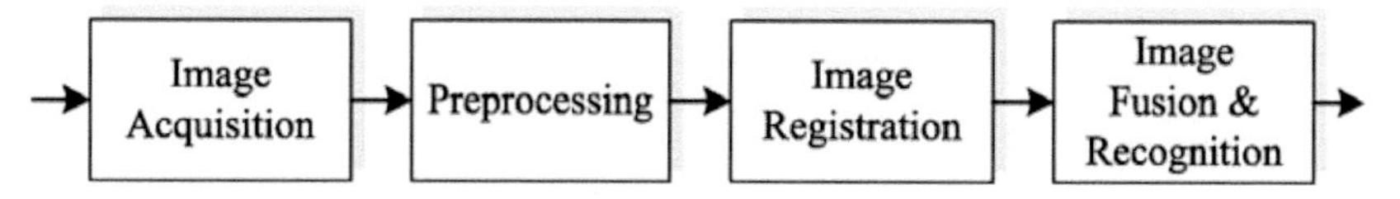


Figure 3.1. Flowchart of multispectral palm image recognition.

interest (ROI), which is further refined through registration. Finally, multispectral images are fused to achieve better recognition performance.

## 3.2 Image Acquisition

Figure 3.2 illustrates the design of multispectral palm image acquisition device, which is composed of six groups of LED arrays ranging from violet to near-infrared (corresponding to 400 to 1000 nm in wavelength), camera, lens, control circuit, single-chip, image grabbing card, and computer. Images are captured in a reflective way under the sheltered environment as shown in the figure. During imaging, the combination and order of wavelengths of active lights are controlled via control circuit according to the user configuration. Active light enters the camera lens after being scattered/reflected by hand skin, and palm image sequences are captured via image grabbing card.

To capture the blood vessel network, a near-infrared sensitive camera is chosen, and Figure 3.3 demonstrates the camera response curve. The response of the camera at 900 nm is approximately 25% of its peak value, which is two-to-three times the response of general purpose cameras.

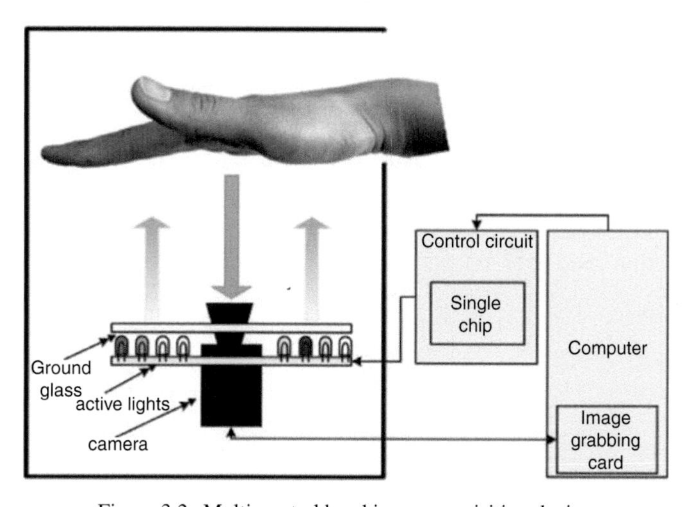


Figure 3.2. Multispectral hand image acquisition device.

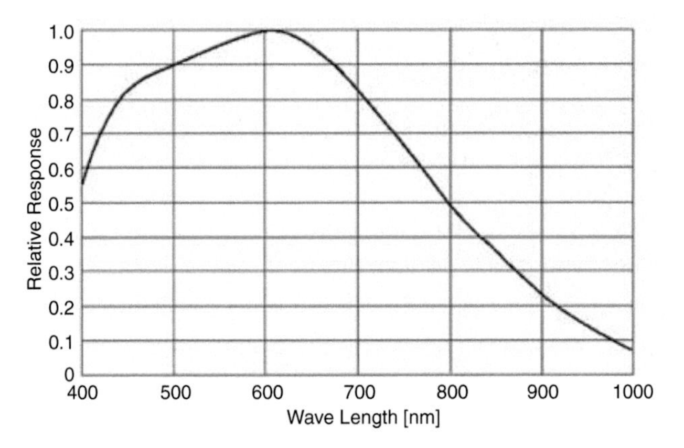


Figure 3.3. Camera response curve.

In a default configuration, the first group of LEDs (WL1) radiates white light, and the remaining groups (WL2–WL6) correspond to 400–1000 nm in ascending order of wavelengths. Each group of lights is arranged on the circuit board in a circular way and scattered by a ground glass before reaching the hand. Because camera response varies as wavelength changes, the circuit board is designed so that the light sources are tunable. To achieve comparable responses for different wavelengths, the light sources, camera gain, and grabbing card are carefully configured. Depending on the wavelength of incident light and skin condition, a different amount of light is reflected by the surface, and the reminder penetrates the skin to different layers, either absorbed or scattered, revealing internal skin structure to the imaging device.

Instead of touching any tangible plane, the subjects need only to naturally stretch their hands, with the palm side facing the camera. The distance between camera and hand is variable and ranges approximately from 20 to 25 cm. The size of CCD is $7.40 \times 5.95$ mm, and it is assumed that the largest palm length is 30 cm. Suppose that $FoV$, $SS$, $f$, and $WD$ denote field of view, sensor size, focal length, and object distance, respectively; then magnification ratio $PMAG$ and focal length $f$ can be derived via Eqs. 3.1 and 3.2:

$$PMAG = \frac{SS}{FoV} = \frac{7.4\,\text{mm}}{300\,\text{mm}} = 0.0246, \tag{3.1}$$

$$f = \frac{WD \times PMAG}{1 + PMAG} = \frac{20\,\text{cm} \times 0.0246}{1.0246} = 0.48\,\text{cm} = 4.8\,\text{mm}. \tag{3.2}$$

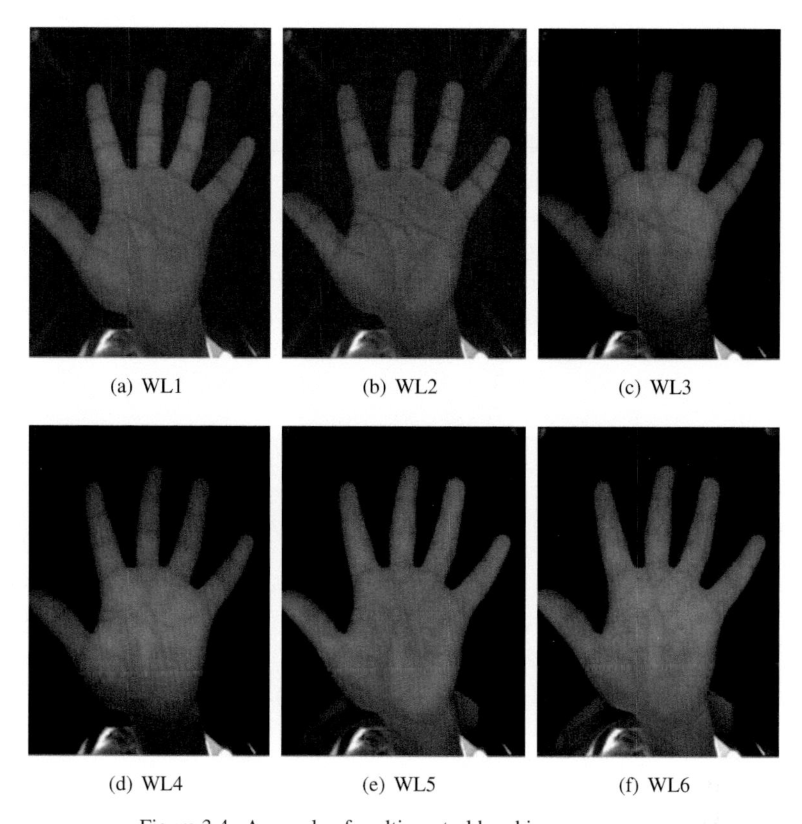

(a) WL1 (b) WL2 (c) WL3

(d) WL4 (e) WL5 (f) WL6

Figure 3.4. A sample of multispectral hand image sequence.

It is obvious that a wide-angle lens (focal length less than 50 mm) will be necessary. Figure 3.4 demonstrates a sample image sequence, and the visual content gradually changes from palmprint to vein image. The above imaging scheme features two characteristics:

(1) Instead of adopting a frequency-division fashion in image acquisition where more than one camera is required, a time-division strategy is adopted. Only one camera is utilized, and different spectral images are obtained during sequential time slots, which provides better spectral scalability and a higher performance price ratio.
(2) The imaging scheme is a contact-free one, which is nonintrusive to users and helps to reduce potential resistance to use. However, preprocessing and registration should be designed to tackle large image variations originating from pose changes.

## 3.3 Preprocessing

A better human-computer interface usually comes together with more hidden computation. In the case of contact-free hand image acquisition, the removal of a restricting plane introduces many more degrees of freedom in hand poses. Camera deformation, large pose variation, and scale change, among others, are the most frequently encountered image variations. Because the cental palm region of the hand is of interest where features will be extracted for recognition, the purpose of preprocessing is to correct camera deformation and robustly segment ROI region in the presence of the image variations mentioned above.

### 3.3.1 Camera Deformation Correction

To capture the whole hand, Eq. 3.2 suggests that a wide-angle lens is required. Therefore, barrel distortion is inevitable in the captured images. Figure 3.5(a) shows a captured image of regular grids.

The barrel distortion is typical for a wide-angle lens and can be compensated via camera calibration with a distortion model. Suppose a real-world object is projected to image plane $(x, y)$ and $r = \sqrt{x^2 + y^2}$. Then the point after distortion can be calculated by Eq. 3.3 (Weng 1992):

$$\begin{bmatrix} x_d \\ y_d \end{bmatrix} = (1 + k_1 r^2 + k_2 r^4 + k_5 r^6) \begin{bmatrix} x \\ y \end{bmatrix} + \begin{bmatrix} 2k_3 xy + k_4(r^2 + 2x^2) \\ k_3(r^2 + 2y^2) + 2k_4 xy \end{bmatrix}, \quad (3.3)$$

where $k_1, k_2, \ldots, k_5$ are parameters to be estimated. A piece of paper with printed regular grids is placed at various positions and with different in-depth rotations, and 10 images are captured (one of them is shown in Figure 3.5[a]). By manual labeling of correspondences, intrinsic parameters can be estimated, and deformation correction can be achieved. We select the Caltech Camera Calibration Toolbox for parameter estimation (Caltech Calib). Figures 3.5(c) and 3.5(d) show the hand images before and after image deformation correction, respectively.

### 3.3.2 Central Palm Region Localization

To locate the central palm, as demonstrated in Figure 3.6(a), each hand image is first binarized with a global threshold determined with Otsu's algorithm, and the foreground region at the bottom of the image is considered to be the wrist. Then the middle point of wrist is regarded as the reference point, and the distance from each contour point to reference point is calculated, forming a one-dimensional signal with five peaks and four valleys, corresponding to five

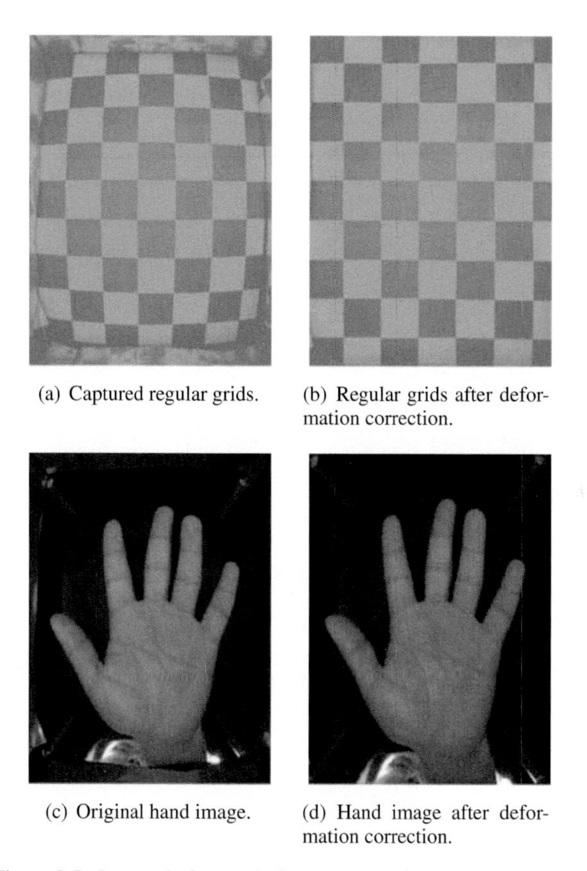

(a) Captured regular grids. (b) Regular grids after deformation correction.

(c) Original hand image. (d) Hand image after deformation correction.

Figure 3.5. Images before and after camera deformation correction.

finger tips and four valleys, respectively. ROI localization rational is demonstrated in Figure 3.6(f). Compared with the traditional palmprint preprocessing method aiming at segmenting images obtained with a contact device, the main difference lies in that the size of the ROI is estimated rather than fixed. A rectangular image region that is 30–80 pixels beneath the reference line is segmented, and the average palm width $PW$ is estimated within this region, which is selected because of its stability under different hand poses. The side length $d$ of ROI is then calculated by $d = 0.6 \times PW$. Afterward, a coordinate system is established, where origin $O$ is set to be the middle point of the reference line, and the direction of horizontal axis is defined to be orthogonal to the reference line. Finally, a square region with side length $d$ is picked out as the ROI. To make the localization result scale invariant, the distance from $O$ to the ROI is also proportional to $PW$. Before feature extraction, the detected ROIs are scaled to predefined size, making different samples comparable.

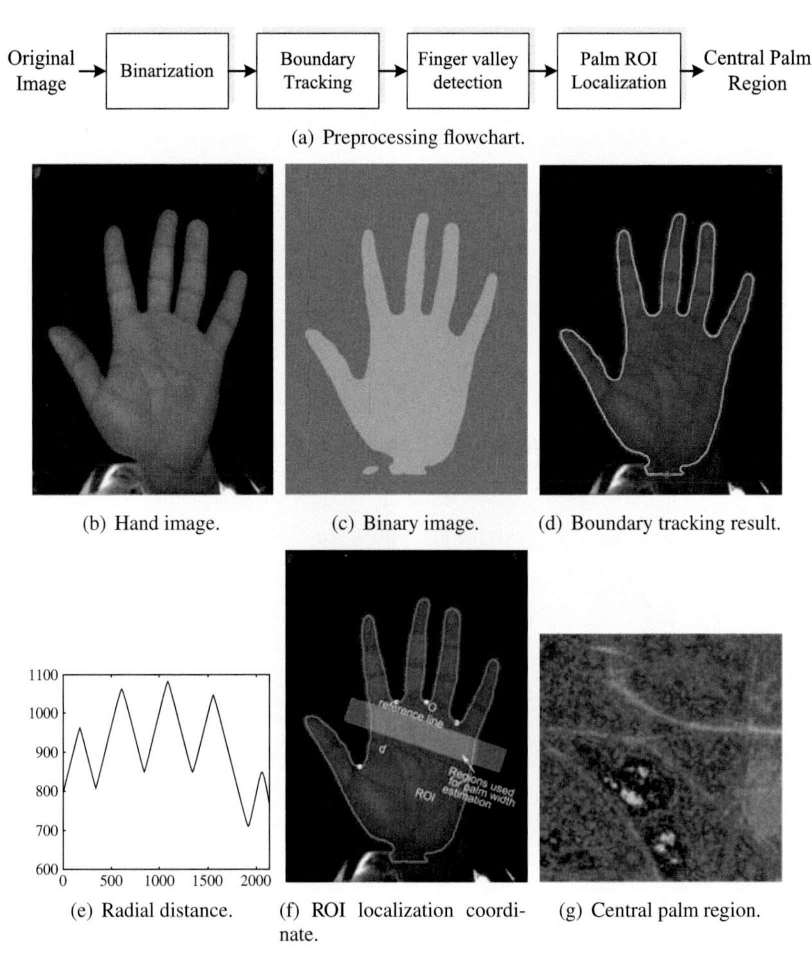


(a) Preprocessing flowchart.

(b) Hand image. (c) Binary image. (d) Boundary tracking result.

(e) Radial distance. (f) ROI localization coordinate. (g) Central palm region.

Figure 3.6. Multispectral palm image preprocessing.

The above preprocessing scheme deals well with scale change and pose variation, while in-depth rotation cannot be removed. Therefore, the subjects are instructed to place their hand horizontally, and in-depth rotation is less than 10 degrees in most cases.

## 3.4 Image Registration

The central palm region localization procedure is performed independently on each image of the multispectral sequence. However, the ROIs detected from

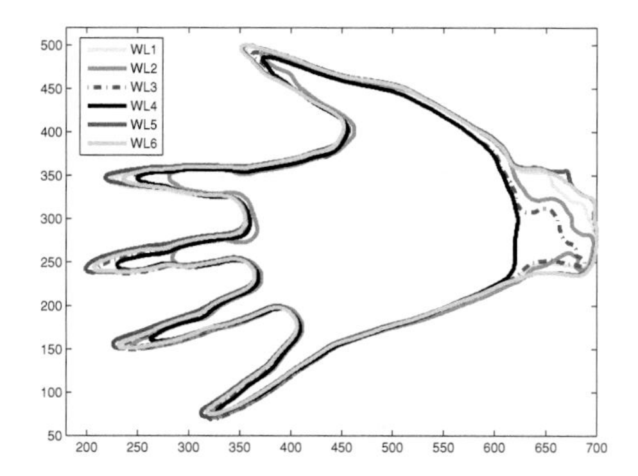


Figure 3.7. Hand contours of a multispectral image sequence.

different wavelengths may not precisely correspond to each other because of the following reasons:

(1) Although the users are required to hold their hand still, hand vibration, pose change, gradual in-depth rotation, and outliers with large movement occur inevitably because the capture of one multispectral sequence lasts approximately 1 minute.
(2) The amount of illumination and camera response of different wavelengths are considerably different, resulting in remarkable distinctions of hand contours, finger valley locations, estimated palm widths, etc.

Figure 3.7 illustrates contours extracted from a multispectral image sequence with each closed curve indicating the contour of one wavelength. Displacement between contours is obvious. Since pixel-level fusion is an important research direction of multispectral images, good alignment of the source images is an essential step.

In the field of remote sensing and medical image analysis, mutual information(MI) is frequently reported to be effective and robust in performaing registration (Maes 1997). However, mutual information works well only in cases that significant geometrical structures exist in images. In contrast, the only universal geometrical structure in palm region is principal lines, but they take only a considerably small portion of image pixels, which remarkably restricts their contribution to registration. Figure 3.8(a) demonstrates the preprocessing results of one image sequence, with the columns indicating the six wavelengths as shown in Figure 3.4. Figure 3.8(b) is the noisy mutual information – based registration surface between the intensities of the first two images in Figure 3.8(a) with regard to two location parameters $x$ and $y$.

Binary textural features, including FusionCode, CompetitiveCode, and ordinal feature (Kong 2004a, b; Sun 2005), have been proved to be very effective in

(a) Preprocessing results of one image sequence (WL1–WL6 from left to right).

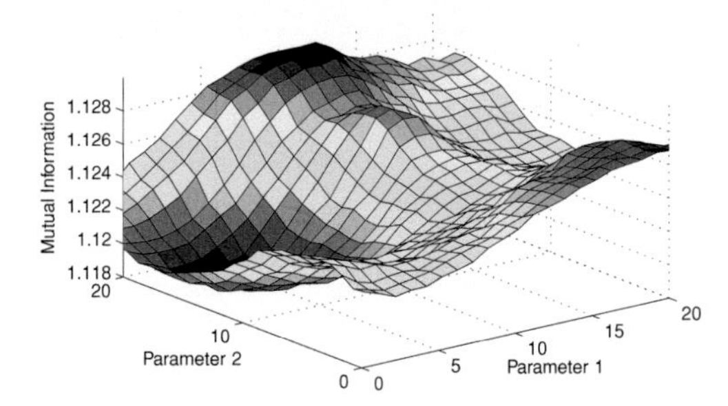


(b) Registration surface based on image intensities.

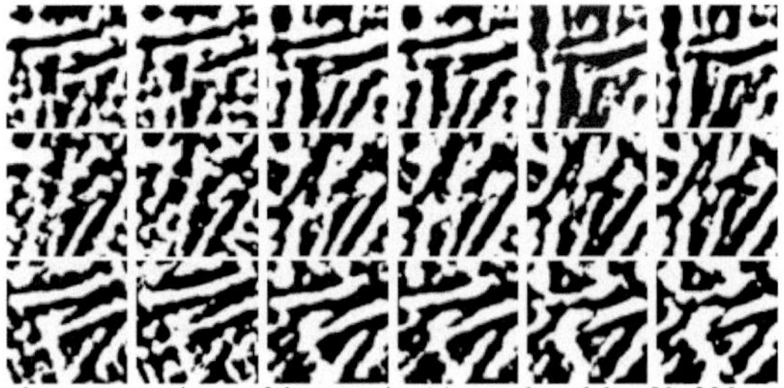

(c) Feature-level representations of images in (a), produced by 0°, 30°, and 60° ordinal filters, respectively.

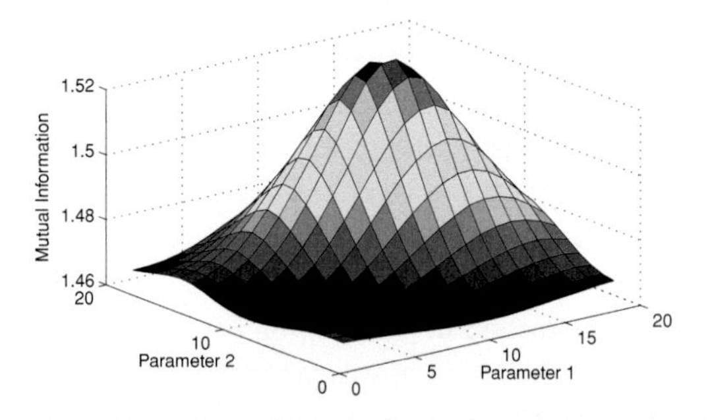


(d) Registration surface based on feature-level representations.

(e) Final ROIs of images in (a) after feature-level registration.

Figure 3.8. Feature-level mutual information-based registration.

palmprint recognition task. These methods seek to robustly, qualitatively, and effectively represent linelike patterns, such as wrinkles, principal lines, and ridges. Figure 3.8(c) illustrates the Orthogonal Line Ordinal Feature (OLOF) (Sun 2005) representations of images in Figure 3.8(a), with the rows corresponding to $0^\circ$, $30^\circ$, and $60^\circ$ filters, respectively. Unlike intensity representation, a large number of structures emerge in feature-level representation, which is more suitable for mutual information – based registration. Moreover, the calculation of mutual information on binary images is quite simple.

Multispectral image registration works under the assumption that there is no in-depth rotation and scale variation across wavelengths, which is valid in most cases. Because the users are instructed not to move their hands during image acquisition, the search space for registration is chosen to to deal with unintentional movement of hands. Furthermore, on account of image quality of the input images as well as preprocessing results, the search space $\Theta$ is reduced to a rigid transformation and is empirically defined as

$$\Theta = \{x, y, \theta | -10 \leq x \leq 10, -10 \leq y \leq 10, -3 \leq \theta \leq 3\},$$

where $x$, $y$, and $\theta$ denote horizontal, vertical translation, and in-plane rotation angle, respectively. Figure 3.8(d) illustrates the mutual information – based registration surface between feature-level representations of the first two images in 3.8(a). It is obvious that the registration surface is much better for registration: It contains a single peak at the expected position (12, 12) and is much smoother than Figure 3.8(b). Registration parameters can be estimated by simply choosing those maximizing the mutual information.

Registration of a multispectral sequence is achieved via sequential processing. Suppose multispectral images are denoted as $I_{WL1}, I_{WL2}, \ldots, I_{WLN}$, where $N = 6$ is the total number of wavelengths. The first image $I_{WL1}$ is first preprocessed, and the resulting ROI is regarded as reference ROI for $I_{WL2}$. Then the same preprocessing is independently performed on $I_{WL2}$ while the output is taken as an initial guess of the ROI. A region with side length 36 pixels larger than this initial guess is picked out and registered with regard to its reference ROI based on feature-level representation. All three directional features are taken into consideration by averaging corresponding registration surfaces. When a successful registration is achieved, the produced ROI is then regarded as reference ROI for $I_{WL3}$, and this process continues until the whole sequence is traversed. Because only images from nearby wavelengths are registered with each other, abrupt image changes, which usually occur when illumination turns from visible light to the infrared spectrum, are circumvented. Figure 3.8(e) presents the final registration result, and displacement of palm regions is successfully corrected.

## 3.5 Image Fusion

The concept of image fusion refers to the idea of integrating information from multiple source images for better visual or computational perception.

The visual contents of hands under different wavelengths may be redundant or complementary to each other, which forms a solid foundation for information fusion (Han 2006). Redundancy means the representation, description, or interpretation of the target in a multispectral images are similar, while complementarity refers to the fact that information that originates from different targets is independent of each other. Multispectral image fusion may:

- Enlarge ranges of use: because of information redundancy, information absence and noise in one wavelength might be compensated by information from other wavelengths.
- Improve recognition performance: multispectral images enrich a raw data source and make recognition performance improvement possible.
- Enable spoof detection: the imaging of vein is based on the absorptivity of deoxidized hemoglobin to near-infrared light and can be possible only when the body is alive.

According to the level of information representation, image fusion can be categorized into pixel-level, feature-level, and decision-level fusion. In the following discussion, pixel-level and decision-level (or more precisely, matching score – level) fusion are studied and compared in the context of identity recognition.

### 3.5.1 Pixel-Level Fusion

Pixel-level fusion takes raw images as input. Therefore the fusion result is apt to uncertainty and instability of the image acquisition procedure. The key issue in pixel-level image fusion is to faithfully preserve domain-specific salient image features.

A pixel-level image fusion scheme normally includes three steps:

1. *Image normalization.* Input images are normalized so that certain criteria are met. For example, most fusion methods require dynamic range or gradient distribution of input images to be similar so that comparable multiscale decomposition coefficients are produced, which facilities activity measure and coefficient combination.

   As described earlier, the power of active light, amount of light entering the CCD camera, and camera response to each wavelength are different,

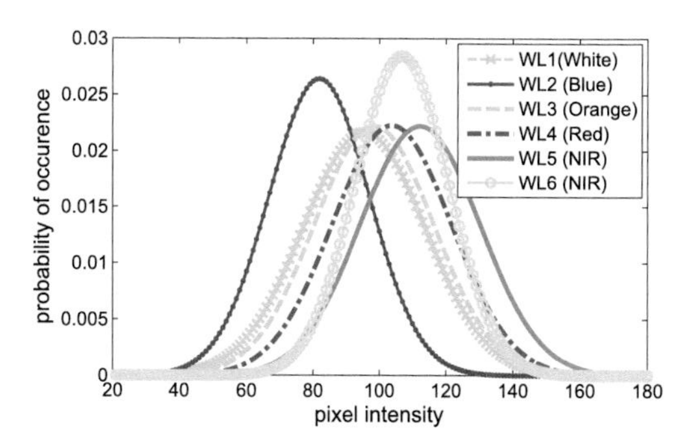


Figure 3.9. Dynamic ranges of multispectral images.

resulting in different dynamic ranges, as illustrated in Figure 3.9. Suppose that the mean and variance of the original image is $m$ and $V$, and the wanted values are $m_T$ and $V_T$. The point process as described in Eq. 3.4 is performed on each wavelength of the multispectral images so that the multiscale decomposition coefficients are comparable across wavelengths:

$$I(x, y) = m_T + (I(x, y) - m) \cdot \sqrt{\frac{V_T}{V}}. \tag{3.4}$$

To further suppress noise and prevent edges from being smoothed, bilateral filtering is adopted as the second step in image normalization.

2. *Multiscale decomposition (MSD).* MSD maps intensity images to more efficient representations of image features. The discriminative features in both palmprint and vein – or more specifically principal lines, wrinkle lines, ridges, and blood vessels – all take the form of linelike patterns. Therefore, Curvelet transform (Curvelet Site), which is designed to efficiently represent edges and other singularities along curves, is selected for pixel-level fusion. Unlike wavelet transform, Curvelet transform has directional parameters, and its coefficients have a high degree of directional specificity. Large coefficients in transform space suggest strong lines on original image, and so Curvelet transform represents linelike structures effectively.
3. *Fusion scheme.* Fusion scheme decides the multiscale decomposition coefficients by weighting relevant coefficients of all input images. According to the generic framework proposed by Zhang et al. (1999), an image fusion scheme is usually composed of (a) the activity measurement that determines the quality of each input, (b) coefficient grouping to define the presense or absence of cross-scale correlation, (c) coefficient combining where a weighted sum of source representations is calculated, and (d) consistency verification to ensure neighboring coefficients are calculated in similar manner.

By means of Curvelet transform, linelike patterns can be represented by a few coefficients, and therefore cross-scale correlation is ignored in coefficient grouping. For base approximation, the average of source images is adopted for coefficient combination, and a weighted sum is chosen for higher frequencies.

The final fused image can be easily obtained via inverse Curvelet transform of the fused coefficients.

### 3.5.2 Matching Score-Level Fusion

Matching score-level fusion takes matching scores of several subsystems as input and outputs a unified score. Matching score-level fusion features robustness to sensors and noises, which makes it the most widely studied direction in image fusion.

In the above multispectral hand image-matching system, the number of classifiers $N \in \{2, 6\}$. $N = 2$ corresponds to a combination of two wavelengths, and $N = 6$ means all six wavelengths. In the verification mode, the number of classes is $c = 2$, with $class1$ denoting intraclass matching and $class2$ representing interclass matching. In the recognition mode, $c = 310$, and each value of $c$ corresponds to one specific hand.

A total number of seven fusion rules are selected, including three fixed rules and four learned rules. A fixed rule treats the matching scores as a posteriori probability. A learned fusion rule regards fusion as a pattern recognition problem. Matching scores from different classifiers are concatenated as features, and the fusion problem is converted to a classifier design aimed at best separating the training data:

- Fixed rules: Three fixed rules (sum rule, product rule, and max rule) are selected for comparison. These fixed rules do not need training and are easy to use.
- Fisher linear discriminant (FLD): Fisher linear discriminant is a classical pattern recognition method. The idea is to project high-dimensional samples of two classes to a one-dimensional line so that projected data are efficient for discrimination. Suppose $x$ is a raw signal and $y = W^T x$ is a projected signal of $x$, then the best projection direction $W$ should maximize the criteria function $J(W)$:

$$J(W) = \frac{|\tilde{m}_1 - \tilde{m}_2|^2}{\tilde{S}_1^2 + \tilde{S}_2^2}, \tag{3.5}$$

where $\tilde{m}_1$, $\tilde{m}_2$, $\tilde{S}_1$, and $\tilde{S}_2$ denote mean and within-class scatter for the two classes after projection, respectively. Suppose $m_1$, $m_2$, $S_1$, and $S_2$ are the corresponding values before projection, then the solution of $W$ is

$$W = (S_1 + S_2)^{-1}(m_1 - m_2). \tag{3.6}$$

- Decision templates (DTs): The Decision templates method was proposed by Duin et al. in 2001 (Kuncheva 2001). Suppose $Z = \{z_1, z_2, \ldots, z_t\}$ is the training set, each training sample $z_j$ is fed to the $N$ classifiers, and the scores $\{s_{1j}, s_{2j}, \ldots, s_{Nj}\}$ are denoted as $s_j$. A decision template $DT_i, i \in [1, c]$ for each of the classes is determined by

$$DT_i(Z) = \frac{\sum_{j=1}^{t} Ind(z_j, i)s_j}{\sum_{j=1}^{t} Ind(z_j, i)}, \tag{3.7}$$

where

$$Ind(z_j, i) = \begin{cases} 1, & z_j \text{ labeled } i; \\ 0, & z_j \text{ not labeled } i. \end{cases}$$

Suppose the matching score for test sample $z_{tj}$ is $s_{tj}$. The similarity of $DT_i, i \in [1, c]$ and $s_{tj}$ can be determined by various fuzzy measures, and sample $z_{tj}$ is classified to the class whose decision template is most similar to $z_{tj}$. In this work, Euclidian distance is chosen as the measure of dissimilarity.
- Dempster-Shafer theory of evidence (DST): The DST method is based on evidence theory and is designed to model reasoning under uncertainty. By avoiding the problem of having to assign unavailable probabilities, it is regarded as a generalization of the Baysian theory (Sentz 2002).

  Suppose $\Theta = \{A_1, \ldots, A_i\}$ is a set of hypotheses. Each subset $A \subseteq \Theta$ is assigned a belief that lies in [0, 1]. If two or more evidences are available, the beliefs are effectively assigned to each subset of $\Theta$.
- Support vector machine (SVM): Support vector machine was proposed to determine the best hyperplane for linearly separable data. The so-called best hyperplane not only separates the two classes without mistake but also maximizes the margin. The former guarantees minimal empirical risk, and the latter suggests best generalization capability.

  Because of its advantages in small sample problems and nonlinear and high-dimensional pattern recognition problems, SVM is widely used in many areas.

The unified matching score produced by matching-level fusion is utilized as the measure of matching.

Table 3.1. *Performances of Multispectral Palm Images*

| | One Session | | | Two Sessions | | |
|---|---|---|---|---|---|---|
| Wavelength | EER (%) | $d'$ | Recognition Rate (%) | EER (%) | $d'$ | Recognition Rate (%) |
| WL1 (white) | **0.67** | 6.0625 | 99.39 | 1.91 | 4.5875 | 97.85 |
| WL2 (blue) | 0.72 | 5.8052 | 98.78 | 2.12 | 4.3920 | 97.20 |
| WL3 (orange) | 0.70 | 5.9127 | 99.29 | 1.72 | 4.8532 | 97.96 |
| WL4 (red) | 0.90 | 5.5068 | 98.98 | 2.46 | 4.4466 | 96.39 |
| WL5 (NIR) | 0.90 | 5.9249 | 98.88 | **1.12** | 5.0875 | 98.02 |
| WL6 (NIR) | 0.72 | 6.1920 | 98.88 | 1.15 | 5.1836 | 98.19 |

## 3.6 Experiments

Experiments are conducted on a multispectral database collected by the Chinese Academy of Sciences, Institute of Automation (CASIA) (Hao 2008). At the first session, 165 volunteers ranging from 20 to 63 years old participated in the data collection. Ninety percent of them are graduate students. For each person, three image sequences of both hands are obtained. The default wavelengths WL1–WL6 are selected (see Section 3.2), thus the first session database contains $165 \times 2 \times 3 \times 6 = 5940$ images. During the second session, 22 out of the 165 volunteers were unavailable for various reasons. To maintain the size of the database, 12 additional subjects were invited thus forming a database containing $155 \times 2 \times 2 \times 3 \times 6 = 11{,}160$ images. The largest session interval was 167 days, and the smallest was 49 days. The device was reconfigured for better imaging effects during the session interval. Each image is of size $768 \times 576$, stored as an eight-bit grayscale image.

The resulting size of ROI varies from 100 to 200 pixels and approximately follows a normal distribution, with mean value $\mu = 166$ and standard deviation $\sigma = 16$. To achieve scale invariance, ROIs after registration are normalized to $128 \times 128$.

### 3.6.1 Baseline Performances

To evaluate the contribution of image fusion to recognition performance, baselines are first established. The orthogonal line ordinal feature (OLOF), as proposed by Sun et al. (2005), is extracted, and the Hamming distance is utilized to measure the dissimilarity between two features. Table 3.1 compares the verification performance of different wavelengths via three important performance

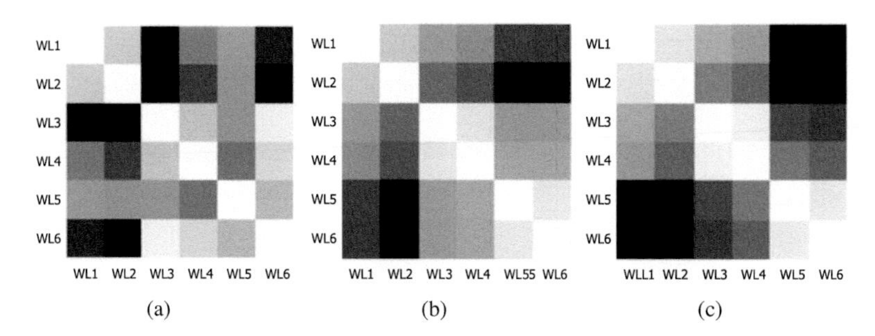


Figure 3.10. Intensity-level (a), intraclass (b), and interclass (c) matching score – level correlation analysis of multispectral palm images.

indices: equal error rate (EER), discriminant index($d'$), and recognition performance.

It is notable that the performance of two sessions is worse than one session. This is predictable because image variations become larger when the second session is included.

Another fact is that at the first session, the white spectrum performs best among others. After the second session, because of hardware adjustment, time-varying texture of hand skin, and larger image variation, the performance of all wavelengths degrades. Among them, inner skin structure, which is captured under near-infrared illumination, is most stable, indicating the stability of inner skin structure in comparison with a superficial structure such as palmprint. This is clearly consistent with our intuition.

### 3.6.2 Division of Wavelengths

The six wavelengths of multispectral hand image sequence are not independent of each other. On the contrary, they are correlated to a certain extent because of the continuity of skin structure. Figure 3.10 demonstrates the correlation coefficients of the six wavelengths with a higher intensity indicating a larger value. Intensity-level correlation in Figure 3.10(a) suggests that the six wavelengths can be roughly divided into three groups: ($WL1$, $WL2$), ($WL3$, $WL4$), and ($WL5$, $WL6$) with high within-group correlation and relatively low intergroup correlation. Matching score – level correlation also displays the same pattern, as Figs. 3.10(b) and 3.10(c) demonstrate.

Enlightened by this observation, wavelength combinations are also divided into correlative groups and complementary groups, with correlative groups corresponding to intragroup image fusion and complementary groups referring to intergroup fusion.

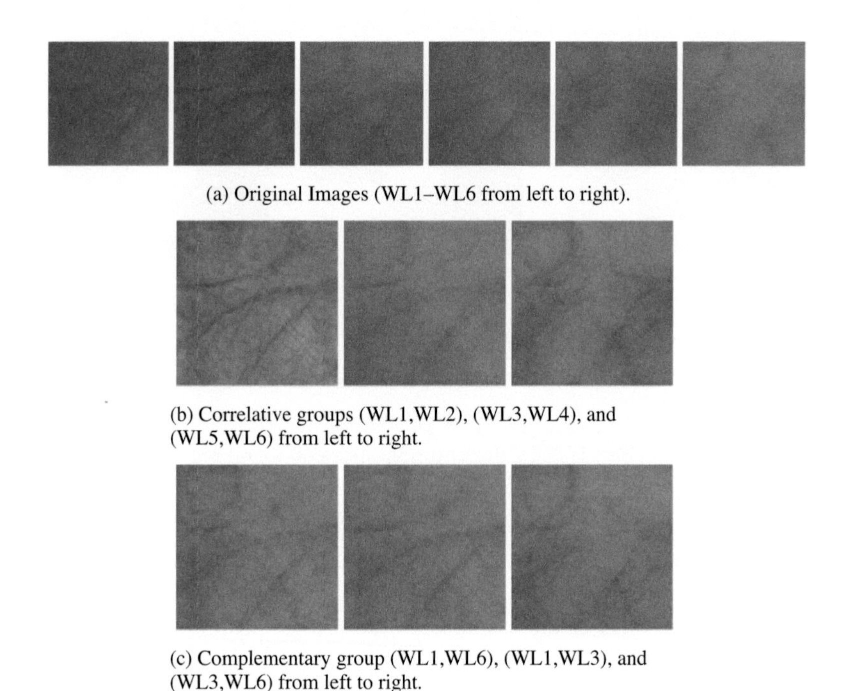

(a) Original Images (WL1–WL6 from left to right).

(b) Correlative groups (WL1,WL2), (WL3,WL4), and (WL5,WL6) from left to right.

(c) Complementary group (WL1,WL6), (WL1,WL3), and (WL3,WL6) from left to right.

Figure 3.11. Pixel-level fusion results of correlative and complementary groups.

### 3.6.3 Pixel-Level Fusion

The palmprint ROIs are fused via the fusion method as detailed in Section 3.5.1. Figure 3.11 demonstrates the original images as well as fused images. It is obvious that fusion of correlative groups enhances salient image features and fused image of complementary groups is a tradeoff between two source images.

Besides visual inspection, objective evaluation of different wavelength combination is established via three recognition performance indicators: equal error rate (EER), discriminant index($d'$), and receiver operating curves (ROC).

The recognition performance of different combinations is demonstrated in Figure 3.12 and Table 3.2. By comparison with the recognition results based on that of the two-session image database, it is observed that all combinations have improved performance with regard to their source wavelengths. In the correlative groups, the combination of WL5 and WL6 improves performance more than other combinations, which is consistent with the conclusion that NIR is most suitable for identity recognition. The underlying reason lies in that fusing WL5 and WL6 helps to reduce the noise level and enhance salient features.

Combination (WL3,WL6) is the best among the complementary groups, which is contradictory to the common perception that fusing WL1 and WL6

Table 3.2. *Performance of Fused Image in Correlative Groups and Complementary Groups*

| Wavelength Combination | | EER (%) | $d'$ |
|---|---|---|---|
| Correlative groups | (WL1,WL2) | 1.61 | 4.6416 |
| | (WL3,WL4) | 1.50 | 4.8232 |
| | (WL5,WL6) | **0.79** | 5.2242 |
| Complementary groups | (WL1,WL6) | 1.12 | 4.8390 |
| | (WL1,WL3) | 1.42 | 4.7902 |
| | (WL3,WL6) | **0.80** | 5.1946 |

improves performance best. From the images in Figure 3.11, it is seen that the texture on palmprint images is richer than other wavelengths, resulting in more large coefficients in the Curvelet domain, which further causes the fused image to reflect more textural information of the palmprint. As a result, the large image variations of the palmprint (WL1) are also conveyed to the fused image. Meanwhile, WL3 is red light and reflects skin structure among surface and vein, which is more stable than a palmprint. These two factors explain why combination (WL3,WL6) outperforms other complementary combinations.

Another observation is that the performance of fused images is better than their sources, which proved the effectiveness of registration. Because the palm region lacks salient features that can be robustly localized by a human being, it

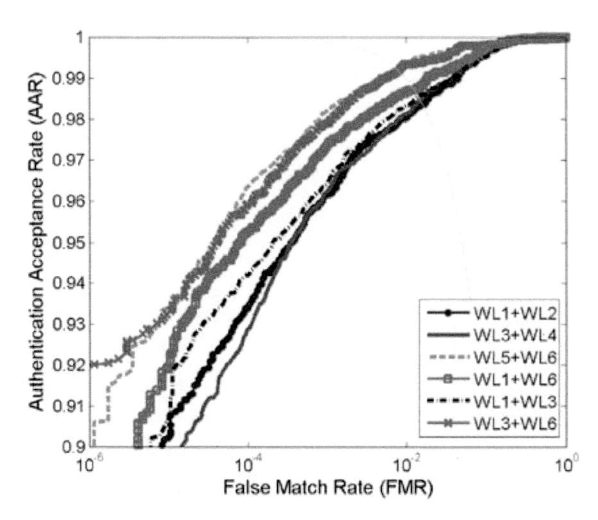


Figure 3.12. Receiver operating characteristics (ROC) of pixel-level fusion.

Table 3.3. *Recognition Rates of Matching Score Fusion with Fixed Rules*

| Wavelength Combinations | | Sum Rule (%) | Product Rule (%) | Max Rule (%) |
|---|---|---|---|---|
| Correlative groups | (WL1,WL2) | 97.91 | 97.89 | 98.04 |
| | (WL3,WL4) | 97.27 | 97.27 | 97.33 |
| | (WL5,WL6) | **98.26** | 98.26 | 98.19 |
| Complementary groups | (WL1,WL6) | **99.29** | 99.27 | 98.75 |
| | (WL1,WL3) | 98.58 | 98.60 | 98.30 |
| | (WL3,WL6) | 98.90 | 98.88 | 98.56 |
| All | | 99.12 | 99.14 | 98.65 |

is very difficult to evaluate the result of registration by labeling ground truth. Suppose that registration succeeds, then the displacement of two source images will be negligible. Thus robust and richer features can be extracted from a fused image, resulting in improved performance.

### 3.6.4 Matching Score-Level Fusion

For matching score-level fusion, each wavelength is matched with its corresponding gallery wavelength, and multispectral matching scores are treated as a feature vector. Table 3.3 compared the performance of fixed rules in combining correlative groups, complementary groups, and all wavelengths.

By choosing the better matching score from two correlative ones, the max rule helps to produce a better intraclass matching score. Therefore, it performs best in combining correlative wavelength groups. In contrast, the sum rule effectively reduces noise level while combining complementary wavelengths.

The complementary groups perform better than the correlative groups as a whole. The recognition rates of combining all wavelengths, as shown in the last row of Table 3.3, are no better than the fusion of two selected wavelengths, such as WL1 and WL6.

For those fusion methods that are designed for two-class problem, such as FLD and SVM, the recognition problem is converted to separating intraclass and interclass matching scores. In a multispectral hand image database, six samples are tokens for each class. Therefore, the number of intraclass matching is $6 \times 5/2 = 15$, and the number of matching two arbitrary classes is $6 \times 6 = 36$. According to the image index of intraclass matching, 15 out of 36 interclass matching scores are selected for the purpose of fusion. Variable numbers of training samples are randomly chosen for training, and the remaining samples

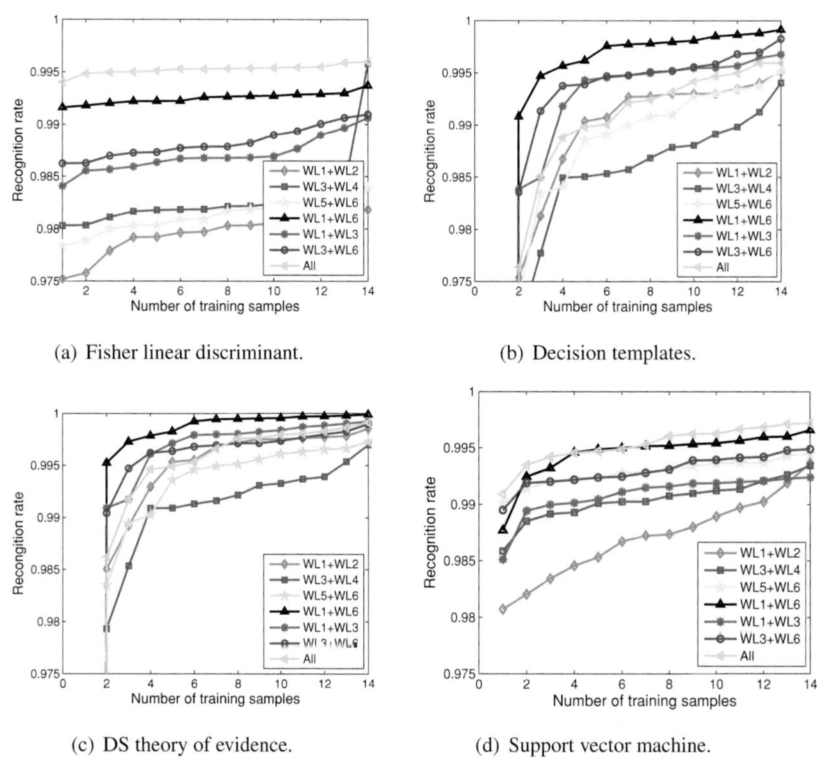


(a) Fisher linear discriminant.

(b) Decision templates.

(c) DS theory of evidence.

(d) Support vector machine.

Figure 3.13. Recognition rates of matching score fusion with learned rules.

are used for testing. The experiments are repeated for 100 times, and the average recognition rates of the four learned rules are demonstrated in Figure 3.13.

For DT and DST methods, combining all six wavelengths is no better than combining two selected wavelengths. The reason lie in the fact that these two methods are multiclass classifiers, and the sample size of 15 is relatively small for a six-dimensional feature vector. The situation is opposite for FLD and SVM, where sample size is sufficient for a two-class problem.

Overall, DST is most suitable for matching score-level fusion of a multispectral palm image because of its capability in combining conflicting evidences. The recognition rate of fusing WL1 and WL6 exceeds 99.9% when the training sample size is six.

## 3.7 Conclusion

In this chapter, acquisition, preprocessing, registration, matching, and fusion of multispectral hand images are exploited. Generally speaking, this is a new direction of research, but a large number of challenging problems still require solution:

- Image acquisition: Imaging is the first step in multispectral image recognition and has substantial influence on consequent processes. The challenges include chromatic dispersion, nonuniform illumination, low camera responses to NIR light, poor vein image quality, etc. These problems can be partially solved by better circuit design and better but more expensive camera and electronically controlled filters.
- Image representation and recognition: The feature extraction method in this chapter is OLOF, which is designed to represent line segments that are randomly distributed over the palm. Visual content under red and NIR light is considerably different with that under visible light. Other representation schemes might exist that are more suitable for sparse pattern such as veins.
- Image fusion: Curvelet transform-based image fusion has proved to be effective for recognition. However, the vein structure is not as clear as the palmprint on fused images. An image feature saliency-based approach might improve the quality of the fused image by focusing more on image areas with salient features.

Undoubtedly, contact-free palmprint recognition is nonintrusive, easier to use, and healthier. Together with these advantages are larger degrees of freedom and larger image variations. Solving these challenging problems is essential for this modality to be accepted by the public.

## References

Camera Calibration Toolbox for Matlab, Software available at http://www.vision.caltech.edu/bouguetj/calib_doc/.

Curvelet transform website. http://www.curvelet.org/.

Doublet, J., M. Revenu, and O. Lepetit. 2007. Robust grayscale distribution estimation for contactless palmprint recognition, *Biometrics: Theory, Applications, and Systems*, 1–6.

Han, C., H. Zhu, and Z. Duan. 2006. *Multi-Source Information Fusion* (in Chinese). Tsinghua University Press.

Han, Y., T. Tan, Z. Sun, and Y. Hao. 2007. Embedded palmprint recognition system on mobile devices, *Lecture Notes in Computer Science: Advances in Biometrics* **4642**, 1184–1193.

Han, Y., Z. Sun, F. Wang, and T. Tan. 2007. Palmprint recognition under unconstrained scenes, *Lecture Notes in Computer Science – ACCV* **4844**, 1–11.

Hao, Y., Z. Sun, T. Tan, and C. Ren. 2008. Multi-spectral palm image fusion for accurate contact-free palmprint recognition, *IEEE Conf. on Image Processing*, 281–284.

Igarashi, T., K. Nishino, and S. K. Nayar. 2005. The appearance of human skin, *Technical Report CUCS-024-05* (Columbia University).

Kong, A., D. Zhang, and M. Kamel. 2009. A survey of palmprint recognition, *Pattern Recognition*, **42**, 1408–1418.

Kong, S. G., J. Heo, F. Boughorbel, Y. Zheng, B. R. Abidi, A. Koschan, M. Yi, and M. A. Abidi. 2007. Multiscale fusion of visible and thermal IR images for illumination-invariant face recognition, *Intl. J. on Computer Vision* **71**, 215–233.

Kuncheva, L. I., C. Bezdek, and R. P. W. Duin. 2001. Decision templates for multiple classifier fusion: an experimental comparison, *IEEE Pervasive Computing* **34**, 299–314.

Maes, F., A. Collignon, D. Vandermeulen, G. Marchal, and P. Suetens. 1997. Multimodality image registration by maximization of mutual information, *IEEE Transaction on Medical Imaging* **16**, 187–198.

Michael, G. K. O., T. Connie, and A. B. J. Teoh. 2008. Touch-less palm print biometrics: novel design and implementation, *Image Vision Computing* **26**, 1551–1560.

Morales, A., M. A. Ferrer, F. Díaz, J. B. Alonso, and C. M. Travieso. 2008. Contact-free hand biometric system for real environments, In *European Signal Processing Conference*.

Sentz, K., and S. Ferson. 2002. Combination of evidence in Dempster-Shafer theory, Sandia Report 2002-0835.

Singh, R., M. Vatsa, and A. Noore. 2008. Integrated multilevel image fusion and match score fusion of visible and infrared face images for robust face recognition, *Pattern Recognition* **41**, 880–893.

Sun, Z., T. Tan, Y. Wang, and S. Z. Li. 2005. Ordinal palmprint recognition for personal identification, *IEEE Conf. on Computer Vision and Pattern Recognition*, 279–284.

Wai-Kin Kong, A., and D. Zhang. 2004. Competitive coding scheme for palmprint verification, *Intl. Conf. on Pattern Recognition*, 520–523.

Wai-Kin Kong, A., and D. Zhang. 2004. Feature level fusion for effective palmprint authentication, *Intl. Conf. on Biometric Authentication*, 761–767.

Wang, J. G., W. Y. Wang, A. Suwandy, and E. Sung. 2007. Fusion of palmprint and palm vein images for person recognition based on 'Laplacian palm' feature, *IEEE Computer Vision and Pattern Recognition Workshop on Biometrics*, 1–8.

Wang, L., and G. Leedham. 2006. Near- and far-infrared imaging for vein pattern biometrics, *Proc. of the IEEE Intl. Conf. on Video and Signal Based Surveillance*.

Weng, J., P. Cohen, and M. Herniou. 1992. Camera calibration with distortion models and accuracy evaluation, *IEEE Trans. Pattern Analysis and Machine Intelligence* **14**, 965–980.

Zhang, Z., and R. S. Blum. 1999. A categorization of multiscale-decomposition-based image fusion schemes with a performance study for a digital camera application, *Proc. of IEEE* **87**, 1315–1326.

# 4

# Face Recognition under the Skin

Pradeep Buddharaju and Ioannis Pavlidis

## 4.1 Introduction

Face recognition stands as the most appealing biometric modality, since it is the natural mode of identification among humans and is totally unobtrusive. At the same time, however, it is one of the most challenging modalities (Zhao et al. 2003). Several face recognition algorithms have been developed in recent years, mostly in the visible and a few in the infrared domains. A serious problem in visible face recognition is light variability, due to the reflective nature of incident light in this band. This can clearly be seen in Figure 4.1. The visible image of the same person in Figure 4.1(a) acquired in the presence of normal light appears totally different from that in Figure 4.1(b), which was acquired in low light.

Many of the research efforts in thermal face recognition were narrowly aiming to see in the dark or reduce the deleterious effect of light variability (Figure 4.1) (Socolinsky et al. 2001; Selinger and Socolinsky 2004). Methodologically, such approaches did not differ very much from face recognition algorithms in the visible band, which can be classified as appearance-based (Chen et al. 2003) and feature-based (Buddharaju et al. 2004). Recently attempts have been made to fuse the visible and infrared modalities to increase the performance of face recognition (Socolinsky and Selinger 2004a; Wang et al. 2004; Chen et al. 2005; Kong et al. 2005).

The authors have presented a physiological facial recognition method that promotes a different way of thinking about face recognition in the thermal infrared (Buddharaju et al. 2006, 2007; Buddharaju and Pavlidis 2008). This work has shown that facial physiological information, extracted in the form of a superficial vascular network, can serve as a good and time-invariant feature vector for face recognition. However, the methodology in that pilot work had some weak points. The recognition performance reported in past experiments

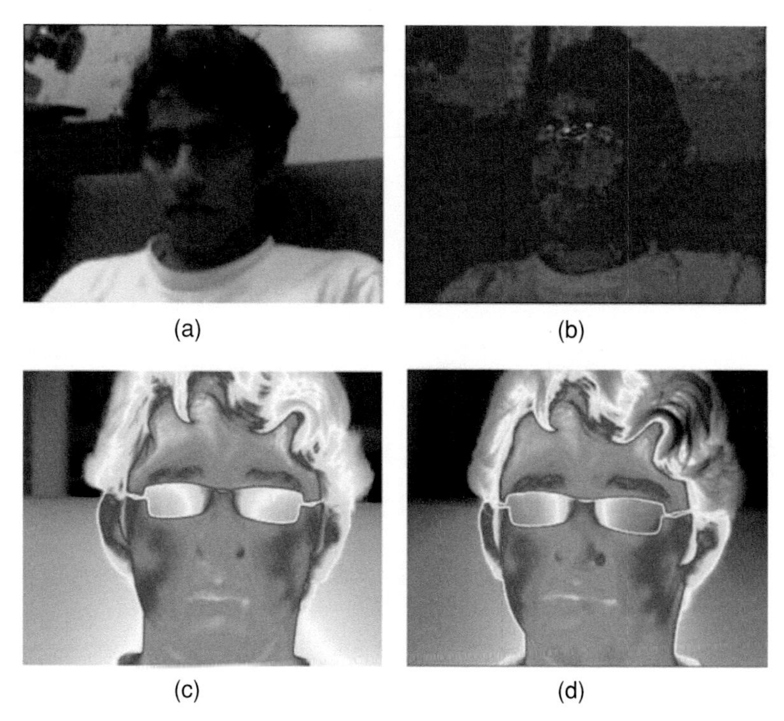


Figure 4.1. Example showing illumination effect on visible and thermal infrared images. All the images were acquired from the same subject at the same time. (a) Visible image in normal light. (b) Visible image in low light. (c) Thermal infrared image in normal light. (d) Thermal infrared image in low light.

(Buddharaju et al. 2007) can be substantially improved by curing these weaknesses. This chapter presents an advanced methodological framework that aspires to transform physiological face recognition from feasible to viable. Specifically, the main contributions in the chapter are:

- A new vessel segmentation post-processing algorithm that removes fake vascular contours detected by the top-hat vessel segmentation method
- A new vascular network matching algorithm that is robust to nonlinear deformations due to facial pose and expression variations
- Extensive comparative experiments to evaluate the performance of the new method with respect to previous methods.

The rest of the chapter is organized as follows. Section 4.2 presents an overview of the new methodology. Section 4.3 presents in detail the vessel segmentation post-processing algorithm. Section 4.4 discusses the new vascular

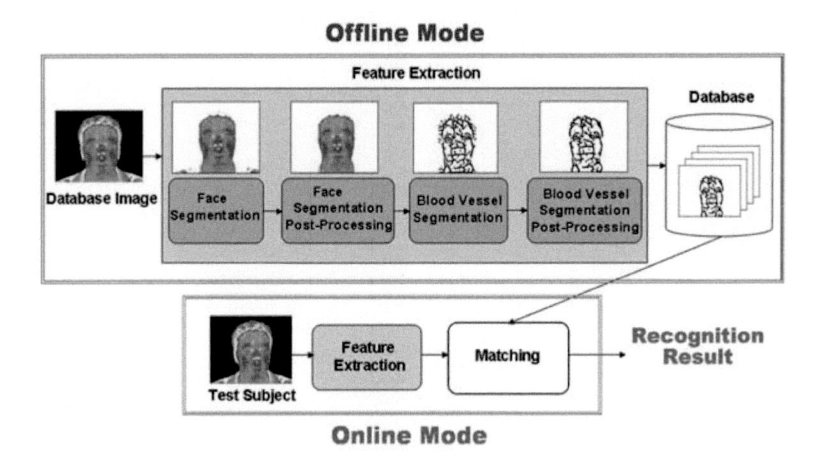


Figure 4.2. Methodological architecture.

network matching algorithm. Section 4.5 presents the experimental results and attempts a critical evaluation. The chapter concludes in Section 4.6.

## 4.2 Methodology

Figure 4.2 shows the methodological architecture. The method operates in the following two modes:

*Off-line Mode:* The thermal facial images are captured by a mid-wave infrared (MWIR) camera. For each subject to be registered in the database, the feature extraction algorithm extracts the feature vector form the facial image and links it to the subject's record. The feature extraction algorithm has four steps:

First, a Bayesian *face segmentation* separates facial tissue from background. Second, *face segmentation post-processing* corrects face segmentation errors, which are due to occasional overlapping between portions of the tissue and background distributions. Third, a top-hat *vessel segmentation* algorithm extracts the vascular network from the facial segment after an anisotropic diffuser clarifies fuzzy edges, due to heat diffusion. These three steps have been adopted from Buddharaju et al. (2007) and are briefly presented in this section. Fourth, a new *vessel segmentation post-processing* algorithm, which is one of this chapter's contributions, corrects vessel segmentation. The vessel segmenter occasionally is fooled by areas of high contrast (e.g., hair-line and skin edges) and reports them as vascular contours. These fake vascular contours participate in the matching process with deleterious effects.

*On-line Mode*: Given a query image, its vascular network is extracted using the feature extraction algorithm outlined in the off-line mode, and it is matched against vascular networks stored in the database. The new matching algorithm, which is another of this chapter's contributions, has two stages.

First, a *face pose estimation* algorithm estimates the pose of the incoming test image, which is required to calculate the vascular network deformation between it and database images. Second, the *dual bootstrap ICP matching* algorithm registers the test and database vascular networks. The matching score between the two depends on the amount of overlapping.

### 4.2.1 Face Segmentation

Because of its physiology, a human face consists of "hot" parts that correspond to tissue areas that are rich in vasculature and "cold" parts that correspond to tissue areas with sparse vasculature. This casts the human face as a bimodal temperature distribution entity, which can be modeled using a mixture of two Normal distributions. Similarly, the background can be described by a bimodal temperature distribution with walls being the "cold" objects and the upper part of the subject's body dressed in clothing being the "hot" object. The consistency of bimodality across subjects and image backgrounds is striking. We approach the problem of delineating facial tissue from background using a Bayesian framework since we have a priori knowledge of the bimodal nature of the scene.

We call $\theta$ the parameter of interest, which takes two possible values (skin $s$ or background $b$) with some probability. For each pixel $x$ in the image at time $t$, we draw our inference of whether it represents skin (i.e., $\theta = s$) or background (i.e., $\theta = b$) based on the posterior distribution $p^{(t)}(\theta|x_t)$ given by

$$p^{(t)}(\theta|x_t) = \begin{cases} p^{(t)}(s|x_t), & \text{when } \theta = s, \\ p^{(t)}(b|x_t) = 1 - p^{(t)}(s|x_t), & \text{when } \theta = b. \end{cases} \tag{4.1}$$

We develop the statistics only for skin, and then the statistics for the background can easily be inferred from Eq. (4.1).

According to Bayes' theorem,

$$p^{(t)}(s|x_t) = \frac{\pi^{(t)}(s) f(x_t|s)}{\pi^{(t)}(s) f(x_t|s) + \pi^{(t)}(b) f(x_t|b)}. \tag{4.2}$$

Here $\pi^{(t)}(s)$ is the prior skin distribution and $f(x_t|s)$ is the likelihood for pixel $x$ representing skin at time $t$. In the first frame ($t = 1$) the prior distributions for skin and background are considered equiprobable:

$$\pi^{(1)}(s) = \frac{1}{2} = \pi^{(1)}(b). \tag{4.3}$$

For $t > 1$, the prior skin distribution $\pi^{(t)}(s)$ at time $t$ is equal to the posterior skin distribution at time $t - 1$:

$$\pi^{(t)}(s) = p^{(t-1)}(s|x_{t-1}). \tag{4.4}$$

The likelihood $f(x_t|s)$ of pixel $x$ representing skin at time $t \geq 1$ is given by

$$f(x_t|s) = \sum_{i=1}^{2} w_{s_i}^{(t)} N\left(\mu_{s_i}^{(t)}, \sigma_{s_i}^{2(t)}\right), \tag{4.5}$$

where the mixture parameters $w_{s_i}$(weight), $\mu_{s_i}$(mean), $\sigma_{s_i}^2$(variance), $i = 1, 2$, and $w_{s_2} = 1 - w_{s_1}$ of the bimodal skin distribution can be initialized and updated using the EM algorithm. For that, we select $N$ representative facial frames (off-line) from a variety of subjects that we call the training set. Then we manually segment, for each of the $N$ frames, skin (and background) areas, which yields $N_s$ skin (and $N_b$ background) pixels.

Sometimes, part of the subject's skin can be erroneously classified as background, and a few background patches can be erroneously marked as facial skin. This is due to occasional overlapping between portions of the skin and background distributions. The isolated nature of these mislabeled patches makes them easily correctable through post-processing. We apply a three-step post-processing algorithm to the binary segmented image. Using foreground (and background) correction, we find the mislabeled pixels in foreground (and background) and reassign them.

### 4.2.2 Blood Vessel Segmentation

Once a face is delineated from the rest of the scene, the segmentation of superficial blood vessels from the facial tissue is carried out in the following steps:

*Step 1:* Process the image to reduce noise and enhance the edges.
*Step 2:* Apply morphological operations to localize the superficial vasculature.

The weak sigmoid edges formed due to heat diffusion at the blood vessels can be handled effectively using anisotropic diffusion. The anisotropic diffusion filter is formulated as a process that enhances object boundaries by performing intraregion as opposed to interregion smoothing.

The mathematical equation that describes this process is

$$\frac{\partial I(\bar{x}, t)}{\partial t} = \nabla(c(\bar{x}, t)\nabla I(\bar{x}, t)). \tag{4.6}$$

In our case $I(\bar{x}, t)$ is the thermal infrared image, $\bar{x}$ refers to the spatial dimensions, $t$ is time, and $c(\bar{x}, t)$ is called the diffusion function. The discrete version of the anisotropic diffusion filter of Eq. (4.6) is as follows:

$$
\begin{aligned}
I_{t+1}(x, y) = I_t + \frac{1}{4} \times [&c_{N,t}(x, y)\nabla I_{N,t}(x, y) \\
&+ c_{S,t}(x, y)\nabla I_{S,t}(x, y) + c_{E,t}(x, y)\nabla I_{E,t}(x, y) \\
&+ c_{W,t}(x, y)\nabla I_{W,t}(x, y)].
\end{aligned}
\tag{4.7}
$$

The four diffusion coefficients and four gradients in Eq. (4.7) correspond to four directions (North, South, East, and West) with respect to the location $(x, y)$. Each diffusion coefficient and the corresponding gradient are calculated in the same manner. For example, the coefficient along the north direction is calculated as follows:

$$
c_{N,t}(x, y) = \exp\left(\frac{-\nabla I^2_{N,t}(x, y)}{k^2}\right), \tag{4.8}
$$

where $I_{N,t} = I_t(x, y+1) - I_t(x, y)$.

Image morphology is then applied on the diffused image to extract the blood vessels that are at a relatively low contrast compared with that of the surrounding tissue. We employ for this purpose a top-hat segmentation method, which is a combination of erosion and dilation operations. Top-hat segmentation takes one of two forms: white top-hat segmentation that enhances the bright objects in the image or black top-hat segmentation that enhances dark objects. In our case, we are interested in the white top-hat segmentation because it helps to enhance the bright ("hot") ridge-like structures corresponding to the blood vessels. In this method the original image is first opened and then this opened image is subtracted from the original image:

$$
\begin{aligned}
I_{\text{open}} &= (I \ominus S) \oplus S, \\
I_{\text{top}} &= I - I_{\text{open}},
\end{aligned}
\tag{4.9}
$$

where $I$, $I_{\text{open}}$, $I_{\text{top}}$ are the original, opened, and white top-hat segmented images respectively, S is the structuring element, and $\ominus$, $\oplus$ are morphological erosion and dilation operations, respectively.

## 4.3 Vessel Segmentation Post-Processing

A vessel's superficial thermal imprint is at a higher temperature than surrounding tissue due to convective heat produced from the flow of "hot" arterial blood.

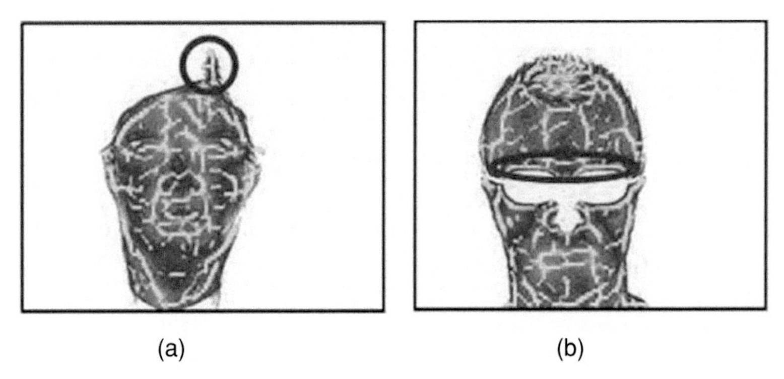
(a) (b)

Figure 4.3. Errors from the top-hat segmentation algorithm for vasculature extraction: (a) outliers due to facial hair; (b) outliers due to glasses.

The top-hat segmentation algorithm is successful in localizing vessels because it targets transitions from hot to cold to hot. In some instances, such transitions are not due to the presence of vessels. Examples include tissue between hair lines or tissue between glasses and eyebrows (see Figure 4.3).

It is essential to detect and remove these outliers from the vascular network before applying a matching algorithm. To study in depth the properties of these outliers, the authors selected 25 representative subjects from the University of Houston dataset and analyzed the segmentation errors. Specifically, the authors identified the locations of both true vessels and outliers. Then they drew measurement lines across each of the vessels and outliers and plotted the corresponding temperature profiles. They noticed that the variance between minimum and maximum temperature values was much larger in outliers than in true vessels. Indeed, the gradient in outliers is quite steep (several degrees C), as it is formed between facial hair or glasses and tissue. By contrast, in true vessels, the gradient is quite small (only tenths of degrees C), as it is formed between the projection of the vessel's lumen and surrounding tissue (Figure 4.4). Figure 4.5 shows the difference between minimum and maximum temperatures ($T_{\max} - T_{\min}$) across all the selected line profiles from the 25 representative subjects.

The new segmentation post-processing algorithm removes outliers based on the above findings. Specifically, it carries out the following steps:

*Step 1:* Skeletonize the vascular network to one pixel thickness.

*Step 2:* Draw a normal parallelogram across each skeleton pixel and gather all the pixels covered by this parallelogram.

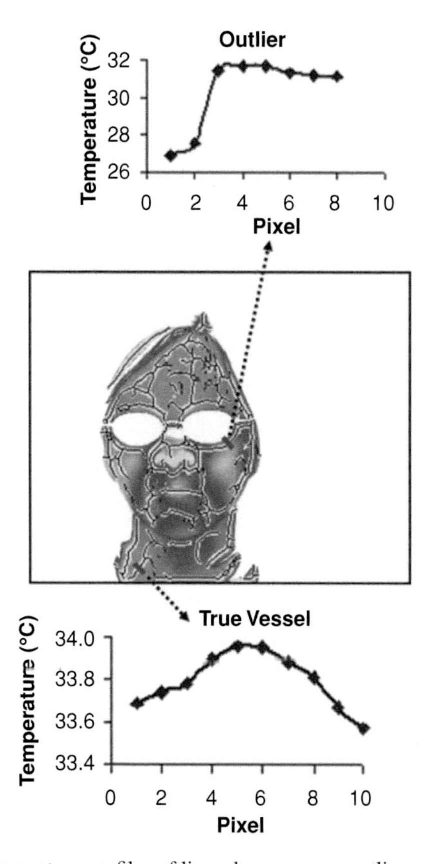


Figure 4.4. Temperature profiles of lines drawn across outliers and true vessels.

*Step 3:* Apply $K$-Means (with $K = 2$) on the pixels covered by this parallelogram. If the difference between the centers of each cluster is greater than 1.5, then mark it as an outlier pixel.

*Step 4:* Remove all the branches from the vascular network that have more than 50% of their pixels marked as outliers.

After deleting the outliers from the vascular network, the remaining vascular map can be stored in the database.

## 4.4 Vascular Network Matching

The matching method presented in Buddharaju et al. (2007) could not cope with nonlinearities in the deformation of the vascular network, because of variations

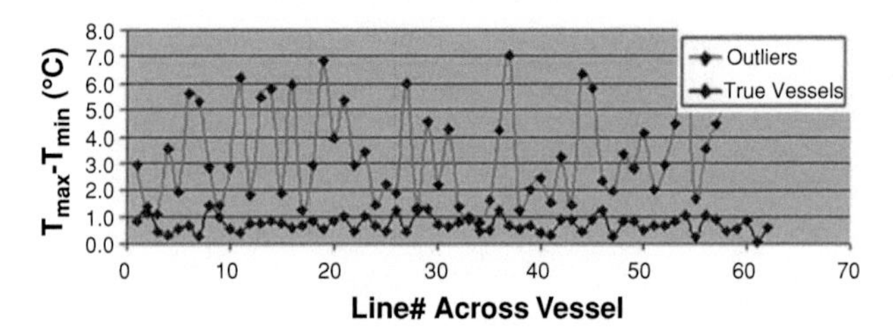


Figure 4.5. Difference between minimum and maximum temperatures for all the selected line profiles.

in facial pose and expressions. This chapter presents a new vascular network matching algorithm that is robust to nonlinear deformations.

### 4.4.1 Registration of Vascular Networks

The aim is to register the vascular network of the test image with that of the database image, so that they can be aligned. The Iterative Closest Point (ICP) algorithm has appealing properties for point-based registration (Besl and McKay 1992). ICP requires proper initialization, as different instantiations of the algorithm use different combinations of image points, distance metrics, and transformation models. In Stewart et al. (2003), developed a variation of the ICP algorithm, called dual bootstrap ICP, that works well when initialization provides just a "toe hold" on the correct estimate of the transformation and successfully registers elongated structures such as vasculature. Specifically, they reported good results from registration of retinal vascular images in the visible band. Since superficial vasculature extracted in the thermal infrared has morphological resemblance to retinal vasculature in the visible, the authors adopted the dual bootstrap algorithm for the registration task at hand.

After successful registration of the test and database vascular images, the matching score is computed based on the number of overlapping vessel pixels. If $I_{\text{test}}$ represents the test vascular image with $N_{\text{test}}$ vessel pixels, and $I_{\text{db}}$ represents the database vascular image with $N_{\text{db}}$ vessel pixels, the matching score is

$$Score = \frac{N_{\text{overlap}}}{\max(N_{\text{test}}, N_{\text{db}})} \times 100, \tag{4.10}$$

where $N_{\text{overlap}}$ represents the number of vessel pixels in $I_{\text{test}}$ with a corresponding vessel pixel in $I_{\text{db}}$ within a certain distance.

Figure 4.6 shows some examples of the performance of the dual bootstrap ICP algorithm in registering vascular images in the thermal infrared. The example at the bottom row of the figure features substantial pose variation between

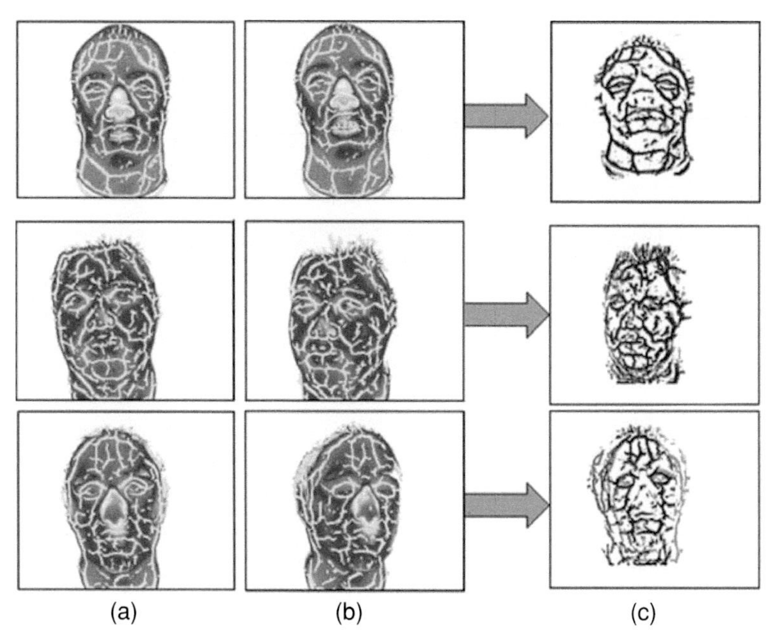


Figure 4.6. Registration performance examples: (a) test vascular networks; (b) database vascular networks; (c) registration results.

the test and database images. The larger the pose variation, the more difficult it becomes for the dual bootstrap ICP to cope successfully. This can be improved by estimating the pose of the test and database images and setting accordingly the threshold value (*Thr*) used to accept or reject the test image. The pose estimation algorithm that was developed for this purpose is presented in the next section.

### 4.4.2 Face Pose Estimation

At a neutral pose ($Pose = 0°$) the nose is at the center of the face; that is, the position of the nose is halfway between the left and right ends of the face. From the face segmentation algorithm presented in Buddharaju et al. (2007), one can find the left and right ends of the face. Hence, if one localizes the nose, he or she can estimate the facial pose.

In a thermal infrared image, the nose is typically at a gradient with its surroundings, as shown in Figure 4.7. This is because of the tissue's shape (tubular cavity), its composition (cartilage), and the forced circulation of air, due to breathing. The combination of all three creates a nasal thermal signature that is different than that of the surrounding solid, soft tissue.

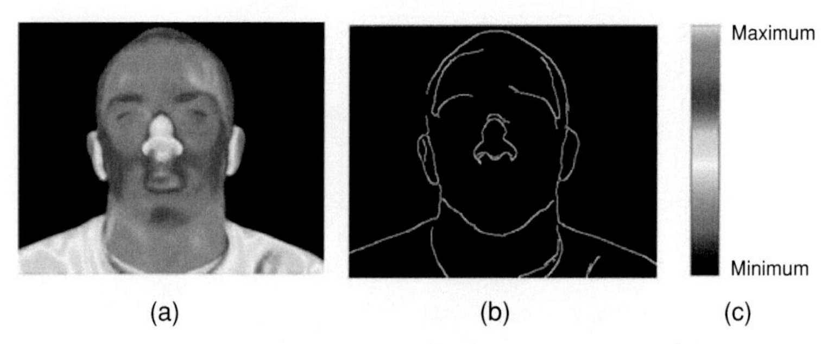


Figure 4.7. Nose edge extraction from thermal facial image: (a) thermal facial image; (b) ridges extracted using the Canny edge detection algorithm; (c) color map.

By using a standard edge detection algorithm, one can extract the nose edges from the facial image. The next step is to search for the nose edge model in the facial edge map. The authors used a Hausdorff-based matching algorithm to localize the nose model in the face edge image (Huttenlocher et al. 1993). Figure 4.8 shows performance examples of the face pose estimation algorithm.

## 4.5 Experiments

The authors conducted several experiments to validate the performance of the new physiological face recognition method. This section presents the experimental setup and results in detail.

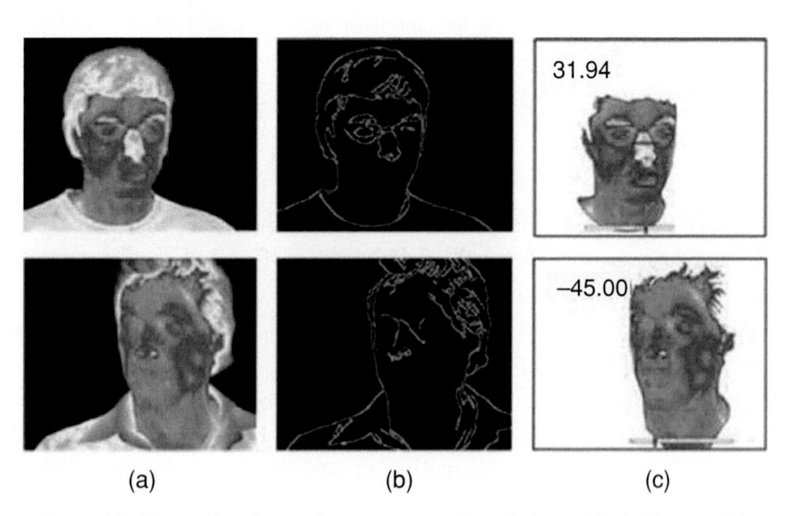


Figure 4.8. Pose estimation performance examples: (a) thermal facial images; (b) nose detection using Hausdorff-based matching; (c) pose estimates.

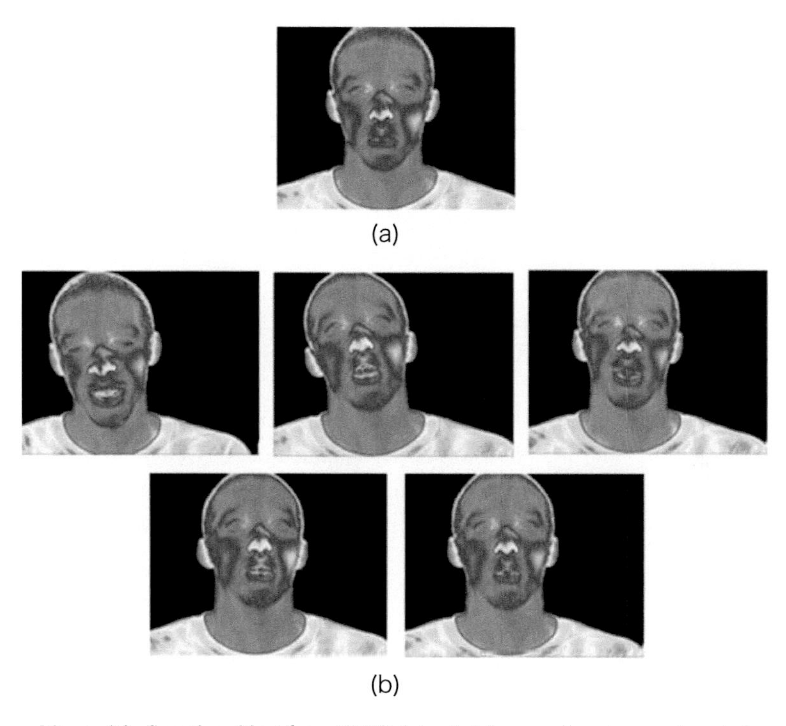


Figure 4.9. Sample subject from FEDS dataset: (a) one gallery image at neutral pose and expression; (b) five probe images at varying facial expressions.

### 4.5.1 Experiments on the University of Houston Database

The authors collected a substantial thermal facial dataset for the purposes of this evaluation. This set, known as the University of Houston (UH) database, has thermal facial images of varying expressions and poses from 300 subjects. The images were captured using a high-quality mid-wave infrared (MWIR) camera.

#### 4.5.1.1 Facial Expression Dataset

To test the performance of the new method in the presence of varying facial expressions between gallery and probe images, the authors created the facial expression dataset (FEDS) out of the UH database as follows: From each of the 300 subjects one frontal facial image at $0^{\circ}$ pose and neutral expression was used as a gallery image. Then five different facial images at $\sim 0^{\circ}$ pose but with varying facial expressions were used as probe images for each subject. Hence, FEDS has a total of 300 gallery images and 1500 probe images from 300 subjects. Figure 4.9 shows a sample subject set from FEDS.

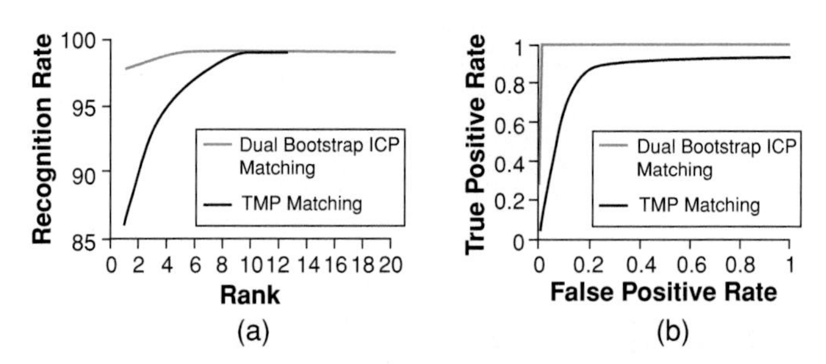


Figure 4.10. Experimental results on the FEDS dataset using dual bootstrap ICP versus TMP matching: (a) CMC curves; (b) ROC curves.

Figures 4.10(a) and 4.10(b) show, respectively, the Cumulative Math Characteristic (CMC) and Receiver Operating Characteristic (ROC) curves of the FEDS experiments using the thermal minutia point (TMP) matching algorithm reported in Buddharaju et al. (2007) (a fingerprinting variety) versus the dual bootstrap ICP matching algorithm.

The results demonstrate that the dual bootstrap ICP outperforms the TMP matching algorithm. In the case of TMP matching, the CMC curve shows that rank 1 recognition is 86%, whereas for the for dual bootstrap ICP is 97%. Also, the dual bootstrap ICP matching method achieves a high positive detection rate at very low false detection rates, as shown in Figure 4.10(b). This indicates that the ICP matching algorithm is highly robust to deformations caused in the vascular network by facial expression variations.

#### 4.5.1.2 Facial Pose Dataset

To test the performance of the new method in the presence of varying poses between gallery and probe images, the authors created the facial pose dataset (FPDS) out of the UH database as follows: From each of the 300 subjects one frontal facial image at $0^{\circ}$ pose and neutral expression was used as a gallery image. Then four different facial images at neutral facial expression but at varying poses between $-30^{\circ}$ and $30^{\circ}$ were used as probe images. Hence, FPDS has a total of 300 gallery images and 1200 probe images from 300 subjects. Figure 4.11 shows a sample subject set from FPDS.

Figures 4.12(a) and 4.12(b)show the results of the FPDS experiments using the dual bootstrap ICP matching algorithm. The results demonstrate that the algorithm copes well with facial pose variations between gallery and probe images. Specifically, the CMC curve shows that rank 1 recognition is 89%, and the ROC curve shows that it requires a false acceptance rate over 5% to reach a positive acceptance rate above the 90% range. One can notice that the false acceptance rate on FPDS experiments is a bit higher than on FEDS

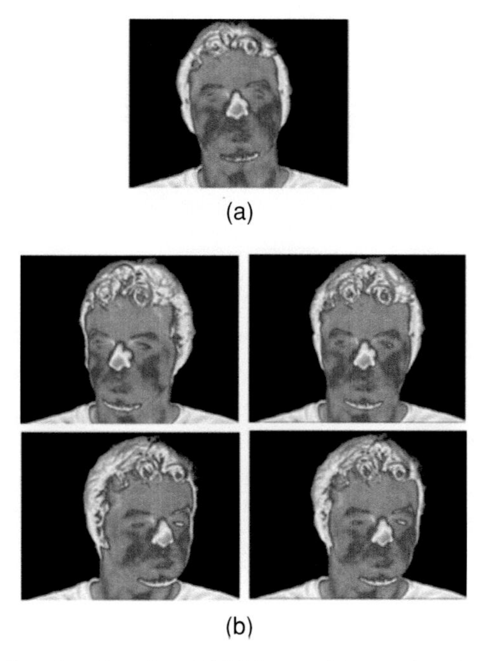


Figure 4.11. Sample subject from FPDS dataset: (a) one gallery image at neutral pose and expression; (b) four probe images at varying poses.

experiments. This is to be expected, as variations in pose typically cause more nonlinear deformations in the vascular network than those caused by variations in facial expressions.

### 4.5.2 Experiments on the University of Notre Dame Database

A major challenge associated with thermal face recognition is recognition performance over time (Socolinsky and Selinger 2004b). Facial thermograms

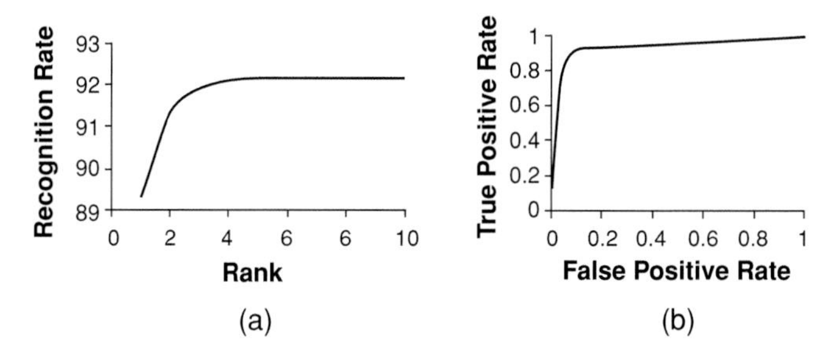


Figure 4.12. Experimental results on the FPDS dataset using the dual bootstrap ICP matching algorithm: (a) CMC curve; (b) ROC curve.

may change depending on the physical condition of the subject, making it difficult to acquire similar features for the same person over time. Previous face recognition methods in the thermal infrared that used raw thermal data reported degraded performance over time (Chen et al. 2003, 2005). Facial physiological information, however, remains invariant to physical conditions because the thermal contrast between the vascular and surrounding pixels is maintained (natural constant).

Since most of the subjects in the UH database had images collected during the same session, no statistically significant quantification of the low-permanence problem was possible. For this reason, the authors obtained clearance to apply the method on another data set, that of the University of Notre Dame (UND) (at the University of Notre Dame n.d.). This database has a large collection of visible and thermal facial images acquired with a time gap. The database consists of 2294 images acquired from 63 subjects during nine different sessions under specific lighting (LF: central light turned off, LM: all three lights on) and facial expression conditions (FA: neutral expression, FB: smiling expression).

The database is divided into four different gallery and probe sets (Chen et al. 2003): LF + FA, LF + FB, LM + FA, and LM + FB. Each of the gallery sets (e.g., LF–FA) can be tested against the other three probe sets (e.g., LF–FB, LM–FA, and LM–FB). Thus, 12 different pairs of gallery and probe sets were used for testing. The performance of the new dual-bootstrap ICP matching algorithm was compared to that of TMP matching (Buddharaju et al. 2007) and PCA matching (Chen et al. 2003) algorithms. Table 4.1 summarizes the rank 1 recognition results of these algorithms on each of the 12 experiments. Each entry in the left column of the table corresponds to a gallery set, and each entry in the top row corresponds to a probe set. From the table, it can be clearly seen that the new matching algorithm yields better recognition results even in the presence of time and temperature variations, thus outperforming the TMP (legacy physiology–based) and PCA (legacy raw thermal–based) recognition algorithms.

### 4.5.3 Experiments on the University of Arizona Database

The authors have also used data from stress experiments carried out at the University of Arizona (UA). These data, although acquired within a few minutes for each subject, feature dramatic changes in the facial thermal map due to the onset of stress. In fact, in a few minutes much more variability is present than the one in the UND, which took months to assemble. The length of each experiment is approximately 20 minutes. For each subject, the authors extracted about five, equally time-spaced frames from the interview. One sample subject

Table 4.1. *Rank1 Recognition Performance of Dual Bootstrap Iterative Closest Point (DBICP) Vascular Network Matching Algorithm, TMP Matching Algorithm (Buddharaju et al. 2007), and PCA Algorithm (Chen et al. 2005) on Each of the 12 Experiments on the UND Database*

| | Probe | | | |
|---|---|---|---|---|
| Gallery | FA–LF | FA–LM | FB–LF | FB–LM |
| FA–LF | –<br>–<br>– | 86.54% (DBICP)<br>82.65% (TMP)<br>78.74% (PCA) | 84.38% (DBICP)<br>80.77% (TMP)<br>76.83% (PCA) | 83.33% (DBICP)<br>81.33% (TMP)<br>75.77% (PCA) |
| FA–LM | 83.65% (DBICP)<br>81.46% (TMP)<br>79.23% (PCA) | –<br>–<br>– | 84.24% (DBICP)<br>79.38% (TMP)<br>75.22% (PCA) | 82.45% (DBICP)<br>80.25% (TMP)<br>73.56% (PCA) |
| FB–LF | 85.48% (DBICP)<br>80.27% (TMP)<br>74.88% (PCA) | 88.87% (DBICP)<br>81.92% (TMP)<br>76.57% (PCA) | –<br>–<br>– | 85.82% (DBICP)<br>80.56% (TMP)<br>74.23% (PCA) |
| FB–LM | 83.39% (DBICP)<br>80.67% (TMP)<br>69.56% (PCA) | 87.34% (DBICP)<br>82.25% (TMP)<br>74.58% (PCA) | 85.56% (DBICP)<br>79.46% (TMP)<br>78.33% (PCA) | –<br>–<br>– |

from the database is shown in Figure 4.13. It can clearly be seen from the visualization on forehead and neck that the thermal map changed significantly between database (Figure 4.13[a]) and test images (Figure 4.13[b]).

Figure 4.14(a) shows the CMC and Figure 4.14(b) the ROC curves of the UA experiments using the dual bootstrap ICP versus the TMP matching algorithms. The results demonstrate that the dual bootstrap ICP outperforms the TMP matching algorithm (Buddharaju et al. 2007). In the case of TMP matching, the CMC curve shows that rank 1 recognition is 83.6%, whereas for ICP it is 93.2%. Also, the dual bootstrap ICP matching method achieves a high positive detection rate at very low false detection rates, as is shown in Figure 4.14(b).

## 4.6 Conclusions

This chapter presents new algorithms that substantially improve the performance of physiology-based face recognition in the thermal infrared. Specifically, a vascular network post-processing algorithm removes fake contours detected by vessel segmentation algorithm. A new vascular network matching algorithm can cope with nonlinear deformations between test and database vascular networks.

The experimental results obtained with the UH, UND, and UA databases, which are nontrivial sets, confirm the superiority of the new method.

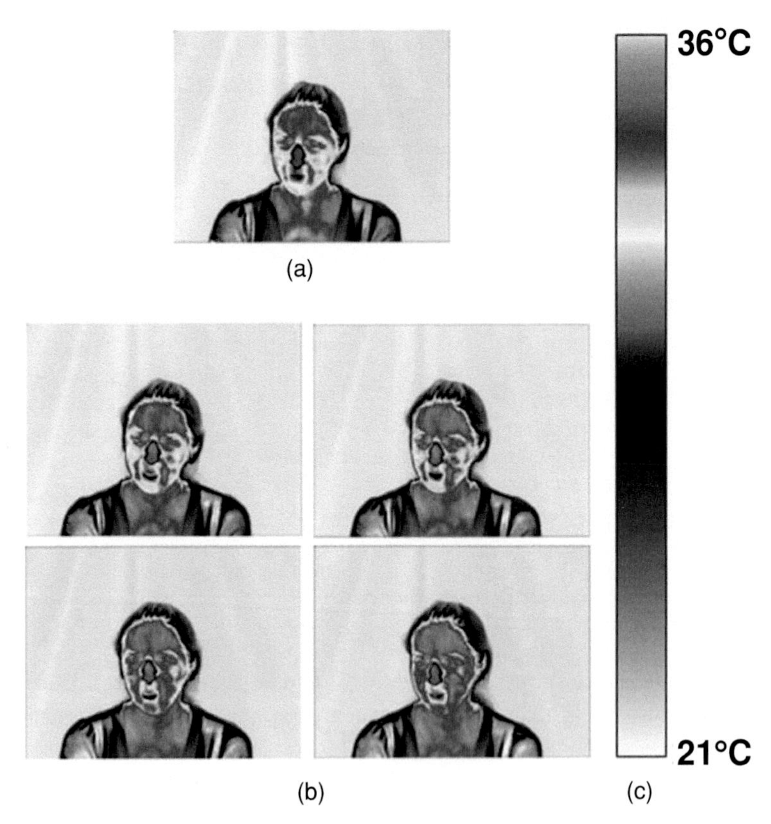


Figure 4.13. Sample subject from UA dataset: (a) one database image extracted at 2 minutes 6 seconds of the interview; (b) four test images extracted at 6 minutes, 9 minutes 18 seconds, 13 minutes 22 seconds, and 17 minutes 40 seconds of the interview, respectively. (c) Thermal color map used for visualization.

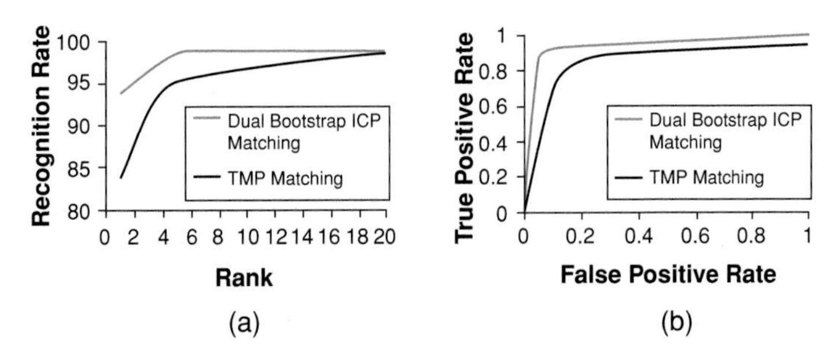


Figure 4.14. Results of the experiments on the UA database using dual bootstrap ICP versus TMP matching: (a) CMC curves; (b) ROC curves.

## Acknowledgments

The authors would like to thank the University of Notre Dame for kindly providing its facial database. They also acknowledge Dr. Judee Burgoon at the University of Arizona for designing and conducting the stress experiments, as part of a collaborative DOD effort. This research was supported in part by a contract from the Defense Academy for Credibility Assessment (DACA). The views expressed in the chapter do not necessarily represent the views of the funding agencies.


## References


T. C. V. L. at the University of Notre Dame. Biometrics database distribution. http://www.nd.edu/ cvrl/.

Besl, P., and N. McKay. 1992. A method for registration of 3-d shapes. *IEEE Transactions on Pattern Analysis and Machine Intelligence*, **14**(2), 239–256.

Buddharaju, P., and I. Pavlidis. 2008. Face recognition beyond the visible spectrum. In N. Ratha and V. Govindaraju, editors, *Advances in Biometrics: Sensors, Algorithms and Systems*, chapter 9, pages 157–180. Springer.

Buddharaju, P., I. Pavlidis, and I. Kakadiaris. 2004. Face recognition in the thermal infrared spectrum. In *Proceedings of the Joint IEEE Workshop on Object Tracking and Classification Beyond the Visible Spectrum*, Washington, D.C.

Buddharaju, P., I. Pavlidis, and P. Tsiamyrtzis. 2006. Pose-invariant physiological face recognition in the thermal infrared spectrum. In *Proceedings of the 2006 IEEE Conference on Computer Vision and Pattern Recognition*, pages 53–60, New York.

Buddharaju, P., I. Pavlidis, P. Tsiamyrtzis, and M. Bazakos. 2007. Physiology-based face recognition in the thermal infrared spectrum. *IEEE Transactions on Pattern Analysis and Machine Intelligence*, **29**(4), 613–626.

Chen, X., P. Flynn, and K. Bowyer. 2003. PCA-based face recognition in infrared imagery: baseline and comparative studies. In *Proceedings of the IEEE International Workshop on Analysis and Modeling of Faces and Gestures*, pages 127–134, Nice, France.

Chen, X., P. Flynn, and K. Bowyer. 2005. IR and visible light face recognition. *Computer Vision and Image Understanding*, **99**(3), 332–358.

Huttenlocher, D. P., G. A. Klanderman, and W. A. Rucklidge. 1993. Comparing images using the Hausdorff distance. *IEEE Transactions on Pattern Analysis and Machine Intelligence*, **15**(9), 850–863.

Kong, S. G., J. H. anf B. R. Abidi, J. Paik, and M. A. Abidi. 2005. Recent advances in visual and infrared face recognition – a review. *Computer Vision and Image Understanding*, **97**(1), 103–135.

Selinger, A., and D. Socolinsky. 2004. Face recognition in the dark. In *Proceedings of the Joint IEEE Workshop on Object Tracking and Classification Beyond the Visible Spectrum*, Washington, D.C.

Socolinsky, D., and A. Selinger. 2004. Thermal face recognition in an operational scenario. In *Proceedings of the IEEE Computer Society Conference on Computer Vision and Pattern Recognition*, volume 2, pages 1012–1019, Washington, D.C.

Socolinsky, D., and A. Selinger. 2004. Thermal face recognition over time. In *Proceedings of the 17th International Conference on Pattern Recognition*, volume 4, pages 23–26.

Socolinsky, D., L. Wolff, J. Neuheisel, and C. Eveland. 2001. Illumination invariant face recognition using thermal infrared imagery. In *Proceedings of the IEEE Computer Society Conference on Computer Vision and Pattern Recognition*, volume 1, pages 527–534, Kauai, Hawaii.

Stewart, C. V., C. Tsai, and B. Roysam. 2003. The dual-bootstrap iterative closest point algorithm with application to retinal image registration. *IEEE Transactions on Medical Imaging*, **22**(11), 1379–1394.

Wang, J.-G., E. Sung, and R. Venkateswarlu. 2004. Registration of infrared and visible-spectrum imagery for face recognition. In *Proceedings of the Sixth IEEE International Conference on Automatic Face and Gesture Recognition*, pages 638–644, Seoul, Korea.

Zhao, W., R. Chellappa, P. J. Phillips, and A. Rosenfeld. 2003. Face recognition: a literature survey. *ACM Computing Surveys (CSUR)*, **35**(4), 399–458.

# PART II

# Fusion Methods in Multibiometric Systems

# 5
# Biometric Authentication: A Copula-Based Approach

Satish G. Iyengar, Pramod K. Varshney,
and Thyagaraju Damarla

## 5.1 Introduction

The process of authentication involves verifying the identity of a person claiming access to one or more resources of a system. Authentication systems can be based on passwords, security tokens, biometrics, or combinations of them (O'Gorman 2003). Passwords are words, phrases, or alphanumeric personal identification numbers (PINs) that serve as short-form indicators of a person's identity. They are usually created by authorized users during the enrollment or registration phase (e.g., creating computer user accounts) and are kept secret from others. Security tokens, on the other hand, are physical devices that the users are required to carry to be allowed access to the system. More recent designs of automatic human recognition systems involve the use of features such as face, fingerprints, iris, or behavioral traits such as gait or rate of keystrokes. For example, in building access control applications, a person's face may be matched to templates stored in a database consisting of all enrolled users. Decision to allow or deny entry is then taken based on the similarity score generated by the face-matching algorithm. Such security systems that rely on biometrics have several advantages over the more conventional ones (passwords or security tokens). For example, a PIN, if leaked, may be used by an unauthorized person causing serious security concerns. However, a person's physical signature belongs only to that individual and is extremely difficult if not impossible to emulate. Further, biometric systems may be more convenient and user friendly because there is no password to remember or any token to carry. See O'Gorman (2003) for a more detailed comparison of the three approaches, especially in terms of security achievable, convenience of use, and the overall cost of the system.

However, several limitations exist. Biometric traits such as face and voice change with age. One may be required to update the systems' database to

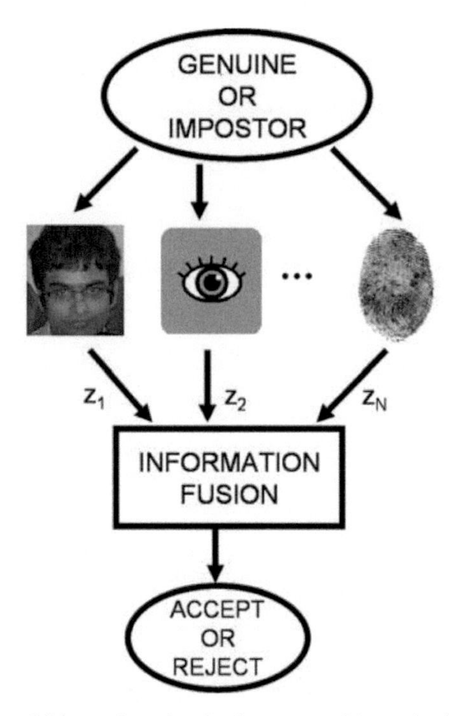


Figure 5.1. A multibiometric authentication system. Biometric signatures of disparate modalities such as face, iris, and fingerprint are fused.

counter this time variabity. Environmental noise and noise in the acquisition system further affect the accuracy and reliability of the system. Overlap between physical features or interclass similarity (e.g., twins with identical facial features) limits the system's ability to distinguish between the classes. There also exist intraclass variations due to differences between the acquired biometric signature of an individual requesting the access and his or her template registered in the database. Apart from noise sources stated above, these differences may also stem from the psychological and behavioral variations of an individual at different instances in time. One method by which to overcome these limitations is to consider combining multiple sources of information. It may include fusing observations of disparate modalities (e.g., voice and face) or multiple features (extracted from the same biometric trait), multiple classifiers, or multiple samples of the same source. This method of fusing several biometric sources is called multibiometrics. Figure 5.1 shows a multimodal biometric system that considers fusion of disparate biometric signatures such as face, iris, and fingerprints.

Fusion of multimodal biometrics offers several advantages and new possibilities for system improvement. For example, in video/image-based person authentication systems for security and access control applications, the system performance degrades when the subjects age or when the lighting conditions are poor. The presence of an audio signature along with video would overcome many of these difficulties. In other words, *noise in one modality may not affect the other* and thus make the system more robust to noise. Second, multiple modalities may contain complementary information relevant to the verification task. The level of detail and the type of information present in one modality may be different from the other. An efficient system design is one that exploits this heterogeneity of the multimodal data set.

In this chapter we concern ourselves with the design of rules for fusing different biometric signatures and describe a new approach based on the statistical theory of copulas (Nelsen 1999). We first discuss how copula functions provide an efficient approach for modeling the joint statistics of data acquired from disparate sources. Fusion algorithms are then developed using the copula-derived models. We also consider the problem of analyzing the effect of intermodal dependence on system performance and describe some of our recent results (Iyengar et al. 2009; Iyengar 2009b). The chapter provides a detailed exposition on copula theory and its applicability to biometric authentication. We also note that although Figure 5.1 implies fusion of multimodal observations, the developed framework is general enough to handle other problems where heterogeneity in the acquired data is due to multiple samples, algorithms, or multiple classifiers; that is, the measurements $\{z_n\}_{n=1}^{N}$ in Figure 5.1 may also denote multiple samples or multiple features (extracted from the same modality) or output of multiple algorithms that are combined (jointly processed) at a fusion center. Thus, copula theory enables the development of a general mathematical framework for heterogeneous information fusion.

## 5.2 Fusion of Multibiometrics

A biometric authentication task is essentially a binary hypotheses-testing problem in which data (biometric signatures) from several modalities are fused to test for the hypothesis $H_1$ against $H_0$, where

$H_0$: claimant an impostor

$H_1$: claimant a genuine user.

Fusion of information from multiple biometric sensors can be classified in three different levels:

- Data- or feature-level fusion: Local observations from each source are processed directly or are transformed so that only relevant features can be extracted and retained for further processing. Resultant features from each source are then combined to obtain a global decision regarding the identity of the human under test. This method is most efficient in terms of performance because it involves minimum information loss. However, feature sets obtained are typically of high dimensionality, and one often suffers from the well-known *curse of dimensionality*. Further, the design of a fusion rule may not be straightforward as the acquired feature set may not be commensurate (e.g., audio and corresponding video features).
- Score-level fusion: Fusion of match scores is second to the feature-level fusion in terms of performance efficiency as the input undergoes moderate information loss in its transformation to similarity scores. Similarity (or dissimilarity) scores are obtained for each modality by matching the input data (or features) to those stored in the system's database. The approach is then to fuse the scores thus obtained by matching the input at each source to its corresponding template. The range of score values may be different for different matching algorithms. One of the challenges in the design of a score-level fusion rule is to incorporate this heterogeneity.
- Decision-level fusion: Local decisions regarding the presence or absence of a genuine user are obtained by independently processing each modality. Binary data thus obtained for each source are subsequently fused to make a global decision. Significant reduction in system complexity can be obtained. However, this is at the cost of potentially high information loss due to the binary quantization of individual features.

Further, methods for multibiometric fusion can be classified into two broad categories (Jain et al. 2005): (a) the classification approach and (b) the combination approach. As an example, consider the problem of fusing information from an audio and a video sensor. Approach a involves training a classifier to jointly process the audiovisual features or matching scores and classify the claimant as a genuine user (Accept) or an impostor (Reject). The classifier is expected to be capable of learning the decision boundary irrespective of how the feature vectors or matching scores are generated, and thus no processing is required before feeding them into the classifier. Several classifiers based on neural networks, k-NN, and support vector machines (SVM) and that based on the likelihood principle have been used in the literature. On the other hand, approach b is to combine all the feature vectors or matching scores to generate a single scalar score, and a global decision regarding the presence or absence of a genuine user is based on this combined score. Thus, to achieve a meaningful combination, the features obtained from disparate modalities must be transformed or normalized to a *common* domain. Design of such a transform is not straightforward and is often data dependent and requires extensive empirical evaluation (Toh et al. 2004; Snelick et al. 2005; Jain et al. 2005).

Our interest in this chapter is in the likelihood ratio–based fusion approach (e.g., Ross et al. 2006; Wang and Bhanu 2006). The method does not require the data to be transformed so as to make them commensurable. Further, the method has a strong theoretical foundation and is proved optimal (in both the Neyman-Pearson [NP] and Bayesian sense) (Lehmann and Romano 2008). However, it requires complete knowledge of the joint probability density functions (PDFs) of multiple genuine and impostor features. Thus, estimation of these PDFs is one major challenge, and optimality suffers if there is mismatch between the true and the estimated joint PDFs.

Next, we discuss statistical modeling of heterogeneous data (features or scores).

## 5.3 Statistical Modeling of Heterogeneous Biometric Data

A parametric approach to statistical signal-processing applications such as detection, estimation, and tracking necessitate complete specification of the joint PDF of the observed samples. However, in many cases, derivation of the joint PDF becomes mathematically intractable. In problems such as fusion of multibiometrics, random variables associated with each biometric trait may follow probability distributions that are different from one another. For example, it is highly likely that features (or match scores) derived from the face and acoustic measurements follow disparate PDFs. The differences in physics governing each modality results in disparate marginal (univariate) distributions. There may also be differences in signal dimensionality, support, and sampling rate requirements across multiple modalities. Moreover, nonzero statistical dependence may exist between the different sources because of complex intermodal interactions. Deriving the underlying dependence structure is thus a challenge and may not always be possible. We can therefore identify the following two challenges when modeling the joint distribution of heterogeneous data:

1. Quantification of intermodal dependence and interactions
2. Derivation of the joint PDF of dependent heterogeneous measurements when each of the underlying marginals follow disparate distributions.

Prabhakar and Jain (2002) use nonparametric density estimation for combining the scores obtained from four fingerprint-matching algorithms and use likelihood ratio–based fusion to make the final decision. Several issues such as the selection of the kernel bandwidth and density estimation at the tails complicate this approach. More recently, Nandakumar et al. (2008) consider the use of multivariate Gaussian mixture models (GMM) for genuine and impostor score densities. They show that GMM models are easier to implement than kernel density estimators (KDE) while also achieving high system performance. However, GMM models require selecting the appropriate number of Gaussian components. The use of too many components may result in data overfitting, while using too few components may not approximate the true density well. The authors use a GMM fitting algorithm developed by Figueiredo and Jain (2002) that automatically estimates the number of components and the component parameters using the expectation-maximization (EM) algorithm and the minimum message length criterion.

We present in this chapter an alternative approach based on copula theory. We show how copula functions possess all the *ingredients* necessary for modeling the joint PDF of heterogeneous data. One of the main advantages of the copula approach is that it allows us to express the log-likelihood ratio as a sum of two terms: one that corresponds to the strategies employed by the individual modalities and the second to cross-modal processing. This allows us to separately quantify system performance due only to the model differences across the two hypotheses and that contributed only by the cross-modal interactions. Thus, it provides an elegant framework by which to study the effects of cross-modal interactions.

We now explain how copula theory can be exploited to address the modeling issues discussed above. We begin with the following definition:

**Definition 1** *A random vector* $\mathbf{Z} = \{Z_n\}_{n=1}^{N}$ *governing the joint statistics of an N-variate data set can be termed heterogeneous if the marginals* $Z_n$ *are nonidentically distributed.*

The goal is to construct the joint PDF $f(\mathbf{z})$ of the heterogeneous random vector $\mathbf{Z}$. Further, the variables $Z_n$ may exhibit statistical dependence so that $f(\mathbf{z}) \neq \prod_{n=1}^{N} f_n(z_n)$.

Characterizing multivariate statistical dependence is one of the most widely researched topics and has always been a difficult problem (Mari and Kotz 2001). The most commonly used bivariate measure, the Pearson's correlation $\rho$, captures only the linear relationship between variables and is a weak measure of dependence when dealing with non-Gaussian random variables. Two random variables $X$ and $Y$ are said to be uncorrelated if the covariance $\Sigma_{X,Y}$ (and thus $\rho$) is zero. Statistical independence has a stricter requirement in that $X$ and $Y$ are independent only if their joint density can be factored as the product of

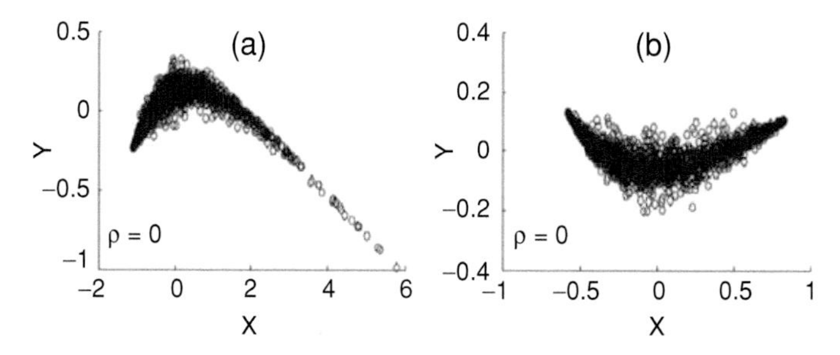


Figure 5.2. Scatter plots show that the correlation coefficient $\rho$ is a weak measure of dependence.

the marginals. In general, a zero correlation does not guarantee independence (except when the variables are jointly Gaussian). For example, we see that though dependence of one variable on the other is evident in the scatter plots (Figure 5.2a and b), the correlation coefficient is zero.

The problem is further compounded when dependent heterogeneous random variables with disparate PDFs are involved. Often one then chooses to assume multivariate Gaussianity or intermodal independence (also called the product model) to construct a tractable statistical model. A multivariate Gaussian model necessitates the marginals to be Gaussian and thus would fail to incorporate the true non-Gaussian marginal PDFs. Assuming statistical independence neglects intermodal dependence, thus leading to suboptimal solutions. It will be evident later (Section 5.6) that a copula-based model for dependent heterogeneous random vectors allows us to retain the marginal PDFs as well as *capture* the intermodal dependence *information*.

### 5.3.1 Copula Theory and Its Implications

Copulas are functions that couple multivariate joint distributions to their component marginal distribution functions. Sklar in 1959 first defined copula functions (Nelsen 1999; Kurowicka and Cooke 2006).

**Theorem 1** *(Sklar's Theorem)*
*Let $F(z_1, z_2, \dots z_N)$ be the joint cumulative distribution function (CDF) with continuous marginal CDFs $F_1(z_1)$, $F_2(z_2), \dots, F_N(z_N)$. Then there exists a copula function $C(\cdot)$ such that for all $z_1, z_2, \dots, z_n$ in $[-\infty, \infty]$,*

$$F(z_1, z_2, \dots, z_N) = C(F_1(z_1), F_2(z_2), \dots, F_N(z_N)) \tag{5.1}$$

*For continuous marginals, $C(\cdot)$ is unique; otherwise $C(\cdot)$ is uniquely determined on $Ran F_1 \times Ran F_2 \times \cdots \times Ran F_N$ where $Ran X$ denotes the range of $X$.*

*Conversely, if $C(\cdot)$ is a copula and $F_1(z_1)$, $F_2(z_2), \ldots, F_N(z_N)$ are marginal CDFs, then the function $F(\cdot)$ in (5.1) is a valid joint CDF with the marginals $F_1(z_1)$, $F_2(z_2), \ldots, F_N(z_N)$.*

Note that the copula function $C(u_1, u_2, \ldots, u_N)$ is itself a CDF with uniform marginals as $u_n = F_n(z_n) \sim \mathcal{U}(0, 1)$ (by probability integral transform).

The copula-based joint PDF of $N$ continuous random variables can now be obtained by taking an $N$th order derivative of (5.1) and is given as

$$f^c(\mathbf{z}) = \underbrace{\left(\prod_{n=1}^{N} f_n(z_n)\right)}_{f^p(\mathbf{z})} c(F_1(z_1), \ldots, F_N(z_N)), \tag{5.2}$$

where $\mathbf{z} = [z_1, z_2, \ldots, z_N]$, and we use the superscript $c$ to denote that $f^c(\mathbf{z})$ is the copula representation of the joint PDF $f(\mathbf{z})$ (i.e., $f(\mathbf{z}) = f^c(\mathbf{z})$). The function $f^p(\mathbf{z})$, in the right-hand side of (5.2), denotes the zero dependence or the product model, and $c(\cdot)$ in the same equation is the copula density function given by

$$c(\cdot) = \frac{\partial^N (C(u_1, u_2, \ldots, u_N))}{\partial u_1, \partial u_2, \ldots, \partial u_N}. \tag{5.3}$$

Thus, the copula function factorizes a joint distribution so that the dependence structure is separated from the product of marginals (5.2). The main advantage of such a representation is that it allows one to define joint distributions of multiple statistically dependent variables with disparate marginals. This is well suited for modeling heterogeneous random vectors. For example, consider two random variables $Z_1$ and $Z_2$ with disparate PDFs, say, *gamma*$(a, b)$ and *beta*$(c, d)$, respectively. The product distribution $f^p(z_1, z_2) = f(z_1) \cdot f(z_2)$ (which retains the marginal PDFs) can be reweighted by $c(\cdot)$ to incorporate statistical dependence that may exist between the two variables.

Note that we need to know the true copula density function $c(\cdot)$ to have an exact representation as in (5.2). We emphasize here that any joint PDF with continuous marginals can be written in terms of its copula density function. However, identifying the true copula is not a straightforward task. A common approach then is to select a copula density $k(\cdot)$ a priori and fit the given marginals (see Section 5.5 for more details). Model mismatch errors are introduced when $k(\cdot) \neq c(\cdot)$. Thus, although copula theory provides an approach, in principle, to derive joint PDFs with arbitrary marginals, the extent to which the intermodal dependence is characterized depends on how well the selected copula density $k(\cdot)$ fits the true dependence structure $c(\cdot)$.

In the following, we first consider system design and its performance analysis assuming the knowledge of the true copula density. This allows us to analyze the effects of intermodal dependence. We defer the discussion on joint PDF construction with potentially misspecified copula functions until Section 5.5.

## 5.4 Copula-Based Multibiometric Fusion

A decision theory problem consists of deciding which of the hypotheses $H_0, \ldots, H_k$ is true based on the acquired observation vector of, say, $L$ samples. As noted before (Section 5.2), a biometric authentication task can be formulated as a binary hypotheses testing problem ($H_1$ vs. $H_0$) for which the optimal rule (in both the Neyman-Pearson (NP) and Bayesian sense) is to compute the log-likelihood ratio ($\Lambda$) and decide in favor of $H_1$ when the ratio is larger than a predefined threshold ($\eta$),

$$\Lambda(\mathbf{z}) = \log \frac{f(\mathbf{z})}{g(\mathbf{z})} \overset{H_0}{\underset{H_0}{\gtrless}} \eta, \tag{5.4}$$

where $f(\mathbf{z})$ and $g(\mathbf{z})$, denote the joint PDFs of the random observation vector $\mathbf{z}$ under the hypotheses $H_1$ and $H_0$, respectively. The two error probabilities associated with a binary hypotheses testing problem are (1) the false alarm rate $P_F$, which is the probability of rejecting $H_0$ when $H_0$ is true ($P_F = Pr(\Lambda > \eta | H_0)$), and (2) probability of miss $P_M$, which indicates the rate of making a decision in favor of $H_0$ when in fact $H_1$ is true ($P_M = Pr(\Lambda < \eta | H_1)$).

In the NP setup, the threshold $\eta$ is selected to constrain $P_F$ to a value $\alpha < 1$ and at the same time minimize $P_M$.

### 5.4.1 Log-Likelihood Ratio Test Based on Copulas (LLRT-cop)

Using copula theory, an equivalent expression for the decision statistic $\Lambda(\mathbf{z})$ in (5.4) can be given as

$$\Lambda^c(\mathbf{z}) = \log \left( \prod_{n=1}^{N} \frac{f_n(z_n)}{g_n(z_n)} \right) + \log \left[ \frac{c_1(F_1(z_1), \ldots, F_N(z_N))}{c_0(G_1(z_1), \ldots, G_N(z_N))} \right], \tag{5.5}$$

where $F_n(z_n)$ ($f_n(z_n)$) and $G_n(z_n)$ ($g_n(z_n)$) denote the CDFs (PDFs) of $z_n$ under the two hypotheses $H_1$ and $H_0$, respectively. The copula density $c_i(\cdot)$ defines the intermodal dependence under each hypothesis $H_i$. The log-likelihood ratio test (LLRT) corresponding to a copula-based decision statistic such as $\Lambda^c(\mathbf{z})$ will henceforth be denoted as LLRT-cop.

### 5.4.2 Log-Likelihood Ratio Test for the Product Model (LLRT-P)

It is interesting to note the form of the test statistic in (5.5). The first term,

$$\Lambda^{p}(\mathbf{z}) = \log\left(\prod_{n=1}^{N} \frac{f_n(z_n)}{g_n(z_n)}\right), \tag{5.6}$$

is the statistic one obtains when the measurements $z_1, z_2, \ldots, z_N$ are statistically independent (under both hypotheses) or when dependence between them is deliberately neglected for simplicity. We denote the test based on the statistic in (5.6) (product model) as LLRT-P. In problems where the derivation of the joint density becomes mathematically intractable, tests are usually employed assuming independence between variables conditioned on each hypothesis. This naturally results in performance degradation.

It is evident from (5.5) and (5.6) that LLRT-cop involves additional computations to incorporate cross-modal interactions (the second term on the right-hand side of [5.5]). An important question then is, How much do we gain by this additional processing? Can we exactly quantify the performance gains (if any) achieved because of the increased computational load? In other words, we would like to know the effect of nonzero statistical dependence between the heterogeneous variables on fusion performance.

We next compare performances of LLRT-cop and LLRT-P detectors.

### 5.4.3 Performance Analysis

The asymptotic performance of a likelihood ratio test can be quantified using the Kullback-Leibler (KL) divergence (Cover and Thomas 2006), $D(f||g)$, between the PDFs $f(\mathbf{z})$ and $g(\mathbf{z})$:

$$D(f||g) = \int f(\mathbf{z}) \log\left(\frac{f(\mathbf{z})}{g(\mathbf{z})}\right) d\mathbf{z}, \tag{5.7}$$

where $D(f||g)$ measures how "different" $f(\mathbf{z})$ is relative to $g(\mathbf{z})$.[1] Further, (1) $D(f||g) \geq 0$ and (2) $D(f||g) = 0 \Leftrightarrow f = g$.

Now, for $L$ (independent) users of the system, through Stein's Lemma (Chernoff 1956; Cover and Thomas 2006, p. 383), we have for a fixed value of $P_M = \beta$, $(0 < \beta < 1)$,

$$\lim_{L\to\infty} \frac{1}{L} \log P_F = -D(f||g). \tag{5.8}$$

[1] The base of the logarithm is arbitrary. In this chapter, $\log(\cdot)$ denotes a natural logarithm unless defined otherwise.

The greater the value of $D(f||g)$, the faster is the convergence of $P_F$ to zero as $L \to \infty$. The KL divergence is thus indicative of the performance of a log-likelihood ratio test. Further, it is additive when the dependence across the heterogeneous observations is zero,

$$D\left(f^p||g^p\right) = \sum_{n=1}^{N} D(f_n||g_n), \tag{5.9}$$

where $D(f_n||g_n)$ is the KL divergence for a single modality $Z_n$.

For the special case of zero dependence between the biometric traits under one of the hypotheses, say, $H_0$ (i.e., $c_0(\cdot) = 1 \implies g(\mathbf{z}) = g^p(\mathbf{z})$), we have the following theorem.

**Theorem 2** *(Iyengar et al. 2009)*
*The KL divergence between the two competing hypotheses ($H_1$ vs. $H_0$) increases by a factor equal to the multi-information (under $H_1$) when dependence between the variables is taken into account:*

$$D(f||g) = D(f^p||g) + \underbrace{\mathcal{I}_1(Z_1; Z_2; \ldots; Z_N)}_{\geq 0}, \tag{5.10}$$

*where $\mathcal{I}_i(Z_1; Z_2; \ldots; Z_N)$ denotes the multi-information under the hypothesis $H_i$.*

Multi-information (Studený and Vejnarová 1999) $I_1(Z_1; Z_2; \ldots; Z_N)$ is given as

$$I_1(Z_1; Z_2; \ldots; Z_N) = \int_{\mathbf{z}} f(\mathbf{z}) \log \frac{f(\mathbf{z})}{f^p(\mathbf{z})} d\mathbf{z}. \tag{5.11}$$

Equation (5.11) can be expressed in terms of the copula density as

$$I_1(Z_1; Z_2; \ldots; Z_N) = \int_{\mathbf{z}} f(\mathbf{z}) \log \frac{f^p(\cdot)c_1(\cdot)}{f^p(\cdot)} d\mathbf{z} \tag{5.12}$$

$$= \mathbb{E}_f \log c_1(\cdot), \tag{5.13}$$

where $\mathbb{E}_f$ denotes the expectation operation with respect to the PDF $f(\mathbf{z})$.

The result in (5.10) is intuitively satisfying as $\mathcal{I}_1(Z_1; Z_2; \ldots; Z_N)$ (which reduces to the well-known mutual information for $N = 2$) describes the complete nature of dependence between the variables.

### 5.4.4 Effect of Statistical Dependence Across Multiple Biometrics on Fusion

Poh and Bengio (2005) on page 4384 note, "Despite considerable efforts in fusions, there is a lack of understanding on the roles and effects of correlation and variance (of both the client and impostor scores of base classifiers/experts)."

Although it is widely accepted that it is essential to correctly account for correlation in classifier design (Roli et al. 2002; Ushmaev and Novikov 2006), the exact link between classification performance and statistical dependence has not been established to the best of our knowledge. Recent contributions in this direction include, apart from Poh and Bengio (2005), Koval et al. (2007) and Kryszczuk and Drygajlo (2008).

Poh and Bengio (2005) studied the problem under the assumption of normality for both genuine and impostor features or scores and concluded that a positive value for the correlation coefficient is detrimental to the system. Contrary to this result, Koval et al. (2007) used error exponent analysis to conclude that a nonzero intermodal dependence always enhances system performance. Recently Kryszczuk and Drygajlo (2008) considered the impact of correlation for bivariate Gaussian features. They used Matusita distance as a measure of separation between the PDFs of the competing hypotheses. They showed that the conclusions of the above two studies do not hold in general; that is, they do not extend to arbitrary distributions.

Copula theory allows us to answer this important question and is general in treatment. The result in Theorem 2 makes no assumptions about the PDFs of biometric features. From Theorem 2,

$$D(f(\mathbf{z})||g(\mathbf{z})) \geq D(f^p(\mathbf{z})||g(\mathbf{z})) \tag{5.14}$$

because of the nonnegativity of the multiinformation. Thus, in addition to the model differences across the hypotheses, the presence of nonzero dependence further increases the interclass distinguishibility. However, the problem is more complicated when the variables exhibit statistical dependence under both hypotheses, and the result that *dependence can only enhance detection performance* is no longer true (Iyengar 2009b).

Next, we discuss methods to construct joint PDFs with potentially misspecified copula functions.

## 5.5 Joint PDF Construction Using Copulas

As pointed out earlier, the copula density $c(\cdot)$ (the true dependence structure) is often unknown. Instead, a copula density $k(\cdot)$ is chosen a priori from a valid set

Table 5.1. *Well-Known Copula Functions*

| Copula | $K(u_1, u_2)$ | Kendall's $\tau$ |
|---|---|---|
| Gaussian | $\Phi_N[\Phi^{-1}(u_1), \Phi^{-1}(u_2); \theta]$ | $\frac{2}{\pi}\arcsin(\theta)$ |
| Clayton | $[u_1^{-\theta} + u_2^{-\theta} - 1]^{-\frac{1}{\theta}}$ | $\frac{\theta}{\theta+2}$ |
| Frank | $-\frac{1}{\theta}\log\left(1 + \frac{(e^{-\theta u_1}-1)(e^{-\theta u_2}-1)}{e^{-\theta}-1}\right)$ | $1 - \frac{4}{\theta}\left[1 - \frac{1}{\theta}\int_0^{\theta}\frac{t}{e^t-1}dt\right]$ |
| Gumbel | $\exp\left[-\left\{(-\log u_1)^{\theta} + (-\log u_2)^{\theta}\right\}^{1/\theta}\right]$ | $1 - \frac{1}{\theta}$ |
| Product | $u_1.u_2$ | 0 |

$\mathcal{A} = \left[k_1(\cdot), \ldots, k_p(\cdot)\right]$ of copula functions. Several copula functions have been defined, especially in the econometrics and finance literature (e.g., Clemen and Reilly 1999); the popular ones among them are the Gaussian copula, Student's $t$ copula, and copula functions from the Archimedean family (see Table 5.1). The copula-based estimate of a joint PDF $f(\mathbf{z})$ has a form similar to (5.2) and is given as

$$\hat{f}(\mathbf{z}) = f^p(\mathbf{z})k(F_1(z_1), F_2(z_2), \ldots, F_n(z_n)) \tag{5.15}$$

$$= f^k(\mathbf{z}), \tag{5.16}$$

where the true but unknown copula density $c(\cdot)$ in (5.2) is replaced by a trial copula density $k(\cdot)$ chosen a priori. Thus, $f^k(\mathbf{z}) = f(\mathbf{z})$ if and only if $k(\cdot) = c(\cdot)$.

As an example, let $Z_1$ and $Z_2$ be the random variables associated with two heterogeneous biometrics; that is, they may follow disparate distributions. We wish to construct a copula-based estimate of the bivariate joint density $f(z_1, z_2)$. Table 5.1 lists some of the well-known bivariate copulas.[2] Each of these functions is parameterized by $\theta$, the "copula dependence" parameter.

The first step is to estimate the marginal PDFs $f_1(z_1)$ and $f_2(z_2)$ individually if they are unknown and then proceed to estimate the parameters of the copula density $k(\cdot)$. Note the reduction in multivariate PDF estimation complexity, as the estimation problem can now be split into two steps:

1. Estimation of the univariate marginal PDFs
2. Estimating the copula parameter $\theta$.

[2] $\Phi_N(\cdot,\cdot)$ and $\Phi(\cdot)$ in Table 5.1 denote standard bivariate and univariate Gaussian CDFs, respectively.

The use of nonparametric measures such as Kendall's $\tau$ (as opposed to maximum likelihood estimation [MLE]) to estimate the copula parameter further reduces the computational complexity.

In the following, we assume that the marginal PDFs are known or have been consistently estimated and concentrate only on copula fitting from the acquired data. The copula parameter $\theta$ can be estimated from the acquired measurements using any one of two methods: (1) estimation using nonparametric dependence measures or (2) maximum likelihood estimation.

### 5.5.1 Estimation Using Nonparametric Dependence Measures

Nonparametric rank correlations such as Kendall's $\tau$ and Spearman's $\rho^s$ measure concordance (a measure of dependence) between two random variables. Let $(z_1(i), z_2(i))$ and $(z_1(j), z_2(j))$ be two observations from a bivariate measurement vector $(Z_1, Z_2)$ of continuous random variables. The observations are said to be concordant if $(z_1(i) - z_1(j))(z_2(i) - z_2(j)) > 0$ and discordant if $(z_1(i) - z_1(j))(z_2(i) - z_2(j)) < 0$. Nelsen (1999) describes how copulas can be used to quantify concordance between random variables. Column three of Table 5.1 shows the relationship between Kendall's $\tau$ and $\theta$ for some of the well-known copula functions (Mari and Kotz 2001; Nelsen 1999; Kurowicka and Cooke 2006).

Now, given $L$ i.i.d. measurements $(z_1(l), z_2(l))$ $(l = 1, 2, \ldots, L)$, the observations are rank ordered, and a sample estimate of Kendall's $\tau$ is computed as

$$\hat{\tau} = \frac{c - d}{c + d}, \tag{5.17}$$

where $c$ and $d$ are the number of concordant and discordant pairs, respectively. Estimates of the copula dependence parameter $\theta$ then can be obtained from $\hat{\tau}$ using the relations given in Table 5.1.

Similar relations hold between $\rho^s$ and different copula functions.

### 5.5.2 Maximum Likelihood Estimation

MLE-based approaches can also be used to estimate $\theta$ and are discussed in Bouyé et al. (2000). As noted earlier, the copula representation allows one to estimate the marginals (if unknown) first and then the dependence parameter $\theta$ separately. This two-step method is known as the method of inference functions for margins (IFM) (Joe and Xu 1996). Given $L$ i.i.d. realizations $(z_1(l), z_2(l))_l$ $(l = 1, 2, \ldots, L)$,

$$\hat{\theta}_{\text{IFM}} = \operatorname{argmax} \sum_{l=1}^{L} \log k\left(F_1(z_1(l)), F_2(z_2(l)); \theta\right). \tag{5.18}$$

When the marginal CDFs in (5.18) are replaced by their empirical estimates,

$$\hat{F}_n(x) = \frac{1}{L} \sum_{l=1}^{L} I(X_l \leq x), \tag{5.19}$$

where $I(\mathcal{E})$ is an indicator of event $\mathcal{E}$, the method is called the canonical maximum likelihood (CML) method. Thus,

$$\hat{\theta}_{CML} = \text{argmax} \sum_{l=1}^{L} \log k \left( \hat{F}_1(z_1(l)), \hat{F}_2(z_2(l)); \theta \right). \tag{5.20}$$

Though we have discussed only the case of two modalities here, the method described above can be extended to construct joint PDFs when more than two modalities are involved. Clemen and Reilly (1999) discuss the multivariate Gaussian copula approach by computing pair-wise Kendall's $\tau$ between the variables. Multivariate Archimedean copulas are studied in Nelsen (1999).

Below we summarize the copula method for joint PDF estimation as a sequence of steps before presenting experimental results in the next section:

1. Estimate one-dimensional margninal PDFs (if unknown) from the acquired data.
2. Select a copula density $k(\cdot)$.
3. Given the multivariate data, estimate the dependence parameter $\theta$ of the selected copula density $k(\cdot)$ directly using (5.20). A second approach based on nonparametric concordance measures where one first computes the sample estimate of Kendall's $\tau$ using (5.17). An estimate of $\theta$ is then obtained using the relationship between Kendall's $\tau$ and $\theta$ (see column three of Table 5.1).

## 5.6 Experimental Results

In this section, we evaluate the performance of the copula-based fusion rules using real data. We use the publicly available NIST-BSSR 1 database (NIST 2004) developed by the National Institute of Standards and Technology. The database includes similarity scores from two commercial face recognizers and one fingerprint system and is partitioned into three sets. We use the NIST-face dataset, which consists of match scores from 3000 subjects in our experiment. Two samples (match scores) are available per subject, thus resulting in a total of $(2 \times 3000)$ genuine and $(2 \times 3000 \times 2999)$ impostor scores. The scores are heterogeneous as the two face recognizers use different algorithms to match the frontal face images of the subjects under test. Face matcher 1 quantifies the similarity between two images using a scale from zero to one, while the second

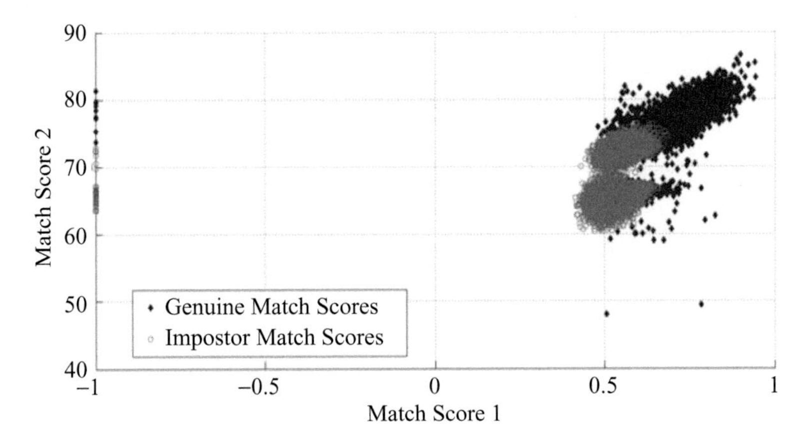


Figure 5.3. Scatter plot of the genuine and impostor scores from the two face matchers.

matcher outputs score values ranging from zero to 100 with higher values indicating a better match between the face image of the subject under test and the template in the database recorded previously. A scatter plot of both the genuine and impostor scores is shown in Figure 5.3. Data (under each hypothesis) are partitioned into two subsets of equal size where the first subset is the training set used for model fitting and the second is the testing set used for the system's performance evaluation. Thirty different training-testing sets (resamples or trials) are obtained from the same data by randomizing the partitioning process described above, and an average system performance across the 30 trials is computed. We consider both the NP and the Bayesian frameworks. We now describe the training and the performance evaluation steps in detail.

Given the training data set (from a single trial), the joint PDF (of scores from the two face matchers) can be estimated by first modeling the marginal PDFs and then estimating the copula dependence parameter. We use a GMM model to fit the scores generated by both face matchers (Figueiredo and Jain 2002). Figure 5.4 shows the estimated marginal PDFs for both impostor ($H_0$) and genuine ($H_1$) scores. We then use the Frank ($k_1(\cdot)$) and Gumbel ($k_0(\cdot)$) copula functions to model dependence between genuine and impostor scores, respectively. Our choice of the copula functions is guided by a KL divergence (between the true and the estimated joint PDFs) criterion Iyengar (2009b). Given the above choice of copula functions, estimates for the corresponding copula dependence parameters ($\theta$) are obtained using the CML approach described in Section 5.5.2. A copula-based joint PDF is thus derived for both the genuine and impostor scores.

Note that the first step of modeling the marginal PDFs is common to both the product- and the copula-based models; both models capture the marginal

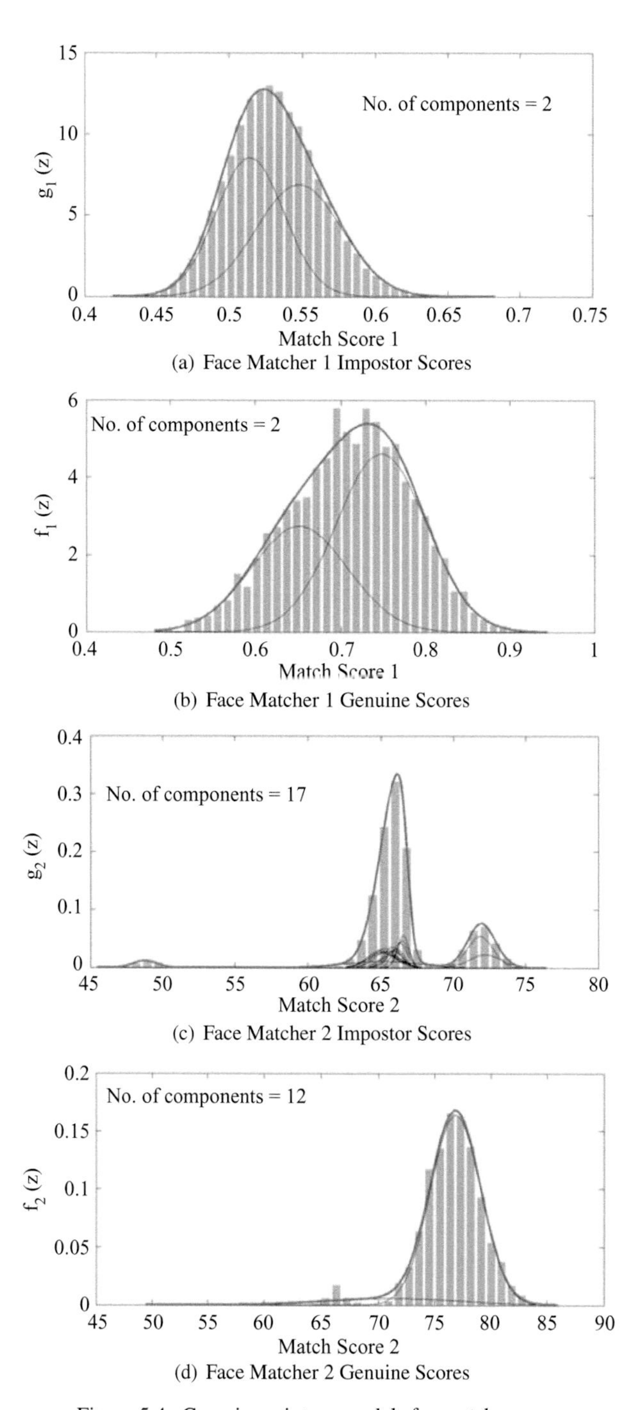


Figure 5.4. Gaussian mixture models for match scores.

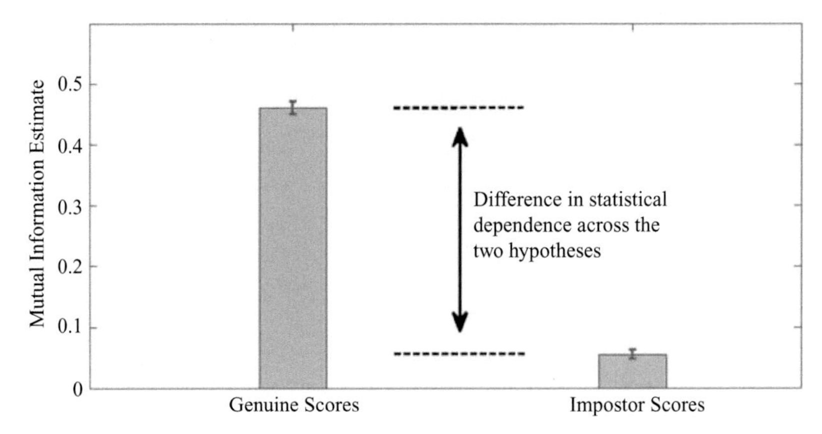


Figure 5.5. Mutual information estimates averaged over 30 resamples. The plot also shows symmetric one standard deviation error bars.

statistics. The product model is derived by just taking the product of the two estimated marginal PDFs and does not model the joint statistics. With the additional step of copula fitting, the goal is to characterize the dependence structure (to a certain extent) that may be present in the data along with the marginal statistics. To show that this is indeed the case, we compute mutual information between scores from the two face matchers using the selected copula functions (Frank and Gumbel functions). The copula-based sample estimate of mutual information between the genuine scores can be given as

$$\hat{\mathcal{I}}_{k_1}(\cdot) = \frac{1}{L}\sum_{l=1}^{L} \log k_1\left(\hat{F}_1(z_1(l)), \hat{F}_2(z_2(l))\right), \tag{5.21}$$

where we approximate the integral over $f(\mathbf{z})$ in (5.12) and (5.13) by a sample expectation and replace the true but unknown copula density $c_1(\cdot)$ by the Frank copula density $k_1(\cdot)$. Mutual information estimates for the impostor scores can also be obtained similarly. It is evident from Figure 5.5, which shows the average (over all 30 resamples) mutual information, that scores under both hypotheses are statistically dependent. The copula model is thus able to capture the dependence structure. Of course, the extent to which the true dependence structure is characterized depends on how well the copula function fits the true model.

Model fitting is then followed by performance evaluation using the testing data. It can be seen from Figure 5.3 that sometimes a score of $-1$ is reported by face matcher 1. Surprisingly, this is true even with some genuine match scores, that is, when the acquired face image of a subject was matched to his own template in the database. This may have been due to errors during data acquisition, image registration, or feature extraction due to the poor quality of the image. Negative one thus serves as an indicator to flag the incorrect working of the matcher. The fusion performance will thus depend on how this anomaly is handled in the decision making. For example, the fusion center can be designed to respond in one of the following ways upon the reception of the error flag:

1. Request for a retrial: The fusion center does not make a global decision upon receiving the error flag. Instead the subject claiming an identity is requested to provide his biometric measurement again. The *request for a retrial* design thus ensures that scores are always in the valid range ($z_1 \in [0, 1]$). We emulate this by deleting all the users whose match scores were reported as $-1$ and present results using $(2 \times 2992)$ genuine and $(2 \times 2992 \times 2991)$ impostor scores. However, there may be applications where the system does not have the liberty to request for a retrial, and the fusion center has to make a decision after each match.
2. Censoring (face matchers that generate the error flag): In our example, face matcher 1 generates the error flag. Upon the reception of the error flag ($z_1 = -1$), the terms of the log likelihood ratio test that depend on $z_1$ are discarded. Thus, the first and the third terms in

$$\Lambda^k(\mathbf{z}) = \underbrace{\log \frac{f_1(z_1)}{g_1(z_1)}}_{=0} + \log \frac{f_2(z_2)}{g_2(z_2)} + \underbrace{\log \frac{k_1(\cdot)}{k_0(\cdot)}}_{=0} \tag{5.22}$$

are set to zero.
3. Accept $H_0$: The system decides in favor of $H_0$ when one or more of the face matchers generate an error flag. This design is conservative and is thus suitable for applications where one desires minimal false alarm rates.
4. Accept $H_1$: The system decides in favor of $H_1$ when one or more error flags are generated.
5. Random decision: Toss a fair coin to decide between $H_0$ and $H_1$.

We show performance results for all five designs in Figure 5.6. A mean receiver operating characteristic (ROC) curve is obtained by averaging $P_D$ values (at equal $P_F$) across the 30 resamples. It can be seen from Figure 5.6 that the product fusion rule outperforms the individual performances of both face matchers, as expected. Further, the superiority of copula-based processing over the product rule is also evident from the plots. The copula fusion rule, in addition to the differences in the marginal PDFs, is able to exploit the differences in the dependence structures across the two hypotheses (see Figure 5.5). Of all the five designs, the "Request for a retrial" approach achieves the best performance as the method ensures input data of *good* quality. The performance of "Censoring" and "Accept $H_0$" are similar. This is because, with a few terms set to zero in the "Censoring" design, the rule decides in favor of $H_0$ in most

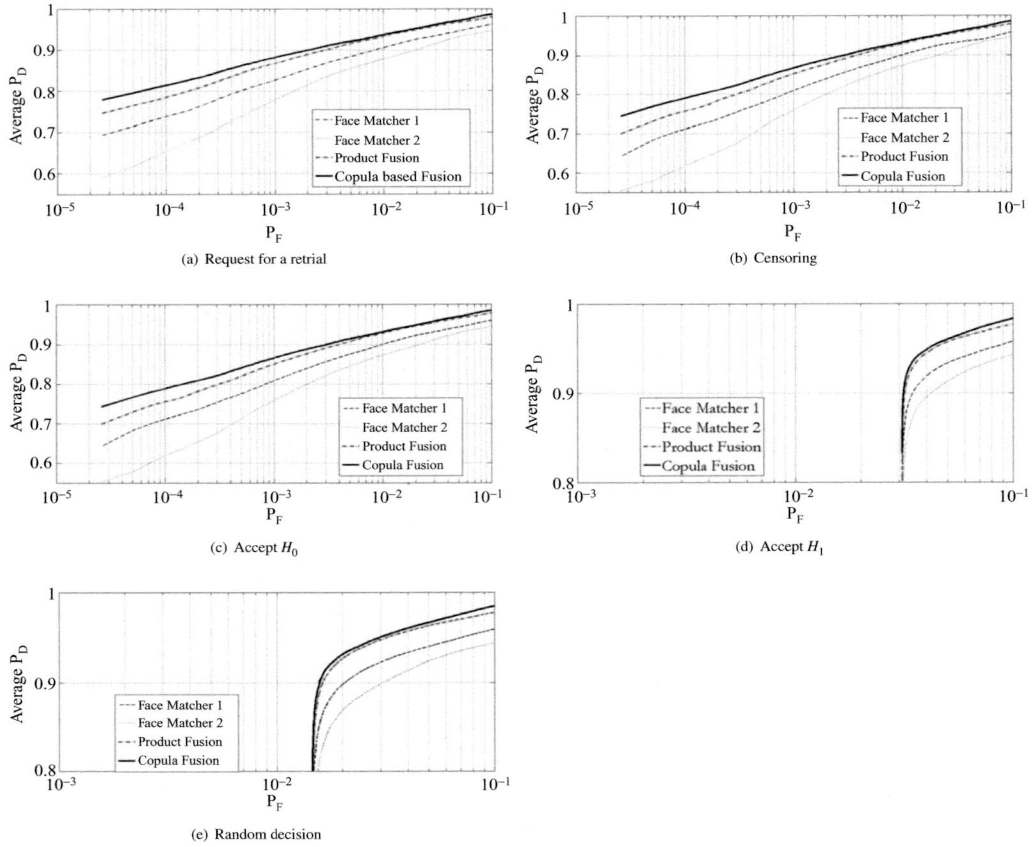
Average P_D
P_F
Face Matcher 1
Face Matcher 2
Product Fusion
Copula based Fusion
(a) Request for a retrial
Copula Fusion
(b) Censoring
(c) Accept $H_0$
(d) Accept $H_1$
(e) Random decision

Figure 5.6. Receiver operating characteristic curves.

Table 5.2. *Peak Increase in $P_D$ Due to Copula Processing ($P_D^k - P_D^p$). Corresponding $P_F$ for "Request for a Retrial", "Censoring," and "Accept $H_0$" Designs is 0.0026%, and that for "Accept $H_1$" and "Random Decision" Designs is 9.9%*

| Fusion Rule | Increase in Average $P_D$ (%) | 95% Confidence Interval |
|---|---|---|
| Request for a retrial | 3.31 | (2.82, 3.81) |
| Censoring | 4.40 | (3.73, 5.07) |
| Accept $H_0$ | 4.38 | (3.71, 5.05) |
| Accept $H_1$ | 0.64 | (0.59, 0.67) |
| Random decision | 0.71 | (0.66, 0.77) |

cases (when the error flag is received). The "Accept $H_1$" and "Random decision" methods are more liberal (or favor $H_1$) and thus show increased false-alarm rates. We also calculate peak improvements in the average $P_D$ as the maximum difference between the copula-based average $P_D$ ($P_D^k$) and that computed using the product rule ($P_D^p$) in Table 5.2. The increase in $P_D$ due to copula processing is maximum at $P_F$ equal to 0.0026% for the "Request for a retrial," "Censoring," and "Accept $H_0$" designs and for a $P_F$ of 9.9% for "Accept $H_1$" and "Random decision" design rules. Table 5.2 also shows 95% confidence intervals for the peak improvements computed using the two-tailed $t$-test (Kreyszig 1970).

We note here that Dass et al. (2005) addressed the biometrics scores fusion problem using copulas and observed no improvement over the product fusion rule. The authors modeled the marginal PDFs as a mixture of discrete and continuous components to account for the error flags (negative ones). However, copula methods require the marginal distributions to be strictly continuous. Further, their analysis was limited to the use of Gaussian copula densities that may be insufficient to model the intermodal dependence. In this chapter we have employed different approaches to handle error flags and have considered the use of a more general family of copula functions with the potential of improving system performance. These reasons could explain the differences between our results and Dass et al. (2005).

We now consider the Bayesian framework. In some problems one is able assign or know a priori the probabilities of occurence for the two competing classes, $H_0$ and $H_1$, denoted by $P(H_0)$ and $P(H_1)$, respectively. The objective of a Bayesian detector is to minimize the probability of error $P_E$ (or more generally, the Bayes risk function) given the priors where

$$P_E = min(P(H_0|z), P(H_1|z)), \tag{5.23}$$

where $P(H_0|z)$ and $P(H_1|z)$ are the posterior probabilities of the two hypotheses given the observations.

In Figure 5.7 we plot $P_E$ averaged over the 30 resamples versus the prior probability $P(H_1)$ for all five strategies. We see that LLRT-cop achieves the best performance over the entire range of priors, showing that our copula-based approach performs better than the one using the product model.

## 5.7 Concluding Remarks

In this chapter we have discussed the statistical theory of copula functions and its applicability to biometric authentication in detail. Copulas are better descriptors of statistical dependence across heterogeneous sources. No assumptions on the source of heterogeneity are required; the same machinery holds for fusion of multiple modalities, samples, algorithms, or multiple classifiers. Another interesting property of the copula approach is that it allows us to separate the cross-modal terms from the unimodal ones in the log likelihood ratio, thus allowing intramodal versus intermodal analyses. Performance analysis in the asymptotic regime proved the intuitive result that when intermodal dependence is accounted for in the test statistic, discriminability between the two competing hypotheses increases over the product rule by a factor exactly equal to the multi-information between the heterogeneous biometric signatures. In all, the copula approach provides a general framework for processing heterogeneous information. Applicability and the superiority of our copula-based approach was shown by applying it to the NIST-BSSR 1 database.

A couple of extensions that are of interest to us include the following:

- *Combination of multiple copula densities*: Different copula functions exhibit different behavior, and a combination of multiple copula functions may better characterize dependence between several modalities than just using a single copula function. It would be interesting to explore this multimodel approach in detail.
- *Joint feature extraction*: The design of a multibiometric identification system includes, apart from information fusion, several preprocessing steps such as feature selection and extraction. In this chapter we focused only on the fusion aspect and chose to entirely omit the discussion on feature selection and extraction methods. Deriving features of reduced dimensionality is an essential step where data are transformed so that only relevant information is extracted and retained for further processing. This alleviates the well-known *curse of dimensionality*. There have been several studies and methods

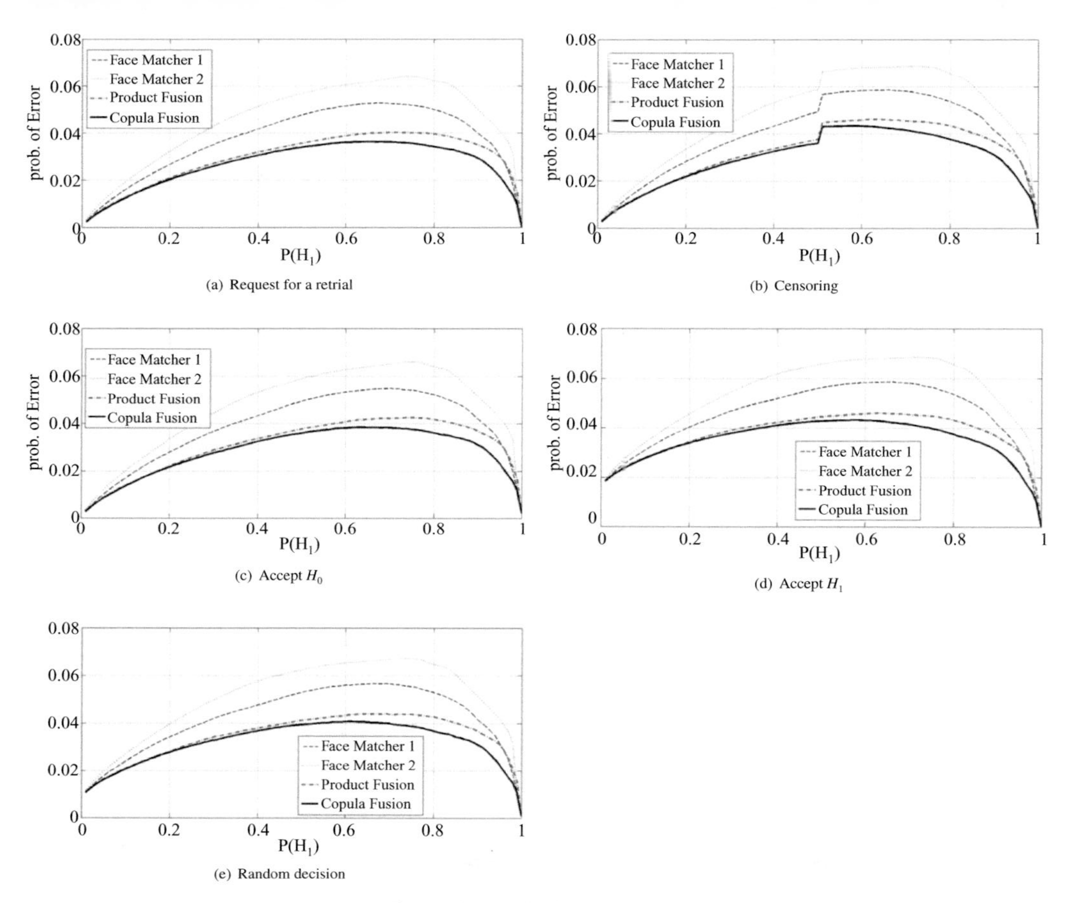


(a) Request for a retrial

(b) Censoring

(c) Accept $H_0$

(d) Accept $H_1$

(e) Random decision

Figure 5.7. Probability of error vs. $P(H_1)$.

proposed for common modality or homogeneous signals. Heterogeneous signal processing offers new possibilities for system improvement. One can envision a joint feature extraction algorithm that exploits the dependence structure between the multimodal signals. Development of feature extraction methods that optimize for intermodal redundancy or synergy could be an interesting direction for future research.

## Acknowledgments

Research was sponsored by the Army Research Laboratory and was accomplished under Cooperative Agreement No. W911NF-07-2-0007. It was also supported by ARO grant W911NF-06-1-0250. The views and conclusions contained in this document are those of the authors and should not be interpreted as representing the official policies, either expressed or implied, of the Army Research Laboratory or the U.S. government. The U.S. government is authorized to reproduce and distribute reprints for government purposes notwithstanding any copyright notation hereon.

The authors thank Dr. Anil K. Jain and Dr. Karthik Nandakumar for their valuable comments and suggestions during the preparation of this chapter.

## References

2004. NIST biometric scores set. http://www.itl.nist.gov/iad/894.03/biometricscores/.

Bouyé, E., V. Durrleman, A. Nikeghbali, G. Riboulet, and T. Roncalli. 2000. Copulas for finance – a reading guide and some applications. *SSRN eLibrary*. http://ssrn.com/paper=1032533.

Chernoff, H. 1956. Large-sample theory: parametric case. *Ann Math. Statist.*, **27**, 1–22.

Clemen, R. T., and T. Reilly. 1999. Correlations and copulas for decision and risk analysis. *Management Sciences*, **45**, 208–224.

Cover, T., and J. Thomas. 2006. *Elements of Information Theory*. 2 ed. John Wiley and Sons.

Dass, S. C., K. Nandakumar, and A. K. Jain. 2005. A principled approach to score level fusion in multimodal biometric systems. In: *Audio and Video based Biometric Person Authentication*.

Figueiredo, M., and A. K. Jain. 2002. Unsupervised learning of finite mixture models. *IEEE Transactions on Pattern Analysis and Machine Intelligence*, **24**, 381–396.

Iyengar, S. G. 2011. Ph.D dissertation in progress. Syracuse University, Syracuse, NY.

Iyengar, S. G., P. K. Varshney, and T. Damarla. 2009. A parametric copula based framework for multimodal signal processing. Pages 1893–1896 of *Proc. of IEEE Conference on Acoustics, Speech and Signal Processing*.

Jain, A. K., K. Nandakumar, and A. Ross. 2005. Score normalization in multimodal biometric systems. *Pattern Recognition*, **38**, 2270–2285.

Joe, H., and J. J. Xu. 1996. *The estimation method of inference functions for margins for multivariate models*. Tech. rept. Department of Statistics, University of British Columbia.

Koval, O., S. Voloshynovskiy, and T. Pun. 2007. Analysis of multimodal binary detection systems based on dependent/independent modalities. In: *IEEE 9th Workshop on Multimedia Signal Processing*.

Kreyszig, E. 1970. *Introductory Mathematical Statistics: Principles and Methods*. John Wiley and Sons.

Kryszczuk, K., and A. Drygajlo. 2008. Impact of feature correlations on separation between bivariate normal distributions. Pages 1–4 of *Proc. of the 19th International Conference on Pattern Recognition*.

Kurowicka, D., and R. Cooke. 2006. *Uncertainty Analysis with High Dimensional Dependence Modeling*. John Wiley and Sons.

Lehmann, E. L., and J. P. Romano. 2008. *Testing Statistical Hypotheses*. 3rd ed. Springer.

Mari, D., and S. Kotz. 2001. *Correlation and Dependence*. Imperial College Press, London.

Nandakumar, K., Y. Chen, S. C. Dass, and A. K. Jain. 2008. Likelihood ratio based biometric score fusion. *IEEE Transactions on Pattern Analysis Machine Intelligence*, **30**(2), 342–347.

Nelsen, R. B. 1999. *An Introduction to Copulas*. Springer.

O'Gorman, L. 2003. Comparaing passwords, tokens, and biometrics for user authentication. *Proceedings of the IEEE*, **91**(12), 2021–2040.

Poh, N., and S. Bengio. 2005. How do correlation and variance of base-experts affect fusion in biometric authentication tasks? *IEEE Transactions on Signal Processing*, **53**(11), 4384–4396.

Prabhakar, S., and A. K. Jain. 2002. Decision-level fusion in fingerprint verification. *Pattern Recognition*, **35**(4), 861–874.

Roli, F., G., Fumera, and J. Kittler. 2002. Fixed and trained combiners for fusion of imbalanced pattern classifiers. Pages 278–284 of *Proc. of International Conference on Information Fusion*.

Ross, A. A., K. Nandakumar, and A. K. Jain. 2006. *Handbook of Multibiometrics*. Springer.

Snelick, R., U. Uludag, A. Mink, and A. K. Jain. 2005. Large scale evaluation of multimodal biometric authentication using state-of-the-art systems. *IEEE Transactions on Pattern Analysis and Machine Intelligence*, **27**(3), 450–455.

Studený, M., and J. Vejnarová. 1999. *Learning in Graphical Models*. The multiinformation function as a tool for measuring stachastic dependence, pages 261–297. MIT Press.

Toh, K. A., X. Jiang, and W. Y. Yau. 2004. Exploiting global and local decisions for multimodal biometrics verification. *IEEE Transactions on Signal Processing, supplement on secure media*, **52**(10), 3059–3072.

Ushmaev, O., and S. Novikov. 2006. Biometric fusion: robust approach. In *2nd Workshop on Multimodal User Authentication*.

Varshney, P. K. 1997. *Distributed Detection and Data Fusion*. Springer.

Wang, R., and B. Bhanu. 2006. Performance prediction for multimodal biometrics. Pages 586–589 of *Proc. of International Conference on Pattern Recognition*.

# 6

# An Investigation into Feature-Level Fusion of Face and Fingerprint Biometrics

Ajita Rattani and Massimo Tistarelli

## 6.1 Introduction

The term "biometrics" defines the analysis of unique physiological or behavioral characteristics to verify the claimed identity of an individual. Biometric identification has eventually assumed a much broader relevance as a new technological solution toward more intuitive computer interfaces (Hong et al. 1999; Jain et al. 1999).

Multibiometric systems Jain and Ross (2004) have been devised to overcome some of the limitations of unimodal biometric systems. In general terms, the combination of multiple biometric traits is operated by grouping multiple sources of information. These systems utilize more than one physiological or behavioral characteristic, or a combination of both, for enrollment and identification. For example, the problem of nonuniversality can be overcome, because multiple traits together always provide a sufficient population coverage. Multibiometrics also offers an efficient countermeasure to spoofing, because it would be difficult for an impostor to spoof multiple biometric traits of a genuine user simultaneously (Jain and Ross 2004). In some cases the sensor data can be corrupted or noisy, the use of multiple biometric traits always allow to reduce the effects of errors and noise in the data.

Ross and Jain (2003) presented a wide overview of multimodal biometrics describing different possible levels of fusion, within several scenarios, modes of operation, integration strategies, and design issues. Evidence in a multibiometrics system can be integrated at several different levels:

(1) Sensor level: The raw data acquired from multiple sensors can be processed and integrated to generate new data from which features are extracted. For example, the fingerprint image acquired from both optical and solid state sensors may be fused to generate a single image.

(2) Feature level: Information extracted from different sources is concatenated into a joint feature vector, which is then compared to a template (which is also a joint feature vector).
(3) Match score level: Feature vectors are created independently for each modality and compared to the enrollment templates, which are stored separately for each biometric trait, generating independent matching scores. The individual scores are finally combined into a total score.
(4) Rank level: This type of fusion is relevant in identification systems where each classifier associates a rank with every enrolled identity. Thus, fusion entails consolidating the multiple ranks associated with an identity and determining a new rank that would aid in establishing the final decision.
(5) Decision level: A separate authentication decision is made for each biometric trait. These decisions are then combined into a final vote.

The most commonly adopted approach in the literature to combine information from multiple biometric traits is to design multiple classifier systems to fuse the scores produced from different matching engines. This methodology can be applied to any combination of biometric traits regardless of their nature, sensing modality, and template representation. The only real requirement is a good computation of each expert's statistics to tailor the fusion machinery. On the other hand, this approach does not fully exploit the richness of information resulting from coupling multiple data sources at an earlier stage. Conversely, a biometric system that integrates information at earlier stages is expected to deliver better performances in terms of accuracy because of the availability of more information.

As reported in the literature a biometric system that integrates information at an earlier stage of processing is expected to provide more accurate results than the systems that integrate information at a later stage because of the availability of more and richer information (Ross and Jain 2003; Fierrez-Aguilar et al. 2003). Figure 6.1 shows an example of an hypothetical multimodal biometric system for face and fingerprint with three levels of fusion: feature level, matching score level, and decision level. Fusion at matching score, rank, and decision levels has been extensively studied in the literature (Chibelushi et al. 1993; Duc et al. 1997; Hong and Jain 1998; Gutschoven and Verlinde 2000; Verlinde et al. 2000; Kittler et al. 1998; Wang et al. 2003; Singh et al. 2004). Despite the abundance of research papers related to multimodal biometrics, fusion at the feature level is a relatively understudied problem. In general terms, fusion at the feature level is relatively difficult to achieve in practice because multiple modalities may have incompatible feature sets, and the correspondence among different feature space may be unknown. Moreover, fused feature vectors

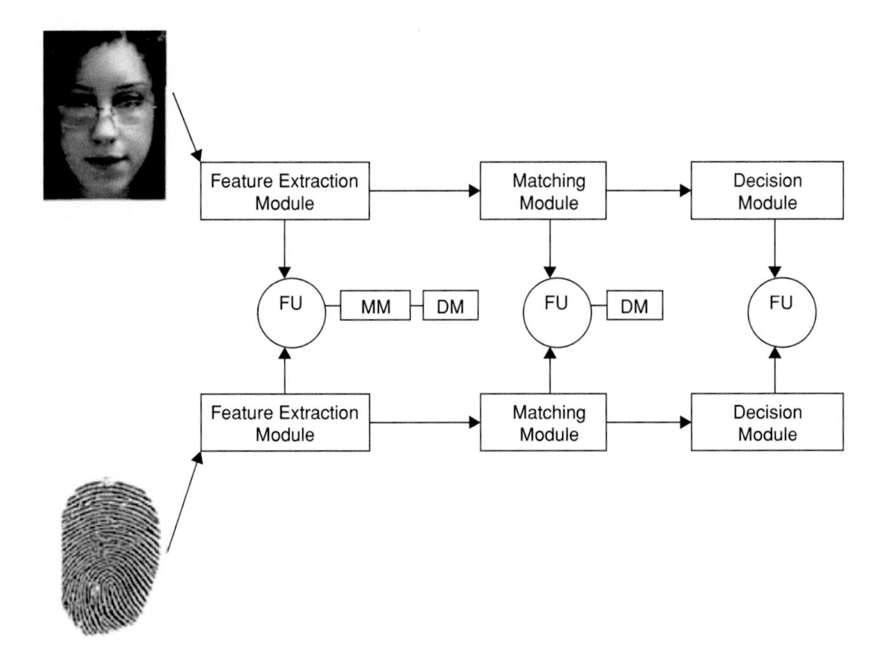


Figure 6.1. The three levels of fusion in a hypothetical multibiometrics system involving face and fingerprint: feature-level, score-level, and decision-level fusion. FU, MM, and DM represent, respectively, the Fusion Unit, the Matching Module, and the Decision Module.

may lead to the problem of a curse of dimensionality, requiring a very complex matcher, and the fused feature vector may contain noisy or redundant data, thus leading to a decrease in the performance of the classifier (Ross and Jain 2003). For these reasons this multimodal fusion approach has been relatively understudied.

Ross and Govindaraju (2005) proposed a method for the fusion of hand and face biometrics at feature extraction level. Kumar et al. (Kumar et al. 2003) attempted to improve the performance of palmprint-based verification system by integrating hand geometry features along with the palmprint features. Zhou and Bhanu (2007) proposed a multibiometric system based on the fusion of face and gait features at the feature level. In Son and Lee (2005) and Gan and Liang (2006) the feature-level fusion of face and iris images is addressed, describing a methodology for feature-level fusion of both. Both have applied projection to lower-dimensional space for feature fusion and reduction using prior training and have used nearest neighbor distance for classification. Even though face and fingerprints represent the most widely used and accepted biometric traits, no methods for feature-level fusion of these modalities have been proposed in the literature. A possible reason is the radically different nature of face and fingerprint images: A face is processed as a pictorial image (holistic approach) or as composed of patches (local analysis), while a fingerprint is typically represented by minutiae points. In this chapter a recently introduced methodology for face modeling (Bicego et al. 2006) is exploited, which is based on the pointwise representation of the face appearance using the scale invariant feature transform (SIFT) (Lowe 1999). SIFT key-point descriptors are extracted from the face image (Bicego et al. 2006), and Gabor features are computed at the location of the fingerprint minutiae points (Jain et al. 1997). Based on these vector representations a novel approach for multimodal feature-level fusion is proposed. Two feature selection techniques are proposed and applied to both the face and fingerprint key-point descriptors individually. The feature-level fusion process is applied to the selected key points. A comparison of the performance obtained with matching score fusion is also presented. Several experiments are reported on both a chimerical and a real multimodal database.

## 6.2 Face and Fingerprint-Based Identification

The difference between the physical characteristics and sensing modalities involved in face and fingerprint requires processing these biometric traits according to different computational schemes. Not only the physical structure of the corresponding body segments is different, but distinctive information must be searched in different subspaces of the raw data as well. This requires modeling a different representation for each of the two data sources, which can be eventually merged in a single, complex representation.

### 6.2.1 Face Recognition Based on the Scale-Invariant Feature Transform

Lowe proposed a method to extract distinctive (Schmid and Mohr 1997) and invariant features from images for object recognition (Lowe 1999). This particular type of feature (also known as scale-invariant feature transform [SIFT]) is invariant to image scale and rotation and provides robust matching across a substantial range of affine distortion, change in three-dimensional (3D) viewpoint, addition of noise, and change in illumination. SIFT features are well localized in both the spatial and frequency domain, reducing the probability of disruption by occlusion, clutter, or image noise. In addition, SIFT features are highly distinctive. This property allows a single feature to be correctly matched with high probability against a large database of features, providing a basis for robust object recognition. The cost of extracting these features is minimized by adopting a cascade filtering approach, in which the more expensive operations are applied only at image locations that have been selected at the initial test. The application of SIFT for face analysis has been recently presented in Bicego et al. (2006).

Each SIFT feature **s** consists of the $(x, y)$ location, orientation, scale, and the key-point descriptor **K** of size $1 \times 128$. As shown in Figure 6.4, from a face image a set of SIFT features $\mathbf{s} = (s_1, s_2, \ldots, s_m)$ is extracted, with $s_i = (x, y, \theta, K)$. The term "point" will be used throughout to denote a key-point descriptor from either the face or fingerprint image.

The main computational steps involved to generate the set of image features are the following:

(1) *Scale-space extrema detection*: The first processing stage searches over all scales and image locations. It is implemented efficiently by using a difference-of-Gaussian (DoG) function to identify potential interest points that are invariant to scale and orientation. Interest points (also called key points) are identified as local maxima or minima of the DoG-filtered images across scales. The value of each pixel in the DoG-filtered images is compared to its eight neighbors at the same scale, plus the nine corresponding neighbors at neighboring scales. If the pixel corresponds to a local maximum or minimum, it is selected as a candidate key point. Figures 6.2 and 6.3 schematically show the process for the scale space filtering and the local extrema detection.

(2) *Key-point localization*: At each candidate location, a detailed model fitting is applied to determine the correct key-point location, scale, and the ratio of principal curvatures. This information allows points to be rejected when having a low contrast (sensitive to noise) or being poorly localized along an edge.

(3) *Orientation assignment*: Based on the local image gradient directions, one or more orientations are assigned to each key-point location. To determine the key-point orientation, a gradient orientation histogram is computed in the neighborhood of the key point, from the Gaussian filtered image at the closest scale to the key point's scale. The contribution of each neighboring pixel is weighted by the gradient magnitude and a Gaussian window with $\theta$ equal to 1.5 times the scale of the key point. Peaks in the histogram correspond to dominant orientations. A separate key point is created for the

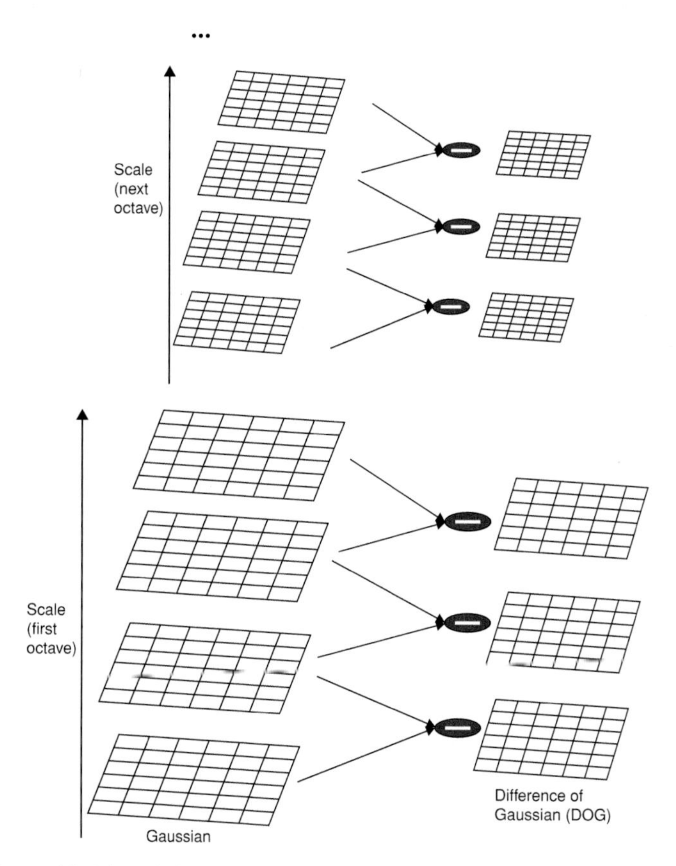


Figure 6.2. Blurred images at different scales and the computation of the difference-of-Gaussian images.

direction corresponding to the histogram maximum, and any other direction within 80 of the maximum value. All the properties of the key point are related to the key-point orientation to enforce invariance to rotation. For each image sample $L(x, y)$, at the chosen scale, the gradient magnitude $m(x, y)$ and the orientation $\theta(x, y)$ are computed using pixel differences: The orientation histogram is composed of 36 bins covering the 360-degree range of orientations with an approximation error equal to 10 degrees.

(4) *Key-point Descriptor*: The local image gradients are computed, at the selected scale, within a region around each key point. Once a key-point orientation has been selected, the feature descriptor is computed as a set of orientation histograms, computed over a $4 \times 4$ pixel neighborhood. The orientation histograms are computed from the Gaussian filtered image that is closest in scale to the key point's scale. As for the previous stage, the

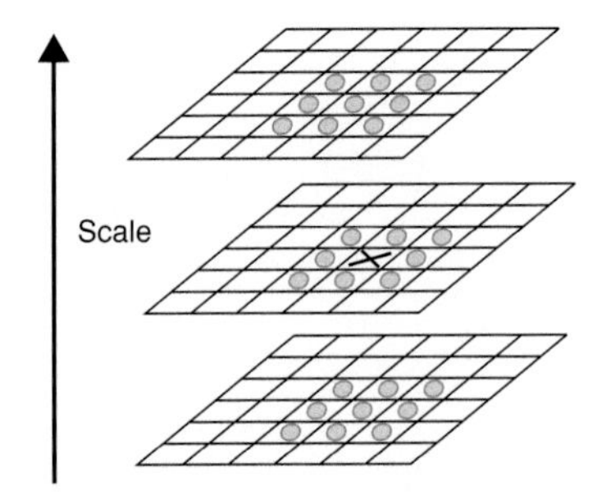


Figure 6.3. Local extrema detection; the pixel marked with an "x" is compared against its 26 neighbors in a $3 \times 3 \times 3$ neighborhood that spans adjacent DoG images.

contribution of each pixel is weighted by the gradient magnitude, and by a Gaussian with $\theta$ equal to 1.5 times the scale of the key point. Each descriptor contains an array of four histograms, each composed by eight bins, computed around the key point.

The final SIFT feature vector is composed of $4 \times 4 \times 8 = 128$ elements. To enforce the invariance to linear or affine changes in illumination, the feature vector is also normalized.

### 6.2.2 Fingerprint Matching Based on Minutiae Representation

Fingerprints are currently the most widely used biometric traits for person verification and identification. The fingerprint of an individual is unique, remains

Figure 6.4. Example face image showing the location and amplitude of the SIFT features.

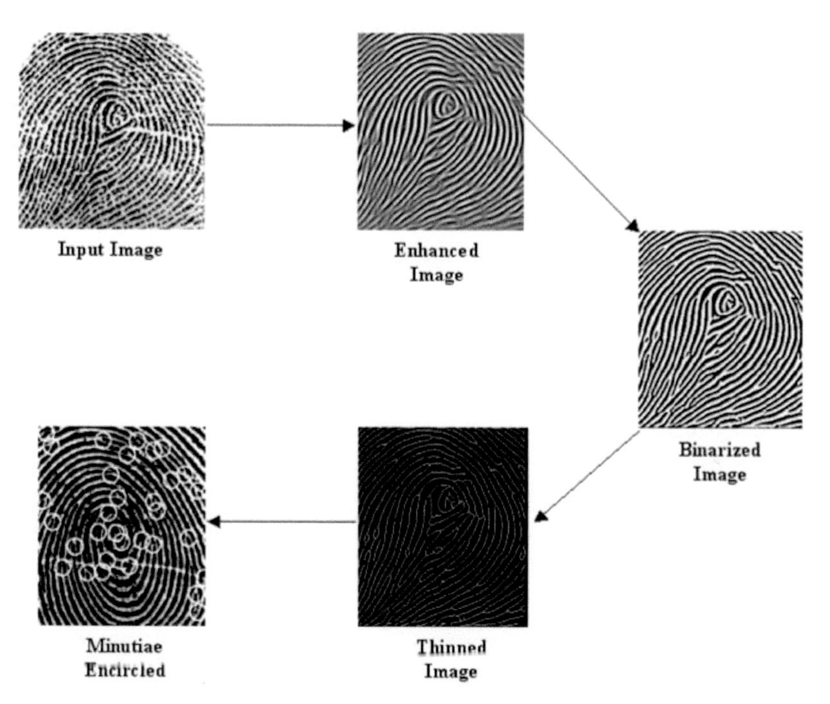


Figure 6.5. Processing steps involved in the fingerprint minutiae extraction and resulting representation.

unchanged over a lifetime, and is formed from an impression of the pattern of ridges of a finger. A ridge is defined as a single curved segment, and a valley is the region between two adjacent ridges. The minutiae, which are the local discontinuities in the ridge flow pattern, provide the basic features that are most often used for verification or identification. Specific details such as the type, orientation, and location are determined to label each individual minutia (Jain et al. 1997; Ratha et al. 1996; Maio et al. 2002). In this chapter only two minutiae types are considered: ridge endings and bifurcations. Ridge endings are the points where the ridge curve terminates. A bifurcation is the point where a ridge splits from a single path to two paths at a Y-junction. A minutia $m$ is described by the triplet $m = \{x, y, \theta\}$, where $(x, y)$ are the minutiae point coordinates and $\theta$ denotes the minutiae orientation.

The fingerprint minutiae extraction is based on four processing steps (see Figure 6.5):

(1) *Image segmentation and rotation invariance*: The input image is segmented to remove noise and to extract the inked region (the foreground part) from

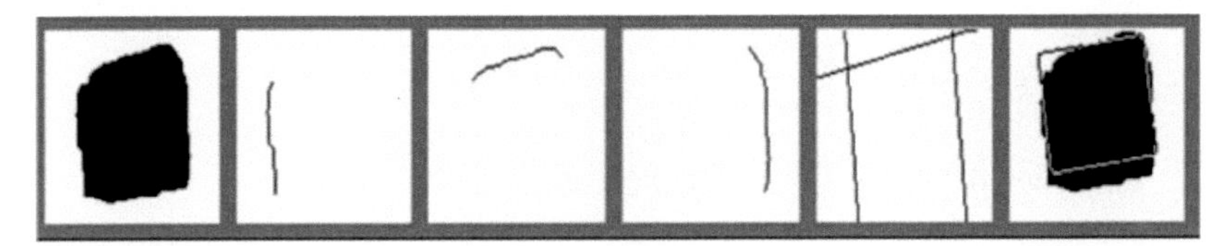

Figure 6.6. Left to right: the six steps to produce rotation invariant fingerprint images.

the background. Rotation invariance is obtained by first fitting straight lines to the left, top, and right edges and then computing the overall slope of the foreground. A linear regression algorithm is applied to fit line segments to the fingerprint edges. The overall slope is computed as the average of the slopes of the left-edge line, the right-edge line, and a line perpendicular to the top-edge line. A rectangle is fit to the segmented region, and the foreground is de-rotated according to the orientation of the rectangle (see Figure 6.6). As the proposed method for rotation invariance operates on a presegmented image, the detection of boundaries is not a critical issue, and the algorithm proved to be robust to noise in the fingerprint images. It is worth noting that as the rectangle is fitted after estimating straight lines on the detected fingerprint boundaries, the algorithm proved to be robust also when applied to the oval fingerprints scans such as in the FVC fingerprint database.

(2) *Image enhancement*: The segmented image is enhanced by using the local ridge orientation $\theta_{xy}$ at the point location $(x, y)$. The orientation is represented by the angle formed by the fingerprint ridge with the horizontal axis. The local spatial frequency $f_{xy}$ at the point location $(x, y)$ is computed as the inverse of the number of ridges per unit length, measured along an hypothetical segment centered at $(x, y)$ and orthogonal to the local ridge orientation $\theta_{xy}$. The fingerprint image is enhanced by filtering the image with a Gabor kernel tuned to the local ridge orientation and frequency.

(3) *Binarization and thinning*: After the enhancement process, the fingerprint image is converted to a binary map. The binary map is thinned to obtain one pixel-wide ridges.

(4) *Minutiae extraction*: The minutiae points are extracted from the thinned image by computing the "crossing number" $C_n(p)$ of each pixel "p":

$$C_n(p) = \frac{1}{2} \sum_{i=1}^{i<9} |val(p_i) - val(p_{i-1})|, \tag{6.1}$$

where $p_0$ to $p_7$ are the pixels belonging to an ordered sequence of pixels defining the eight neighborhood of $p$ and $val(p)$ is the binary pixel value.

A value of the crossing number equal to 1 and 3 correspond, respectively, to a ridge ending and a ridge bifurcation. An intermediate ridge point is defined by a crossing number equal to 2. The minutiae obtained from this algorithm are filtered to preserve only the true minutiae.

## 6.3 Feature-Level Fusion

Feature-level fusion is based on building a new representation for a set of biometric modalities that is obtained combining together the feature representations from each individual modality. Let $\mathbf{X} = (x_1, x_2, \ldots, x_m)$ and $\mathbf{Y} = (y_1, y_2, \ldots, y_n)$ denote the normalized feature vectors extracted from two different sources. The fused vector $\mathbf{Z}$ is obtained by the concatenation of the two feature sets $\mathbf{X}$ and $\mathbf{Y}$. The concatenation can be either serial or parallel. Serial concatenation implies that the two vectors are appended together. Parallel concatenation implies that each element of the first vector $\mathbf{X}$ is concatenated with the feature of the second vector $\mathbf{Y}$. Often feature selection techniques are applied to reduce the dimensionality of the concatenated vector accompanied by removal of the redundant features. Finally, the concatenated feature vector $\mathbf{Z}$ is fed to the matcher to compute the proximity between the database and the query-concatenated feature vectors (Ross and Govindaraju 2005). In the following sections these processing steps are described in full detail.

### 6.3.1 Feature Set Compatibility

The SIFT feature key-point set is translation and rotation invariant. The minutiae feature point set is made compatible with the SIFT feature key-point set by making each feature both translation and rotation invariant. The feature rotation invariance is handled during the preprocessing step, while the translation invariance is obtained by registering a reference point location in the database image with the query images (Jain et al. 2000). Scale invariance is achieved as per the dots per inch (dpi) specification of the sensors. The smooth flow pattern of ridges and valleys in a fingerprint can be viewed as an oriented texture field (Jain et al. 2000). Textured regions with different spatial frequency, orientation, or phase can be easily extracted by decomposing the image texture into several spatial frequency and orientation channels. Frequency-tuned Gabor filtering is applied to capture texture information in specific band-pass channels as well as to decompose this information into bi-orthogonal components of the spatial frequency spectrum. The local structure of the texture is extracted around each minutiae point by applying a Gabor filtering tuned to eight orientations

Figure 6.7. Extracted fingerprint reference point (marked with **X**) used for image registration.

(0, 22.5, 45, 67.5, 90, 112.5, 135, 157.5), eight different scales, and two phases (0 and $\pi/2$). By combining the filter responses at each minutia point, a 128 valued key-point descriptor is obtained. The feature rotation invariance is handled during the preprocessing step, and the feature translation invariance is obtained by registering a reference point location in the database image with the query images, as shown in Figure 6.7. Scale invariance is achieved as per the dpi specification of the sensors.

### 6.3.2 Feature Normalization

The SIFT and Gabor feature sets lie in different scale and range spaces. Therefore the key-point descriptors computed as SIFT feature $\mathbf{s} = (s_1, s_2, \ldots, s_m)$ and as minutiae $\mathbf{m} = (m_1, m_2, \ldots, m_n)$ are normalized, applying the *min-max* algorithm (Jain et al. 2005). This procedure reduces the vectors to the same scale and range, thus enforcing the compatibility between the two key-point sets. All 128 values of the key point descriptors are mapped to the range $[0:1]$, producing two normalized feature key-point sets $\mathbf{s}_{\text{norm}}$ and $\mathbf{m}_{\text{norm}}$. After normalization a single threshold can be applied to discriminate the concatenated face and fingerprint key-point sets extracted from the gallery and probe images.

### 6.3.3 Feature Selection

The curse-of-dimensionality (Ross and Govindaraju 2005), related to feature-level fusion, states that the concatenated feature vector will not necessarily improve the matching performance of the system because some of the feature values may be noisy and redundant compared to the others. Therefore a feature selection strategy is applied to get the optimal subset of features of size $k$ that improves the performance of the classifier. In the literature, feature selection techniques have been applied either before Zhou and Bhanu (2007) or after Ross and Govindaraju (2005) feature concatenation, with varying motivations and results. In our approach the feature selection process is applied to the individual feature vectors *before* performing the feature concatenation.

To better understand the influence of the feature selection process, two different selection strategies are adopted. The first feature selection strategy is based on *k-means* clustering (Jain and Dubes 1988). The second technique aims at selecting key points belonging to regions centered on discriminative landmarks such as the eyes, nose, and mouth for the face images and the singular points for the fingerprints. The two feature selection algorithms are described here:

(1) *K-means clustering*: *k-means* is one of the simplest unsupervised learning algorithms to solve the data-clustering problem. The procedure follows a simple and easy way to classify a given data set through a certain number of clusters (assume $k$ clusters) fixed a priori. The *k-means* algorithm employs $k$ key points to represent clusters. Starting from randomly chosen representative points, two steps are iteratively performed until convergence. (1) each key point is assigned to the nearest representative and (2) representatives are re-computed by averaging all the key points assigned to it. The feature selection is performed by applying the *k-means* technique to the key-point set of face and fingerprint individually and retaining only the point from each cluster with the maximum similarity to the other key points. The point retained from each cluster is included in the fused feature vector. As the key points falling within the same cluster share similar characteristics, by reducing the number of key points redundant information is also removed.

(2) *Points belonging to specific regions*: Only the key points belonging to specific regions of the face and the fingerprint images are retained as reduced point sets. In the case of face images, the SIFT features belonging to an area centered on specific landmarks such as the eyes, the nose, and the mouth are retained. In the case of fingerprints, the minutiae points lying inside a circular region around the global core point are retained. As the central region of the fingerprint is the least effected by skin deformation, the selection of minutiae points around this region also compensate for the effect of skin elasticity and pressure distortion. The optimal radius of the circular regions for the face and fingerprint feature selection has been experimentally determined on two independent unimodal training data sets, as a tradeoff between maximal feature reduction and minimal

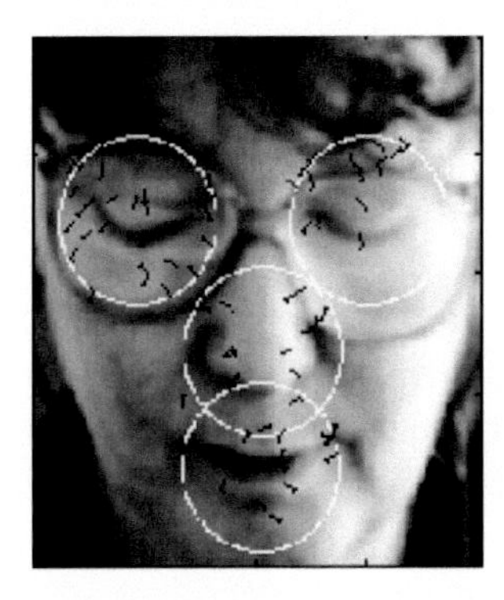

Figure 6.8. Selection of features belonging to selected regions. Left: The landmark points and associated regions of the face image considered for the SIFT points selection. Right: The region of the fingerprint image defined for selection of minutiae points.

performance degradation. The resulting optimal values are equal to 5.4% of the image area for the face regions and 38.4% of the image area for fingerprints. The pictures in Figure 6.8 show two example images with the regions considered for face and fingerprint. In the performed experiments the manually annotated landmark coordinates provided with the datasets have been used.

### 6.3.4 Merging Feature Vectors

Once the feature selection strategy is applied to obtain the discriminant key points from face and fingerprint, these selected feature point sets are then concatenated together in a serial mode; that is, face and fingerprint point sets are appended together to a super fused point set. This concatenated feature point sets are processed by the matcher to compute the similarity score. If there are $N$ and $M$ selected key-point descriptors from face and fingerprint modalities, the face and fingerprint key-point sets are merged in a serial fashion, producing a combined vector with the structure shown in Figure 6.9.

## 6.4 Matching Feature Vectors

The concatenated features key-point sets of the gallery and the probe images are matched to compute the similarity score. The point pattern matching has been applied. This technique aims at finding the percentage of points "paired" between the fused feature point set of the gallery and probe images. Two points are paired if and only if the Euclidean distance of the corresponding key-point

```
Fusedpoint-set={Face_keydescriptor_1,
                Face_keydescriptor_2,
                ...,
                ...,
                Face_keydescriptor_N,
                Finger_keydescriptor_1,
                Finger_keydescriptor_2,
                ...,
                ...,
                Finger_keydescriptor_M
               }
```

Figure 6.9. Structure of the vector obtained by merging the face and fingerprint feature set. The resulting feature vector is made by serial concatenation of the feature vectors extracted from the face and fingerprint data.

descriptors $D_K$ is within a predetermined threshold $k_0$:[1]

$$D_K(i, j) = \sqrt{\sum_i concat(i) - concat(j)^2} \leq k_0, \quad (6.2)$$

where two points $i$ and $j$ are represented by two key-point descriptors $\mathbf{k}$ with $\mathbf{k} = k_1 \ldots k_{256}$ of the concatenated feature sets. In the case of multiple candidate points satisfying (6.2) an ambiguity occurs. Since the key-point descriptor captures most of the local information, the correspondence ambiguity is solved by selecting the point, among the candidate points, having a minimum Euclidean distance between the key-point descriptors of the gallery and the probe point sets. As the face and fingerprint features are preregistered before concatenation, there is no need to compute the transformation parameters to align the concatenated database and query point sets. The final matching score $S_M$ is computed from the number of matched key-point pairs extracted from the two sets as

$$S_M = \frac{M_{PQ}}{M \times N} \times 100, \quad (6.3)$$

where $M_{PQ}$ is the number of paired points between the gallery and the probe concatenated point sets, and $M$ and $N$ are the number of points in the concatenated feature point sets, respectively, in the gallery and probe images. Multiple assignments are avoided by labeling the concatenated feature point set in the

[1] This value has been experimentally determined and set equal to six pixels.

gallery image when it has been paired with another feature key-point descriptor from the probe image.

## 6.5 Experimental Results

To test the performance of feature-level fusion applied to face and fingerprint data, several experiments have been designed. All tests were performed by computing genuine and impostor scores according to the leave-one-out standard testing as described in the Lausanne and BANCA protocols (Luettin and Maitre October 1998; Bailly-Baillire et al. 2003). Given a database with $N$ subjects, genuine and impostor scores are generated as follows:

(1) Genuine scores are computed by comparing each image of each subject with all the other images of the same individual resulting in $N \times 5 \times 4$ comparisons.
(2) Impostor scores are generated by comparing each image of the genuine users to all the images of all other clients. The total number of comparisons is $N \times (N - 1) \times 5$.

Two databases have been used to perform the experiments:

- Dataset 1: a chimerical (artificially assembled) database composed of 50 subjects with five samples per subject. The face images are taken from the Matched Controlled session of the BANCA database (Bailly-Baillire et al. 2003), and the fingerprint data was collected by the authors, using an optical sensor at 500 dpi.
- Dataset 2: a real multimodal database collected by the authors. The database consists of 100 subjects with five samples (face and fingerprint instances) per subject.

In all the experiments performances are reported by means of False Acceptance Rate (FAR), False Rejection Rate (FRR), and accuracy of the system. The accuracy $A$ is defined as

$$A = max_i \left\{ \left( 100 - \frac{FAR(i) + FRR(i)}{2} \right) \right\}, \tag{6.4}$$

where $i$ is the particular threshold point, and $FAR(i)$ and $FRR(i)$ are the $FAR$ and $FRR$ values at threshold $i$. Accuracy values are computed for each $FAR$ and $FRR$ corresponding to all possible matching thresholds, and the computed maximum accuracy value is reported for each system.

Table 6.1. *Results of the Tests Performed on the Individual Modalities. FRR, FAR, and Accuracy Values computed from Dataset 1 on the Individual Modalities*

| Modality and Features | FRR | FAR | Accuracy |
|---|---|---|---|
| Face SIFT | 11.47 | 10.52 | 88.90 |
| Fingerprint minutiae | 7.43 | 12.19 | 90.18 |
| Fingerprint minutiae with key descriptor | 5.384 | 10.97 | 91.82 |

To better understand the discrimination power of different feature representations, with unimodal and multimodal biometrics, as well as the impact of the feature selection techniques, two experimental sessions were performed:

(1) *Analysis of monomodal systems*: The two monomodal recognition systems were tested without any modification in the feature sets, that is, SIFT features (vector $k$) and minutiae. The individual system performances were recorded, and the results were computed for each modality. As can be noted from Tables 6.1 and 6.2, fingerprint verification always performed better than face. Figure 6.10(a) shows the ROC curve obtained testing both the face and fingerprint unimodal systems on Dataset 1. Finally, the effect of introducing the key descriptor with each minutiae point is examined. According to the proposed algorithm, the SIFT and the minutiae point sets extracted from the fingerprint data are normalized using the min-max technique. As reported in Tables 6.1 and 6.2 the introduction of the key descriptor in the fingerprint template already increased the verification accuracy of this modality.

(2) *Multimodal fusion*: In this phase, the main goal was to compare the performance of the monomodal systems with the feature-level fusion and the score-level fusion based on the sum rule.[2] All reported fusion experiments were performed by using the fingerprint features, including the SIFT key descriptor extracted at minutiae points. The face and fingerprint point sets are concatenated together after using the *k-means* clustering feature selection technique. The reduced feature sets are serially concatenated, that is, point sets of face and fingerprint modalities are appended together into a common point set. To compare the performance of feature-level fusion with score-level fusion, the sum rule score-level fusion (Ross and Jain 2003) technique was applied to the scores produced by the face and fingerprint

[2] The product, average, and min-max fusion rules also were tested, but the sum rule always performed better than the others.

Table 6.2. *Results of the Tests Performed on the Individual Modalities. FRR, FAR, and Accuracy Values Computed from Dataset 2 on the Individual Modalities*

| Modality and Features | FRR | FAR | Accuracy |
|---|---|---|---|
| Face SIFT | 7.47 | 10.43 | 91.05 |
| Fingerprint minutiae | 4.36 | 6.91 | 94.36 |
| Fingerprint minutiae with key descriptor | 5.86 | 4.87 | 94.64 |

modalities. Even with the application of other matching score-level fusion techniques such as the min and max rule (Ross and Jain 2003), similar results were obtained. The classification results obtained by applying the feature-level and the score-level fusion are reported in Tables 6.3, 6.4, and 6.5. The results reported in Tables 6.1, 6.2 and 6.3 consistently demonstrate an enhancement in the accuracy applying the feature-level fusion scheme in comparison to both the score-level and the individual modalities.

The same multimodal fusion experiments were performed applying the feature selection technique based on points belonging to specific regions. The results presented in in Table 6.4 demonstrate that feature-level fusion coupled with this feature selection scheme improves the matching performance. Figure 6.10(b) compares the best fingerprint scores and the multimodal fusion at score and feature level as obtained from Dataset 1. In this case the *k-means* feature selection technique was applied.

Table 6.3. *Results of the Fusion Tests. FRR, FAR, and Accuracy Values Computed Applying the Score-Level and the Feature-Level Fusion*

| Test Results from Dataset 1 | | | |
|---|---|---|---|
| Fusion Method | FRR | FAR | Accuracy |
| Score level | 5.66 | 4.78 | 94.77 |
| Feature level | 1.98 | 3.18 | 97.41 |
| Test Results from Dataset 2 | | | |
| Fusion Method | FRR | FAR | Accuracy |
| Score level | 6.11 | 3.82 | 95.03 |
| Feature level | 4.62 | 1.43 | 96.97 |

Table 6.4. *Results of the Fusion Tests. Comparison of the FRR, FAR, and Accuracy Values Computed from the Two Databases Applying the Feature-Level Fusion and the Feature Selection Based on Points Belonging to Specific Regions*

| Database | FRR | FAR | Accuracy |
|---|---|---|---|
| Dataset 1 | 0 | 4.54 | 97.72 |
| Dataset 2 | 3.14 | 1.84 | 97.12 |

A comparison of the performance of the feature-level multimodal fusion obtained from the two datasets is shown in Figure 6.10(c). In this case the feature selection was performed applying the points belonging to a specific region technique. Table 6.5 shows the statistics for the number of points retained by the two feature selection techniques applied.

The reported experimental results clearly show that multimodal fusion performed at higher levels (either at sensor, data, or feature level) consistently improves the classification performance. Even though it may appear that the two fusion methods exploit the same information, by processing the data at an earlier stage allows us to exploit the full discrimination capability by better tailoring the data selection techniques.

Table 6.5. *Statistics Regarding the Number of Points Retained by Applying the Two Feature Selection Techniques (*k-Means *and Points Belonging to Specific Regions)*

| Test Data from Dataset 1 | | | |
|---|---|---|---|
| | Face | Fingerprint | Fused Point Set |
| Total extracted features | 145 | 50 | 195 |
| *k-means* clustering technique | 145 | 50 | 89 |
| Points belonging to specific regions | 47 | 20 | 67 |
| **Test Data from Dataset 2** | | | |
| | Face | Fingerprint | Fused Point Set |
| Total extracted features | 158 | 63 | 221 |
| *k-means* clustering technique | 158 | 63 | 94 |
| Points belonging to specific regions | 58 | 28 | 86 |

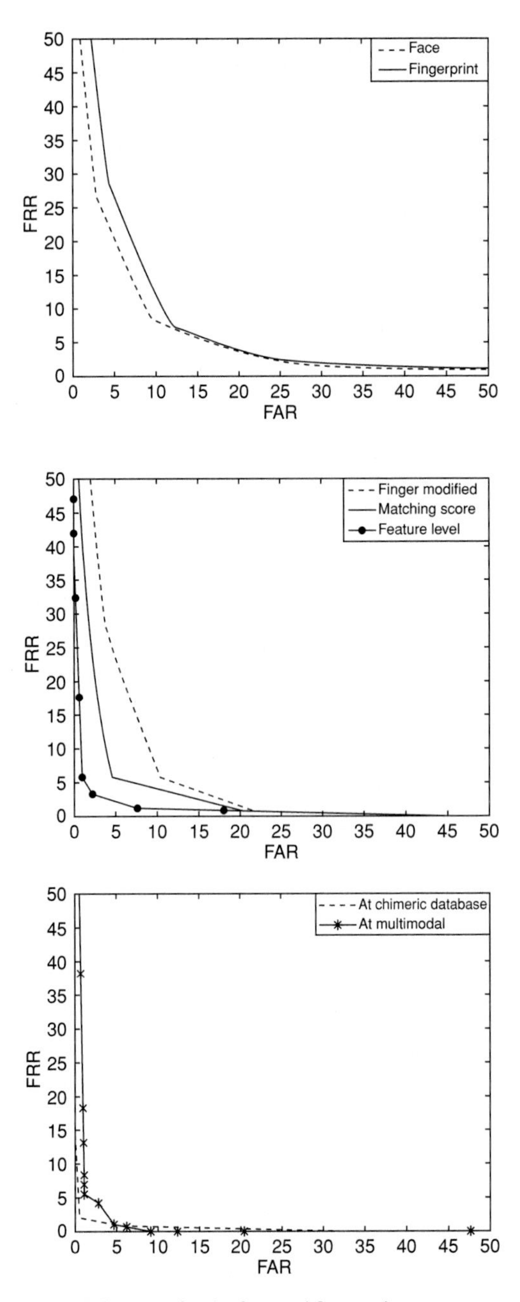


Figure 6.10. Top: ROC curves for the face and fingerprint systems computed from Dataset 1. Middle: ROC curves for the fingerprint system (with introduced key-point descriptor around minutiae points) and the fusion with face at score and feature level. Bottom: ROC curves for the feature-level fusion after applying the point belonging to specific region feature selection technique.

## 6.6 Conclusion

A multimodal biometric system based on the integration of face and fingerprint traits at the feature extraction level was presented. These two traits are the most widely accepted biometrics in most applications. There are also other advantages in multimodal biometric systems, including case of use, robustness to noise, and availability of low-cost, off-the-shelf hardware for data acquisition. From a system point of view, redundancy can always be exploited to improve accuracy and robustness. This is achieved in many living systems as well. Human beings, for example, use several perception cues for recognition of other living creatures, including visual, acoustic, and tactile perception. Starting from these considerations, this chapter outlined the possibility of augmenting the verification accuracy by integrating multiple biometric traits. In most of the examples presented in the literature, fusion is performed either at the score level or at the decision level, always improving the performance of each single modality. In this chapter a novel approach has been presented where both fingerprint and face images are processed with compatible feature extraction algorithms to obtain comparable features extracted from the raw data. Reported results show that a remarkable improvement in the accuracies is obtained when feature sets are properly selected and merged together. The presented approach does not constitute an end in itself, but rather suggests an attempt to perform multimodal data fusion as early as possible in the data-processing chain. Possibly this may even imply a normalization of the data at the sensor acquisition level to allow fusion at the data level. The actual feasibility of this approach may heavily depend on the physical nature of the acquired signal. Several experiments, performed with different algorithmic solutions, have been presented on both a chimeric and a real multimodal database. Further experiments, on multimodal databases composed of more subjects, will allow better validation, from a statistical point of view, of the overall identification and verification performances of the presented multibiometric system.

## References

Bailly-Baillire, E., S. Bengio, F. Bimbot, M. Hamouz, J. Kittler, J. Marithoz, J. Matas, K. Messer, V. Popovici, F. Pore, B. Ruiz, and J. P Thiran. 2003. The banca database and evaluation protocol. In *Proceedings of 4th AVBPA*, volume LNCS 2688, pages 625–638. Springer.

Bicego, M., A. Lagorio, E. Grosso, and M. Tistarelli. 2006. On the use of sift features for face authentication. In *Proc. of Intl. Workshop on Biometrics in Association with CVPR*.

Chibelushi, C. C., J. S. Mason, and F. Deravi. 1993. Integration of acoustic and visual speech for speaker recognition. In *EUROSPEECH '93*, pages 157–160.

Duc, B., G. Maitre, S. Fischer, and J. Bigun. 1997. Person authentication by fusing face and speech information. In *Proceedings of First AVBPA*, volume LNCS. Springer.

Fierrez-Aguilar, J., J. Ortega-Garcia, and J. Gonzalez-Rodriguez. 2003. Fusion strategies in biometric multimodal verification. In *Proceedings of International Conference on Multimedia and Expo–ICME 2003.*

Gan, J., and Y. Liang. 2006. A method for face and iris feature fusion in identity authentication. *IJCSNS*, **6**(2B).

Gutschoven, B., and P. Verlinde. 2000. Multi-modal identity verification using support vector machines. In *Proceedings of 3rd Intl. Conf. on Information Fusion.*

Hong, L., and A. Jain. 1998. Integrating faces and fingerprints for personal identification. *IEEE Transactions on PAMI*, **20**(12), 1295–1307.

Hong, L., A. Jain, and S. Pankanti. 1999. Can multi-biometrics improve performance? In *Proc. of AutoID*, pages 59–64.

Jain, A., and R. Dubes. 1988. *Algorithms for Clustering Data*. Prentice Hall.

Jain, A., L. Hong, and R. Bolle. 1997. On-line fingerprint verification. *IEEE Transactions on PAMI*, **19**(4), 302–314.

Jain, A., R. Bolle, and S. Pankanti. 1999. *Biometrics: Personal Identification in a Networked Society*. Kluwer Academic Publishers.

Jain, A., S. Prabhakar, L. Hong, and S. Pankanti. 2000. Filterbank-based fingerprint matching. *IEEE Transactions on Image Processing*, **9**(5), 846– 859.

Jain, A., and A. Ross. 2004. Multi-biometric systems. *Communications of the ACM*, **47**(1), 34–40.

Jain, A., K. Nandakumar, and A. Ross. 2005. Score normalization in multimodal biometric systems. *Pattern Recognition*, **38**(12), 2270–2285.

Kittler, J., M. Hatef, R. P. W. Duin, and J. Matas. 1998. On combining classifiers. *IEEE Transactions on PAMI*, **20**(3), 226–239.

Kumar, A., D. C. M. Wong, H. C. Shen, and A. K. Jain. 2003. Personal verification using palmprint and hand geometry biometric. In *Proceedings of 4th AVBPA*, pages 668–678.

Lowe, D. G. 1999. Object recognition from local scale invariant features. In *International Conference on Computer Vision*, pages 1150–1157, Greece.

Luettin, J., and G. Maitre. 1998. Evaluation protocol for the the xm2fdb database (lausanne protocol). Technical report IDIAP COM-05, IDIAP, Martigny, October.

Maio, D., D. Maltoni, R. Cappelli, J. L. Wayman, and A. K. Jain. 2002. Fvc2002: Second fingerprint verification competition. In *16th Int.l Conf. on Pattern Recognition*, pages 811–814, Quebec City, August 11–15.

Ratha, N. K., K. Karu, S. Chen, and A. K. Jain. 1996. A real-time matching system for large fingerprint databases. *IEEE Transactions on PAMI*, **18**(8), 799–813.

Ross, A., and A. K. Jain. 2003. Information fusion in biometrics. In *Pattern Recognition Letters*, **24**, 2115–2125.

Ross, A., and R. Govindaraju. 2005. Feature level fusion using hand and face biometrics. In *Proc. of SPIE Conference on Biometric Technology for Human Identification II*, pages 196–204, Orlando, FL.

Schmid, C., and R. Mohr. 1997. Local gray value invariants for image retrieval. *IEEE Transactions on PAMI*, **19**(5), 530–534.

Singh, S., G. Gyaourova, and I. Pavlidisu. 2004. Infrared and visible image fusion for face recognition. In *SPIE Defense and Security Symposium*, pages 585–596.

Son, B., and Y. Lee. 2005. Biometric authentication system using reduced joint feature vector of iris and face. In *AVBPA*, pages 513–522.

Verlinde, P., G. Chollet, and M. Acheroy. 2000. Multi-modal identity verification using expert fusion. *Information Fusion*, **1**, 17–33.

Wang, Y., T. Tan, and A. K. Jain. 2003. Combining face and iris biometrics for identity verification. In *Proc. of 4th Int' Conf. on Audio- and Video-Based Biometric Person Authentication (AVBPA)*, pages 805–813.

Zhou, X., and B. Bhanu. 2007. Integrating face and gait for human recognition at a distance in video. *IEEE SMC-B*, **37**(5), 1119–1137.

# 7

# Adaptive Multibiometric Systems

Luca Didaci, Gian Luca Marcialis, and Fabio Roli

## 7.1 Introduction

Personal identification and verification by using biometric traits, such as fingerprints and faces, cover a large variety of applications. However, performance of current systems is still far from humans' (Sinha et al. 2006a, b).

The core of a biometric recognition system is the so-called enrollment stage. For each client, one or more biometric traits (e.g., a fingerprint and face images) are acquired and processed to represent it with a feature set (e.g., minutiae points). This feature set, labeled with the user's identity, is called a template and stored as a prototype of user's biometric trait in the system's database. The template is used in the recognition stage by comparing it with the input biometric(s), thus obtaining the so-called matching score, a real value into [0,1], which is the degree of similarity between the input sample and the given template.

As pointed out clearly in Uludag et al. (2004), in real operational scenarios, we have to handle substantial variations of each person's appearance. This large intraclass variability is due to changes of the environment conditions (e.g., illumination changes), aging of the biometric traits, variations of the interaction between the sensor and the individual (e.g., variations of the person pose), etc. Therefore, the enrolled templates could be poorly representative of the biometric data to be recognized, resulting in poor recognition performance. For example, experiments on several face databases (Tan et al. 2006; Roli and Marcialis 2006) showed that the performance of an eigenface-based face recognizer drops quickly when the enrolled templates become poorly representative.

Although multiple templates can be collected during the enrollment session and stored in the user's gallery, this does not necessarily solve the problem of large intraclass variability. In fact, some of the mentioned variations above are due to the nonstationary nature of the stochastic process generating the biometric patterns, that is, they can change over time. It is nearly impossible to capture examples of such temporal variations during a single enrollment session over a short period. Using multiple (re)enrolment sessions, separated by a given interval of time, can surely help in tracking the temporal variations of biometric traits, but frequent reenrolment sessions are expensive, and such a system's administration policy can be difficult to adopt.

Moreover, because reenrolment is supervised, it cannot take into account intraclass variations, for example, cuts on fingerprints, which are significant only in a very small period. In other cases, biometric images could be considered by the supervisor to be poor quality images. This is correct from the point of view of the human supervisor, who has to perform the quality assessment by visual inspection of images, but can be strongly wrong from the point of view of the matcher, which may take advantage of such intraclass variations. In fact, the current scientific definition of a "quality measure" in biometrics is that it must be a good predictor of the matching performance (Tabassi et al. 2004). This is not always the case with the quality assessed by visual inspection, but even neglecting temporal variations of biometric data, the collection of a representative set of templates can be a challenging task. In fact, the intraclass variability of a biometric trait can be extremely large in the stationary case as well. Therefore, collecting a representative templates set can require an effort by the administrator and the enrolled users, a storage capability, a length of the enrolment session, and other factors, which are not compatible with the requirements of many applications.

With regard to this issue, it is worth noting that much new biometric data are made available during the system operation over time. As pointed out in Roli et al. (2008), attempting to exploit this data stream is a reasonable strategy to implement template adaptive systems. This is confirmed by several works (Jiang and Ser 2002; Ryu et al. 2006; Liu et al. 2003; Roli and Marcialis 2006; Rattani et al. 2008a; Freni et al. 2008b; Didaci et al. 2009b). As the data acquired during the system's operation are unlabeled, the design of an adaptive biometric system can be regarded as a learning task in which one tries to exploit jointly a small set of labeled biometric data, collected during an initial enrolment session, and a large batch of unlabeled data, acquired during the system operation (Seeger 2002; Zhu 2006).

Although the state of the art on semisupervised approaches has grown over the last few years, and much experimental evidence has reported about their effectiveness, no significant improvement has been reached to make them suitable for practical use. From this point of view, this field of research is still in its infancy. In particular, a few trials have described the behavior of this system in a systematic form. This chapter's goal is to review the state of the art and introduce a possible formulation for modeling the behaviour of semisupervised approaches exploiting multiple biometrics (Didaci et al. 2009a, b).

The chapter is organized as follows. Section 2 presents a critical review of previous works that have addressed the issue of designing adaptive biometric systems, especially by focusing on the kind of "adaptivity" proposed. In Section 3 the so-called template co-update algorithms are presented. Initially proposed for two matchers, the algorithm is extended here to multiple matchers. A theoretical modeling of this algorithm is the main focus of Section 3. Experiments are proposed in Section 4 and show that the behavior of template co-update algorithm is well fitted by the proposed model. Section 5 discusses some pros and cons of this algorithm and the limitation of this model as to vulnerabilities, robustness, and parameter estimation that are worthy of investigation. Section 6 concludes the chapter.

## 7.2 Self-adaptive Biometric Systems: A Review

A recent report of the U.S. General Accounting Office stated: "The quality of the templates is critical in the overall success of the biometric application. Because biometric features can change over time, people may have to re enrol to update their reference template. Some technologies can update the reference template during matching operations." (p. 5, Rhodes 2004).

However, adaptive biometric systems are not in the current mainstream of basic research in biometrics, probably for several reasons, among others: the lack of appropriate databases, containing a large number of biometric data collected over the time, and the intrinsic difficulty of this topic, also due to the lack of a precise formulation of the problem. It should be noted that a similar situation holds for the general theme of adaptive pattern recognition and for the field of document image analysis (Kelly et al. 1999; Nagy 2004a; Hand 2006).

It is worth noting that the concept of "adaptation" does not refer to a peculiar characteristic of a biometric system. By considering the state of the art, this term can refer to:

- Changing the system parameters (e.g., the eigenfaces) (Liu et al. 2003; Roli and Marcialis 2006)
- Selecting the best templates from a given set of candidates (Uludag et al. 2004; Freni et al. 2008b)
- Updating the features characterizing the templates (Jiang and Ser 2002; Ryu et al. 2006)
- Increasing the gallery size with novel, "highly genuine" samples as templates (Suthankar and Stockton 2001; Roli et al. 2007)

- Assigning the correct label to each input sample (Okada and von der Malsburg 1999; Rattani et al. 2008a).

It is worth noting that all these features are usually attributed to the human supervisor. Accordingly, adaptation is referred to the "substitution" of (or the support to) the human supervisor. A certain module of the system is coupled with or substitutes for the human supervisor. In this chapter we focus on the concept of "template update" by involving the last two features above.

For a recent review of adaptive biometric systems, the reader is referred to Roli et al. (2008). Another survey, focusing in particular on template update, has been proposed in Rattani et al. (2009a).

The idea of making "adaptive" the biometric systems comes from previous works (Okada and von der Malsburg 1999; Jiang and Ser 2002; Liu et al. 2003). In particular, Okada and von der Malsburg (1999) described a prototype system for face recognition in video that implements an automatic incremental update of the galleries containing views of the users' faces. Views recognized with high "reliability" in the input video are added to the galleries. When the input is rejected, that is, the identity of the face image is unknown, a new entry, corresponding to a new identity, is added to the person's gallery. It is easy to see that this self-training approach may work well if the number of recognition errors stays low, otherwise a system's performance can degrade over the time. Jiang and Ser (2002) proposed an algorithm for online template updating. This algorithm can update templates by a fusion process with impressions acquired online that are recognized as genuine with high reliability. The fusion process recursively generates a "super-template," and it can allow removing some spurious minutiae and recovering some missing minutiae. Liu et al. (2003) proposed an algorithm to update incrementally the eigenspace of a PCA-based face recognition system by exploiting unlabeled data acquired during the system's operation. The proposed updating algorithm uses decay parameters to give more weight to recent samples of face images and less to the older ones, thus implementing a mechanism to forget gradually outdated training examples. As an individual eigenspace is used for each identity, the updating algorithm requires that identity labels are assigned to the input face images; when a test image arrives, it is projected into each individual eigenspace, and the identity label of the eigenspace that gives the minimal residue (which is defined by the difference between the test image and its projection in the eigenspace) is assigned to the image.

From these pionierising works, research on adaptive biometric systems has grown, and other approaches, several of them inspired by the semisupervised learning theory, have been published, involving single matchers (Ryu et al.

2006; Roli and Marcialis 2006; Rattani et al. 2008b; Freni et al. 2008a) and multiple matchers (Roli et al. 2007; Rattani et al. 2008a). A first trial to critically review and taxonomize works that are the state of the art has been done in Rattani et al. (2009a), while an analysis of the possible research directions has been given in Poh et al. (2009).

For the purposes of this chapter, we will briefly focus on the multibiometric approaches, which are substantially represented by the so-called template co-update algorithm.

The key idea behind biometric co-updating can be regarded as a generalization to the learning task of the basic idea behind multimodal biometrics. In fact, the complementary performances of biometric recognisers using distinct biometric traits, such as face and fingerprints, are one of the fundamental motivations for multimodal biometrics (Ross et al. 2006). Intuitively, each recognizer is expected to assign correct labels to certain input data that are difficult for the other. In turn, each matcher works as "supervisor" for the other one and "selects" samples in the batch to be added into the gallery. Co-updating has been investigated in several experimental works. In Roli et al. (2007), it has been compared with methods based on single matchers (self-updating). Experiments have shown that galleries obtained are averagely larger than those obtained by using a single matcher approach. In Rattani et al. (2008a), the advantages of self-updating have been better investigated by considering that co-updating is less prone to misclassification error than self-update. In Didaci et al. (2008, 2009a), a preliminary model for describing the behavior of the co-update has been presented. Finally, in Didaci et al. (2009b), the possible extension to ensembles of multiple matchers has been considered. The following section is devoted to the detailed description of such models.

## 7.3 A Theoretical Model for the Template Co-update Algorithm

### 7.3.1 The Template Co-update Algorithm

Recently, a semisupervised template update has been proposed (Zhu 2006; Roli and Marcialis 2006; Didaci et al. 2009a; Roli et al. 2008). In this approach, unlabeled samples (that is, collected during system operations) showing very strong similarity to existing templates are added to the gallery of the related subject. The aim is to increase the representativeness of related sets of templates. The core of the template update approach is the insertion of new samples without external supervision. Template update solutions involve both monomodal and multimodal verification systems (Uludag et al. 2004; Jiang and Ser 2002;

**Algorithm 1** Co-update

(i) In the enrolment (supervised) session, collect a set $D_L$ of face and fingerprint images. A couple of face and fingerprint images are acquired for each user.
(ii) Create the fingerprint and face templates using the set $D_L$.
(iii) Loop for $H$ iterations (or until some stop criterion is met):
  (a) Collect a set $D_U$ without supervision. Each element of $D_U$ is a pair of face and fingerprint samples $\{x^{(\text{face})}, x^{(\text{finger})}\}$ from the same individual
  (b) $D_L^{'} \leftarrow \{\}$
  (c) For each element $\{x^{(\text{face})}, x^{(\text{finger})}\} \in D_U$
    1. If $x^{(\text{face})}$ is verified, the sample $x^{(\text{finger})}$ is added to $D_L^{'}$
    2. If $x^{(\text{finger})}$ is verified, the sample $x^{(\text{face})}$ is added to $D_L^{'}$
  (d) $D_L \leftarrow D_L \bigcup D_L^{'}$
  (e) Update face and fingerprint templates using the augmented labeled set $D_L$

Ryu et al. 2006; Didaci and Roli 2006; Roli and Marcialis 2006; Roli et al. 2007, 2008; Rattani et al. 2008a; Didaci et al. 2008). In particular, the so-called co-update algorithm showed that the mutual help of noncorrelated biometrics (e.g., fingerprints and faces) can increase the gallery representativeness more quickly than systems adopting only one biometric (Roli et al. 2007, 2008), thus improving the overall performance. Intuitively, each recognizer is expected to assign correct labels to certain input data that are difficult for the other.

Description of the co-update algorithm is given in Algorithm 1. Let $D_L$ be a set of labeled biometric data extracted from two biometrics, face and fingerprint. These data are the templates enrolled by human supervision, and thus they are labeled with users' identities (clients' names). A batch $D_U$ (usually much larger than $D_L$) of data is acquired during system operations. Each element of $D_U$ is a pair of biometric samples from the same individual. During the off-line co-update phase, each matcher is applied to the batch $D_U$ to verify the identity of each couple of biometric samples. A biometric sample is added to the set $D_L$ if and only if the identity of the other biometric sample of the couple has been verified.

Let $x^{(b)}$ be an unlabeled sample of the biometric $b$, where $b \in$ {face, fingerprint}. To verify the claimed identity of $x^{(b)}$, a function $f_{\text{SCORE}}^{(b)}(x^{(b)}, y^{(b)})$ computes the similarity between $x^{(b)}$ and a labeled sample $y^{(b)}$. Details about $f_{\text{SCORE}}^{(b)}(\bullet, \bullet)$ depend on the biometric at hand. Let $G_h^{(b)} = \{x_{h,1}^{(b)}, \ldots, x_{h,n}^{(b)}\}$ be the gallery of labeled samples of the biometric $(b)$ for the client $h$. In the verification stage the claimed identity of $x^{(b)}$will be verified if and only if $s^{(b)} = \max_k(f^{(b)}_{\text{SCORE}}(x^{(b)}, x^{(b)}_{h,k}\})) > s^{(b)*}$, that is, if the maximum similarity score between $x^{(b)}$ and the templates in the gallery exceeds a threshold $s^{(b)*}$. A more general function other than max can also be used.

It is worth noting that in the co-update process the two biometrics play complementary role. One biometric verifies the claimed identity, assuming the role of supervisor and allowing the gallery of the other biometric to be augmented. Let us call *master* the biometric that assumes the supervisor's role, and *slave* the biometric whose gallery is augmented due to the master biometric. During the co-training process both biometrics assume, alternatively, master and slave roles. Both matchers are retrained with this augmented data set (e.g., by updating the face and fingerprint template galleries), and the process is repeated a specified number of times.

Co-updating is expected to work because each matcher may assign correct labels to certain examples, considered as difficult for the other. This is due to the "diversity" of matchers involved, as fingerprint-based and face-based ones.

Because the co-update algorithm introduces new samples without external supervision, it is necessary to avoid missclassified samples. This might introduce misclassified samples in the gallery. For this reason, only "confident samples" are added by a very high co-update threshold value at which no false matches occur. A way to do this is where an acceptance threshold such that FAR $= 0\%$ can be used. Let us consider the supervisor's role in a (supervised) enroll phase. For each sample presented to the system, the supervisor must (1) verify the identity and (2) verify the informative contribution of the new acquisition. Subtask (1) ensures that the gallery will be made up only of samples of the true identity. The aim of subtask (2) is to avoid that noninformative samples are added to the gallery. Noninformative samples include, but are not limited to, low-quality samples or samples very similar to those already present in the gallery. In the co-update algorithm the matcher that acts as a "master" plays the role of supervisor only for issues that concern subtask (1). Subtask (2) is not esplicitely performed, even if the biometrics "complementarity" allows us to suppose that informative samples are inserted, on average.

Some observations can be made about this version of the algorithm. First, it is possible to use a lower threshold, at the cost of introducing into the galleries a certain number of "impostors" (Roli et al. 2008). This is a common problem in all co-update and self-update algorithms. The update method used in this work consists of adding a new template to the gallery, but more sophisticated methods are possible, such as, by obtaining a new template "fusing" different samples (Freni et al. 2008a).

### 7.3.2 The Proposed Model

In the following we propose a mathematical model that allows us to point out the relationships between the gallery size increase and the error rate reduction achieved. This model can be adopted by designers for the preliminary assessment of template co-update algorithms in real environments.

#### 7.3.2.1 Terminology

In this section, we introduce all variables adopted in the model and during the working hypothesis. Some of them are better clarified later.

*Problem settings:*

- $N_{\text{TOT}}$: maximum number of templates that a gallery can contain
- $n$: size of the template gallery
- $D_U$: set of unlabeled biometric samples presented to the co-update system at each co-update step
- $k$: size of $D_U$.

*Terms that describe the gallery size increase:*

- $n_{(i)}$: size of the template gallery at the $i$th update step
- $\Delta n$: expected increase of the gallery size at each co-update step.

*Terms that describe the error rate achieved (FRR):*

- $m$: for a biometric sample $x$, this is the number of other samples belonging to the same client that produce a score value over the updating threshold. $m$ can be regarded as the as the representativeness degree of the sample. A sample is representative when related to $m > 0$.
- $f_c$: percentage of representative sample. A sample is representative when its $m$ is more than 0.
- $f_I$: $1 - f_c$.

*Terms involved in the co-update model description:*

- $k_{\text{ver}}$: number of samples whos identity is correctly verified. $k_{\text{ver}} = k$ in a supervised system, and $k_{\text{ver}} \leq k$ in a co-update system.
- $k_d$: number of distinct (unique) elements among the $k$ elements in $D_U$.
- $k_{dn}$: number of elements (among the $k_d$) that are not present in gallery.
- $w_{\text{sup}}$: parameter that determines the system's dynamic in a supervised system.
- $w$: parameter that determines the system dynamic in a co-update system.

#### 7.3.2.2 Working Hypothesis

The main assumption in the co-update approach is that the two biometric traits are conditionally independent given the identity. For each couple of biometric samples $\{\widehat{x}^{(\text{face})}, \widehat{x}^{(\text{finger})}\}$ from the same individual,

$$p\left(x^{(\text{face})} = \widehat{x}^{(\text{face})} | x^{(\text{finger})} = \widehat{x}^{(\text{finger})}\right) = p\left(x^{(\text{face})} = \widehat{x}^{(\text{face})}\right) \tag{7.1}$$

and similarly,

$$p\left(x^{(\text{finger})} = \widehat{x}^{(\text{finger})} | x^{(\text{face})} = \widehat{x}^{(\text{face})}\right) = p\left(x^{(\text{finger})} = \widehat{x}^{(\text{finger})}\right). \tag{7.2}$$

For instance, we are assuming that the face appearance and the related client's fingerprint image are independent of each other. This assumption is identical to that used in (Blum and Mitchell 1998).

The hypothesis holds if there is no correlation between the biometrics at hand, for instance, face and fingerprint. In other cases, for example, in a multiple algorithm approach, where a different set of features are extracted from the same biometry, the hypothesis should be carefully evaluated.

Let $n$ be the number of different templates contained in a gallery, for a given identity. Let $N_{\text{TOT}}$ be the maximum number of templates that a gallery can contain. The role, master or slave, of the two biometrics is highlighted by superscripts $M$ and $S$.

Some assumptions are made to propose a mathematically tractable model.

The first assumption concerns the finite discrete space used to represent different biometric impressions. The proposed model assumes that each identity can produce a maximum of $N_{\text{TOT}}$ different observations. The main consequence of this assumption is that a new example acquired by the system does not necessarily lead to a substantial performance improvement, because the new example can be considered already present in the gallery. It is worth highlighting the rationale of this assumption. Actually, each identity can produce a potentially infinite number of different observations of the face and fingerprint biometrics, respectively, but the template gallery in a real biometric system can store only a finite number of templates. In the literature, it has been suggested to "fuse" such similar variations to obtain a super-template (Roli and Marcialis 2006; Rattani et al. 2008a).

The second assumption states that all biometric impressions are equally probable (as usually stated in biometric applications). This hypothesis may be supported in uncontrolled environments.

#### 7.3.2.3 Gallery Size Increase with Supervisor

As pointed out in the previous section, the term "adaptation" refers to substituting the supervisor role. Therefore, in this section we model the human "supervisor" in the updating process. The goal of the model is to describe how the gallery size increase due to the human supervisor. Since in co-updating one of matchers takes the role of supervisor, the co-update modeling is simplified by first considering the "ideal" supervisor. Our aim is to give the expected increase of the gallery size due to this supervisor.

In the update stage, a set $D_U$ of $|D_U| = k$ biometric samples for each identity are presented to the system. The $k$ samples are acquired from $k_g$ "genuine" users and from $k_i$ "impostor" users, $k = k_g + k_i$. Due to the human supervision no impostor can be added to the gallery. Thus, $k_i = 0$ without loss of generality. Moreover, we can assume that a supervisor can correctly verify the identity of each genuine samples, so the number of verified samples will be $k_{\text{ver}} = k$.

Although all the samples can be potentially added to the gallery due to the human validation, only a fraction of these provides a contribution to the size of the gallery. Each of the $k_{\text{ver}}$ samples can be considered as drawn with replacement from a homogeneous population of $N_{\text{TOT}}$ elements, so the set $D_U$ could contain both identical samples and samples already present in the gallery. According to the above hypothesis, to calculate how many samples provide informative contribution to the gallery, we must specify:

- The number $k_d$ of distinct elements, over $k_{\text{ver}}$
- The number $k_{dn}$ of elements not present in gallery, over $k_d$.

The expected value of $k_{dn}$ corresponds to the expected increase $\Delta n$ of the gallery size due to the ideal supervisor. Given $k_d$ and $k_{dn}$ r.vs., it can be proven that

$$\Delta n \cong E\left[k_{dn}\right] = (N_{\text{TOT}} - n) \cdot \left[1 - \left(1 - \frac{1}{N_{\text{TOT}}}\right)^{k_{\text{ver}}}\right].$$

In fact, the quantities $k_{dn}$ and $k_d$ can be viewed as random variables with pdf $p(k_{dn})$ and $p(k_d)$, respectively. According to the law of total probabilities:

$$p(k_{dn}) = \sum_{k_d=0}^{k} p(k_{dn}|k_d) \cdot p(k_d).$$

The pdf $p(k_d)$ – the probability of obtaining exactly $k_d$ distinct elements in a set of $k_{\text{ver}}$ elements drawn with replacement from a homogeneous population of $N_{\text{TOT}}$ elements – can be modeled using a multinomial distribution:

$$p(k_d) = \binom{N_{\text{TOT}}}{k_d} \sum_{i=0}^{k_d} (-1)^i \binom{k_d}{i} \left(\frac{k_d - i}{N_{\text{TOT}}}\right)^{k_{\text{ver}}}. \tag{7.3}$$

The expected value is

$$E\left[k_d\right] = \sum_{k_d=0}^{k} k_d \cdot p(k_d) = N_{\mathrm{TOT}}\left[1 - \left(1 - \frac{1}{N_{\mathrm{TOT}}}\right)^{k_{\mathrm{ver}}}\right]. \quad (7.4)$$

The pdf $p(k_{dn}|k_d)$ – the probability that a set of $k_d$ distinct elements drawn from a homogeneous population of $N_{\mathrm{TOT}}$ elements contains exactly $k_{dn}$ elements not present in gallery – can be modeled using a hypergeometric distribution:

$$p\left(k_{dn}|k_d\right) = \frac{\binom{N_{\mathrm{TOT}} - n}{k_{dn}}\binom{n}{k_d - k_{dn}}}{\binom{N_{\mathrm{TOT}}}{k_d}} \quad (7.5)$$

The expected value is

$$E\left[k_{dn}|k_d\right] = \sum_{k_{dn}=0}^{k_d} k_{dn} \cdot p(k_{dn}|k_d) = k_d \cdot \frac{N_{\mathrm{TOT}} - n}{N_{\mathrm{TOT}}} \quad (7.6)$$

since

$$E\left[k_{dn}\right] = \sum_{k_{dn}=0}^{k_{\mathrm{ver}}} k_{dn} \cdot p\left(k_{dn}\right) = \sum_{k_{dn}=0}^{k_{\mathrm{ver}}} k_{dn} \cdot \left[\sum_{k_d=0}^{k_{\mathrm{ver}}} p\left(k_{dn}|k_d\right) \cdot p\left(k_d\right)\right]. \quad (7.7)$$

Recalling (1.6):

$$E\left[k_{dn}\right] = \sum_{k_d=0}^{k_{\mathrm{ver}}} p\left(k_d\right)\left[\sum_{k_{dn}=0}^{k_d} k_{dn} \cdot p\left(k_{dn}|k_d\right)\right] = \sum_{k_d=0}^{k_{\mathrm{ver}}} p\left(k_d\right) \cdot E\left[k_{dn}|k_d\right], \quad (7.8)$$

we obtain

$$E\left[k_{dn}\right] = \sum_{k_d=0}^{k_{\mathrm{ver}}} p\left(k_d\right)\left[k_d \cdot \frac{N_{\mathrm{TOT}} - n}{N_{\mathrm{TOT}}}\right] = \left(\frac{N_{\mathrm{TOT}} - n}{N_{\mathrm{TOT}}}\right) \cdot \sum_{k_d=0}^{k_{\mathrm{ver}}} k_d \cdot p\left(k_d\right) \quad (7.9)$$

from (7.4):

$$E\left[k_{dn}\right] = \left(N_{\mathrm{TOT}} - n\right) \cdot \left[1 - \left(1 - \tfrac{1}{N_{\mathrm{TOT}}}\right)^{k_{\mathrm{ver}}}\right]. \quad (7.10)$$

We assume that, for each update step, the number of new and distinct samples added to the template gallery, namely, $\Delta n$, is equal to its expected value $E[k_{dn}]$:

$$\Delta n \cong E\left[k_{dn}\right] = \left(N_{\mathrm{TOT}} - n\right) w_{\mathrm{sup}}, \quad (7.11)$$

where the term

$$w_{\text{sup}} = \left(1 - \frac{1}{N_{\text{TOT}}}\right)^{k_{\text{ver}}} \tag{7.12}$$

is related to the number of samples $k_{\text{ver}}$ verified by the supervisor and determines the system's dynamics. This assumption is supported by the fact that the correspondent variance $var[k_{dn}]$ is very small.

It is worth recalling that, due to the human supervision, $k_{\text{ver}} = k$, that is, all the identity of the samples in the $D_U$ set will be verified.

Let $n_0$ be the initial size of the gallery, and $n_{(i)}$be the size of the gallery at the $i$th update step. The length of the gallery at the $i$th step can be written as:

$$\begin{aligned} n_{(0)} &= n_0, \\ n_{(i)} &= n_{(i-1)} \cdot w_{\text{sup}} + N_{\text{TOT}} \cdot \left(1 - w_{\text{sup}}\right). \end{aligned} \tag{7.13}$$

The size of the gallery at the $i$th update step is the weighted mean between the maximum allowed size $N_{\text{TOT}}$ and the size at the previous step. It is easy to see that the weight $w_{\text{sup}}$ is a monotonically decreasing function of $k_{\text{val}}$. High values of $k_{\text{val}}$ determine low values of $w_{\text{sup}}$, so the size of the gallery at the $i$th update step depends principally on $N_{\text{TOT}}$. Low values of $k_{\text{val}}$ determine high values of $w_{\text{sup}}$, so the size of the gallery at the $i$th update step is more related to the size at the previous step.

#### 7.3.2.4 Gallery Size Increase without Supervisor

In the present section we will propose a model that describes how the gallery size increases using a co-update technique.

In the co-update stage, a set $D_U$ of $|D_U| = k$ pairs of biometric samples (i.e., face and fingerprint) are presented to the system. As illustrated in the previous section, the $k$ samples are acquired from $k_g$"genuine" users and from $k_i$ "impostor" users, $k = k_g + k_i$.

As described in Section 7.3.1 the "master" biometric takes the role of the supervisor.

The difference with Section 7.3.2.3 is that (1) impostors may be introduced in the gallery (basically, $FAR \neq 0$) and (2) some genuine users can be rejected (basically, $FRR \neq 0$). With regard to point 1, we may impose that systems are working on the FAR = 0% operational point, also called zeroFAR. Using this operational point no impostor will be added to the gallery, so without loss of generality we can develop the model assuming that $k_i = 0$.

Let us call $k_{\text{ver}}$, $k_{\text{ver}} \leq k$, the number of samples of the master biometric whose identity has been verified (i.e., its score is over the updating threshold in practice).

The set $D_U$ is composed of pairs of biometric samples (master and slave), and each sample in the couple is acquired by the same individual, so the value $k_{\text{ver}}$ represents both the number of samples of the master biometric correctly validated by the matcher and the number of samples, whose identity has been validated due to the master biometry, that can be potentially added to the gallery.

The value $k_{\text{ver}}$ can be easily computed by considering that each of $k$ biometric samples of the master biometric can be considered as drawn with replacement from a homogeneous population of $N_{\text{TOT}}^{(M)}$ elements.

The probability that a "master" sample will be verified is

$$p = 1 - FRR^{(M)}, \tag{7.14}$$

where $FRR^{(M)}$ is the False Rejection Rate for the master biometric computed at the operational point FAR $= 0\%$. The probability that $m$ samples will be verified can be modeled using a binomial distribution:

$$p(m) = \binom{k_{\text{ver}}}{m} p^m (1-p)^{(k_{\text{ver}}-m)}. \tag{7.15}$$

Thus, the expected value of verified samples is

$$E[m] = k_{\text{ver}} \cdot p = k_{\text{ver}} \cdot \left(1 - FRR^{(M)}\right). \tag{7.16}$$

Let us assume that for each co-update step the number of verified samples $k_{\text{ver}}$ is about equal to its expected value $E[m]$, since the correspondent variance $var[m]$ is very small:

$$k_{\text{ver}} \cong E[m] = k \cdot \left(1 - FRR^{(M)}\right). \tag{7.17}$$

It is worth highlighting difference and similarities between the supervised update and co-update.

In the supervised update approach all the $k$ samples could be potentially added to the gallery due to the human validation that ensures the true identity of these samples, so $k_{\text{ver}} = k$. Each of these $k_{\text{ver}}$ samples can be considered as drawn with replacement from a homogeneous population of $N_{\text{TOT}}$ elements. This assumption has been used in Section 7.3.2.3 to develop the model.

In the co-update approach the matcher based on the master biometric can validate the identity of only $k_{\text{ver}} = k \cdot \left(1 - FRR^{(M)}\right)$ samples. At least as regards subtask (1) of a human supervisor (identity verification), the master matcher plays the role of a supervisor whose effectiveness is related to the $FRR$ value. The more the $FRR$ value decreases, the more the effectiveness of the matcher tends to that of the human supervisor.

The $k$ samples of the master biometric are drawn with replacement from a homogeneous population of $N_{\text{TOT}}^{(M)}$ elements, and the $k_{\text{ver}}$ samples of the slave biometric are the samples that were coupled with master samples correctly validated. So the $k_{\text{ver}}$ samples of the slave biometric are selected by the master matcher. Because the two biometrics at hand are conditionally independent (7.1, 7.2), even the $k_{\text{ver}}$ samples of the slave biometric can be considered as drawn with replacement from a homogeneous population of $N_{\text{TOT}}^{(S)}$ elements. Due to the conditional independence of the two biometrics we can describe the increase of the gallery size using results obtained in the supervised update model.

Recalling (7.11) we can write the (expected) enlargement of the slave gallery due to the collection of $k$ couple of biometric samples:

$$\Delta n \cong E\left[k_{dn}\right] = (N_{\text{TOT}} - n) \cdot \left[1 - \left(1 - \frac{1}{N_{\text{TOT}}}\right)^{k_{\text{ver}}}\right]. \tag{7.18}$$

Recalling the expected value of $k_{\text{ver}}$ in a co-update system,

$$\Delta n = (N_{\text{TOT}} - n) \cdot \left[1 - \left(1 - \frac{1}{N_{\text{TOT}}}\right)^{k\left[1-FRR^{(M)}\right]}\right], \tag{7.19}$$

let $n_0^{(S)}$ be the initial size of the slave gallery, and $n_{(i)}^{(S)}$ be the size of the gallery at the $i$th update step. The length of the gallery at the $i$th step can be written as

$$\begin{aligned} n_{(0)}^{(S)} &= n_0^{(S)}, \\ n_{(i)}^{(S)} &= n_{(i-1)}^{(S)} \cdot w + N_{\text{TOT}}^{(S)} \cdot (1 - w), \end{aligned} \tag{7.20}$$

and the term $w$ is

$$w = \left(1 - \frac{1}{N_{\text{TOT}}^{(S)}}\right)^{k_{\text{ver}}} = \left(w_{\text{sup}}\right)^{\left[1-FRR^{(M)}\right]}. \tag{7.21}$$

The length of the gallery at the $i$th step, $n_{(i)}^{(S)}$, is the weighted average between the length at the previous step, $n_{(i-1)}^{(S)}$, and the maximum length of the gallery, $N_{\text{TOT}}^{(S)}$. The weight $w$, that depends on the $FRR^{(M)}$value, determines the system's dynamics.

If $FRR^{(M)} = 1$, $w = 1$ and $n_{(i)}^{(S)} = n_{(0)}^{(S)}$. No genuine sample will be correctly accepted by the matcher, and the co-update approach will be unable to enlarge the slave gallery.

If $FRR^{(M)} = 0$, $w = w_{\text{sup}} < 1$. The matcher can accept all the genuine samples presented to the system, as a human supervisor. The size of the slave gallery increases as in the case of supervised update.

If $0 < FRR^{(M)} < 1$, $w = (w_{\text{sup}})^{[1-FRR^{(M)}]}$, so $w_{\text{sup}} < w < 1$. The co-update approach can enlarge the slave gallery, even if more slowly than in the case of supervised update.

To sum up, the system dynamic equation is the same as in the supervised case, but while the human supervisor guarantees correctly verifying all "genuine" identities (so $FRR = 1$ and $k_{\text{ver}} = k$), in the co-update approach the human supervisor is replaced by a matcher characterized by $FRR \leq 1$ and $k_{\text{ver}} \leq k$.

It can be noticed that

$$\lim_{i\to\infty} n_{(i)}^{(S)} = \begin{cases} N_{\text{TOT}}^{(S)} & \text{if } w < 1, \\ n_{(0)}^{(S)} & \text{if } w = 1 \end{cases} \tag{7.22}$$

that is, if the co-update process is able to acquire new samples ($w < 1$), the gallery will reach its maximum size $N_{\text{TOT}}^{(S)}$.

As both biometrics act as a "master" or a "slave," we can report in a compact form the enlargement of both galleries during the co-update process:

$$\mathbf{n}_{(i)} = \left[\mathbf{n}_{(i-1)}\right]^t \cdot \mathbf{w} + [\mathbf{N}_{\text{TOT}}]^t \cdot [1 - \mathbf{w}], \tag{7.23}$$

where

$$w^{(\text{finger})} = \left(1 - \frac{1}{N_{\text{TOT}}^{(\text{finger})}}\right)^{k[1-FRR^{(\text{face})}]}, \tag{7.24}$$

$$w^{(\text{face})} = \left(1 - \frac{1}{N_{\text{TOT}}^{(\text{face})}}\right)^{k[1-FRR^{(\text{finger})}]}, \tag{7.25}$$

$$\mathbf{w} = \begin{bmatrix} w^{(\text{finger})} & 0 \\ 0 & w^{(\text{face})} \end{bmatrix}, \tag{7.26}$$

$$\mathbf{n}_{(i)} = \begin{bmatrix} n_{(i)}^{(\text{finger})} \\ n_{(i)}^{(\text{face})} \end{bmatrix}, \tag{7.27}$$

$$\mathbf{N}_{\text{TOT}} = \begin{bmatrix} N_{\text{TOT}}^{(\text{finger})} \\ N_{\text{TOT}}^{(\text{face})} \end{bmatrix}. \tag{7.28}$$

#### 7.3.2.5 False Rejection Rate Modeling

Here $w$ depends on $FRR^{(M)}$. To model this value, each client is characterized by two parameters, $f_I$ and $m$, defined as follows. This is done for each biometric at hand.

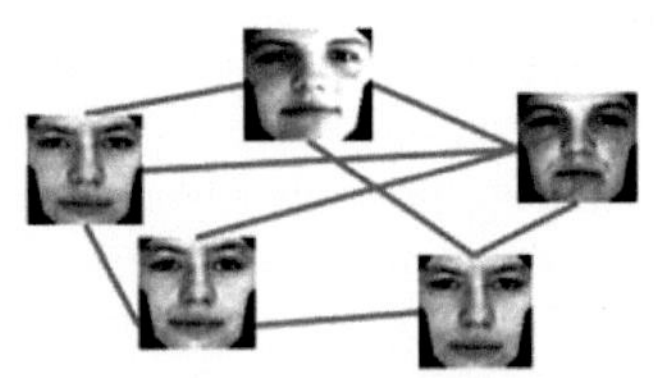


Figure 7.1. An example of "easy" and "difficult" clients that exhibit different connection degrees.

Let us define the "connection degree" $m(x)$ for a biometric sample $x$ as the number of other samples belonging to the same client that produce a score value over the updating threshold.

There is a subset of samples for which this connection degree is zero: samples that, even if in the template set, cannot improve the system's performances. Let $f_I$ be the fraction of these "isolated" samples, and $m$ the average connection degree computed only for nonisolated samples. In other words, the value $f_I$ represents the fraction of outlier samples. Morevoer, let $m$ be the average connection degree computed only for the nonoutlier. Therefore, "difficult" clients are modeled by a low value of $m$ and high value of $f_I$, while a high value of $m$ and a low value of $f_I$ are adopted for "easy" clients (see Figure 7.1). Parameters $m$ and $f_I$ depend on the dataset and on the employed matchers.

Figure 7.1 exemplifies the concept of "easy" and "difficult" clients in terms of their connection degree.

Isolated samples contribute to the $FRR$ value with a constant value equal to 1, because they cannot "match" other samples. A gallery that contains only outliers will lead to a system with $FRR = 1$. The contribute of nonisolated samples is computed as follows. Let $x$ be a sample with connection degree $m$. The identity of $x$ will be correctly verified if at least one among these $m$ samples is in the master gallery. Let $r$ be the number of these samples in the master gallery, $0 \leq r \leq m$; thus the identity of $x$ will be correctly verified if $r > 0$, that is, $FRR = 0$. Otherwise, this sample will be rejected definitely, and thus $FRR = 1$. The value $r$ is a random variable with pdf $p(r)$. Accordingly,

$$FRR^{(M)} = f_I \cdot 1 + (1 - f_I) \cdot [0 \cdot p(r = 0) + 1 \cdot p(r > 0)]. \qquad (7.29)$$

Since $p(r)$ is the probability that exactly $r$ samples on $m$ are present in a gallery of size $n$, $r$ can be modeled by the hypergeometric distribution when

**Algorithm 2** Algorithm for Co-updating of multiple matchers

(i) Define $c$ matchers, one for each "view"
(ii) Set the size of the ensemble, $DIM_E$
(iii) Set the number of possible ensembls, $N_E = \binom{c}{DIM_E}$
(iv) In the enrollment (supervised) session, collect a multimodal set of sample $D_L$ for each client
(v) Create templates using the set $D_L$
(vi) Loop for $H$ iterations:
(vii) (a) Collect a set $D_U$ without supervision. Each element of $D_U$ is a set of $c$ biometric samples $\{\mathbf{x}_1, \ldots, \mathbf{x}_c\}$ from the same client.
(b) For each ensemble $E_i, i \in \{1, \ldots, N_E\}$
(c) 1. "Master" matcher $\leftarrow E_i$
2. "Slave" views $\leftarrow \mathbf{x}_j, j \neq i$
3. If $\mathbf{x}_i$ is verified by $E_i$, samples $\mathbf{x}_j, j \neq i$ are added to $D_L$
(d) Update templates using the augmented labeled set $D_L$

$n < (N_{\text{TOT}}^{(M)} - m)$:

$$p(r) = h\big(r; N_{\text{TOT}}^{(M)}, m, n\big).$$

Worth noting is that as the gallery reaches the size $n = (N_{\text{TOT}}^{(M)} - m)$, $FRR^{(M)}$ depends only on the fraction of outliers, $f_I$:

$$FRR^{(M)} = \begin{cases} f_I \cdot 1 + (1 - f_I) \cdot 0 & \text{if } n \geq N_{\text{TOT}}^{(M)} - m \\ f_I \cdot 1 + (1 - f_I) \cdot h\big(r = 0; N_{\text{TOT}}^{(M)}, m, n\big) & \text{if } n < N_{\text{TOT}}^{(M)} - m. \end{cases} \tag{7.30}$$

#### 7.3.2.6 Ensemble of Matchers

Let us consider a biometric identification problem characterized by the use of $c$ sets of features (here called "views") $\{\mathbf{x}_1, \ldots, \mathbf{x}_c\}$. Each view can correspond to one biometry, or several views can be obtained from the same biometry, provided that each view is conditionally independent of each other. Under these assumption it is easy to generalize the proposed model in a general framework involving more than two matchers. The system is made up of $c$ matchers, one matcher for each view. Due to the independence assumption, each recognizer is expected to assign correct "labels" to certain input data that are difficult for the other. The description of the generalized co-update is given by Algorithm 2.

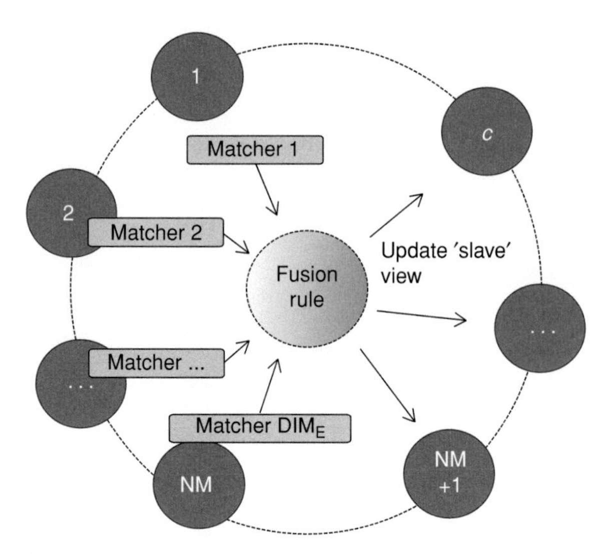


Figure 7.2. The scheme of the template co-update algorithm extended to multiple matchers.

Matchers can be combined in different kinds of ensembles (Kittler 1998). Without loss of generality, we can neglect the particular kind of adopted fusion rule. Setting the size of the ensemble, $DIM_E$, the number of possible ensembles will be $N_E = \binom{c}{DIM_E}$. The main difference from the co-update approach is that the role of "master" is played by an ensemble of matchers instead of a single matcher, and the role of "slave" – that is, galleries that are augmented due to the master ensemble – is played by all the views that are not used by the master ensemble. Figure 7.2 shows the extension to multiple matchers of the template co-update algorithm.

During the off-line co-update phase, each ensemble is applied to the batch $D_U$. As in the co-update algorithm, the results of matching is a value that can be interpreted as a similarity value between the input sample and related template set. If this value exceeds a given "updating threshold," the match is verified, and samples related to the group of $c$ slave matchers are added to the set $D_L$. All views assume, alternatively, master and slave roles. The process is repeated a specified number of times. It is worth highlighting two particular cases: (1) $DIM_E = 1$: The ensemble is made up of only one matcher at time, and the other ones are "slaves." (2) $DIM_E = c - 1$: The ensemble is made up of $c - 1$ matchers at time, and the remaining one is "slave." Under the same assumption made for the co-update process, the length of the $j$th slave gallery at the $i$th step can be written as

$$\begin{aligned} n_{(0)}^{(S_j)} &= n_0^{(S_j)}, \\ n_{(i)}^{(S_j)} &= n_{(i-1)}^{(S_j)} \cdot w + N_{\text{TOT}}^{(S_j)} \cdot (1-w). \end{aligned} \tag{7.31}$$

$FRR^M$ depends on the particular kind of adopted fusion rule.

On the basis of the above generalization, we believe that generalized co-updating can be also supported by hypothesizing the dichotomy master–slave, where both are an ensemble of matchers. Therefore, the final behavior should be quite similar to that of the analyzed two-matchers case.

## 7.4 Experimental Results

### 7.4.1 The Data Set

The data set adopted consists of 42 individuals composed of 20 face and fingerprint images for each individual, keeping in mind the independence of face and fingerprint traits. The time of both collected data sets spans over one year. Forty-two frontal face images with 20 instances representing significant illumination changes and variations in facial expressions per person were used from the Equinox Corporation database (Equinox). The fingerprint data set has been collected by the authors using the Biometrika Fx2000 optical sensor. The images are acquired with variations in pressure, moisture, and time interval to represent large intraclass variations. The results are computed on five random coupling of face and fingerprint datasets and are averaged. While minutiae are simply extracted from the fingerprint images after commonly used processing algorithms (Maltoni et al. 2003), PCA is computed for the whole data set and applied to face images to reduce the size of the overall feature space. According to the current literature (Li and Jain 2005), 95 % of energy is retained.

It is worth noting that fingerprint and face data sets are strongly different in terms of environmental conditions: The face one is notably simpler than the fingerprint one. We adopted so different data sets to show the effect of intraclass variations on the model prediction ability.

### 7.4.2 Experimental Protocol

To investigate the correctness of the proposed model, we first implemented a simple bimodal identification system made up of a PCA-based face matcher and a fingerprint matcher using the String matching algorithm. (String is based

Table 7.1. *Average and Standard Deviation Values of the Model Parameters. Note that Values Confirm the Difference Among Adopted Data Sets as to the "Intrinsic" Difficulty of Clients, Depending on the Given Biometric. In the Table, $f_I$ is the Fraction of Isolated Samples and m is the Connection Degree*

| | Face | | Fingerprint | |
|---|---|---|---|---|
| | Mean | Standard Deviation | Mean | Standard Deviation |
| $m$ | 0.524 | 0.246 | 0.365 | 0.274 |
| $f_I$ | 0.231 | 0.138 | 0.818 | 0.144 |

on minutiae points.) We used the standard versions of these two recognition algorithms (Turk and Pentland 1991; Jain et al. 1997). Then we implemented the template co-update algorithm. Both the eigenspace of the PCA-based face matcher and the co-update threshold value at FAR $= 0\%$ are computed using the whole dataset and has not been updated during the co-update process. The update of face and fingerprint templates is performed simply by adding new examples to the user's gallery.

In the experiments and in the model, $m_i$ has been set as follows. We considered all samples for each client $i$, and computed $m_i$ as the average number of samples exceeding the updating threshold. Then we selected, as the initial template in $D_l$, the image near to $m_i$ samples. The rationale behind this choice is to exclude outliers from the initial gallery, similar to what happens in real situations, where the initial template is chosen in completely supervised fashion.

To simulate the acquisition of a batch set $Du$, several sets of $k = 10$ couples face and fingerprint of "genuine" examples are drawn with replacement from a homogeneous population of $N_{\text{TOT}}^{\text{face}} = N_{\text{TOT}}^{\text{fingerprint}} = 20$ samples and used as batches collected during the system operations. We are aware that adopted database size may not be very well appropriate for the task, but it respects, on average, the size adopted in other template update work reported in the literature (Ryu et al. 2006; Jiang and Ser 2002; Liu et al. 2003).

### 7.4.3 Results

To set the correct parameters in the proposed model, for each client and for each biometric we computed (1) the value $f_I$, that is, the fraction of samples that produce a score' under the updating threshold, and (2) the value $m$, that is, the integer nearest to the average connection degree of the connected samples. Table 7.1 shows the computed parameters. Results are averaged on 10 trials (experimental values).

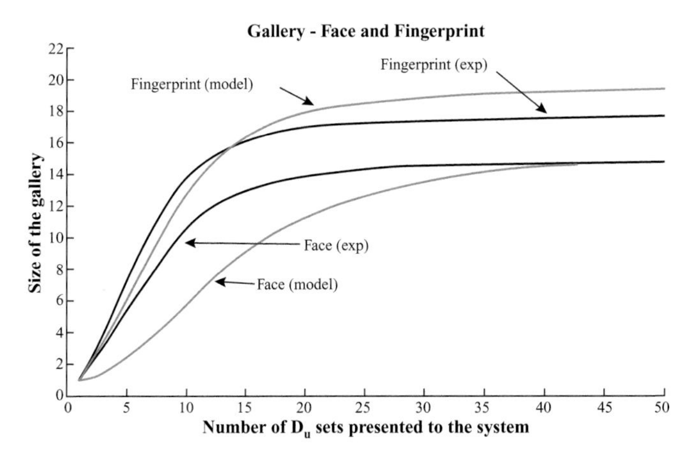


Figure 7.3. Predicted and experimental curves showing the differences between the proposed model and the "real" system. The gallery size increase at each co-update iteration is shown.

Table 7.1 reports the mean and standard deviation of $f_I$ and $m$ values for all clients. Fingerprint and face matchers have been considered, and the difference between these two matchers can be seen. This is mainly due to the "difficulty" of an adopted data set. In particular, the fingerprint data set, also called "Extreme," exhibits several strong intraclass variations in terms of moisture and pressure, thus making it quite difficult and a good test reference for stressing fingerprint matchers.

Figures 7.3–7.4 plot the predicted and experimental curves related to the gallery size increase (Eqs. [7.20] and [7.30]).

The model is able to predict the experimental performance, with a negligible difference. As can be seen, in the real scenario, due to the presence of isolated samples, the true value of FRR will be greater than 0 (FRR = 1 if all the samples in gallery are isolated). As can be noticed from Figs. 7.3–7.4, this drawback is taken into account in the present model.

The saturation of theoretical and experimental curves is obviously due to the form of Eqs. (7.20)–(7.30). In particular, the weight $w$ tends to decrease as the gallery size of both matchers increases, depending on the value of their FRR. Thus, the size of galleries must converge to $N_{\text{TOT}}$ if $m_i$ is not zero. According to the model, at the end of co-update process, $FRR(n = N_{\text{TOT}}) = f_I$. It is worth noting that the correct prediction of FRR values is matter of primary importance both for the validation of the model and for the designers, who need relevant information about the performance of the system.

Some issues have not yet been investigated: (2) In real environments $N_{\text{TOT}}$ is unknown. This problem can be overcame by considering $N_{\text{TOT}}$ as the number

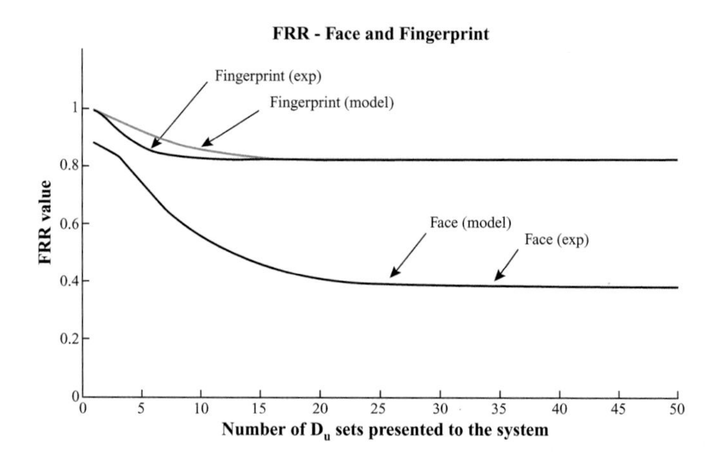


Figure 7.4. Predicted and experimental curves showing the differences between the proposed model and the "real" system. The False Rejection Rate at each co-update iteration is shown.

of samples in the batch exhibiting, for each client, a score above the zeroFAR threshold adopted. (2) The same for the estimation of $m$. These assumptions do not consider the problem of impostor insertion, a still open issue as remarked in (Poh et al. 2009; Rattani et al. 2008a). Therefore, the impact of $N_{TOT}$ and $m$ predicted for a batch of samples even including impostors, on a larger, nonchimerical data set, will be investigated in a future work.

Finally, we show in Figure 7.5 the plot of accuracy achieved by co-updating fingerprint and face matchers against the one obtained by simply self-updating

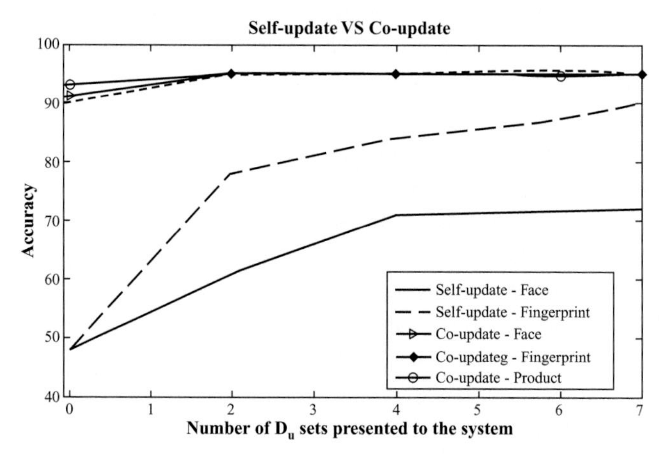


Figure 7.5. Experimental comparison between self-update and co-update in the "identification" modality. The term "accuracy" refers to the identification rate.

both matchers. With the term "self-updating," we mean that the role of the supervisor is taken by the matcher itself. In Figure 7.5 the so-called "identification" modality is adopted. This means that a sample must be recognized in the set of clients already registered in the system. Reported plots clearly show that co-update allows us to achieve much better performance than that achieved by self-updating the individual matchers.

## 7.5 Discussion

In this section, we discuss the main results reported in the chapter. Some of the topics that should be better investigated can be also extended to other algorithms for adaptive biometric systems.

In our opinion, three issues must be pointed out before closing the chapter:

(1) The security breaches introduced by the co-updating algorithm
(2) The relationship between the highly genuine samples and the image quality
(3) The robustness of parameters estimation, which can be also dependent on the intrinsic characteristics of clients.

As pointed out in previous sections, the proposed model assumes a quite reliable estimation of the zeroFAR operational point. This is a strong assumption because it is well known that a large sample size is necessary to estimate this point. A small error in the threshold could lead to a FAR more than zero. On the other hand, such an estimation error does not ensure that the corresponding FRR will be reduced, since these kinds of errors involve a unreliable estimation of both curves (FAR and FRR). Even by assuming that FRR decreases, the correspondent FAR impacts on the system performance and, thus, on the co-updating algorithm's performance. In particular, since the probability of misclassifying impostors is not zero, some impostors, according to the rationale of the algorithm, could be introduced into the gallery. As a consequence, they could be considered as novel "templates" and could attract novel impostor samples. This aspect has been investigated in Rattani et al. (2008a) by experiments. Although that paper has shown that co-updating is less prone than self-updating to introduction, of impostors the problem still exists also for co-updates. This obviously must be taken into account even in the proposed model, when an extension aimed at considering the probability of impostor introduction must be added and is currently a matter of ongoing research.

The second aspect is related to the criterion for introducing "highly genuine" samples to the gallery. For instance, even if the "master" biometric selected the highly genuine users according to the matching scores, a problem can arise if the "slave" biometric received corrupted data or bad quality samples. These are not necessarily desirable as intraclass variations. For example, they could lead to a bad estimation of zeroFAR after updating. Therefore, the decision process should be improved. In Poh et al. (2009), the image quality has been suggested as an additional criterion, to try avoiding the problem of "undesired" intraclass variations insertion. No experiments have been done so far for exploring the benefits that an additional feature can add to adaptive biometric systems.

The third issue is more related to the proposed model and to the working effect of the template co-update algorithm. It is worth noting that a ROC curve can be plotted for each client. Therefore, an appropriate threshold should be tuned. This is motivated also by the presence of clients that are intrinsically "difficult," which tend to be confused with other clients. This aspect has been recently investigated for "self-updating" systems in Marcialis et al. (2008) and Rattani et al. (2009b). Under certain environmental conditions, it has been shown that using a client-specific threshold allows one to add fewer impostors than using a global threshold, as is done in this chapter.

A similar problem arises, in our opinion, in the co-update algorithm and in the estimation of parameters of the proposed model. In fact, it should be pointed out that, in the reported experiments, the parameters have been estimated for the whole data set. Thus, the hypothesis is the reliable estimation of the degree of connection and the fraction of connected samples as well as that of zeroFAR. This can be performed only on a small part of the data that are labeled data (at the starting iteration) and, gradually, to data added into the galleries. Therefore, several experiments must be performed to evaluate how the reliability of the parameters impacts the prediction ability of the model, in particular, by studying the user population characteristics, as recently done in Rattani et al. (2009b), in the case of self-updates.

## 7.6 Conclusions

In this chapter, we reviewed the approaches proposed in the literature aimed at adding to biometric systems some characteristic of "adaptation." In particular, we focused on the "adaptation," or "updating," of templates, and the problem of deciding when to exploit unlabeled samples from a batch of data – in other words, how to model the supervisor in an automatic form, explicitely conceived for multibiometric systems.

This investigation led us to present the so-called template co-update algorithm. We also proposed a theoretical model aimed at explaining its behavior in terms of the amount of samples added to the galleries at each iteration and the related expected performance. The model assumes that no impostors can be wrongly classified, that is, the system is working on a reliable estimation of the zeroFAR operational point. The model has been finally extended to multibiometric systems, that is, systems exploiting more than two matchers. Experiments on a chimerical bimodal data set have shown the predictive ability of the model.

Although it has been shown that the use of multibiometric adaptive systems can further improve recognition performance, the role of the human supervisor can be avoided with difficulty. The potential introduction of impostors in the clients' gallery and the crucial settings of the updating parameters (e.g., the threshold) must be strongly taken into account – especially because it can be argued that even "genuine" biometric images can be "dangerous" if affected by a strong lack of quality. However, the introduction of some "adaptability" properties can also help the human supervisor. From this point of view, we believe that the proposed model can be extended and adapted to other algorithms. To sum up, it can potentially give biometric system designers interesting guidelines for the introduction of automatic adaptation capabilities.

## References


Blum, A., and T. Mitchell. 1998. Combining labeled and unlabeled data with co-training. Proc. of the Workshop on Computational Learning Theory, pp. 92–100.

Didaci, L., and F. Roli, 2006. Using co-training and self-training in semi-supervised multiple classifier systems, *Joint IAPR Int. Work. on S+SSPR06*, Springer LNCS 4109, 522–530.

Didaci, L., G. L. Marcialis, and F. Roli. 2008. A theoretical and experimental analysis of template co-update in biometric verification systems, *Joint IAPR Int. Workshop on Structural and Syntactical Pattern Recognition and Statistical Techniques in Pattern Recognition S+SSPR08*, December 4–6, 2008, Orlando (FL), N de Vitora-Lobo et al. eds., Springer LNCS5342, pp. 775–784.

Didaci, L., G. L. Marcialis, and F. Roli. 2009a. Modelling FRR of biometric verification systems using the template co-update algorithm, *3rd IAPR/IEEE Int. Conference on Biometrics ICB* 2009, June 2–5, 2009, Alghero (Italy), M. Tistarelli and M. Nixon eds., Springer LNCS 5558, pp.765–774.

Didaci, L., G. L. Marcialis, and F. Roli. 2009b. Semi-supervised co-update of multiple matchers, IAPR *Int. Workshop on Multiple Classifiers Systems MCS* 2009, Rejkiavik (Iceland), Springer LNCS, in press.

Freni, B., G. L. Marcialis, and F. Roli. 2008. Replacement algorithms for fingerprint template update, *5th Int. Conf. on Image Analysis and Recognition ICIAR08*, June, 25–27, 2008, Povoa de Varzim (Portugal), A. Campihlo and M. Kamel eds., Springer LNCS 5112, pp. 884–893.

Freni, B., G. L. Marcialis, and F. Roli. 2008. Template selection by editing algorithms: a case study in face recognition, *Joint IAPR Int. Workshop on Structural and Syntactical Pattern Recognition and Statistical Techniques in Pattern Recognition S+SSPR08*, December 4–6, 2008, Orlando (FL), N de Vitora-Lobo et al. eds., Springer LNCS5342, pp. 755–764.

Hand, D. J. 2006. Classifier technology and the illusion of progress. *Statistical Science*, **21**(1), 1–15.

http://www.equinoxsensors.com/products/HID.html.

Jain, A. K., L. Hong, and R. Bolle. 1997. On-line fingerprint verification, *IEEE Transactions on Pattern Analysis and Machine Intelligence*, **19**(4), 302–314.

Jiang, X., and W. Ser. 2002. Online fingerprint template improvement, *IEEE Transactions on Pattern Analysis and Machine Intelligence*, **24**(8), 1121–1126.

Kelly, M. G., D. J. Hand, and N. M. Adams. 1999. The impact of changing populations on classifier performance. In *Proc 5th ACM SIGDD International Conference on Knowledge Discovery and Data Mining*, pp. 367–371, San Diego, CA, ACM Press.

Kittler, J., M. Hatef, R. Duin, and J. Matas. 1998. On combining classifiers, *IEEE Trans. on PAMI*, **20**(3), 226–239.

Li, S. Z., and A. K. Jain. 2005. *Handbook of Face Recognition*. Springer.

Liu, X., T. Chen, and S. M. Thornton. 2003. Eigenspace updating for non-stationary process and its application to face recognition, *Pattern Recognition*, pp. 1945–1959.

Maltoni, D., D. Maio, A. K. Jain, and S. Prabhakar. 2003. *Handbook of Fingerprint Recognition*. Springer.

Marcialis, G. L., A. Rattani, and F. Roli. 2008. Biometric template update: an experimental investigation on the relationship between update errors and performance degradation in face verification, *Joint IAPR Int. Workshop on Structural and Syntactical Pattern Recognition and Statistical Techniques in Pattern Recognition S+SSPR08*, December 4–6, 2008, Orlando (FL), N. de Vitora-Lobo et al. eds., Springer LNCS5342, pp. 694–703.

Nagy, G. 2004a. Classifiers that improve with use, *Proc. Conference on Pattern Recognition and Multimedia, IEICE Pub.*, **103**(658), Tokyo, pp. 79–86.

Nagy, G. 2004b. Visual pattern recognition in the years ahead, *Proc. of International Conference on Pattern Recognition* XVII, vol. IV, Cambridge, UK, August, pp. 7–10.

Okada, K., and C. von der Malsburg. 1999. Automatic video indexing with incremental gallery creation: integration of recognition and knowledge acquisition, *Proc. ATR Symposium on Face and Object Recognition*, pp. 153–154, Kyoto, July 19–23.

Poh, N., R. Wong, J. Kittler, and F. Roli. 2009. Challenges and research directions for adaptive biometric recognition systems, *3rd IAPR/IEEE Int. Conference on Biometrics ICB* 2009, June 2–5, 2009, Alghero (Italy), M. Tistarelli and M. Nixon eds., Springer LNCS 5558, pp. 753–764.

Rattani, A., G. L. Marcialis, and F. Roli. 2008a. Capturing large intra-class variations of biometric data by template co-updating, *IEEE Workshop on Biometrics, Int. Conf. on Vision and Pattern Recognition CVPR08*, Anchorage, Alaska, USA (2008).

Rattani, A., G. L. Marcialis, and F. Roli. 2008b. Biometric template update using the graph-mincut algorithm: a case study in face verification, *IEEE Biometric Symposium BioSymp08*, September 23–25, 2008, Tampa (FL), IEEE, ISBN 978-1-4244-2567-9, pp. 23–28.

Rattani, A., B. Freni, G. L. Marcialis, and F. Roli. 2009a. Template update methods in adaptive biometric systems: a critical review, *3rd IAPR/IEEE Int. Conference on Biometrics ICB* 2009, June 2–5, 2009, Alghero (Italy), M. Tistarelli and M. Nixon eds., Springer LNCS 5558, pp. 847–856.

Rattani, A., G. L. Marcialis, and F. Roli. 2009b. An experimental analysis of the relationship between biometric template update and the Doddington's Zoo in face verification, *Proc. of IEEE/IAPR Int. Conf. on Image Analysis and Processing*, Springer LNCS, in press.

Rhodes, K. A. 2004. Aviation security, challenges in using biometric technologies. U.S.A. General Accounting Office.

Roli, F., and G. L. Marcialis. 2006. Semi-supervised PCA-based face recognition using self-training, *Joint IAPR Int. Work. on S+SSPR06*, Springer LNCS 4109, 560–568.

Roli, F., L. Didaci, and G. L. Marcialis. 2007. Template co-update in multimodal biometric systems, *IEEE/IAPR 2nd International Conference on Biometrics ICB* 2007, August 27–29, 2007, Seoul (Korea), S.-W. Lee and S. Li eds., Springer LNCS 4642, pp. 1194–1202.

Roli, F., L. Didaci, and G. L. Marcialis. 2008. Adaptive biometric systems that can improve with use, in N. Ratha and V. Govindaraju eds., *Advances in Biometrics: Sensors, Systems and Algorithms*, Springer, pp. 447–471, 2008

Ross, A., K. Nandakumar, and A. K. Jain. 2006. *Handbook of Multibiometrics*. Springer.

Ryu, C., K. Hakil, and A. Jain. 2006. Template adaptation based fingerprint verification, *Proc. ICPR*, **4**, 582–585, Hong Kong.

Seeger, M. 2002. Learning with labeled and unlabeled data, Technical Report, University of Edinburgh, Institute for Adaptive and Neural Computation, pp. 1–62.

Sinha, P., B. J. Balas, Y. Ostrovsky, and R. Russell. 2006. Face recognition by humans: 19 results all computer vision researchers should know about. Proceedings of IEEE, vol. 94, no. 11, 1948–1962.

Sinha, P., B. J. Balas, Y. Ostrovsky, and R. Russell. 2006. Face recognition by humans. In *Face Recognition: Models and Mechanisms*. Academic Press.

Sukthankar, R., and R. Stockton. 2001. Argus: the digital doorman, *IEEE Intelligent Systems*, March/April, pp. 14–19.

Tabassi, E., C. L. Wilson, and C. I. Watson. 2004. Fingerprint image quality, NIST Technical Report NISTIR 7151, August, 2004.

Tan, X., S. Chen, Z.-H. Zhou, and F. Zhang. 2006. Face recognition from a single image per person: a survey. *Pattern Recognition*, **39**(9), 1725–1745.

Turk M., and A. Pentland. 1991. Eigenfaces for face recognition. *Journal of Cognitive Neuroscience*, **3**(1), 71–86, 1991.

Uludag, U., A. Ross, and A. K. Jain. 2004. Biometric template selection and update: a case study in fingerprints, *Pattern Recognition*, **37**(7), 1533–1542.

Zhu, X. 2006. Semi-supervised learning literature survey, Technical report, Computer Sciences TR 1530, Univ. Wisconsin, Madison, USA.

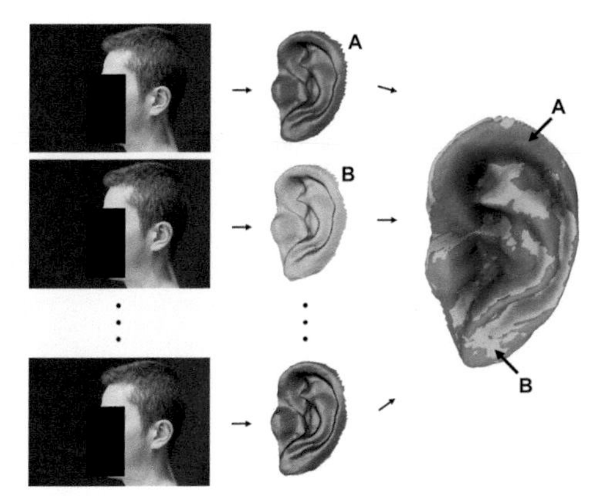


Figure 1.3. The 3D ear models obtained from the video frame set are globally aligned using ICP.

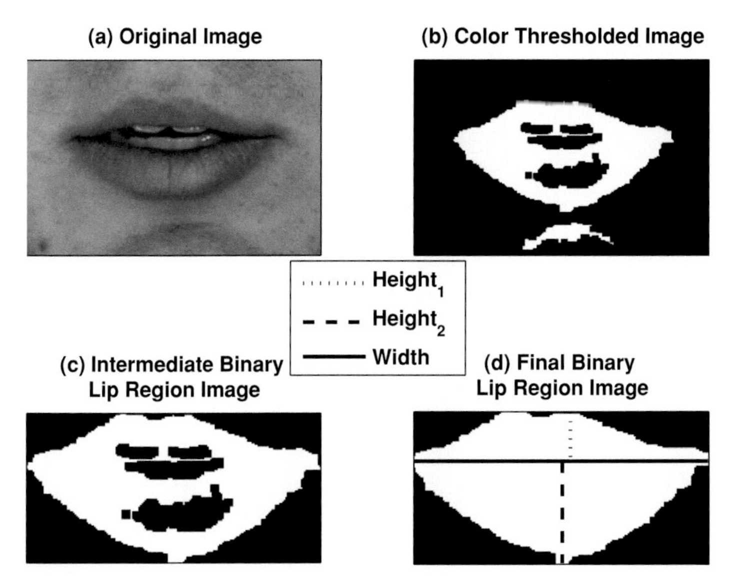


Figure 2.2. Visual feature extraction in "System-1" for an image frame of the AVPF corpus; see also Kumar et al. (2007).

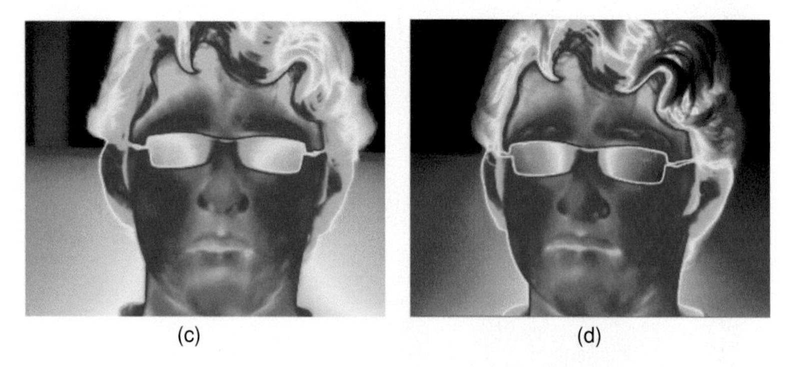


Figure 4.1. Example showing illumination effect on visible and thermal infrared images. All the images were acquired from the same subject at the same time. (c) Thermal infrared image in normal light. (d) Thermal infrared image in low light.

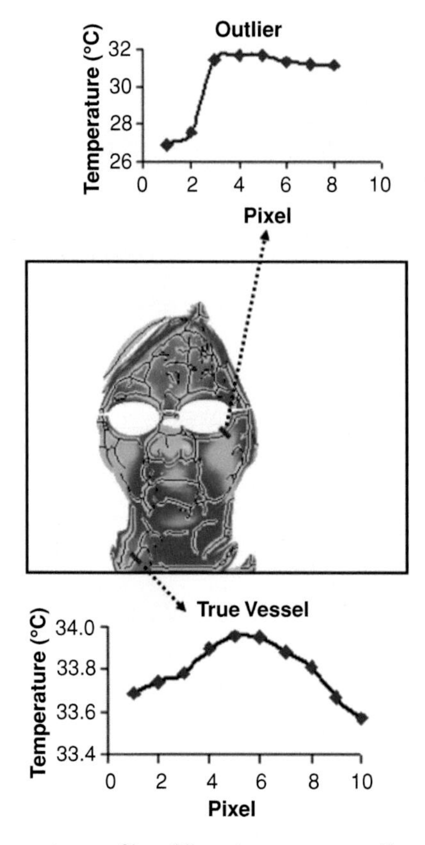


Figure 4.4. Temperature profiles of lines drawn across outliers and true vessels.

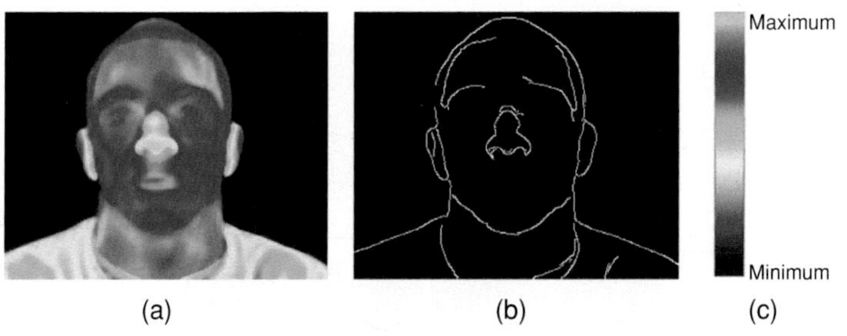


Figure 4.7. Nose edge extraction from thermal facial image: (a) thermal facial image; (b) ridges extracted using the Canny edge detection algorithm; (c) color map.

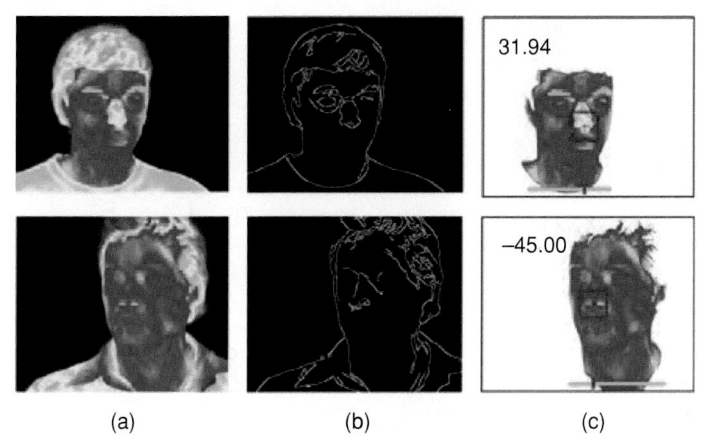


Figure 4.8. Pose estimation performance examples: (a) thermal facial images; (b) nose detection using Hausdorff-based matching; (c) pose estimates.

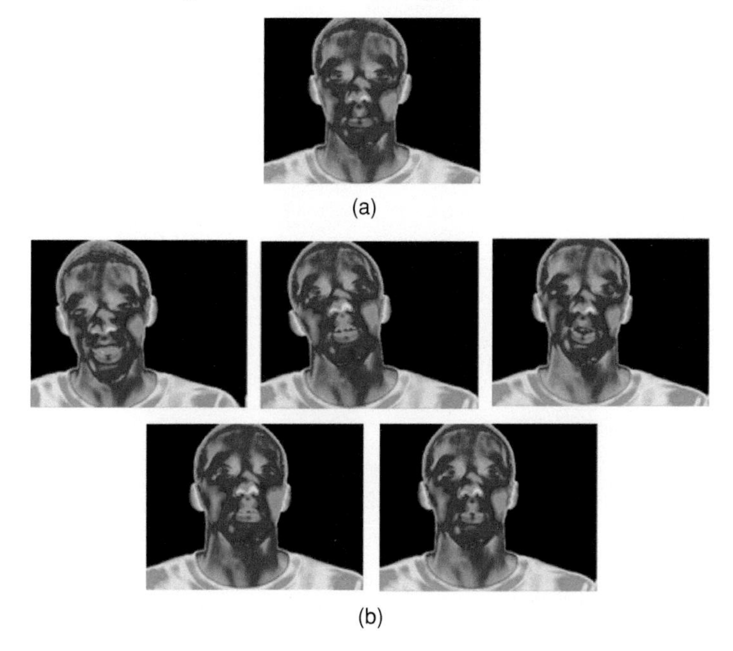


Figure 4.9. Sample subject from FEDS dataset: (a) one gallery image at neutral pose and expression; (b) five probe images at varying facial expressions.

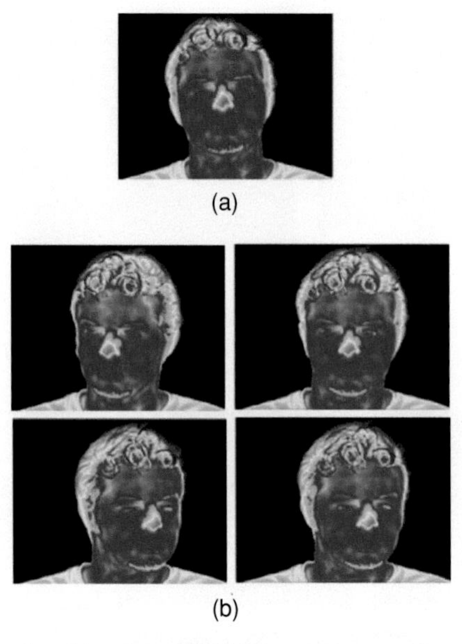


Figure 4.11. Sample subject from FPDS dataset: (a) one gallery image at neutral pose and expression; (b) four probe images at varying poses.

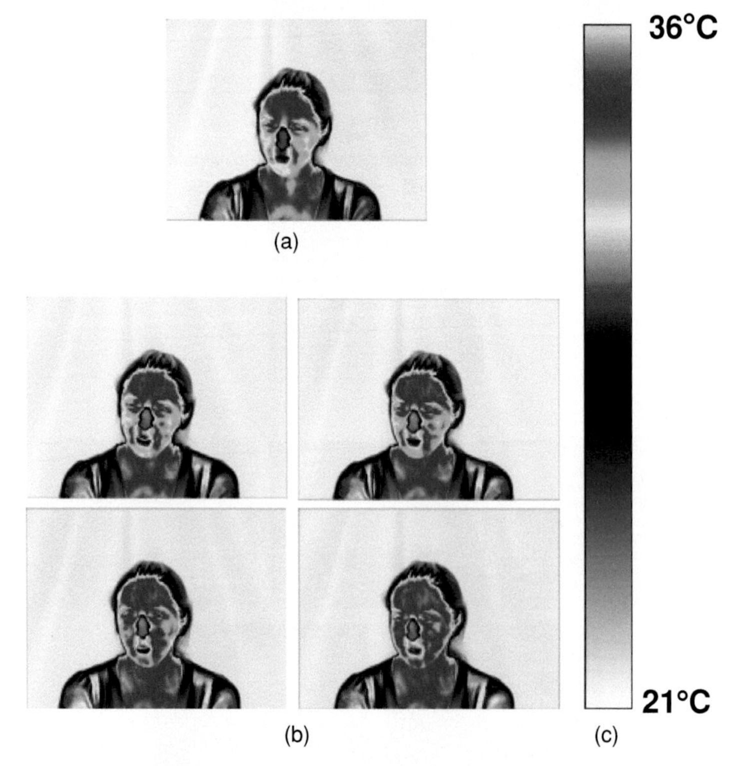


Figure 4.13. Sample subject from UA dataset: (a) one database image extracted at 2 minutes 6 seconds of the interview; (b) four test images extracted at 6 minutes, 9 minutes 18 seconds, 13 minutes 22 seconds, and 17 minutes 40 seconds of the interview, respectively. (c) Thermal color map used for visualization.

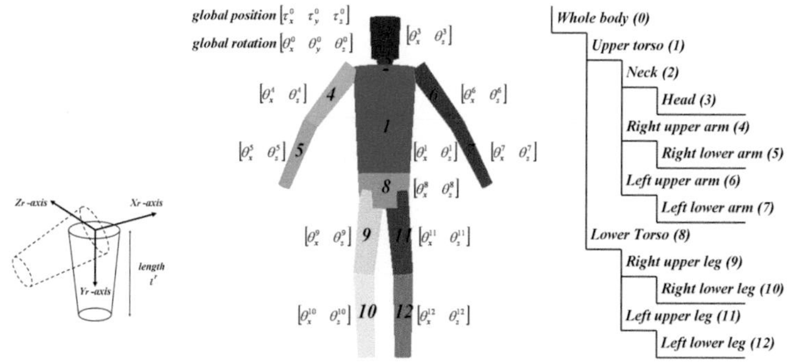


(a) Tapered cylinder (b) Kinematic model (c) Hierarchical structure

Figure 8.19. 3D human body model.

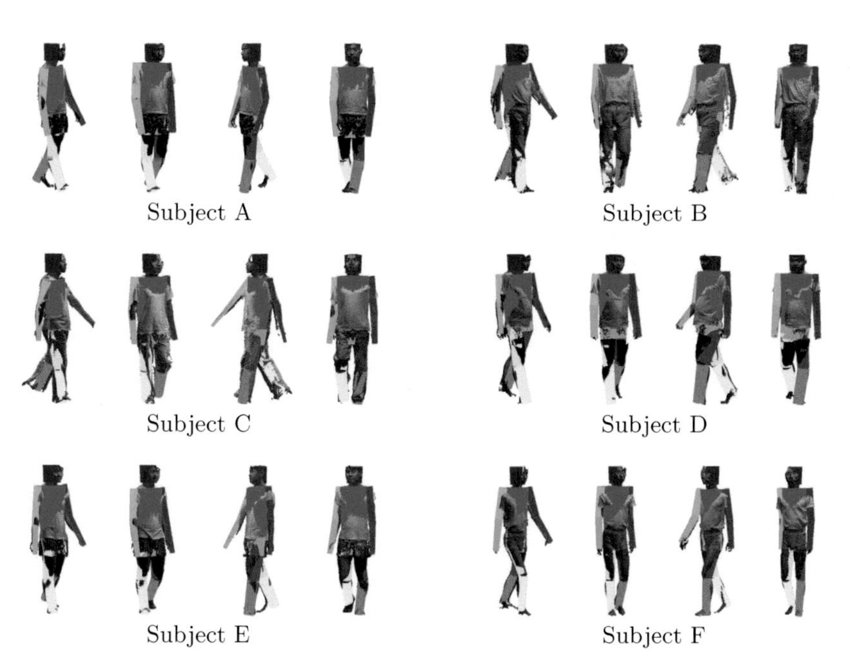


Figure 8.21. 3D human body model fitted to four poses.

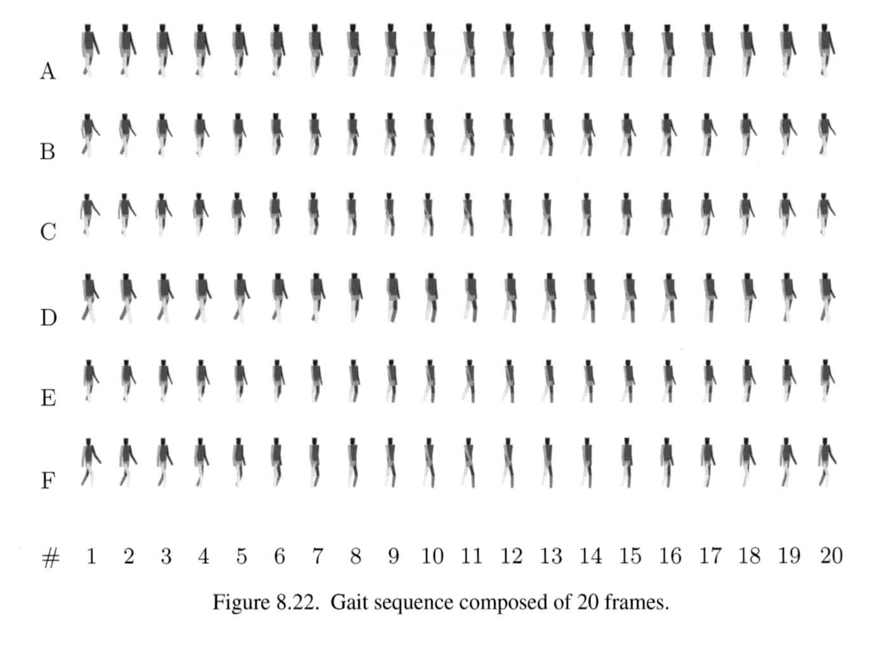


Figure 8.22. Gait sequence composed of 20 frames.

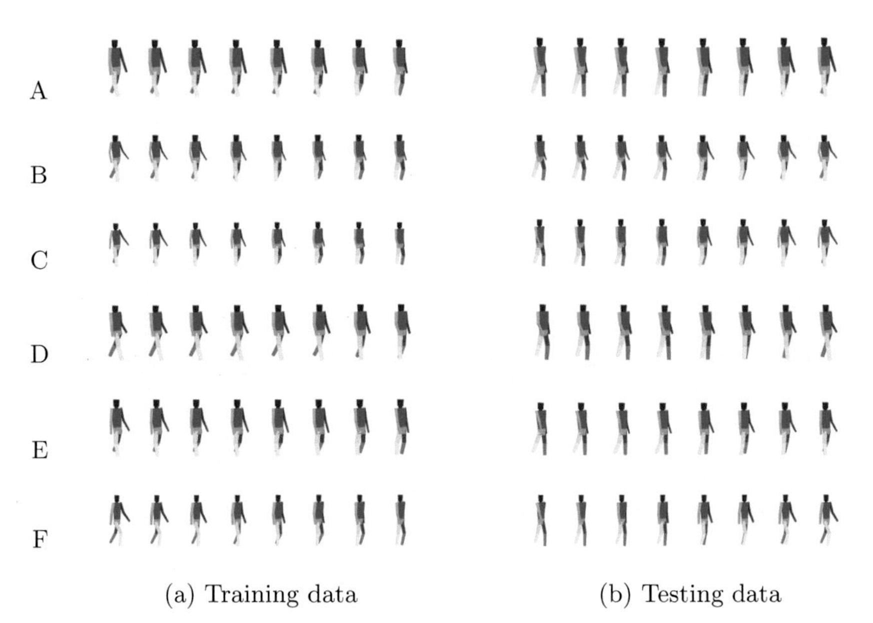


Figure 8.23. Examples of training data and testing data.

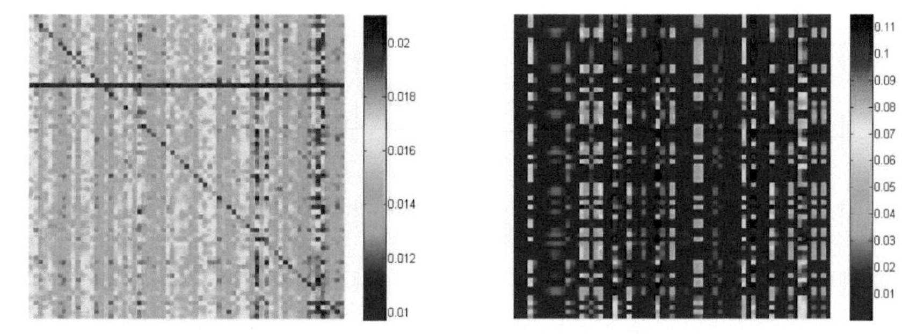


Figure 9.7. Similarity matrices for ventral and dorsal pathway approaches on probe A.

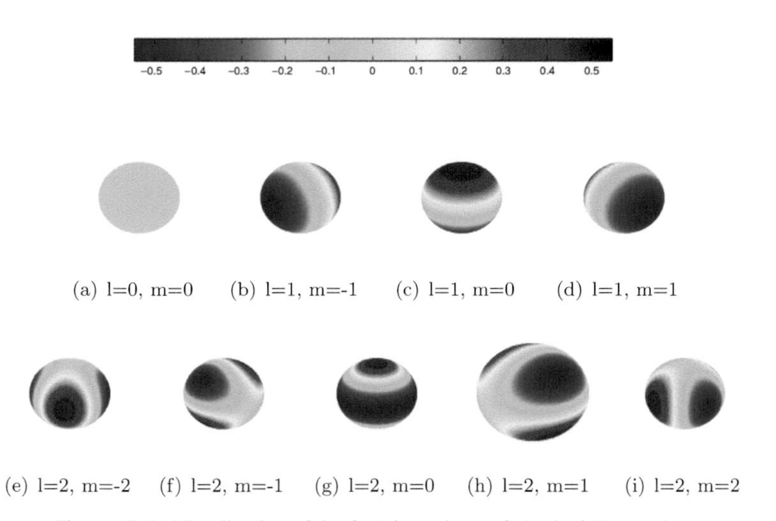


(a) l=0, m=0 (b) l=1, m=-1 (c) l=1, m=0 (d) l=1, m=1

(e) l=2, m=-2 (f) l=2, m=-1 (g) l=2, m=0 (h) l=2, m=1 (i) l=2, m=2

Figure 10.5. Visualization of the first three-degree Spherical Harmonics.

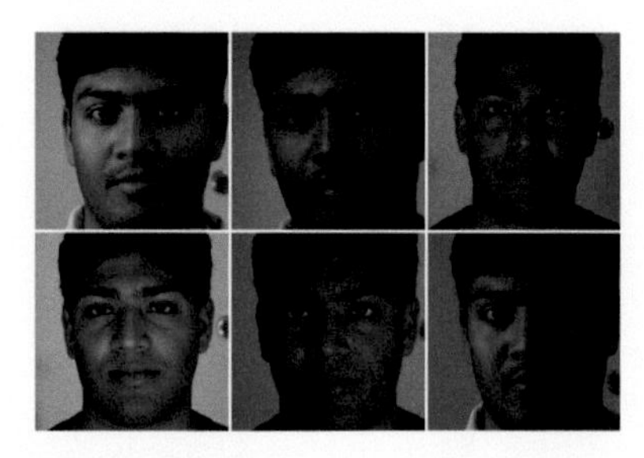

Figure 11.7. Examples from Database A: Six 2D images captured with varying lighting conditions for the same subject.

Figure 12.3. Synchronized images captured by gait cameras.

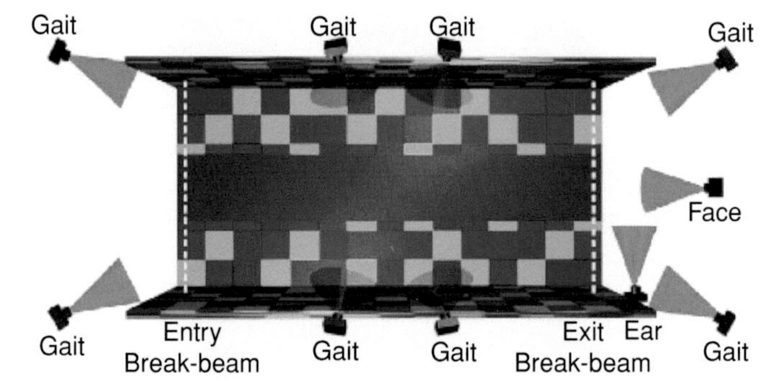


Figure 12.4. Placement of cameras and break-beam sensors in system.

# PART III

# Hybrid Biometric Systems

# 8

# Multiple Projector Camera System for Three-Dimensional Gait Recognition

Koichiro Yamauchi, Bir Bhanu, and Hideo Saito

## 8.1 Introduction

The human body has fascinated scientists for thousands of years. Studying the shape of the human body offers opportunities to open up entirely new areas of research. The shape of the human body can be used to infer personal characteristics and features. Body type and muscle strength, for instance, can be used to distinguish gender. The presence or absence of wrinkles around the eyes and loose facial skin suggests a person's age. In addition, the size and shape of a person's face, belly, thighs, and arms can determine a body habitus: slim, healthy, or overweight. The length of individual limbs such as legs and their postural sway when a person walks suggests an underlying misalignment of the bone structure. It is, in fact, possible to identify people by their physical body shape of the entire body. Unlike traditional physical measures of height, width, and length of body parts, the body shape is represented by a closed surface of the entire human body as a 2-manifold. The surface is digitally captured and described by geometric primitives such as vertices, lines, and curves. It is useful for health professionals and technical experts to retrieve personal data from a shared database whenever the need arises. Using a large number of body shape measurements, valuable personal characteristics can be statistically analyzed. If there is a strong correlation between body shape and medical disease, for instance, we can avoid invasive diagnostic procedures such as medical imaging methods that utilize electromagnetic radiation. Measurement of the shape of the human body also plays a leading role in medical diagnosis; it may even be possible to discover unexpected diseases through studying body shape. The differences among people of both sexes, young and old vary considerably in size and volume. In addition, the target is not just body parts such as face, ears, and fingers, but the entire body, including all of them. The focal issue involved in the use of the entire body is how to exploit a vast amount of information.

Therefore, it is challenging to compute the underlying mechanism from the appearance of the human body and establish basic technologies for human understanding.

## 8.2 Structured Light System

The pair of one camera and one projector, that is, a structured light system, is the minimum configuration for range imaging. The geometry of the structured light system is approximated by either a simple or a complex model. The simple model represents the system by simplifying the geometry with the small number of parameters. In contrast, the complex model represents the system by complicating the geometry with the large number of parameters. Naturally, the geometric model is designed for high-accuracy measurement against the loss of versatility. A typical geometric model encapsulates two separate models: the camera model and the projector model (Bolles et al. 1981). Generally, the pinhole model is the most commonly used representation (Zhang et al. 2007). The camera geometry is represented by a $3 \times 4$ matrix having 11 degrees of freedom, and the projector geometry is represented by a $2 \times 4$ matrix having 7 degrees of freedom. The two matrices provide range data by the principle of binocular stereo. Although the pinhole model is suited for the camera geometry, it is not applicable to the projector geometry. For example, light stripes do not always pass through the optical center of the projector using a rotatable mirror, for instance, a galvanometer mirror and a polygon mirror. Subsequently, the triangulation principle based on the baseline is also utilized. Given one side and two angles of a triangle, these determine the position of a target object. One side is the baseline, which is defined as the distance between the camera and the projector. One of the angles indicates the camera view and the other indicates the projector view. The invariable baseline model (Matsuki and Ueda 1989) fails to represent some projectors using a rotatable mirror, but the variable baseline model (Reid 1996) eases this problem. However, these models assume that all light stripes are vertical to the baseline. It is preferable to express the light stripe by a three-dimensional (3D) plane disregarding the inner structure of the projector. In this section, the problem of geometric model for a structured light system is addressed. The geometric model is defined such that the camera model is based on the pinhole model, and the projector model is based on the equation of a plane model. If light stripes are projected in different directions, their projections are expressed accurately. Furthermore, the camera and projector parameters are estimated by observing a planar object from three viewpoints. Unlike other approaches using cube objects (Wakitani et al. 1995;

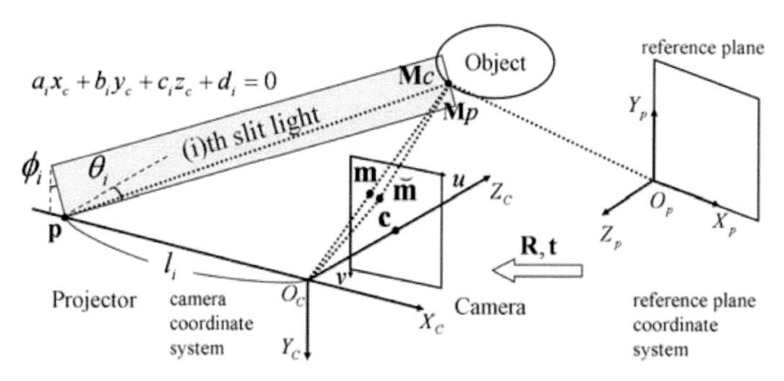

Figure 8.1. Geometric model of a structured light system.

Lu and Li 2003), it facilitates the procedure of the user's tasks and provides a high degree of accuracy.

### 8.2.1 Geometric Model

A structured light system consists of a camera and a projector. The system captures a range of data by the camera observing a target object illuminated from the projector. Figure 8.1 is the geometric model of a structured light system. The camera model is based on the pinhole model, and the projector model is based on the equation of a plane model. The geometric model is represented in the camera coordinate system, and the reference plane is represented in the reference plane coordinate system.

#### 8.2.1.1 Camera Model

A pinhole model is defined as the case that light rays from an object pass through the optical center $O_c$ for imaging. The principal point **c** at the intersection of the optical axis with the image plane is denoted by $[u_0, v_0]$. The $X_c$-axis, $Y_c$-axis, and $Z_c$-axis are parallel to horizontal axis, vertical axis, and optical axis, respectively, of the image plane. Here a two-dimensional (2D) point, that is, image coordinates, **m** is denoted by $[u, v]$ in the image plane, and a 3D point, camera coordinates, $\mathbf{M}_c$ is denoted by $[x_c, y_c, z_c]$ in the camera coordinate system ($O_c$-$X_c$-$Y_c$-$Z_c$). In addition, the $X_p$-axis, $Y_p$-axis, $Z_p$-axis, and $O_p$ are defined as horizontal axis, vertical axis, orthogonal axis, and coordinate origin of the reference plane, respectively. Here a 3D point, that is, reference plane coordinates, $\mathbf{M}_p$ is denoted by $[x_p, y_p, z_p]$ in the reference plane coordinate system ($O_p$-$X_p$-$Y_p$-$Z_p$). The perspective projection that maps the reference plane coordinates onto the image coordinates is given by

$$\tilde{\mathbf{m}} \simeq \mathbf{A}\left[\mathbf{R}\ \mathbf{t}\right]\tilde{\mathbf{M}}_p \tag{8.1}$$

with

$$\mathbf{A} = \begin{bmatrix} \alpha & \gamma & u_0 \\ 0 & \beta & v_0 \\ 0 & 0 & 1, \end{bmatrix},$$

where $\mathbf{A}$ is the camera intrinsic matrix with the scale factors, $\alpha$, $\beta$, $\gamma$, and the principal point, $u_0$, $v_0$, that is, the intrinsic parameters, and $[\,\mathbf{R}\ \mathbf{t}\,]$ combines the rotation matrix and the translation vector, that is, the extrinsic parameters. The tilde indicates the homogeneous coordinate by adding 1 for the additional element: $\widetilde{\mathbf{m}} = [u, v, 1]$ and $\widetilde{\mathbf{M}}_p = [x_p, y_p, z_p, 1]$. The radial distortion causes the inward or outward displacement of the image coordinates from their ideal locations. This type of distortion is mainly caused by flawed radial curvature curve of the lens elements (Weng et al. 1992). Here a distorted 2D point, that is, real image coordinates, $\breve{\mathbf{m}}$ is denoted by $[\breve{u}, \breve{v}]$. The discrepancy between the ideal image coordinates and the real image coordinates considering first two terms of radial distortion is given by $k_1$ and $k_2$.

#### 8.2.1.2 Projector Model

The projector emits one to hundreds of light stripes for the measurement. We consider the case in which the light stripes are projected in different directions. It is difficult to assume that the projector model is based on the pinhole model, because they do not pass through the optical center. Therefore, we use the equation of a plane model to accurately represent the projector instead of considering the projection of the light stripes, which depend on the type of projector. In the camera coordinate system, the light stripe can be written as

$$a_i x_c + b_i y_c + c_i z_c + d_i = 0, \tag{8.2}$$

where $i$ is the light stripe number, and $a_i C b_i C c_i C d_i$ are the coefficients of the equation. There are an equal number of equations of planes and light stripes. Intuitively, the intersection of the $X_c$-axis and the light stripe, $\mathbf{p}$, moves from the left to the right on the axis. We define $l_i$ is the baseline, that is, the distance between the optical center of the camera and the light stripe of the projector, $\theta_i$ is the projection angle, that is, the angle between $Z_c$-axis and the light stripe, and $\phi_i$ is the tilt angle, that is, the angle between $Y_c$-axis and the light stripe. From the coefficients of the equation, these explicit parameters can be written as

$$l_i = d_i / a_i, \tag{8.3}$$

$$\theta_i = \arctan(-c_i / a_i), \tag{8.4}$$

$$\phi_i = \arctan(-b_i / a_i). \tag{8.5}$$

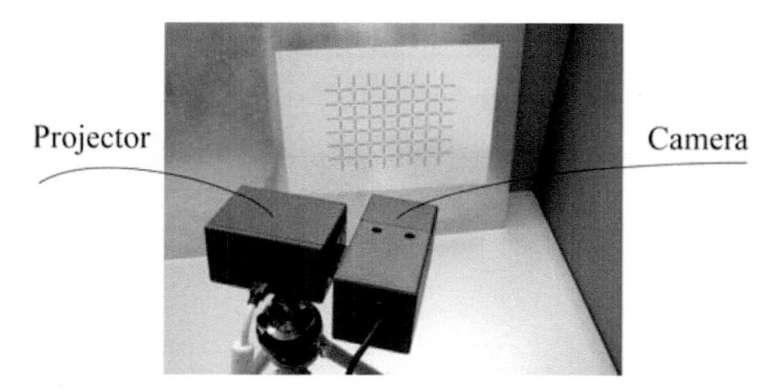


Figure 8.2. Calibration scene.

Projector parameters are expressed by both implicit and explicit representations. The coefficients are used for computation of range data, but their values do not exhibit distinct features. In contrast, the baselines, projection angles, and tilt angles provide characteristic distributions.

#### 8.2.1.3 Triangulation Principle

To achieve range data, the projector emits light stripes to a target object, and then the camera observes the illuminated object. So the camera coordinates are the intersection of the viewpoint of the camera and the equation of a plane of the projector. The triangulation principle based on one side and two angles of a triangle can be written as

$$x_c = \frac{(u - u_0) - \frac{\gamma}{\beta}(v - v_0)}{\alpha} z_c, \tag{8.6}$$

$$y_c = \frac{v - v_0}{\beta} z_c, \tag{8.7}$$

$$z_c = \frac{\frac{d_i}{a_i}}{-\frac{c_i}{a_i} - \frac{(u-u_0)-\frac{\gamma}{\beta}(v-v_0)}{\alpha} - \frac{b_i}{a_i}\frac{(v-v_0)}{\beta}}. \tag{8.8}$$

The coordinate $z_c$ is computed by the relationship between the viewpoint of the camera and the equation of a plane of the projector. Then, the coordinate $x_c$ and the coordinate $y_c$ are computed by the similar triangle related to the camera. Therefore, the camera coordinates can be recovered by the camera and projector parameters.

### 8.2.2 Calibration Method

In this section we present a calibration method for a structured light system by observing a planar object from three viewpoints. Figure 8.2 is the calibration

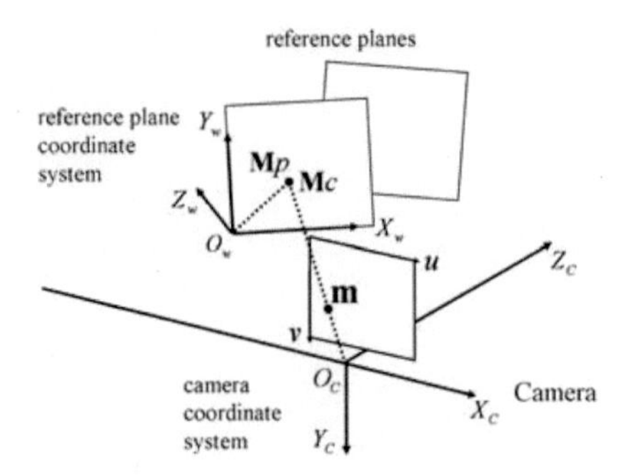


Figure 8.3. Camera calibration.

scene of a structure light system. The planar object, called the reference plane, contains a checkered pattern, so that calibration points are detected as the intersection of line segments. To perform the calibration, the reference plane coordinates are assigned to the calibration points. Three sets of color images and stripe images, which capture calibration points and light stripes on the reference planes, respectively, are required. Our approach incorporates two separate stages: camera calibration and projector calibration.

#### 8.2.2.1 Camera Calibration

In the camera calibration stage, camera parameters are obtained by Zhang's method (Zhang 2000). Figure 8.3 shows the relationship between the reference plane and the image plane. The camera parameters are estimated by the correspondence between the reference plane coordinates and the image coordinates. Note that three color images must be captured from different positions changing orientations. If the reference plane undergoes pure translation, the camera parameters cannot be estimated.

#### 8.2.2.2 Projector Calibration

In the projector calibration stage, projector parameters are estimated by a image-to-camera transformation matrix based on the perspective projection and the Euclidian transformation of the camera parameters that encapsulate the position and orientation of the reference planes. Figure 8.4 shows the relationship among the reference plane, the image plane, and the light stripe. The transformation matrix that maps the image coordinates into the camera coordinates is given by

$$\widetilde{\mathbf{M}}_c \simeq \begin{bmatrix} \mathbf{I} \\ (\mathbf{r}_3^T \mathbf{t})^{-1} \mathbf{r}_3^T \end{bmatrix} \mathbf{A}^{-1} \widetilde{\mathbf{m}} \tag{8.9}$$

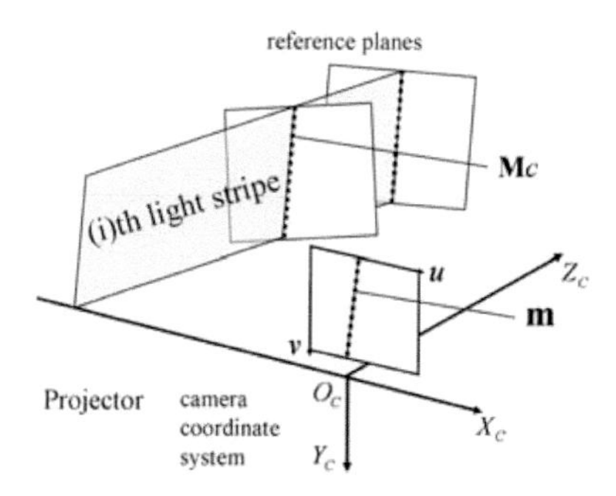


Figure 8.4. Projector calibration.

with

$$\mathbf{R} = [\mathbf{r}_1\ \mathbf{r}_2\ \mathbf{r}_3] \quad \mathbf{I} = diag(1, 1, 1) \quad \mathbf{b} = [0, 0, 1],$$

where $(T)$ indicates the transpose of a matrix and $(-1)$ indicates the inverse of a matrix. This matrix is directly estimated by camera parameters unlike other methods that necessitate recalculations (Chen and Kak 1987; Huynh et al. 1999). For each light stripe, the image coordinates is transformed to the camera coordinates, so that the coefficients of the equation of a plane can be computed by the least square method of at least three image coordinates. If the image coordinates of the light stripe are obtained from one reference plane, the equation of a plane cannot be computed. This is how all the light stripes are estimated.

### 8.2.3 Experimental Results

The data are captured by a structured light system, Cartesia 3D Handy Scanner of SPACEVISION. This system captures range data in 0.5 seconds with 8 mm focal length, 640 × 480 pixels, and 256 light stripes by the space encoding method (Hattori and Sato 1996). Here, two light stripes are not used for measurement. The light stripes based on the gray coded pattern are scanned by a single light stripe and a rotatable mirror. The reference plane with the checkered pattern includes 48 calibration points with 20 mm horizontal and vertical intervals.

#### 8.2.3.1 Calibration

Three sets of color images and stripe images are used for calibration as shown in Figure 8.5. For the color images, one straight line is fitted to two horizontal line segments, and the other straight line is fitted to two vertical segments. The calibration point is detected as the intersection of two straight lines. For stripe

Table 8.1. *Camera Parameters*

| | |
|---|---|
| **A** | $\begin{bmatrix} 1061.71 & -0.562002 & 350.08 \\ 0 & 1064.09 & 286.547 \\ 0 & 0 & 1 \end{bmatrix}$ |
| $k_1$ | −0.140279 |
| $k_2$ | −0.0916363 |

images, luminance values from 1 to 254 correspond to the light stripe number. The light stripes are projected to the reference plane vertically. Table 8.1 shows the camera intrinsic matrix and the coefficients of the radial distortion of the camera parameters. Figure 8.6 shows the baselines, projection angles, and tilt angles of the projector parameters. When the light stripe number increases, the baselines gradually decrease, the projection angles increase, and the tilt angles remains almost constant. The camera and projector parameters enable the system to recover the camera coordinates of a target object.

#### 8.2.3.2 Evaluation

We evaluated the measurement accuracy using five spheres with 25 mm radius placed in front of the system. They are numbered from top left to bottom right. In our evaluation, the system captures range data and then fits the ideal spheres to them. The measurement accuracy, which is defined as the distance between

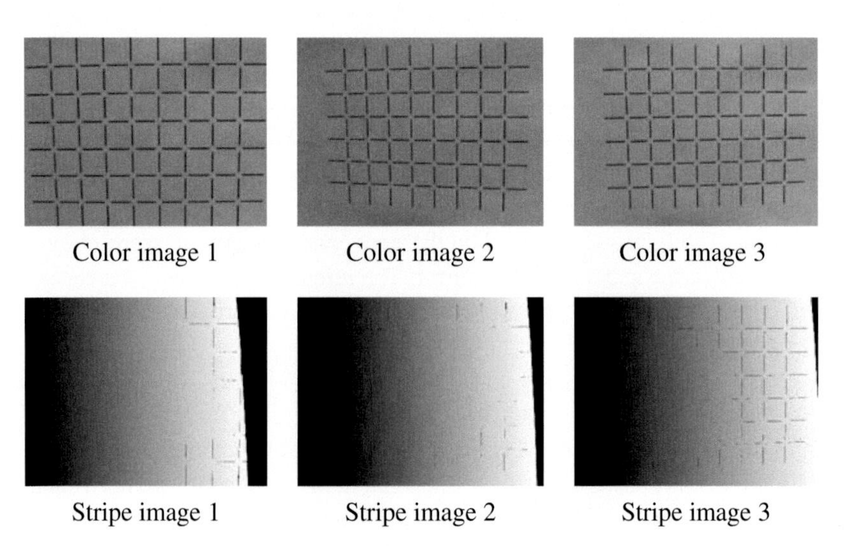


Figure 8.5. Three sets of color images and stripe images.

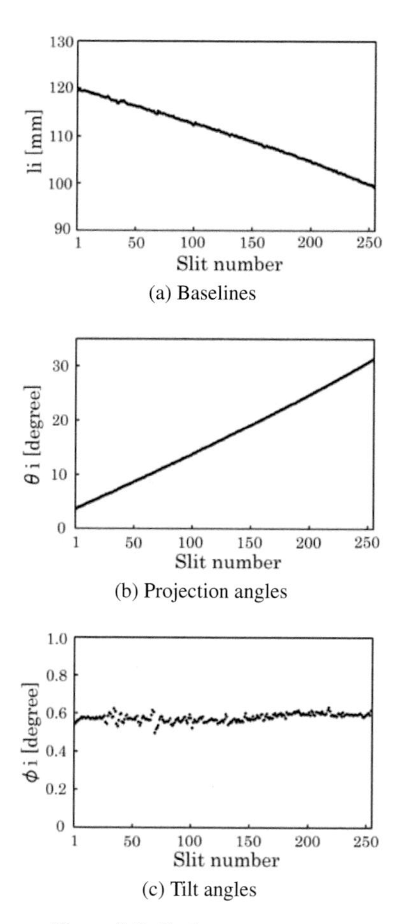


(a) Baselines



(b) Projection angles



(c) Tilt angles

Figure 8.6. Projector parameters.

the ideal radius $\hat{r}$ and the real radius $r_j$, is given by

$$E_s = \frac{1}{N_s} \sum_{j=1}^{N_s} (r_j - \hat{r})^2, \tag{8.10}$$

where $N_s$ is the number of measuring points. To show the effectiveness, we evaluated our approach by comparing it with two conventional approaches:

(1) *The pinhole model calibrated by slide stage:* The camera is modeled by the $3 \times 4$ projection matrix, and the projector is modeled by the $2 \times 4$ projection matrix. The camera and projector parameters are estimated using the slide stage.

Approach ( 1 )

Approach (2)

Approach (3)

Figure 8.7. Measurement results of five spheres.

(2) *The equation of a plane model calibrated by slide stage:* The camera model is based on the pinhole model, and the projector model is based on the equation of a plane model. The camera parameters are obtained by Tsai's method (Tsai 1987), and the projector parameters are estimated using the reference plane.
(3) *The equation of a plane model calibrated by reference plane:* The camera model is based on the pinhole model, and the projector model is based on the equation of a plane model. The camera and projector parameters are estimated using the reference plane.

Figure 8.7 is the measurement results of five spheres. In approach 1, the left two spheres and the ground are distorted in contrast with the approaches

Table 8.2. *Measurement Accuracy of Structured Light System*

| | Sphere | | | | |
|---|---|---|---|---|---|
| | No. 1 | No. 2 | No. 3 | No. 4 | No. 5 |
| Measuring points | 15,629 | 15,629 | 19,405 | 19,861 | 19,861 |
| Approach 1 ($mm^2$) | 0.41 | 0.38 | 0.26 | 0.26 | 0.31 |
| Approach 2 ($mm^2$) | 0.22 | 0.31 | 0.19 | 0.13 | 0.20 |
| Approach 3 ($mm^2$) | 0.23 | 0.32 | 0.21 | 0.15 | 0.21 |

2 and 3. Table 8.2 shows the measurement accuracy of the structured light system. In approach 1, the measurement accuracy is higher than approaches 2 and 3. Approaches 2 and 3 achieve similar performance. Therefore, the equation of a plane model is applicable to the structured light system. In addition, the reference plane as a planer object provides a high degree of accuracy and has a high degree of availability compared with the slide stage as a cubic object. The experimental results demonstrate the effectiveness and efficiency of our approach.

## 8.3 3D Human Body Measurement

Human body measurement system is classified as either a multicamera system or a projector-camera system. We emphasize the advantages and drawbacks of both systems. The multicamera system captures a whole human body data in real time with low resolution and low accuracy. In contrast, the projector-camera system captures whole human body data over a couple of seconds with high resolution and high accuracy. These systems are used to make distinctions depending on application needs. For example, motion tracking systems require real-time data compared with biometrics recognition systems require high resolution and highly accurate data. The following are representative human body measurement systems using multiple cameras or projector-camera pairs. Moezzi et al. (1997) proposed a system for generating and replying photorealistic 3D digital video sequences of real events and performances by two or more cameras. The volume intersection method recovers an object's 3D shape by determining whether the corresponding pixel location is part of the object or the background. The model of a single person in any pose has about 17,000 voxels or 70,000 triangles. Saito et al. (2003) proposed a method for shape reconstruction and virtual view generation from multiple cameras. The multi-camera system, called 3D room, is consisted of 49 cameras, 10 of which are mounted on each of four walls and nine of which are mounted on the ceiling in the room. The system acquires 10,000 triangles in the mesh to represent a subject on the sofa in real time. Koo et al. (2004) presented a contour triangulation-based shape reconstruction from multiple projector-camera pairs. The projector-camera system, called 3D Model Studio, consists of four projector-camera pairs. Each projector-camera pair, which is mounted in the pole, moves from the top to the bottom. The system acquires 200,000 triangles in the mesh to represent a standing subject in 16.7 seconds. Treleaven (2004) reported a whole body scanner and its applications using multiple projector-camera pairs. The projector-camera system, which is the product of $(TC)^2$, consists of six projector-camera pairs. Each projector-camera pair is assigned around a subject. The system acquires 200,000 points located on the subject's surface within 10 seconds. However, there are not enough viewpoints to capture whole human body data because of occlusion. In this section, a compact and high-speed human body measurement system is proposed. Four projector-camera pairs are installed in a pole as a measuring unit that covers the range from head to toe. Each pair captures partial body data in 0.5 seconds with 2.0 mm measurement accuracy. Three pole units, which have a total of 12 projector-camera pairs, are assigned around a subject. Two of them are positioned diagonally forward right and left, and the other one is positioned backward. The system acquires whole human body data in 2 seconds with 1.88 mm measurement accuracy.

## 8.3.1 Human Body Measurement System

We present a method for shape reconstruction of the entire body using multiple projector-camera pairs. The small number of projector-camera pairs cannot completely cover the entire body and resolve occlusion problems. In addition, it is preferable to finish the measurement in the shortest possible time, because the body sway of a subject affects measurement accuracy. In our system, whole human body data are captured from multiple viewpoints by simultaneously measurement.

### 8.3.1.1 Projector-Camera Pair

Figure 8.8 is the structured light system consisting of one camera and one projector. This system captures range data in 0.5 seconds with 6 mm focal length, $640 \times 480$ pixels, and 256 light stripes by the space-encoding method (Hattori and Sato 1996). The light stripes based on the gray coded pattern are generated by scanning and switching of a single light stripe emitted from the semiconductor laser. The wavelength and power of the laser light are 650 nm and

Figure 8.8. Projector-camera pair.

50 mW, respectively. Using a 650 nm bandpass filter, the projector-camera pair is insensitive to illuminations such as fluorescent lights. The measurement error is within 2.0 mm when a target object is located 1 meter ahead.

#### 8.3.1.2 Pole Unit

In our system, four projector-camera pairs are installed in a pole and used as a measuring unit. Figure 8.9 is the pole unit and control computer. For each projector-camera pair, the projector is assigned over the camera. The baseline, which is the distance between the camera and the projector, is 330 mm. The control computer with Intel D865 GRH motherboard, Pentium 4 2.4 GHz, and 512 MB memory is installed in the pole unit. The pole unit is 300 mm wide, 265 mm long, 2135 mm high and weights 30 kg. The measurement range is 800 mm wide and 1800 mm high when a target object is located 1 meter ahead. It is much wider than the range of one projector-camera pair. Each

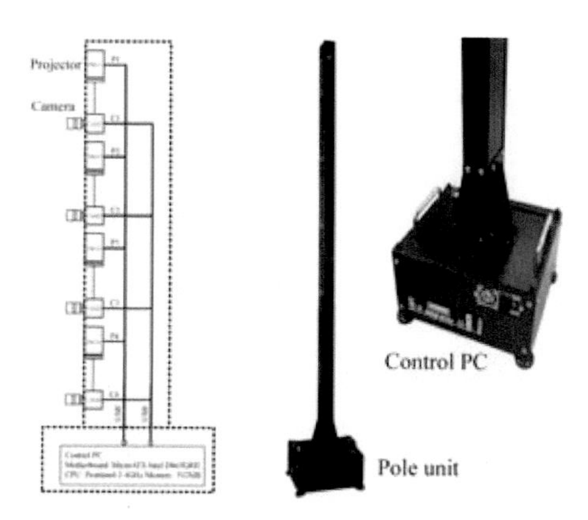


Figure 8.9. Pole unit and control computer.

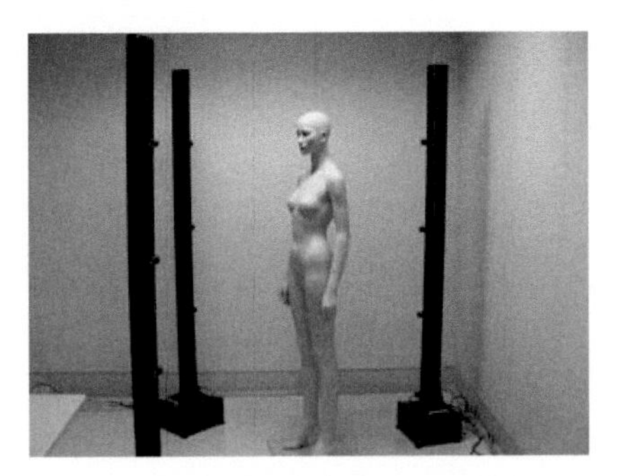

Figure 8.10. Human body measurement system.

projector-camera pair is connected to the control computer through two USB 2.0 cables. The computer synchronizes the actions of the camera and projector and generates range data from four sets of color images and stripe images.

#### 8.3.1.3 System Configuration

Let us consider human body measurement and its occlusion problem. The large number of projector-camera pairs can capture the range data of an entire body, but their measurement ranges are severely overlapped. In contrast, the small number of projector-camera pairs cannot cover well particular body parts, such as the submental region, axillary region, groin region, and side of a human body. Therefore, we appropriately assign multiple projector-camera pairs around a subject. Figure 8.10 is the human body measurement system consisting of three pole units. Twelve projector-camera pairs allow shape reconstruction of the entire body. The system is 1200 mm wide and 2000 mm long to cover both men and women of standard proportions. The distance between the pole unit and a subject is approximately 1000 mm, and the measurement range is 800 mm round. The number of measuring points is about $1/2$ to one million depending on the subject and its pose. The three pole units are movable to change the measurement range. The measurement accuracy is improved by increasing the number of pole units. In contrast, the installation space is reduced by decreasing the number of pole units. Therefore, we freely construct the system according to the circumstances.

#### 8.3.1.4 Measurement Time

During the measurement, subjects need to keep their posture as still as possible. The body sways increase every second, so that the measurement should be finished within 1 second, preferably in real time. If we operate a total of 12 projector-camera pairs one by one, the measurement time will be lengthened. If we operate some projector-camera pairs simultaneously, range data will not be

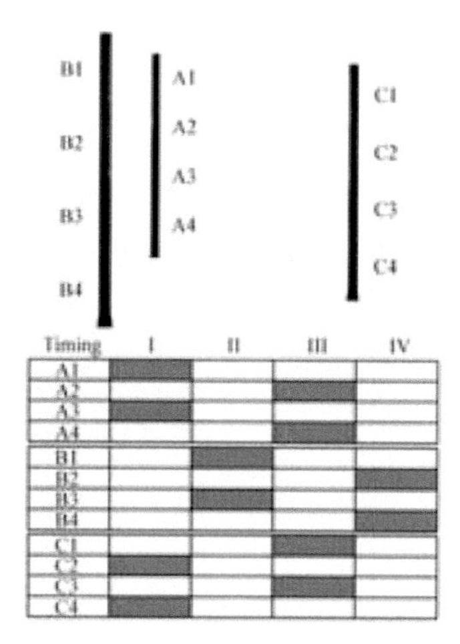


Figure 8.11. Timing diagram.

acquired because of light interference. Figure 8.11 is the timing diagram. Here three pole units are indicated by A, B, C, and four projector-camera pairs of the pole unit are numbered from top to bottom. Two or four projector-camera pairs are used simultaneously, so that whole human body data are captured only four times. In timing I, four projector-camera pairs, A1, A3, C2, C4, differ in height and are opposite each other, so that we can avoid light interference. Since the measurement time for each timing is 0.5 seconds, the measurement time is approximately 2 seconds.

## 8.3.2 Calibration

We present a calibration method of a projector-camera pair and its coordinate system alignment. For the projector-camera pair, the camera parameters are estimated by Tsai's (1987) method, and the projector parameters are determined by mechanical specification. After that, coordinate systems of projector-camera pairs are integrated together.

### 8.3.2.1 Projector-Camera Pair

The projector-camera pair consists of one camera and one projector. The camera model is based on the pinhole model. The camera parameters – intrinsic, extrinsic, and radial distortion parameters – are obtained by Tsai's method (Tsai 1987). The projector model is based on the baseline model. The baseline is defined by product drawing, and the projection angles are computed by the clock speed of the polygon mirror. Therefore, the projector-camera pair allows

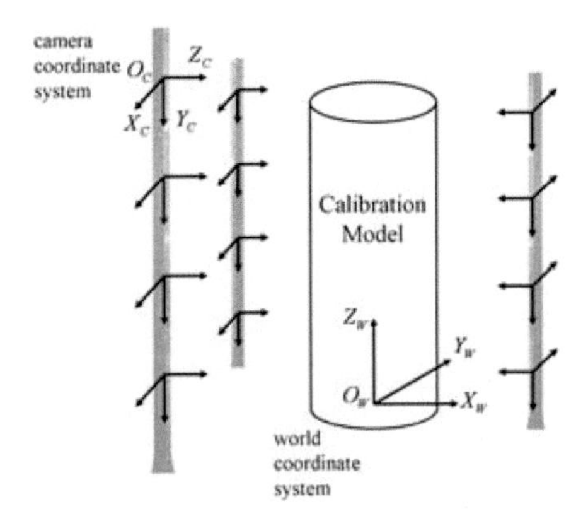


Figure 8.12. Integration into world coordinate system.

us to capture range data by the triangulation principle in the camera coordinate system.

#### 8.3.2.2 Coordinate System Alignment

The human body measurement system consists of three pole units with 12 projector-camera pairs. Each projector-camera pair is represented in the camera coordinate system, so that 12 camera coordinate systems are integrated into the world coordinate system as shown in Figure 8.12. For the coordinate system alignment, a calibration object, which is represented in the world coordinate system such as a cylinder and a cube, is required. Here a 3D point, that is, camera coordinates, $\mathbf{M}_c$ is denoted by $[x_c, y_c, z_c]$ in the camera coordinate system ($O_c$-$X_c$-$Y_c$-$Z_c$), and a 3D point, that is, world coordinates, $\mathbf{M}_w$ is denoted by $[x_w, y_w, z_w]$ in the world coordinate system ($O_w$-$X_w$-$Y_w$-$Z_w$). The affine transformation that transforms the camera coordinates to the world coordinates is given by

$$\widetilde{\mathbf{M}}_w = \mathbf{H}_a \widetilde{\mathbf{M}}_c, \tag{8.11}$$

with

$$\mathbf{H}_a = \begin{bmatrix} h_{11} & h_{12} & h_{13} & h_{14} \\ h_{21} & h_{22} & h_{23} & h_{24} \\ h_{31} & h_{32} & h_{33} & h_{34} \\ 0 & 0 & 0 & 1 \end{bmatrix},$$

where $\mathbf{H}_a$ is the affine transformation matrix. The tilde indicates the homogeneous coordinate by adding 1 for the additional element: $\widetilde{\mathbf{M}}_c = [x_c, y_c, z_c, 1]$

Figure 8.13. Calibration cylinder.

and $\widetilde{\mathbf{M}}_w = [x_w, y_w, z_w, 1]$. An affine transformation that has a total of 12 degrees of freedom encapsulates a Euclid transformation, which has a total of 6 degrees of freedom describing rotation and translation. The 12 parameters $[h_{11}, \ldots, h_{34}]$ can be estimated by the least square method of at least four camera coordinates. To achieve accurate range data, it is necessary to use many camera coordinates. Since 12 camera coordinate systems are integrated into the world coordinate system, the system captures whole human body data. The assignment and the number of pole units have no constraints as long as all of the projector-camera pairs observe a calibration object.

## 8.3.3 Experimental Results

The data are captured by our human body measurement system consisting of three pole units with 12 projector-camera pairs. We calibrated the system in two separate steps and then evaluated the system using representative projector-camera pairs. Furthermore, three subjects are measured to indicate the performance of the system.

### 8.3.3.1 Calibration

The calibration method incorporates two separate stages: projector-camera pair calibration and coordinate system alignment calibration. The camera and projector parameters of 12 projector-camera pairs are estimated, and then their camera coordinate systems are integrated to the world coordinate system. The world coordinate system needs to be defined on a cubic object to perform Tsai's method and estimate the affine transformation matrix. Thus, we utilize the calibration cylinder with 415 mm round and 1800 mm height as shown in Figure 8.13. The cylinder is slightly similar in form and size to a subject compared with cubes and cones, so that it is expected to improve the measurement

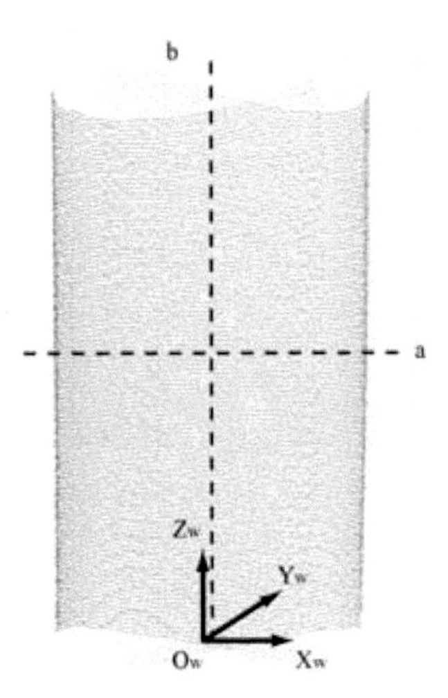


Figure 8.14. Measurement result of the cylinder.

accuracy. The pole units are located around the cylinder to observe the curved surface at any views. The calibration cylinder contains a checkered pattern, that is, line segments, with 50 mm horizontal and vertical intervals whose vertices are invisible by erasing a part of lines. The calibration point is detected as the intersection of two straight lines, one of which is fitted to two horizontal line segments and the other one of which is fitted to two vertical segments. Finally, about 80 to 100 calibration points are used for the calibration process.

#### 8.3.3.2 Evaluation

We evaluated the measurement accuracy using the calibration cylinder. Figure 8.14 is the measurement result of the cylinder captured by two projector-camera pairs. In the figure, the symbol a indicates the horizontal cross section, and the symbol b indicates the vertical cross section. Here a 3D point captured by left projector-camera pair is denoted by $\mathbf{M}^l_w$, and a 3D point captured by right projector-camera pair is denoted by $\mathbf{M}^r_w$. The measurement accuracy, which is defined by observing the same calibration points from two projector-camera pairs, is given by

$$E_h = \frac{1}{N_h} \sum_{k=1}^{N_h} \|\mathbf{M}^l_{w,k} - \mathbf{M}^r_{w,k}\|, \tag{8.12}$$

where $N_h$ is the number of calibration points. Table 8.3 shows the measurement accuracy of the human body measurement system. We used 33 calibration

Table 8.3. *Measurement Accuracy of Human Body Measurement System*

| | |
|---|---|
| Calibration points | 33 |
| Average error (mm) | 1.88 |
| Standard deviation (mm) | 0.79 |

points and obtained the result with 1.88 mm average error and 0.79 mm standard deviation. The error is within 0.2 percent of the distance to a subject. Figure 8.15 is the horizontal cross section of the cylinder. The overlapped range of two projector-camera pairs is $x_w = -130{\sim}130$ mm. Subjectively, mapped points are depicted as a smooth curve. Figure 8.16 is the vertical cross section of the cylinder. The ideal value is $y_w = 0$ mm. Almost mapped points are distributed around $y_w = -2{\sim}2$ mm. However, on both $z_w = 0{\sim}200$ mm and $z_w = 700{\sim}900$ mm, mapped points are distorted because of radial lens distortion. It turns out that the maximum error is approximately 6 mm.

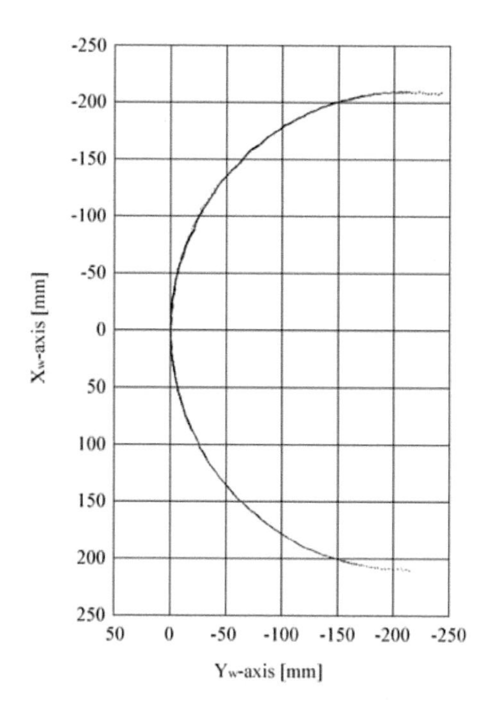


Figure 8.15. Horizontal cross section.

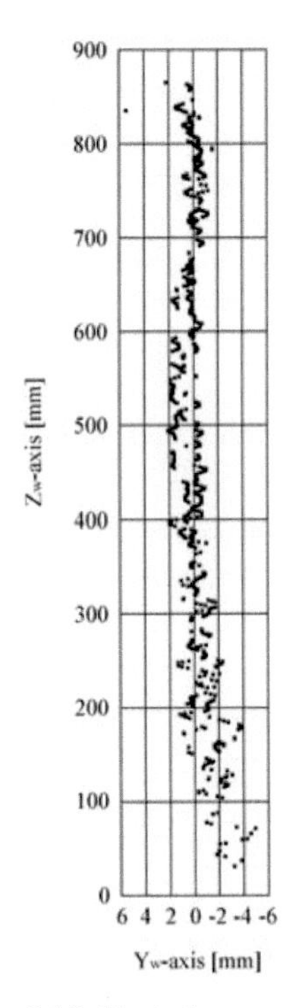


Figure 8.16. Vertical cross section.

#### 8.3.3.3 Measurement

Figure 8.17 shows the measurement result of a 165 cm–tall mannequin and a 175 cm – tall man. The system successfully acquires range data of the entire body, especially occluded parts, that is, the submental region, axillary region, groin region, and side of a human body. The body sways increase gradually when capturing, but the system remains nearly unaffected because of simultaneously measurement. However, it is difficult to obtain range data of head hair because of low reflectance of structured lights emitted from the projector. We consider the effect of a structured light on the retina. In our system, the structured light is emitted from class 3B semiconductor laser. Even if the distance between the laser and the eye is 50 mm, the energy density incident upon the pupil is a thousandth less than the legal standard. Since the structured light is generated by expanding the laser beam and scanning it at high speed, the irradiance level per unit area per unit time is substantially lower.

## 8.4 Human Gait Recognition

Biometrics systems generally use a single or multi camera and extract individual features for human recognition. They are successfully gaining ground and

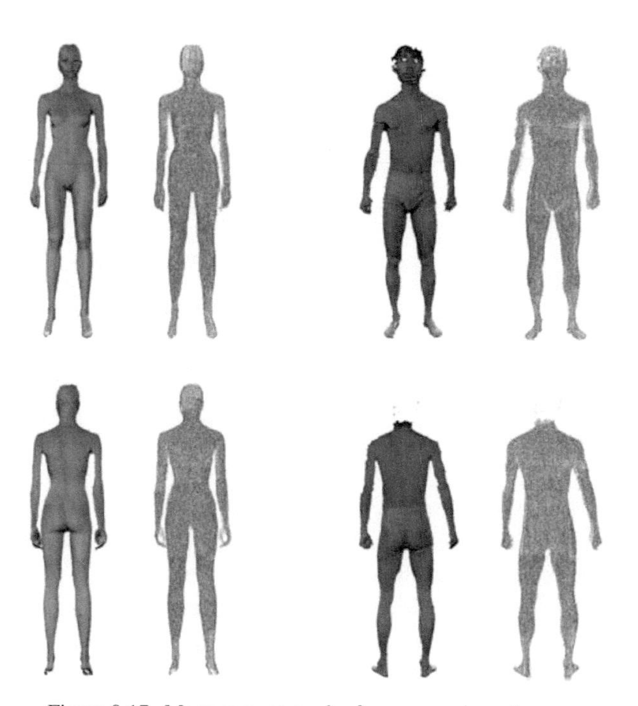

Figure 8.17. Measurement result of a mannequin and a man.

are available for security applications. Biometrics modalities with depth information are an attractive resource. The following are representative recognition approaches using 3D biometrics. Samir et al. (2006) developed a geometric approach for comparing the shapes of facial surfaces via the shapes of facial curves. The facial surface is represented by a union of level curves of the height function. The metric on shapes of facial surfaces is derived by accumulating distances between corresponding facial curves. Malassiotis et al. (2006) presented an authentication system based on measurements of 3D finger geometry using a real-time and low-cost sensor. The similarity between the training and testing set are computed by the finger width and curvature measurements sampled by the finger length. Chen and Bhanu (2007) proposed a complete human recognition system using 3D ear biometrics. The ear helix/antihelix representation and the local surface patch representation are used to estimate the initial rigid transformation between a gallery-probe pair. A modified iterative closest point algorithm is performed to iteratively refine this transformation. Multimodal 3D biometrics approaches have been developed in recent years. Tsalakanidou et al. (2007) presented an authentication system based on the fusion of 3D face and finger biometrics. Theoharis et al. (2008) presented a unified approach to fuse 3D facial and ear data. These methods achieve a high recognition rate when

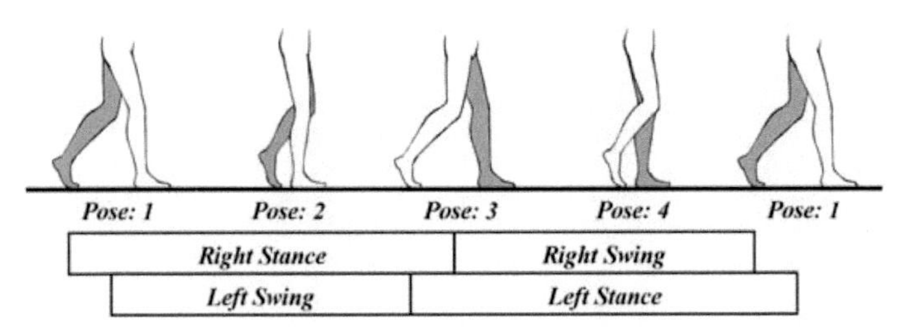


Figure 8.18. Gait cycle expressed by swing phase and stance phase.

compared with a single modality approach. Although biometrics approaches using 3D face, finger, ear, and their multimodal data have been proposed, gait recognition methods still utilize video sequences. Therefore, we attempt to tackle human recognition using 3D gait biometrics where both the modeling and the test data are obtained in 3D. In this section, we present a recognition method using 3D gait biometrics from a projector-camera system. Here 3D human body data consisting of representative poses over one gait cycle are captured. A 3D human body model is fitted to the body data using a bottom-up approach. Since the body data are dense and at a high resolution, we can interpolate the entire sequence to fill in between gait acquisitions. Gait features are defined by both dynamic and static features. The similarity measure based on gait features is used for recognition of a subject and its pose.

### 8.4.1 3D Human Body Data

Gait has two distinct periods: a swing phase, when the foot does not touch the ground moving the leg forward, and a stance phase, when the foot touches the ground. Figure 8.18 is the gait cycle expressed by the swing phase and the stance phase. The cycle begins with a *foot touch*, which marks the start of the swing phase. The body weight is transferred onto the other leg, and the leg swings forward to meet the ground in front of the other foot. The cycle ends with the foot touch. The start of the stance phase is when the heel strikes the ground. The ankle flexes to bring the foot flat on the ground and the body weight transferred onto it. The end of the stance phase is when the heel leaves the ground. We measure four poses during the cycle with a projector-camera system. The human body measurement system captures high-resolution and highly accurate range data of the entire body. It includes approximately one million points in a couple of seconds. A subject has the following posture conditions:

1. Right foot touches the ground. Right leg (left hand) is in front of the torso, and left leg (right hand) is at the back of the torso. The length of stride is the longest during walking.

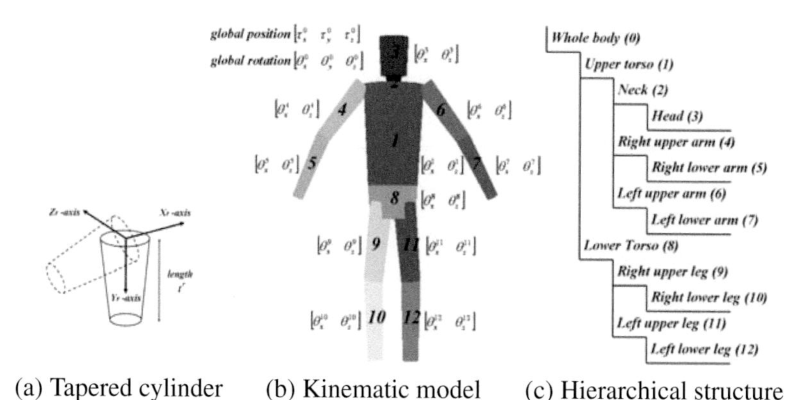


(a) Tapered cylinder (b) Kinematic model (c) Hierarchical structure

Figure 8.19. 3D human body model.

2. Right foot touches the ground, and left foot leaves the ground. Right leg is vertical to the ground, and left leg is at the back of the torso. Both hands are along the sides.
3. Left foot touches the ground. Left leg (right hand) is in front of the torso, and right leg (left hand) is at the back of the torso. The length of stride is the longest during walking.
4. Left foot touches the ground, and right foot leaves the ground. Left leg is vertical to the ground, and right leg is at the back of the torso. Both hands are along the sides.

Currently, gait databases have tens of images during a gait cycle (Gross and Shi 2001; Sarkar et al. 2005). We assumed that the measured poses are four.

### 8.4.2 3D Human Body Model

The model of the human body is based on a kinematic tree consisting of 12 segments, as illustrated in Figure 8.19. The body segment, $r$, is approximated by a 3D tapered cylinder that has one free parameter, $\iota^r$: the cylinder length. It has two degrees of the freedom rotational joint, $[\theta_x^r, \theta_z^r]$, in the local coordinate system ($O_r$-$X_r$-$Y_r$-$Z_r$). The upper torso is the root segment, that is, the parent of lower torso, right upper leg, and left upper leg. Similarly, other segments are linked to parent segments by the rotational joints. The whole body is rotated around three axes, and other segments are rotated around two axes. Here the neck is the fixed segment between head and upper torso, so that we do not consider the neck joint angles. The articulated structure of the human body has a total of 40 degrees of freedom (DOFs). The pose is described by a 6D vector,

$\mathbf{p}$, representing global position and rotation, a 22D vector, $\mathbf{q}$, representing the joint angles, and a 12D vector, $\mathbf{r}$, representing the lengths of body parts as follows:

$$\mathbf{p} = \left[\tau_x^0, \tau_y^0, \tau_z^0, \theta_x^0, \theta_y^0, \theta_z^0\right], \tag{8.13}$$

$$\begin{aligned}\mathbf{q} = \big[&\theta_x^1, \theta_z^1, \theta_x^3, \theta_z^3, \theta_x^4, \theta_z^4, \theta_x^5, \theta_z^5, \theta_x^6, \theta_z^6, \theta_x^7, \theta_z^7,\\ &\times \theta_x^8, \theta_z^8, \theta_x^9, \theta_z^9, \theta_x^{10}, \theta_z^{10}, \theta_x^{11}, \theta_z^{11}, \theta_x^{12}, \theta_z^{12}\big],\end{aligned} \tag{8.14}$$

$$\mathbf{r} = [\iota^1, \iota^2, \iota^3, \iota^4, \iota^5, \iota^6, \iota^7, \iota^8, \iota^9, \iota^{10}, \iota^{11}, \iota^{12}]. \tag{8.15}$$

The combination of the representative four poses is denoted by $s$. Joint DOF values concatenated along the kinematic tree define the kinematic pose, $\mathbf{k}$, as a tuple, $[\mathbf{p}, \mathbf{q}, \mathbf{r}, s]$, where $\mathbf{p} \in \mathbb{R}^6$, $\mathbf{q} \in \mathbb{R}^{22}$, $\mathbf{r} \in \mathbb{R}^{12}$, $s = \{s_1, s_2, s_3, s_4\}$. In the previous works, segments are linked to parent segments by either 1-DOF (hinge), 2-DOF (saddle), or 3-DOF (ball and socket) rotational joints (Vondrak et al. 2008). We use only 2-DOF rotational joints, because the 3D tapered cylinder has rotational symmetry along the direction orthogonal to the radial direction. As a result, we eliminate the twist of body parts as a unnecessary variable.

### 8.4.3 Model Fitting

Let us consider human body modeling and its problems. Modeling methods, which use ideal data, sometimes fail when applied to real data (Yu et al. 2007). The real data captured by projector-camera systems have some problems. For example, the projector-camera system cannot cover well particular body parts, such as the groin region, axillary region, and side of a human body, so that the real data are not independently and identically distributed (Nurre et al. 2000). In addition, the body sways, and dark-colored clothes also have detrimental effects, such as holes and gaps. In this section, a modeling method for dealing with the problems occurring in real data is proposed. Our approach to modeling a walking human incorporates four separate steps: body axes estimation, torso detection, arms/legs detection, and head/neck detection. The first step is body axes estimation. The principle component analysis is applied to determine coronal axis, vertical axis, sagittal axis, and the centroid of a human body (Jolliffe 2005). First, we compute the eigenvectors and the mean vector using whole human body data. The first eigenvector and the mean vector define the vertical axis and the centroid. Then we compute the eigenvectors using torso data. The second eigenvector and the third eigenvector define the coronal axis and the sagittal axis. The second step is upper torso and lower torso detection. We extract torso cross sections along the vertical axis from head to toe and calculate the cross sectional areas. The height of the centroid is defined as the boundary between upper torso and lower torso. Here a threshold value is defined by the cross-sectional area of the boundary. Then, all of the cross-sectional areas are compared with the threshold value in a vertical direction. When the cross-sectional area is smaller than the threshold value, its height is the top of the upper torso (or the bottom of lower torso). Therefore, upper torso and lower torso can be detected. The third step is arms and legs detection. The eight body parts, right/left-upper/lower-arm and right/left-upper/lower-leg, are detected by using the same method. Thus, two of them are called the *upper part* and *lower part* (e.g., a pair of right upper arm and right lower arm). Two tapered cylinders are fitted to 3D points of the upper part and lower part to minimize the distance between them. The joint angles and the lengths of the tapered cylinders are determined, so that the upper part and lower part can be detected. The fourth step is head and neck detection. Let us consider the difference between the head and other body parts. It is sometimes difficult to capture the shape of hair, because of the low sensitivities to dark color. In fact, we cannot obtain more than half of the head shape, so that face shape is used only for the detection. First, the lengths of the head and neck are estimated from the distributions of 3D points projected into the two planes. Next, joint angles are estimated by fitting the tapered cylinder to the head. However, the tapered cylinder is not fitted to the neck, because the neck is the fixed segment, as previously described.

### 8.4.4 Gait Reconstruction

A gait sequence composed of tens or hundreds of poses is required to be analyzed and recognized. The representative four poses obtained by fitting body models to body data are used to recover the other poses. Assuming that the motion between pose $\alpha$ and pose $\beta$ varies linearly, kinematic pose, $\mathbf{k}_f = [\mathbf{p}_f, \mathbf{q}_f, \mathbf{r}_f, s]$, at frame $f$ ($\alpha < f < \beta$) can be written as

$$\mathbf{p}_f = \mathbf{p}_\alpha + (f - \alpha)\mathbf{v}, \tag{8.16}$$

$$\mathbf{q}_f = \mathbf{q}_\alpha + \frac{f - \alpha}{\beta - \alpha}(\mathbf{q}_\beta - \mathbf{q}_\alpha), \tag{8.17}$$

$$\mathbf{r}_f = (\mathbf{r}_{s_1} + \mathbf{r}_{s_2} + \mathbf{r}_{s_3} + \mathbf{r}_{s_4})/4, \tag{8.18}$$

where $\mathbf{v}$ is velocity vector, which includes speed and direction, and the combination of $\alpha$ and $\beta$ is expressed by $\{\alpha, \beta\} \in \{\{s_1, s_2\}, \{s_2, s_3\}, \{s_3, s_4\}, \{s_4, s_1\}\}$.

The equations allow interpolation of joint angles and lengths of body parts. Therefore, arbitrary poses between representative poses can be recovered.

### 8.4.5 Feature Matching

Gait features are divided into two types: (1) dynamic features and (2) static features. For example, the length of stride is one of the significant features of human gait. It can be computed by the leg length and its varying angles between poses. In addition, all of the joint positions can be computed by using the same method. Therefore, both dynamic and static features are used for recognition. We define the dynamic feature as joint angles, $\mathbf{q}_{m,n}$, and static feature as lengths of the body parts, $\mathbf{r}_{m,n}$. Here $m$ is the personal identification number, and $n$ is the pose index. To transform these values into a common domain, the normalization is given by

$$\mathbf{q}'_{m,n} = \frac{\mathbf{q}_{m,n} - \boldsymbol{\mu}_q}{\boldsymbol{\sigma}_q}, \tag{8.19}$$

$$\mathbf{r}'_{m,n} = \frac{\mathbf{r}_{m,n} - \boldsymbol{\mu}_r}{\boldsymbol{\sigma}_r}, \tag{8.20}$$

where

$$\boldsymbol{\mu}_q = \frac{1}{M}\frac{1}{N}\sum_m^M\sum_n^N \mathbf{q}_{m,n} \quad \boldsymbol{\mu}_r = \frac{1}{M}\frac{1}{N}\sum_m^M\sum_n^N \mathbf{r}_{m,n},$$

$$\boldsymbol{\sigma}_q = \left(\frac{1}{M}\frac{1}{N}\sum_m^M\sum_n^N (\mathbf{q}_{m,n} - \boldsymbol{\mu}_q)(\mathbf{q}_{m,n} - \boldsymbol{\mu}_q)^T \cdot \mathbf{E}\right)^{1/2} \cdot \mathbf{d},$$

$$\boldsymbol{\sigma}_r = \left(\frac{1}{M}\frac{1}{N}\sum_m^M\sum_n^N (\mathbf{r}_{m,n} - \boldsymbol{\mu}_r)(\mathbf{r}_{m,n} - \boldsymbol{\mu}_r)^T \cdot \mathbf{E}\right)^{1/2} \cdot \mathbf{d}.$$

In the formulations, $\boldsymbol{\mu}_q$, $\boldsymbol{\mu}_r$ are the arithmetic means of dynamic and static features, and $\boldsymbol{\sigma}_q$, $\boldsymbol{\sigma}_r$ are the standard deviations of dynamic and static features, $M$, $N$ are the numbers of people and poses, with the matrix $\mathbf{E} = diag(1, 1, 1, \ldots, 1)$ and the vector $\mathbf{d} = [1, 1, 1, \ldots, 1]$. Both features are concatenated on a feature vector $\boldsymbol{\phi}_{m,n} = [\mathbf{q}'_{m,n}, \mathbf{r}'_{m,n}]$. If only the dynamic feature is used, a feature vector is defined as $\boldsymbol{\phi}_{m,n} = [\mathbf{q}'_{m,n}]$. Suppose that an unknown feature vector, $\boldsymbol{\phi}_U$, is one of $M \times N$ feature vectors, $\boldsymbol{\phi}_{m,n}$. The minimum value of matching scores can be written as

$$E_r = \min_{m,n} \|\boldsymbol{\phi}_U - \boldsymbol{\phi}_{m,n}\|. \tag{8.21}$$

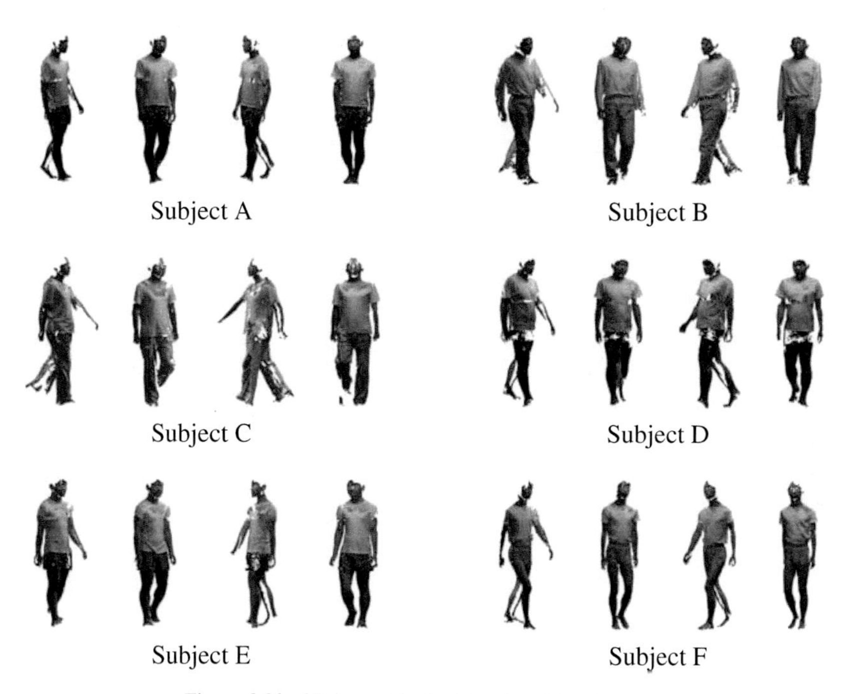


Figure 8.20. 3D human body data of walking humans.

The matching score is computed as $L_2$ distance. For unknown data, the personal identification number and pose index are recognized.

### 8.4.6 Experimental Results

The experiments were performed on the body data set collected by the human body measurement system. It contains 24 body data from the representative four poses of six subjects $X \in \{A, B, C, D, E, F\}$.

#### 8.4.6.1 Sensing and Modeling

The body data of representative poses are captured by a human body measurement system, Cartesia 3D Body Scanner of SPACEVISION. The system consisted of nine projector-camera pairs, which acquires nine range data in 3.6 seconds with 640 × 480 pixels, 3 mm depth resolution, and 3 mm measurement accuracy. Yamauchi and Sato (2006) have developed this commercial product based on research results achieved until now. Projector-camera pairs are calibrated by the proposed geometric model and calibration method, and their camera coordinate systems are integrated by the improved alignment approach. Figure 8.20 shows the measurement results of walking humans. The

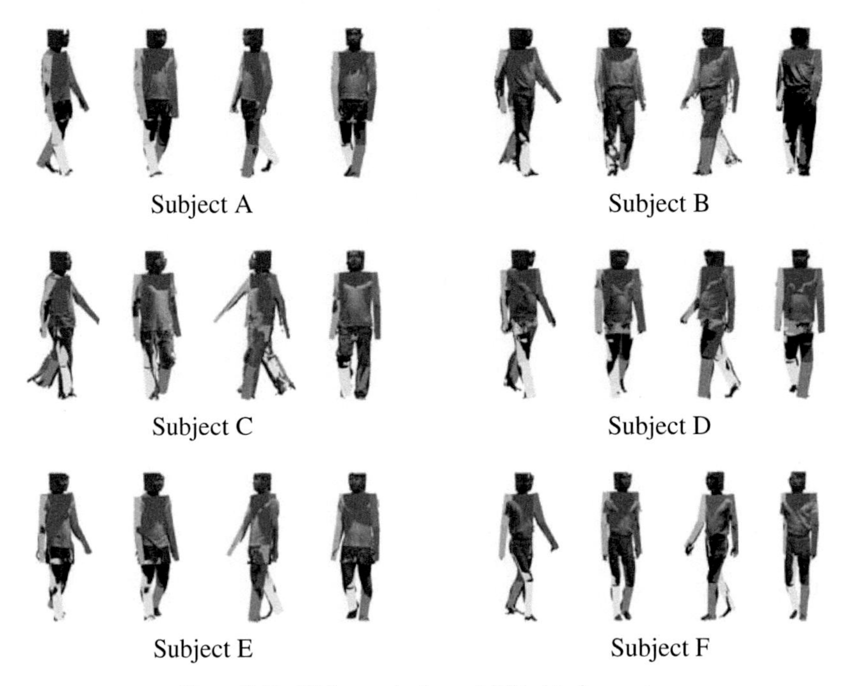


Figure 8.21. 3D human body model fitted to four poses.

number of measuring points is about 1/2 to one million depending on the subject and the pose. Figure 8.21 shows the results of human body modeling. For the modeling in the experiment we used three parameters: $R = 36$, $\delta_{ut} = 0.25$, and $\delta_{lt} = 0.5$. The body model is fitted to the captured body data, so that their joint angles and lengths of body parts are obtained.

#### 8.4.6.2 Gait Reconstruction

Figure 8.22 shows the results of gait reconstruction. We define that the one gait cycle is composed of 20 frames $Y \in \{1, 2, \ldots, 20\}$. The speed is given by dividing the stride length by the number of poses, and the direction is given manually. Four of them are representative poses, indicated by the frame index 1, 6, 11, and 16, and the others are interpolated poses, indicated by the frame index 2–5, 7–10, 12–15, and 17–20.

#### 8.4.6.3 Recognition

The representative poses $s = \{s_1, s_2, s_3, s_4\}$ and their symmetric poses $\bar{s} = \{\bar{s}_1, \bar{s}_2, \bar{s}_3, \bar{s}_4\}$ are used for the experiment. The symmetric poses $\bar{s}_1$, $\bar{s}_2$, $\bar{s}_3$, $\bar{s}_4$ are symmetric to $s_3$, $s_4$, $s_1$, $s_2$, respectively. They are synthesized by allocating

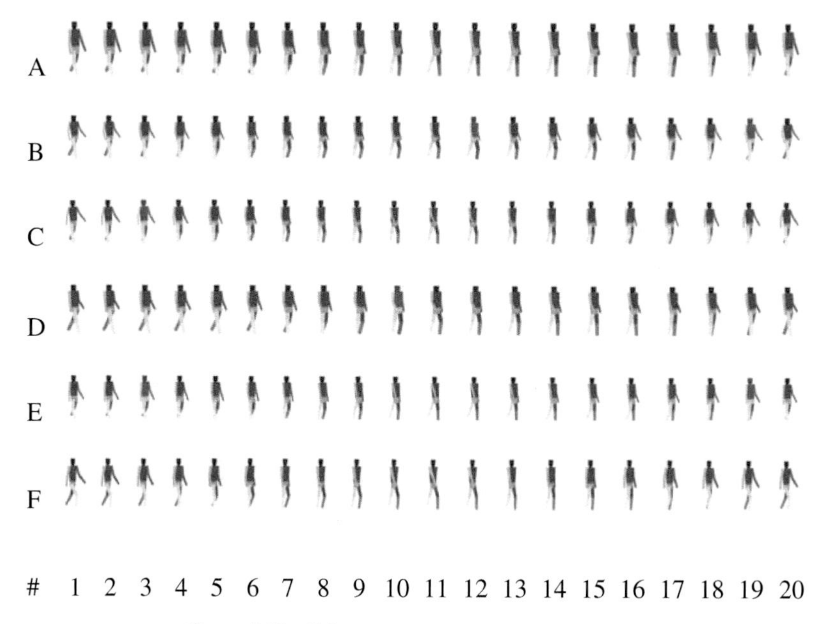


Figure 8.22. Gait sequence composed of 20 frames.

right (or left) side parameters of representative poses to left (or right) side parameters of symmetrical poses. For the training data, two gait sequences are recovered by using two combinations of representative poses and symmetrical poses. Figure 8.23(a) shows the training data of six subjects. One gait sequence is recovered by four poses $\eta_1 = \{s_1, \bar{s}_2, s_3, \bar{s}_4\}$, and the other is recovered by four poses $\eta_2 = \{\bar{s}_1, s_2, \bar{s}_3, s_4\}$. Each subject has 40 poses, so that training data contain a total of 240 kinematic poses. For the testing data, one gait sequence is recovered by representative poses $\eta_3 = \{s_1, s_2, s_3, s_4\}$. Figure 8.23(b) shows the testing data of six subjects. This sequence includes the representative four poses and 16 interpolated poses. The 16 interpolated poses are unique, and so they are not included in the training data. Therefore, we utilize 96 kinematic poses of six subjects for testing. There is absolutely no overlap between the training and testing data. To evaluate the proposed method, identification rate and average pose error are obtained. The identification rate is obtained by dividing the number of recognized subject by the number of testing data. The pose error is the frame difference between the estimated pose and the ideal pose. Table 8.4 shows that we achieve 98.96% using dynamic feature and 100.0% using both dynamic and static features for the identification rate. When only the dynamic feature is used, the method fails to recognize testing data Subject D with pose 14, who should not be recognized as the training data for Subject

Table 8.4. *Identification Rate and Average Pose Error*

| Features | Identification Rate (%) | Average Pose Error (Frame) |
|---|---|---|
| Dynamic | 98.96 | 0.41 |
| Dynamic and static | 100.0 | 1.31 |

B with pose 13. Although body types between two subjects are different, their joint angles, that is, leg and arm swings, are quite similar. In contrast, we achieve 0.41 using the dynamic feature and 1.31 using both features for the average pose error. The experiment using the dynamic feature has acceptable results, because it focuses on estimating poses, that is, the dynamic feature cannot consider lengths of body parts. Therefore, both dynamic and static features are useful for gait recognition.

## 8.5 Conclusion

We presented a framework for measurement and its application using range data of entire human body. The first part is the mechanism for calibration of

(a) Training data (b) Testing data

Figure 8.23. Examples of training data and testing data.

structured light system. A structured light system consists of one camera and one projector. The geometric model is defined such that the camera model is based on the pinhole model, and the projector model is based on the equation of a plane model. The measurement accuracy is improved by 19–44% compared with the traditional method. Next, both camera and projector parameters are estimated by observing a planar object from three arbitrary viewpoints. Unlike other approaches using cube objects, it facilitates the procedure of the user's tasks. The second part is the formulation of human body measurement system for acquiring the range data of the entire body. A projector-camera pair is one of the sophisticated structured light systems. In our system, four projector-camera pairs are installed in the pole as a measuring unit. The human body measurement system consists of three pole units with 12 projector-camera pairs. This system obtains whole human body data including about 1/2 to one million points in 2 seconds with 1.88 mm average error. We advocate that the high-resolution, highly accurate range data are well suited for security applications. The third part is the introduction of gait biometrics for identification of individuals and their poses. Whole human body data that comprises representative poses during a gait cycle are captured, and then the positions of joints and body parts are inferred by fitting kinematic models to the data set. Unlike attempts that utilize silhouette images that have been affected by clothing and self-occlusions, we use range data of the entire body to directly extract gait features. In the experiments, we achieve 98.96% using the dynamic feature and 100.0% using both dynamic and static features for the identification rate.

## References


Bolles, R. C., J. H. Kremers, and R. A. Cain. 1981. A simple sensor to gather three-dimensional data. Technical Report 249.

Chen, C. H., and A. C. Kak. 1987. Modeling and calibration of a structured light scanner for 3-D robot vision. *Proceedings of International Conference on Robotics and Automation*, 807–815.

Chen, H., and B. Bhanu. 2007. Human ear recognition in 3D. *IEEE Transactions on Pattern Analysis and Machine Intelligence*, **29**(4), 718–737.

Gross, R., and J. Shi. 2001. The CMU motion of body (MoBo) database. *Technical Report CMU-RI-TR-01-18*.

Hattori, K., and Y. Sato. 1996. Accurate rangefinder with laser pattern shifting. *Proceedings of International Conference on Pattern Recognition*, **3**, 849–853.

Huynh, D. Q., R. A. Owens, and P. E. Hartmann. 1999. Calibrating a structured light stripe system: a novel approach. *International Journal of Computer Vision*, **33**(1), 73–86.

Jolliffe, I. T. 2005. *Principal Component Analysis*. Springer.

Koo, B. K., Y. K. Choi, and S. I. Chien. 2004. 3D human whole body construction by contour triangulation. *IEICE Transactions on Information and Systems*, **E87-D**(1), 233–243.

Lu, R. S., and Y. F. Li. 2003. Calibration of a 3D vision system using pattern projection. *Sensors and Actuators A: Physical*, **104**(1), 94–102.

Malassiotis, S., N. Aifanti, and M. G. Strintzis. 2006. Personal authentication using 3-D finger geometry. *IEEE Transactions on Information Forensics and Security*, **1**(1), 12–21.

Matsuki, M., and T. Ueda. 1989. A real-time sectional image measuring system using time sequentially coded grating method. *IEEE Transactions on Pattern Analysis and Machine Intelligence*, **11**(11), 1225–1228.

Moezzi, S., L. C. Tai, and P. Gerard. 1997. Virtual view generation for 3D digital video. *IEEE Multimedia*, **4**(1), 18–26.

Nurre, J. H., J. Connor, E. A. Lewark, and J. S. Collier. 2000. On segmenting the three-dimensional scan data of a human body. *IEEE Transactions on Medical Imaging*, **19**(8), 787–797.

Reid, I. D. 1996. Projective calibration of a laser-stripe range finder. *Image and Vision Computing*, **14**(9), 659–666.

Saito, H., S. Baba, and T. Kanade. 2003. Appearance-based virtual view generation from multicamera videos captured in the 3-D room. *IEEE Transactions on Multimedia*, **5**(3), 303–316.

Samir, C., A. Srivastava, and M. Daoudi. 2006. Three-dimensional face recognition using shapes of facial curves. *IEEE Transactions on Pattern Analysis and Machine Intelligence*, **28**(11), 1858–1863.

Sarkar, S., P. J. Phillips, Z. Liu, I. R. Vega, P. Grother, and K. W. Bowyer. 2005. The humanID gait challenge problem: data sets, performance, and analysis. *IEEE Transactions on Pattern Analysis and Machine Intelligence*, **27**(2), 162–177.

Theoharis, T., G. Passalis, G. Toderici, and I. A. Kakadiaris. 2008. Unified 3D face and ear recognition using wavelets on geometry images. *Pattern Recognition*, **41**(3), 796–804.

Treleaven, P. 2004. Sizing us up. *IEEE Spectrum*, **41**(4), 28–31.

Tsai, R. Y. 1987. A versatile camera calibration technique for high-accuracy 3D machine vision metrology using off-the-shelf TV cameras and lens. *IEEE Journal of Robotics and Automation*, **3**(4), 323–344.

Tsalakanidou, F., S. Malassiotis, and M. G. Strintzis. 2007. A 3D face and hand biometric system for robust user-friendly authentication. *Pattern Recognition Letters*, **28**(16), 2238–2249.

Vondrak, M., L. Signal, and O. C. Jenkins. 2008. Physical simulation for probabilistic motion tracking. *Proceedings of IEEE Conference on Computer Vision and Pattern Recognition*, 1–8.

Wakitani, J., T. Maruyama, T. Morita, T. Uchiyama, and A. Mochizuki. 1995. Wrist-mounted laser rangefinder. *Proceedings of IEEE/RSJ International Conference on Intelligent Robots and Systems*, **3**, 362–367.

Weng, J., P. Cohen, and M. Herniou. 1992. Camera calibration with distortion models and accuracy evaluation. *IEEE Transactions on Pattern Analysis and Machine Intelligence*, **14**(10), 965–980.

Yamauchi, K., and Y. Sato. 2006. 3D human body measurement by multiple range images. *Proceedings of International Conference on Pattern Recognition*, **4**, 833–836.

Yu, H., S. Qin, D. K. Wight, and J. Kang. 2007. Generation of 3D human models with different levels of detail through point-based simplification. *Proceedings of International Conference on "Computer as a Tool,"* 1982–1986.

Zhang, B., Y. F. Li, and Y. H. Wu. 2007. Self-recalibration of a structured light system via plane-based homography. *Pattern Recognition*, **40**(4), 1368–1377.

Zhang, Z. 2000. A flexible new technique for camera calibration. *IEEE Transactions on Pattern Analysis and Machine Intelligence*, **22**(11), 1330–1334.

# 9

# Gait Recognition Using Motion Physics in a Neuromorphic Computing Framework

Ricky J. Sethi, Amit K. Roy-Chowdhury, and Ashok Veeraraghavan

## 9.1 Introduction

Interpreting how people walk is intuitive for humans. From birth, we observe physical motion in the world around us and create perceptual models to make sense of it. Neurobiologically, we invent a framework within which we understand and interpret human activities like walking (Kandel et al. 2000). Analogously, in this chapter we propose a computational model that seeks to understand human gait from its neural basis to its physical essence.

We thus started by examining the basis of all human activities: motion. The rigorous study of motion has been the cornerstone of physics for the last 450 years, over which physicists have unlocked a deep, underlying structure of motion. We employ ideas grounded firmly in fundamental physics that are true for the motion of the physical systems we consider in gait analysis.

Using this physics-based methodology, we compute *Hamiltonian Energy Signatures (HES)* for a person by considering all the points on their contour, thus leading to a multidimensional time series that represents the gait of a person. These HES time-series curves thus provide a model of the gait for each person's style of walking. It can also be shown, using basic physical principles, that the HES is invariant under a special affine transformation, as shown in Appendix 9.A.1.3. This allows us to use the HES to *categorize* the activities of different people across different domains (high resolution, low resolution, etc.) in a moderately view-invariant manner. The HES time series, therefore, can characterize the walking styles of individuals. Note that these HES curves can be computed in either the image plane, yielding the Image HES as used in this chapter, or in the three dimensional (3D) world, giving the Physical HES, depending on the application domain and the nature of the tracks extracted. In either case, the Hamiltonian framework gives a highly abstract,

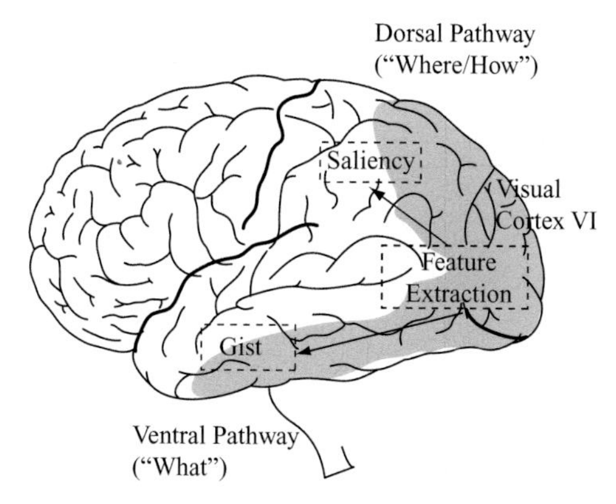


Figure 9.1. Neuromorphic model for the dorsal and ventral pathways: the computational modules are superimposed onto the parts of the brain that perform similar functions, where we follow the NMC labeling convention discussed in Section 9.2.2.

compact representation for a system and can yield the energy of the system being considered under certain conditions.

Since the perception of gait involves the interpretation of motion by the brain, we embed the above physics-based motion models within a framework inspired by Neurobiology and Neuromorphic Computing (NMC). The latest models for the perception and interpretation of motion by the brain are employed to present a novel technique for the representation and recognition of human walking styles. These models indicate that visual processing in the brain, as shown in Figure 9.1, bifurcates into two streams at V1: a Dorsal Motion Energy Pathway and a Ventral Form/Shape Pathway (Sigala et al. 2005; Jhuang et al. 2007).

In the Itti-Koch NMC model (Peters and Itti 2007; Siagian and Itti 2007), an input image is filtered in a number of low-level visual feature channels, including orientation and motion energies, as computed in the Dorsal Pathway; in our case we use the HES to get the motion energies of a person's gait, as outlined in Section 9.3.1. In the NMC model (Siagian and Itti 2007), the same low-level feature detectors as the Dorsal Pathway acquired over very short time frames are used to classify the scene by computing a holistic, low-level signature from the Ventral Pathway; in our case we thus use the shape features to classify a person's gait as the Ventral Pathway component, as outlined in Section 9.3.2.

In the NMC approach, these two pathways are combined in the *Integration* module, as shown in Figure 9.2. Recent research, building upon the neurobiology of object recognition, suggests the brain uses the same, or at least similar, pathways for motion recognition as it does for object recognition (Giese and Poggio 2003; Goddard 1992; Sigala et al. 2005; Riesenhuber and Poggio

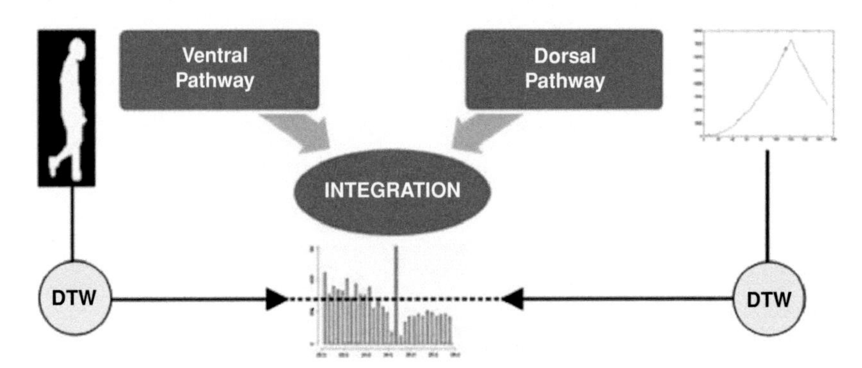


Figure 9.2. The neuromorphic computing-inspired model: the ventral and dorsal pathways' processing is combined in the integration module using variants of feature integration and biased competition. The output of each pathway is a feature vector that is compared to the query/test using Dynamic Time Warping (DTW).

1999; Jhuang et al. 2007). Although existing neurobiological models for motion recognition do posit the existence of a coupling or integration of these two pathways, they leave any specific mechanism for combination of the two pathways as an open question (Giese and Poggio 2003; Giese 2004).

Building upon this and recent work in the neurobiological community, which shows the dorsal and ventral processes could be integrated through a process of *feature integration* (Treisman and Gelade 1980) or *biased competition* (Deco and Rolls 2005; Beck and Kastner 2008; Kastner and Ungerleider 2001; Yang and Jabri 2003; Deco and Lee 2004) as originally outlined by Desimone and Duncan (1995) and Reynolds et al. (1999), we propose a computational model for the integration of the two pathways in the NMC framework by implementing this integration in a statistical framework, creating *Total Integration* (only the winners from both pathways survive), *Partial Integration* (intermediate values are pointwise correlations of normalized measures), and *Weighted Integration* (Ventral values are weighted by Dorsal values and do no worse than Ventral values) models, all using the *bootstrap*. The bootstrap is used to find the variance of a statistic on a sample; the statistic, in our case is the quantiles. After a sample is collected from an experiment, we can calculate a statistic on it (such as the mean or quantiles, for example), and then use the bootstrap to figure out the variance in that statistic (e.g., via a confidence interval). The bootstrap itself works by resampling with replacement, as described in Section 9.3.3.

### 9.1.1 Overview of Chapter

Building upon the fundamental principles of the physics of motion and the NMC model of perception, we present a novel framework for the modeling and recognition of humans based on their gait in video. The HES curves, developed in Section 9.3.1, give us an immediate sense of a person's gait, as required for the motion energy aspect of the Dorsal Pathway. For the Ventral Pathway, as described in Section 9.3.2, we use shape features with DTW, but we also have the freedom to use different features (e.g., image features using HMM (Veeraraghavan et al. 2004) or gait energy image (Han and Bhanu 2003)). Finally, in Section 9.3.3 we incorporate the Integration module by using the neurobiological ideas of feature integration and biased competition, which we implement with a Total Integration, Partial Integration, and Weighted Integration framework using the bootstrap. This approach provides flexibility since new approaches in low-level feature extraction can be employed easily within our framework. We present detailed validation of our proposed techniques and show results on the USF gait dataset in Section 9.4.

## 9.2 Related Work

We build liberally upon theoretical thrusts from several different disciplines, including Analytical Hamiltonian Mechanics, Neuromorphic Computing and Neurobiology, and, of course, gait analysis. The models developed for robotics in Peters and Itti (2007) provide the basic NMC architecture but are used more for object recognition and analysis. Similarly, Energy-Based Models (EBMs) (LeCun et al. 2007) capture dependencies between variables for *image recognition* by associating a scalar "energy" to each configuration of the variables. Still others Bruhn et al. (2005) take local and global optical flow approaches and compute confidence measures. Researchers have proposed computational frameworks for integration, for example, Tu et al. (2001), but they have also been restricted to the analysis of single images. The use of DDMCMC shown in Yuille and Kersten (2006) might be an excellent Integration module application for future NMC-based research thrusts, and we will consider such MCMC-based approaches in the future.

### 9.2.1 Related Work on Fusion of Multiple Features in Activity Recognition

For representing the motion energy processes of the Dorsal Pathway, we propose a unique descriptor, the HES, that models the global motion of the objects involved in the activities. Our conception of the HES is based upon fundamental ideas in Classical Dynamics (Landau and Lifshitz 1976) and Quantum Mechanics (Shankar 1994), especially Hamilton's Variational Principle (Landau and Lifshitz 1976).

In terms of activity recognition (Hu et al. 2004; Turaga et al. 2008), some of the cutting-edge research uses the fusion of multiple features (e.g., Liu et al. 2008). Their approach to features fusion comes closest to the idea of combining features that express both the form and motion components. Our approach also draws inspiration from the method employed in Hu et al. (2008), which detects global motion patterns by constructing supertracks using flow vectors for tracking high-density crowd flows in low resolution. Our methodology, on the other hand, works in both high and low resolution and for densely and sparsely distributed objects because all it requires is the $(x, y, t)$ tracks for the various objects. Also, our physical model goes well beyond an examination of Eulerian or Lagrangian fluid flows, which yield only local (vector) rather than global (integral) properties.

### 9.2.2 Related Work in Neurobiology and NMC

Humans exhibit the ability to quickly understand and summarize a scene in less than 100 ms. When visual information comes in from the retina, the brain seems to do some initial processing in the V1 visual cortex. Subsequently, that information bifurcates and travels along two parallel pathways in the neural model, the so-called What (Ventral) pathway and the Where (Dorsal) pathway (Peters and Itti 2007). Some NMC models (Siagian and Itti 2007; Peters and Itti 2007; Itti et al. 1998) relate the ventral and dorsal processing to the ideas of gist and saliency, where the saliency component is based on low-level visual features such as luminance contrast, color contrast, orientation, and motion energies, while the gist component is a relatively low-dimensional scene representation that is acquired over very short time frames and computed as a holistic low-dimensional signature, by using the same low-level feature detectors as the saliency model. However, we use the standard notation for these two pathways (Dorsal and Ventral) as outlined in the latest neurobiological models of motion recognition (Giese and Poggio 2003; Giese 2004, 2000).

Eventually, or perhaps concurrently (Yang and Jabri 2003), the results of these two pathways are integrated, as shown in Figure 9.1; although existing neurobiological models for motion recognition do posit the existence of a coupling or integration of these two pathways, they leave any specific mechanism for combination of the two pathways as an open question (Giese and Poggio 2003; Giese 2004). Recent work in the neurobiological community shows the dorsal and ventral processes could be integrated through a process of *feature integration* (Treisman and Gelade 1980) or *biased competition* (Deco and Rolls 2005; Beck and Kastner 2008; Kastner and Ungerleider 2001; Yang and Jabri 2003; Deco and Lee 2004).

### 9.2.3 Related Work in Gait Recognition

Recently, significant effort has been devoted to the study of human gait, driven by its potential use as a biometric for person identification. We outline some of the methods in gait-based human identification, and a comprehensive review on gait recognition can be found in Nixon et al. (2005).

#### 9.2.3.1 Role of Shape and Kinematics in Human Gait

Johansson (1973) attached light displays to various body parts and showed that humans can identify motion with the pattern generated by a small set of moving dots. Muybridge (1901) captured photographic recordings of humans in his study on animal locomotion. He used high-speed photographic images to study locomotion in humans and animals. Since then, considerable effort has been made in the computer vision, artificial intelligence, and image processing communities to the understanding of human activities from videos. A survey of work in human motion analysis can be found in Gavrilla (1999).

Several studies have been done on the various cues that humans use for gait recognition. Hoenkamp (1978) studied the various perceptual factors that contribute to the labeling of human gait. Medical studies Murray et al. (1964) suggest that there are 24 different components to human gait. If all these different components are considered, then it is claimed that the gait signature is unique. Because it is very difficult to extract these components reliably, several other representations have been used. It has been shown (Cutting and Kozlowski 1977) that humans can do gait recognition even in the absence of familiarity cues. A dynamic array of point lights attached to the walker was used to record the gait pattern. It was found that static or very brief presentations are insufficient for recognition while longer displays are sufficient. Cutting and Kozlowski (1977) also suggest that dynamic cues such as speed, bounciness, and rhythm are more important for human recognition than static cues such as height. Cutting and Proffitt (1981) argue that motion is not the simple compilation of static forms and claim that it is a dynamic invariant that determines event perception.

#### 9.2.3.2 Shape-Based Methods

Niyogi and Adelson (1994) obtained spatio-temporal solids by aligning consecutive images and use a weighted Euclidean distance to obtain recognition. Phillips et al. (2002) provide a baseline algorithm for gait recognition using silhouette correlation. Han and Bhanu (2003) use the gait energy image, while Wang et al. (2002) use Procrustes shape analysis for recognition. Foster et al.

(2003) use area-based features. Bobick and Johnson (2001) use activity specific static and stride parameters to perform recognition. Collins et al. (2002) build a silhouette-based nearest neighbor classifier to do recognition. Several researchers have used Hidden Markov Models (HMM) for the task of gait-based identification. For example Kale et al. (2004) built a continuous HMM for recognition using the width vector and the binarized silhouette as image features. A model-based method for accurate extraction of silhouettes using the HMM is provided in Lee et al. (2003). They use these silhouettes to perform recognition. Another shape-based method for identifying individuals from noisy silhouettes is provided in (Tolliver and Collins 2003). Finally, Zou and Bhanu (2006) take a unique shape-based approach based on gait energy image (GEI) and co-evolutionary genetic programming (CGP) for human activity classification.

#### 9.2.3.3 Kinematics-Based Methods

Apart from these image-based approaches Cunado et al. (1994) model the movement of thighs as articulated pendulums and extract a gait signature using this model. But in such an approach robust estimation of thigh position in a video can be very difficult. In another kinematics-based approach (Bissacco et al. 2001), trajectories of the various parameters of a kinematic model of the human body are used to learn a representation of a dynamical system. The parameters of the linear dynamical system are used to classify different kinds of human activities.

## 9.3 Proposed Framework for Gait Analysis

We take an NMC-inspired approach for recognizing the walking style of people by integrating the motion signature of the objects for the Dorsal Pathway (the Hamiltonian Energy Signatures) and shape features for the Ventral Pathway via the Integration module using a variant of the neurobiological ideas of biased competition and feature integration (see below for detailed discussion). The overall approach is shown diagrammatically in Figure 9.2.

### 9.3.1 Dorsal Pathway: Hamiltonian Energy Signatures (HES)

One of the most fundamental ideas in theoretical physics is the *Principle of Stationary Action*, also known variously as Principle of Least Action as well as Hamilton's Variational Principle (Landau and Lifshitz 1976). This is a variational principle that can be used to obtain the equations of motion of a system and is the very basis for most branches of physics, from Analytical

Mechanics to Statistical Mechanics to Quantum Field Theory. Building upon the work of Lagrange, W. R. Hamilton applied the idea of a function whose value remains constant along any path in the configuration space of the system (unless the final and initial points are varied) to Newtonian mechanics to derive Lagrange's equations, the equations of motion for the system being studied.

Following Hamilton's approach, we define *Hamilton's Action*,[1] $S$, for motion along a worldline between two fixed physical events (not events in activity recognition) as

$$S \equiv \int_{t_1}^{t_2} L(q(t), \dot{q}(t), t)dt \tag{9.1}$$

with $q$ the generalized coordinates,[2] and $L$, in this case, the *Lagrangian*, which, for a conservative system, is defined as

$$L = T - U, \tag{9.2}$$

where $T$ is the *Kinetic Energy* and $U$ is the *Potential Energy*. The *Hamiltonian function*, derived from *Hamilton's Variational Principle* (see Appendix 9.A.1.1), is usually stated most compactly, in generalized coordinates, as (Goldstein 1980)

$$H(q, p, t) = \sum_i p_i \dot{q}_i - L(q, \dot{q}, t), \tag{9.3}$$

where $H$ is the Hamiltonian, $p$ is the generalized momentum, and $\dot{q}$ is the time derivative of the generalized coordinates, $q$. If the transformation between the Cartesian and generalized coordinates is time independent, then the Hamiltonian function also represents the total mechanical energy of the system:

$$H(q(t), p(t)) = T(p(t)) + U(q(t)). \tag{9.4}$$

In general, we compute (9.3), which depends explicitly on time, but if we have generalized coordinates and transformations from the image plane to the 3D world, we can make the assumption (9.4) as a first approximation.[3]

[1] To avoid confusion, we will use the term Action to exclusively refer to Hamilton's Action and not action as it is normally understood in Gait Analysis.

[2] Generalized coordinates are the configurational parameters of a system: the natural, minimal, complete set of parameters by which you can completely specify the configuration of the system. In this chapter we deal only with Cartesian coordinates, although we can deal with the more general case by using a methodology as in Dobrski (2007).

[3] In this first approximation, the system can be idealized as a holonomic system, unless we deal with velocity-dependent or time-varying potentials. In fact, even when we cannot make those idealizations (e.g., viscous flows), we can define "generalized potentials" (Goldstein 1980) and retain the standard Lagrangian, as in (9.2).

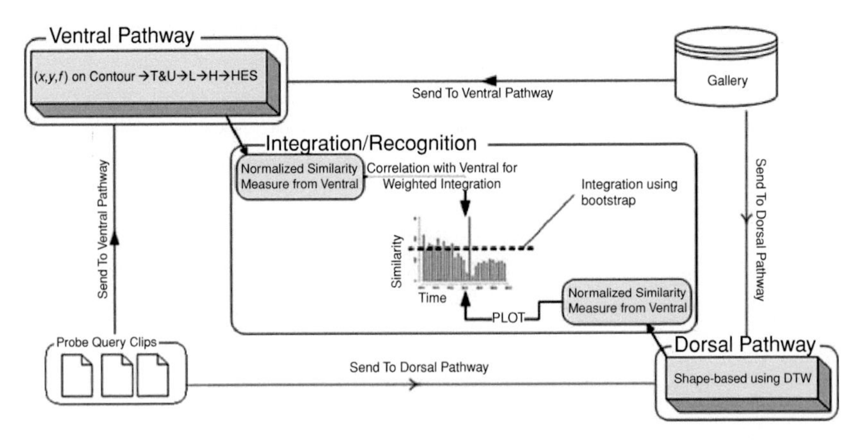


Figure 9.3. Proposed NMC-inspired framework for gait analysis of USF dataset: final recognition decision is made in the Integration module. Here a probe clip of a person walking is sent to both the Ventral and Dorsal Pathways; similarly, clips from the gallery are also sent to both pathways. Similarity measures between the probe clip and the clips in the gallery are computed from each pathway, and the results integrated in the Integration module, where final recognition occurs.

#### 9.3.1.1 Application to Gait Analysis

This Hamiltonian is exactly what we utilize as the Hamiltonian Energy Signature (HES) of a system or subsystem observed in the given video. We end up with a quantity that provides a motion energy description of the gait: the *HES* (9.6), which gives a simple, intuitive expression for an abstract, compact representation of the system; that is, the characteristic time-series curves for each person. We thus segment the video into systems and subsystems (e.g., the whole body of a person, parts of the body, etc.) and, for each of those, get their tracks, from which we compute $T$ and $U$, and use that to get the HES curve signature, which can then be evaluated further and the results analyzed accordingly, as shown in Figure 9.3.

A system, in this sense, is defined according to the constraints of the video and the people whose walking style we are trying to identify. Thus, a system could be points on the joints of a person, points on the contour of a person, subsampled points on a contour, etc. More generally, the HES can be used to characterize any system or subsystem. Similarly, a human could be represented as a singular, particulate object that is part of a system of objects or as a system composed of subsystems; for example, when we can characterize their legs, arms, hands, fingers, etc.

Thus, we use the video to gain knowledge of the physics and use the physics to capture the essence of the person being observed via the HES (defined below). So, now the question is how to compute the HES from the tracks in the video. We solve this problem by using these tracks to compute the kinematic quantities that drop out of the Lagrangian formalism, thus giving a theoretical basis for examination of their energy from $(x, y, t)$.

#### 9.3.1.2 Examples

For example, in the general case when $U \neq 0$, the Lagrangian, $T - U$, of a single person acting under a constant force, $F$ (e.g., for a gravitational field, $g$, $F = mg$) over a distance, $x$, is:

$$L(x(t), \dot{x}(t)) = \frac{1}{2}mv^2 - Fx,$$

with

$$x = x_o + v_o t + \frac{1}{2}at^2 \quad \text{and} \quad a = \frac{F}{m}. \tag{9.5}$$

We now use this Lagrangian to calculate Hamilton's Action for the general system:

$$\begin{aligned} S &= \int_{t_a}^{t_b} L dt = \int_{t_a}^{t_b} \left( \frac{1}{2}m\left(v_o^2 + 2v_o \frac{F}{m}t\right) - F\left(x_o + v_o t\right)\right) dt \\ &= \frac{1}{2}mv_o^2(t_b - t_a) - Fx_o(t_b - t_a). \end{aligned} \tag{9.6}$$

Using Hamilton's Variational Principle on (9.6) for a gravitational force yields (with $y$ being the vertical position, which can be determined from the tracks):

$$H = T + U = \frac{1}{2}mv_o^2 + mgh = \frac{1}{2}mv_o^2 + mg(y_b - y_a). \tag{9.7}$$

Here, as a first approximation, we treat $m$ as a scale factor and set it to unity; in the future, we can estimate mass using the shape of the object or other heuristics, including estimating it as a Bayesian parameter. In addition, mass is not as significant when we consider the same class of objects. For more complex interactions, we can even use any standard, conservative model for U (e.g., as a spring with $U = \frac{1}{2}kx^2$ for elastic interactions). In addition, we can compute more complex interactions between the points on a person's contour.

#### 9.3.1.3 Advantages

The approach we utilize to compute $H$ and $S$ (which are used to calculate the HES curves) is relatively straightforward: We find tracks for the points on the contour of a silhouette, construct distance and velocity vectors from those tracks for all the relevant points on a person's contour and use these to compute HES versus time curves for each system or subsystem observed in the video. These HES curves thereby yield a compact signature for the gait of an individual and allow us to characterize different walking styles. For comparing the gaits of different people, we use the HES for each person; because the HES is already a time series, we can compare their characteristic HES curves using a Dynamic Time Warping (DTW) algorithm.

The main advantage of using the Hamiltonian formalism is that it provides a robust framework for theoretical extensions to more complex physical models. More immediately, it offers form-invariant equations, exactly as in the Lagrangian formalism, which leads to view-invariant metrics. In addition, it can be shown that the Image HES allows us to recognize activities in a moderately view-invariant manner while the 3D Physical HES is completely view invariant; the invariance of both comes from the invariance of the HES to affine transformations, as explained in detail in Appendix 9.A.1.3 with experimental validation shown in Sethi et al. (2009).

### 9.3.2 Ventral Pathway: Shape-Based Features

Our construction provides flexibility because new approaches in low-level feature extraction can be employed easily within our framework. For the present work, we use shape features with DTW. In general, the neurobiology literature suggests that orientation, shape, and color might serve as the best form-based components (Kandel et al. 2000). In particular, we used the approach in (Veeraraghavan et al. 2005). The integration is directly on the similarity matrices, so the exact same method can be used for other low-level features. Thus, many of the low-level approaches mentioned in Section 9.2.3 could have been used instead.

Specifically, Veeraraghavan et al. (2005) presents an approach for comparing two sequences of deforming shapes using both parametric models and nonparametric methods. In their approach, Kendall's definition of shape is used for feature extraction. Since the shape feature rests on a non-Euclidean manifold, they propose parametric models such as the autoregressive model and autoregressive moving average model on the tangent space. The nonparametric model is based on Dynamic Time-Warping, but they employ a modification of the Dynamic Time-Warping algorithm to include the nature of the non-Euclidean space in which the shape deformations take place. They apply this algorithm for gait-based human recognition on the USF dataset by exploiting the shape deformations of a person's silhouette as a discriminating feature and then providing recognition results using the nonparametric model for gait-based person authentication.

### 9.3.3 NMC Integration and Gait Analysis

The usual NMC tack is to integrate the Dorsal and Ventral Pathways via the Integration module, usually by weighting them, as shown in Figure 9.2. NMC and neurobiologically based approaches have examined different integration methodologies, including simple pointwise multiplication, as well as exploring more standard neurobiological integration mechanisms such as *feature integration* (Treisman and Gelade 1980), in which simple visual features are analyzed pre-attentively and in parallel, and *biased competition* (Desimone and Duncan 1995; Reynolds et al. 1999), which "proposes that visual stimuli compete to be represented by cortical activity. Competition may occur at each stage along a cortical visual information processing pathway."

There are a variety of different approaches that might be useful in simulating this Integration, including multiple hypothesis testing such as Tukey HSD, MCMC techniques mentioned earlier, etc. We propose a computational approach to integration that is a variant of these different methods and develop a computational framework that approximately mimics the neurobiological models of feature integration and biased competition (Kandel et al. 2000; Deco and Rolls 2005; Kastner and Ungerleider 2001). Our final NMC implementation is outlined in Figure 9.3.

We simulate the integration via a framework in which we develop three different integration variations using the bootstrap to establish the quantile analysis (explained below). To implement any of the integration variants, we biased the Ventral Pathway with the Dorsal Pathway by using "feature maps" (as discussed in Yang and Jabri (2003), as well as Treisman's feature integration theory (Treisman and Gelade 1980)), where a feature map is the distribution of features with matching peaks using a similarity measure between features.

The integration is accomplished within the overall gait recognition framework, as outlined in Algorithm 1. We start by first creating a distance matrix for each person in a given Probe with each person in the Gallery using the method for the Ventral Pathway, which, in our case, was using shape features with DTW. We also created a distance matrix for each person in that same Probe with each person in the Gallery using our method for the Dorsal Pathway, the HES characteristic curves using DTW. Finally, we apply the integration model to the two matrices to get the result matrix, which contains our final matches. We implement the different Integration variants within a Hypothesis

---

**Algorithm 1** Main steps of the Integration module in gait analysis

---

Objective of the Integration Module: Given a probe clip of people walking and a gallery of people walking, match each person in the probe clip to the people in the gallery.

```
Objective: For each Probe in list of Probes, do Integration
function NMC_IT {{}
for all (Persons in the Probe) do
   for all (Persons in the Gallery) do
      distanceMatrixVentralPathway(i,j) =
      matchVentral(Person_Probe, Person_Gallery)
      distanceMatrixDorsalPathway(i,j) =
      matchDorsal(Person_Probe, Person_Gallery)
   end for
end for
resultMatrix = INTEGRATION(distanceMatrixDorsalPathway, distance-
MatrixVentralPathway)
}
```

The resultMatrix returned from the INTEGRATION function contains the final distance measures between each Person in the Probe versus each Person in the Gallery. The Integration module is implemented using the bootstrap as Total Integration, Partial Integration, and Weighted Integration.

---

Testing framework in which, as seen above, we also use the bootstrap to ensure reasonable limits.

#### 9.3.3.1 Hypothesis Testing

Hypothesis testing can be considered a five-step process, given a set of distance scores of a probe sequence against all elements of the gallery:

(1) Establish a null hypothesis, $H_o$, and an alternative hypothesis, $H_a$. In our case, the null hypothesis would be that a distance measure is not significant while the alternative would be that it is.
(2) Establish a significance level, $\alpha$, which is usually set to 0.05 (Kochanski 2005).
(3) Collect the data, select the test statistic, and determine its value (observed) from the sample data (in our case, this is creating the distance matrix).
(4) Determine the criterion for acceptance/rejection of the null hypothesis by comparing the observed value to the critical value. In our case, this critical value threshold is determined via the appropriate Confidence Interval. The

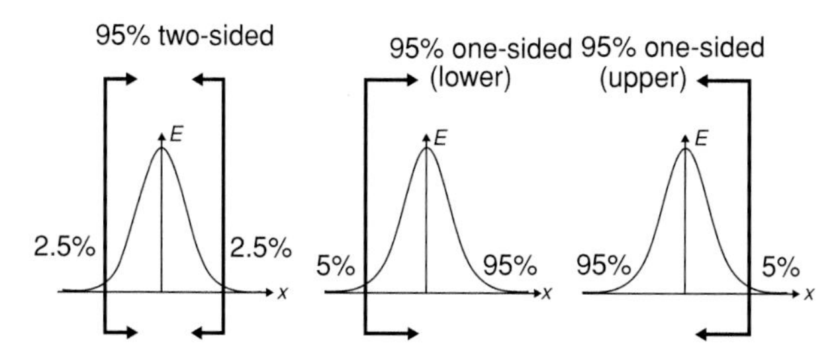


Figure 9.4. Two- and one-sided confidence intervals (CI): the first diagram shows a two-sided CI showing the confidence interval in the middle and the critical regions to the left and right; the second diagram shows a one-sided lower bound with the critical region to the left; the final diagram shows a one-sided upper bound with the critical region to the right; the E just indicates the mean expectation value.

two-sided Confidence Interval will have a lower critical value of the 0.025 quantile and an upper critical value of the 0.975 quantile for $\alpha = 0.05$. In our implementation, we use the bootstrap to find the variance of these quantiles (see below for details of the bootstrap and confidence intervals).

(5) Conclusion: Reject the null hypothesis if the observed value falls within the critical region (i.e., falls outside the Confidence Interval determined by the quantiles). In our case, the null hypothesis would be that all quantiles are equally significant, and the alternative hypothesis would be that at least one quantile is different (i.e., is statistically significant); these significant quantiles would be the ones that fall in the critical region.

#### 9.3.3.2 Bootstrap

Following the work in Efron and Tibshiriani (1993), Zio and Maio (2008), and Zoubir and Boashash (1998), we use the bootstrap to find the variance of the desired quantile threshold used within the various BC models. Bootstrap is a nonparametric method that lets us compute some statistics when distributional assumptions and asymptotic results are not available. In statistics, it is more appealing to compute the two-sided $\alpha$ significance threshold (confidence interval) via bootstrapping because of its accuracy and lack of assumptions.

A confidence interval is a range of values that tries to quantify the uncertainty in the sample. A confidence interval can be two-sided or one-sided, as shown in Figure 9.4; for example, the 95% two-sided confidence interval shows the bounds within which one finds 95% of the population (similarly for the one-sided upper and lower confidence bounds). Confidence intervals are also equivalent to encapsulating the results of many hypothesis tests; if the confidence interval does not include $H_o$, then a hypothesis test will reject $H_o$, and vice versa (Kochanski 2005); in fact, both confidence intervals and hypothesis testing are key elements of inferential statistics. This is important

Table 9.1. *Outline of Bootstrap Quantile Analysis*

**Step 1**: *Experiment*: Get DistanceMatrix
$DM = 2.41, 4.86, 6.06, 9.11, 10.20, 12.81, 13.17, 14.10, 15.77, 15.79$
(these numbers are randomly generated numbers for illustrative purposes only as the actual distance matrices are too big to list in this example).

**Step 2**: *Resample*:
Using a pseudo-random number generator, draw a random sample of *length(DM)* values, with replacement, from DM. Thus, one might obtain the bootstrap resample
$DM' = 9.11, 9.11, 6.06, 13.17, 10.20, 2.41, 4.86, 12.81, 2.41, 4.86$.
Note that some of the original sample values appear more than once, and others not at all.

**Step 3**: *Calculate the bootstrap estimate*: Compute the *bootstrap percentile intervals* $(1 - \alpha)100\%$ for either the upper or the lower quantile for the resample; in this example, we might be computing the upper quantile and get $q_1^u = 13.008$ for the upper quantile of the first bootstrap run (if we were computing the lower quantile, we would get $q_1^l$ for the lower quantile computed for the first bootstrap run).

**Step 4**: *Repetition*: Repeat Steps 2 and 3 $N$ (say, 1000) times to obtain a total of $N$ bootstrap estimates: $q_1^u, q_2^u, \ldots, q_N^u$ and sort in increasing order (if we were computing the lower quantile, we would instead have $q_1^l, q_2^l, \ldots, q_N^l$).

**Step 5**: *Parameter estimation*: The desired quantile threshold is then derived from the bootstrap confidence interval, which is given as a two-sided confidence interval:
$CI = (q_{\text{lower}}^u, q_{\text{upper}}^u)$, where $lower = \lfloor N\alpha/2 \rfloor$ and $upper = N - lower + 1$ (if we were computing the lower quantile, the bootstrap confidence interval would instead be
$CI = (q_{\text{lower}}^l, q_{\text{upper}}^l)$, where $lower = \lfloor N\alpha/2 \rfloor$ and $upper = N - lower + 1$).
Alternatively, some methodologies use the mean of $q_1^u, q_2^u, \ldots, q_n^u$ for the desired quantile threshold of the upper quantile and the mean of $q_1^l, q_2^l, \ldots, q_n^l$ for the desired quantile threshold of the lower quantile.

in our method as we utilize a hypothesis testing framework, within which we use the bootstrap to estimate the confidence intervals.

The bootstrap works by resampling with replacement to find the variance of a statistic on a sample, as shown for our specific case in Table 9.1. We may use this algorithm twice, depending on the BC variant we are computing: once for the upper quantile and once for the lower quantile. One way to estimate confidence intervals from bootstrap samples is to take the $\alpha$ and $1 - \alpha$ quantiles of the estimated values, called bootstrap percentile intervals. For example, for the upper quantile, this confidence interval would then be given as $CI = (q_{\text{lower}}^u, q_{\text{upper}}^u)$, with $lower = \lfloor N\alpha/2 \rfloor$ and $upper = N - lower + 1$, where N

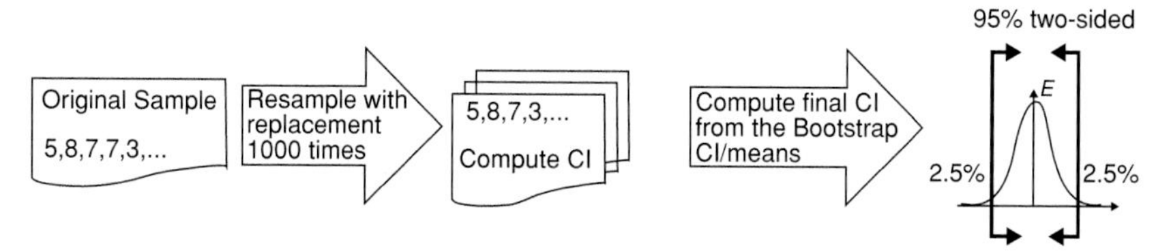


Figure 9.5. Overview of bootstrap. This figure shows how the original sample is resampled (with replacement), say, 1000 times. In each resampling, a confidence interval is computed based on that sample. Eventually, the final confidence interval is estimated from either the bootstrap confidence interval (on the CI computed on each resample) or the means (again, of the CI computed on each resample).

is the number of bootstrap samples and $(q^u_{\text{lower}}, q^u_{\text{upper}})$ are the lower and upper critical values of the bootstrap confidence interval bounds.

So, in our case we use the hypothesis testing framework to establish the critical region quantiles for the confidence interval associated with our significance level, $\alpha$, for each probe in the Distance Matrix. To find the variance of the desired quantiles (both lower and upper), we use the bootstrap method from Example 9.1 and Figure 9.5. We use the same significance level, $\alpha$, as before and derive the bootstrap critical region, $CI = (q^u_{\text{lower}}, q^u_{\text{upper}})$, for the upper quantile and $CI = (q^l_{\text{lower}}, q^l_{\text{upper}})$ for the lower quantile. We also use the alternate method (using just the mean of the quantile threshold) from the bootstrap for comparison.

#### 9.3.3.3 Integration Variants

It is important to note there can be different approaches to integration as this is at the cutting edge of neurobiological research. In this chapter, we develop three different computational models for integration: Total Integration (using a one-sided upper bound CI), Partial Integration (two-sided CI), and Weighted Integration (two-sided CI).

*Total Integration (TI)*: In this case, only the winners survive. First, the observed distance matrix is converted into a similarity matrix; then the bootstrap quantile analysis (shown in Example 9.1) is done on both the Dorsal Pathway measures and the Ventral Pathway measures for the upper quantile only. If the value of either the Ventral or Dorsal Pathway is lower than its upper bootstrap quantile analysis confidence bound, then its value is set to 0; if both are higher than their upper bootstrap quantile analysis, the resultant value is set to the pointwise correlation between the normalized Dorsal and Ventral Pathway measures (only the values that "survive" in both are returned as the final result).

*Partial Integration (PI)*: A two-sided CI is used in which the observed distance measure is lowered to 0 if it is less than the lower distance quantile or changed to the max value if it is greater than the upper distance quantile;

intermediate values are set to the pointwise correlation between the normalized Dorsal and Ventral Pathway measures.

*Weighted Integration (WI)*: The Ventral Pathway values are weighted based on the Dorsal Pathway values; if the observed distance value of the Ventral and the Dorsal Pathway is lower than the lower distance quantile obtained from the bootstrap quantile analysis for both, then the value is set to 0; if either is higher than the upper quantile analysis, it is set to the max value. All other values are set to the unaltered Ventral Pathway value.

## 9.4 Experimental Results

We experimented with videos from the standard USF gait dataset consisting of 67 people walking on different surfaces (grass and concrete) with different shoe types and different camera views. The Gallery contains video of four cycles of walking by all 67 people under standard conditions. There are also videos of different combinations of the 67 people (between 40 and 67) in the seven different probes, labeled Probe A to Probe G. The goal is then to compare the gait of each person in a probe with the gait of all the people in the Gallery to determine which one(s) it matches most closely. This is done for each of the probes in turn.

Tracking and basic object detection was already available (Kale et al. 2004), and we utilized these $(x, y, t)$ tracks to compute the Kinetic (T) and Potential (U) energies of each point on the contour of each person (mass can be idealized to unity or computed from shape, and, when we assume gait is characterized only by the horizontal motion of the body, U is set to zero). The distance and velocity vectors derived from the tracks are thereby used to compute the HES curves, which are then used as the Dorsal Pathway component of the NMC framework.

The HES curve generated for each person is actually a multidimensional vector composed of HES curves for all the points on the contour of that person's silhouette, as shown in Figure 9.6. We then utilized Weighted Integration to bias the Ventral Pathway component with the Dorsal Pathway component and then used the bootstrap to set the threshold for peaks in the distributions that might compete for selection/matching. We biased these peaks by doing pointwise multiplication with the Dorsal Pathway values computed earlier to make our final selections/matches. The results are then plotted as both heatmaps of the distance matrices as well as Cumulative Match Score (CMS) graphs, which plot probability versus rank.

Figure 9.8 shows the similarity matrices and Figure 9.9 the CMS curves generated via the Weighted Integration (WI) methodology. The number of

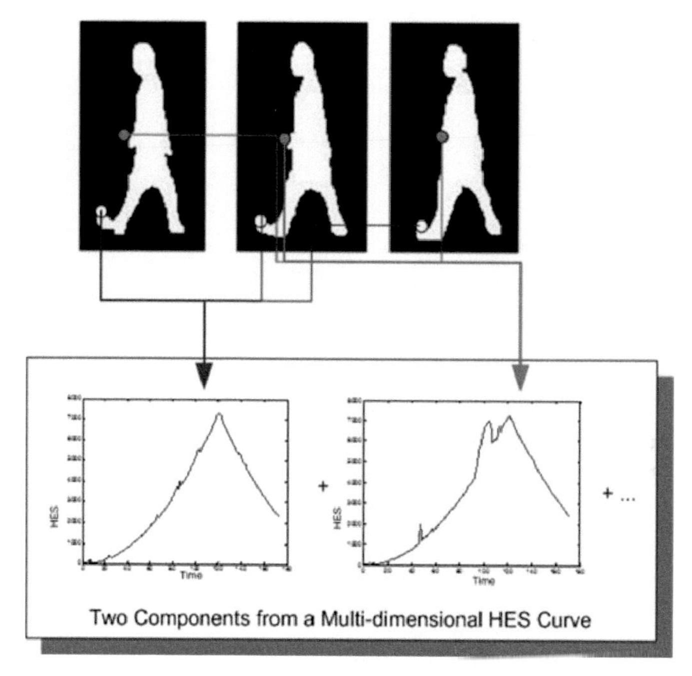


Figure 9.6. Representative samples of the Multidimensional Vector of HES curves for each person's silhouette.

matches reported as similar, as well as the order of these matches, in each row of the Ventral Pathway method determines which method (TI, PI, or WI) does better, as reflected in the CMS curves and similarity matrices, above. For example, the CMS curves for the NMC similarity matrices for Probe A in Figure 9.8 all miss the first couple of matches (e.g., person1 to person1) because the Ventral Pathway method misses them in the first place, as seen in Figure 9.7.

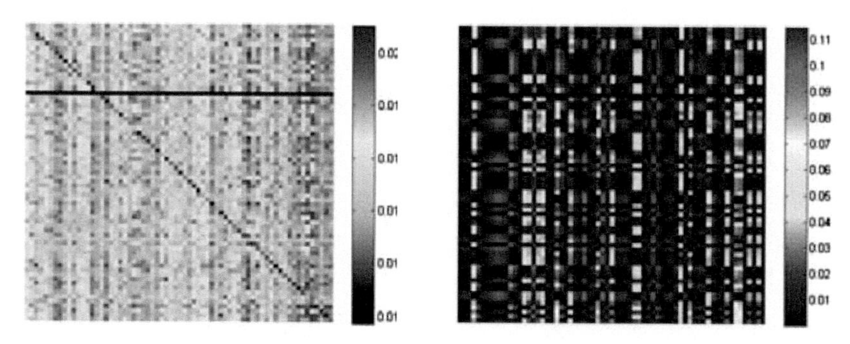


Figure 9.7. Similarity matrices for ventral and dorsal pathway approaches on probe A.

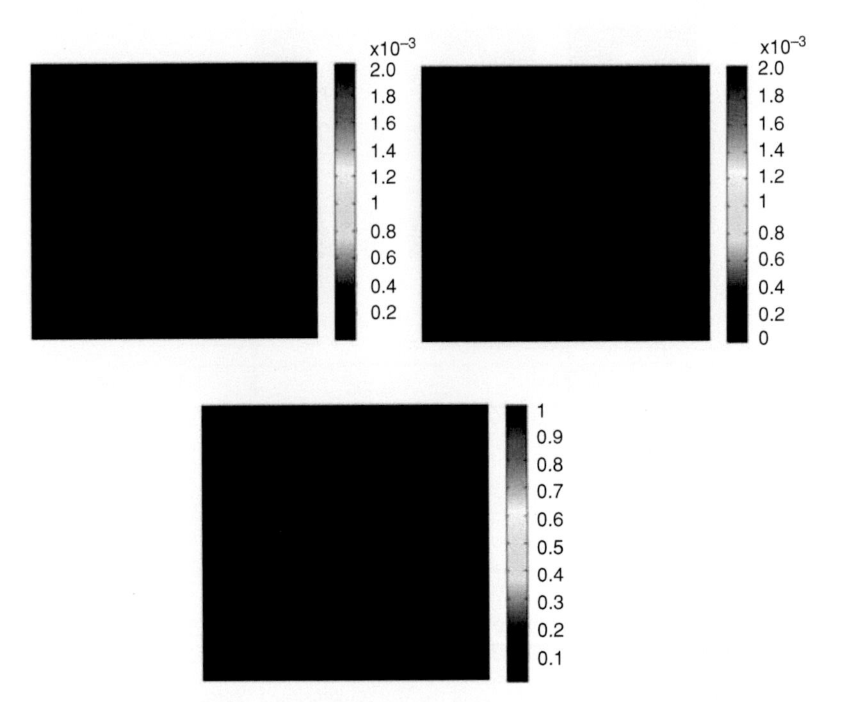


Figure 9.8. Similarity matrices for total integration, partial integration, and weighted integration on probe A.

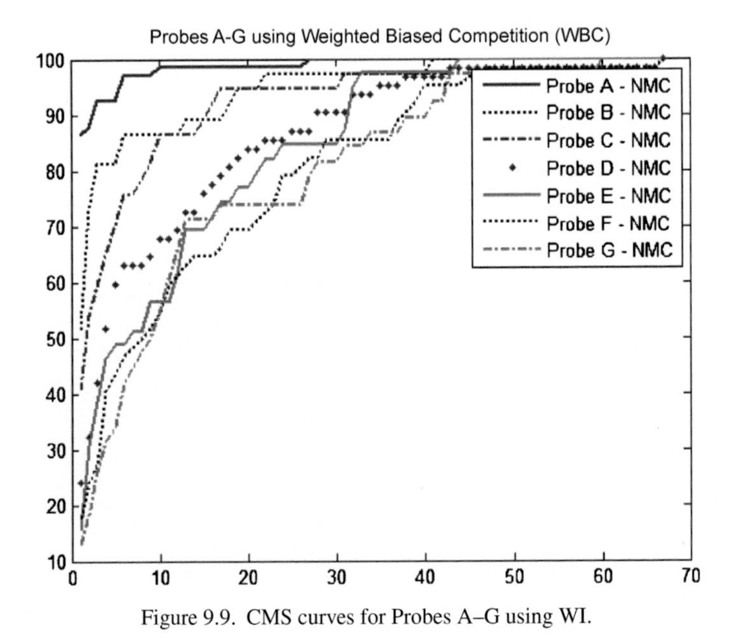


Figure 9.9. CMS curves for Probes A–G using WI.

Table 9.2. *Comparison of Ventral Pathway and NMC Integration Rank 1 and Rank 5 Match Probabilities for Probes A–G*

| | Rank 1 | | Rank 5 | |
|---|---|---|---|---|
| Probe | Ventral | NMC | Ventral | NMC |
| A | 81.8 | 86.4 | 92.4 | 92.4 |
| B | 59.5 | 51.4 | 81.1 | 83.8 |
| C | 40.5 | 40.5 | 70.3 | 70.3 |
| D | 21.0 | 24.2 | 54.8 | 58.1 |
| E | 15.4 | 15.4 | 46.2 | 46.2 |
| F | 16.1 | 17.7 | 41.9 | 43.6 |
| G | 13.2 | 13.2 | 34.2 | 34.2 |

Finally, we see the NMC approach consistently outperforms the Ventral Pathway approach alone, as seen in Table 9.2. The singular exception is Probe B in rank 1; this is because the Weighted Integration favors the Ventral Pathway method more heavily than the Dorsal Pathway method, and, in this case, the Ventral Pathway method misses the real match and actually guesses matches that are far removed from the real match, as seen in the similarity matrix in Figure 9.7. In fact, analyses like this and quantile-quantile plots readily demonstrate the presence of a shift between two distributions for most of the probes and show that the NMC always does at least as well as the Ventral Pathway method for all the probes and, in fact, usually performs better. For example, in Probe A, the Ventral Pathway method ranked 81.8% of the people correctly in rank 1 whereas the NMC approach ranked 86.4% in rank 1; in Probe D, the Ventral Pathway ranked 54.8% in rank 5 while the NMC ranked 58.1% there; in Probe F, the Ventral Pathway got 54.8% in rank 10 whereas NMC ranked 60%. Note that although these results are specific to our Ventral Pathway approach, it is expected that similar improvements would be realized using other approaches for the pathway.

## 9.5 Conclusion

The NMC framework and architecture provides a structured approach to gait analysis within a single, unifying framework that mimics the processing in the dorsal and ventral pathways of the human brain, as understood in the neurobiology community, and is moderately view-invariant. Our formulation takes an altogether novel approach whereby we attempt to create a theoretical framework inspired by the biological model and rooted in pure physics to gain insight into the problem of gait analysis in video. We also developed a new

Dorsal Pathway feature that characterizes walking styles based on their global properties (Hamiltonian Energy Signature [HES]).

## Acknowledgments

This work was partially supported by NSF grant IIS-0712253 and ARO grant W911NF-07-1-0485. We would like to acknowledge Utkarsh Gaur of the UCR Video Computing Group for many interesting discussions and feedback.

## 9.A.1 Appendix

### 9.A.1.1 Hamilton's Variational Principle

Hamilton's Variational Principle states that the integral, $S$, taken along a path of the possible motion of a physical system, is a minimum (technically, an extremum (Landau and Lifshitz 1976)) when evaluated along the actual path of motion. This variation can be expressed as

$$\delta S = \delta \int_{t_1}^{t_2} L(q, \dot{q}, t)dt = 0. \tag{9.8}$$

Here $\delta$ is an operation that represents a variation of any system parameter by an infinitesimal amount away from the value taken by that parameter when (9.3) is an extremum. If we express $L$ in terms of generalized coordinates, $q = q(t)$, then the change in $S$ when $q$ is replaced by $q + \delta q$ is arrived at by requiring that the *first variation* be zero (Landau and Lifshitz 1976) to yield, after integration by parts:

$$\delta S = \left[\frac{\partial L}{\partial \dot{q}} \delta q\right]_{t_1}^{t_2} + \int_{t_1}^{t_2} \left(\frac{\partial L}{\partial q} - \frac{d}{dt}\frac{\partial L}{\partial \dot{q}}\right) \delta q dt = 0. \tag{9.9}$$

This can only be true if the integrand is zero identically, which gives rise to the so-called *Euler-Lagrange* equations of the Lagrangian formalism:

$$\frac{\partial L}{\partial q} - \frac{d}{dt}\frac{\partial L}{\partial \dot{q}} = 0. \tag{9.10}$$

The Hamiltonian formalism is related to the Lagrangian formalism by the *Legendre transformation*, from generalized coordinates and velocities $(q, \dot{q})$ to generalized coordinates and momenta $(q, p)$, using the $\dot{q}_i$. Thus, the *Hamiltonian function* is usually stated most compactly, in generalized coordinates, as Goldstein (1980)

$$H(q, p, t) = \sum_i p_i \dot{q}_i - L(q, \dot{q}, t), \tag{9.11}$$

where $H$ is the Hamiltonian, $p$ is the generalized momentum, and $\dot{q}$ is the time derivative of the generalized coordinates, $q$.

### 9.A.1.2 Deriving the Hamiltonian

The procedure for deriving the Hamiltonian (Goldstein 1980) is to first write out the Lagrangian, $L$, from equation (9.2) in generalized coordinates, expressing $T$ and $U$ in the normal manner for Lagrange's equation. Then the generalized momenta are calculated by differentiating the Lagrangian with respect to the generalized velocity:

$$p_i = \frac{\partial L}{\partial \dot{q}_i}. \tag{9.12}$$

Now we can express the generalized velocities in terms of the momenta by simply inverting the result of (9.12) and using those generalized velocities in (9.11). Finally, we derive *Hamilton's Equations of Motion* from the Hamiltonian equivalent of the Euler-Lagrange equations:

$$\frac{\partial H}{\partial p_i} = \dot{q}_i, \frac{\partial H}{\partial q_i} = F_i - \dot{p}_i, \frac{\partial H}{\partial t} = -\frac{\partial L}{\partial t}, \tag{9.13}$$

where, for a free particle with no external forces, the $F_i$ term goes to zero, leaving:

$$\frac{\partial H}{\partial p_i} = \dot{q}_i, \quad \frac{\partial H}{\partial q_i} = -\dot{p}_i, \quad \frac{\partial H}{\partial t} = -\frac{\partial L}{\partial t}. \tag{9.14}$$

The first two relations give 2n first-order differential equations and are called Hamilton's canonical equations of motion. This effectively results in expressing first-order constraints on a $2n$-dimensional phase space, whereas the Lagrangian method expresses second-order differential constraints on an $n$-dimensional coordinate space.

Furthermore, if the total energy is conserved then the work, $W$, done on the particle had to have been entirely converted to potential energy, $U$. This implies that $U$ is solely a function of the spatial coordinates $(x, y, z)$; equivalently, $U$ can be thought of as purely a function of the generalized configuration coordinates, $q_i$. Rarely, $U$ is also a function of $\dot{q}_i$, making for a velocity-dependent potential, but is still independent of the time $t$. Noether's theorem, in fact, guarantees that any conserved quantity (e.g., energy) corresponds to a symmetry: thus, the system can then be thought of as being independent with respect to some variable or coordinate. In this case, Noether's theorem implies the independence of the Lagrangian with respect to time, as long as energy is conserved in this process.

### 9.A.1.3 Invariance of HES under Affine Transformations

In this section, we show the invariance of the Action which, by Equations (9.8)–(9.11), applies to $H$ and thus, by extension, to HES, as well. We start off by using the invariance properties of the Lagrange equations; in particular, one of the properties of the Lagrange equations is their form invariance under coordinate transformations, especially under translations and rotations. This, in turn, implies the Action is also invariant under a *Euclidean Transform* (translation and rotation). We can also see this invariance from first principles by starting with the three fundamental facts of the physical world:

1. Homogeneity of Time: any instant of time is equivalent to another
2. Homogeneity of Space: any location in space is equivalent to another
3. Isotropy of Space: any direction in space is equivalent to another.

Two consequences follow from these three facts, for which there is no evidence of the contrary:

1. The mechanical properties of a closed system are unchanged by any parallel displacement of the entire system in space.
2. The mechanical properties of a closed system do not vary when it is rotated as a whole in any manner in space.

And so, three properties of the Lagrangian follow:

1. The Lagrangian of a closed system does not depend explicitly on time.
2. The Lagrangian of a closed system remains unchanged under translations.
3. The Lagrangian of a closed system remains unchanged under rotations.

We use these basic principles in the following approach. For Lagrangian Invariance under Special Affine Transformations (translation and rotation), let the solution of the Lagrange Equations in the original coordinate system be

$$x = x(t), v = v(t) \Rightarrow S = \int_{t_1}^{t_2} L(x(t), v(t))dt. \tag{9.15}$$

The solution of the Lagrange equations for a displaced system therefore is

$$\tilde{x} = x_0 + Rx(t), \tilde{v} = Rv(t). \tag{9.16}$$

The Action calculated on the solution of the displaced system is

$$\Rightarrow \tilde{S} = \int_{t_1}^{t_2} L(\tilde{x}, \tilde{v})dt = \int_{t_1}^{t_2} L(x_0 + Rx(t), Rv(t))dt. \tag{9.17}$$

Invariance of the Lagrangian under translation gives

$$\Rightarrow \int_{t_1}^{t_2} L(Rx(t), Rv(t))dt. \tag{9.18}$$

Invariance of the Lagrangian under rotation gives

$$\Rightarrow \int_{t_1}^{t_2} L(x(t), v(t))dt = S. \tag{9.19}$$

Since S is the Action calculated on the solution in the original system of coordinates, this shows the invariance of the Action under rotational and translational transformations:

$$\tilde{S} = S. \tag{9.20}$$

This also applies, by Equations (9.8)–(9.11), to H and hence shows that the HES computed from 3D points is invariant to rigid translational and rotational transformations. The HES computed from image parameters is invariant to 2D translations, rotations, and skew on the image plane as these properties are further proven for the Lagrangian in Section 9.A.1.3.1. We thus show that the 3D Hamiltonian is invariant to rigid 3D transformations, and the Image Hamiltonian is invariant to 2D transformations.

#### 9.A.1.3.1 Affine Invariance of the Lagrangian and the Action

The previous section depends on the rotational and translational invariance of the Lagrangian, and so here we show that the Lagrangian is invariant under an arbitrary affine transform of World Coordinates (e.g., any combination of scaling, rotation, transform, and/or shear). This also applies to the Hamiltonian by the Legendre Transform of (9.11) because, as shown in Section 9.A.1.1, the Legendre Transform is used in classical mechanics to derive the Hamiltonian formulation from the Lagrangian formulation and vice versa. Thus, we have the Lagrangian:

$$L = T - U \tag{9.21}$$

with Kinetic Energy, $T$, and Potential Energy, $U$. The Lagrangian is a function:

$$L = L\left(x_1, x_2, x_3, \dot{x}_1, \dot{x}_2, \dot{x}_3\right), \tag{9.22}$$

where $x_1, x_2, x_3$ are the world coordinates, and $\dot{x}_i = \frac{dx_i}{dt}$ are the time derivatives. We first do an affine transform:

$$y_i = \sum_j C_{ij} x_j + d_i. \tag{9.23}$$

Because this is an affine transform, the determinant of the matrix $C_{ij}$ is nonzero; that is, $|C| \neq 0$. Then, the inverse matrix exists:

$$A = C^{-1}. \tag{9.24}$$

Now we can get the formulae for $x_i$

$$x_i = \sum_j A_{ij} y_j + b_i. \tag{9.25}$$

The new Lagrangian is a complex function:

$$L'(y_1, y_2, y_3, \dot{y}_1, \dot{y}_2, \dot{y}_3) = L(x_1, x_2, x_3, \dot{x}_1, \dot{x}_2, \dot{x}_3), \tag{9.26}$$

where $x_1, x_2, x_3, \dot{x}_1, \dot{x}_2, \dot{x}_3$ are functions of $y_1, y_2, y_3, \dot{y}_1, \dot{y}_2, \dot{y}_3$:

$$x_1 = x_1(y_1, y_2, y_3), \tag{9.27}$$

$$x_2 = x_2(y_1, y_2, y_3), \tag{9.28}$$

$$x_3 = x_3(y_1, y_2, y_3), \tag{9.29}$$

$$\dot{x}_1 = \dot{x}_1(\dot{y}_1, \dot{y}_2, \dot{y}_3), \tag{9.30}$$

$$\dot{x}_2 = \dot{x}_2(\dot{y}_1, \dot{y}_2, \dot{y}_3), \tag{9.31}$$

$$\dot{x}_3 = \dot{x}_3(\dot{y}_1, \dot{y}_2, \dot{y}_3). \tag{9.32}$$

As we can see, the Lagrangian stays invariant: $L = L'$, as it is just a substitution of variables and it does not change the Lagrangian value. Now we prove that Euler-Lagrange equation and Action principle are invariant under an affine transform. In Lagrangian mechanics, the basic principle is not Newton's equation but the Action principle: the Action is a minimal, as per (9.8). The Action principle then leads to the Euler-Lagrange equation:

$$\frac{d}{dt}\frac{\partial L}{\partial \dot{x}_i} = \frac{\partial L}{\partial x_i}, \tag{9.33}$$

where $i = 1, 2, 3$ , $x_1$ $x_2$ $x_3$ are the world coordinates, and $\dot{x}_i = \frac{dx_i}{dt}$ are the time derivatives.

We now show that the Action principle, and then Euler-Lagrange equations, are invariant under an affine transform. We have an affine transform, as in (9.23): $y_i = \sum_j C_{ij} x_j + d_i$. Again, because this is an affine transform, the determinant of the matrix $C_{ij}$ is nonzero $|C| \neq 0$. Then, the inverse matrix exists, once again: $A = C^{-1}$, and we can get the formulae for $x_i$: $x_i = \sum_j A_{ij} y_j + b_i$. The new Lagrangian is again a complex function:

$$L'(y_1, y_2, y_3, \dot{y}_1, \dot{y}_2, \dot{y}_3) = L(x_1, x_2, x_3, \dot{x}_1, \dot{x}_2, \dot{x}_3), \tag{9.34}$$

where $x_1, x_2, x_3, \dot{x}_1, \dot{x}_2, \dot{x}_3$ are functions of $y_1, y_2, y_3, \dot{y}_1, \dot{y}_2, \dot{y}_3$as in (9.27)–(9.32) with time derivatives:

$$\dot{x}_i = \sum_j A_{ij} \dot{y}_j. \tag{9.35}$$

Note that

$$\frac{\partial x_i}{\partial y_j} = A_{ij}, \tag{9.36}$$

$$\frac{\partial \dot{x}_i}{\partial \dot{y}_j} = A_{ij}. \tag{9.37}$$

We now multiply equation (9.33) by $A_{ij}$ and sum over $i$:

$$\sum_i \frac{d}{dt}\frac{\partial L}{\partial \dot{x}_i} A_{ij} = \sum_i \frac{\partial L}{\partial x_i} A_{ij}, \tag{9.38}$$

$$\sum_i \frac{d}{dt}\frac{\partial L}{\partial \dot{x}_i}\frac{\partial \dot{x}_i}{\partial \dot{y}_j} = \sum_i \frac{\partial L}{\partial x_i}\frac{\partial x_i}{\partial y_j}. \tag{9.39}$$

Using the rule of derivatives of complex functions:

$$\sum_i \frac{\partial L}{\partial x_i}\frac{\partial x_i}{\partial y_j} = \frac{\partial L'}{\partial y_j}, \tag{9.40}$$

$$\sum_i \frac{\partial L}{\partial \dot{x}_i}\frac{\partial \dot{x}_i}{\partial \dot{y}_i} = \frac{\partial L'}{\partial \dot{y}_i}. \tag{9.41}$$

Then

$$\frac{d}{dt}\frac{\partial L'}{\partial y_j} = \frac{\partial L'}{\partial \dot{y}_j}, \tag{9.42}$$

which is the same equation as (9.33); hence it is invariant under an affine transform, and thus the Action principle is also invariant under an affine transform. Thus, Lagrangian Invariance implies Action Invariance which implies the invariance of the Euler-Lagrange equations, which, in turn, implies the invariance of the HES.

## References


Beck, D. M., and S. Kastner. 2008. *Top-down and bottom-up mechanisms in biasing competition in the human brain, Vision Research.*

Bissacco, A., A. Chiuso, Y. Ma, and S. Soatto. 2001. *Recognition of human gaits*, 52–57.

Bobick, A. F., and A. Johnson. 2001. *Gait recognition using static activity-specific parameters.*

Bruhn, A., J. Weickert, and C. Schnorr. 2005. *Lucas/Kanade meets Horn/Schunck: combining local and global optic flow methods, IJCV*, pp. 211–231.

Collins, R., R. Gross, and J. Shi. 2002. *Silhoutte based human identification using body shape and gait, Intl. Conf. on AFGR*, 351–356.

Cunado, D., M. J. Nash, S. M. Nixon, and N. J Carter. 1994. *Gait extraction and description by evidence gathering, Intl. Conf. on AVBPA*, 43–48.

Cutting, J. E., and L. T. Kozlowski. 1977. *Recognizing friends by their walk: Gait perception without familiarity cues, Bulletin of the Psychonomic Society* **9(5)**, 353–356.

Cutting, J. E., and D. R. Proffitt. 1981. *Gait perception as an example of how wemay perceive events, Intersensory Perception and Sensory Integration.*

Deco, G., and E. Rolls. 2005. *Neurodynamics of biased competition and cooperation for attention: a model with spiking neurons, J. Neurophysiol.*, 295–313.

Deco, G., and T. S. Lee. 2004. *The role of early visual cortex in visual integration: a neural model of recurrent interaction, European Journal of Neuroscience*, 1–12.

Desimone, R., and J. Duncan. 1995. *Neural mechanisms of selective visual attention, Annu. Rev. Neurosci.* **18**, 193–222.

Dobrski, M. 2007. *Constructing the time independent Hamiltonian from a time dependent one, Central European Journal of Physics* **5**(3), 313–323.

Efron, B., and R. J. Tibshiriani. 1993. *An Introduction to the Bootstrap, Monographs on Statistics and Applied Probability 57*, Chapman & Hall.

Foster, J. P., M. S. Nixon, and A. Prugel-Bennett. 2003. *Automatic gait recognition using area-based metrics., Pattern Recognition Letters* **24**, 2489–2497.

Gavrilla, D. M. 1999. *The visual analysis of human movement: A survey*, no. 1, 82–98.

Giese, M. A. 2000. *Neural model for the recognition of biological motion, in Dynamische Perzeption* **2**.

Giese, M. A., and T. Poggio. 2003. *Neural mechanisms for the recognition of biological movements and action, Nature Reviews Neuroscience* **4**, 179–192.

Giese, M. A. 2004. *Neural model for biological movement recognition, in Optic Flow and Beyond*, pp. 443–470.

Goddard, N. H. 1992. *The perception of articulated motion: recognizing moving light displays*, Ph.D. thesis, University of Rochester.

Goldstein, H. 1980. *Classical Mechanics*, Addison-Wesley.

Han, J., and B. Bhanu. 2003. *Individual recognition using gait energy image, Workshop on MMUA*, 181–188.

Hoenkamp, E. 1978. *Perceptual cues that determine the labelling of human gait, Journal of Human Movement Studies* **4**, 59–69.

Hu, M., S. Ali, and M. Shah. 2008. *Detecting global motion patterns in complex videos, ICPR.*

Hu, W., T. Tan, L. Wang, and S. Maybank. 2004. *A survey on visual surveillance of object motion and behaviors, IEEE Transactions on Systems, Man and Cybernetics* **34**, 334–352.

Itti, L., C. Koch, and E. Niebur. 1998. *A model of saliency-based visual attention for rapid scene analysis, PAMI*, pp. 1254–1259.

Jhuang, H., T. Serre, L. Wolf, and T. Poggio. 2007. *A biologically inspired system for action recognition, ICCV.*

Johansson, G. 1973. *Visual perception of biological motion and a model for its analysis, PandP* **14**(2), 201–211.

Kale, A., A. N. Rajagopalan, A. Sundaresan, N. Cuntoor, A. Roy-Chowdhury, V. Krueger, and R. Chellappa. 2004. *Identification of humans using gait IEEE Trans. on Image Processing* 1 vol. 13, pp. 1163–1173.

Kandel, E., J. Schwartz, and T. Jessell. 2000. *Principles of Neural Science*, 4th ed., McGraw-Hill Medical.

Kastner, S., and L Ungerleider. 2001. *The neural basis of biased competition in human visual cortex, Neuropsychologia*, 1263–1276.

Kochanski, G. 2005. *Confidence intervals and hypothesis testing.*

Landau, L., and E. Lifshitz. 1976. *Course of Theoretical Physics: Mechanics*, 3rd ed., Pergamon Press, Moscow.

LeCun, Y., S. Chopra, M. A. Ranzato, and F. Huang. 2007. *Energy-based models in document recognition and computer vision, ICDAR.*

Lee, L., G. Dalley, and K. Tieu. 2003. *Learning pedestrian models for silhoutte refinement Proc. Int'l Conf. Computer Vision*, pp. 663–670.

Liu, J., S. Ali, and M. Shah. 2008. *Recognizing human actions using multiple features.*

Murray, M., A. Drought, and R. Kory. 1964. *Walking patterns of normal men, Journal of Bone and Joint Surgery* **46-A**(2), 335–360.

Muybridge, E. 1901. *The Human Figure in Motion*, Dover.

Nixon, M., T. Tan, and R. Chellappa. 2005. *Human Identification Based on Gait*, Springer.

Niyogi, S. A., and E. H. Adelson. 1994. *Analyzing and recognizing walking figuresin xyt*, Tech. Report 223, MIT Media Lab Vision and Modeling Group.

Peters, R. J., and L. Itti. 2007. *Beyond bottom-up: in corporating task-dependent influences into a computational model of spatial attention, CVPR.*

Phillips, J., S. Sarkar, I. Robledo, P. Grother, and K. W. Bowyer. 2002. *The gait identification challenge problem: data sets and baseline algorithm. Proceedings International Conference on Pattern Recognition*, vol. 1, pp. 385–388.

Reynolds, J. H., L. Chelazzi, and R. Desimone. 1999. *Competitive mechanisms subserve attention in macaque areas v2 and v4, J. Neurosci.* **19**, 1736–1753.

Riesenhuber, M., and T. Poggio. 1999. *Hierarchical models for object recognition in cortex, Nat. Neuroscience* **2**, 1019–1025.

Sethi, R., A. Roy-Chowdhury, and S. Ali. 2009. *Activity recognition by integrating the physics of motion with a neuromorphic model of perception, WMVC.*

Shankar, R. 1994. *Principles of Quantum Mechanics*, 2nd ed. Springer.

Siagian, C., and L. Itti. 2007. *Biologically-inspired robotics vision Monte-Carlo localization in the outdoor environment.* IROS.

Sigala, R., T. Serre, T. Poggio, and M. Giese. 2005. *Learning features of intermediate complexity for the recognition of biological motion, Artificial Neural Networks: Biological Inspirations*, ICANN. Springer.

Tolliver, D., and R. T. Collins. 2003. *Gait shape estimation for identification, 4th Intl. Conf. on AVBPA.*

Tu, Z., S. Zhu, and H. Shum. 2001. *Image segmentation by data driven Markov chain Monte Carlo, ICCV.*

Turaga, P., R. Chellappa, V. S. Subrahmanian, and O. Udrea. 2008. *Machine recognition of human activities: a survey, IEEE Transactions on Circuits and Systems for Video Technology.*

Treisman, A. M., and G. Gelade. 1980. *A feature-integration theory of attention, Cogn. Psychol.* **12**, 97–136.

Veeraraghavan, A., A. K. Roy-Chowdhury, and R. Chellappa. 2004. *Role of shape and kinematics in human movement analysis, CVPR.*

Veeraraghavan, A., A. K. Roy-Chowdhury, and R. Chellappa. 2005. *Matching shape sequences in video with applications in human motion analysis, PAMI*, 1896–1909.

Wang, L., H. Ning, W. Hu, and T. Tan. 2002. *Gait recognition based on Procrustes shape analysis, Proceedings International Conference on Image Processing*, vol. 3, pp. III-433-III-436.

Yang, L., and M. Jabri. 2003. *Sparse visual models for biologically inspired sensorimotor control, Proceedings Third International Workshop on Epigenetic Robotics*, pp. 131–138.

Yuille, A., and D. Kersten. 2006. *Vision as Bayesian inference: analysis by synthesis, Trends in Cognitive Sciences* **10**(7), 301–308.

Zio, E., and F. Di Maio. 2008. *Bootstrap and order statistics for quantifying thermal-hydraulic code uncertainties in the estimation of safety margins, Science and Technology of Nuclear Installations.*

Zou, X., and B. Bhanu. 2006. *Human activity classification based on gait energy image and coevolutionary genetic programming, ICPR* **3**, 556–559.

Zoubir, A. M., and B. Boashash. 1998. *The bootstrap and its application in signal processing, IEEE Signal Processing Magazine* **15**, 56–76.

# 10

# Face Tracking and Recognition in a Camera Network

Ming Du, Aswin C. Sankaranarayanan, and Rama Chellappa

## 10.1 Introduction

Multicamera networks are becoming increasingly common in surveillance applications given their ability to provide persistent sensing over a large area. Opportunistic sensing and nonintrusive acquisition of biometrics, which are useful in many applications, come into play. However, opportunistic sensing invariably comes with a price, namely, a wide range of potential nuisance factors that alter and degrade the biometric signatures of interest. Typical nuisance factors include pose, illumination, defocus blur, motion blur, occlusion, and weather effects. Having multiple views of a person is critical for mitigating some of these degradations.

In particular, having multiple viewpoints helps build more robust signatures because the system has access to more information. For face recognition, having multiple views increases the chances of the person being in a favorable frontal pose. However, to use the multiview information reliably, we need to estimate the pose of the person's head. This could be done explicitly by computing the actual pose of the person to a reasonable approximation, or implicitly by using a view selection algorithm. Solving for the pose of a person's head presents a difficult problem, especially when images have poor resolution and the calibration of cameras (both external and internal) is not sufficiently precise to allow robust multiview fusion. This holds especially true in surveillance applications when the subjects under surveillance often appear in the far- field of the camera.

Face recognition from a multicamera network is the focus of this chapter. It is worth noting that the problem exceeds just that of face recognition across pose. In our setting, at a given time instant and the localization of the head, we obtain multiple images of the face in different poses. These images could

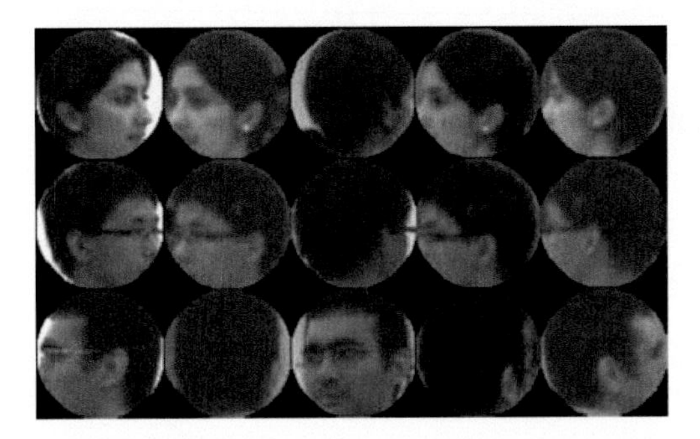

Figure 10.1. Images acquired by a multicamera network. Each column corresponds to a different camera, and each row corresponds to a different time instant and subject. Note that, under unconstrained acquisition, it is entirely possible that none of the images are frontal in spite of using five cameras to observe the subject.

include a mix of frontal, nonfrontal images of the face or, in some cases, a mix of nonfrontal images (see Figure 10.1, where all the images are normalized to the size of $80 \times 80$ pixels). This makes registration of the faces extremely important. If we decide to impose a three-dimensional (3D) model onto the face, then registration is possible. However, even once the face is registered across views using a 3D model, to align it to other models of the face we need to estimate the global pose of the head with respect to a 3D model (essentially, align eyes to eyes, nose to nose, etc.).

We propose rotation-invariant features for multiview-based face tracking and recognition. For a given set of multiview video sequences, we first use a particle filter to track the location of the head using multiview information. At each time instant, we then build the texture map associated with the face under a spherical model. Having multiview information (and the location of the head) allows us to back-project image intensity values onto the surface of the spherical model and construct a texture map for the whole face. We then compute a spherical harmonic (SH) transform of the texture map, and we construct rotation-invariant features based on the properties of the SH projection. Building rotational invariance into our features allows us to bypass the pose estimation step completely. We show that the proposed feature is highly effective for recognition of faces, and that it also exhibits improved class separability in terms of intraclass and between-class variations. The SH features are extracted through video-based head tracking. Recognition can be achieved either by frame-based recognition or by exploiting additional temporal structure in the video.

The chapter is organized as follows. We first discuss related work in Section 10.2. A particle-filtering framework for multicamera tracking of head location is described in Section 10.3. In Section 10.4 we introduce a rotation-invariant feature based on properties of SH transformation and present experiments on recognition in Section 10.5. Finally, we discuss future research extensions in Section 10.6.

## 10.2 Prior Work

In this section we discuss prior art in multiview tracking, multiview recognition, and spherical harmonics separately.

### 10.2.1 Multiview Tracking

Multiview tracking has received considerable attention as a research topic given its applicability to a wide range of scenarios. If the subject undergoes planar motion, then the homography induced by the plane can be used to track the person's feet and/or legs (Sankaranarayanan and Chellappa 2008; Fleuret et al. 2006; Khan and Shah 2006; Fillbrandt and Kraiss 2005; Kim and Davis 2006). However, such algorithms work under the assumption that the leg/head is a point viewable in far-field settings. In a closer setup, it is important to model the face and the texture associated with it. Markerless motion capture techniques (Sundaresan and Chellappa 2008; Gavrilla 1999; Gavrila and Davis 1996) estimate the locations and orientations of all the limbs and joints in the body and, as a consequence, estimate the head's location and potentially its 3D shape. However, motion capture typically has stringent requirements on acquisition setup as well as in subsequent processing to obtain motion parameters. Head pose tracking is also useful in video conferencing (Yang and Zhang 2004; Lepetit and Fua 2005; Aggarwal et al. 2005), smart rooms, and entertainment applications. Most of these approaches estimate the location as well as orientation of the head.

Histogram features are extremely useful for location tracking, as they are inherently robust to changes in the pose of the object and in-plane rotation. The popular mean-shift tracker (Comaniciu et al. 2000; Yilmaz 2007) uses histogram features to track two-dimensional (2D) locations on the image plane. Nummiaro et al. (Nummiaro et al. 2003) describe a particle filtering framework at each view, and they use epipolar geometry for track association across views. Jin et al. (Jin et al. 2006) describe a 3D location tracking system using color histograms and a Kalman filter, followed by a local search algorithm to estimate the location of the head. The algorithm used in this chapter is similar in that we use color histograms as the feature for tracking. However, we use a particle filter to estimate the posterior density of the tracking state vector and a spherical model for the head.

### 10.2.2 Multiview Recognition

Face recognition across pose has been well studied, and we refer the reader to a survey on face recognition (Zhao et al. 2003) for a comprehensive review of pose-invariant recognition of faces. However, a systematic algorithm for handling multiple images of a face under different poses has not been developed to the best of our knowledge. As mentioned earlier, face recognition using multiview images differs from the traditional pose problem where we have only one image of a person in a known/unknown pose.

Xie et al. (2006, 2007) present a method in which they select features (such as eyes and mouth) across views to build a normalized face. Experiments are performed with two cameras, with the person looking frontally or close to frontally at the cameras. However, in a more unconstrained setting with larger baselines between cameras, it is possible that none of the images obtained approaches a frontal pose.

Face recognition from video has received increasing interest in recent years. Decision based on majority voting of recognition results of individual frames has been the natural choice for many systems (Park et al. 2005), (Pnevmatikakis and Polymenakos 2009). More complicated methods for video-based face recognition utilize Sequential Importance Sampling (Zhou et al. 2003), AR process (Aggarwal and Roy 2004), or manifolds (Turaga et al. 2008; Lee et al. 2003). Most of these methods are designed for single-view videos and can handle pose variations only to a limited extent.

### 10.2.3 Spherical Harmonics

Spherical harmonics (Hobson 1931) are orthonomal basis functions defined over the sphere and can be viewed as an extension of the Fourier transform for the spherical functions. In computer vision literature, SH has been extensively used for modeling illumination and its effects on images (Zhang and Samaras 2006), following the work of Basri and Jacobs (Basri and Jacobs 2001). We build texture maps on the spherical head model, and SH develops as a natural choice to describe these texture maps. In particular, the choice of SH (in comparison to other bases) is motivated by the property of SH under rotations (Ivanic and Ruedenberg 1996; Green 2003). This property is similar to the phase-shift property of the Fourier transform, and we will discuss it in detail in Section 10.4. SHs have also been used extensively for matching 3D shapes (Saupe and Vranic 2001; Vranic et al. 2001; Kazhdan et al. 2003), mainly to exploit the rotational invariance that can be obtained by using the property appropriately.

## 10.3 Multiview Tracking of Faces

In this section we describe a multiview tracking algorithm for estimating the location of a head in a video sequence. We use the Sequential Importance Resampling (SIR) particle filtering method for multiview head/face tracking. A detailed introduction to SIR can be found in (Arulampalam et al. 2002). The filtering algorithm can be described in terms of the following aspects: the state space, the state transition model, and the observation model.

### 10.3.1 State Space

To describe a 3D object's pose fully, we usually need a six-dimensional $R^3 \times SO(3)$ representation, where the 3D real vector space represents the object's location, and the special orthogonal group $SO(3)$ represents the object's orientation. This holds especially true when we want to use the object's appearance as a feature in the particle filter framework. However, this leads to the following problems: (1) The feature vector space will be high dimensional; (2) the appearance of object is sensitive to translations, rotations, and nonrigid deformations; and (3) the dimensionality of the state space is also high, in the sense that even a large number of particles will necessarily be sparse in such a space. Considering these issues, we model the human head as a sphere and use histogram-based features for tracking. This rotation-invariant feature allows us to explore a low-dimensional state space $\mathcal{S} = R^3$. In this space, each state vector $\mathbf{s} = [x, y, z]$ represents the 3D position of a sphere's center, disregarding the orientation. The radius of the sphere is a constant obtained through initialization.

For initialization and registration of the head model, we select the head center and one point at the rim of the head in the first frames of all cameras' views. The initial position of the head center and the radius of the sphere can then be estimated through triangulation, given that all the cameras are calibrated. Note that reliable object detectors, such as those trained by the Adaboost algorithm (Viola and Jones 2002), may lead to an automatic initialization.

### 10.3.2 State Transition Model

The state transition model $P(\mathbf{s}_t|\mathbf{s}_{t-1})$ is set as a normal distribution $\mathcal{N}(\mathbf{s}_t|\mathbf{s}_{t-1}, \Sigma)$, where $\Sigma$ is diagonal, and we have found that the tracking result is relatively insensitive to the specific value of $\Sigma$. In this work we fix the standard deviation along each axis at 50 mm.

### 10.3.3 Observation Model

The observations for the filter are the multiview video frames $I_t^j$, where $j$ is the camera index and $t$ is the frame index. This information is redundant for the goal of tracking. As we have already mentioned, adopting histogram features offers advantages in terms of both robustness and efficiency. To this end we need to back-project $I_t^j$ onto the spherical head model and establish the histogram over the texture map. The observation likelihood is modeled as follows:

$$P\left(O_t|\mathbf{s}_\mathbf{t}^{(\mathbf{i})}\right) = P\left(I_t^1, I_t^2, \ldots, I_t^K|\mathbf{s}_\mathbf{t}^{(\mathbf{i})}\right) \propto 1 - D(H(M_{t,i}), H_{\text{template}}), \quad (10.1)$$

where $\mathbf{s}_t^{(i)}$ is the $i$th particle at the $t$th frame; $H(M_{t,i})$ is the histogram of the texture map built from the particle $\mathbf{s}_t^{(i)}$, and $H_{\text{template}}$ is the histogram of template texture map. The template texture map is computed after initializing head position at the first frame, then updated by back-projecting the head region in the image, which is fixed by the maximum a posteriori (MAP) estimate onto the sphere model. The $D(H_1, H_2)$ function calculates the Bhattacharyya distance between two normalized histograms as

$$D(H_1, H_2) = \sqrt{1 - \sum_i \sqrt{H_1^T H_2}}. \quad (10.2)$$

Here the summation is over the bin index $i$ and $D(H_1, H_2) \in [0, 1]$.

We now describe the procedure for obtaining texture map on the surface of the head model. First, we uniformly sample the spherical surface according to the following procedure:

1. Uniformly sample within the range $[-R, R]$, where $R$ is the radius of the sphere, to get $z_n, n = 1, 2, \ldots, N$.
2. Uniformly sample $\alpha_n$ within the range $[0, 2\pi]$, and independent of $z_n$.
3. $x_n = \sqrt{R^2 - z_n^2} \cos \alpha_n$, $y_n = \sqrt{R^2 - z_n^2} \sin \alpha_n$.

Then for the $j$th camera, the world coordinates of sample points $[x_n, y_n, z_n]$, $n = 1, 2, \ldots, N$ are transformed into coordinates in that camera's reference frame $[x_n^{C_j}, y_n^{C_j}, z_n^{C_j}]$ to determine their visibility in that camera's view. Only unoccluded points (i.e., those satisfying $z_n^{C_j} \le z_0^{C_j}$, where $z_0^{C_j}$ is the distance from the head center to the $j$th camera center) will be projected onto the image plane. By relating these model surface points $[x_n, y_n, z_n]$ to the pixels at

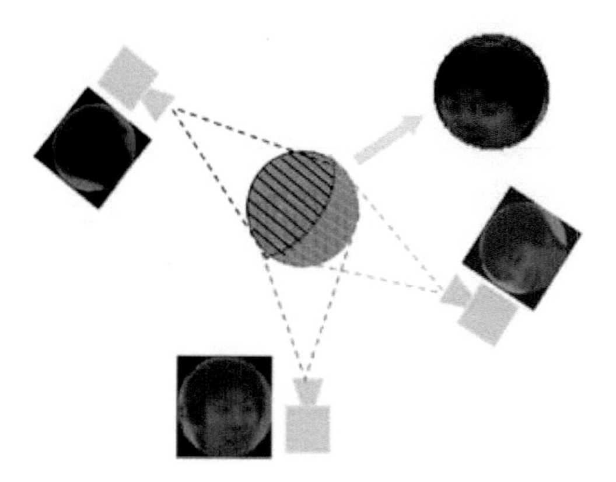

Figure 10.2. Texture map of the head model is built through back-projection of multiple view images. The overlapped region is fused using a weighting strategy.

their projected image coordinates $I(x_n^{P_j}, y_n^{P_j})$, we build the texture map $M^j$ of the visible hemisphere for the $j$th camera view. This continues until we have transformed the texture maps obtained from all camera views to the spherical model. For the points in the overlapped region, we fuse them using a weighting strategy: Thinking of the texture map of the $j$th camera view as a function of locations of surface points, $M^j(x, y, z)$. We assign the function value at point $[x_n, y_n, z_n]$ a weight:

$$W_{n,j} = e^{-\sqrt{\left(x_n^{P_j} - x_0^{P_j}\right)^2 + \left(y_n^{P_j} - y_0^{P_j}\right)^2}/R}, \tag{10.3}$$

where $\left[x_0^{P_j}, y_0^{P_j}\right]$ is the projection of head center on the $j$th image plane, and thus roughly the center of all the projections. In other words, the weight of each point, $W_{n,j}$, is determined by the point's proximity to the projection center. This is based on the fact that, on the rim of a sphere, a large number of surface points tend to project to the same pixel, so image pixels corresponding to those points are not suitable for back-projection. The intensity value at the point $[x_n, y_n, z_n]$ of the resulting texture map will be

$$M(x_n, y_n, z_n) = M^{j_{\max}}(x_n, y_n, z_n), \tag{10.4}$$

where

$$j_{\max} = \arg\max W_{n,j}, \quad j = 1, 2, \ldots, K. \tag{10.5}$$

The texture mapping and back-projection processes are illustrated in Figure 10.2.

Figure 10.3. Tracking example for the Frame 99, 147, 151, 159, 193 of a multiview video sequence. The images in each row are captured by the same camera, while those in the same column are captured at the same time instant.

### 10.3.4 Tracking Results

Figure 10.3 shows an example of a tracking result. We also plot the 3D trajectory of the subject's head for this sequence in Figure 10.4. Every video sequence we captured is 200 frames in length. The tracker is able to locate the subject's head in all of them without failure, despite the frequent occurrences of rotation, translation, and scaling of the human head, and some abrupt motions, as shown in Figure 10.3. The occasionally observed inaccuracies in bounding circles happen mostly because of the difference between sphere and the exact shapes of a human head. As a result of successful tracking, we can attach a smooth texture map to the head model, which guarantees that we always have full observation of the face even when it appears partially and in nonfrontal poses in all cameras' views. This paves the way for accomplishing the subsequent recognition task.

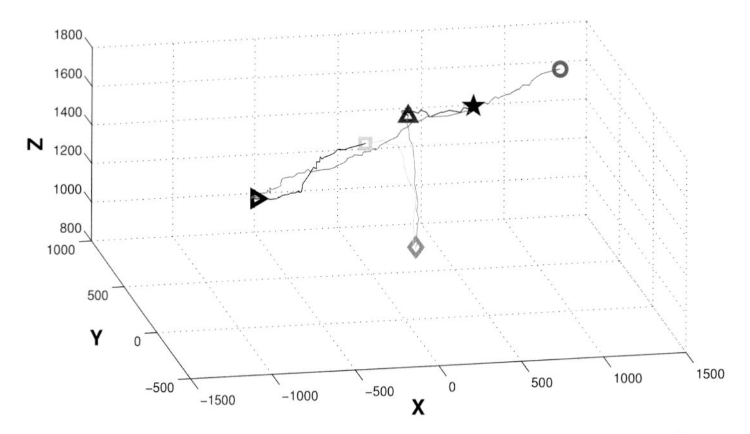


Figure 10.4. The subject's head motion trajectory in the video sequence shown in Figure 10.3. For clarity, we divide the whole trajectory into five segments, which are jointed by abrupt turning points. Those points are marked with different symbols. The trajectory starts from the red circle and ends at the dark green pentagram. The subject's sudden squat can be seen clearly from the trajectory.

## 10.4 Spherical Harmonics and Rotational Invariance

After tracking as described in Section 10.3, we obtain texture maps on the unit sphere's surface. We can regard them as functions on $S^2$. Spherical harmonics (Hobson 1931) are a set of orthonormal basis functions over the sphere. Just like Fourier basis functions in classical signal processing, SHs can be used to linearly expand any square-integrable function $f$ on $S^2$ as

$$f(\theta, \phi) = \sum_{l=0}^{\infty} \sum_{m=-l}^{l} f_{lm} Y_{lm}(\theta, \phi), \tag{10.6}$$

where $Y_{lm}(\cdot, \cdot)$ defines the SH basis function of degree $l \geq 0$ and order $m$ in $(-l, -l+1, \ldots, l-1, l)$, so $2l+1$ basis functions exist for a given order $l$. Note that we use the spherical coordinate system. Here $\theta \in (0, \pi)$ and $\phi \in (0, 2\pi)$ are the zenith and azimuth angles, respectively. Here $f_{lm}$ is the coefficient associated with the basis function $Y_{lm}$ for the function $f$ and can be computed as

$$f_l^m = \int_\theta \int_\phi f(\theta, \phi) Y_l^m(\theta, \phi) d\theta d\phi. \tag{10.7}$$

The basis function has the following form:

$$Y_{lm}(\theta, \phi) = K_{lm} P_l^m(\cos\theta) e^{im\phi}, \tag{10.8}$$

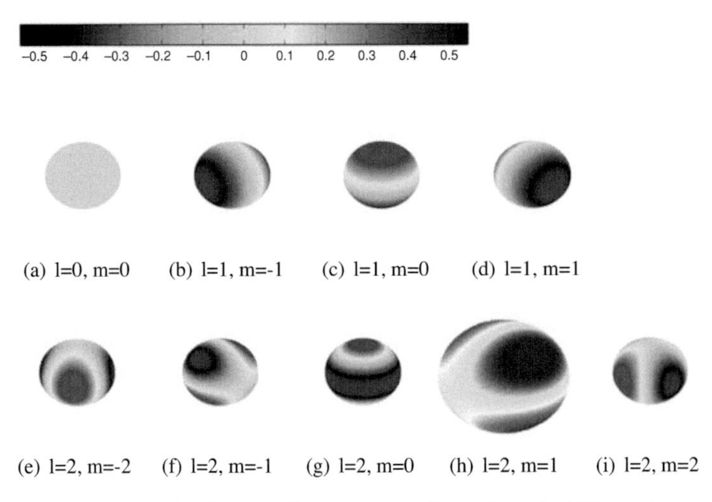


Figure 10.5. Visualization of the first three-degree Spherical Harmonics.

where $K_{lm}$ denotes a normalization constant such that

$$\int_{\theta=0}^{\pi}\int_{\phi=0}^{2\pi} Y_{lm}Y_{lm}^{*}d\phi d\theta = 1. \tag{10.9}$$

Here $P_l^m(x)$ are a set of 1D orthonomal polynomial functions with the name-associated Legendre functions. For details about the associated Legendre functions and the recurrence relations to calculate them, readers can refer to (Green 2003) and (Arfken and Weber 2001).

However, the spherical functions determined by the texture map are real functions, so we are more interested in the Real Spherical Harmonics (or Tesseral Spherical Harmonics):

$$Y_l^m(\theta,\phi) = \begin{cases} Y_{l0} & \text{if } m = 0 \\ \frac{1}{\sqrt{2}}(Y_{lm} + (-1)^m\, Y_{l,-m}) = \sqrt{2}N_{lm}\,P_l^m(\cos\theta)\cos m\phi & \text{if } m > 0, \\ \frac{1}{\sqrt{2}i}(Y_{l,-m} - (-1)^m\, Y_{lm}) = \sqrt{2}N_{lm}\,P_l^{-m}(\cos\theta)\sin m\phi & \text{if } m < 0 \end{cases} \tag{10.10}$$

where the normalization factor $N_{l,m}$ is

$$N_{lm} = \sqrt{\frac{2l+1}{4\pi}\frac{(l-|m|)!}{(l+|m|)!}}. \tag{10.11}$$

The Real SHs are also orthonormal, and they share most of the major properties of the general SHs. Hereafter the word "Spherical Harmonics" shall refer only to the Real Spherical Harmonics. We visualize the SHs for, $l = 0, 1, 2$ in Figure 10.5.

For the subspace $E_l$ spanned by $Y_l^m(\theta, \phi)$, $m = -l \dots l$, (i.e., the SHs of the same degree), we have the following fact (Kazhdan et al. 2003) (Brocker and Dieck 2003):

**Lemma 10.1** *$E_l$ is an irreducible representation for the rotation group SO(3).*

This lemma can be used to prove a crucial property of SH expansion coefficients:

**Proposition 1** *If two functions defined on $S^2$: $f(\theta, \phi)$ and $g(\theta, \phi)$ are related by a rotation $R \in SO(3)$, that is, $g(\theta, \phi) = R(f(\theta, \phi))$, and their SH expansion coefficients are $f_l^m$ and $g_l^m$ ($l = 0, 1, \dots$ and $m = -l, \dots, l$), respectively, the following relationship exists:*

$$g_l^m = \sum_{m'=-l}^{l} D_{mm'}^l f_l^{m'}, \tag{10.12}$$

and the $D_{mm'}^l s$ satisfy

$$\sum_{m'=-l}^{l} \left(D_{mm'}^l\right)^2 = 1. \tag{10.13}$$

In other words, after rotation, the SH expansion coefficients at a certain degree $l$ are actually linear combinations of those before the rotation, and coefficients at different degrees do not affect each other.

The proof is as follows: Let us denote the $l$th-degree frequency component as $f_l(\theta, \phi)$:

$$f_l(\theta, \phi) = \sum_{m=-l}^{l} f_l^m Y_l^m(\theta, \phi), \tag{10.14}$$

then $f_l(\theta, \phi) \in E_l$. According to the lemma:

$$\begin{aligned}
g_l(\theta, \phi) &= R(f_l(\theta, \phi)) = R\left(\sum_{m=-l}^{l} f_l^m Y_l^m(\theta, \phi)\right) \\
&= \sum_{m=-l}^{l} f_l^m R(Y_l^m(\theta, \phi)) \\
&= \sum_{m=-l}^{l} f_l^m \sum_{m'=-l}^{l} D_{mm'}^l Y_l^{m'}(\theta, \phi) \\
&= \sum_{m'=-l}^{l} \sum_{m=-l}^{l} f_l^m D_{mm'}^l Y_l^{m'}(\theta, \phi).
\end{aligned} \tag{10.15}$$

Equation (10.12) follows by comparing (10.15) with

$$g_l(\theta, \phi) = \sum_{m'=-l}^{l} g_l^{m'} Y_l^{m'}(\theta, \phi). \tag{10.16}$$

As for Equation (10.13), notice that $Y_l^m$s and $Y_l^{m'}$ are both orthonormal basis:

$$\begin{aligned} RHS = 1 &= \int_{\theta=0}^{\pi} \int_{\phi=0}^{2\pi} Y_l^m Y_l^m \, d\phi d\theta \\ &= \sum_{m'=-l}^{l} (D_{mm'}^l)^2 \int_{\theta=0}^{\pi} \int_{\phi=0}^{2\pi} Y_l^{m'} Y_l^{m'} \, d\phi d\theta \\ &= \sum_{m'=-l}^{l} (D_{mm'}^l)^2 = LHS. \end{aligned} \tag{10.17}$$

The property can also be represented in a matrix form (Green 2003):

$$\begin{pmatrix} f_0^0 \\ f_1^{-1} \\ f_1^0 \\ f_1^1 \\ f_2^{-2} \\ \vdots \\ \vdots \\ f_2^2 \\ \vdots \end{pmatrix} = \left[\begin{array}{c|ccc|ccccc|c} 1 & 0 & 0 & 0 & 0 & 0 & 0 & 0 & 0 & . \\ \hline 0 & x & x & x & 0 & 0 & 0 & 0 & 0 & . \\ 0 & x & x & x & 0 & 0 & 0 & 0 & 0 & . \\ 0 & x & x & x & 0 & 0 & 0 & 0 & 0 & . \\ \hline 0 & 0 & 0 & 0 & x & x & x & x & x & . \\ 0 & 0 & 0 & 0 & x & x & x & x & x & . \\ 0 & 0 & 0 & 0 & x & x & x & x & x & . \\ 0 & 0 & 0 & 0 & x & x & x & x & x & . \\ 0 & 0 & 0 & 0 & x & x & x & x & x & . \end{array}\right] \begin{pmatrix} g_0^0 \\ g_1^{-1} \\ g_1^0 \\ g_1^1 \\ g_2^{-2} \\ \vdots \\ \vdots \\ g_2^2 \\ \vdots \end{pmatrix}, \tag{10.18}$$

where the $x$ denotes nonzero entries corresponding to appropriate $D_{mm'}^l$ values.

Thus, rotation-invariant matching of two spherical texture maps $f$ and $g = R(f)$ can be done in two ways:

1. Given a texture map $f(\theta, \phi)$ and its corresponding SH coefficient $\{f_l^m, l = 0, 1, 2, \ldots, m = -l, \ldots, l\}$, we can formulate the energy vector associated with $f$ as

$$e_f = (\|f_0\|_2, \|f_1\|_2, \|f_2\|_2, \ldots, \|f_l\|_2, \ldots), \tag{10.19}$$

where

$$\|f_l\|_2 = \sqrt{\sum_{m=-l}^{l} (f_l^m)^2}. \tag{10.20}$$

Figure 10.6. Comparison of the reconstruction qualities of head/face texture map with different number of spherical harmonic coefficients. The images from left to right are: the original 3D head/face texture map, the texture map reconstructed from 40-degree, 30-degree, and 20-degree SH coefficients, respectively.

The property we have presented guarantees this feature is invariant to rotation. We refer to $e_f$ as the SH Energy feature.

2. An alternate procedure involves matching $\{f_l^m\}$ and $\{g_l^m\}$ using the relationship in (10.18). However, matching under such constraints is computationally complex and, in a sense, is equivalent to estimating the pose of the head.

The remaining issue concerns obtaining a suitable band-limited approximation using SHs for our application. As SHs are a complete set of orthonormal basis, once we use all of them (i.e., $l = 0, 1, \ldots, +\infty$), we are guaranteed to reconstruct the original spherical function perfectly. However, this is impractical in real applications. The trade-off between representational accuracy and computational efficiency must be taken into consideration. In Figure 10.6, we show a 3D head texture map and its reconstructed version with 20-, 30-, and 40-degree SH transform, respectively. The ratio of computation time for the three cases is roughly 1:5:21. (The exact time varies with configuration of the computer, for example, on a PC with Xeon 2.13 GHz CPU, it takes roughly 1.2 seconds to do a 20-degree SH transform for 18,050 points.) We have observed that the 30-degree transform achieves the best balance: The 40-degree transform takes a long time to compute, whereas the 20-degree transform produces a blurred reconstruction of the texture map.

## 10.5 Experiments

### 10.5.1 Multiview Face Recognition Using Spherical Harmonics Features

Generally speaking, with multiple cameras in the scene, we are able to locate the human head more accurately, even when some cameras fail to capture it. However, we must then estimate the pose of head correctly to match and recognize the face. Otherwise, even if a 3D model is built and its textures mapped, no common reference frame will exist to compare them.

As introduced in Section 10.4, SH coefficients possess an energy distribution that is invariant to rotation. This implies that although the SH coefficients change with the pose of a subject's head, the energy distribution across degrees of the SHs will remain the same. This also explains why we can disregard the orientation of the head model in Section 10.3 and track it in a 3D state space.

Based on such analysis, we design a multiview face recognition scheme as follows: The system tracks the human head using a spherical models, based on the histogram of the texture map on the model's surface, as described in Section 10.3. The texture map is updated through back-projection according to the tracking output. This texture map is regarded as a discrete function defined on a spherical surface. We apply the SH transform to this function and compute the SH energy feature at each frame. The recognition result is obtained through majority voting.

### 10.5.2 Experiment Settings

The data we used in this work are multiview video sequences captured with five video cameras, collected in two different sessions: one for building a gallery set and the other for constructing a probe set. To test the robustness of our recognition system, we arrange the two sessions to be on two different days, approximately one week apart. The data set comprises 20 subjects, and the gallery video is 200 frames in length. The orientation of the subject's head varies frequently in each gallery video. In each probe sequences, the subjects walk in a straight path, and the length of the each sequence is 100 frames. The data are collected in a indoor environment. Figure 10.7 shows some example frames from gallery and probe video sequences. The appearance of some subjects changes significantly between the two sessions. For example, the first subject in Figure 10.7 wears different head dresses, and the fourth subject cut his hair between the two sessions. This will pose challenges to our face recognition system, as SH coefficients are derived from the texture map of the subject's head model.

### 10.5.3 Comparison of Discrimination Power of Features

To verify the normalized energy feature's discrimination power, we conducted the following experiment. We calculated distances for each unordered pair of feature vectors $\{x_i, x_j\}$ in the gallery. If $\{x_i, x_j\}$ belongs to the the same subject,

Figure 10.7. Example of gallery and probe video frames. Images in the top row are gallery frames, and those in the bottom row are probe frames. Some subjects appear quite different in gallery and probe videos.

then the distance is categorized as being *in-class*. If $\{x_i, x_j\}$ originates from two different classes, then the distance is categorized as being *between-class*. We approximate the distribution of the two kinds of distances as:

$$P(o_i) = \frac{\sum_{n=1}^{N} k(d_n - o_i)}{N}, \tag{10.21}$$

where

$$k(u) = \begin{cases} 1, & \text{if } |u| < u_d, \\ 0, & \text{otherwise.} \end{cases} \tag{10.22}$$

In the above equations, $o_i$ is the fixed $i$th bin center at which the distribution is evaluated, $d_n$ is the $n$th distance, and $u_d$ is a fixed half-bin width.

Intuitively, if a feature has good discrimination power, then the in-class distances evaluated using that feature tend to take smaller values, as opposed to the between-class distances. If the two distributions mix, then it will be difficult to use this feature for classification. Quantitatively, we use the KL divergence to evaluate the difference between the two distributions:

$$KL(p\|q) = \sum_{i=1}^{N} p(x_i) \log \frac{p(x_i)}{q(x_i)}, \tag{10.23}$$

where $x_i$ are evaluation points. The KL divergence is not a distance metric because of its asymmetry; instead, we calculate $KL(p\|q) + KL(q\|p)$. Thus a large KL divergence indicates a significant discrepancy between the two distributions. We summarize the KL divergences in Table 10.1 and plot the

Table 10.1. *KL Divergence of in-Class and Between-Class Distances for Different Features*

| Intensity | Intensity+PCA | SH | SH+PCA | SH Energy | Normalized SH Energy |
|---|---|---|---|---|---|
| 0.1454 | 0.1619 | 0.2532 | 0.2843 | 0.1731 | 1.1408 |

distributions in each case in Figure 10.8. In all cases, we calculate the two kinds of distances with Euclidean metric. As clearly shown in Figure 10.8, in-class distances for the normalized SH energy feature are concentrated in the low-value bins, whereas the between-class ones tend to have higher values, and

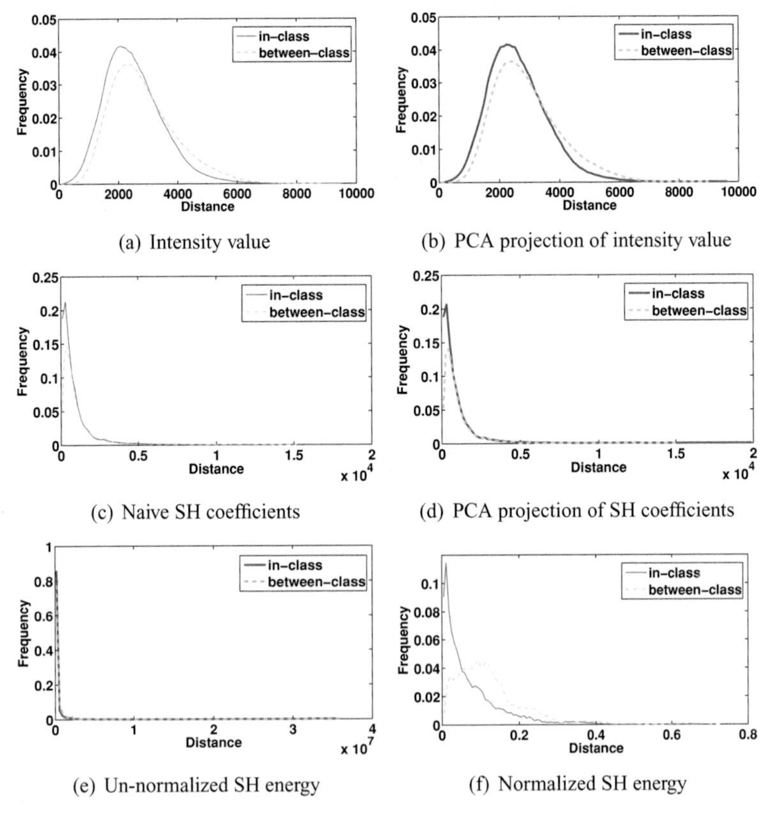


(a) Intensity value
(b) PCA projection of intensity value
(c) Naive SH coefficients
(d) PCA projection of SH coefficients
(e) Un-normalized SH energy
(f) Normalized SH energy

Figure 10.8. Comparison of the discriminant power of different features. The green curve is between-class distance distribution, and the red is in-class distance distribution. The number of bins is 100.

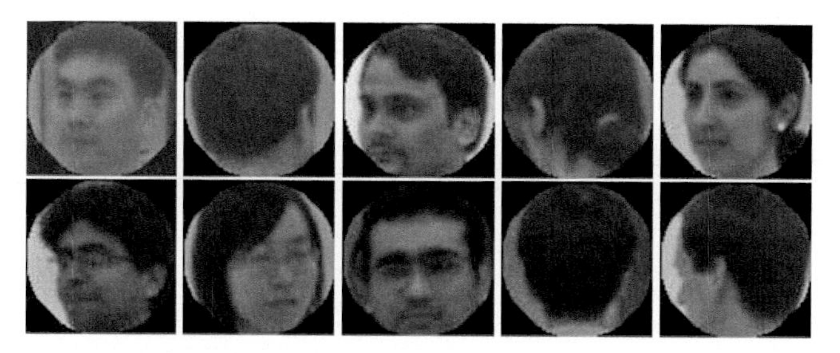

Figure 10.9. Examples of training images of an intensity-value–based recognition system in our experiments.

their modes are obviously separated from each other. For all other features, the between-class distances do not show a clear trend of being larger than the in-class ones, and their distributions are mixed. The symmetric KL-divergence suggests that, in the normalized SH energy feature case, the two distributions' difference exceeds that of other cases by a large margin.

### 10.5.4 Comparison of Recognition Performance

We compare the performance of a number of different human face recognition algorithms. The inputs to all these face recognition systems are the same tracking results obtained with the tracking procedure described in Section 10.3. For a fair comparison, we also make the gallery (in these experiments we do not differ between gallery and training) set size and the probe set the same for all systems. Every fourth frame in the tracked gallery videos is used. For any system based on raw image intensity value, we use only the head region that is cropped by a circular mask generated by the tracking result. All the head images are scaled to the same size. Examples of masked head images appear in Figure 10.9.

A typical recognition algorithm has feature extraction and classification stages. In the face recognition field, frequently used feature extraction and selection methods include Principal Component Analysis (PCA) (Sirovich and Kirby 1987) (Turk and Pentland 1991), Linear Discriminant Analysis (LDA) (Etemad and Chellappa 1997) (Belhumeur et al. 1996), and Locality Preserved Projection (LPP) (He et al. 2003). The most popular classifiers for face recognition are based on Nearest Neighbor (NN) (Turk and Pentland 1991) (Etemad and Chellappa 1997) (Belhumeur et al. 1996) (He et al. 2003), Support Vector Machine (SVM) (Heisele et al. 2001) (Guo et al. 2000), and Kernel Density Estimation (KDE) (Ahonen and Pietikainen 2009). We investigate the performance of five features and five classifiers. Each tested system is a combination of them. The five features the following:

1. Intensity+PCA. We use all gallery frames to train a PCA subspace (Sirovich and Kirby 1987). Eigenvectors that preserve the top 95% energy are kept. The projection of image on this subspace is used as a feature.
2. Intensity+LDA. We project the images onto a subspace trained using Linear Discriminant Analysis (Etemad and Chellappa 1997) (Belhumeur et al. 1996). The gallery images are preprocessed using PCA to avoid the rank deficiency in the within-class separation matrix.
3. SH+PCA. We first construct a texture map on the spherical head model for every multiview frame group (each consists of the five frames captured at the same time). Then for every texture map, we perform a 30-degree SH transform to extract 961 coefficients. The dimensionality is further reduced by the PCA, and the reduced feature vector is used as signature.
4. SH Energy. We calculate the energy of SH coefficients at each degree according to (10.19), Section 10.4, but the result is not normalized with regard to the total energy. The feature vector's length is 31.
5. Normalized SH Energy. Again, the SH energy is computed, but now it is normalized with respect to the total energy.

The classifiers are the following:

1. NN. The Nearest Neighbor classifier. We tried both L-1 and L-2 distances for each system. In most trials, the L-2 distance yields a better result. The results shown use the L-2 norm except for the Intensity+PCA case and the SH+PCA case, since their results with L-1 norm are better than with L-2 norm.
2. NV. The Nearest View classifier. Frames of five views captured at the same time (they certainly belong to the same subject) are grouped and treated as a whole. We find the nearest neighbor for each of the five members of the group. Among these nearest neighbors for the five members, we further choose the one with the shortest distance as the Nearest View and use its label to classify all the members.
3. KDE. The Kernel Density Estimation classifier using Gaussian kernel.
4. SVM-Linear. The multiclass Support Vector Machine classifier (one-against-one) with linear kernel. The kernel is defined as an inner-product between two input vectors. The parameters are selected using a four fold cross-validation process.
5. SVM-RBF. The multiclass Support Vector Machine classifier (one-against-one) with RBF kernel. The parameters are also selected through cross-validation. RBF kernel is defined by the following equation:

$$K(u, v) = e^{-\gamma \|u-v\|^2}. \tag{10.24}$$

Table 10.2. *Comparison of Recognition Performance*

| Feature | NN (%) | NV (%) | KDE (%) | SVM-Linear (%) | SVM-RBF (%) |
|---|---|---|---|---|---|
| Intensity PCA | 45 | **55** | 45 | 45 | 55 |
| Intensity LDA | 40 | 35 | 20 | 35 | 35 |
| SH PCA | 35 | N/A | 20 | 15 | 40 |
| SH energy | 50 | N/A | 45 | 50 | 60 |
| Normalized SH energy | **65** | N/A | **70** | **75** | **85** |

After classifying of individual frames of the probe video, recognition for the entire video sequence is done based on majority voting:

$$ID_k = \underset{i}{\operatorname{argmax}}\, N_{i,k}, \tag{10.25}$$

where $N_{i,k}$ is the number of frames of probe video $k$ that are classified as the $i$th person in gallery. The rank-1 recognition results appear in Table 10.2. For each classifier, we highlight the recognition rate of the best features in bold. In fact, we have conducted more experiments with different settings, but we present only representative results. For example, for intensity-based recognition methods, we also tried to normalize all the intensity values for each image to compensate for illumination variations but observed no improvement. We also experimented with a $k$-NN classifier where $k > 1$, but it performed less well.

### 10.5.5 Analysis of Results

The linear subspace methods can be regarded as baseline algorithms. As we can see from Table 10.2, the correct classification rate of intensity-value–based methods does not exceed the limit of 55%. We would like to highlight the difference between the nature of single-view approach and the special structure of multiview image data: Most of the time, a camera is always pointing at the back of subject's head. We can expect that view's image to be misclassified almost always, because the backs of human heads look similar, and the between-class variation is smaller than the in-class variation. Figure 10.10 shows the mean face and the first five eigenfaces obtained. In comparison to the single-view face recognition case, we cannot separate the facial features from these images. Moreover, many eigenfaces simply represent the back of head. When we classify a probe, its match to a gallery image is dominated by pose similarity instead of facial feature similarity. This is the consequence of

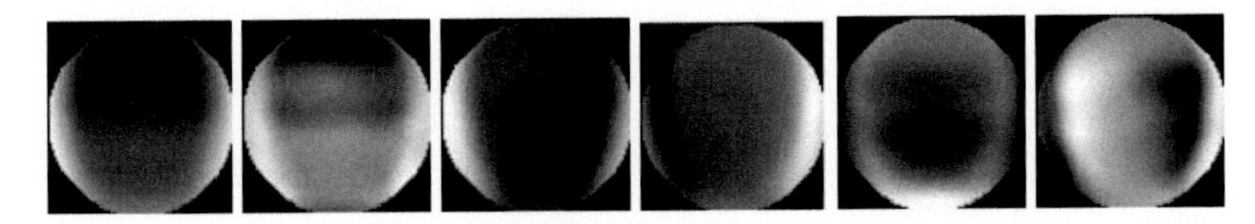

Figure 10.10. Mean face and the first five eigenfaces in the Intensity+PCA case.

applying a single-view based face recognition algorithm directly to the multiview scenario without having pose information. The NV classifier aims to alleviate this problem, in the hope that the best match to a nonback view of the subject can be found in the gallery and that the distance between them will be smaller than the distance between the backs of heads of different subjects. As we can see, this strategy does increase the rank-1 recognition rate from 45% to 55% in the PCA case and is even equivalent to the performance of the SVM classifier. In the LDA case, however, we obtain an opposite result. The problem may be solved only through the use of a multiview approach, which systematically accounts for information from multiple cameras. This also explains why the SH energy feature based on head texture map proves effective in the multicamera scenario. As shown in Table 10.2, the normalized SH energy feature, performs the best among the features; even the simple Nearest Neighbor classifier achieves a 65% recognition rate, which is already higher than that of any other features. When using the SVM-RBF classifier, the performance further improves to 85%. We also observed that the unnormalized energy feature brings only limited improvement to traditional intensity-value based feature in the SVM case. This suggests that a normalization step is always desired when using the SH energy feature. Moreover, the low recognition rate achieved in the SH+PCA case indicates that the SH coefficient by itself is not an effective recognition feature. As previously mentioned, we do not adopt the head model's texture- map as a feature because it requires either alignment between two unregistered spherical surfaces in the recognition stage or a higher dimension of state vector space and observation vector space in the tracking algorithm.

## 10.6 Conclusions and Future Work

In this chapter we proposed a face tracking and recognition algorithm for a camera network. It achieves robust multiview head tracking, then takes advantage of the rotational invariance property of the SHs for pose-invariant face recognition. Experiments show that it has improved performance when compared to traditional methods.

In the future, we would like to extend our work along the following lines:

- In the current system, the recognition result of a video is based on majority voting. Modeling the temporal structure of videos will provide dynamic information that is often helpful to recognition (Zhou et al. 2003).
- There is also more information in the SH feature than has been exploited in this chapter. For example, by calculating the transformation matrix of two SH coefficient vectors, we can obtain estimates of poses.
- Finally, SHs have been applied to illumination-invariant face recognition problem for years (Basri and Jacobs 2001) (Zhang and Samaras 2006). We would like to place its traditional application with our work in a unified face recognition system that can achieve invariance to both pose and illumination variations.

## References

Aggarwal, G., and A. K. Roy. 2004. A system identification approach for video-based face recognition, *Proceedings of International Conference on Pattern Recognition*, Cambridge, UK, pp. 175–178, August.

Aggarwal, G., A. Veeraraghavan, and R. Chellappa. 2005. 3D facial pose tracking in uncalibrated videos, *Lecture Notes in Computer Science*, **3776**, 515–520.

Ahonen, T., and M. Pietikainen. 2009. Pixelwise local binary pattern models of faces using kernel density estimation, *Lecture Notes in Computer Science*, **5558**, 52–61.

Arfken, G., and H. Weber. 2001. *Mathematical Methods for Physicists*. Academic Press.

Arulampalam, S., S. Maskell, N. Gordon, and T. Clapp. 2002. A tutorial on particle filters for on-line non-linear/non-Gaussian Bayesian tracking, *IEEE Transactions on Signal Processing*, **50**, 174–188.

Basri, R., and D. Jacobs. 2001. Lambertian reflectance and linear subspaces, *Proceedings of IEEE International Conference on Computer Vision*, Vancouver, British Columbia, Canada, **2**, 383–390, July.

Belhumeur, P., J. Hespanha, and D. Kriegman. 1996. Eigenfaces vs. Fisherfaces: recognition using class specific linear projection, *Proceedings of European Conference on Computer Vision*, Cambridge, UK, pp. 45–58, April.

Brocker, T., and T. Dieck. 2003. *Representations of Compact Lie Groups*, pp. 87–90, Springer.

Comaniciu, D., V. Ramesh, and P. Meer. 2000. Real-time tracking of non-rigid objects using mean shift, *Proceedings of IEEE Conference on Computer Vision and Pattern Recognition*, Hilton Head, South Carolina, pp. 142–149, June.

Etemad, K., and R. Chellappa. 1997. Discriminant analysis for recognition of human face images, *Journal of the Optical Society of America*, **14**, 1724–1733.

Fillbrandt, H., and K. H. Kraiss. 2005. Tracking people on the ground plane of a cluttered scene with a single camera, *WSEAS Transactions on Information Science and Applications*, **2**, 1302–1311, September.

Fleuret, F., J. Berclaz, and R. Lengagne. 2006. Multi-camera people tracking with a probabilistic occupancy map, Technical Report EPFL/CVLAB2006.07.

Gavrilla, D. 1999. The visual analysis of human movement: a survey, *Computer Vision and Image Understanding*, **73**, 82–98.

Gavrila, D., and L. Davis. 1996. 3D model-based tracking of humans in action: a multi-view approach, *Proceedings of IEEE Conference on Computer Vision and Pattern Recognition*, San Francisco, California, pp. 73–80, June.

Green, R. 2003. Spherical harmonic lighting: the gritty details, *Archives of the Game Developers Conference*, San Jose, California, March.

Guo, G., S. Z. Li, and K. Chan. 2000. Face recognition by support vector machines, *Proceedings of IEEE International Conference on Automatic Face and Gesture Recognition*, Grenoble, France, pp. 196–201, March.

He, X., S. Yan, Y. Hu, and H. J. Zhang. 2003. Learning a locality preserving subspace for visual recognition, *Proceedings of IEEE International Conference on Computer Vision*, Nice, France, **2**, 385–392.

Heisele, B., P. Ho, and T. Poggio. 2001. Face recognition with support vector machines: global versus component-based approach, *Proceedings of IEEE International Conference on Computer Vision*, Vancouver, British Columbia, Canada, **2**, 688–694, July.

Hobson, E. W. *The theory of Spherical and Ellipsoidal Harmonics*, Cambridge University Press.

Ivanic, J., and K. Ruedenberg. 1996. Rotation matrices for real spherical harmonics: direct determination by recursion, *Journal of Physical Chemistry*, **100**, 6342–6347.

Jin, H., G. Qian, and S. Rajko. 2006. Real-time multi-view 3D object tracking in cluttered scenes, *Lecture Notes in Computer Science*, **4292**, 647–656.

Kazhdan, M., T. Funkhouser, and S. Rusinkiewicz. 2003. Rotation invariant spherical harmonic representation of 3D shape descriptors, *Proceedings of Eurographics/ACM SIGGRAPH symposium on Geometry processing*, Aachen, Germany, pp. 156–164, June.

Khan, S. M., and M. Shah, 2006 A multi-view approach to tracking people in crowded scenes using a planar homography constraint, *Proceedings of European Conference on Computer Vision*, Graz, Austria, **4**, 133–146, May.

Kim, K., and L. Davis. 2006. Multi-camera tracking and segmentation of occluded people on ground plane using search-guided particle filtering, *Proceedings of European Conference on Computer Vision*, Graz, Austria, **3**, 98–109, May.

Lee, K. C., J. Ho, M. H. Yang, and D. Kriegman. 2008. Video-based face recognition using probabilistic appearance manifolds, *Proceedings of IEEE Conference on Computer Vision and Pattern Recognition*, Madison, Wisconsin, **1**, 313–320, June.

Lepetit, V., and P. Fua. 2005. Monocular model-based 3D tracking of rigid objects: a survey, *Foundations and Trends in Computer Graphics and Vision*, **1**, 1–89.

Nummiaro, K., E. K. Meier, T. Svoboda, D. Roth, and L. V. Gool. 2003. Color-based object tracking in multi-camera environments, *Lecture Notes in Computer Science*, **2781**, 591–599.

Park, U., H. Chen, and A. K. Jain. 2005. 3D model-assisted face recognition in video, *Proceedings of 2nd Workshop on Face Processing in Video*, Victoria, British Columbia, Canada, pp. 322–329, May.

Pnevmatikakis, A., and L. Polymenakos. 2009. Subclass linear discriminant analysis for video-based face recognition, *Journal of Visual Communication and Image Representation*, **20**, 543–551.

Sankaranarayanan, A. C., and R. Chellappa. 2008. Optimal multi-view fusion of object locations, *Proceedings of IEEE Workshop on Motion and Video Computing*, Copper Moutain, Colorado, pp. 1–8, January.

Saupe, D., and D. V. Vranic. 2001. 3D model retrieval with spherical harmonics and moments, *Lecture Notes in Computer Science*, **2191**, 392–397.

Sirovich, L., and M. Kirby. 1987. A low-dimensional procedure for the characterization of human faces, *Journal of the Optical Society of America A*, **4**, 519–524.

Sundaresan, A., and R. Chellappa. 2008. Model driven segmentation and registration of articulating humans in Laplacian eigenspace, *IEEE Transactions on Pattern Analysis and Machine Intelligence*, **30**, 1771–1785.

Turaga, P., A. Veeraraghavan, and R. Chellappa. 2008. Statistical analysis on Stiefel and Grassmann manifolds with applications in computer vision, *Proceedings of IEEE Conference on Computer Vision and Pattern Recognition*, Anchorage, Alaska, pp. 1–8, June.

Turk, M., and A. Pentland. 1991. Eigenfaces for recognition, *Journal of Cognitive Neuroscience*, **3**, 71–86.

Viola, P., and M. Jones. 2002. Robust real-time object detection, *International Journal of Computer Vision*, **57**, 137–154.

Vranic, D. V., D. Saupe, and J. Richter. 2001. Tools for 3D-object retrieval: Karhunen-Loeve transform and spherical harmonics, *Proceedings of IEEE Workshop on Multimedia Signal Processing*, Cannes, France, pp. 293–298, October.

Xie, B., T. Boult, V. Ramesh, and Y. Zhu. 2006. Multi-camera face recognition by reliability-based selection, *Proceedings of IEEE International Conference on Computational Intelligence for Homeland Security and Personal Safety*, Venice, Italy, pp. 18–23, October.

Xie, B., V. Ramesh, Y. Zhu, and T. Boult. 2007. On channel reliability measure training for multi-camera face recognition, In *Proceedings of IEEE Workshop on the Application of Computer Vision*, Austin, TX, pp. 41–41, February.

Yang, R., and Z. Zhang. 2004. "Eye gaze correction with stereovision for video-teleconferencing," *IEEE Transactions on Pattern Analysis and Machine Intelligence*, **26**, 956–960.

Yilmaz, A. 2007. Object tracking by asymmetric kernel mean shift with automatic scale and orientation selection, *Proceedings of IEEE Conference on Computer Vision and Pattern Recognition*, Minneapolis, Minnesota, pp. 1–6, June.

Zhang L., and D. Samaras. 2006. Face recognition from a single training image under arbitrary unknown lighting using spherical harmonics, *IEEE Transactions on Pattern Analysis and Machine Intelligence*, **28**, 351–363.

Zhao, W., R. Chellappa, P. J. Phillips, and A. Rosenfeld. 2003. Face recognition: a literature survey, *ACM Computing Surveys*, **35**, 399–458.

Zhou S., V. Krueger, and R. Chellappa. 2003. Probabilistic recognition of human faces from video, *Computer Vision and Image Understanding*, **91**, 214–245.

# 11

# Bidirectional Relighting for 3D-Aided 2D Face Recognition

G. Toderici, G. Passalis, T. Theoharis, and I. A. Kakadiaris

## 11.1 Introduction

Face recognition is one of the most widely researched topics in computer vision because of a wide variety of applications that require identity management. Most existing face recognition studies are focused on two-dimensional (2D) images with nearly frontal-view faces and constrained illumination. However, 2D facial images are strongly affected by varying illumination conditions and changes in pose. Thus, although existing methods are able to provide satisfactory performance under constrained conditions, they are challenged by unconstrained pose and illumination conditions.

FRVT 2006 explored the feasibility of using three-dimensional (3D) data for both enrollment and authentication (Phillips et al. 2007). The algorithms using 3D data have demonstrated their ability to provide good recognition rates. For practical purposes, however, it is unlikely that large scale deployments of 3D systems will take place in the near future because of the high cost of the hardware. Nevertheless, it is not unreasonable to assume that an institution may want to invest in a limited number of 3D scanners, if having 3D data for enrollment can yield higher accuracy for 2D face authentication/identification.

In this respect we have developed a face recognition method that makes use of 3D face data for enrollment while requiring only 2D data for authentication. During enrollment, different from the existing methods (e.g., Blanz and Vetter 2003) that use a 2D image to infer a 3D model in the *gallery*, we use 2D+3D data (2D texture plus 3D shape) to build subject-specific annotated 3D models. To achieve this, we first fit an Annotated Face Model (AFM) to the raw 2D+3D data using a subdivision-based deformable framework (Kakadiaris et al. 2007). A geometry image representation is extracted using the UV parameterization of the model. In the authentication phase, we use a single 2D image as the input to map the subject-specific 3D AFM. Given the pose in the 2D image, an Analytical Skin Reflectance Model (ASRM) is then applied to the *gallery* AFM to transfer the lighting from the probe to the texture in the gallery. The matching score is computed using the relit *gallery* texture and the probe texture.

Our contributions are the following: (1) using 2D+3D data to build the subject-specific 3D model during enrollment, which is able to more accurately characterize the subject identity than the existing 2D/3D methods that use a 2D image to infer the 3D gallery model; (2) a bidirectional face *relighting* algorithm that allows us to achieve better face recognition performance than the traditional *unlighting* methods; (3) a new view-dependent distance metric; and (4) a newly collected 3D database with probe images under large variations of pose and illumination. To the best of our knowledge, the existing publicly available 3D face databases, including the FRGC v.2, do not include probe images under both lighting variation and pose variation. Our 3D database is available through the website http://www.cbl.uh.edu/URxD/.

This chapter is organized as follows: In Section 11.2 we briefly review related methods. In Section 11.3 we present the methods for enrollment using 3D+2D data and for authentication using 2D images, and in Section 11.4 we provide qualitative and quantitative results.

## 11.2 Related Work

The literature on 3D and 2D+3D face recognition has rapidly increased in recent years. An excellent survey is given by Bowyer et al. (2006). The most closely related work is by Riccio and Dugelay (2007), who proposed using geometric invariants on the face to establish a correspondence between the 3D *gallery* face and the 2D *probe*. Some of the invariants are manually selected. This algorithm does not use the texture information registered with the 3D data from the scanner and thus does not take full advantage of the input data. Blanz and Vetter (2003) employed a morphable model technique to acquire the geometry and texture of faces from 2D images. Zhang and Samaras (2006) use a spherical harmonic representation (Basri and Jacobs 2003) with the morphable model for 2D face recognition. In contrast with our method that uses 2D+3D data to build 3D subject-specific model for the gallery, their methods used a 2D image to build a 3D model for the gallery based on a 3D statistical morphable model. Yin and Yourst (2003) used frontal and profile 2D images to construct 3D shape models. Compared with these methods, our approach is able to more accurately model the subject identity because of the use of more information (2D+3D). Smith and Hancock (2005) presented an approach for albedo estimation from 2D images also based on a 3D morphable model. The normals of the fitted model are then used for the computation of shading, assuming a Lambertian reflectance model. Biswas et al. (2007) proposed a method for albedo estimation for face recognition using two-dimensional images. However, their approach makes the assumption that the image does not contain shadows, and the method does not handle specular light. The relighting approach of Lee et al. (2005) also suffers from the self-shadowing problem.

The proposed method, having significantly fewer constraints and limitations than previous approaches, widens the applicability of such methods. Especially when compared with relighting methods designed for face recognition (e.g., Tsalakanidou et al. 2007), the proposed method offers significantly higher visual quality in cases where specular highlights oversaturate the images.

## 11.3 Methods

### 11.3.1 2D+3D Enrollment

We employ the Annotated Face Model (AFM) proposed by Kakadiaris et al. (2007) to generate geometry images (regularly sampled 2D images that have three channels) encoding geometric information ($x$, $y$, and $z$ components of a vertex in $R^3$). In this paper the number of channels in the geometry image is seven (three channels for representing the actual geometry of the face, three for representing the texture information, and one for the visibility map). In all experiments we used a resolution of 256 × 256 for the AFM.

Specifically, we first fit the AFM to the input 3D data (Kakadiaris et al. 2007). Once the fitting is complete, we represent the AFM as a geometry image. For each vertex in the geometry image, we compute the closest point

---

**Algorithm 1** Enrollment with 3D data

**Input:** 3D facial mesh, 2D facial image, subject ID. linenosize=, linenodelimiter=.

1: Pre-process the 3D facial mesh.
2: Register AFM to the 3D facial mesh.
3: Fit AFM to 3D facial mesh.
4: Lift texture from the 2D facial image based on the fitted AFM.
5: Compute visibility map.
6: Store the fitted AFM, texture and visibility map in the enrollment database as metadata for subject ID.

---

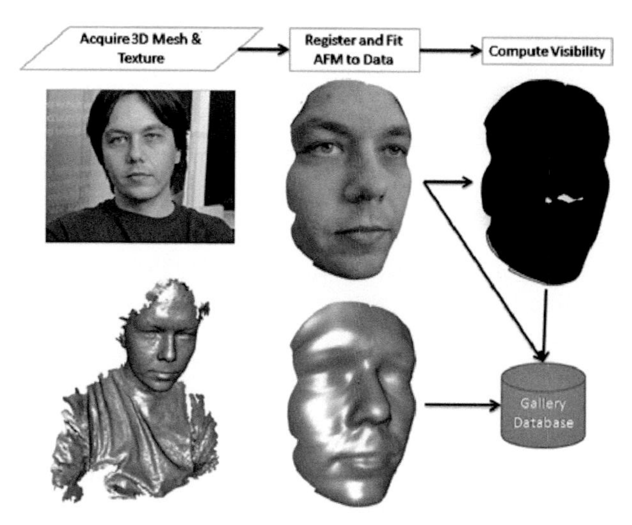


Figure 11.1. Depiction of the enrollment procedure for our 3D-aided 2D face recognition system. The first column depicts the input data, and the second column depicts the fitted AFM with texture on the top and without texture on the bottom.

on the data. The texel corresponding to this point in the data is used to create the corresponding texture image for the fitted AFM. Additionally, we compute a visibility map (Algorithm 1). If the closest point on the data does not have a valid texel assigned (i.e., if the 3D point was not visible to the 2D image sensor), we assign the value 1 to the corresponding location in the visibility map. Otherwise, we assign a value of 0. The enrollment pipeline is depicted in Figure 11.1.

### 11.3.2 2D Authentication

In the authentication stage (Algorithm 2, the input to our method is a 2D image. Seven fiducial landmarks (two eye inner corners, two eye outer corners, nose tip, and two nose corners) are manually labeled. Numerous approaches exist that allow automatic localization of landmarks (Gu and Kanade 2008; Saragih et al. 2009; Liang et al. 2008). Then the pose is estimated based on these landmarks and their corresponding locations on the AFM. Once the pose is known, the texture is mapped onto the AFM (Figure 11.2). We use an analytical skin reflectance model to bidirectionally relight the *gallery* texture using the stored AFM mesh, to match the illumination of the *probe* texture (Figure 11.3).

#### 11.3.2.1 Analytical Skin Reflectance Model

We use a hybrid bidirectional reflectance distribution function (BRDF) to model skin reflectance. We did not use a bidirectional surface scattering

**Algorithm 2** Authentication with 2D data

**Input:** 2D facial image and claimed subject ID. linenosize=, linenodelimiter=.

1: Retrieve from the enrollment database the AFM that corresponds to the claimed ID.
2: Determine a set of seven landmarks on the 2D facial image.
3: Register the AFM to the 2D facial image using the corresponding landmarks (Figure 11.2).
4: Compute the visibility map.
5: Bidirectionally relight the enrollment 2D facial texture to match the probe 2D facial texture.
6: Compute the CW-SSIM (Section 11.3.2.3) score between the relit texture and the probe texture using the visibility information from both to discard invisible areas from the comparison.
7: Threshold the score to make an ACCEPT/REJECT decision.

reflection distribution function (BSSRDF) model because the test data that we used do not have sufficient resolution to estimate a subsurface scattering component. The ASRM uses the Lambetian BRDF to model the diffuse component and the Phong BRDF to model the specular component. The Lambertian BRDF (Lambert 1760) is the simplest and most widely used physics-based model for diffuse reflectance. The model assumes that the surface is equally bright from all directions. The intensity of the light at a surface point, $I_d$, is

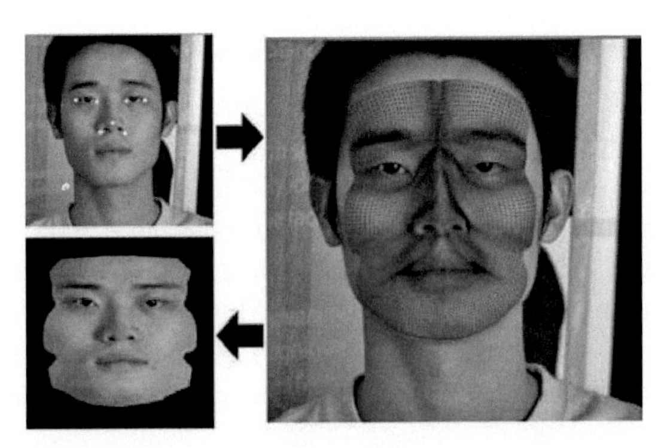

Figure 11.2. Converting raw 2D images to textures in geometry image space: Starting from a raw 2D image, the fitted AFM of the same subject is registered and superimposed over the image, which allows us to lift the texture to the geometry image space.

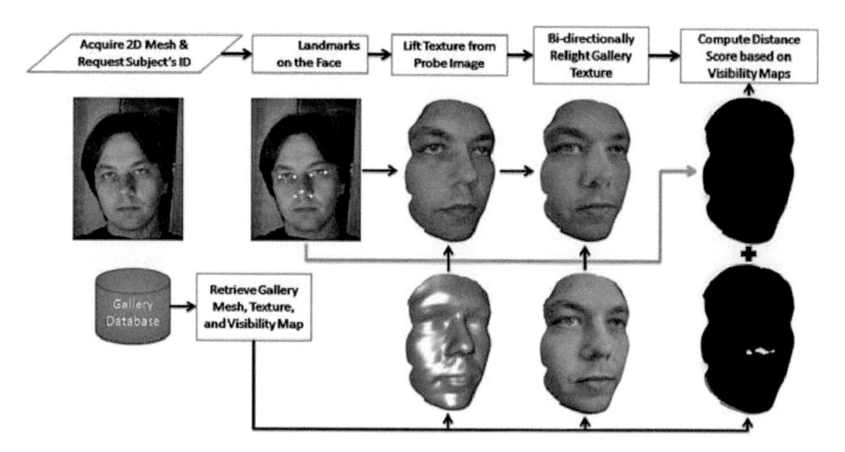


Figure 11.3. The authentication phase of the 3D-aided 2D face recognition system.

proportional to the angle between surface normal and incident light directions (denoted as $\theta$): $I_d = E \cos\theta$, where $E$ is the intensity of the light source. The Lambertian BRDF does not take into account the specular reflections caused by the oily layer of the skin. To accommodate this we use the BRDF proposed by Phong (1975). The intensity of the specular reflection at a surface point is $I_s = E \cos^n \phi$, where $\phi$ is the angle between the view vector and the reflected light and $n$ is a parameter that controls the size of the highlight. Note that each facial area has different specular properties, and thus we use a specular map based on the annotation of the AFM (for details see Kakadiaris et al. 2007).

#### 11.3.2.2 Bidirectional Relighting

The illumination parameters and the ASRM can be optimized in two different ways: estimate the albedo (unlighting; see our past study (Toderici et al. 2007)) and transfer illumination (relighting). In both cases the texture must be represented in the AFM's UV space.

Generally, the texture $M_T$ is the result of the lighting applied on the unknown albedo $M_A$ and is given by

$$M_T = I_s + (I_d + I_a) \cdot M_A, \tag{11.1}$$

where $I_a$ is the ambient component, $I_d$ the diffuse component, and $I_s$ the specular component (assuming white specular highlights). By solving this equation for the albedo, we obtain

$$M_A = \frac{M_T - I_s}{I_d + I_a}. \tag{11.2}$$

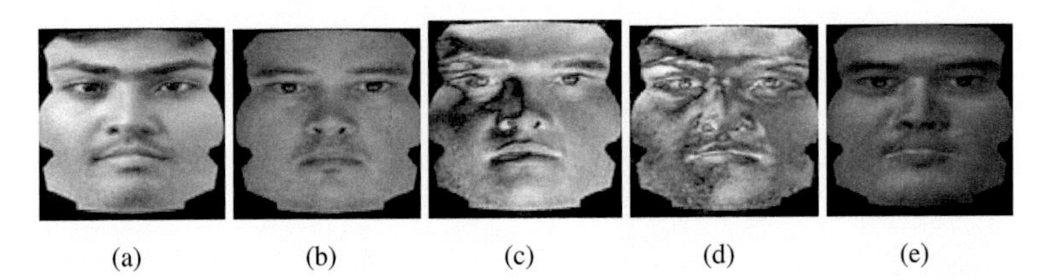

(a) (b) (c) (d) (e)

Figure 11.4. Optimization for relighting (textures are in geometry image space): (a) $M'_T$: texture of subject A; (b) $M_T$: texture of subject B; (c) texture difference between subjects (before optimization); (d) $D$: texture difference between subjects (after optimization); (e) subject B with subject's A illumination $(I'_s + (I'_d + I'_a)\frac{M_T - I_s}{I_d + I_a})$.

For many practical applications, the albedo itself is not required and is used only as an intermediate step for relighting. We advocate the use of bidirectional relighting without first estimating the albedo. This means that the optimization directly estimates the parameters for two lights (one that *removes* the illumination from the *gallery* image and one that *adds* the illumination from the *probe* image). The goal is to match the illumination conditions of a *gallery* texture to that of a *probe* texture. The following metric is minimized:

$$D = \left| M'_T - I'_s - (I'_d + I'_a)\frac{M_T - I_s}{I_d + I_a} \right|, \tag{11.3}$$

where $I_a$, $I_d$, and $I_s$ are the parameters of the light illuminating the *gallery*, $I'_a$, $I'_d$, and $I'_s$ are the parameters of the second light illuminating the *probe*, and $M'_T$ is the target texture. This process is depicted in Figure 11.4. The relighting method is bidirectional, meaning that *probe* and *gallery* textures can be interchanged.

To improve performance under low lighting conditions, instead of computing the difference in the RGB color space, we chose to use a Hue-Saturation-Intensity (HSI) model with the intensity weighed at twice the amount of hue and saturation. We observed both visually and quantitatively improved relighting performance when using this color space and weighting scheme instead of simply computing an $L_2$ norm in RGB color space.

The above equations describe an ASRM for a single point light and the objective function to be minimized. The ASRM is implemented as a Cg shader, and for self-shadowing the shadow mapping technique (Everitt et al. 2001) is used. To model multiple point lights, the contribution of each light's ASRM must be summed. The full implementation runs on consumer-level graphics hardware and is able to bidirectionally relight a texture to a target within, on average, five seconds.

#### 11.3.2.3 Distance Metric

For face recognition, a distance metric between 2D images is needed. We introduce a simple distance metric to evaluate the benefits of using unlit or relit images versus raw images in a face recognition scenario. We first apply a wavelet transform to the texture channel from the geometry images. This transform decomposes the images using the complex version (Portilla and simoncelli 2000) of the steerable pyramid transform (Simoncelli et al. 1992) (CWSPT), a linear multiscale, multi-orientation image decomposition algorithm.

The image is first divided into highpass and lowpass subbands. The lowpass subband is fed into a set of steerable bandpass filters that produce a set of oriented subbands and a lower-pass subband. This lower-pass subband is subsampled by 2 and recursively applied to the same set of steerable bandpass filters. Such a pyramid wavelet representation is translation-invariant and rotation-invariant.

To maintain reasonable image resolution and computational complexity, our algorithm applies a three-scale, 10-orientation complex steerable pyramid transform to decompose each component of the image. Only the oriented subbands at the farthest scale are stored, allowing us to compare the subband coefficients of the two images directly, without the overhead of reconstruction. These coefficients are compared using the Complex Wavelet Structural Similarity (CW-SSIM) index algorithm (Wang et al. 2004). It is a translational, insensitive image similarity measure inspired by the SSIM index algorithm.

CW-SSIM iteratively measures the similarity indices between the two sliding windows placed in the same positions of the two images and uses the weighted sum as a final similarity score. This score is measured by a variation of the CW-SSIM index equation originally proposed by Wang and Simoncelli (2005).

To be able to handle variations in pose we compute the normal map of the AFM when registered to the 2D input. The normal map is used to determine which pixels are not visible to the camera. The hidden pixels are used to create a thresholding map in the UV space of the AFM. We compute the CWSPT of the resulting image, which allows us to determine the contribution of each hidden pixel in the final score of the CW-SSIM. Because the CW-SSIM is computed using a sliding window, we use only those pixels for which the magnitude of the thresholded CWSPT map is below the upper bound $\tau = 0.5$, which was experimentally determined.

A window of size $3 \times 3$ traverses the image one step at a time. At each step, we extract all wavelet coefficients, resulting in two sets of coefficients $p_w = \{p_{w,i} | i = 1, \ldots, N\}$ and $g_w = \{g_{w,i} | i = 1, \ldots, N\}$, drawn from the *probe* image and the *gallery* image, respectively. For the same window, the coefficients from the visibility map are $m_w = \{m_{w,i} | i = 1, \ldots, N\}$. The distance metric can be written as follows:

$$\tilde{S}(p_w, g_w) = 1 - \left( \frac{2 \sum_{i=1}^{N} |p_{w,i}||g_{w,i}| + K}{\sum_{i=1}^{N} |p_{w,i}|^2 + \sum_{i=1}^{N} |g_{w,i}|^2 + K} \right) \tag{11.4}$$

$$\cdot \left( \frac{2 | \sum_{i=1}^{N} p_{w,i} g_{w,i}^{*} | + K}{2 \sum_{i=1}^{N} |p_{w,i} g_{w,i}^{*}| + K} \right)^{r} \cdot Q, \tag{11.5}$$

where $w$ is the current step of the window, $N$ is the number of coefficients in the window, and $r$ is an experimentally determined exponent. The parameter $K$ is a small positive value that is used to make the result numerically stable. The complex conjugate of $g_{w,i}$ is denoted as $g_{w,i}^{*}$, and $|m_w|$ is the cardinality of the set $m_w$. The variable Q is defined as $\frac{|\{m_{w,i} | m_{w,i} > \tau\}|}{|m_w|}$. The first component (of the subtracted term) measures the equivalence of the two coefficient sets, while the second reflects the consistency of phase changes. If $p_{w,i} = g_{w,i}$ for all $i$, the distance is 0. The weighted sum of the local scores from all windows provides the distance score: $Score(P, G) = \sum_{w} (b_w \cdot \tilde{S}(p_w, g_w))$ where $b_w$ is a predefined weight depending on which subband the local window lies on. In computing the set of weights $b_w$ we took into account the annotated regions of the AFM, assigning large weights to the rigid regions (upper portion of the face), and very small weights to the flexible regions of the face (mouth region).

## 11.4 Results

### 11.4.1 Bidirectional Relighting

We provide two examples, one demonstrating bidirectional relighting, and the second demonstrating the relighting of a *gallery* (2D facial images) to multiple *probe* textures. In all cases, textures from the same subject are used.

Figures 11.5(a), and 11.5(b) depict two textures of the same subject. Note that only 11.5(a) has a corresponding 3D mesh, whereas 11.5(b) is a simple 2D image and uses the mesh of 11.5(a). We performed bidirectional relighting to transfer the illumination conditions from one to the other. The result is two synthetic textures depicted in Figs. 11.5(c), and 11.5(d). The difference of the synthetic textures from the respective target textures is depicted in Figs. 11.5(e), and 11.5(f). After a visual inspection, no significant visible artifacts were introduced by the relighting process.

Figure 11.6 depicts a multiple relighting example. Again, only the source texture (top row) has a corresponding 3D mesh; the remaining textures are using

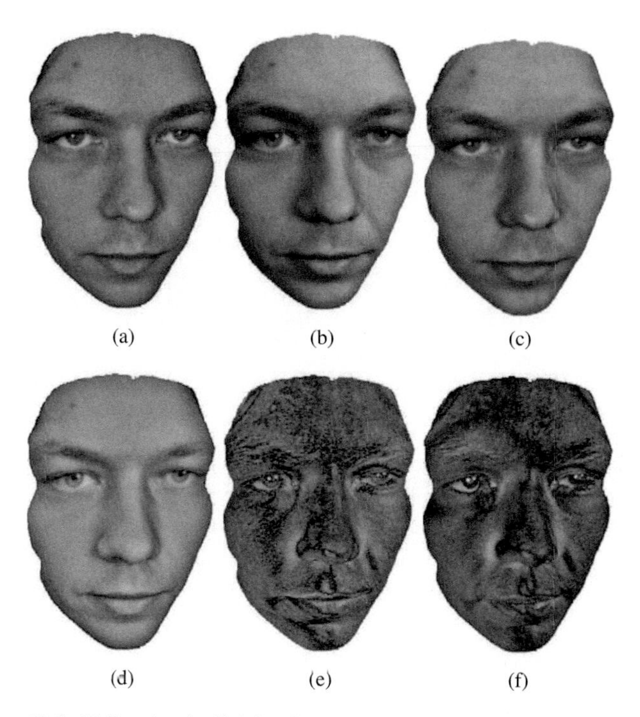


Figure 11.5. Bidirectional relighting for a specific subject: (a) real texture 1 (RT1); (b) real texture 2 (RT2); (c) synthetic texture 1 (ST1): RT1 with RT2's illumination; (d) synthetic texture 2 (ST2): RT2 with RT1's illumination; (e) RT1 minus ST2; (f) RT2 minus ST1.

the source's 3D mesh. Four textures with different illumination conditions are depicted (Figure 11.6 [bottom row]) as target textures. The proposed method estimates the four synthetic relighted images depicted in Figure 11.6 (middle row). These results show that the proposed method is robust under varying lighting conditions, since in all cases the relighting was qualitatively successful.

### 11.4.2 Face Recognition

In this scenario, 2D+3D data are acquired during enrollment and 2D data during authentication (one-to-one matching). This is a reasonable installation where only a few enrollment stations are needed (which may be expensive), along with many authentication stations (which must be inexpensive). To make the problem more challenging, we use a database with varying lighting conditions to evaluate the robustness of the proposed method. We show that in an authentication experiment, a face recognition algorithm benefits more from using relit images than unlit images.

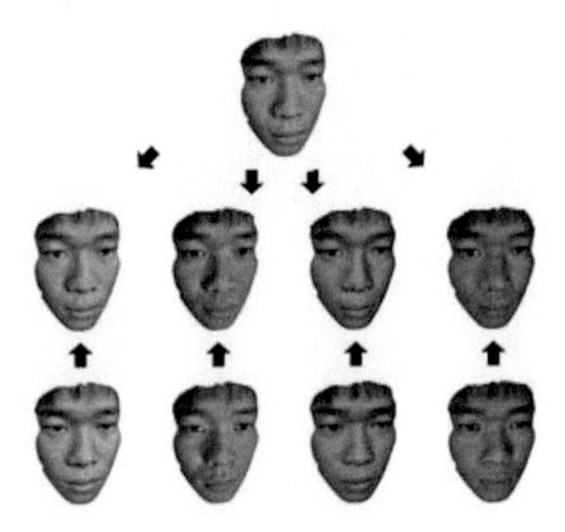

Figure 11.6. Multiple relighting. Top row: source texture. Middle row: synthetic relighted texture. Bottom row: target texture.

#### 11.4.2.1 Databases

***Database A:*** We have constructed a database with varying lighting conditions that includes both 3D and 2D data. The 3D data were captured by a 3dMD two-pod optical scanner, and the 2D data were captured by a commercial Canon DSLR camera. The system has six diffuse lights that allow the variation of the lighting conditions. For each subject there is a single 3D scan (and the associated 2D texture) that is used as a *gallery* dataset, and several 2D images that are used as *probe* datasets. All 2D images have one of the six possible lighting conditions depicted in Figure 11.7. There are 26 subjects, resulting in 26 *gallery* datasets (3D plus 2D) and 800 *probe* datasets (2D only). For *gallery* datasets we used the images with the "best" illumination.

***Database B:*** To analyze the impact of variation in both pose and lighting, we acquired data from 23 subjects under six illumination conditions. For each illumination condition, we asked the subject to face four different points inside the room. This generated rotations on the $y$ axis. For each rotation on $y$, we also acquired three images with rotations on the $z$ axis (assuming that the $z$ axis goes

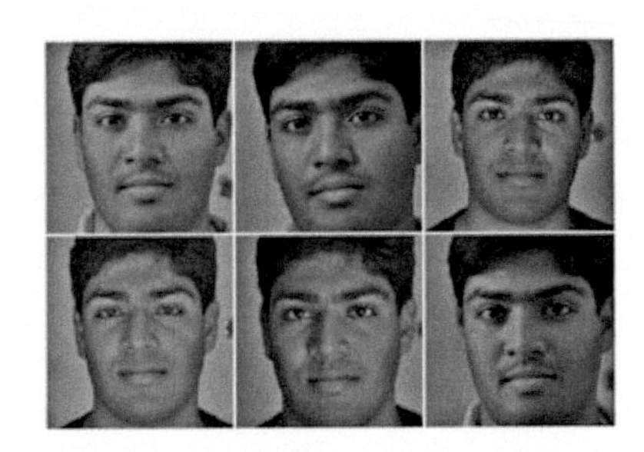

Figure 11.7. Examples from Database A: Six 2D images captured with varying lighting conditions for the same subject.

Table 11.1. *Statistics of Database A and B*

| | Database A | Database B |
|---|---|---|
| Subjects | 26 | 23 |
| 2D+3D in gallery | 26 | 23 |
| 2D in probe | 800 | 1602 |

from the back of the head to the nose, and that the $y$ axis is the vertical axis through the subject's head). Thus, we acquired images under six illumination conditions, four $y$ rotations, and three $z$ rotations per subject. For each image we concurrently acquired the 3D mesh as well. We will refer to this database as Database B. Figure 11.8 depicts the variation in pose and illumination for one of the subjects from Database B. The *gallery* set was created by selecting the 3D mesh and the 2D texture corresponding to the frontal face with the "best" illumination in our set. The statistics of Database A and B are summarized in Table 11.1.

**Authentication Experiments:** We performed an authentication experiment using the above algorithm in which evaluated both relighting and unlighting. In the unlighting case, both *gallery* and *probe* images were unlit (thus became albedos). In the relighting case, the *gallery* image was relit according to the *probe* image. In all cases the 2D images used were described in the geometry image so that they were directly comparable. The results for Database A are summarized using a Receiver Operating Characteristic (ROC) curve (Figure 11.9). In this figure, it is clearly shown that face recognition benefits more from relit images than from unlit images. It achieves a 10% higher authentication rate at $10^{-3}$ False Accept Rate (FAR) than unlighting. The performance using the raw texture is also included as a baseline. Even though these results depend on the database and the distance metric used, they indicate clearly that *relighting is more suitable for face recognition than unlighting*. The reason behind this is

Figure 11.8. Examples from Database B with the variation of lighting and pose.

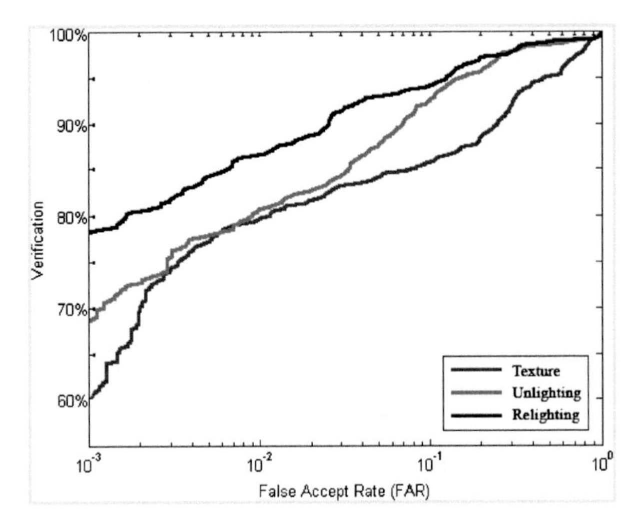


Figure 11.9. ROC curve for authentication experiment on Database A (varying illumination).

that any unlighting method produces an albedo for which the ground truth is not known; therefore the optimization procedure is more prone to errors.

To assess the robustness of the 3D-aided 2D face recognition approach with respect to both lighting and pose variation, we employed Database B. To demonstrate that our method can significantly improve the performance of 2D face recognition algorithms on difficult data, we selected as the baseline a commercial 2D face recognition system that achieved the leading performance in 2D experiments at the Face Recognition Grand Challenge 2006. This selection is to ensure that we have a strong and realistic baseline.

Figure 11.10 depicts the ROC curve for Database B. In this figure we present the results for four different variants of 3D-aided 2D face recognition algorithms. Two of the variants use the *z-normalization* method of the scores, and two employ *median absolute deviation* (MAD) normalization (Jain et al. 2005). The scores obtained with the standard CW-SSIM exhibit lower performance than those that use the visibility map (view-dependent computation denoted as "OPT" in the graphs). The ROC (Figure 11.10) depicts the fact that our 3D-aided 2D face recognition algorithm performs better overall on the ROC and has a lower Equal Error Rate (EER). In the lower false accept rates, the commercial face recognition software has a slight advantage (3% performance advantage at 0.1% FAR). However, the EER of our 3D-aided 2D face recognition algorithm is less than half of that of the commercial product, thus making it more suitable in situations where low EER is desirable.

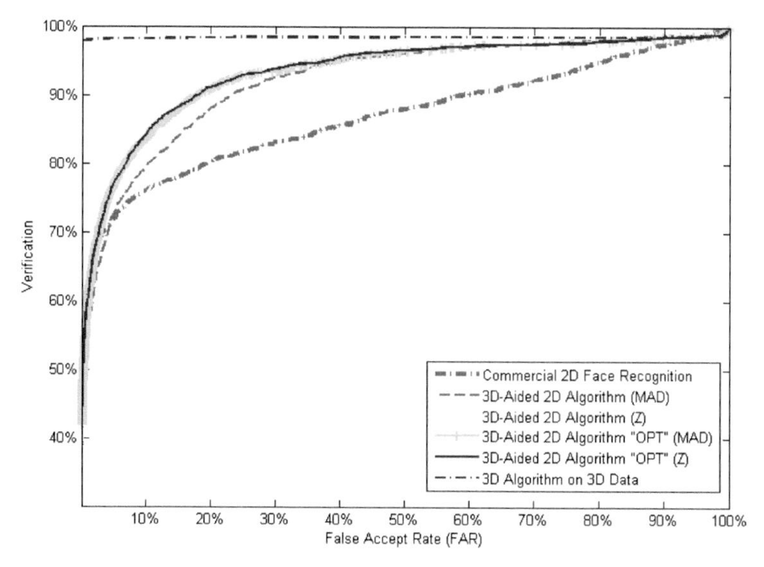


Figure 11.10. ROC curve for authentication experiment on Database B (varying illumination and pose). This shows that the Equal Error Rate that the 3D-aided 2D face recognition algorithm achieves is half that of the leading commercial product available at this time. The results, denoted by "OPT," use the view-dependent CW-SSIM.

**2D/3D Identification Experiment:** We also constructed an identification experiment based on Database B. The results are provided in a Cumulative Matching Characteristic (CMC) curve on 23 subjects of Database B (Figure 11.11). The 3D-aided 2D face recognition approach outperforms the commercial 2D-only product throughout the entire CMC curve.

*Note that the commercial 2D system had 100% identification rate when only frontal images were used.*

## 11.5 Conclusions

We have developed a new system for face recognition that uses 2D+3D data for enrollment and 2D data for authentication. This system fits an annotated deformable model to the 3D data and by using an analytical skin reflectance model to relight the 2D data while using the fitted AFM from the *gallery*. The qualitative and quantitative evaluation indicates that the proposed 3D-aided 2D face recognition algorithm is robust to pose and light variations. Testing was conducted on two databases representing variation of pose and illumination. The experiments demonstrate that the 2D/3D method with relighting process

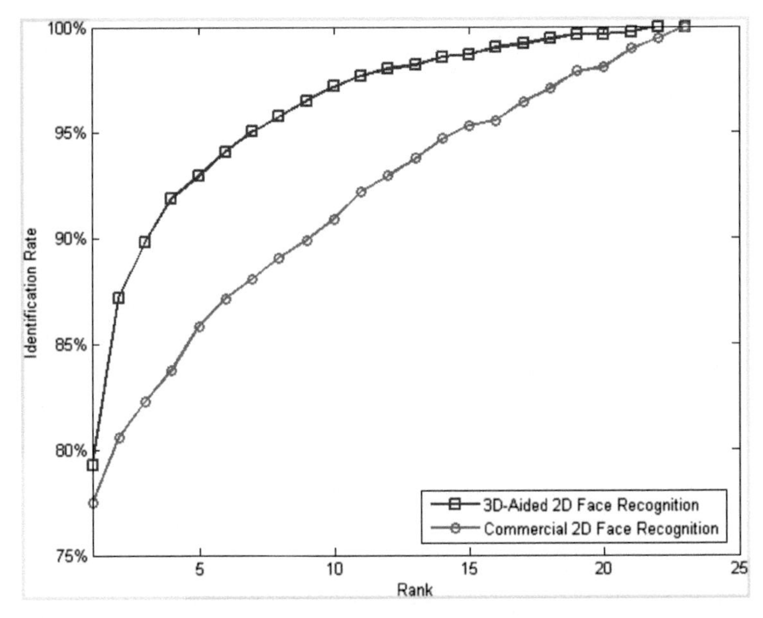


Figure 11.11. Identification performance of the 3D-aided 2D face recognition approach versus the performance of a leading commercial 2D face recognition product. The results are reported on Database B.

provides robust face recognition performance under varying pose and lighting conditions.

## References

Basri, R., and D. Jacobs. 2003. Lambertian reflectance and linear subspaces. *IEEE Transactions on Pattern Analysis and Machine Intelligence*, **25**(2), 218–233.

Biswas, S., G. Aggarwal, and R. Chellappa. 2007. Robust estimation of albedo for illumination-invariant matching and shape recovery. In *Proc. IEEE International Conference on Computer Vision*, pages 1–8, Rio de Janeiro, Brazil, Oct. 14–20.

Blanz, V., and T. Vetter. 2003. Face recognition based on fitting a 3D morphable model. *IEEE Transactions on Pattern Analysis and Machine Intelligence*, **25**(9), 1063–1074.

Bowyer, K., K. Chang, and P. Flynn. 2006. A survey of approaches and challenges in 3D and multi-modal 3D+2D face recognition. *Computer Vision and Image Understanding*, **101**(1), 1–15.

Everitt, C., A. Rege, and C. Cebenoyan. 2001. Hardware shadow mapping. Technical report, NVIDIA Corporation.

Gu, L., and T. Kanade. 2008. A generative shape regularization model for robust face alignment. In *Proc. European Conference on Computer Vision*, pages 413–426, Marseille, France, Oct. 12–18.

Jain, A., K. Nandakumar, and A. Ross. 2005. Score normalization in multimodal biometric systems. *Pattern Recognition*, **38**(12), 2270–2285.

Kakadiaris, I., G. Passalis, G. Toderici, M. Murtuza, Y. Lu, N. Karampatziakis, and T. Theoharis. 2007. Three-dimensional face recognition in the presence of facial expressions: an annotated deformable model approach. *IEEE Transactions on Pattern Analysis and Machine Intelligence*, **29**(4), 640–649.

Lambert., J., 1760. *Photometria sive de mensure de gratibus luminis, colorum umbrae*. Eberhard Klett.

Lee, J., R. Machiraju, H. Pfister, and B. Moghaddam. 2005. Estimation of 3D faces and illumination from single photographs using a bilinear illumination model. In *Proc. Eurographics Symposium on Rendering*, pages 73–82, Konstanz, Germany, June 29–Jul. 1.

Liang, L., R. Xiao, F. Wen, and J. Sun. 2008. Face alignment via component-based discriminative search. In *Proc. European Conference on Computer Vision*, pages 72–85, Marseille, France, Oct. 12–18.

Phillips, J., T. Scruggs, A. O'Toole, P. Flynn, K. Bowyer, C. Schott, and M. Sharpe. 2007. FRVT 2006 and ICE 2006 large-scale results. *National Institute of Standards and Technology Internal Report*, 7408.

Phong., B., 1975. Illumination for computer generated pictures. *Communications of the ACM*, **18**(6), 311–317.

Portilla, J., and E. Simoncelli. 2000. A parametric texture model based on joint statistic of complex wavelet coefficients. *International Journal of Computer Vision*, **40**, 49–71.

Riccio, D., and J.-L. Dugelay. 2007. Geometric invariants for 2D/3D face recognition. *Pattern Recognition Letters*, **28**(14), 1907–1914.

Saragih, J., S. Lucey, and J. Cohn. 2009. Face alignment through subspace constrained mean-shifts. In *Proc. IEEE Computer Society Conference on Computer Vision and Pattern Recognition*, Miami Beach, FL, June 20–25.

Simoncelli, E., W. Freeman, E. Adelson, and D. Heeger. 1992. Shiftable multi-scale transforms. *IEEE Transactions on Information Theory*, **38**(2), 587–607.

Smith, W., and E. Hancock. 2005. Estimating the albedo map of the face from a single image. In *Proc. IEEE International Conference on Image Processing*, **3**, 780–783, Genoa, Italy, Sept. 11–14.

Toderici, G., G. Passalis, T. Theoharis, and I. Kakadiaris. 2007. An automated method for human face modeling and relighting with application to face recognition. In *Proc. Workshop on Photometric Analysis For Computer Vision*, Rio de Janeiro, Brazil, Oct. 14–21.

Tsalakanidou, F., S. Malassiotis, and M. Strintzis. 2007. A 2D+3D face identification system for surveillance applications. In *Proc. IEEE International Conference on Advanced Video and Signal based Surveillance*, London, UK, Sept. 5–7.

Wang, Z., A. Bovik, H. Sheikh, and E. Simoncelli. 2004. Image quality assessment: From error visibility to structural similarity. *IEEE Transactions on Image Processing*, **13**(4), 600–612.

Wang, Z., and E. Simoncelli. 2005. Translation insensitive image similarity in complex wavelet domain. In *Proc. IEEE International Conference on Acoustics, Speech and Signal Processing*, **volume** II, 573–576, Philadelphia, Mar. 18–25.

Yin, L., and M. Yourst. 2003. 3D face recognition based on high-resolution 3D face modeling from frontal and profile views. In *Proc. ACM SIGMM Workshop on Biometrics Methods and Applications*, pages 1–8, New York.

Zhang L., and D. Samaras. 2006. Face recognition from a single training image under arbitrary unknown lighting using spherical harmonics, IEEE Transactions on Pattern Analysis and Machine Intelligence, 28, 351–363.

# PART IV

## Databases and Security

# 12

# Acquisition and Analysis of a Dataset Comprising Gait, Ear, and Semantic Data

Sina Samangooei, John D. Bustard, Richard D. Seely, Mark S. Nixon, and John N. Carter

## 12.1 Introduction

### 12.1.1 Multibiometrics

With the ever increasing demand for security and identification systems, the adoption of biometric systems is becoming widespread. There are many reasons for developing multibiometric systems; for example, a subject may conceal or lack the biometric a system is based on. This can be a significant problem with noncontact biometrics in some applications (e.g., surveillance). Many noncontact biometric modalities exist. Of these face recognition has been the most widely studied, resulting in both its benefits and drawbacks being well understood. Others include gait, ear, and soft biometrics. Automatic gait recognition is attractive because it enables the identification of a subject from a distance, meaning that it will find applications in a variety of different environments (Nixon et al. 2005). The advantage of the ear biometric is that the problems associated with age appear to be slight, though enrolment can be impeded by hair (Hurley et al. 2008). There are also new approaches to using semantic descriptions to enhance biometric capability, sometimes known as soft biometrics (Samangooei et al. 2008). The semantic data can be used alone, or in tandem with other biometrics, and are suited particularly to analysis of surveillance data.

The deployment of mutilbiometric systems is largely still at a research phase (Ross et al. 2006). Of the biometrics discussed here, some approaches fuse face with gait (Shakhnarovich and Darrell 2002; Liu and Sarkar 2007; Zhou and Bhanu 2007; Yamauchi et al. 2009) and some that fuse ear with face (Chang et al. 2003). No approach has fused gait and ear data. One of the first biometric portals was based on iris data and mentioned use of face in early marketing material, but the current literature does not mention this

(Matey et al. 2006). To assess recognition capability, ideally we require a database wherein the biometrics were recorded concurrently, though it appears acceptable to consider disparate sets of data (different biometrics acquired at different times), especially when seeking to establish fusion performance, rather than biometric performance. Naturally, when the effect of age is the target of analysis, then concurrent acquisition of multiple biometrics will be the only practicable way to handle what is otherwise an enormous and challenging metadata labeling and reconciliation approach.

### 12.1.2 Multibiometric Data

There have been many calls for acquisition of multiple biometric data dating from the inception of biometrics (Carter and Nixon 1990). The major multimodal databases currently available include the XMVTS, BANCA, WVU, and MBGC databases.

The XM2VTSDB multimodal face database project contains four recordings of 295 subjects taken over a period of four months (Messer et al. 1999). Each recording contains a speaking head shot and a rotating head shot. Sets of data taken from this database are available, including high-quality color images, 32 kHz 16-bit sound files, video sequences, and a 3D model.

The BANCA database is a large, realistic, and challenging multimodal database intended for training and testing multimodal verification systems (Popovici et al. 2003). The BANCA database was captured in four European languages in two modalities (face and voice). For recording, high- and low-quality microphones and cameras were used. The subjects were recorded in three different scenarios, controlled, degraded, and adverse over 12 different sessions spanning three months. In total 208 people were captured, half men and half women.

The WVU multimodal biometric dataset collection, BIOMDATA, collects iris, fingerprint, palmprint, voice, and face data from over 200 people (Ross et al. 2006). The data were collected using standard enrolment devices, where possible, such as the SecuGen optical fingerprint biometric scanner, the OKI IRISPASS-h handheld device for the iris, and the IR Recognition Systems HandKey II for hand geometry with image and sound recordings for face and voice, respectively. The dataset also includes soft biometrics such as height and weight for subjects of different age groups, ethnicity, and gender with variable number of sessions or subject.

The Multiple Biometric Grand Challenge (MBGC) data build on the data-challenge and evaluation paradigm of FRGC, FRVT 2006, ICE 2005, and ICE 2006 and address requirements that focus on biometric samples taken under less than ideal conditions. As such, the data include low-quality still images, high- and low-quality video imagery, and face and iris images taken under varying illumination conditions as well as off-angle and occluded images. There is no established literature yet, but there is an extensive website with many presentations, especially from the early (recent) workshops.[1] The primary goal of the MBGC is to investigate, test, and improve performance of face and iris recognition technology on both still and video imagery through a series of challenge problems and evaluation. The MBGC seeks to reach this goal through several technology development areas:

1. Face recognition on still frontal, real-world-like high- and low-resolution imagery
2. Iris recognition from video sequences and off-angle images
3. Fusion of face and iris (at score and image levels)
4. Unconstrained face recognition from still and video imagery
5. Recognition from near-infrared (NIR) and high-definition (HD) video streams taken through portals
6. Unconstrained face recognition from still images and video streams.

One of the purposes of the data is for fusion of face and iris as subjects walk through a biometric portal, which is a likely deployment scenario for biometrics.

The Biosecure database is now available.[2] The databases include hand, iris, signature, fingerprint, still face, and audio video for around 200 to 300 subjects (Fierrez-Aguilar et al. 2007). The main characteristics of the databases accommodate different application scenarios, such as:

1. An internet dataset (PC-based, on-line, internet environment, unsupervised conditions) with voice and face data
2. A desktop dataset (PC-based, off-line, desktop environment, supervised conditions), including voice, face, signature, fingerprint, hand, and iris and
3. A mobile dataset (mobile device-based, indoor/outdoor environment, uncontrolled conditions), including voice, face, signature, and fingerprint.

None of these databases include specific concentration on gait and ear. There are separate databases available for these biometrics. To advance our research agenda in gait, ear, and semantic biometrics and to further our investigations into the effects of covariates (exploratory variables) on performance, we sought to acquire a database that included face, gait, and ear, as well as to investigate, via semantic data, potential relating to surveillance applications.

[1] http://face.nist.gov/mbgc/.
[2] http://biosecure.it-sudparis.eu/AB.

### 12.1.3 Noncontact Biometrics

In this section we discuss the biometrics gathered by our new database.

#### 12.1.3.1 Gait Biometrics

Gait as a biometric can be used alone, to cue acquisition of other biometrics, or fused with other biometric data. It is suited to deployment in portals, since this is where a subject must walk through.

There have been many previous approaches to gait that rely on data where a subject walks in a plane normal to the camera's view (Nixon et al. 2005). These offer encouragement of the use in a portal arrangement because with laboratory data recognition performance approaches that of many other biometrics. There are several datasets recording such data in indoor and outdoor scenarios, in particular the HumanID (Sarkar et al. 2005), (CASIA n.d.), and Southampton datasets (Seely et al. 2008). Because Multiview data are available, view-dependent and viewpoint-invariant approaches are possible. Work has been done on fusing gait with other biometrics (Liu and Sarkar 2007; Shakhnarovich et al. 2001), particularly faces, though there has been none fusing gait and ear/face. Little work has been done on recognition in pure 3D, which our dataset allows.

#### 12.1.3.2 Ear Biometrics

Ears are a particularly appealing approach to noncontact biometrics because they are unaffected by expressions and vary less with age when compared to faces. Also, reported levels of recognition are promising (Hurley et al. 2005). Although automated ear biometrics is a relatively recent development, the use of ears for forensics dates back to the 1800s, when they formed part of the system developed by Alphonse Bertillon (1889). However, it was not until 1955 that a criminologist, Alfred Iannarelli, developed a practical recognition process based solely on the ear (Iannarelli 1989). In developing this process, he gathered and analyzed over 10,000 ear photographs to demonstrate they could be used for accurate recognition. Like fingerprints, ear prints have been used in the police service as a forensic tool, and in 1967 their analysis provided key evidence in a criminal prosecution (Osterburgh 1989). Ear prints have continued to be used in cases as recently as 2008. However, at least one conviction has been overturned on appeal because of insufficient ear print quality (State vs. Kunze 1999).

In 1998, Burge and Burger proposed the first computerized ear recognition system. Although their paper had no recognition results, it led to a range of further studies into the effectiveness of ears as a biometric. Many approaches have been used to achieve accurate recognition on small collections of ear images taken under controlled conditions. Recent work has focused on improving the robustness to achieve recognition in less constrained environments that contain background clutter, occlusion and lighting, and pose variation (Bustard and Nixon 2009).

#### 12.1.3.3 Semantic Biometrics

The description of humans based on their physical features has been explored for several purposes including medicine (Rosse and Mejino 2003), biometric fusion (Jain et al. 2004), eyewitness analysis (Koppen and Lochun 1997), and human identification (Interpol 2008). Descriptions chosen vary in levels of visual granularity and include visibly measurable features as well as those measurable only using specialized tools. One of the first attempts to systematically describe people for identification based on their physical traits was the anthropometric system developed by (Bertillon 1889) in 1896. His system used 11 precisely measured traits of the human body, including height, length of right ear, and width of cheeks. This system was quickly superseded by other forms of forensic analysis such as fingerprints. More recently, description of anthropometric traits have been used along side primary biometrics in *soft biometric fusion* to improve recognition rates (Wayman 1997; Jain et al. 2004; Nandakumar et al. 2004; Zewail et al. 2004). Jain et al. (2004) present an example where, using a general Bayesian framework, they fuse fingerprints with the soft features of gender, ethnicity, and height to achieve improved identification rates.

Meaningful words (semantic terms) that humans use to describe one another by their visually discernible traits can also be used as a soft biometric. In the Southampton Multi-Biometric Tunnel, selected semantic terms describing visual traits of subjects are collected from human observers. The traits described are those discernible by humans at a distance, complementing the primary biometrics gathered in the Multi-Biometric Tunnel (i.e., gait, face, and ear). Furthermore, the traits and descriptive terms are chosen for their *consistent* and *accurate* mention by humans in various scenarios (Samangooei et al. 2008).

### 12.1.4 On Our New Database

In outdoor scenarios such as surveillance where there is very little control over the environments, complex computer vision algorithms are often required for analysis. However, constrained environments, such as walkways in airports where the surroundings and the path taken by individuals can be controlled, provide an ideal application for such systems. Figure 12.1 depicts an idealized constrained environment. The path taken by the subject is restricted to a narrow path and once inside is in a volume where lighting and other conditions are controlled to facilitate biometric analysis. The ability to control the surroundings

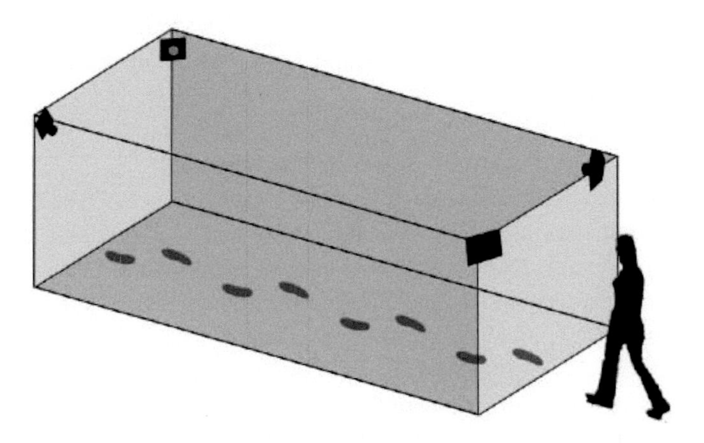

Figure 12.1. A controlled environment with fixed cameras provides an ideal scenario for automatic gait recognition. The subject is constrained to walk through the middle; controlled lighting and background facilitate analysis.

and the flow of people greatly simplifies the computer vision task, compared with typical unconstrained environments. Even though biometric datasets with greater than 100 people are increasingly common, very little is still known about the inter- and intrasubject variation in many biometrics. This information is essential to estimate the recognition capability and limits of automatic recognition systems. To accurately estimate the inter- and the intra class variance, substantially larger datasets are required (Veres et al. 2006). Covariates such as facial expression, headwear, footwear type, surface type, and carried items are attracting increasing attention, although considering the potentially large impact on an individual's biometrics, large trials need to be conducted to establish how much variance results.

This chapter is the first description of the multibiometric data acquired using the University of Southampton's Multi-Biometric Tunnel (Middleton et al. 2006; Seely et al. 2008), a biometric portal using automatic gait, face, and ear recognition for identification purposes. The tunnel provides a constrained environment and is ideal for use in high-throughput security scenarios and for the collection of large datasets. We describe the current state of data acquisition of face, gait, ear, and semantic data and present early results showing the quality and range of data that have been collected. The main novelties of this dataset in comparison with other multibiometric datasets are the following:

1. Gait data exist for multiple views and are synchronized, allowing 3D reconstruction and analysis

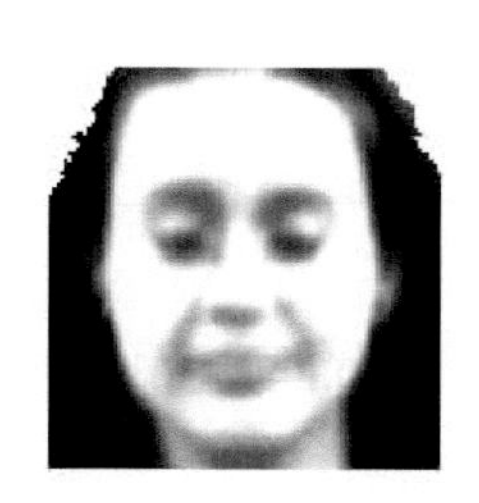

Figure 12.2. Example face samples. All are taken from the same gait sequence showing the 1st (76 × 76), 11th (101 × 101), and 21st (150 × 150) samples out of 24.

2. The face data are a sequence of images allowing for face recognition in video
3. The ear data are acquired in a relatively unconstrained environment, as a subject walks past and
4. The semantic data are considerably more extensive than has been available previously.

We shall aim to show the advantages of these new data in biometric analysis, though the scope for such analysis is considerably greater than time and space allows for here.

## 12.2 Data Collection

The main components of our new multibiometric database are separate, synchronized, and integratable sample databases of gait, face, ear, and semantic descriptions. Gait samples are from 12 (and some early experiments using eight) multiview overhead cameras and suitable for per camera analysis as well as 3D reconstruction. Face samples are taken as the user walks down the tunnel, resulting in a sequence of frames per sample, where the subject's face is automatically extracted and the background removed. Example face samples can be seen in Figure 12.2. Ear samples are comprised of a single snapshot, one taken per gait sample. Finally, semantic descriptions of subjects in the form of self-annotations and observed descriptions are captured on a subset of the subjects. The exact contents of these datasets are summarized in Tables 12.1–12.4. Note, in the description of the gait database contents, that the total number of unique subjects is 192, which is less than the subjects recorded. This is due to some subjects providing repeat samples.

Table 12.1. *Gait Dataset Samples*

| | |
|---|---|
| Total sequences | 2070 (∼84 invalid) |
| Total subjects | 192 (∼5 invalid subjects) |
| Average sequences/subject | 10 |
| 12 sensors | 895 samples across 89 subjects (∼31 invalid sequences from 4 subjects) |
| 8 sensors | 1175 samples across 117 subjects (∼53 invalid sequences from 5 subjects) |
| Repeat walks | 120 samples across 12 subjects |

### 12.2.1 Gait Tunnel

The Multi-Biometric Tunnel, a unique research facility situated at the University of Southampton, has been specifically designed as a noncontact biometric access portal (Middleton et al. 2006), providing a constrained environment for people to walk through, while facilitating recognition. The system has been designed with airports and other high-throughput environments in mind, where contact-based biometrics would prove impractical. Such a system could be set up in a very unobtrusive manner where individuals might not even be aware of its presence. It also enables the automated collection of large amounts of noncontact biometric data in a fast and efficient manner, allowing very large datasets to be acquired in a significantly shorter timeframe than previously possible.

The Multi-Biometric Tunnel is able to detect the entry and exit of a subject, allowing a high degree of automation. While a subject is inside the tunnel their gait is recorded by 12 Point Grey Dragonfly cameras, allowing the reconstruction of 3D volumetric data. The gait cameras all have a resolution of $640 \times 480$ and capture at a rate of 30 FPS (frames per second); they are connected together over an IEEE1394 network employing commercial synchronization units[3] to ensure accurate timing between cameras. Figure 12.3 shows a single frame as captured by the cameras. Video is also captured of the subject's face and upper body using a high-resolution ($1600 \times 1200$) IEEE1394 camera, enabling face recognition. A single snapshot is taken as the subject exits the tunnel, of the side of the subject's head, for ear biometrics. As shown in Figure 12.4, the facility has a central region that participants walk along, with the face and ear cameras placed at the end of the walkway and the gait video cameras positioned around the upper perimeter of the tunnel. The walls of the tunnel are painted with a

[3] PTGrey Camera Synchronization unit, part No. SYNC, http://www.ptgrey.com.

Table 12.2. *Ear Dataset Samples*

| | |
|---|---|
| Total samples | 2070 |
| Total subjects | 192 |
| Average samples/subject | 10 |
| Completely occluded ears | 49 |
| Occlusion due to hair | 45 |
| Occlusion due to hats | 4 |

nonrepeating rectangular pattern to aid automatic camera calibration. Saturated colors have been chosen to ease background and foreground separation. These choices are mandated by the nature of the facility. After the subject has walked 10 times through the tunnel, taking on average 5 minutes per person, they are asked to record semantic data associated with the database, which include questions about gender, age, ethnicity, and physical parameters.

Upon arrival, the purpose and procedure for database acquisition was explained to each potential participant, and on agreement they signed a consent form to confirm that they were willing to participate in the experiment. To ensure privacy, the consent forms had no unique identifiers, and as such they are the only record of the participant's identity. Each participant was asked to choose a unique identifier at random, which could then be associated with any data collected from that individual. Before commencing the experiment, each subject was asked to walk through the tunnel as a trial run; this was not recorded and was watched by the supervisor to ensure that the subject understood their instructions. Normally subjects were not supervised, with the aim of collecting a natural gait and facial expression.

The tunnel is equipped with a status light mounted outside the visible area; participants were asked to wait until it indicated that the system was ready. Before each sample the gait and face cameras captured 1 second of video footage while the tunnel area was empty; this was used later for the background estimation and subtraction. Upon entering the tunnel, the subject would walk

Table 12.3. *Face Dataset Samples*

| | |
|---|---|
| Total sequences | 2070 |
| Total subjects | 192 |
| Average sequences/subject | 10 |
| Average face frames/sequence | 31.8<br>(min = 6 and max = 48 depending on speed of walk and subject height) |

Table 12.4. *Semantic Dataset Samples*

| | |
|---|---|
| Total annotations | 2828 |
| Total self-annotations | 193 |
| Total observed annotations | 2635 |
| In set 1 | 1367 (∼93 users of 15 subjects) |
| In set 2 | 845 (∼59 users of 15 subjects) |
| In set 3 | 288 (∼22 users of 15 subjects) |
| In set 4 | 135 (∼9 users of 15 subjects) |

through a break-beam sensor, starting the capture process. Toward the end of the tunnel another breakbeam sensor stopped the capture process. After capture, the recorded data was saved (unprocessed) to disk. The entire process of induction, walking through the tunnel, and answering questions, took on average 30 minutes per participant. The result is that data are collected for three noncontact biometrics from camera sensors synchronized using commercial IEEE-1394 bus synchronization devices. Before describing analysis of the biometric data and its fusion, we shall describe some special considerations of the separate biometrics.

#### 12.2.1.1 Gait Data

The volume of data acquired when subjects walk through the tunnel currently forces the acquisition procedure to store the unprocessed data straight to disk, and further processing is conducted afterwards. With modern processors and storage, the recognition process can actually be complete a few steps after the subject has exited the tunnel, and we have performed this for the BBC (UK 2009). Our purpose here is more the use of the tunnel to acquire a database, and for this purpose, the images from the multiple gait cameras are reconstructed into a 3D silhouette that can then be viewed from any angle. There are several

Figure 12.3. Synchronized images captured by gait cameras.

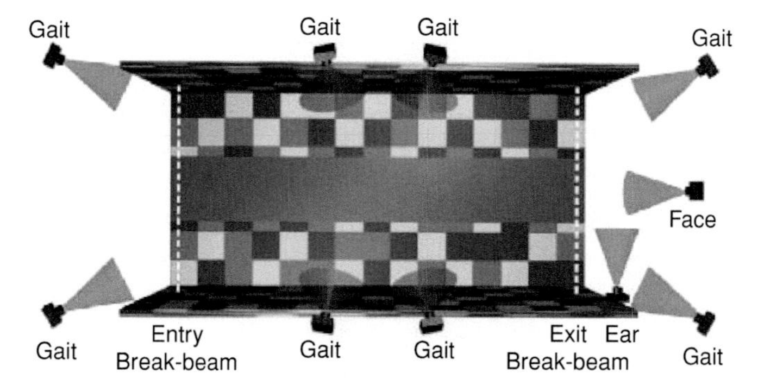


Figure 12.4. Placement of cameras and break-beam sensors in system.

stages to processing the gait video data. Separate background and foreground images are used to facilitate background subtraction and shadow suppression. This is followed by some post-processing using simple morphological operators to clean up the silhouette data. The resulting silhouettes are corrected for radial distortion and then used as the basis for shape from silhouette reconstruction. Shape from silhouette reconstruction is simply the calculation of the intersection of projected silhouettes (see Figure 12.5), and it can be expressed mathematically as

$$V(x, y, z) = \begin{cases} 1 & \text{if} \quad \Sigma_{i=n}^{N} I_n \left(M_n (x, y, z)\right) \geq k \\ 0 & \text{otherwise.} \end{cases}$$

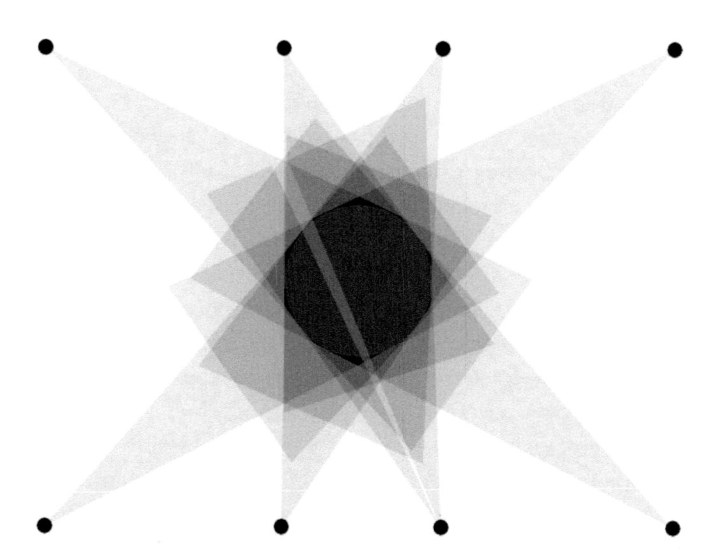

Figure 12.5. 3D reconstruction is performed by taking the intersection of the reprojected silhouettes from each camera.

Figure 12.6. A three-dimensional volumetric frame created by the Multi-Biometric tunnel using shape from silhouette reconstruction.

Here $V$ is the derived 3D volume, $k$ is the number of cameras required for a voxel to be marked as valid, and $N$ is the total number of cameras. $I_n$ is the silhouette image from camera $n$, where $I_n(u, v) = 0, 1$, and $M_n(x, y, z : u, v)$ is a function that maps the 3D world coordinates to the coordinate system of camera $n$. $M_n$ is calculated using the calibration information derived for each camera. In a conventional implementation of shape from silhouette, a voxel may be considered valid only if all cameras have silhouette pixels at its location; therefore $k = N$ must be satisfied. Using a value of $k$ that is lower than $N$ results in a less selective criteria, which adds a degree of resilience against background segmentation errors, although the reconstructed shape is not as accurate. The use of high-intensity colors for the background means that very little segmentation error occurs, allowing the use of a $k = N$ criteria. A small amount of post-processing is carried out on the resulting 3D volumes using binary morphology to improve the accuracy of the reconstructed volumes. An example volume created by shape from silhouette reconstruction is shown in Figure 12.6.

Figure 12.7. Example ear sample.

#### 12.2.1.2 Ear Data

To record the ear a digital photograph was taken when a subject passed through the light beam at the end of the tunnel. The camera uses a wide field of view to ensure ears were visible with a large range of subject heights and walking speeds. The photograph was taken with a high-shutter speed to minimize motion blur. In addition, two flash cameras were used to provide sufficient light for a high shutter speed and reduce any shadows caused by hair or headgear. The flash guns were positioned to point from above and below the ear.

It should also be noted that subjects were not instructed to explicitly reveal their ears. This was to record subjects with a realistic degree of ear occlusion, representative of a real usage scenario. Of the 187 subjects recorded by the system, 6% walked too fast to be captured by the ear camera. A further 26% had their ears completely obscured by hair or headgear. We intend to include metadata in the database indicating where this occurs. An example ear from the dataset can be seen in Figure 12.7.

#### 12.2.1.3 Semantic Data

The collection of semantic terms is integrated with the Southampton Multi-Biometric Tunnel. Participants are asked to annotate themselves and a set of 15 other subjects according to a set of traits using a set of predefined terms, listed in Table 12.5.

The annotation-gathering process was designed carefully to avoid (or allow the future study of) inherent weaknesses and inaccuracies present in

Table 12.5. *Physical Traits and Associated Semantic Terms*

| **Body** | |
|---|---|
| 0. Arm length | (0.1) Very short<br>(0.2) Short<br>(0.3) Average<br>(0.4) Long<br>(0.5) Very long |
| 1. Arm thickness | (1.1) Very thin<br>(1.2) Thin<br>(1.3) Average<br>(1.4) Thick<br>(1.5) Very thick |
| 2. Chest | (2.1) Very slim<br>(2.2) Slim<br>(2.3) Average<br>(2.4) Large<br>(2.5) Very large |
| 3. Figure | (3.1) Very small<br>(3.2) Small<br>(3.3) Average<br>(3.4) Large<br>(3.5) Very large |
| 4. Height | (4.1) Very short<br>(4.2) Short<br>(4.3) Average<br>(4.4) Tall<br>(4.5) Very tall |
| 5. Hips | (5.1) Very narrow<br>(5.2) Narrow<br>(5.3) Average<br>(5.4) Broad<br>(5.5) Very broad |
| 6. Leg length | (6.1) Very short<br>(6.2) Short<br>(6.3) Average<br>(6.4) Long<br>(6.5) Very long |
| 7. Leg direction | (7.1) Very bowed<br>(7.2) Bowed<br>(7.3) Straight<br>(7.4) Knock kneed<br>(7.5) Very knock kneed |
| 8. Leg thickness | (8.1) Very thin<br>(8.2) Thin<br>(8.3) Average<br>(8.4) Thick<br>(8.5) Very thick |
| 9. Muscle build | (9.1) Very lean<br>(9.2) Lean<br>(9.3) Average<br>(9.4) Muscly<br>(9.5) Very muscly |
| 10. Proportions | (10.1) Average<br>(10.2) Unusual |
| 11. Shoulder shape | (11.1) Very rounded<br>(11.2) Rounded<br>(11.3) Average<br>(11.4) Square<br>(11.5) Very square |

| **Global** | |
|---|---|
| 12. Weight | (12.1) Very thin<br>(12.2) Thin<br>(12.3) Average<br>(12.4) Big<br>(12.5) Very big |
| 13. Age | (13.1) Infant<br>(13.2) Pre-Adolescence<br>(13.3) Adolescence<br>(13.4) Young adult<br>(13.5) Adult<br>(13.6) Middle aged<br>(13.7) Senior |
| 14. Ethnicity | (14.1) European<br>(14.2) Middle Eastern<br>(14.3) Indian/Pakistan<br>(14.4) Far Eastern<br>(14.5) Black<br>(14.6) Mixed<br>(14.7) Other |
| 15. Sex | (15.1) Female<br>(15.2) Male |
| **Head** | |
| 16. Skin color | (16.1) White<br>(16.2) Tanned<br>(16.3) Oriental<br>(16.4) Black |
| 17. Facial hair color | (17.1) None<br>(17.2) Black<br>(17.3) Brown<br>(17.4) Red<br>(17.5) Blond<br>(17.6) Gray |
| 18. Facial hair length | (18.1) None<br>(18.2) Stubble<br>(18.3) Moustache<br>(18.4) Goatee<br>(18.5) Full beard |
| 19. Hair color | (19.1) Black<br>(19.2) Brown<br>(19.3) Red<br>(19.4) Blond<br>(19.5) Gray<br>(19.6) Dyed |
| 20. Hair length | (20.1) None<br>(20.2) Shaven<br>(20.3) Short<br>(20.4) Medium<br>(20.5) Long |
| 21. Neck length | (21.1) Very short<br>(21.2) Short<br>(21.3) Average<br>(21.4) Long<br>(21.5) Very long |
| 22. Neck thickness | (22.1) Very thin<br>(22.2) Thin<br>(22.3) Average<br>(22.4) Thick<br>(22.5) Very thick |

human-generated descriptions. The error factors that the system was designed to deal with include the following:

- *Memory (Ellis 1984):* Passage of time may affect a witness's recall of a subject's traits. Memory is affected by variety of factors, such as the construction and utterance of featural descriptions rather than more accurate (but indescribable) holistic descriptions. Such attempts often alter memory to match the featural descriptions.
- *Defaulting (Lindsay et al. 1994):* Features may be left out of descriptions in free recall, often not because the witness failed to remember the feature, but rather because the feature has some default value. Race may be omitted if the crime occurs in a racially homogenous area, Sex may be omitted if suspects are traditionally male.
- *Observer variables (Flin and Shepherd 1986; O'Toole 2004):* A person's own physical features, namely, their self-perception and mental state, may affect recall of physical variables. For example, tall people have a skewed ability to recognize other tall people but will have less ability when it comes to the description of shorter individuals, not knowing whether they are average or very short.
- *Anchoring (Chapman and Johnson 2002):* When a person is asked a question and is initially presented with some default value or even seemingly unrelated information, the replies given are often weighted around those initial values. This is especially likely when people are asked for answers which have some natural ordering (e.g., measures of magnitude)

The data-gathering procedure employed in the tunnel was designed to account for all these factors. Memory issues are addressed by allowing annotators to view videos of subjects multiple times, also allowing them to repeat a particular video if necessary. Defaulting is avoided by explicitly asking individuals for each chosen trait meaning that even values for apparently *obvious* traits are captured. This style of interrogative description where constrained responses are explicitly requested is more complete than free-form narrative recall but may suffer from inaccuracy, though not to a significant degree (Yarmey and Yarmey 1997). Subject variables can never be completely removed, so instead we allow the study of differing physical traits across various annotators. Users are asked to self-annotate based on self-perception; also, certain subjects being annotated are themselves annotators. This allows for some concept of the annotator's own appearance to be taken into consideration when studying their descriptions of other subjects. Anchoring can occur at various points of the data capture process. We have accounted for anchoring of terms gathered for individual traits by setting the default term of a trait to a neutral

"Unsure" rather than any concept of "Average." Table 12.4 shows the current annotations collected in this manner from the Southampton Multi-Biometric Tunnel.

## 12.3 Recognition

Considerable scope is afforded by these data for analysis of recognition potential. We have yet to analyze performance of all the data in a fusion schema, and we have yet to analyze face recognition performance alone. In concert with our research agendas in new approaches to gait, ear, and semantic biometrics, we have addressed the following:

1. Gait recognition in 3D
2. Robust ear recognition using a planar approximation
3. Recognition and recall by semantic labels.

We have also shown how fusion of these data can achieve significantly improved performance over the single data, thus demonstrating the capability of this new dataset to support fusion as well as individual biometric recognition.

### 12.3.1 Gait

Because gait is a periodic signal, we consider only one period for analysis: the image samples taken between heel strike of one foot until the next heel strike of the same foot. An automatic process was used to locate a complete gait cycle; this was achieved by analyzing the variation in the size of the subject's bounding box. Several different variants of the average silhouette gait analysis technique were used to evaluate the dataset collected from the Multi-Biometric Tunnel: the normalized side-on average silhouette, the (nonnormalized) side-on average silhouette, and the combination of side-on, front-on, and top-down average silhouettes. The dataset used for analysis comprised 187 subjects, where 85 subjects were viewed by 12 cameras, and 103 subjects were viewed viewed by 8 cameras (Seely et al. 2008). The set contained 2070 samples, of which 1986 were valid. Reasons for a sample being invalid include clipping from where the subject was outside the reconstruction area and the automatic gait cycle finder being unable to reliably identify a complete cycle. The database is made up of 76% male and 24% female subjects, and the average age was 27 years. All three gait analysis techniques discussed below have similarities with the work of (Shakhnarovich et al. 2001), in that the 3D volumetric data are used to synthesize silhouettes from a fixed viewpoint relative to the subject. The resulting silhouettes are then analyzed by using the average silhouette approach.

The advantage of using three-dimensional data is that silhouettes from any arbitrary viewpoint can be synthesized, even if the viewpoint is not directly seen by a camera. For example, silhouettes from an orthogonal side-on viewpoint can be synthesized from the volumetric data by

$$J_i(y,z) = \bigcup_{x=x_{MIN}}^{x_{MAX}} V_i(x,y,z).$$

In other words, the side-on orthogonal viewpoint $J_i$ for frame $i$ is synthesized by taking the union of voxels in volume $V_i$ along the $x$ axis, where the $x$ axis spans left to right, $y$ spans front to back, and $z$ spans from the top to the bottom. In a similar manner, the front-on and top-down orthogonal viewpoints can be synthesized by taking the union of the voxels along the $y$ or the $z$ axis, respectively. In the first analysis, silhouettes are taken from a side-on orthogonal viewpoint so that normal gait recognition could be assessed. This view is not seen by any camera and so can only be synthesized. The use of a side-on viewpoint facilitates comparison with previous results. The average silhouette is calculated wherein the center of mass $C_i = (C_{i,x}, C_{i,y})$ is found for each frame $i$. This is calculated by rendering the 3D reconstruction to an image and estimating its center of mass by defining each image pixel within the silhouette to have a unit mass. The average silhouette is then found by summing silhouettes after they have been aligned using the value

$$A(xy) = \frac{1}{M} \sum_{i=0}^{M-1} J_i(x - C_{i,x}, y - C_{i,y}),$$

where $A$ is the average silhouette and $M$ is the number of frames in the gait cycle. The derived average silhouette is normalized in size so that it is 64 pixels high, while preserving the aspect ratio. The average silhouette is treated as the feature vector and used for leave-one-out recognition, using nearest-neighbor classification and the Euclidean distance as the distance metric between samples. A recognition rate of 97.9% was achieved. No feature-set transformation or selection was performed in this and subsequent analysis. This result is then similar in performance to current state-of-art approaches to gait biometrics, yet allows other views to be analyzed in future. Because the silhouette data can be synthesized from an orthogonal viewpoint, the subject's distance from the viewpoint will not affect the silhouette size, thus meaning that scale normalization is unnecessary and removes valuable information. For this reason a second analysis was conducted using nonscale-normalized average silhouettes, and the average silhouettes were downsampled by a factor of four to reduce the computational workload. The non-normalized average silhouette

Table 12.6. *Performance of Various Average Silhouette Signatures Measured Using Equal Error Rate (EER) and Correct Classification Rate (CCR)*

| Average silhouette | CCR (%) | EER (%) |
|---|---|---|
| Side (Scale-normalized) | 97.9 | 6.8 |
| Side | 99.8 | 1.8 |
| (Side, front, top) | 100 | 1.9 |

retains information such as the subject's build and height. The same viewpoint as the previous normalized variant was used, achieving an improved recognition rate of 99.8%.

The above analysis methods only utilize one viewpoint, meaning that very little of the additional information contained within the three-dimensional data was exploited. Therefore one additional analysis technique was performed, using non-normalized average silhouettes derived from three orthogonal viewpoints: side-on, front-on, and top-down. The features from the three average silhouettes were simply concatenated, and the resulting feature vector used for recognition, achieving an even better recognition rate of 100%. Again this is comparable with state-of-the-art approaches. Several different analysis methods have been carried out to evaluate the quality of the collected data. The correct classification rate and equal error rate were found for each analysis method; a summary of the results is presented in Table 12.6. The respective cumulative match scores are shown in Figure 12.8; it can be seen that the normalized average signature yields relatively poor performance, most likely due to the loss of information such as height and build. This is confirmed by the much improved classification performance of the non-normalized average silhouette. Classification performance using the concatenated average silhouettes proves better than both other methods, although the improvement in the equal error rate is marginal; this suggests that the additional information contained within 3D data is useful for recognition.

In addition, receiver operating characteristic (ROC) curves demonstrating the system's capability to verify identity are shown in Figure 12.9. These confirm that normalized side-on average silhouettes are clearly inferior. However, the situation is less clear between the other two cases, where the method using multiple viewpoints proves more selective than that of a single viewpoint. These results together suggest that the gait data alone are as worthy as a contender for evaluation of gait as a biometric, as in a multibiometric system.

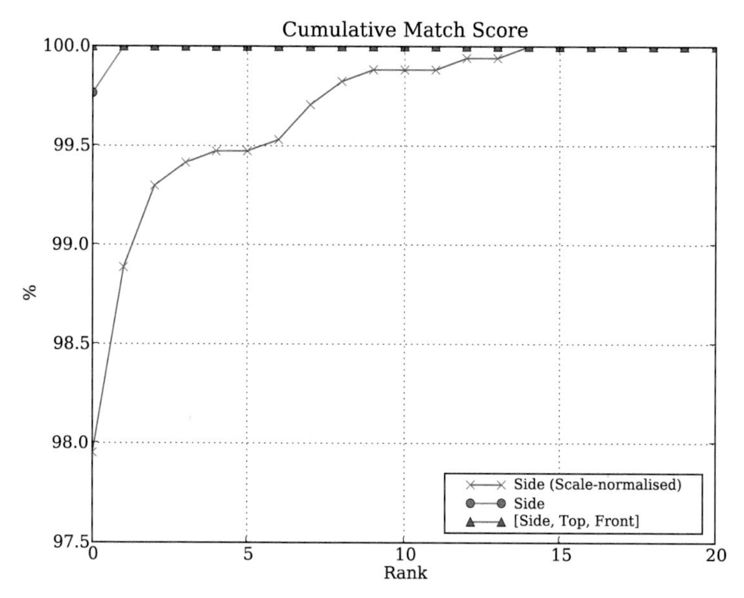


Figure 12.8. Cumulative match score plots for gait silhouettes derived from 3D.

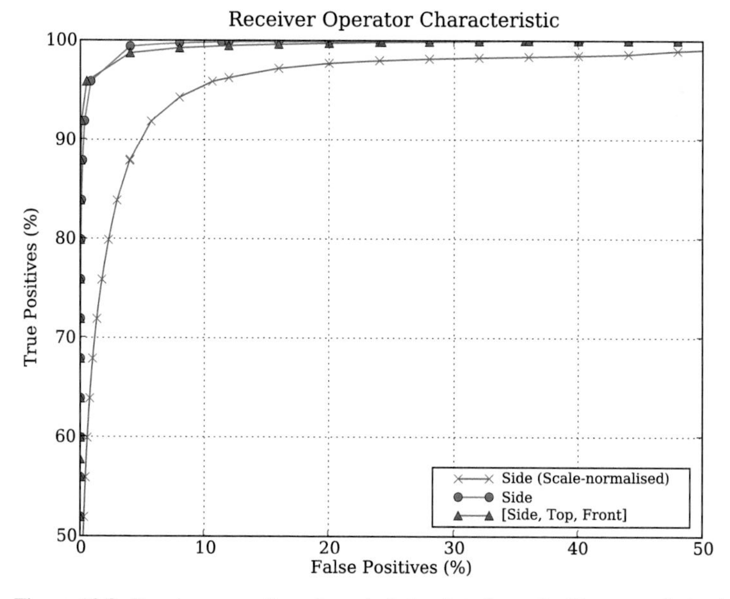


Figure 12.9. Receiver operating characteristic plots for gait silhouettes derived from 3D.

### 12.3.2 Ear

The recorded ear images were used to recognize the subjects using the technique developed by Bustard and Nixon (2009). The technique uses SIFT feature points (Lowe 1999) to detect and align known samples of a subjects' ears with an image to be identified. SIFT points are a highly robust means of matching distinctive points between images. They define both a location, which includes a position, scale, and orientation, and an associated signature calculated from the image region around the point. SIFT points have been shown to retain similar signatures under a wide range of variations, including pose, lighting, field of view, and resolution (Mikolajczyk and Schmid 2005). Any four matching points between a gallery and probe image are sufficient to align and recognize an ear. This enables the technique to remain accurate even when significantly occluded. In addition, by requiring that each point's relative location conforms to the same configuration as that in an existing ear gallery, the detection is precise. Therefore, nonear images are rarely misclassified as ears. This precision is further enhanced by using the points to align the sample image with the unknown ear and robustly comparing the two images. If the images are not similar, the match is rejected. The difference between the images then forms an estimate of similarity for matching ears and enables the most likely identity to be determined. These steps enable the algorithm to recognize ears accurately, even in the presence of brightness and contrast differences, image noise, low resolution, background clutter, occlusion, and small pose variation. The ear recognition accuracy was evaluated using a "leave one out" strategy, with each image removed from the gallery and tested against the rest of the dataset in turn.

As can be seen in Figure 12.10, the rank 1 recognition performance for visible ears was 77%. This is lower than the performance in previous publications and reflects the less constrained ear images, which include a greater degree of occlusion (Figure 12.11) than the original publication.

### 12.3.3 Score-Based Fusion

We have also performed a fusion approach to investigate the suitability of these data for fusion purposes. Score fusion was used to combine the multiple biometric recognition results. When high-quality camera data are available, gait recognition provides almost perfect recognition performance, making fusion unnecessary. This is useful when subjects are both recorded and recognized using the tunnel. When subjects are recorded by the tunnel but recognized using existing security cameras, the quality of recordings will be reduced.

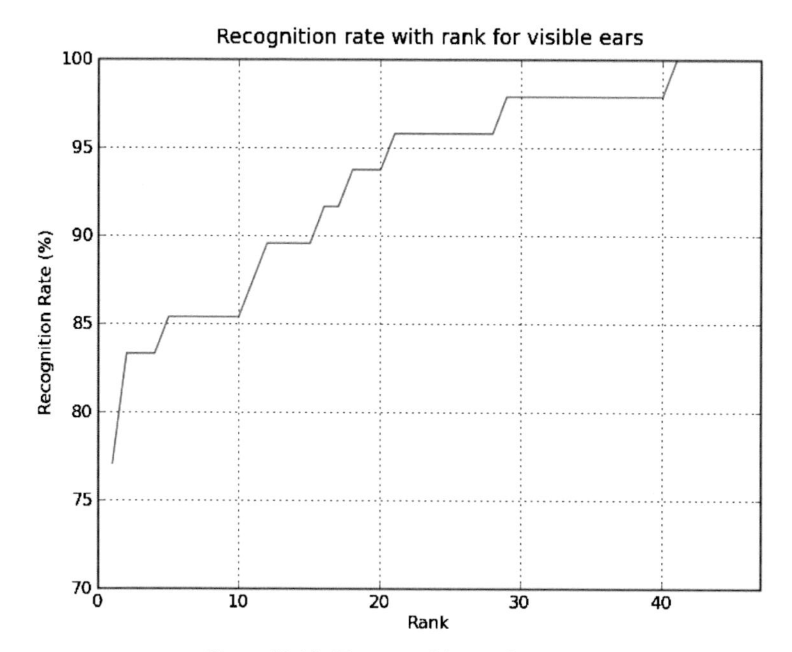


Figure 12.10. Ear recognition performance.

This can be simulated in the dataset by degrading the camera data to produce lower-quality gait signatures. Under these circumstances performance is reduced, making fusion desirable.

The distance measures returned by each algorithm were normalized using an estimate of the offset and scale of the measures between different subjects. For each algorithm these values were calculated using the mean and standard deviation of the distance between subjects in the gallery set. In addition, missing distance values were also estimated. If subjects walked too quickly

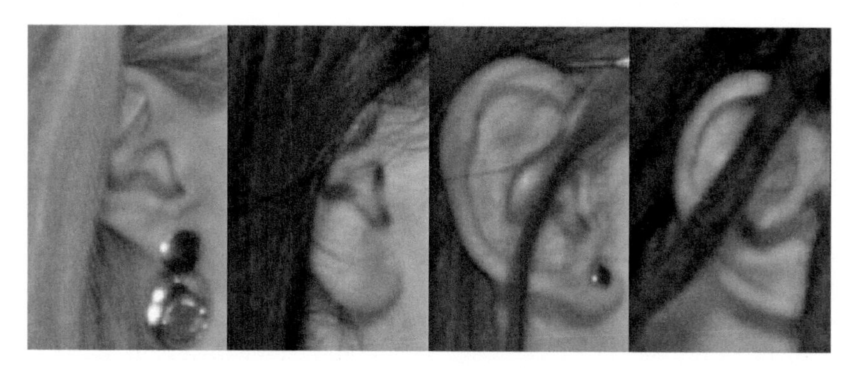

Figure 12.11. Occluded ears.

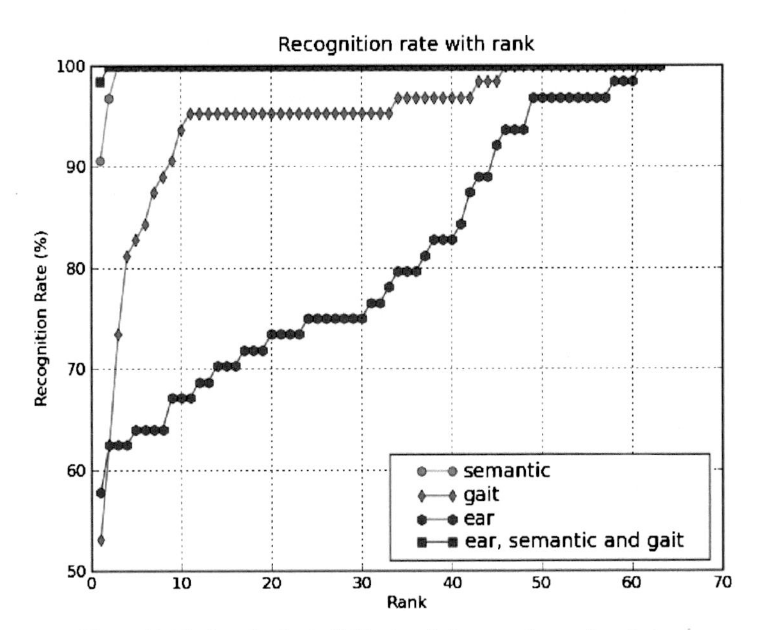


Figure 12.12. Results for individual techniques and complete fusion.

to be captured by the ear camera, their distance to each gallery probe was estimated to be the mean distance for all matched ears. Also, when the recognition algorithm did not find a match between a gallery image and a probe, the distance measure was estimated to be the maximum value of the recorded distances. The normalized gait, semantic, and ear data scores were then combined using the sum rule (Jain et al. 2007).

This fusion approach was evaluated using a "leave one out" recognition test, applied to a subset of the database that contained biometric data across all modalities. Figure 12.12 shows the recognition rates for each biometric and the results obtained when their results are fused. Using the fusion algorithm a 98% rank 1 recognition rate can be obtained. Figure 12.13 shows the results of separately fusing each of the modalities; in all cases the recognition results improve significantly with fusion. As such, the semantic data can be used on their own or in fusion.

## 12.4 Conclusions

We have developed a new database for noncontact biometrics. The data are largely complete, and we are currently finalizing their distribution, which will be arranged via our current gait database.[4] We already distribute one of the world's

[4] www.gait.ecs.soton.ac.uk.

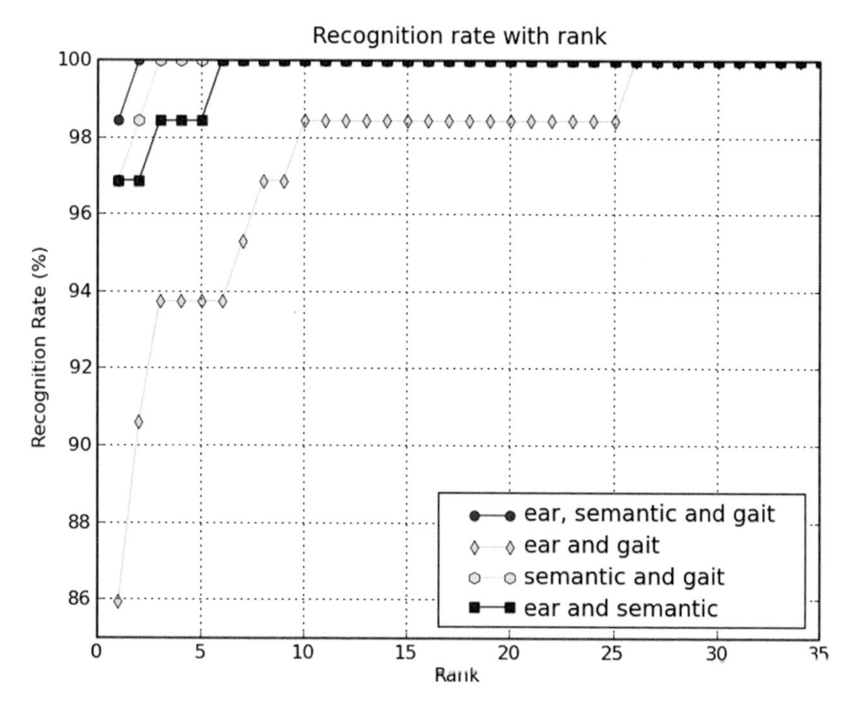


Figure 12.13. Results for all fusion combinations.

largest gait databases (sot on 2003), and we shall make our new database available there. The database comprises data recorded as subjects pass through the portal. The data include sequences of face images, sequences of gait recorded from multiple synchronized cameras affording 3D data, ear images, and semantic descriptions. We have shown already that these data are a promising avenue for investigation for noncontact biometrics, either alone or fused.

## References

Aug. 2003. URL http://www.gait.ecs.soton.ac.uk/.

Bertillon, A. 1889. *Instructions for taking descriptions for the identification of criminals and others, by means of anthropometric indications.* American Bertillon Prison Bureau.

Burge, M., and W. Burger. 1998. *Biometrics*, personal identification in networked society: personal identification in networked society, chapter in *Ear Biometrics*. Kluwer Academic Publishers.

Bustard, J. D., and M. S. Nixon. 2009. Towards unconstrained ear recognition from 2D images. *IEEE Trans. SMC(A)*, vol. 40, no. 3.

Carter, J., and M. Nixon. 1990. An integrated biometric database. In *IEE Colloq. on Electronic Images and Image Processing in Security and Forensic Science*, pages 4/1–4/5.

CASIA. CASIA gait database, http://www.sinobiometrics.com.

Chang, K., K. Bowyer, S. Sarkar, and B. Victor. 2003. Comparison and combination of ear and face images in appearance-based biometrics. *IEEE Trans. PAMI*, **25**(9), 1160–1165.

Chapman, G. B., and E. J. Johnson. 2002. Incorporating the irrelevant: anchors in judgments of belief and value. Pages 120–138. *Heuristics and Biases: The Psychology of Intuitive Judgment*. Cambridge University Press.

Ellis, H. D. 1984. Practical aspects of facial memory. Section 2, pages 12–37. In *Eyewitness Testimony: Psychological Perspectives*. Cambridge University Press.

Fierrez-Aguilar, J., J. Ortega-Garcia, D. T. Toledano, and J. Gonzalez-Rodriguez. 2007. Biosec baseline corpus: a multimodal. *Pattern Recognition*, **40**(4), 1389–1392.

Flin, R. H., and J. W. Shepherd. 1986. Tall stories: Eyewitnesses' ability to estimate height and weight characteristics. *Human Learning*, **5**.

Hurley, D. J., M. S. Nixon, and J. N. Carter. 2005. Force field feature extraction for ear biometrics. *Computer Vision and Image Understanding*, **98**, 491–512.

Hurley, D. J., B. Arbab-Zavar, and M. S. Nixon. 2008. The ear as a biometric. In *Handbook of Biometrics*. Springer.

Iannarelli, A. 1989. *Ear Identification*. Paramount.

Interpol. 2008. *Disaster Victim Identification Form (Yellow)*. Booklet.

Jain, A., S. Dass, and K. Nandakumar. 2004. Can soft biometric traits assist user recognition. In *Proc. SPIE*.

Jain, A. K., K. Nandakumar, X. Lu, and U. Park. 2004. Integrating faces, fingerprints, and soft biometric traits for user recognition. In *Proc. BioAW*, pages 259–269.

Jain, A. K., P. Flynn, and A. A. Ross. 2007. *Handbook of Biometrics*. Springer.

Koppen, P. V., and S. K. Lochun. 1997. Portraying perpetrators; the validity of offender descriptions by witnesses. *Law and Human Behavior*, **21**(6), 662–685.

Lindsay, R., R. Martin, and L. Webber. 1994. Default values in eyewitness descriptions. *Law and Human Behavior*, **18**(5), 527–541.

Liu, Z., and S. Sarkar. 2007. Outdoor recognition at a distance by fusing gait and face. *Image Vision Comput.*, **25**(6), 817–832.

Lowe, D. G. 1999. Object recognition from local scale-invariant features. *IEEE International Conference on, Computer Vision*, **2**, 1150.

Matey, J., O. Naroditsky, K. Hanna, R. Kolczynski, D. LoIacono, S. Mangru, M. Tinker, T. Zappia, and W. Zhao. 2006. Iris on the move: acquisition of images for iris recognition in less constrained environments. *Proceedings of the IEEE*, **94**(11), 1936–1947.

Messer, K., J. Matas, J. Kittler, and K. Jonsson. 1999. XM2VTSDB: the extended M2VTS database. In *AVBPA*, pages 72–77.

Middleton, L., D. K. Wagg, A. I. Bazin, J. N. Carter, and M. S. Nixon. 2006. Developing a non-intrusive biometric environment. In *IEEE Conf. IROS*.

Mikolajczyk, K., and C. Schmid. 2005. A performance evaluation of local descriptors. *IEEE Trans. PAMI*, **27**(10), 1615–1630.

Nandakumar, K., S. C. Dass, and A. K. Jain. 2004. Soft biometric traits for personal recognition systems. In *Proc. ICBA*, pages 731–738.

Nixon, M. S., T. N. Tan, and R. Chellappa. 2005. *Human Identification Based on Gait*. International Series on Biometrics. Springer.

Osterburgh, J. W. 1989. *Crime Laboratory*. Paramount.

O'Toole, A. J. 2004. Psychological and neural perspectives on human face recognition. In *Handbook of Face Recognition*. Springer.

Popovici, V., J. Thiran, E. Bailly-Bailliere, S. Bengio, F. Bimbot, M. Hamouz, J. Kittler, J. Mariethoz, J. Matas, K. Messer, B. Ruiz, and F. Poiree. 2003. The BANCA database and evaluation protocol. In *Proc. AVBPA*, **2688**, 625–638.

Ross, A. A., K. Nandakumar, and A. K. Jain. 2006. *Handbook of Multibiometrics (International Series on Biometrics)*. Springer.

Rosse, C., and J. L. V. Mejino. 2003. A reference ontology for biomedical informatics: the foundational model of anatomy. *J. Biomed. Informatics*, **36**(6), 478–500.

Samangooei, S., B. Guo, and M. S. Nixon. 2008. The use of semantic human description as a soft biometric. In *Proc. IEEE BTAS*.

Sarkar, S., P. J. Phillips, Z. Liu, I. R. Vega, P. Grother, and K. W. Bowyer. 2005. The humanid gait challenge problem: data sets, performance, and analysis. *IEEE Transactions on Pattern Analysis and Machine Intelligence*, **27**(2), 162–177.

Seely, R. D., S. Samangooei, L. Middleton, J. N. Carter, and M. S. Nixon. 2008. The University of Southampton Multi-Biometric Tunnel and introducing a novel 3D gait dataset. In *Proc. IEEE BTAS*.

Shakhnarovich, G., and T. Darrell. 2002. On probabilistic combination of face and gait cues for identification. In *IEEE Proc. FGR*, page 176.

Shakhnarovich, G., L. Lee, and T. Darrell. 2001. Integrated face and gait recognition from multiple views. In *IEEE CVPR*, pages 439–446.

State vs. David Wayne Kunze. 1999. Court of Appeals of Washington, Division 2.

Veres, G., M. Nixon, and J. Carter. 2006. Is enough enough? what is sufficiency in biometric data? *Lecture Notes in Computer Science*, **4142**, 262.

Wayman, J. L. 1997. Benchmarking large-scale biometric system: issues and feasibility. In *Proc. CTST*.

Yamauchi, K., B. Bhanu, and H. Saito. 2009. Recognition of walking humans in 3d: initial results. *Computer Vision and Pattern Recognition Workshop*, pages 45–52.

Yarmey, A. D., and M. J. Yarmey. 1997. Eyewitness recall and duration estimates in field settings. *J. App. Soc. Psych.*, **27**(4), 330–344.

Zewail, R., A. Elsafi, M. Saeb, and N. Hamdy. 2004. Soft and hard biometrics fusion for improved identity verification. *MWSCAS*, **1**, 225–228.

Zhou, X., and B. Bhanu. 2007. Integrating face and gait for human recognition at a distance in video. *IEEE Trans. Systems, Man and Cybernetics, Part B*, **37**(5), 1119–1137.

# 13

# Dynamic Security Management in Multibiometrics

Ajay Kumar

## 13.1 Introduction

Biometrics-based personal identification systems offer automated or semiautomated solutions to various aspects of security management problems. These systems ensure controlled access to the protected resources and provide higher security and convenience to the users. The security of the protected resources and information can be further enhanced with the usage of multibiometrics systems. The multibiometric systems are known to offer enhanced security and antispoofing capabilities while achieving higher performance. These systems can utilize multiple biometric modalities, multiple biometric samples, multiple classifiers, multiple features, and/or normalization schemes to achieve performance improvement (refer to chapter x for more details). However, the higher security and reliability offered by multibiometrics systems often come with additional computational requirements and user inconvenience, which can include privacy and hygienic concerns. Therefore the deployment of multibiometrics systems for civilian and commercial applications is often a judicious compromise between these conflicting requirements. The management of multibiometric systems to adaptively ensure the varying level of security requirements, user convenience, and constraints has invited very little attention in the literature. Very little work has been done on the theory, architecture, implementation, or performance estimation of multibiometrics that dynamically ensure the varying level of security requirements.

## 13.2 Why Dynamic Security Management?

The expected security requirements from the multibiometrics systems are typically expressed in terms of error rates and reliability of the employed system.

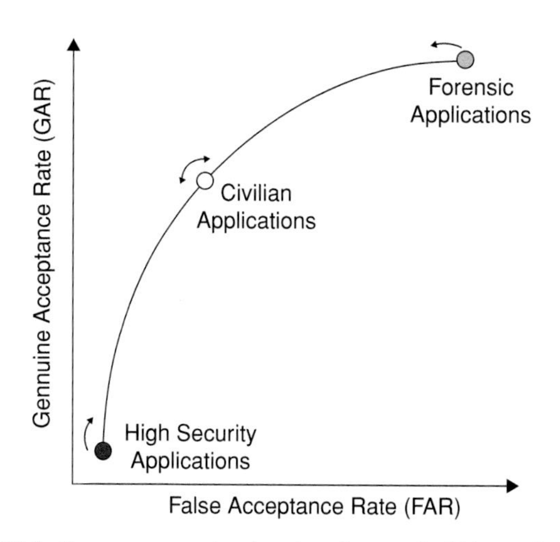


Figure 13.1. Common operational regions for a typical biometric system.

These error rates correspond to false acceptance rate (FAR), which is the rate at which imposters are accepted as genuine users, or false rejection rate (FRR), which is the rate at which genuine users are rejected by the system as imposters. The reliability of biometrics systems largely depends on those controllable factors that directly affect the confidence and stability of decisions (performance measures). These include the ability of multibiometrics systems to resist spoof attempts and the stability of performance measures with respect to environmental changes such as illumination, humidity and temperature, lifecycle of components, etc.

The multibiometrics systems that employ score- and decision-level combinations to consolidate individual scores or decisions are most common in the literature (Jain et al. 2004; Ross et al. 2006). These systems typically employ a fixed combination rule and a fixed decision threshold to achieve a desired level of performance. The desired level of performance is often the average equal error rate (EER) or the false acceptance rate (FAR). Figure 13.1 shows a typical Receiver Operating Characteristics (ROC) for a multibiometrics system. The highlighted points on this plot show the desired operating points for different applications. It can be observed from this plot that those multibiometrics system that offer a fixed level of security, such as low FAR, have to cope up with an associated high false rejection rate (FRR). The higher level of rejection (FRR) by the multibiometrics system for the genuine users causes high inconvenience to users and slows the average flow of traffic. The average traffic flow refers to the average number of genuine users successfully authenticated by the multibiometrics system per unit time. Figure 13.2 illustrates the effect of increasing

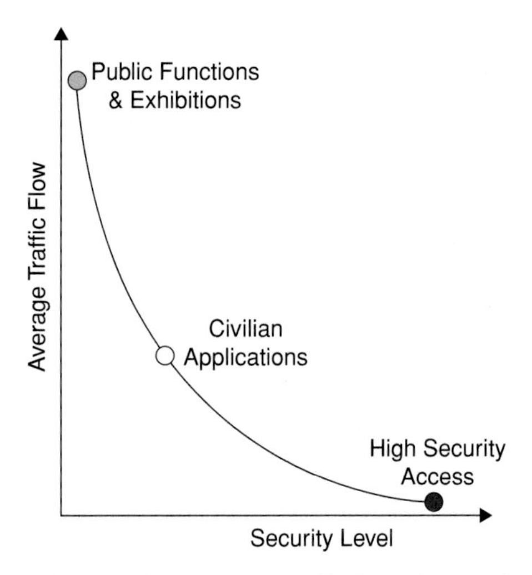


Figure 13.2. Reduction in average traffic flow with security level.

the security-level requirement from a multibiometrics system on the average flow of traffic. It can be observed from this figure that the average traffic flow is highest when there is no security requirement, and it decreases gradually with the increasing requirements of security. The reduction in average traffic flow could be due to an increase in the required or average number of attempts from genuine users (due to higher FRR rather than FTE), or due to the increase in average time required to authenticate the genuine user, resulting mainly from the added complexity of multibiometrics systems (added acquisition or processing time). Therefore the conflicting requirements of higher security and average traffic flow require the development of multibiometrics systems that can adaptively adjust to the security requirements based on perceived threats. Such systems are expected to automatically adjust the parameters (required number of modalities, fusion parameters, decision threshold, etc.) and offer multiple levels of security.

### 13.2.1 Objectives

There are a potentially large number of applications and scenarios in which a different level of security is expected from the same multibiometrics system. Ideally, these systems should be highly flexible to adapt with varying user constraints and expectations. Let us assume that a multibiometrics system that uses multiple (more than one) modalities for user authentication is deployed to ensure a fixed, a minimum, level of security. This system should be designed in such a way that that it is flexible enough to accommodate absence of a particular biometric modality (resulting from poor image/biometric[1] quality or physical challenges) and substitute another available modality while ensuring the desired (minimum) level of security. This capability requires automated computation and selection of different fusion rules or mechanisms for this substitute modality(s), its parameters, and the new decision threshold to ensure the desired level of performance. Such systems can also generate adaptive tradeoffs for the poor biometric or image quality by demanding additional biometric samples from the same or different modalities. These systems may also accommodate privacy and hygienic concerns from a user that allow them to refuse a particular (or set of) biometric for the authentication. The design and development of such multibiometrics systems that are flexible and can accommodate a range of such constraints have a large number of civilian and commercial applications.

There are wide-ranging applications when the security level of a multibiometrics system should be set depending on perceived threats. The multilevel color-coded citizen advisory system (http://www.dhs.gov/xlibrary/assets/CitizenGuidanceHSAS2.pdf.) developed by the Homeland Security Department represents a typical example of qualitative assessment of the adaptive security requirement. Depending upon perceived threats or risk of attack, this system recommends to citizens a set of appropriate actions. These qualitative threat assessments can be employed to set the security level of the deployed multibiometrics system, which is capable of adapting to multiple levels of security.

## 13.3 Summary of Related Work

The development of multibiometrics system has attracted much attention, and several fusion strategies have been proposed in the literature (Kittler et al. 1998; Tax et al. 2000; Roli et al. 2002; Veeramachaneni et al. 2005; Frischholz and Deickmann 2000; Tronci et al. 2007; Bradlow and Everson 2002; Tulyakov and Govindaraju 2007). Kittler et al. (1998) have experimented with several fixed combination strategies for performance improvement on real biometrics data. In the context of a multibiometrics system, it has been shown (Tax et al. 2000; Roli et al. 2002) that the trainable fusion strategies do not necessarily perform better than fixed combination rules. Authors in Sim et al. (2007) proposed an interesting approach to achieve high security using multimodal biometrics. Their approach involves performing continuous verification using users' passively collected fingerprint and face biometric data. However, this approach requires continued the physical presence of the user and therefore is not

[1] Poor biometric quality may not be necessarily be due to poor image quality (Kumar and Zhang 2008).

suitable for certain kinds of applications, including the popular access control applications. Frischholz and Deickmann (2000) details a multimodal system that offers multiple levels of security by employing different decision strategies for the three biometric modalities (face, lip motion, and voice), which can be combined. When the required security level is low, it may well be enough to make a decision based on the agreement of two out of three modalities. On the other hand, for high-security applications, this system demands agreement for all three modalities. However, this BioID system does not provide a systematic way to vary the level of security. Instead, a system administrator makes a decision on the decision strategies to be adopted to achieve the desired performance. Another approach to dynamically achieve higher security is to employ the dynamic selection of matchers as detailed in a paper by Tronci et al. (2007). The best match score from a set of match scores is selected based on the likelihood of input user being genuine or an impostor. The experimental results shown in the paper by Tronci et al. (2007) are quite interesting but require further work because the (1) performance achieved is not consistent as improvement is achieved only for two cases out of four cases considered, and (2) the performance improvement shown is very little.

An interesting architecture for the dynamic security management involving multiple biometrics modalities/sensors and multiple fusion rules has been discussed by Bradlow and Everson (2002). This work envisions a scenario in which a secured building is partitioned into various zones (this can be different rooms), and the access rights for each of the users are different for each of these zones. The access decisions in a particular zone may further depend on the outcome of decisions made for access attempts in other zones. In addition, the number of biometric modalities acquired or required in each zone could vary, and so is the employed fusion rule. Authors in Bradlow and Everson (2002) employ decision-level fusion strategies and argue that the moderate level of correlation among different biometric sensors can be safely ignored without any significant impact on accuracy. Another aspect of multibiometrics security lies in adaptively ensuring the desired performance while automatically responding to user preference, user constraints, and aging Poh et al. (2009). The research challenges for such problems are related to the dynamic selection of fusion models, model updating, and inference with the models. Kumar and Passi (2008) have suggested a semisupervised learning approach to such adaptive biometrics systems and explores possible research directions.

The adaptive management of multiple modalities or sensors to automatically ensure the desired level of security has been detailed in a paper by Veeramachaneni et al. (2005). This approach is certainly promising and probably the first work that employed the decisions from the individual biometric sensors to adaptively select the decision rule that can meet the desired performance or security constraint. The work by Veeramachaneni et al. (2005) and Kanhangad el al. (2008) provides theoretical framework for the multibiometrics sensor fusion model and is highly promising but also has some limitations. First, the decision-level combination approach has higher performance variations and therefore generates relatively unstable results that require a significantly higher number of iterations (the average of the results from the 100 runs is employed). In addition, the decision level has least information content among other fusion levels (feature level and match score level). Therefore the performance from the combination of abstract labels at the decision level is expected to be quite limited. Matching scores, on the other hand, contain more information than the resulting decisions, and therefore adaptive combination of matching scores can lead to better performance. The distribution of matching scores in the paper by Jain et al. (2004) is assumed to be Gaussian, which may not be true for several biometric sensors. The iris is one of the most promising biometrics for large-scale user identification, and its imposter match score distribution has been shown (Daugman 2006) to closely follow the binomial distribution. The Poisson distribution $P_P(m, \lambda)$ of matching score $m$ can be used as convenient approximation to binomial distribution $P_B(m; n, \tau)$ when $n$ is large and $\tau$ is small. Another important problem in the paper by Veeramachaneni et al. (2005) relates to using only simulated data. No effort has been made to investigate the performance of the adaptive multibiometrics system on real biometric data, which makes it very difficult to ascertain its utility. The adaptive score-level framework discussed in this chapter attempts to alleviate many of the shortcomings in the paper by Veeramachaneni et al. (2005) which employs decision-level framework.

## 13.4 Quantifying the Security Level

The security of a multibiometrics system can be quantified in terms of the performance indices, that is, in terms of error rates. The equal error rate (EER) is another commonly employed performance index for a biometrics system. However, depending upon applications, the operating point of the multibiometrics system can be different, that is, not necessarily EER, which is the operating point at which FAR is same as FRR. For high-security applications, the cost of accepting imposters as genuine users (FAR) is much higher than the cost (or loss) incurred by rejecting a genuine user as imposters. Therefore, the security-level requirements to be achieved (or the expectations) from a multibiometrics systems, in a Bayesian sense, are often quantified using following two parameters:

The global cost of falsely accepting an imposter $= C_{\text{FA}} \in [0, \ldots 1]$
The global cost of falsely rejecting a genuine user $= C_{\text{FR}} \in [0, \ldots 1]$

The overall or global performance from a multibiometrics system can be quantified using above two costs. The Bayesian cost $E$ to be minimized by the multimodal biometrics system is the weighted sum of $F_{\mathrm{AR}}$ and $F_{\mathrm{RR}}$:

$$E = C_{\mathrm{FA}} F_{\mathrm{AR}}(\eta) + C_{\mathrm{FR}} F_{\mathrm{RR}}(\eta), \quad \text{where} \quad C_{\mathrm{FA}} + C_{\mathrm{FR}} = 2, \tag{13.1}$$

where $F_{\mathrm{AR}}(\eta)$ is the global or the combined false acceptance rate and $F_{\mathrm{RR}}(\eta)$ is the combined false rejection rate at decision threshold $\eta$ from the multibiometrics system. One of the key objectives for the adaptive security management using a multibiometrics system is to minimize the overall (global) cost $E$, while knowing that the individual FAR and FRR characteristics from the multibiometrics component sensors are fixed. This can be minimized by selecting (1) the appropriate operating points for the individual multibiometrics component sensors and (2) the appropriate combination mechanism rule.

## 13.5 Framework for Dynamic Multibiometrics Management

A generalized framework that can adaptively combine multiple biometric modalities in such a way that the desired level of security (which can vary with time and space) is always ensured has a range of applications. Figure 13.3 shows the block diagram of such a generalized system that responds to the changing needs, that is, system requirements, and accordingly authenticates the users. The multibiometrics sensor data from $N$ sensors are employed to first extract the corresponding $F_1, F_2, \ldots, F_{\mathrm{N}}$ feature vectors. These feature vectors are then utilized to generate respective matching scores $s_1, s_2, \ldots, s_n$ from the corresponding templates acquired during the registration. The key objective of this system is to select one of the $n$ possible, predefined, score combination rules and a respective decision threshold in such a manner that the security requirements injected into system (from an external source) are satisfied. In other words, this multibiometrics system attempts to minimize the (global) cost $E$, as illustrated in equation (13.1), by selecting (1) the appropriate score-level combination rule, (2) its parameters, and (3) the decision threshold. The multidimensional search among the various operating points from individual biometrics and their corresponding combination, to optimize the minimum global cost $E$, can be achieved by the particle swarm optimization (PSO) approach. Therefore a brief introduction to PSO is provided in section 5.1.

### 13.5.1 Particle Swarm Optimization

The PSO is employed to find the solution for the adaptive selection of a combination of individual points, which are referred to as the particles in

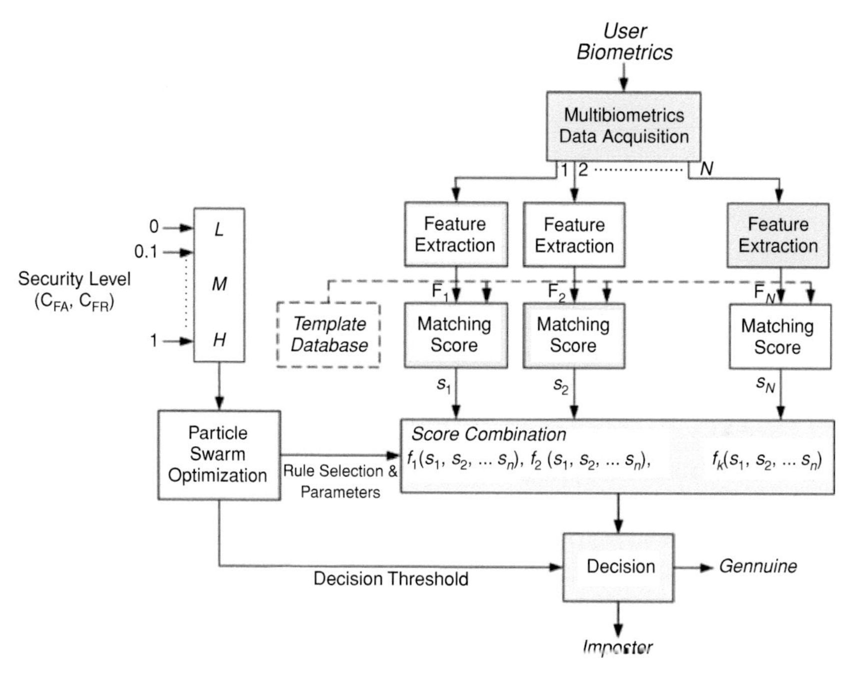


Figure 13.3. Dynamic security management using adaptive combination of component matching scores.

multidimensional search space. Each particle, characterized by its position and velocity, represents the possible solution in search space. The particle moves to a new position in multidimensional solution space depending upon the particle's best position ($p_{ak}$) and global best position ($p_{gk}$). The $p_{ak}$and $p_{gk}$ are updated after each iteration whenever a suitable, that is, lower-cost, solution is located by the particle. The velocity vector of each particle determines the forthcoming motion details. The velocity update equation Clerc and Kennedy (2002) of particle $a$ of the PSO, for instance, ($t$+1), can be represented as follows:

$$v_{ak}(t+1) = \omega v_{ak}(t) + c_1 r_1 \left[\rho_{ak}(t) - x_{ak}(t)\right] + c_2 r_2 [\rho_{gk}(t) - x_{ak}(t)], \quad (13.2)$$

where $\omega$ is the inertia weight between 0 and 1 and provides a balance between global and local search abilities of the algorithm. The accelerator coefficients $c_1$ and $c_2$ are positive constants, and $r_1$ and $r_2$ are two random numbers in the 0–1 range. The corresponding position vector is updated by

$$x_{ak}(t+1) = x_{ak}(t) + v_{ak}(t+1). \quad (13.3)$$

Equation (13.2) indicates that the new velocity of a particle in each of its dimensions is dependent on the previous velocity and the distances from previously observed best solutions (positions of the particle).

### 13.5.2 Score-Level Combinations

The combination matching scores generated from the multibiometrics sensors require candidate potential score-level combination strategies for the consideration of the optimizer (PSO). These matching scores are expected to be uncorrelated. However, this assumption may not be true in a real-world multibiometrics system, and some moderate level of correlation between matching scores is expected. Therefore, the combination strategies that are effective for both correlated and uncorrelated matching scores deserve consideration. In general, the candidate score-level combination strategies to be evaluated by the optimizer (PSO) can be described as follows:

$$S_g = \beta_g(S_j, w_j) \quad j = 1, 2, \ldots n, g = 1, 2, \ldots K, \tag{13.4}$$

where $\beta_g$ is some nonlinear or linear function of component matching scores and $w_j$ represents corresponding weights. The experimental results on the score-level combination have suggested (Tax et al. 2000) that the sum rule is expected to perform better when some degree of correlation is expected among the matching scores, whereas the product rule is expected to perform better on the assumption of independence among the matchers. In the context of the score-level framework in Figure 13.3, let us consider four ($n = 4$) possible score-level combinations from sum or average, product, exponential sum, and tan-hyperbolic sum. The combined matching score $S_g$ from each of these combinations is obtained as follows:

$$S_1 = \sum_{j=1}^{n} s_j w_j,\ S_2 = \prod_{j=1}^{n} s_j^{w_j},\ S_3 = \sum_{j=1}^{n} e^{s_j} w_j,\ S_4 = \sum_{j=1}^{n} \tanh(s_j) w_j. \tag{13.5}$$

The PSO is employed to dynamically select the appropriate decision threshold and the weights ($w_j$) to minimize the fitness function, that is, Bayesian cost in equation (13.1), from each of the possible score-level combinations. In the context of the score-level framework shown in figure 13.3, each particle is characterized by three continuous variables, the parameters of the score-level fusion rule $w_1$ and $w_2$, decision threshold *thr*, and a two-bit discrete binary variable representing four different score-level fusion rules. The number of decision combination rules required when decisions, rather than scores in (13.5)–(13.8), are combined is very high ($2^{2^N}$) and depends on number of modalities ($N$) employed in the decision rule–based framework in (Veeramachaneni et al. 2005). This results in a large search space for locating possible optimal solutions using PSO and the likelihood that PSO could converge to suboptimal (or local) solutions. This is the potential limitation of the decision-level based approach to meet dynamically changing security requirements in a multibiometrics system.

## 13.6 Experimental Validation and Discussion

The dynamic security management using a score-level and the decision-level framework can be ascertained from the experimental validation on the real multibiometrics data. First, the experimental results on the publically available National Institute of Standards and Technology, Biometric Score Set Release 1 (NIST BSSR1) database are presented. This is followed by another set of experimental results for a publically available iris and palm database.

### 13.6.1 NIST BSSR1 Database

The first partition of the NIST BSSR1 database consists of matching scores from 517 subjects. In this evaluation all the matching scores from 517 subjects, corresponding to two different face matchers (referred as C and G), are employed as multibiometrics matching scores. The experimental evaluations using the score- and decision-level approach are presented to demonstrate the effect of varying the security level on the selection of fusion strategies and the performance, that is, error in achieving the expected security level (equation [13.1]). The PSO parameters $c_1$, $c_2$, and $\omega$ are empirically selected and fixed at 1, 1, and 0.8, respectively, for all the experimental evaluations. The initial positions of the particle are randomly selected in the search space (uniform distribution assumption). Therefore the PSO generates varying results from each run, and the experimental results from the average of the results in 100 runs are shown.

The ROC from the two face matchers are shown in Figure 13.4, and the distribution of genuine and imposter matching scores is shown in Figure 13.5 (a)–(b). Figure 13.5(e) shows the average of the minimum *weighted error rate*, achieved from the score-level–based adaptive combination scheme, for varying security requirements. This *security level* is essentially the sum of cost of false acceptance ($C_{\text{FA}}$) and cost of false rejection ($C_{\text{FR}}$). This figure also illustrates the average of minimum error when the decision-level approach (Veeramachaneni et al. 2005) is employed. It can be observed from this figure that the average error rate is always at minimum, for all the selected costs or security level, using the score-level framework shown in Figure 13.3 as compared with the error rate obtained from the decision-level approach detailed in (Veeramachaneni et al. 2005). Figure 13.5(f) shows the standard deviation of the minimum error, from each run, for the decision-level approach and those from the score-level approach. The dynamic security management framework formulated in Figure 13.3 generates a more stable solution than the one that can be achieved by a decision-level framework. This can be ascertained from Figure 13.5(f), which

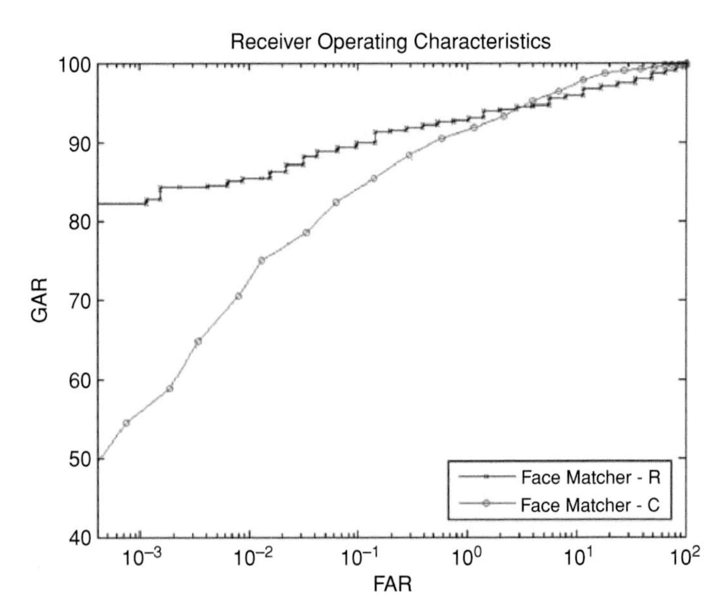


Figure 13.4. Receiver operating characteristics from two face matchers using NIST BSSR1 database.

illustrates the comparative variations in the minimum of the costs achieved from each of the 100 runs. The smaller standard deviation from the score level framework in Figure 13.5(f) means that the large number of iterations are essentially not required for the score-level approach. The experimental observations have suggested that only a single run may be adequate to achieve the stable results from score-level combination. The adaptability property required for the dynamic security management is clearly demonstrated from the results in Figure 13.5(c). For example, when the required security level is increased from 0 to 2, different fusion rules (equation [13.5]) are selected by the system. When the input security level is in the 0–0.2 range, the tan-hyperbolic fusion rule dominates (appears the most number of times), the weighted sum rule appears when the security level is in the range 0.8–1.3, and so on. The corresponding selection of 16 decision-level rules (Veeramachaneni et al. 2005) is shown in Figure 5(d). This explains how the framework for the dynamic management of the security level adaptively selects appropriate combination rules.

### 13.6.2 Iris and Palm Database

Another set of publically available database employed to demonstrate the effectiveness of the dynamic security management consisted of iris and palmprint images. The iris has emerged as one of the most promising modalities for the

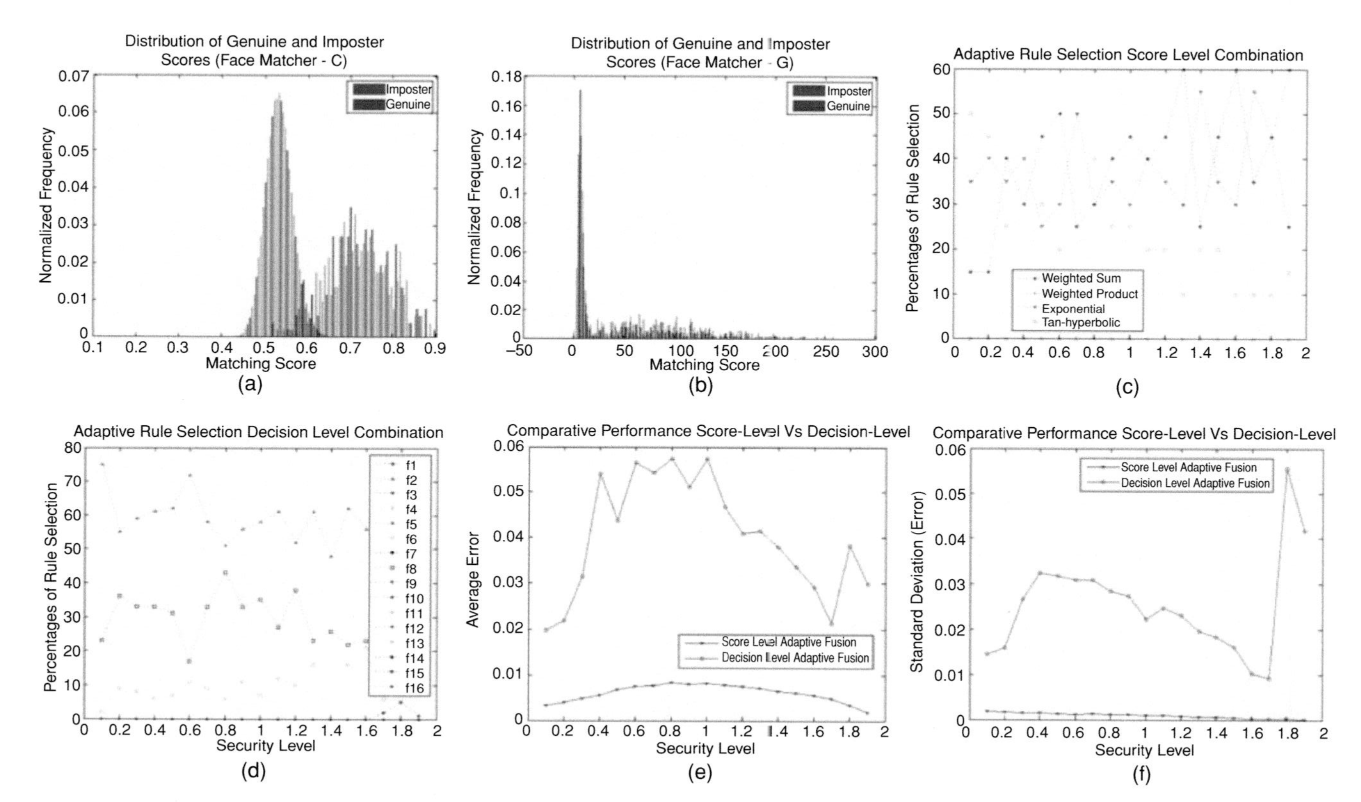


Figure 13.5. Distribution of matching scores from two face matchers in NIST BSSR1 database in (a) and (b); adaptive selection of fusion rules using score level and decision level in (c) and (d), respectively; the average and standard deviation of minimum error from the adaptive score and decision level combination in (e) and (f), respectively.

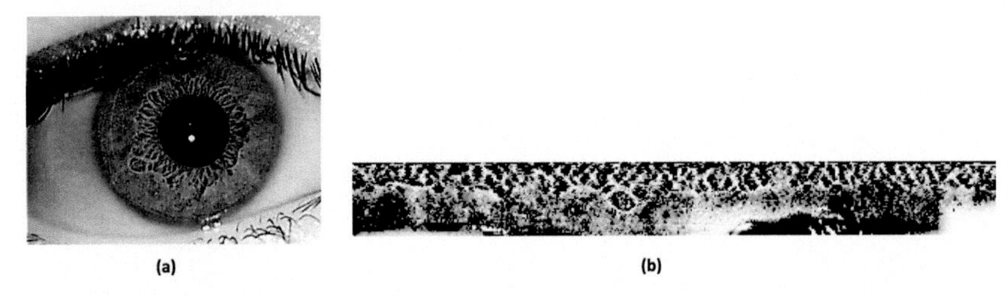


Figure 13.6. Image sample from the employed iris images and corresponding normalized enhanced image.

large-scale user identification and a highly suitable candidate for any multi-biometrics system. The literature on palm identification (Sun et al. 2005; Jain and Demirkus 2008; Zhang et al. 2003; Kumar 2008) has suggested reliable performance on the large databases. This has been the key motivation in selecting iris and palm modalities for dynamic security management. The database employed for the performance evaluation is publicly available on (IITD Iris Database) and (PolyU Palmprint Database), respectively. The IITD iris database (IITD Iris Database) consists of low-resolution 320 × 240 pixel iris images from 224 users. Therefore the first 224 palm images from the PolyU palm database were randomly paired and employed in this evaluation. The mutual independence of biometric modalities allows us to randomly augment these biometric modalities that are collected individually. The normalization, enhancement, and feature extraction steps on the iris images are the same as detailed in a paper by Kumar and Passi (2008). Figure 13.6 shows a sample of iris images along with the enhanced normalized image from the IITD database. The combination of log-Gabor and Haar wavelet filters, as detailed in the paper by Kumar and Passi (2008), was used to extract the features from each of the 48 × 432 pixels normalized iris images. The steps employed for the segmentation of palm images from the database images were similar, as detailed in a paper by Zhang et al. (2003). Figure 13.7 shows a sample of palm images and the corresponding normalized region of interest employed for the feature extraction. In this set of experiments, 35 × 35 ordinal mask with $\delta_x = 3, \delta_y = 10$ are employed to extract the ordinal features from every 128 × 128 pixel normalized palmprint image. Sun et al. (2005) provides further details of the feature extraction and matching criteria employed for the palm images.

The ROC curve corresponding to the iris and palm biometric samples evaluated in this set of experiments is shown in Figure 13.8. The dynamic selection score- and decision-level rules are shown in Fig 13.9. This selection is adaptive to the expected level of security desired from the system. The average of the minimum *weighted error rate*, achieved from the score-level–based adaptive

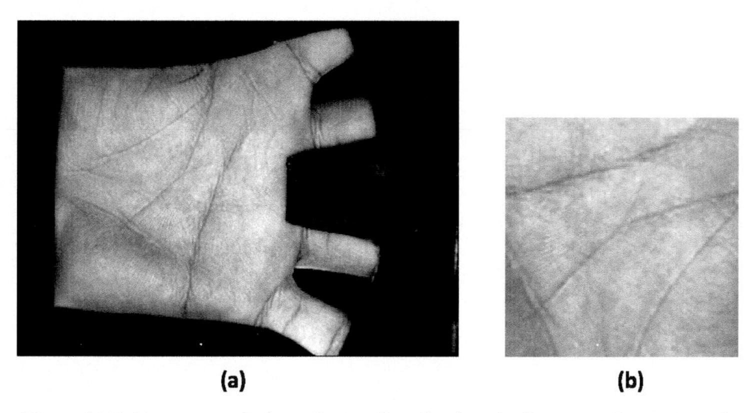


Figure 13.7. Image sample from the employed palmprint images and corresponding normalized enhanced.

combination scheme, for variation in the expected level of security is shown in Figure 13.10. This figure also includes the average of minimum error using the decision-level approach. The comparative results in Figure 13.10 suggests that the dynamic security framework using a score-level framework achieves a minimum average error for each of the chosen costs or desired security level, as compared with the decision-level approach in the paper by Veeramachaneni

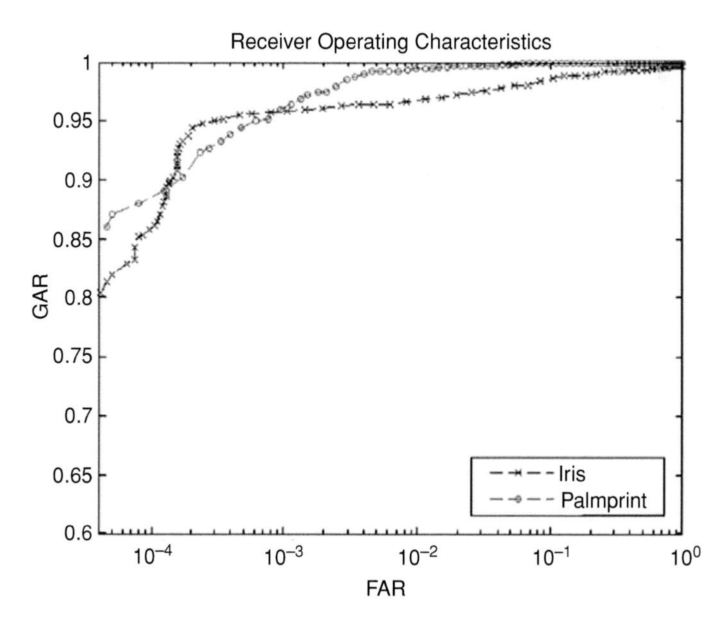


Figure 13.8. Receiver operating characteristics from the iris and palmprint matching scores.

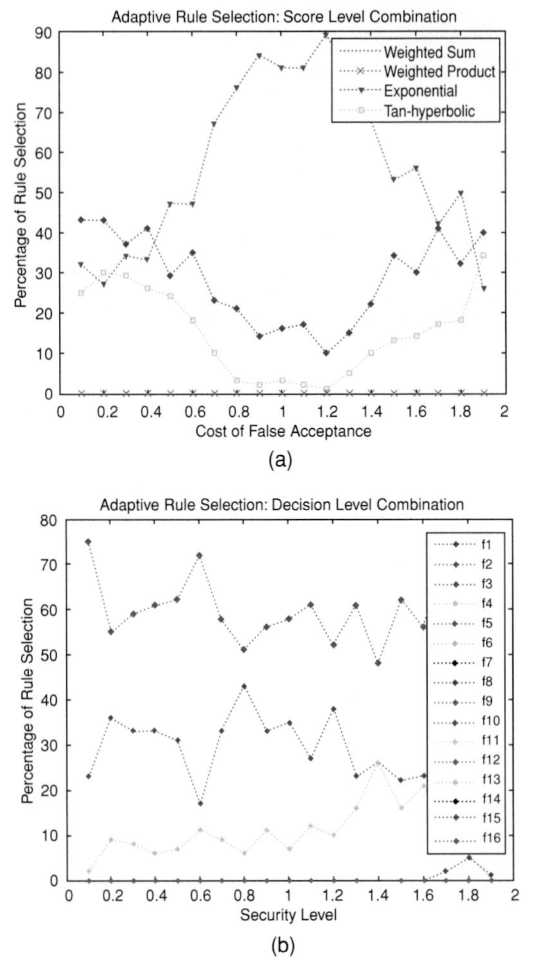


Figure 13.9. Adaptive selection of fusion rules using score-level combination (a) and decision-level combination (b).

et al. (2005). The summary of experimental evaluation using the iris and palm dataset again confirms the effectiveness and the advantages of dynamic security management.

## 13.7 Summary and Further Directions

The security level and the traffic flow offered by a multibiometrics system can be dynamically managed using adaptive combinations of matching scores. The framework illustrated in Figure 13.3 has been experimentally evaluated on real and simulated biometric data, some of which were discussed in section 6,

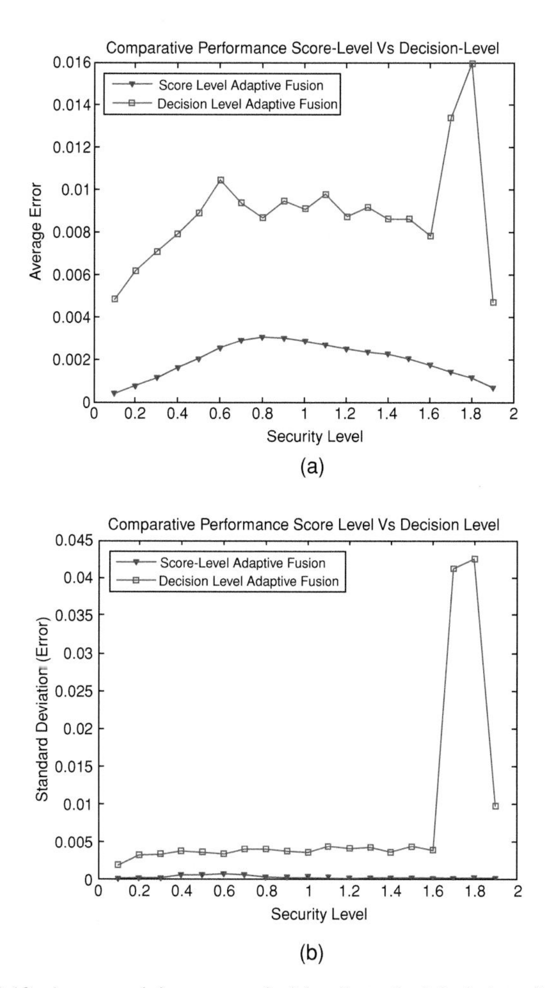


Figure 13.10. Average minimum error in (a) and standard deviation of minimum error in (b) from the score-level and decision-level approach using the adaptive combination of iris and palmprint modalities.

to ascertain their effectiveness. The experimental evaluations have consistently suggested the superiority of using such a score-level framework over the decision-level–based approach. The success of this new framework can be attributed to the usage of score-level combinations with accompanying nonlinearities, which helps to minimize the weighted sum of errors, and to the usage of PSO, which is employed in a rather hybrid configuration. The PSO is such a configuration that is required to optimize the selection of the score-level combination, its corresponding parameters/weights, and the decision threshold. This PSO shares the majority of the computational requirements of the dynamic multibiometrics system. However, all such computations with PSO can be performed offline and stored in a look-up table for the online access and usage. In this chapter the score-level framework suggested in Figure 13.3 has been evaluated on four score-level combinations (equation [13.5]). There could be several other score-level combination approaches that may perform better, that is, achieve minimum cost $E$ (equation [13.1]) and can be easily incorporated in the proposed framework. In this context, the likelihood-based score-level combination suggested in (Nandakumar et al. 2008) has shown promising results and could be a potential addition among the score-level fusion rules to be considered by PSO.

The dynamic security management using score-level combinations has been experimentally evaluated for the bimodal case, and further evaluations of large multibiometrics datasets are required. Another aspect of managing the dynamically changing security requirements is related to user preferences, constraints and limitations. Therefore further experimental evaluations are required to examine the possibility of employing the alternative biometric modalities, from a given set, while maintaining the desired level of security. A range of other open problems require the consideration of the user-specific, algorithm-specific, and sensor-specific biometric characteristics, for dynamically managing multibiometrics security. The management of dynamic security requirements using the framework discussed in this chapter offers a promising addition in the literature for further multibiometrics research. However, much more needs to be done before the deployment of multibiometrics systems that can dynamically ensure changing security requirements becomes a reality.

## References


Bradlow, E. T., and P. J. Everson. 2002. Bayesian inference for the beta-binomial distribution via polynomial expansions, *J. Comput. & Graphical Statistics,* **11**(1), 200–207.

Clerc, M., and J. Kennedy. 2002. The particle swarm-explosion, stability, and convergence in a multidimensional somplex space, *IEEE Trans. Evolutionary Comp.*, **6**, 58–73.

Daugman, J. 2006. Probing the uniqueness and randomness of IrisCodes: results from 200 billion iris pair comparisons, *Proc. IEEE,* **94**(11), 1927–1935.

Frischholz, R. W., and U. Deickmann. 2000. BioID: a multimodal biometric identification system, *IEEE Comput.,* **33**(2).

http://www.dhs.gov/xlibrary/assets/CitizenGuidanceHSAS2.pdf.

IITD Iris Database, http://web.iitd.ac.in/∼ .biometrics/Database_Iris.htm.

Jain, A. K., A. Ross, and S. Pankanti. 2004. An introduction to biometric recognition, *IEEE Trans. Circuits & Sys. Video Tech.*, **14**(1), 4–20.

Jain, A. K., and M. Demirkus. 2008. On latent palmprint matching, MSU Technical Report.

Kanhangad, V., A. Kumar, and D. Zhang. 2008. Comments on 'an adaptive multimodal biometric management algorithm, *IEEE Trans. Sys. Man & Cybern., Part-C*, **38**(5), 438–440.

Kittler, J., M. Hatef, R. P. W. Duin, and J. Matas. 1998. On combining classifiers, *IEEE Trans. Patt. Anal. Machine Intell.*, **20**, 226–239.

Kumar, A. 2008. Incorporating cohort information for reliable palmprint authentication, *Proc. 6th Indian Conf. Computer Vision, Graphics, and Image Processing*, Bhubaneswar, India, pp. 583–590.

Kumar, A., and A. Passi. 2008. Comparison and combination of iris matchers for reliable personal identification, *Proc. CVPR 2008*, pp. 21–27, Anchorage, Alaska.

Kumar, A., and D. Zhang. 2008. Incorporating user quality for performance improvement in hand identification, *Proc. ICARCV 2008*, Hanoi, pp. 1133–1136.

Nandakumar, K., Y. Chen, S. C. Dass, and A. K. Jain. 2008. Likelihood ratio based biometric score fusion, *IEEE Trans. Patt. Anal. Machine Intell.*, **30**(2), 342–347.

NIST BSSR1 biometric score set, http://www.nist.gov/biometricscores.

The PolyU Palmprint Database (version 2.0); http://www.comp.polyu.edu.hk/ ~ biometrics.

Poh, N., R. Wong, J. Kittler, and F. Roli. 2009. Challenges and research directions for adaptive biometric recognition systems, *Proc. ICB*, Alghero, Italy.

Roli, F., S. Raudys, and G. L. Marcialis. 2002. An experimental comparison of fixed and trained fusion rules for crisp classifier outputs, *3rd Intl. Workshop on Multiple Classifier Systems*, MCS 2002, Cagliari (Italy), Springer.

Ross, A., K. Nandakumar, and A. K. Jain. 2006. *Handbook of Multibiometrics*. Springer.

Sim, T., S. Zhang, R. Janakiraman, and S. Kumar. 2007. Continuous verification using multimodal biometrics, *IEEE Trans. Patt. Anal. Machine Intell.*, **29**(4), 687–700.

Sun, Z., T. Tan, Y. Yang, and S. Z. Li. 2005. Ordinal palmprint representation for personal identification, *Proc. CVPR 2005*, pp. 279–284.

Tax, D. M. J., M. V. Breukelen, R. P. W. Duin, and J. Kittler. 2000. Combining multiple classifiers by averaging or multiplying, *Pattern Recognition*, **33**, 1475–1485.

Tronci, R., G. Giacinto, and F. Roli. 2007. Dynamic score selection for fusion of multiple biometric matchers, *Proc. 14th IEEE International Conference on Image Analysis and Processing*, ICIAP 2007, Modena, Italy, pp. 15–20.

Tulyakov, S., and V. Govindaraju. 2007. Use of identification trial statistics for combination of biometric matchers, *IEEE Trans. Info. Security Forensics*, **3**(4), 719–733.

Veeramachaneni, K., L. A. Osadciw, and P. K. Varshney. 2005. An adaptive multimodal biometric management algorithm, *IEEE Trans. Sys. Man & Cybern., Part-C*, **35**(3), 344–356.

Zhang, D., W. K. Kong, J. You, and M. Wong. 2003. On-line palmprint identification, *IEEE Trans. Patt. Anal. Machine Intell.*, **25**, 1041–1050.

# PART V

# Performance of Multibiometric Systems

# 14

# Prediction for Fusion of Biometrics Systems

Rong Wang and Bir Bhanu

## 14.1 Introduction

To increase the accuracy of an individual human recognition, sensor fusion techniques (Bhanu and Govindaraju 2009; Kuncheva 2006; Ross et al. 2004) for multimodal biometrics systems are widely used today. For example, for a biometrics system, one can combine a face recognition system and a fingerprint recognition system to perform better human recognition. By fusing different biometrics, we may achieve the following benefits with the availability of more meaningful information: improved recognition/identification; reduction of false alarm, and broadening the range of populations for which the fused system will function satisfactorily.

There are four levels of fusion possibilities in a multimodal biometrics system (Waltz and Llinas 1990; Hall and Llinas 2001): data level, feature level, score level, and decision level. Data-level fusion is the combination of unprocessed data to produce new data expected to be more informative and synthetic than the single biometric data (Borghys et al. 1998). This kind of fusion requires a pixel-level registration of the raw images. When the sensors are alike, we can consider all data at the data-level fusion, but it is more complicated when several different sensors are used because of the problems associated with resolution, registration, etc. (Han and Bhanu 2007; Nadimi and Bhanu 2004). Feature level is believed to be promising because feature sets can provide more information about the input biometrics than other levels (Ross and Jain 2004). However, sometimes different feature sets are in conflict and may not be available, which makes the feature-level fusion more challenging than other levels of fusion (Ross and Govindarajan 2005; Zhou and Bhanu 2008). Fusion at the score level is widely used because match scores and nonmatch scores from different biometrics can be normalized and combined by different score-level techniques (Shakhnarovich and Darrell 2002). These techniques include product of likelihood ratios, logistic regression, simple sum of normalized scores (Kale et al. 2004), maximum of the normalized scores, and weighted sum of normalized scores (Ulery et al. 2006), etc. Decision-level fusion combines decisions of different classifiers or experts. Decision fusion methods include the the statistical method, voting method, fuzzy logic–based method, etc. (Dasarthy 1994).

Given the characteristics of individual biometrics (e.g., face, fingerprint, ear, voice, gait), how can we find the optimal combination that gives the best recognition performance? The traditional approach is to try all the possible combinations by performing exhaustive experiments to determine the optimal combination. This brute-force approach could be very time consuming. In this chapter we present two theoretical approaches to predict the fusion performance that allows us to select the optimal combination of biometrics.

The first approach develops a prediction model based on the $\Phi$ transformation. Given the characteristics of each biometrics, we compute the match-score and non–match-score distributions, which are modeled as a mixture of Gaussians. Based on this assumption, we decompose the *area under the ROC curve (AUROC)* of the fusion system to a set of *AUROCs* that is obtained from the combinations of the components from the match-non–match-score distribution. The modeling of the score distributions as a mixture of Gaussians is more consistent with the real data than a single Gaussian assumption. We use an explicit $\Phi$ transformation that maps a *ROC* curve to a straight line in 2D space whose axes are related to the false alarm rate and the correct recognition rate. Finally, using this representation, we derive a metric to evaluate the sensor fusion performance and find the optimal sensor combination.

The second approach develops a prediction model based on the Neyman-Pearson theory. Like the first approach, we use match-non–match-score distributions, which are modeled as a mixture of Gaussians. Then we get the likelihood ratio of each sensor/biometric. Finally, we use a measurement that considers not only the mean and variance but also the skewness of the log-likelihood ratio of the fusion system as the discriminability measurement to evaluate the performance of the system. Unlike the traditional application of the Neyman-Pearson theory in the classification field, we apply this theory in the performance prediction of the fused sensor system to find the optimal sensor fusion combination.

The chapter is organized as follows. The related work and the contributions of this chapter are presented in Section 14.2. The two prediction models are presented in Section III. This section includes the decomposition of the *AUROC* for the Gaussian mixture model, $\Phi$ transformation that maps a *ROC* curve to a straight line in the 2D space, and the metric used to estimate the fusion system performance. Further, it includes the Neyman-Pearson theory, mean, variance, and skewness of the fusion system, and the discriminability measurement used to predict the performance of biometrics fusion. Experimental results, which verify the two prediction approaches on the publicly available XM2VTS database, and a mixed database (fingerprint, ear, and video databases [face and gait]), are described in Section IV. The performance comparison of the two approaches on the XM2VTS database is shown in this section. Finally, the conclusions are presented in Section V.

## 14.2 Related Work and Contributions

### 14.2.1 Related Work

A variety of methods for the fusion of multibiometrics have been reported in the literature (Bhanu and Govindaraju 2009; Ross et al. 2004). Kittler et al. (1998) develop a theoretical framework for fusing the decision of multiple sensors. Using the Bayesian theory, for different assumptions, the recognition problem is expressed as the product rule or the sum rule, which constitute the core of the sensor fusion strategies. They prove that many commonly used combination rules such as the min rule, max rule, median rule, and majority vote rule can be developed from the basic (product and sum) decision rules. Verlinde et al. (2000) compare a large number of fusion algorithms for the decision-level fusion in the multimodal biometric verification systems. They consider parametric and nonparametric techniques for the fusion of the binary decisions. Jain et al. (2005) applied different normalization techniques and fusion rules to fingerprint, face, and hand geometry biometrics. They showed that the min-max, $z$-score, and tanh normalization methods followed by the sum fusion rule have better performance than other normalization methods and fusion rules. More research on the biometric fusion methods can be found in Ben-Yacoub (1998), Giacinto and Roli (2001), Griffin (2004), and Varshney (1997).

Keller et al. (2001) analyze sensor fusion by using the fuzzy set theory at the decision level. They use the *d-metric*, which is the ratio of the probability of detection to the probability of false alarm to predict the sensor fusion performance. Daugman (2000) discusses the sensor fusion at the decision level. He gives the probability of a false alarm under the disjunction rule and the probability of a false reject under the conjunction rule. He concludes that a strong sensor is better to be used alone than in combination with a weaker one. Poh and Bengio (2004; 2005) propose a measurement F-ratio that is related to the *Equal Error Rate* (*EER*) to find the optimal fusion candidate under the assumption that the match/non-match score have a single Gaussian distribution. They verify their approach on the BANCA multimodal database. Wang and

Table 14.1. *Approaches for the Choice of Sensor Fusion Combinations*

| Authors | Approach | Comments |
|---|---|---|
| Daugman (2000) | Provide the probability of false alarm and false reject under the conjunction rule and disjunction rule based on the statistical decision theory | Decision-level fusion |
| Keller et al. (2001) | Derive a metrics based on the fuzzy theory. | Decision-level fusion |
| Poh and Bengio (2004) | Derive $F$-ratio metrics based on the statistical approach | Score-level, single Gaussian distribution assumption |
| Wang and Bhanu (2006) | Derive a Fisher measurement for the sensor fusion system | Score-level, single Gaussian distribution assumption |
| This chapter | Two approaches:<br>• Derive a set of metrics based on $\Phi$ transformation and *ROC* curve decomposition<br>• Derive a measurement that considers mean, variance, and skewness of log-likelihood ratio of the fusion system | Score-level, Gaussian mixture model assumption |

Bhanu (2006) present a prediction model that is based on the likelihood ratio. They derive the Fisher measurement for the sensor fusion system to predict its performance. In their approach, they model the match/non-match score as single Gaussian distributions. Table 14.1 provides a summary of the above methods and compares them with the proposed approaches in this chapter.

### 14.2.2 Contributions

The specific contributions of this chapter are the following:

(1) We present two approaches for predicting performance of biometrics fusion. These approaches are based on the score-level fusion. We model match-non–match-score distributions as mixtures of Gaussians. This assumption is shown to be more appropriate for the real-world data than a single Gaussian.

(2) In the $\Phi$ transformation-based prediction approach, we decompose the *AUROC* of the fusion system to a set of *AUROCs* that is obtained from the combinations of the components from the match-score and the non–match-score distribution. Because *AUROC* can be used to evaluate the recognition system performance and is not easy to compute it analytically, we use an explicit $\Phi$ transformation that maps a *ROC* curve to a straight line in the 2D space whose axes are related to the false alarm rate and the correct recognition rate. We derive a metric to evaluate the sensor fusion performance and find the optimal biometrics combination.
(3) In the Neyman-Pearson theory–based prediction approach, we use the theory in a novel manner to predict the sensor fusion performance. We compute the log-likelihood ratio for each sensor. Then we develop a measurement that considers not only the mean and variance (Wang and Bhanu 2006) but also the skewness of the log-likelihood ratio of the similarity scores of the fusion system. We use this measurement to predict the fusion system performance. By using this prediction model, we can find the optimal fusion combination instead of doing the brute-force experiments.
(4) We verify our prediction approaches on the publicly available XM2VTS database, a mixed database that consists of NIST-4 fingerprint database, and our 3D ear and video (face and gait) databases. We compare performances of the proposed two approaches on the XM2VTS database.

## 14.3 Performance Prediction Models

### 14.3.1 Performance Measurements

There are two classes in an object recognition system: match and non-match. A similarity score is used to evaluate the similarity between the two objects (training and test samples). When the two sample objects are the instances of the same object, then the similarity score is called a *match score*. When the two sample objects are from different objects, then the similarity score is called a *non-match score*. We denote $f(x)$ as the match score distribution, and $g(x)$ as the non–match-score distribution (see Figure 14.1) In this chapter we assume that higher the similarity score, the better is the match between the stored (training) object and a test object.

Given a similarity score criterion $k$ as shown in Figure 14.1, we have four measures of probabilities:

- False Alarm Rate (*FAR*): The probability that the non-match scores exceed the threshold $k$. *FAR* can be expressed as $FAR(k) = \int_k^\infty g(x)dx$.
- Correct Reject Rate (*CRR*): the probability that the non-match scores fall below the threshold $k$. *CRR* can be expressed as $CRR(k) = \int_{-\infty}^k g(x)dx$.

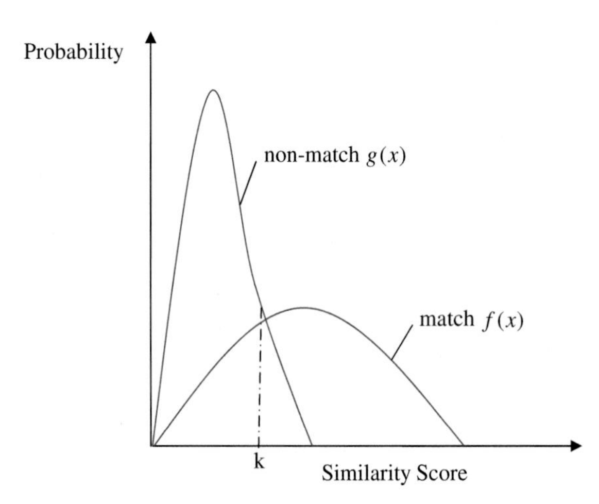


Figure 14.1. The match-score and the non–match-score distributions.

- Correct Accept Rate (*Hit*): the probability that the match scores exceed the threshold $k$. *Hit* can be expressed as $Hit(k) = \int_k^\infty f(x)dx$.
- False Reject Rate (*FRR*): the probability that the match scores fall below the threshold $k$. *FRR* can be expressed as $FRR(k) = \int_{-\infty}^k f(x)dx$.

According to the definitions of these four probabilities, for a criterion $k$, we have $FAR(k) + CRR(k) = 1$ and $FRR(k) + Hit(k) = 1$.

The *FAR* and the *Hit* have the same decision region. Thus, it is not possible to increase the *Hit* and decrease the *FAR* at the same time. There is a tradeoff between these two probabilities. Note that the *FAR* and the *Hit* are functions of the criterion $k$. The variations of *FAR* and *Hit* with different criterion $k$ can be expressed by the *Receiver Operating Characteristic* (*ROC*) curve. It is a graphic plot whose $x$-axis is the *FAR* and the $y$-axis is the *Hit* (Marzban 2004). The *ROC* curve is used to evaluate the performance of a recognition system because it represents the changes in *FAR* and *Hit* with different discrimination criteria (thresholds). Given a match score $k$, the *Probability of Correct Identification* (*PCI*) is computed by

$$\begin{aligned} PCI &= P[f(x=k)] \cdot P[g(x<k)] \\ &= \int_{-\infty}^{\infty} f(k) \cdot \left[1 - \int_k^\infty g(t)dt\right] dk \\ &= \int_{-\infty}^{\infty} f(k) \cdot [1 - FAR(k)]dk \\ &= \int_0^1 [1 - FAR(k)]d\,Hit(k). \end{aligned} \tag{14.1}$$

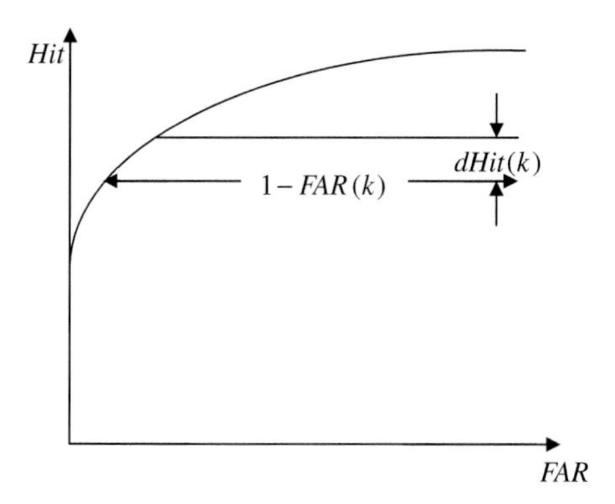


Figure 14.2. An example of the *ROC* curve.

Figure 14.2 is an example of the *ROC* curve. From Figure 14.2, we conclude that the area under the *ROC* curve is equal to the *PCI* (Green and Swets 1966).

The performance of an object recognition system can be evaluated by the *Equal Error Rate* (*ERR*) where the *FAR* equals to the *FRR*. The positions of the *EER* on a *ROC* curve is shown in Figure 3. In general, if the value of the *ERR* is lower, then the performance is better. Since the *FAR* and the *FRR* are functions of criterion $k$, we can find

$$k^* = \underset{k}{\text{argmin}} \, |FAR(k) - FRR(k)| \,. \tag{14.2}$$

The *Half Total Error Rate* (*HTER*), which is defined as

$$HTER = \frac{FAR(k^*) + FRR(k^*)}{2}, \tag{14.3}$$

can be used to evaluate the system performance. The lower the *HTER* value, the higher the recognition accuracy of the system.

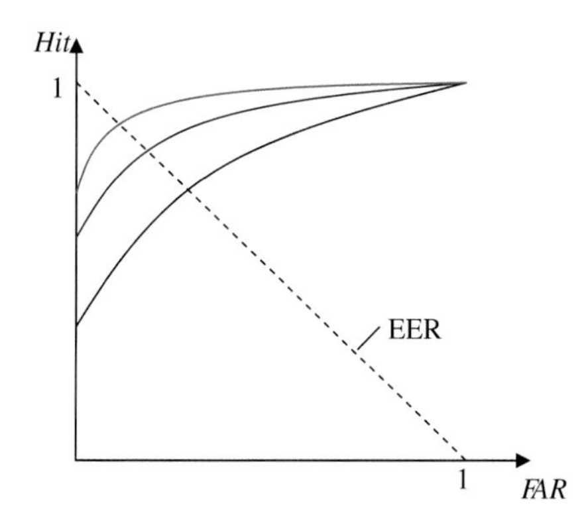


Figure 14.3. Equal error rate positions on the *ROC* curve.

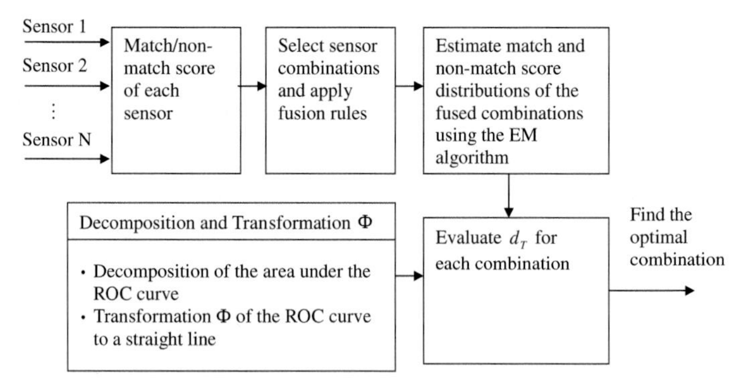


Figure 14.4. Diagram of the prediction model based on Φ transformation.

## 14.3.2 Prediction Model Based on the Φ Transformation

Given $N$ sensors or biometrics, the procedure for the performance prediction is shown in Figure 14.4.

### 14.3.2.1 Decomposition of the Area under the *ROC* Curve

We assume that the match score distribution $f(x)$ and the non–match-score distribution $g(x)$ are mixtures of Gaussian with $m$ and $n$ components, respectively. Then we have

$$f(x) = \sum_{i=1}^{m} \alpha_i f_i(x), \quad \text{and} \quad g(x) = \sum_{j=1}^{n} \beta_j g_j(x), \tag{14.4}$$

where $\alpha_i, \beta_j$ are component proportions such that $\sum_{i=1}^{m} \alpha_i = 1$ and $\sum_{j=1}^{n} \beta_j = 1$. For each component, we have $f_i(x) \sim N(m_{s_i}, \delta_{s_i}^2)$ and $g_j(x) \sim N(m_{n_j}, \delta_{n_j}^2)$, where $m_{s_i}$ and $\delta_{s_i}$ are the mean and standard deviation of the $i$th component of the match-score distribution, and $m_{n_j}$ and $\delta_{n_j}$ are mean and standard deviation of the $j$th component of the non–match-score distribution. For the criterion $k$, the *FAR* for the Gaussian mixture models is,

$$FAR(k) = \int_k^{\infty} \sum_{j=1}^{n} \beta_j g_j(x)dx = \sum_{j=1}^{n} \int_k^{\infty} \beta_j g_j(x)dx = \sum_{j=1}^{n} \beta_j FAR_j(k). \tag{14.5}$$

The *Hit* for the Gaussian mixture models is

$$Hit(k) = \int_k^{\infty} \sum_{i=1}^{m} \alpha_i f_i(x)dx = \sum_{i=1}^{m} \int_k^{\infty} \alpha_i f_i(x)dx = \sum_{i=1}^{m} \alpha_i Hit_i(k), \tag{14.6}$$

where $FAR_j(k) = \int_k^{\infty} \beta_j g_j(x)dx$ and $Hit_i(k) = \int_k^{\infty} \alpha_i f_i(x)dx$.

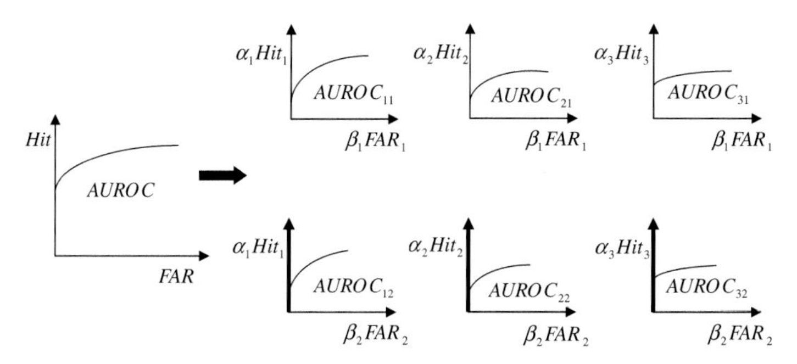


Figure 14.5. Decomposition of the area under the *ROC* curve for the Gaussian mixture distribution.

After simplifying the notations in equation (14.1) and using equations (14.5) and (14.6), we have

$$\begin{aligned} AUROC &= \int_0^1 (1 - FAR(k))d\,Hit(k) \\ &= \int_0^1 \left(1 - \sum_{j=1}^{n} \beta_j FAR_j(k)\right) d\left(\sum_{i=1}^{m} \alpha_i Hit_i(k)\right) \\ &= \sum_{i=1}^{m}\sum_{j=1}^{n} \int_0^1 (1 - \beta_j FAR_j(k))d(\alpha_i Hit_i(k)) - \sum_{i=1}^{m} \int_0^1 \alpha_i d(Hit_i(k)) \\ &= \sum_{i=1}^{m}\sum_{j=1}^{n} AUROC_{ij} - 1, \end{aligned} \tag{14.7}$$

where

$$AUROC_{ij} = \int_0^1 (1 - \beta_j FAR_j(k))d(\alpha_i Hit_i(k)). \tag{14.8}$$

For example, if $m = 3$, $n = 2$, then the *AUROC* curve can be decomposed as the sum of six *AUROC* curves whose axes are the component combinations of the match score distribution and the non–match-score distribution. Figure 14.5 shows this decomposition of the area under the *ROC* curve for Gaussian mixtures. We can see that the *AUROC* whose axes are *FAR* and *Hit* can be decomposed as $AUROC_{11}$, $AUROC_{21}$, $AUROC_{31}$, $AUROC_{12}$, $AUROC_{22}$, and $AUROC_{32}$ whose axes are $\beta_1 FA_1$ and $\alpha_1 Hit_1$, $\beta_1 FAR_1$ and $\alpha_2 Hit_2$, $\beta_1 FAR_1$ and $\alpha_3 Hit_3$, $\beta_2 FAR_2$ and $\alpha_1 Hit_1$, $\beta_2 FAR_2$ and $\alpha_2 Hit_2$, $\beta_2 FAR_2$ and $\alpha_3 Hit_3$. At the same time, we should minus the overlap $\sum_{i=1}^{3} \int_0^1 \alpha_i d(Hit_i)$, which are the bold parts in Figure 14.5.

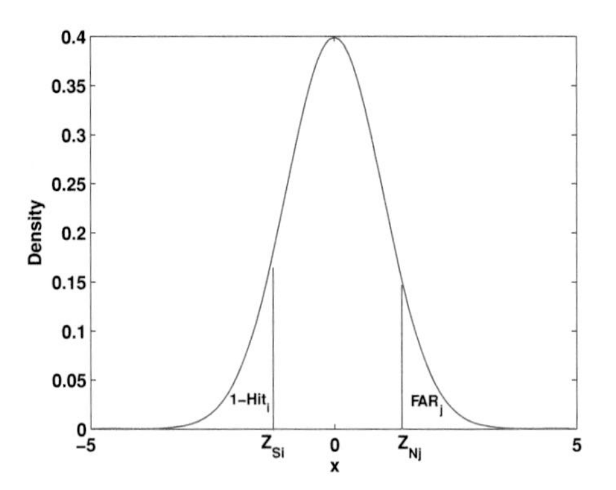


Figure 14.6. Standard normal distribution.

#### 14.3.2.2 Fusion Prediction

In the previous section, we proved that *AUROC* can be used to evaluate the recognition system performance. Both parametric and nonparametric approaches can be used to estimate the *AUROC* (Dorfman and Alf 1969; Yousef et al. 2006; Ataman et al. 2006; Yan et al. 2003; Cortes and Mohri 2004). Instead of estimating the *AUROC* directly, we propose using a transformation to map a *ROC* curve into a 2D straight line whose axes are related with the *FAR* and *Hit* (Wang and Bhanu 2007). We consider $AUROC_{ij}$ whose axes are $\beta_j FAR_j$ and $\alpha_i Hit_i$. We know that

$$\beta_j FAR_j(k) = \beta_j \int_k^{\infty} \frac{1}{\sqrt{2\pi\delta_{n_j}^2}} \exp\left[-\frac{(x-m_{n_j})^2}{2\delta_{n_j}^2}\right] dx = \beta_j \Phi\left(\frac{k-m_{n_j}}{\delta_{n_j}}\right), \tag{14.9}$$

$$\alpha_i Hit_i(k) = \alpha_i \int_k^{\infty} \frac{1}{\sqrt{2\pi\delta_{s_i}^2}} \exp\left[-\frac{(x-m_{s_i})^2}{2\delta_{s_i}^2}\right] dx = \alpha_i \Phi\left(\frac{k-m_{s_i}}{\delta_{s_i}}\right), \tag{14.10}$$

where $\Phi$ is an integral of the standard normal distribution with zero mean and unit variance. Figure 14.6 shows a standard normal distribution. $\Phi$ is defined as $\Phi(t) = \int_t^{\infty} \frac{1}{\sqrt{2\pi}} \exp(-\frac{x^2}{2})dx$.

We denote

$$Z_{Nj} = \frac{k-m_{n_j}}{\delta_{n_j}}, \tag{14.11}$$

$$Z_{Si} = \frac{k-m_{s_i}}{\delta_{s_i}}. \tag{14.12}$$

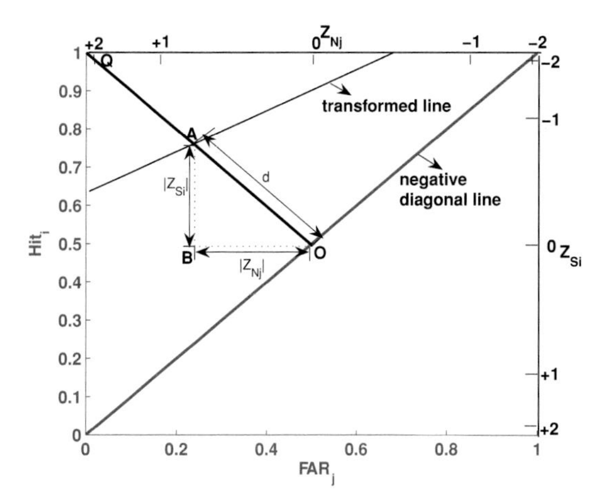


Figure 14.7. Transformation of the *ROC* curve to a 2D straight line.

Then, equation (14.9) and equation (14.10), can be written as

$$\beta_j FAR_j(k) = \beta_j \Phi(Z_{Nj}), \tag{14.13}$$

$$\alpha_i Hit_i(k) = \alpha_i \Phi(Z_{Si}). \tag{14.14}$$

In Figure 14.6, the area beyond $Z_{Nj}$ is $FAR_j$ and the area below $Z_{Si}$ is $1 - Hit_i$. According to equations (14.11) and (14.12), we can get the linear relationship between $\beta_j Z_{Nj}$ and $\alpha_i Z_{Si}$:

$$\alpha_i \cdot Z_{Si} = \frac{\alpha_i}{\beta_j} \cdot \frac{\delta_{n_j}}{\delta_{s_i}}(\beta_j \cdot Z_{Nj}) + \alpha_i \cdot \frac{m_{nj} - m_{si}}{\delta_{s_i}} \tag{14.15}$$

Thus, the *ROC* curve is transformed to a 2D straight line whose $x$-axis is $\beta_j Z_{Nj}$, $y$-axis is $\alpha_i Z_{Si}$, slope is $\frac{\alpha_i \delta_{n_j}}{\beta_j \delta_{s_i}}$, and $y$-intercept is $\alpha_i \cdot \frac{m_{nj} - m_{si}}{\delta_{s_i}}$. Figure 14.7 shows the transformation of the *ROC* curve to a 2-D straight line. In this figure, the left and bottom axes are the $Hit_i$ and $FAR_j$, and the top and right axes are $Z_{Nj}$ and $Z_{Si}$. According to Figure 14.6, when the $Hit_i$ is 0.5, then $Z_{Si} = 0$. There we find the same relationship between the $FAR_j$ and $Z_{Si}$.

In Figure 14.7, we connect the points where the $FAR_j$ is equal to the $Hit_i$ and get a line called a negative diagonal line. The points on the negative diagonal line have the property of $Z_{Nj} = Z_{Si}$. Then we connect the point $Q$ where $Hit_i$ is 1 and $FAR_j$ is 0 and the point $O$ where $Hit_i$ is 0.5 and $FAR_j$ is 0.5. Line $QO$ is called the diagonal line. The points on the diagonal line have the property of $Z_{Nj} = -Z_{Si}$. Assume that the intersection point of the transformed line and the line $QO$ is $A$. Then $|AB| = |Z_{Si}|$, $|OB| = |Z_{Nj}|$, $d = |OA| = \sqrt{2}|Z_{Nj}|$. We know that the points on the line $QO$ have the property of $Z_{Nj} = -Z_{Si}$, then $d = \frac{\sqrt{2}}{2}|Z_{Nj} - Z_{Si}|$. If the point $A$ is closer to the point $Q$, then $|Z_{Nj}|$ is increased and $|Z_{Si}|$ is decreased. From Figure 14.6, we can see that if $|Z_{Nj}|$ is increased, then the $FAR_j$ is decreased, and if $|Z_{Si}|$ is increased, then the $Hit_i$ is increased. That means if the point $A$ is closer to the point $Q$, that is, the distance $d$ is larger, then the area under the *ROC* is greater. Thus, we use $\Delta Z = Z_{Nj} - Z_{Si}$ to represent the relationship between $FAR_j$ and $Hit_i$. For the same reason, the relationship between $\beta_j FAR_j$ and $\alpha_i Hit_i$ can be represented by $\beta_j Z_{Nj} - \alpha_i Z_{Si}$, which is proportional to the $AUROC_{ij}$.

Thus, the $AUROC_{ij}$ can be evaluated in the transformed 2D space, which is much easier to handle. The transformed area into distance $d_{ij}$ can be measured as

$$d_{ij} = \beta_j Z_{Nj} - \alpha_i Z_{Si}. \tag{14.16}$$

It is proportional to the $AUROC_{ij}$.

From equations (14.11) and (14.12), when $Z_{Nj} = -Z_{Si}$, that is, the *FAR* is equal to the *FRR*, the specific value of $k$ is $k^* = \frac{\delta_{s_i} m_{nj} + \delta_{n_j} m_{si}}{\delta_{s_i} + \delta_{n_j}}$ can be obtained. Now substituting the value of $k = k^*$ into equation (14.16) and using equations (14.11) and (14.12), we have

$$d_{ij} = (\alpha_i + \beta_j)\frac{m_{si} - m_{nj}}{\delta_{s_i} + \delta_{n_j}}. \tag{14.17}$$

Thus, according to equation (14.7) (and ignoring $-1$), the *AUROC* can be evaluated by a fusion metric:

$$d_T = \sum_{i=1}^{m}\sum_{j=1}^{n} d_{ij} = \sum_{i=1}^{m}\sum_{j=1}^{n}(\alpha_i + \beta_j)\frac{m_{si} - m_{nj}}{\delta_{s_i} + \delta_{n_j}}. \tag{14.18}$$

Equation (14.18) can be used to evaluate the sensor fusion system performance instead of performing the exhaustive experiments to determine the optimal sensor combination. In this prediction approach, we apply a $\Phi$ transformation, which maps a *ROC* curve to a straight line in the 2D space where the *AUROC* can be evaluated by the distance in the 2D space.

#### 14.3.2.3 Summary

We summarize our prediction approach based on $\Phi$ transformation in the following:

(1) For each sensor system, we normalize the match scores and the non-match scores so as to get the normalized $f(x)$ and $g(x)$.
(2) We randomly pick a number of sensors/biometrics and combine them by different fusion rules such as sum rule, product rule, etc.

(3) For each combination, we apply the expectation-maximization (EM) algorithm to estimate the distributions of the match score and the non-match score. Thus, we get the number of components and the proportion of each component, its mean, and variance.
(4) For each of the sensor combination, we use equation (14.18) to compute $d_T$, which is used to predict the fusion system performance.
(5) We sort $d_T$ values in the decreasing order and find the optimal sensor combination corresponding to the highest value of $d_T$.

### 14.3.3 Prediction Model Based on the Neyman-Pearson Theory

We know that there is a tradeoff between the *FAR* and *Hit*. The Neyman-Pearson criterion states that we should construct the decision rule that allows the maximum *Hit* while the *FAR* does not exceed a certain value $\alpha$. We can use the likelihood ratio $l(x)$, where $l(x) = \frac{f(x)}{g(x)}$, to express the Neyman-Pearson theory:

$$l(x) = \frac{f(x)}{g(x)} \geq \gamma, \mathit{FAR} = \int_k^\infty g(x)dx = \alpha, \quad 0 \leq \alpha \leq 1, \qquad (14.19)$$

where $\gamma$ is the criterion of the likelihood ratio. We can see that the likelihood ratio does not depend on the a priori probabilities of match and non-match. It depends on the distributions of match score and non-match score and the constant value $\alpha$.

#### 14.3.3.1 Prediction Model for Fusion

Assume that we have $q$ independent sensors/biometrics, $x_1, x_2, \ldots, x_q$, where each biometrics represents an independent recognition system. Let their match-score distributions be $f_1(x)$, $f_2(x)$, $\ldots$, $f_q(x)$ and non–match-score distributions be $g_1(x)$, $g_2(x)$, $\ldots$, $g_q(x)$. If we fuse these $q$ biometrics, then the likelihood ratio of the fusion system is $l(x_1, x_2, \ldots, x_q)$. Because these biometrics are independent, then we have $l(x_1, x_2, \ldots, x_q) = l(x_1) \ldots l(x_q)$. According to the Neyman-Pearson theory, the performance of the fusion system can be expressed as the likelihood ratio that is equal to or greater than a threshold $\gamma$, that is, $l(x_1) \ldots l(x_q) \geq \gamma$. Taking the natural logarithm for both sides, we get

$$\textstyle\sum_{i=1}^{q} \ln l(x_i) \geq \ln \gamma, \qquad (14.20)$$

where $\ln l(x_i) = \ln \frac{f_i(x)}{g_i(x)}$.

We observe that the distribution of $\sum_{i=1}^{q} \ln l(x_i)$ depends on the distributions of match score and non-match score of the biometrics $x_1, x_2, \ldots, x_q$. We assume that the distributions of the match score and non-match score are mixtures of Gaussian, then for biometrics $i$, where $i = 1, 2, \ldots, q$, we have

$$f_i(x) = \sum_{j=1}^{s_i} \alpha_{ij} f_{ij}(x) \tag{14.21}$$

and

$$g_i(x) = \sum_{t=1}^{n_i} \beta_{it} g_{it}(x), \tag{14.22}$$

where $s_i$ and $n_i$ are the number components. For different sensors, the component numbers may be different. Here $\alpha_{ij}$, $\beta_{it}$ are component proportions such that, $\sum_{j=1}^{s_i} \alpha_{ij} = 1$ and $\sum_{t=1}^{n_i} \beta_{it} = 1$. For each component, we have $f_{ij}(x) \sim N(m_{s_{ij}}, \delta_{s_{ij}}^2)$ and $g_{it}(x) \sim N(m_{n_{it}}, \delta_{n_{it}}^2)$, where $m_{s_{ij}}$ and $\delta_{s_{ij}}$ are the mean and standard deviation for the match-score distribution of sensor $i$. Similarly, $m_{n_{it}}$ and $\delta_{n_{it}}$ are the mean and standard deviation for the non–match-score distribution of sensor $i$. We use the EM algorithm to estimate the match-score distribution and the non–match-score distribution.

After we get the distributions of the match score and the non-match score for the biometric $i$, we can compute the log-likelihood ratio of biometric $i$, where

$$\ln l(x_i) = \ln \frac{f_i(x)}{g_i(x)} = \ln \frac{\sum_{j=1}^{s_i} \alpha_{ij} f_{ij}(x)}{\sum_{t=1}^{n_i} \beta_{it} g_{it}(x)}. \tag{14.23}$$

Because these biometrics are independent, then we have

$$\sum_{i=1}^{q} \ln l(x_i) = \ln \frac{\sum_{j=1}^{s_1} \alpha_{1j} f_{1j}(x)}{\sum_{t=1}^{n_1} \beta_{1t} g_{1t}(x)} + \cdots + \ln \frac{\sum_{j=1}^{s_q} \alpha_{qj} f_{qj}(x)}{\sum_{t=1}^{n_q} \beta_{qt} g_{qt}(x)}. \tag{14.24}$$

Now we compute the mean, variance, and skewness for $\sum_{i=1}^{q} \ln l(x_i)$. If the hypothesis *non-match* is true, then the mean of $\sum_{i=1}^{q} \ln l(x_i)$ is

$$\mu_n = E\left(\sum_{i=1}^{q} \ln l(x_i)\right) = \sum_{i=1}^{q} \int_{-\infty}^{\infty} (\ln l(x_i)) g_i(x) dx, \tag{14.25}$$

where $\ln l(x_i)$ is obtained from equation (14.23), and $g_i(x)$ can be estimated by the EM algorithm.

The variance of $\sum_{i=1}^{q} \ln l(x_i)$ is

$$\sigma_n^2 = E\left[\left(\sum_{i=1}^{q} \ln l(x_i)\right)^2\right] - \mu_n^2 = \sum_{i=1}^{q} \int_{-\infty}^{\infty} (\ln l(x_i))^2 g_i(x) dx - \mu_n^2. \tag{14.26}$$

We can get $(\ln l(x_i))^2$ from equation (14.23).

The skewness of $\sum_{i=1}^{q} \ln l(x_i)$ is

$$S_n = \frac{E[(\sum_{i=1}^{q} \ln l(x_i) - \mu_n)^3]}{\sigma_n^3} = \frac{E((\sum_{i=1}^{q} \ln l(x_i))^3) - 3\mu_n\sigma_n^2 - \mu_n^3}{\sigma_n^3}, \tag{14.27}$$

where

$$E\left(\left(\sum_{i=1}^{q} \ln l(x_i)\right)^3\right) = \sum_{i=1}^{q} \int_{-\infty}^{\infty} (\ln l(x_i))^3 g_i(x) dx. \tag{14.28}$$

Like in equations (14.25) and (14.26), we can get $(\ln l(x_i))^3$ from equation (14.23)

If hypothesis *match* is true, then we can get the mean, variance, and skewness of $\sum_{i=1}^{q} \ln l(x_i)$ by the process similar to the case when *non-match* is true. The mean of $\sum_{i=1}^{q} \ln l(x_i)$ is

$$\mu_s = E\left(\sum_{i=1}^{q} \ln l(x_i)\right) = \sum_{i=1}^{q} \int_{-\infty}^{\infty} (\ln l(x_i)) f_i(x) dx, \tag{14.29}$$

where $f_i(x)$ is estimated by the EM algorithm. The variance of $\sum_{i=1}^{q} \ln l(x_i)$ is

$$\sigma_s^2 = E\left[\left(\sum_{i=1}^{q} \ln l(x_i)\right)^2\right] - \mu_s^2 = \sum_{i=1}^{q} \int_{-\infty}^{\infty} (\ln l(x_i))^2 f_i(x) dx - \mu_s^2. \tag{14.30}$$

The skewness of $\sum_{i=1}^{q} \ln l(x_i)$ is

$$S_s = \frac{E[(\sum_{i=1}^{q} \ln l(x_i) - \mu_s)^3]}{\sigma_s^3} = \frac{E((\sum_{i=1}^{q} \ln l(x_i))^3) - 3\mu_s\sigma_s^2 - \mu_s^3}{\sigma_s^3}, \tag{14.31}$$

where

$$E\left(\left(\sum_{i=1}^{q} \ln l(x_i)\right)^3\right) = \sum_{i=1}^{q} \int_{-\infty}^{\infty} (\ln l(x_i))^3 f_i(x) dx. \tag{14.32}$$

Because different decision criteria lead to different probabilities of *FAR* and *Hit*s, we need to define a measurement to evaluate the fusion system performance. Fisher measurement is a discriminability measurement, which is based on the mean and variance of the match score and the non–match-score distributions. When these distributions are not symmetric, we need a measurement that considers this asymmetry to evaluate the system performance. We know that the skewness can be used to measure the asymmetry of a distribution. For a distribution, if the right tail is longer than the other, then this distribution is right-skewed and its skewness is positive; otherwise if the the left tail is longer than the other, then this distribution is left-skewed and its skewness is negative. So we define a measurement $d_S$ that considers the skewness of the match-score and the non–match-score distributions to be our discriminability measurement, where

$$d_S = \frac{(m_s - m_n)^2 + (S_s - S_n)^2}{\delta_s^2 + \delta_n^2}. \tag{14.33}$$

We observe that if the match-score and non–match-score distributions are symmetric, then the measurement $d_S$ is the Fisher measurement. Also note that (Wang and Bhanu 2006) did not account for skewness, which is important for performance prediction.

#### 14.3.3.2 Summary

We summarize our prediction approach based on Neyman-Pearson theory by the following:

(1) For each combination of multibiometrics we apply equations (14.25), (14.26), and (14.27) to get the mean, variance, and skewness when the hypothesis non-match is true.
(2) Like in (1) we use equations (14.29), (14.30), and (14.31) to get the mean, variance, and skewness when the hypothesis *match* is true.
(3) We apply equation (14.33) for each combination of biometrics to compute the measure for the fusion system performance. The higher the value of $d_S$, the better is the performance of the fusion system.
(4) We rank the measurements $d_S$ that we get from the prediction model in decreasing order and find the optimal sensor combination corresponding to the highest value of $d_S$.

## 14.4 Experimental Results

### 14.4.1 Databases

We evaluate the two prediction approaches on two databases: the XM2VTS database and the Mixed database. The **XM2VTS Database** contains face and speech data from 295 subjects that are divided into a set of 200 clients, 25 evaluation impostors, and 70 test imposters (Poh and Bengio 2004a). There are eight baseline systems. The features of the face baseline systems are FH (face image concatenated with its RGB histogram), DCTs (DCTmod2 features extracted from $40 \times 32$ pixel face image), and DCTb (DCTmod2 features extracted from $80 \times 64$ pixel face image). The features of the speech baseline systems are LFCC (linear filter-bank cepstral coefficient), PAC (phase autocorrelation), and SSC (spectral subband centroid). The classifiers used in these experiments are the *multilayer perceptron* (MLP) and *Gaussian mixture model* (GMM). The data used in this chapter are based on the Lausanne Protocol I (LP1). There are three training shots per client for LP1. Thefore, we have 600 ($3 \times 200$) match scores and 40,000 ($8 \times 25 \times 200$) non-match scores for each of the baseline systems. Table 14.2 shows these baseline systems and their features, classifiers, and labels. The **Mixed Database** consists of fingerprint (*NIST Special Database 4* (Bhanu and Tan 2004)), 3D ear (Chen and Bhanu 2007; Chen et al. 2005), and gait/face video databases (Zhou and Bhanu 2007). The NIST-4 database consists of 2000 pairs of fingerprints. Each of the fingerprints is labeled with an ID number preceded by an "f" or an "s" that represents different impressions of the same fingerprint. The images are collected by scanning inked fingerprints from paper. The resolution of a fingerprint image is 500 DPI, and the size of an image is $480 \times 512$ pixels. The data in the 3D ear database are captured by a Minolta Vivid 300 camera (Chen and Bhanu 2007; Chen et al. 2005). The camera outputs 3D range images that contain $200 \times 200$ grid points. There are 155 subjects, which include 17 females, six subjects have earrings, and 12 subjects have their ears partially occluded by hair (with less than 10% occlusion). Six images per subject are recorded, and a total of 902 shots are used for the experiments because some shots are not properly recorded. Every person has at least four shots. There are three different poses in the collected data: frontal, left and right. Video data (Zhou and Bhanu 2007) are obtained by a Sony DCR-VX1000 digital video camera recorder operating at 30 f/s. There are 45 subjects who are walking in the outdoor condition and expose a side view to the camera. Each subject has two video sequences. The number of sequences per person varies from two to three. The resolution of each frame is $720 \times 480$. The video data include gait data and side face data. Table 14.3 shows these systems and their features, classifiers, and labels.

### 14.4.2 Verification of the Match/Non-match Score Distributions as Mixtures of Gaussian

Figure 14.8 shows the match-score and non–match-score histograms and distributions of the baseline systems in the XM2VTS database. The left columns are the histograms, and the right columns are the distributions estimated by the EM algorithm. The component numbers for the eight match-score distributions are 1, 1, 1, 1, 5, 4, 1, 2, and for the eight non–match-score distributions are 1, 13, 18, 1, 15, 17, 18, and 18. Figure 14.9 shows the match-score and non–match-score histograms and distributions for the mixed database. The component numbers

Table 14.2. *Baseline Systems of XM2VTS Database and Their Features, Classifiers, and Labels*

| Name, Classifier | Features | Classifiers | Labels Used in Figure/Text |
|---|---|---|---|
| (FH, MLP) | RGB histogram of the normalized face image | 20 hidden units in the MLP | b1 |
| (DCTs, GMM) | DCTmod2 features computed from 40 × 32 face images | 64 Gaussian components in the GMM | b2 |
| (DCTb, GMM) | DCTmod2 features computed from 80 × 64 face images | 512 Gaussian components in the GMM | b3 |
| (DCTs, MLP) | DCTmod2 features computed from 40 × 32 face images | 32 hidden units in the MLP | b4 |
| (DCTb, MLP) | DCTmod2 features computed from 80 × 64 face images | 20 hidden units in the MLP | b5 |
| (LFCC, GMM) | LFCC speech features computed with a window length of 20 ms, and each window moved at a rate of 10 ms (Poh and Bengio 2004a) | 200 Gaussian components in the GMM | b6 |
| (PAC, GMM) | PAC speech features computed with a window length of 20 ms, and each window moved at a rate of 10 ms (Poh and Bengio 2004a) | 200 Gaussian components in the GMM | b7 |
| (SSC, GMM) | SSC speech features obtained from 16 coefficients (Poh and Bengio 2004a) | 200 Gaussian components in the GMM | b8 |

Table 14.3. *Mixed Database: Data, Features, Classifiers, and Labels*

| Systems | Features | Classifiers | Labels Used in Figure/Text |
|---|---|---|---|
| Fingerprint | Features based on minutiae triangles (Bhanu and Tan 2003) | Nearest neighbor | e1 |
| Ear | Geometric features (Chen et al. 2005) | Nearest neighbor | e2 |
| Gait | PCA and MDA combined scheme (Zhou and Bhanu 2007) | Nearest neighbor | e3 |
| Face | PCA and MDA combined scheme (Zhou and Bhanu 2007) | Nearest neighbor | e4 |

for the four match-score distributions are 12, 11, 9, 9 and for the four non–match-score distributions are 1, 17, 1, and 1. From Figs. 14.8 and 14.9, one can verify that our assumption about match-non–match-score distributions as mixtures of Gaussian is appropriate.

### 14.4.3 Normalization of Scores

Before fusion we need to normalize the match/non-match scores to ensure that no single system will dominate the fusion combination. We denote the match score and non-match score as $\{ms\}$ and $\{ns\}$, respectively. We use three normalization methods: Min-Max, Z-score, and Tanh.

(1) Min-Max: This method maps the scores into [0, 1] range:

$$ms_{\text{norm}} = \frac{ms - \min(\{ms\})}{\max(\{ms\}) - \min(\{ms\})}$$

$$ns_{\text{norm}} = \frac{ns - \min(\{ns\})}{\max(\{ns\}) - \min(\{ns\})}$$

where *min*() and *max*() denote the minimum and the maximum value, and $ms_{\text{norm}}$ and $ns_{\text{norm}}$ denote the normalized match score and non-match score, respectively.

(2) Z-score: This method maps the scores to a standard normal distribution:

$$ms_{\text{norm}} = \frac{ms - \text{mean}(\{ms\})}{\text{std}(\{ms\})}$$

$$ns_{\text{norm}} = \frac{ns - \text{mean}(\{ns\})}{\text{std}(\{ns\})},$$

where mean() and std() denote the mean and standard deviation.

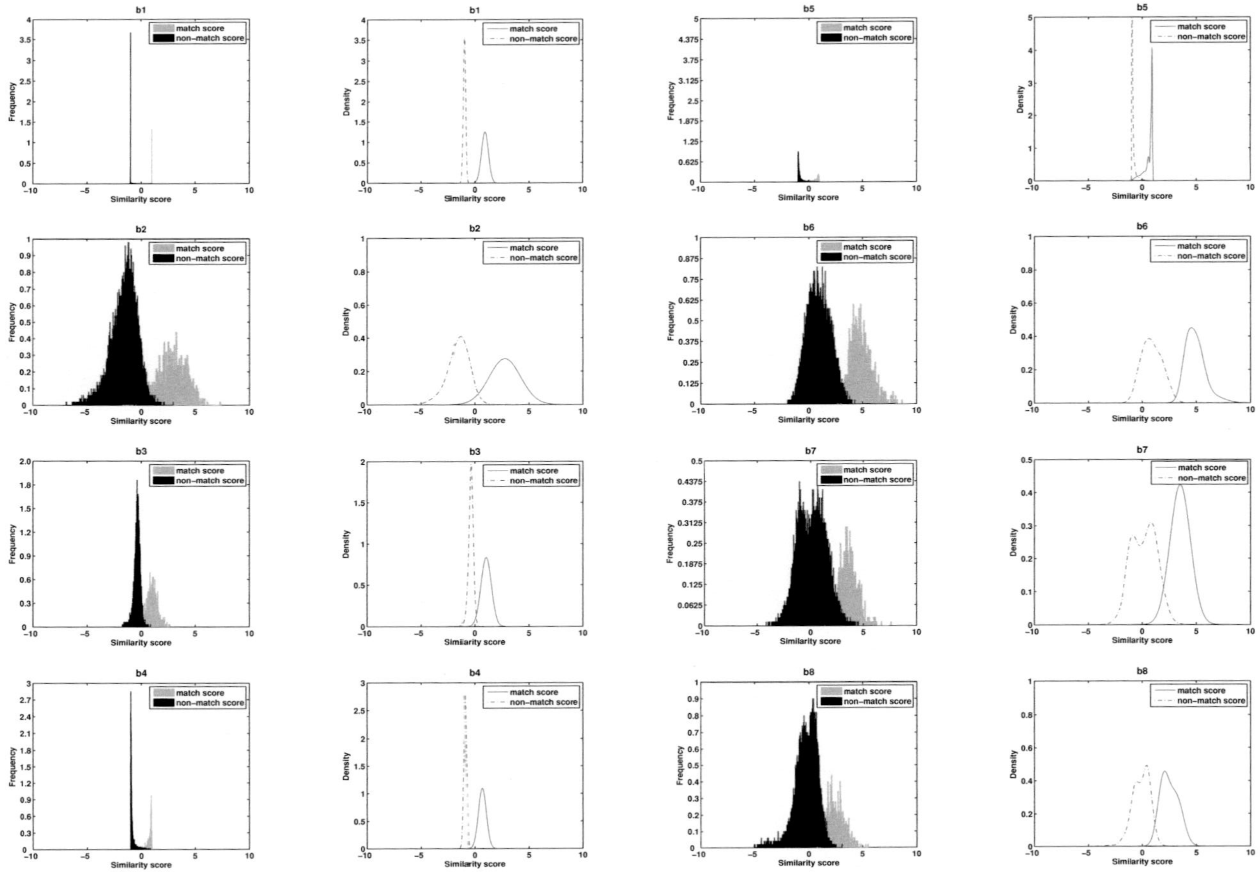

Figure 14.8. Match score and nonmatch score histograms and distributions for the baseline systems in the XM2VTS database.

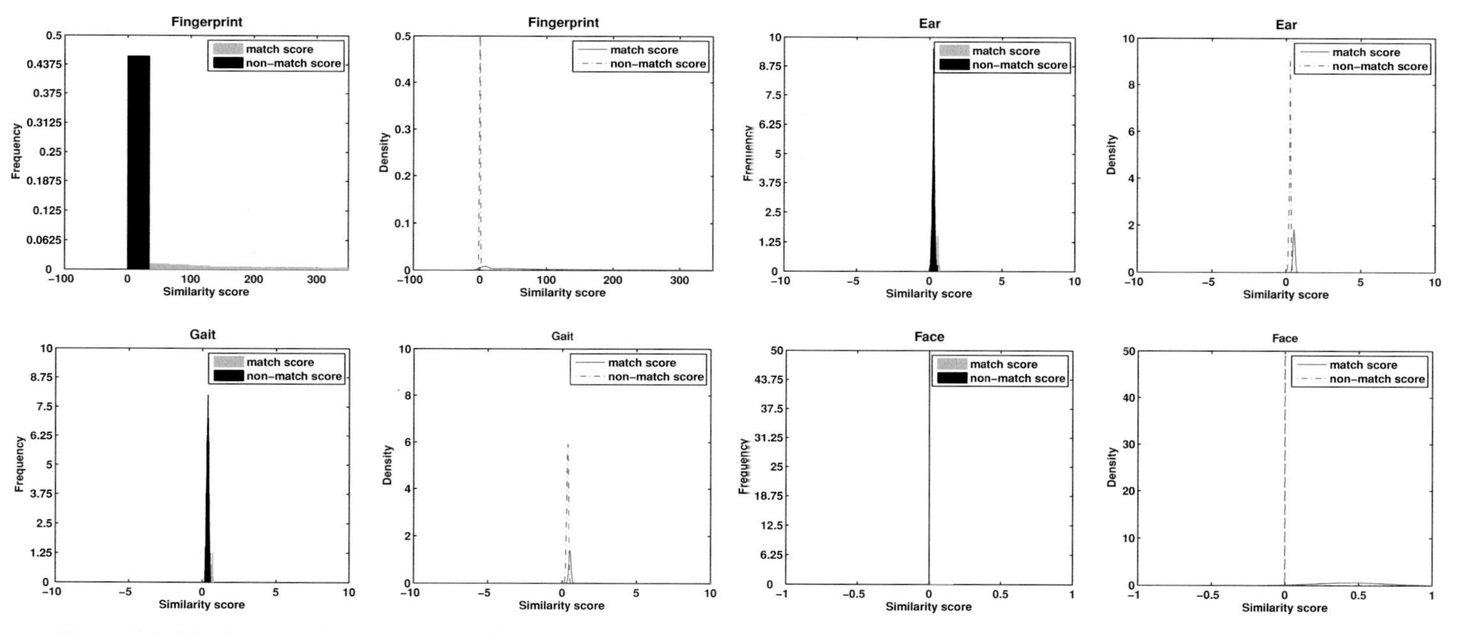


Figure 14.9. Match-score and nonmatch-score histograms and distributions for the mixed database.

Table 14.4. *Combinations of Two-Sensor Fusion*

| 1 | 2 | 3 | 4 | 5 | 6 | 7 |
|---|---|---|---|---|---|---|
| {b2, b3} | {b1, b7} | {b2, b8} | {b4, b6} | {b5, b6} | {b3, b8} | {b3, b5} |
| 8 | 9 | 10 | 11 | 12 | 13 | 14 |
| {b4, b5} | {b1, b8} | {b1, b5} | {b6, b7} | {b1, b4} | {b2, b7} | {b1, b6} |
| 15 | 16 | 17 | 18 | 19 | 20 | 21 |
| {b3, b6} | {b4, b7} | {b2, b6} | {b2, b5} | {b3, b7} | {b1, b2} | {b7, b8} |
| 22 | 23 | 24 | 25 | 26 | 27 | 28 |
| {b2, b4} | {b5, b7} | {b6, b8} | {b4, b8} | {b1, b3} | {b3, b4} | {b5, b8} |

(3) Tanh: Like the minmax this method maps the scores into (0, 1) but has a different effect (Ross and Jain 2004):

$$ms_{\text{norm}} = \frac{1}{2} \cdot \left\{ \tanh\left[0.01 \cdot \frac{(ms - \text{mean}(\{ms\}))}{\text{std}(\{ms\})}\right] + 1 \right\},$$

$$ns_{\text{norm}} = \frac{1}{2} \cdot \left\{ \tanh\left[0.01 \cdot \frac{(ns - \text{mean}(\{ns\}))}{\text{std}(\{ns\})}\right] + 1 \right\},$$

where tanh denotes the hyperbolic tangent.

### 14.4.4 Performance of the Prediction Model Based on the Φ Transformation

#### 14.4.4.1 Prediction for the XM2VTS Database

We use the methods described above to normalize the eight baseline systems. We randomly combine two of the eight baseline systems and get $C_2^8 = 28$ combinations, as shown in Table 14.4. For example, the combination 1 is the baseline system $b2$ that combines with the baseline system $b3$. Similarly, we randomly combine three of the eight baseline systems and get $C_3^8 = 56$ combinations. Table 14.5 is the list of the three sensor combinations. For each combination, we fuse the baseline systems by the sum rule, product rule, min rule, max rule, and median rule. Also for each combination, we use the EM algorithm to estimate the match-score and the non–match-score distributions to get the component numbers, mean, variance, and weight for each component. Further, for each combination we apply equation (14.18) to obtain the $d_T$ metric which is used to predict the fusion system performance. Finally, we rank $d_T$ metric values to find the optimal combination that has the maximum value. We list the top seven optimal baseline systems (from space considerations) for the two-sensor fusion systems in Table 14.6. We can see that for the Min-Max normalization method, the optimal fusion combination (rank 1) from the

Table 14.5. *Combinations of Three-Sensor Fusion*

| 29 | 30 | 31 | 32 | 33 | 34 | 35 | 36 |
|---|---|---|---|---|---|---|---|
| {b4, b7, b8} | {b1, b3, b8} | {b1, b2, b7} | {b4,b5, b6} | {b2, b3, b6} | {b2, b3, b4} | {b4, b6, b8} | {b2, b6, b8} |
| 37 | 38 | 39 | 40 | 41 | 42 | 43 | 44 |
| {b3, b4, b5} | {b1, b3, b4} | {b3, b4, b8} | {b1, b3, b5} | {b1, b5, b6} | {b1, b3, b7} | {b1, b4, b8} | {b3, b6, b7} |
| 45 | 46 | 47 | 48 | 49 | 50 | 51 | 52 |
| {b5, b6, b7} | {b2, b4, b8} | {b2, b6, b7} | {b4, b5, b8} | {b4, b5, b7} | {b3, b4, b7} | {b4, b6, b7} | {b5, b6, b8} |
| 53 | 54 | 55 | 56 | 57 | 58 | 59 | 60 |
| {b2, b4, b6} | {b3, b5, b7} | {b6, b7, b8} | {b1, b6, b7} | {b2, b3, b5} | {b2, b5, b8} | {b1, b2, b6} | {b2, b5, b7} |
| 61 | 62 | 63 | 64 | 65 | 66 | 67 | 68 |
| {b2, b4, b5} | {b1, b7, b8} | {b1, b3, b6} | {b3, b6, b8} | {b3, b4, b6} | {b1, b4, b5} | {b1, b2, b3} | {b1, b2, b5} |
| 69 | 70 | 71 | 72 | 73 | 74 | 75 | 76 |
| {b1, b5, b7} | {b1, b4, b6} | {b2, b4, b7} | {b2, b8, b7} | {b1, b5, b8} | {b3, b5, b6} | {b1, b6, b8} | {b2, b3, b8} |
| 77 | 78 | 79 | 80 | 81 | 82 | 83 | 84 |
| {b2, b3, b7} | {b1, b4, b7} | {b3, b5, b8} | {b2, b5, b6} | {b1, b2, b4} | {b5, b7, b8} | {b1, b2, b8} | {b3, b7, b8} |

Table 14.6. *Top Seven Optimal Combinations of Two Sensor-Fusion Systems for the XM2VTS Database: Evaluation vs. Prediction Based on the Φ Transformation*

(a) Min-Max

| | Evaluation | | | | | Prediction | | | | |
|---|---|---|---|---|---|---|---|---|---|---|
| Rank | Sum | Product | Min | Max | Median | Sum | Product | Min | Max | Median |
| 1 | 17 | 4 | 14 | 12 | 12 | 17 | 9 | 9 | 12 | 12 |
| 2 | 13 | 16 | 26 | 10 | 10 | 13 | 2 | 2 | 10 | 14 |
| 3 | 8 | 25 | 2 | 8 | 4 | 11 | 14 | 14 | 14 | 9 |
| 4 | 11 | 27 | 4 | 4 | 14 | 21 | 20 | 20 | 26 | 26 |
| 5 | 24 | 5 | 16 | 14 | 16 | 8 | 26 | 26 | 20 | 2 |
| 6 | 15 | 14 | 20 | 2 | 25 | 1 | 12 | 12 | 9 | 20 |
| 7 | 19 | 2 | 9 | 5 | 27 | 15 | 16 | 16 | 2 | 10 |

(b) $Z$-score

| | Evaluation | | | | | Prediction | | | | |
|---|---|---|---|---|---|---|---|---|---|---|
| Rank | Sum | Product | Min | Max | Median | Sum | Product | Min | Max | Median |
| 1 | 17 | 4 | 8 | 12 | 12 | 19 | 12 | 12 | 12 | 12 |
| 2 | 12 | 16 | 4 | 10 | 10 | 17 | 14 | 10 | 14 | 14 |
| 3 | 19 | 25 | 12 | 14 | 4 | 12 | 2 | 8 | 10 | 2 |
| 4 | 13 | 27 | 5 | 4 | 14 | 13 | 10 | 14 | 9 | 10 |
| 5 | 24 | 15 | 16 | 9 | 8 | 21 | 4 | 4 | 2 | 9 |
| 6 | 8 | 17 | 15 | 8 | 16 | 8 | 26 | 26 | 26 | 26 |
| 7 | 15 | 19 | 27 | 2 | 5 | 15 | 9 | 5 | 20 | 20 |

(c) Tanh

| | Evaluation | | | | | Prediction | | | | |
|---|---|---|---|---|---|---|---|---|---|---|
| Rank | Sum | Product | Min | Max | Median | Sum | Product | Min | Max | Median |
| 1 | 17 | 12 | 8 | 12 | 12 | 19 | 12 | 12 | 12 | 12 |
| 2 | 12 | 10 | 4 | 10 | 10 | 17 | 14 | 10 | 14 | 14 |
| 3 | 19 | 4 | 12 | 14 | 4 | 12 | 2 | 8 | 10 | 2 |
| 4 | 13 | 14 | 5 | 4 | 14 | 13 | 10 | 14 | 9 | 10 |
| 5 | 24 | 8 | 16 | 9 | 8 | 21 | 9 | 4 | 2 | 9 |
| 6 | 8 | 16 | 15 | 8 | 16 | 8 | 26 | 26 | 26 | 26 |
| 7 | 15 | 5 | 27 | 2 | 5 | 15 | 20 | 5 | 20 | 20 |

evaluation is the same as the prediction for the sum rule, max rule, and median rule. Similar observations can be made for the other normalizations.

We list the top 10 optimal baseline system combinations that we get from the performance evaluation and prediction model for the three-sensor fusion systems in Table 14.7. We observe that for the Min-Max normalization method,

Table 14.7. *Top 10 Optimal Combinations of Three-Sensor Fusion Systems for the XM2VTS Database: Evaluation vs. Prediction Based on the Φ Transformation*

(a) Min-Max

| | Evaluation | | | | | Prediction | | | | |
|---|---|---|---|---|---|---|---|---|---|---|
| Rank | Sum | Product | Min | Max | Median | Sum | Product | Min | Max | Median |
| 1 | 33 | 62 | 63 | 66 | 66 | 77 | 83 | 62 | 66 | 43 |
| 2 | 77 | 29 | 59 | 41 | 43 | 33 | 31 | 63 | 38 | 78 |
| 3 | 36 | 75 | 56 | 40 | 70 | 76 | 59 | 31 | 70 | 66 |
| 4 | 51 | 71 | 75 | 70 | 78 | 64 | 30 | 59 | 63 | 70 |
| 5 | 47 | 56 | 42 | 65 | 38 | 84 | 62 | 42 | 40 | 38 |
| 6 | 76 | 53 | 30 | 32 | 73 | 36 | 42 | 83 | 41 | 81 |
| 7 | 44 | 63 | 67 | 63 | 69 | 38 | 43 | 56 | 81 | 73 |
| 8 | 84 | 51 | 31 | 42 | 81 | 74 | 78 | 30 | 59 | 69 |
| 9 | 64 | 46 | 62 | 37 | 41 | 44 | 56 | 75 | 31 | 41 |
| 10 | 72 | 39 | 65 | 31 | 32 | 47 | 63 | 67 | 78 | 68 |

(b) $Z$-score

| | Evaluation | | | | | Prediction | | | | |
|---|---|---|---|---|---|---|---|---|---|---|
| Rank | Sum | Product | Min | Max | Median | Sum | Product | Min | Max | Median |
| 1 | 66 | 65 | 51 | 66 | 70 | 77 | 70 | 66 | 70 | 70 |
| 2 | 77 | 51 | 65 | 40 | 66 | 66 | 78 | 70 | 81 | 43 |
| 3 | 52 | 50 | 53 | 68 | 43 | 33 | 66 | 63 | 66 | 66 |
| 4 | 33 | 53 | 45 | 38 | 78 | 34 | 43 | 65 | 38 | 78 |
| 5 | 82 | 39 | 50 | 73 | 38 | 52 | 41 | 32 | 43 | 41 |
| 6 | 47 | 71 | 71 | 70 | 41 | 35 | 81 | 41 | 78 | 38 |
| 7 | 36 | 46 | 66 | 41 | 32 | 82 | 69 | 38 | 59 | 32 |
| 8 | 35 | 45 | 74 | 81 | 81 | 58 | 38 | 53 | 75 | 73 |
| 9 | 64 | 29 | 44 | 69 | 73 | 36 | 59 | 56 | 63 | 81 |
| 10 | 32 | 35 | 33 | 43 | 40 | 64 | 31 | 51 | 56 | 69 |

(c) Tanh

| | Evaluation | | | | | Prediction | | | | |
|---|---|---|---|---|---|---|---|---|---|---|
| Rank | Sum | Product | Min | Max | Median | Sum | Product | Min | Max | Median |
| 1 | 66 | 70 | 51 | 66 | 70 | 77 | 70 | 66 | 70 | 70 |
| 2 | 77 | 41 | 65 | 40 | 66 | 66 | 78 | 70 | 81 | 43 |
| 3 | 52 | 66 | 53 | 68 | 43 | 33 | 43 | 63 | 66 | 66 |
| 4 | 33 | 78 | 45 | 38 | 78 | 52 | 41 | 65 | 38 | 78 |
| 5 | 82 | 43 | 50 | 73 | 38 | 82 | 66 | 32 | 43 | 41 |
| 6 | 36 | 38 | 71 | 70 | 41 | 35 | 73 | 41 | 78 | 38 |
| 7 | 47 | 73 | 66 | 41 | 32 | 58 | 69 | 38 | 59 | 32 |
| 8 | 35 | 69 | 74 | 81 | 81 | 34 | 38 | 53 | 75 | 73 |
| 9 | 64 | 32 | 44 | 69 | 73 | 36 | 59 | 56 | 63 | 81 |
| 10 | 32 | 81 | 33 | 43 | 40 | 64 | 63 | 51 | 56 | 69 |

the optimal fusion combinations (rank 1) that we get from the evaluation are the same as the results that we get from the prediction for the max rule.

Note that because our measurement $d_T$ is derived from the transformation of the *ROC* curve and it is related with the *AUROC*, we are not directly concerned with the *ROC* curve of each biometric combination. We use three criteria: Rand statistic $(R)$, Jaccard coefficient $(J)$, and Fowlkes and Mallows index $(FM)$ (Theodoridis and Koutroumbas 1998) to measure the degree of the agreement between the fusion performance evaluation and prediction. We regard the fusion performance evaluation and prediction as two classes. For each class, there are two clusters. The first cluster is a set of top optimal combinations, and the second cluster is the other combinations. For example, if we compare the agreement between the fusion performance evaluation and prediction for top 2, then $evaluation = \{\{rank1, rank2\}, \{\text{other combinations}\}\}$, $prediction = \{\{rank1, rank2\}, \{\text{other combinations}\}\}$. We pair the combinations as a vector. Then we find the number of vectors **(1)** both belong to the same cluster in the evaluation and the prediction, denoted as $a$, **(2)** both belong to the different cluster in the evaluation and the prediction, denoted as $b$, **(3)** belong to the same cluster in the evaluation and different cluster in the prediction, denoted as $c$, and **(4)** belong to the different cluster in the evaluation and the same cluster in the prediction, denoted as $d$. We define these three criteria as

$$R = \frac{(a+d)}{(a+b+c+d)}; \quad J = \frac{a}{(a+b+c)}; \quad FM = \sqrt{\frac{a}{a+b}\frac{a}{a+c}}. \tag{14.34}$$

The values of these criteria are between 0 and 1. The larger the value, the greater is the agreement between them. Figure 14.10 shows these criteria values for the top seven combinations of two-sensor fusion systems for the three normalization methods and the sensors fused by the sum and max rules (product, min, and median rules, not shown for lack of space). Similarly, Figure 14.11 shows these criteria values for top 10 combinations of three-sensor fusion systems for the three normalization methods and the sensors fused by the sum and max rules. Since the combination numbers are limited (28 for two-sensor fusion and 56 for three-sensor fusion), the curves in Figs. 14.10 and 14.11 are not smooth. We find that the prediction performance of the sum and max rules is better than the other fusion rules. Also the normalization methods have less effect on the prediction performance than fusion rules.

#### 14.4.4.2 Prediction for the Mixed Database

Because the number of subjects, for each of the databases in the mixed database (see Section 14.4.1) are different, we repeat the data to make sure that each

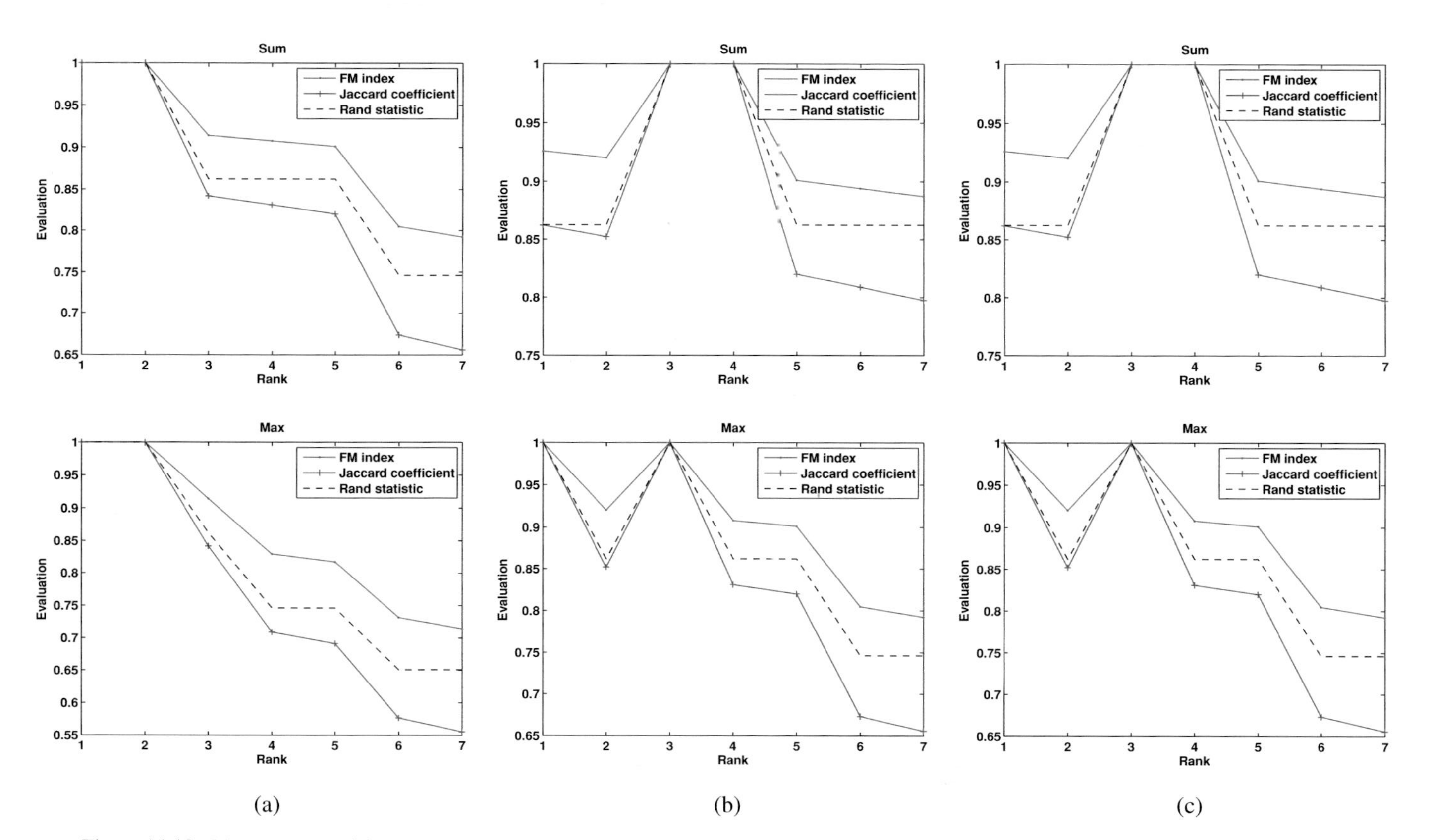


Figure 14.10. Measurement of the agreement degree between the actual results and the prediction based on the Φ transformation for two-sensor fusion systems with different fusion rules and normalization methods for the XM2VTS database: (a) Min-Max; (b) *z*-score; (c) Tanh.

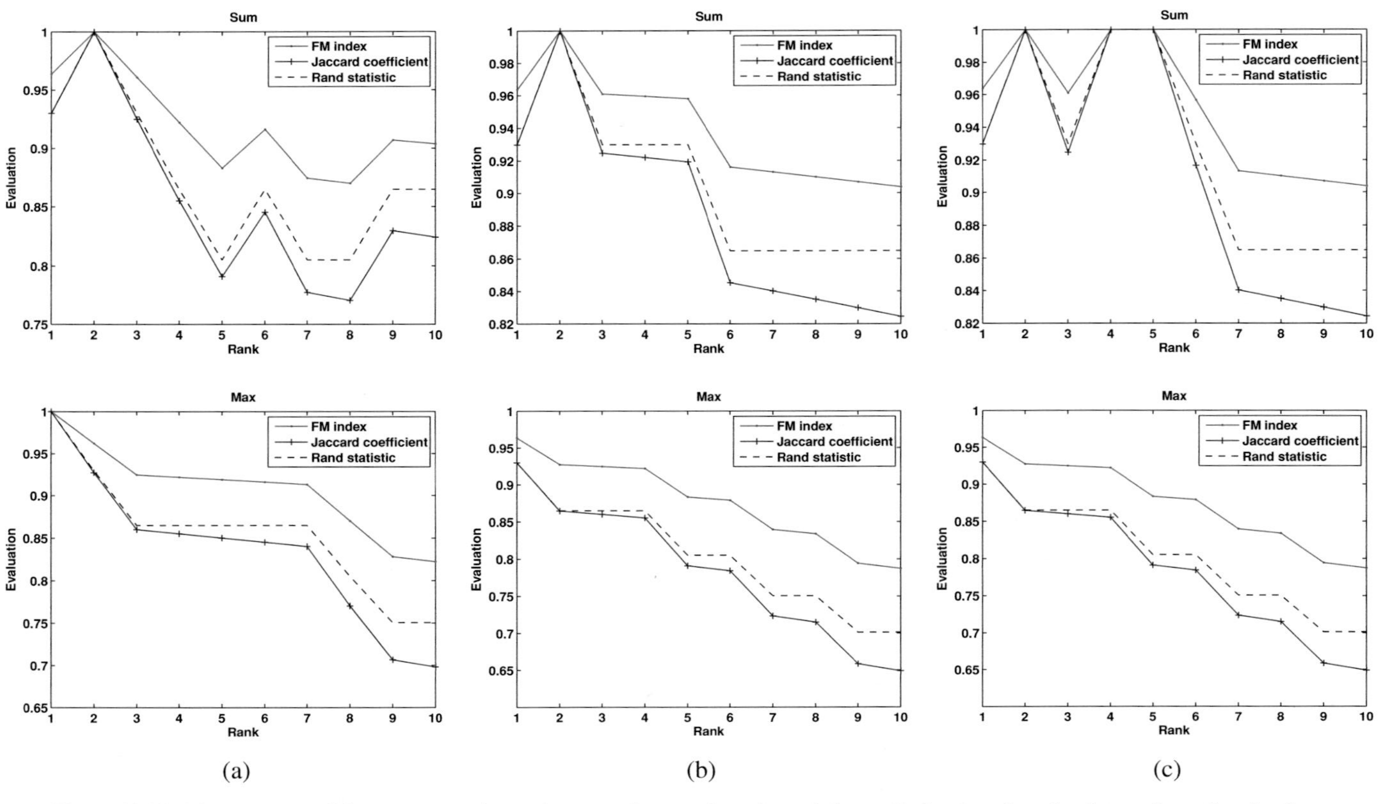


Figure 14.11. Measurement of the agreement degree between the actual results and the prediction based on the Φ transformation for three sensor fusion systems with different fusion rules and normalization methods for the XM2VTS database: (a) Min-Max; (b) $z$-score; (c) Tanh.

subject has the fingerprint, ear, gait, and face data. As the fusion system evaluation and prediction on the XM2VTS database, we apply the Min-Max, $z$-score, and Tanh normalization methods to normalize the four baseline systems. We randomly combine two of the baseline systems and get, $C_2^4 = 6$ combinations: $\{e2, e4\}$, $\{e2, e3\}$, $\{e3, e4\}$, $\{e1, e2\}$, $\{e1, e4\}$, $\{e1, e3\}$. We number them as $1, 2, \ldots, 6$, respectively. We randomly combine three baseline systems and get $C_3^4 = 4$ combinations: $\{e1, e2, e3\}$, $\{e2, e3, e4\}$, $\{e1, e2, e4\}$, $\{e1, e3, e4\}$. We number them as 7, 8, 9, 10, respectively.

We perform experiments similar to those on the XM2VTS database. We list the top six optimal baseline system combinations, which we get from the performance evaluation and performance prediction model for the two-sensor fusion systems in Table 14.8. We can see that for the Min-Max normalization method, the optimal fusion combinations (rank 1) that we get from the evaluation are the same as the results that we get from the prediction for all the five fusion rules. Similar results are obtained for other normalizations.

We list the top four optimal baseline system combinations for three-sensor fusion systems in Table 14.9. We can see that for the Min-Max normalization method, the optimal fusion combinations (rank 1) that we get from the evaluation are the same as the results we get from the prediction for the product rule and min rule. Similar results are obtained for other combinations. Figure 14.12 shows the three criteria values (equation [34]) for the top six combinations of two-sensor fusion systems for the three normalization methods and the sum and product rules (min, max, and median fusion rules are not shown). The performance of the product rule normalized by the Min-Max method is better than other fusion rules normalized by different methods. Figure 14.13 shows these criteria values for the top four combinations of three-sensor fusion systems for the three normalization methods and the sum and product rules. We find that the prediction performance of the sum rule normalized by the $z$-score and Tanh and product rule normalized by the Min-Max and Tanh are the same as the actual performance. We note that the curves in Figs. 14.12 and 14.13 are not smooth because the combination numbers are limited (six for two sensor fusion and four for three sensor fusion).

### 14.4.5 Performance of Prediction Model Based on the Neyman-Pearson Theory

We follow the procedure summarized in the last section to verify the prediction model based on the Neyman-Pearson theory for the XM2VTS database. To verify our prediction model, we needed extensive experiments to evaluate the

Table 14.8. *Top Six Optimal Combinations of Two-Sensor Fusion Systems for the Mixed Database: Evaluation vs. Prediction Based on the Φ Transformation*

(a) Min-Max

| | Evaluation | | | | | Prediction | | | | |
|---|---|---|---|---|---|---|---|---|---|---|
| Rank | Sum | Product | Min | Max | Median | Sum | Product | Min | Max | Median |
| 1 | 4 | 2 | 2 | 2 | 4 | 4 | 2 | 2 | 2 | 4 |
| 2 | 2 | 4 | 6 | 1 | 2 | 2 | 4 | 6 | 4 | 2 |
| 3 | 1 | 6 | 4 | 4 | 1 | 1 | 6 | 4 | 1 | 1 |
| 4 | 5 | 1 | 5 | 5 | 5 | 6 | 1 | 3 | 5 | 6 |
| 5 | 6 | 3 | 3 | 3 | 6 | 5 | 3 | 1 | 3 | 5 |
| 6 | 3 | 5 | 1 | 6 | 3 | 3 | 5 | 5 | 6 | 3 |

(b) $Z$-score

| | Evaluation | | | | | Prediction | | | | |
|---|---|---|---|---|---|---|---|---|---|---|
| Rank | Sum | Product | Min | Max | Median | Sum | Product | Min | Max | Median |
| 1 | 4 | 2 | 2 | 4 | 4 | 4 | 2 | 2 | 2 | 4 |
| 2 | 2 | 4 | 5 | 2 | 2 | 2 | 4 | 4 | 4 | 2 |
| 3 | 1 | 1 | 4 | 1 | 1 | 1 | 1 | 1 | 1 | 1 |
| 4 | 5 | 3 | 1 | 6 | 5 | 6 | 6 | 5 | 6 | 6 |
| 5 | 6 | 6 | 6 | 3 | 6 | 5 | 3 | 6 | 5 | 5 |
| 6 | 3 | 5 | 3 | 5 | 3 | 3 | 5 | 3 | 3 | 3 |

(c) Tanh

| | Evaluation | | | | | Prediction | | | | |
|---|---|---|---|---|---|---|---|---|---|---|
| Rank | Sum | Product | Min | Max | Median | Sum | Product | Min | Max | Median |
| 1 | 4 | 4 | 2 | 4 | 4 | 4 | 2 | 2 | 2 | 4 |
| 2 | 2 | 2 | 5 | 2 | 2 | 2 | 4 | 4 | 4 | 2 |
| 3 | 1 | 1 | 4 | 1 | 1 | 1 | 1 | 1 | 1 | 1 |
| 4 | 5 | 5 | 1 | 6 | 5 | 6 | 6 | 5 | 6 | 6 |
| 5 | 6 | 6 | 6 | 3 | 6 | 5 | 5 | 6 | 5 | 5 |
| 6 | 3 | 3 | 3 | 5 | 3 | 3 | 3 | 3 | 3 | 3 |

fusion system performance. For each combination, we apply the sum rule, product rule, min rule, max rule, and median rule to get the match score and non-match score for the fusion system. We compute the mean, variance, and skewness of the match score and non-match score and apply equation (14.33) to get the actual measurement for each combination. We rank the

Table 14.9. *Top Four Optimal Combinations of Two-Sensor Fusion Systems for the Ear Database, Video (Face and Gait) Database, and NIST-4 Database: Evaluation vs. Prediction Based on the* $\Phi$ *Transformation*

(a) Min-Max

| | Evaluation | | | | | Prediction | | | | |
|---|---|---|---|---|---|---|---|---|---|---|
| Rank | Sum | Product | Min | Max | Median | Sum | Product | Min | Max | Median |
| 1 | 9 | 7 | 7 | 8 | 9 | 7 | 7 | 7 | 7 | 8 |
| 2 | 7 | 8 | 10 | 7 | 8 | 9 | 8 | 8 | 8 | 7 |
| 3 | 8 | 9 | 9 | 9 | 7 | 8 | 9 | 10 | 9 | 10 |
| 4 | 10 | 10 | 8 | 10 | 10 | 10 | 10 | 9 | 10 | 9 |

(b) *Z*-score

| | Evaluation | | | | | Prediction | | | | |
|---|---|---|---|---|---|---|---|---|---|---|
| Rank | Sum | Product | Min | Max | Median | Sum | Product | Min | Max | Median |
| 1 | 7 | 8 | 8 | 7 | 7 | 7 | 7 | 7 | 7 | 7 |
| 2 | 9 | 7 | 7 | 9 | 8 | 9 | 8 | 8 | 9 | 8 |
| 3 | 8 | 9 | 9 | 8 | 9 | 8 | 9 | 9 | 8 | 9 |
| 4 | 10 | 10 | 10 | 10 | 10 | 10 | 10 | 10 | 10 | 10 |

(c) Tanh

| | Evaluation | | | | | Prediction | | | | |
|---|---|---|---|---|---|---|---|---|---|---|
| Rank | Sum | Product | Min | Max | Median | Sum | Product | Min | Max | Median |
| 1 | 7 | 7 | 8 | 7 | 7 | 7 | 7 | 7 | 7 | 7 |
| 2 | 9 | 9 | 7 | 9 | 8 | 9 | 9 | 8 | 9 | 8 |
| 3 | 8 | 8 | 9 | 8 | 9 | 8 | 8 | 9 | 8 | 9 |
| 4 | 10 | 10 | 10 | 10 | 10 | 10 | 10 | 10 | 10 | 10 |

measurements that we get from the actual performance in decreasing order. We list the top seven optimal baseline system combinations, which we get from the performance evaluation and performance prediction model for the two-sensor fusion systems in Table 14.10. Similarly, we list the top 10 optimal baseline system combinations that we get from the performance evaluation and performance prediction model for three-sensor fusion systems in Table 14.11.

In the brute-force experiments for the evaluation of actual performance, we need to normalize the match scores and the non-match scores before fusing the multimodal biometrics. However, the prediction approach based on the Neyman-Pearson does not need to normalize the baseline systems. The values

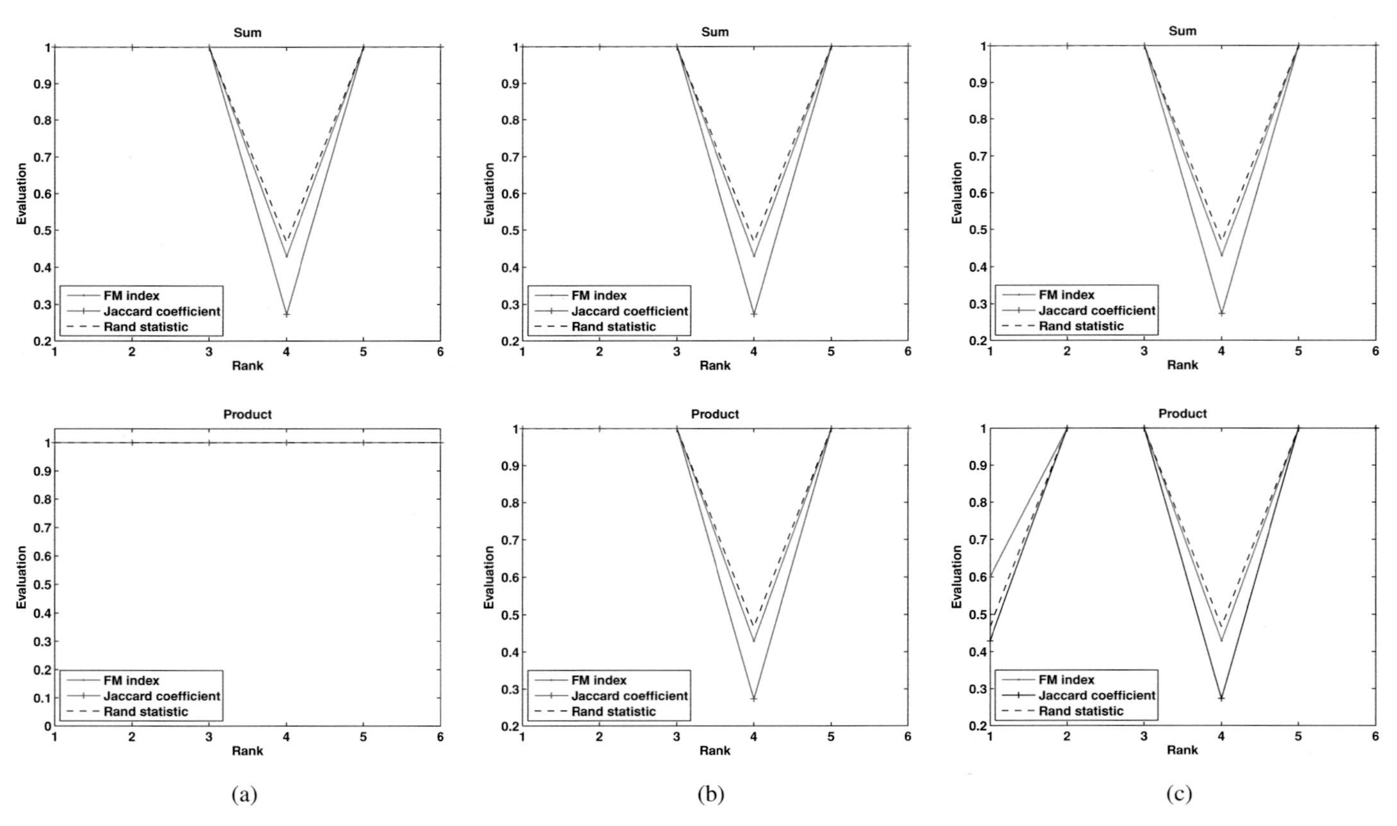


Figure 14.12. Measurement of the agreement degree between the actual results and the prediction based on the $\Phi$ transformation for two-sensor fusion systems with different fusion rules and normalization methods for the the NIST-4 database, ear database, video gait, and face databases: (a) Min-Max; (b) $z$-score; (c) Tanh.

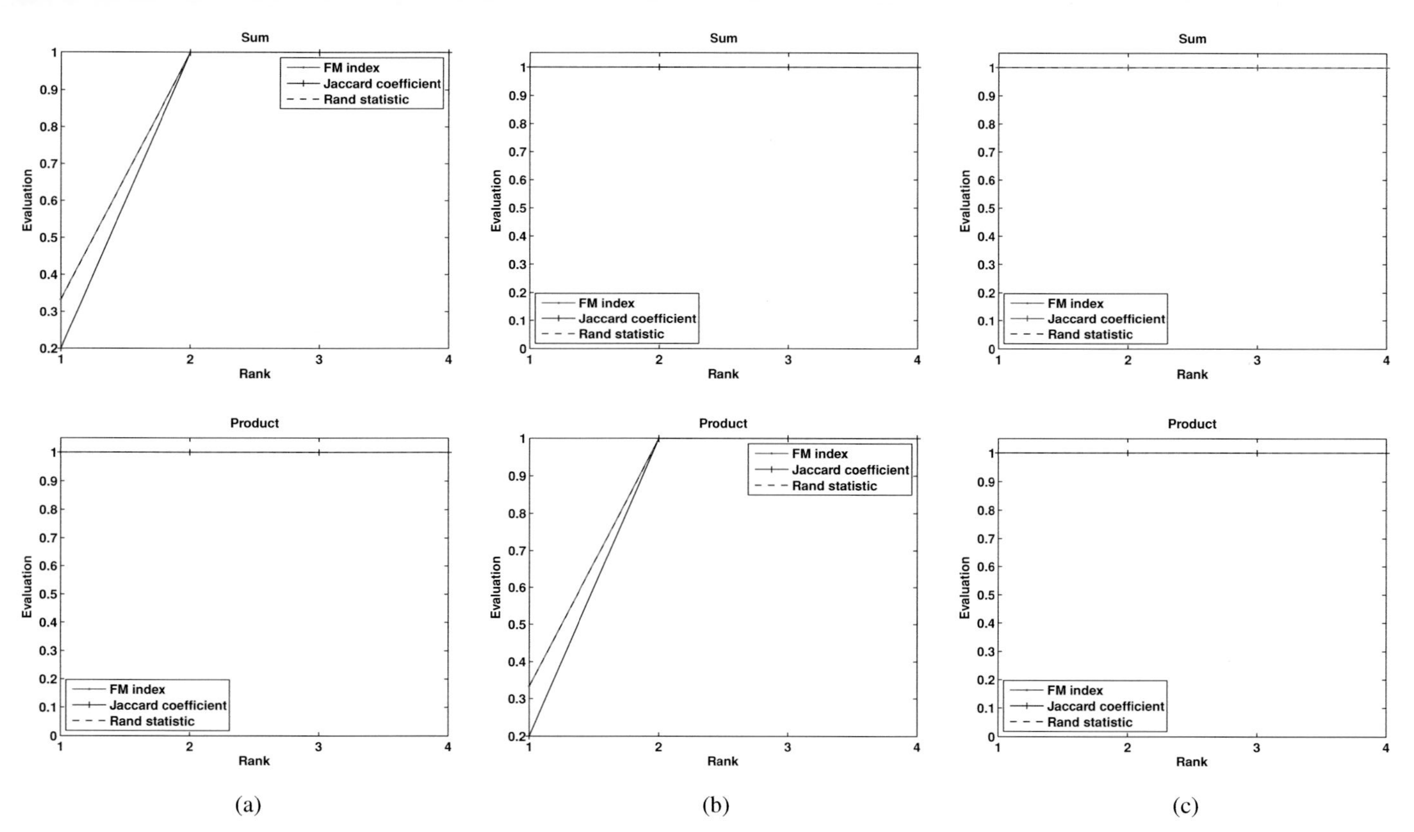


Figure 14.13. Measurement of the agreement degree between the actual results and the prediction based on the $\Phi$ transformation for three-sensor fusion systems with different fusion rules and normalization methods for the NIST-4 database, ear database, video gait, and face databases: (a) Min-Max; (b) $z$-score; (c) Tanh.

Table 14.10. *Top Seven Optimal Combinations of Two-Sensor Fusion Systems for the XM2VTS Database: Evaluation vs. Prediction Based on the Neyman-Pearson Theory*

| | Min-Max | | | | | | Z-score | | | | | |
|---|---|---|---|---|---|---|---|---|---|---|---|---|
| | | Evaluation | | | | | | Evaluation | | | | |
| Rank | Prediction | Sum | Product | Min | Max | Median | Prediction | Sum | Product | Min | Max | Median |
| 1 | 9 | 26 | 14 | 2 | 26 | 12 | 14 | 12 | 12 | 12 | 12 | 12 |
| 2 | 10 | 12 | 2 | 9 | 12 | 10 | 26 | 14 | 10 | 10 | 10 | 10 |
| 3 | 2 | 14 | 10 | 20 | 14 | 26 | 8 | 2 | 14 | 8 | 2 | 14 |
| 4 | 20 | 20 | 12 | 14 | 20 | 14 | 2 | 10 | 2 | 14 | 14 | 9 |
| 5 | 14 | 9 | 9 | 26 | 9 | 8 | 10 | 9 | 20 | 9 | 9 | 26 |
| 6 | 16 | 2 | 20 | 12 | 2 | 20 | 12 | 20 | 8 | 4 | 20 | 20 |
| 7 | 25 | 10 | 26 | 10 | 10 | 2 | 7 | 4 | 26 | 2 | 26 | 2 |

Table 14.11. *Top 10 Optimal Combinations of Three-Sensor Fusion Systems for the XM2VTS Database: Evaluation vs. Prediction Based on the Neyman-Pearson Theory*

| | Min-Max | | | | | | Z-score | | | | | |
|---|---|---|---|---|---|---|---|---|---|---|---|---|
| | | Evaluation | | | | | | Evaluation | | | | |
| Rank | Prediction | Sum | Product | Min | Max | Median | Prediction | Sum | Product | Min | Max | Median |
| 1 | 69 | 38 | 41 | 31 | 66 | 38 | 81 | 70 | 70 | 66 | 66 | 81 |
| 2 | 31 | 70 | 70 | 83 | 43 | 40 | 73 | 78 | 78 | 43 | 70 | 66 |
| 3 | 68 | 43 | 69 | 62 | 78 | 66 | 43 | 43 | 66 | 63 | 43 | 43 |
| 4 | 62 | 78 | 78 | 42 | 70 | 63 | 30 | 41 | 41 | 73 | 78 | 70 |
| 5 | 73 | 81 | 73 | 63 | 81 | 70 | 42 | 69 | 43 | 48 | 41 | 38 |
| 6 | 83 | 63 | 43 | 59 | 38 | 41 | 38 | 66 | 81 | 62 | 38 | 78 |
| 7 | 41 | 59 | 66 | 56 | 73 | 81 | 68 | 73 | 69 | 65 | 81 | 68 |
| 8 | 56 | 30 | 38 | 30 | 69 | 68 | 66 | 59 | 38 | 70 | 32 | 73 |
| 9 | 59 | 41 | 81 | 75 | 48 | 43 | 40 | 63 | 59 | 56 | 73 | 41 |
| 10 | 75 | 83 | 68 | 67 | 68 | 78 | 67 | 38 | 31 | 75 | 69 | 40 |

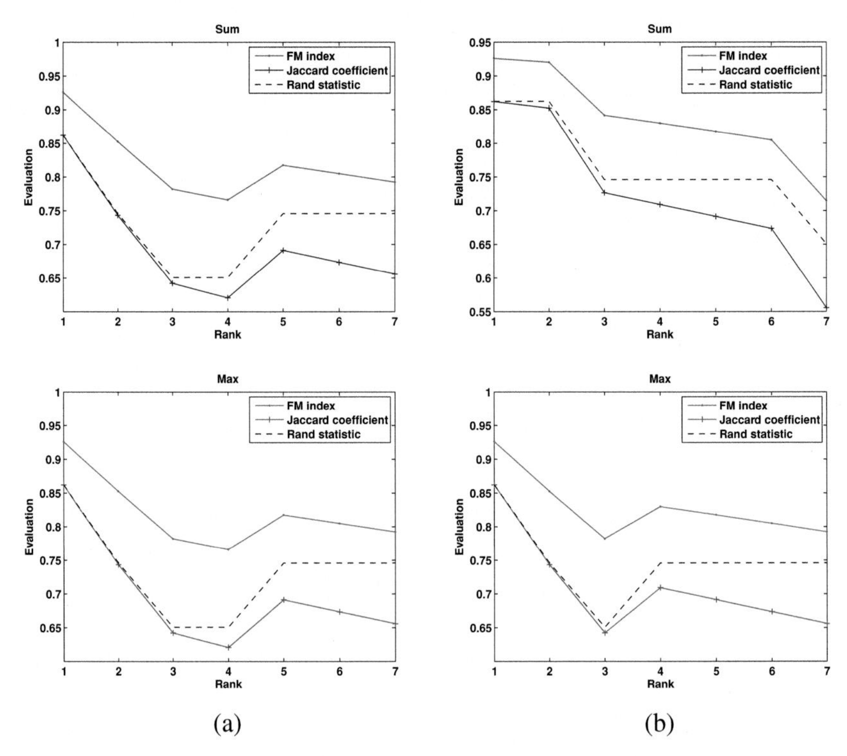


Figure 14.14. Measurement of the agreement degree between the actual results and the prediction based on the Neyman-Pearson theory for two-sensor fusion systems with different fusion rules and normalization methods for the XM2VTS database: (a) Min-Max; (b) z-score.

of $d_S$ from the brute-force experiments and the prediction approach cannot compare directly. We use the criteria $R$, $J$, and $FM$ (Theodoridis and Koutroumbas 1998) to measure the degree of the agreement between the fusion performance evaluation and prediction. Figure 14.14 shows these criteria values for the top seven combinations of the two-sensor fusion systems for Min-Max and $z$-score normalization methods and the sum and max fusion rules. Figure 14.15 shows these criteria values for the top 10 combinations of the three-sensor fusion systems for Min-Max and $z$-score normalization methods and the sum and product fusion rules. Because of the limited combination numbers (28 for two-sensor fusion and 56 for three-sensor fusion), the curves in Figs. 14.14 and 14.15 are not smooth. From Figs. 14.14 and 14.15 and the experiments with other fusion rules, we conclude that different fusion rules and normalization methods have a quite similar effect on the prediction performance. It means that the prediction model is independent of fusion rules.

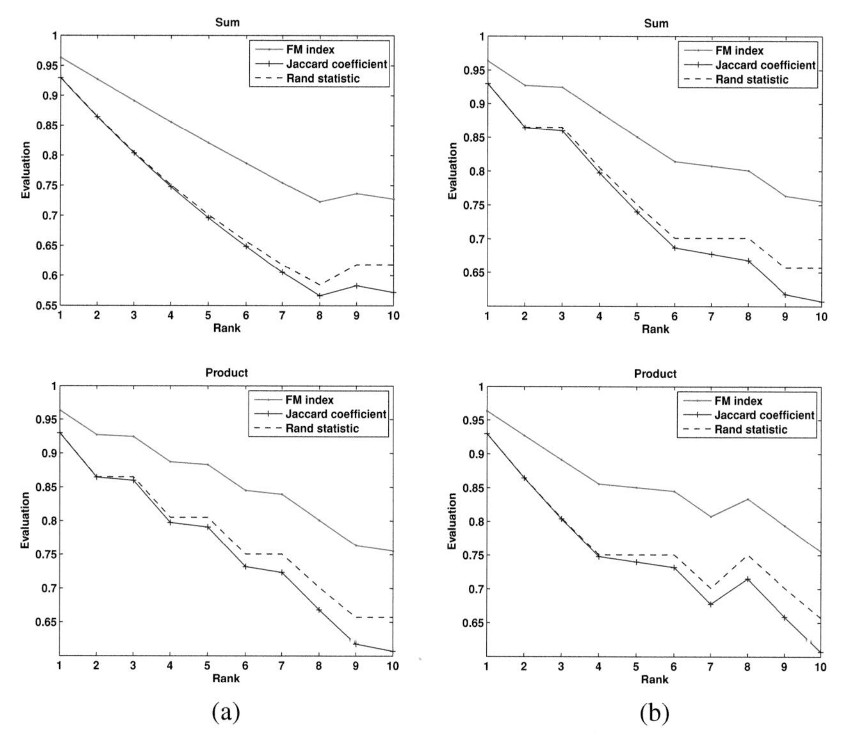


Figure 14.15. Measurement of the agreement degree between the actual results and the prediction based on the Neyman-Pearson theory for three-sensor fusion systems with different fusion rules and normalization methods for the XM2VTS database: (a) Min-Max; (b) z-score.

### 14.4.6 Performance Comparison of the Different Prediction Models

Comparing the criteria values in Figs. 14.10, 14.11, 14.14, and 14.15, we can see that the prediction model that is based on the $\Phi$ transformation has better performance and higher accuracy than the model based on the Neyman-Pearson theory.

## 14.5 Conclusions

In this chapter, we presented two theoretical approaches that predict the performance of fusion of biometrics that allows us to select the optimal combination. Given the characteristics of each biometrics, we compute the object match-score and non–match-score distributions. We model these distributions as mixtures of

Gaussians. In the first approach, we use a transformation to map a *ROC* curve to a 2D straight line whose axes are related to the false alarm rate and the correct recognition rate. Using this representation, we develop a metric to evaluate the sensor fusion performance and find the optimal sensor combination. In the second approach, the prediction model is based on the Neyman-Pearson theory. We define a measurement that considers not only the mean and variance but also the skewness of the log-likelihood ratio of similarity scores of the fusion system as our measurement for discrimination. Then we use this measurement to predict the sensor fusion system performance.

We verify the two prediction approaches on the multimodal XM2VTS database and a mixed database. We use the $R$, $J$, and $FM$ metrics to evaluate the degree of the agreement between the evaluation and prediction of fusion performance. From the experimental results, we conclude that the prediction model based on the $\Phi$ transformation has a better performance than the prediction model based on the Neyman-Pearson theory. By using the proposed prediction models, one can find the optimal combination of biometrics instead of performing the exhaustive experiments. The technical approaches presented here are applicable not only to biometrics fusion but also to various other fusion problems in signal processing, computer vision, and pattern recognition.

## References

Ataman, K., W. N. Street, and Y. Zhang. 2006. Learning to rank by maximizing AUC with linear programming. *Proc. International Joint Conference on Neural Networks*, pages 123–129.

Ben-Yacoub, S. 1998. Multi-modal data fusion for person authentication using SVM. *IDIAP-PR 7*.

Bhanu, B., and V. Govindaraju, editors. 2009. *Multibiometrics for Human Identification*. Cambridge University Press.

Bhanu, B., and X. Tan. 2003. Fingerprint indexing based on novel features of minutiae triplets. *IEEE Trans. on Pattern Analysis and Machine Intelligence*, **25**(5), 616–622.

Bhanu, B., and X. Tan. 2004. *Computational Algorithms for Fingerprint Recognition*. Kluwer Academic Publishers.

Borghys, D., P. Verlinde, C. Perneel, and M. Acheroy. 1998. Multi-level data fusion for the detection of targets using multi-spectral image sequences. *SPIE Optical Engineerings Special Issue on Sensor Fusion*, **37**(2), 477–484.

Chen, H., and B. Bhanu. 2007. Human ear recognition in 3D. *IEEE Trans. on Pattern Analysis and Machine Intelligence*, **29**(4), 718–737.

Chen, H., B. Bhanu, and R. Wang. 2005. Performance evaluation and prediction for 3D ear recognition. *Proc. Audio- and Video-based Biometric Person Authentication*, pages 748–757.

Cortes, C., and M. Mohri. 2004. Confidence intervals for the area under the ROC curve. *Advances in Neural Information Processing Systems*, **17**.

Dasarthy, B. 1994. *Decision Fusion*. IEEE Computer Society Press.

Daugman, J. 2000. Biometric decision landscapes. *Technical Report No. TR482*.

Dorfman, D. D., and E. Alf. 1969. Maximum likelihood estimation of parameters of signal detection theory and determination of confidence intervals. *Journal of Mathematical Psychology*, **6**, 487–496.

Giacinto, G., and F. Roli. 2001. Dynamic classifier selection based on multiple classifier behaviour. *Pattern Recognition*, **34**, 1879–1881.

Green, D. M., and J. A. Swets. 1966. *Signal Detection Theory and Psychophysics*. John Wiley and Sons.

Griffin, P. 2004. Optimal biometric fusion for identity verification. no. RDNI-03-0064, Indentix Corporate Research Center.

Hall, D. L., and J. Llinas. 2001. *Handbook of Multisensor Data Fusion*. CRC Press.

Han, J., and B. Bhanu. 2007. Fusion of color and infrared video for moving human detection. *Pattern Recognition*, **40**(6), 1771–1784.

Jain, A., K. Nandakumar, and A. Ross. 2005. Score normalization in multimodal biometric systems. *Pattern Recognition*, **38**, 2270–2285.

Kale, A., A. Roy-chowdhry, and R. Chellappa. 2004. Fusion of gait and face for human identification. *Proc. Acoustics, Speech, and Signal Processing*, **5**, 901–904.

Keller, J. M., S. Auephanwiriyakul, and P. D. Gader. 2001. Experiments in predictive sensor fusion. *Proc. SPIE*, **4394**, 1047–1058.

Kittler, J., M. Hatef, R. P. W. Duin, and J. Matas. 1998. On combining classifiers. *IEEE Trans. on Pattern Analysis and Machine Intelligence*, **20**(3), 226–239.

Kuncheva, L. 2006. *Combining Pattern Classifiers: Methods and Algorithms*. Springer.

Marzban, C. 2004. The ROC curve and the area under it as performance measures. *Weather and Forecasting*, **19**, 1106–1114.

Nadimi, S., and B. Bhanu. 2004. Adaptive fusion for diurnal moving object detection. *Proc. Intl. Conf. on Pattern Recognition*, **3**(696–699).

Poh, N., and S. Bengio. 2004. Database, protocol and tools for evaluation score-level fusion algorithms in biometric authentication. *IDIAP Research Report*.

Poh, N., and S. Bengio. 2004. Towards predicting optimal fusion candidates: a case study on biometric authentication tasks. *Proc. Machine Learning and Multimodal Interaction Workshop*, pages 159–172.

Poh, N., and S. Bengio. 2005. How do correlation and variance of base classifiers affect fusion in biometric authentication tasks. *IEEE Trans. on Signal Processing*, **53**(11), 4384–4396.

Ross, A., and A. K. Jain. 2004. Multimodal biometrics: an overview. *Proc. 12th European Signal Processing Conferencee*, pages 1221–1224.

Ross, A., K. Nandakumar, and A. Jain. 2004. *Handbook of Multibiometrics*. John Wiley.

Ross, A. A., and R. Govindarajan. 2005. Feature level fusion of hand and face biometrics. *Proc. SPIE Conf. on Biometric Technology for Human Identification II*, pages 196–204.

Shakhnarovich, G., and T. Darrell. 2002. On probabilistic combination of face and gait cues for identification. *Proc. Automatic Face Gesture Recognition*, pages 169–174,

Theodoridis, S., and K. Koutroumbas. 1998. *Pattern Recognition*. Academic Press.

Ulery, B., A. Hicklin, C. Watson, W. Fellner, and P. Hallinan. 2006. Studies of biometric fusion. *NISTIR 7346*.

Varshney, P. K. 1997. Multisensor data fusion. *Electronics and Communications Engineering Journal*, **9**, 245–253.

Verlinde, P., G. Chollet, and M. Acheroy. 2000. Multi-modal identity verification using expert fusion. *Information Fusion*, **1**, 17–33.

Waltz, E., and J. Llinas. 1990. *Multisensor Data Fusion*. Artech House.

Wang, R., and B. Bhanu. 2006. Performance prediction for multimodal biometrics. *Proc. Intl. Conf. on Pattern Recognition*, **3**, 586–589.

Wang, R., and B. Bhanu. 2007. On the performance prediction and validation for multisensor fusion. *IEEE. Conf. on Computer Vision and Pattern Recognition*, pages 1–6, June 17–22.

Yan, L., R. Dodier, M. C. Mozer, and R. Wolniewicz. 2003. Optimizing classifier performance via an approximation to the Wilcoxon-Mann-Whitney statistic. *Proc. International Conference on Machine Learning*, pages 848–855.

Yousef, W. A., R. F. Wagner, and M. H. Loew. 2006. Assessing classifiers from two independent data sets using ROC analysis: a nonparametric approach. *IEEE Trans. on Pattern Analysis and Machine Intelligence*, **28**(11), 1809–1817.

Zhou, X., and B. Bhanu. 2007. Integrating face and gait for human recognition at a distance in video. *IEEE Trans. on Systems, Man, and Cybernetics-Part B: Cybernetics*, **37**(5), 1119–1137.

Zhou, X., and B. Bhanu. 2008. Feature fusion of side face and gait for video-based human identification. *Pattern Recognition*, **41**(3), 778–795.

# 15
# Predicting Performance in Large-Scale Identification Systems by Score Resampling

Sergey Tulyakov and Venu Govindaraju

## 15.1 Introduction

With the wider deployment of biometric authentication systems and the increased number of enrolled persons in such systems, the problem of correctly predicting the performance has become important. The number of available testing samples is usually smaller than the number of enrolled persons that the biometric system is expected to handle. The accurate performance prediction allows system integrators to optimally select the biometric matchers for the system, as well as to properly set the decision thresholds.

Research in predicting the performance in large-scale biometric systems is still limited and mostly theoretical. Wayman (1999) introduced multiple operating scenarios for biometric systems and derived the equations for predicted performance assuming that the densities of genuine and impostor scores are known. Jarosz et al. (2005) presented an overview of possible performance estimation methods including extrapolation of large-scale performance given the performance on smaller-scale databases, binomial approximation of performance, and the application of extreme value theory. Bolle et al. (2005) derived the performance of identification systems (CMC curve) assuming that the performance of the corresponding biometric verification system (ROC curve) is known. The major assumption used in all these works is that the biometric match scores are independent and identically distributed, that is, genuine scores are randomly drawn from a genuine score distribution, and impostor scores are randomly and independently drawn from an impostor score distribution. As we will show in this chapter, this assumption does not generally hold, and using it leads to the underestimation of identification performance.

The need to account for match score dependencies was previously noted in Johnson et al. (2003) and Grother and Phillips (2004). Grother and Phillips (2004) proposed two practical methods to deal with score dependencies:

conditioning impostor scores used in the prediction on corresponding genuine scores obtained in the same test identification trial and applying T-normalization to test scores (Auckenthaler et al. 2000). We will discuss these methods and evaluate their performance.

The research on predicting the biometric system performance on a single test sample (Wang and Bhanu 2007) can be considered as related to our topic because the accurate modeling of matching score dependencies in identification trials is required. The problem of estimating identification system performance was also previously studied in the area of handwritten word recognition (Xue and Govindaraju 2002; Marti and Bunke 2001).

Because we will use the results of experiments throughout the chapter, we will introduce the problem statement and experimental setup at the beginning, in Section 15.2. Sections 15.3 and 15.4 describe two major factors influencing the prediction results: score mixing effect and binomial approximation effect. Sections 15.5 and 15.6 analyze two previously proposed methods for predicting large-scale identification system performance: binomial model and T-normalization. In Section 15.7 we present our prediction method of resampling and utilizing identification trial statistics. Finally, Sections 15.8 and 15.9 will include additional discussion and our conclusion.

## 15.2 Experimental Setup

We have used the biometric matching score set BSSR1 distributed by NISTbss (n.d). This set contains matching scores for a fingerprint matcher and two face matchers "C" and "G." Fingerprint matching scores are given for the left index "li" finger matches and right index "ri" finger matches. Because the performance of fingerprint matcher is different for the two fingers, we consider these datasets as being two separate identification systems. Thus, we consider the predictions in four possible identification systems corresponding to each of these score subsets: "C," "G," "li," and "ri."

Each of these sets contains matching scores for 6000 identification trials, and each trial has scores for either 3000 (for face sets) or 6000 (for fingerprints) enrollees. One score in each trial is genuine, and the remaining are impostors related to different enrollees. To avoid dealing with different numbers of enrollees we restricted the number of scores in identification trials for fingerprints to 3000. Furthermore, some enrollees and some identification trials had to be discarded because of apparent enrollment errors. Finally, we obtained four datasets of 5982 identification trials, with each trial having 2991 matching scores.

We used a bootstrap testing procedure (Bolle et al. 2004): For 100 iterations, we randomly split the data in two parts of 2991 identification trials of separate prediction and testing sets. Because our purpose is to predict the performance in larger identification systems using the performance in smaller systems, for each identification trial in the prediction set we retained only 100 randomly selected impostor scores. Therefore our objective is the following: by using 2991 identification trials with 100 impostor scores in each, try to predict the performance on the test set of 2991 trials and 2990 impostor scores in each trial (one score in each trial is genuine). The results of 100 bootstrap prediction/testing iterations are averaged to obtain the final result.

In this research we have concentrated on predicting the *closed set identification* performance. The identification trial is considered *successful* if a genuine score is higher than all impostor scores of this trial. The *correct identification rate*, that is, a probability of successful identification trials, is a measure of closed set identification performance. Most of the previous works in predicting the identification system performance also consider the scenario of *open set identification*, where, in addition to being the top score, the genuine score is required to be higher than some threshold. We chose not to consider open set identification scenario in this chapter because of the increased complexity of the analysis and our previous observation that simple thresholding of top score might not deliver the optimal performance (Tulyakov and Govindaraju 2005a; see section 15.8.3).

We also do not consider the more general $k$th rank identification performance measured by CMC curve, though our proposed prediction methods can be easily extended to measure such performance. Our goal is to investigate the general mechanisms of the functioning of identification systems, rather than to consider all possible operating and decision-making scenarios.

## 15.3 The Score Mixing Effect

One of the important characteristics of the identification system is the dependence between matching scores assigned to different classes in a single identification trial. For example, in one identification trial all the matching scores might be relatively high, and in another trial all the scores might be low. Such dependence can be a result of multiple factors: the quality of the input biometrics, the density of biometric templates around the input template, the particulars of the matching score calculation algorithms, etc.

Limited research has been carried out so far in investigating score dependencies in identification trials. Li et al. (2005) connect the measures derived

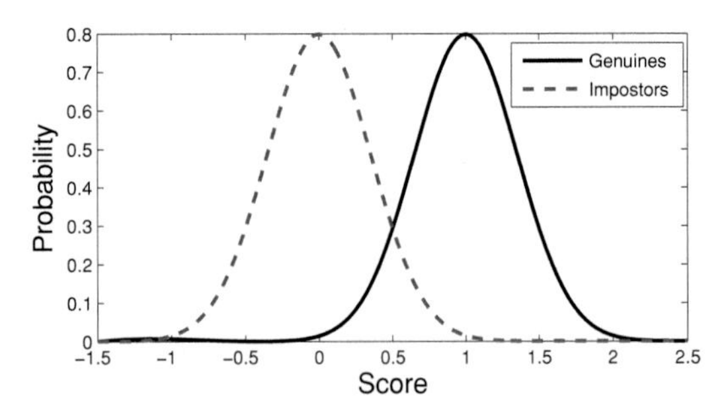


Figure 15.1. Hypothetical densities of matching(genuine) and nonmatching (impostors) scores.

from matching scores with the quality of the image. Wang and Bhanu (2007) investigate the possibility of success of the fingerprint match through the properties of a fingerprint-matching algorithm. Xue and Govindaraju (2002) try to predict the performance of the handwritten word recognizer based on the density of the lexicon but do not consider any other factors, such as quality of the word image. The explicit modeling of score dependencies presented in these approaches might be useful, but in our current investigation we are not associating the score dependence with particular characteristics of a test template or the matching algorithm. The employed dataset (NIST BSSR1) contains only matching scores and does not allow such analysis of matching algorithms.

The following example illustrates the necessity for accounting of matching score dependencies when attempting to predict the identification system performance.

### 15.3.1 Example of Identification Systems

Consider a following two-class identification system. In each identification trial we have only one genuine and one impostor score. Suppose that genuine and impostor scores are distributed according to score densities shown in Figure 15.1.

Consider two possible scenarios on how the matching scores are generated during an identification attempt:

1. Both scores $s_{\text{gen}}$ and $s_{\text{imp}}$ are sampled independently from genuine and impostor distributions.
2. In every identification attempt, $s_{\text{imp}} = s_{\text{gen}} - 1$.

If our identification system follows the first scenario, there will be identification trials with impostor score higher than the genuine score. Consequently, the

Table 15.1. *Identification System Performance Using Original Identification Trials ("True Performance") and Using Random Impostors in Identification Trials ("Randomized Impostors")*

| Matchers | True Performance | Randomized Impostors |
|---|---|---|
| C | 0.811 | 0.738 |
| G | 0.774 | 0.669 |
| li | 0.823 | 0.777 |
| ri | 0.885 | 0.850 |

correct identification rate for such system will be less than 100%. In the second scenario the identification system always correctly places the genuine sample on top and has a correct identification rate of 100%. Score distributions of Figure 15.1 do not reflect this difference. So, if we want to predict identification system performance, we need to learn the dependencies between the matching scores produced in a single identification trial. Using genuine and impostor score densities alone might not be sufficient for correct prediction.

### 15.3.2 Performance of Systems with Randomized Impostor Scores

To confirm the presence of score dependencies in our experimental systems and the necessity to account for this dependence, we conduct the following experiment. Instead of original sets of identification trial scores, we considered identification trials with randomly chosen impostor scores belonging to different trials. We implemented such random sampling by randomly permuting the impostor matching scores from different identification trials. Such randomization converts our original identification systems into a identification system having the same distributions of genuine and impostor scores, but impostor scores in identification trials become independent and identically distributed. Comparing with the example of the previous section, we convert the identification system with dependent scores of the second scenario into an identification system with independent scores of the first scenario.

Table 15.1 compares the performances of our original identification systems and corresponding identification systems with randomized impostor scores (the numbers in the table are the *correct identification rate*). For all matchers the difference in performances of the corresponding identification systems is rather significant.

In all cases we observe that the performance of the original systems is higher. This might be explained by the positive correlations between the genuine and impostor scores for all the considered matchers. When matching scores are positively correlated, we have particular identification trials having both high genuine and high impostor scores. By distributing the high impostor scores to other trials we might make them unsuccessful. This explains the lowered performance of identification systems with randomized scores.

### 15.3.3 Score Mixing Effect

When we try to predict the performance of large-scale identification systems, we could be calculating some parameters or functions using matching scores from separate training identification trials. For example, most of the previous work utilizes the density of the impostor scores $n(x)$ or the cumulative distribution function of impostor scores $N(t) = \int_{-\infty}^{t} n(x)dx$ (we are using the notation of Grother and Phillips [2004]). If we use all our training impostor scores to estimate these distributions, then our prediction will be a prediction of the identification system with randomized scores (as in previous section), rather than the prediction of the performance in the original system.

The *score mixing effect* is the result of considering scores from different identification trials simultaneously instead of considering the sets of matching scores from each training identification trial as separate entities for calculating prediction. The presence of the score mixing effect becomes apparent as soon as practical experiments on real data are performed (see (Grother and Phillips 2004), section 4.2), instead of making purely theoretical predictions (Wayman 1999) or experimenting with synthetic data.

When we try to predict the performance of large scale identification systems, we might have only samples of training identification trials with a small number of impostors. In our experimental setup we predict performance in a systems with 2990 impostors by using training identification trials with only 100 impostors. Given 100 impostors of a single identification trial we have a great difficulty to correctly estimate the distribution of a highest score in a set of 2990 impostors. To make any meaningful predictions, instead of a single trial with 100 impostors, we also have to use scores from other trials. So it seems inevitable that we have to mix the scores from different trials, and we need to learn how to minimize the score mixing effect.

## 15.4 The Binomial Approximation Effect

To perform a further analysis, we will temporarily for this section assume that the scores in identification trials are independent and identically distributed according to either genuine or impostor distributions. The systems with randomized scores of previous section will serve as our test systems here.

Assuming the independence of matching scores in identification trials, the closed set identification performance in a system with $G$ enrollees is represented by the following formula (Grother and Phillips 2004):

$$R = \int_{-\infty}^{\infty} N^{G-1}(x)m(x)dx, \tag{15.1}$$

where $N(x)$ is the cumulative distribution function of impostor (nonmatching) scores and $m(x)$ is the density of genuine (matching) scores. This formula also assumes that largest score corresponds to identification result ("larger score" = "better score"), which is true for all four matchers we have for experiments. Note that this formula can be considered as a specific case of more general formula for calculating the probability of genuine score to be in rank $k$ (or CMC curve) (Grother and Phillips 2004). Because of involvement of binomial terms in the formula for CMC, the prediction approach utilizing equation (15.1) is called the binomial approximation prediction method.

Formula (15.1) can be interpreted as an expectation of function $N^{G-1}(x)$ with respect to genuine samples $x$, and the traditional approximation of the expectation is given by the mean of function values over the set of genuine samples in the training set:

$$R \approx \frac{1}{L}\sum_{i=1}^{L} N^{G-1}(x_i), \tag{15.2}$$

where $L$ is the number of training identification trials and is the same as the number of training genuine score samples ($L = 2991$ in our experiments). It is also traditional to approximate the cumulative distribution function $N(x)$ by the empirical distribution function:

$$N(x) \approx \hat{N}(x) = \frac{1}{K}\sum_{j=1}^{K} I(y_j < x), \tag{15.3}$$

where $K$ is the number of impostor scores $y_j$ used for approximating $N(x)$ and $I$ is the identity function (1 if input parameter is true, 0 if false). After substituting (15.3) into (15.2) we obtain

$$R \approx \frac{1}{L}\sum_{i=1}^{L}\left(\frac{1}{K}\sum_{j=1}^{K} I(y_j < x_i)\right)^{G-1}. \tag{15.4}$$

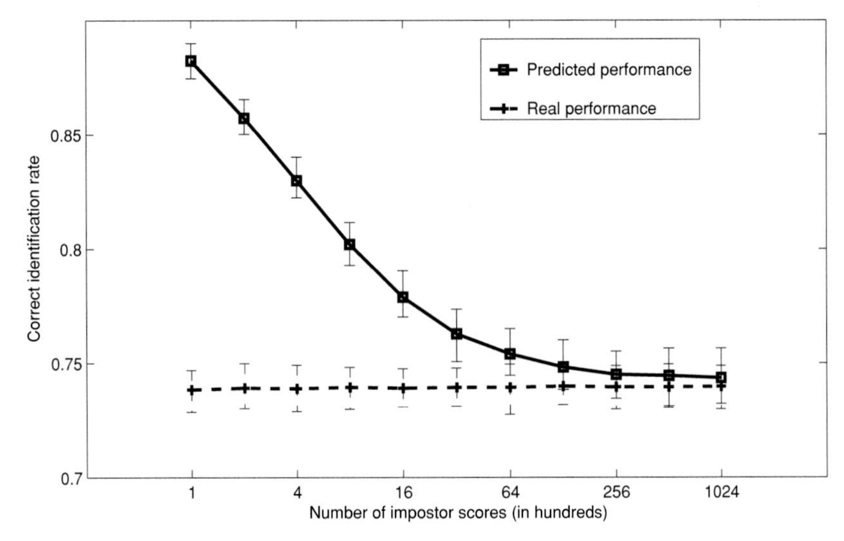


Figure 15.2. Dependence of predicted performance on the number of impostor scores used in binomial approximation for matcher "C" with randomized scores.

This formula can be alternatively derived using combinatorial methods similar to Johnson et al. (2003), but in our derivation we explicitly state used approximations of the theoretically correct prediction equation (15.1).

Using our experimental setup and and randomized training score sets of section 15.3.2, we evaluated the prediction capabilities of binomial approximation method (15.4) on all four of our matchers. Note that because the scores are randomized, the independence condition is satisfied, and the binomial approximation method should be theoretically optimal.

Figure 15.2 shows the predicted performance of matcher "C" using binomial approximation method (15.4) for different numbers of training impostor scores $K$ used for approximating $N(x)$. The experiments on the other three matchers showed a similar dependence of prediction on the number of used impostor samples, and we are omitting their graphs from the chapter.

As we expected, the predicted performance indeed converges to the true performance of the system with randomized scores with the increase in the number of impostor scores used. But this convergence is rather slow and requires a large number of training impostor samples. When the number of used impostors is small, we see a significant overestimation of the identification system performance.

To understand why such overestimation occurs, let us consider the case of $K = 100$ impostor scores used to predict performance in our system with

$G - 1 = 2990$ impostors. From equation (15.3) the values of function $\hat{N}(x)$ will be multiples of $\frac{1}{K}$. If, according to equation (15.4), we consider powers $\hat{N}(x)^{G-1}$, we will see that the values of these powers will be negligible with the exception of the case when $\hat{N}(x) = 1$. For example, if $\hat{N}(x) = \frac{K-1}{K} = \frac{99}{100}$, then $\hat{N}(x)^{G-1} = 0.99^{2990} \approx 8.9 \times 10^{-14}$. Effectively, in this case the application of binomial approximation (15.4) will simply count the number of genuine scores that are bigger than all impostors (for which $\hat{N}(x) = 1$), and the calculated performance will be close to the performance of identification system with $K = 100$ impostors instead of the desired performance of a system with $G - 1 = 2990$ impostors.

Note that the overestimation of performance by binomial approximation occurs not only when $K < G - 1$, but also for larger numbers of training impostor samples $K$. Doddington et al. (2000) proposed using the following rule of thumb when evaluating the performance of biometric systems: to be 90% confident that the true error rate is within ±30% of the observed error rate, there must be at least 30 errors. The imprecision in predicting identification system performance is mostly explained by the errors in approximating the impostor distribution $N(x) \rightarrow \hat{N}(x)$ in the area of high values of $x$. In this area we might have approximated $\hat{N}(x) = 1$, which implies that for a given $x$ we did not find any training impostor value higher than it. But the rule of thumb suggests that we need at least 30 errors (or impostors higher than $x$) to correctly estimate $N(x)$.

So for the precise estimation of $N(x)$ in the area of $x$ where we would normally get only one error (impostor) in our predicted system with $G - 1$ impostors, we would need to have around 30 errors (impostors). This means we would need around $30(G - 1)$ impostors to make predictions for a system with $G - 1$ impostors using binomial approximation, and the results of Figure 15.2 seem to confirm this reasoning. Hence, we can restate the rule of thumb of Doddington et al. (2000) with respect to predicting identification system performance by a binomial approximation: The number of impostor training samples should be at least 30 times bigger than the size of identification system for which the prediction is made – $K/G > 30$.

## 15.5 The Combination of Score Mixing and Binomial Approximation Effects

In the last section we considered identification systems with randomized scores and thus bypassed the existence of the score mixing effect. What happens if we try to predict the performance of original identification systems, and both effects, score mixing effect and binomial approximation effect, influence our predictions?

The first effect underestimates identification system performance, and the second effect overestimates it. It might turn out that we will accidentally predict correctly the performance in larger identification systems with binomial approximation and mixed scores. Note that the true performance of system "C" given in Table 15.1 is 0.811, and from Figure 15.2 the performance of identification system with randomized scores is around the same number when the number of impostors used in binomial approximation is 600. So if we simply considered binomial approximation (15.4), took $K = 600$, and chose random impostors $y_j$, our predicted performance would have coincided with the true performance.

We suspect that the influence of both effects contributed to the good prediction results reported in Johnson et al. (2003). Though in that paper the training sets of impostors are retained, each impostor set is used with all training genuine samples. Thus the score mixing effect should be present in this approach. Also, the binomial formula for calculating prediction (7) of Johnson et al. (2003) involves term $(i/K)^{G-1}$ where $K = 100$, and, as in the analysis of previous section, we expect the binomial approximation effect to be significant. In our experiments we were not able to obtain good prediction results using the approach of Johnson et al. (2003), and thus we do not report its performance.

One of the approaches considered in Grother and Phillips (2004) to deal with the dependence of scores in identification trials is to condition the cumulative distribution function $N(x)$ of impostor scores on the values of genuine scores obtained in the same identification trials. Let us denote $n(y|x)$ as a density of impostor scores with the condition that impostor scores belong to identification trials having genuine score $x$ and let $N_x(t) = \int_{-\infty}^{t} n(y|x)dy$ denote the corresponding conditional distribution function of impostor scores. Then, assuming that impostor scores in each identification trial are independent and identically distributed according to $n(y|x)$, we can derive the following closed set identification performance prediction similar to (15.1):

$$R = \int_{-\infty}^{\infty} N_x^{G-1}(x)m(x)dx. \tag{15.5}$$

To approximate $N_x(x)$, Grother and Phillips (2004) split the training identification trials into $B$ bins of equal size according to their genuine scores. Then they approximated $N_x(x)$ using only training impostor samples from the identification trials of one bin. By increasing the number of bins $B$ they were trying to control the dependence between matching scores, but they disregarded the

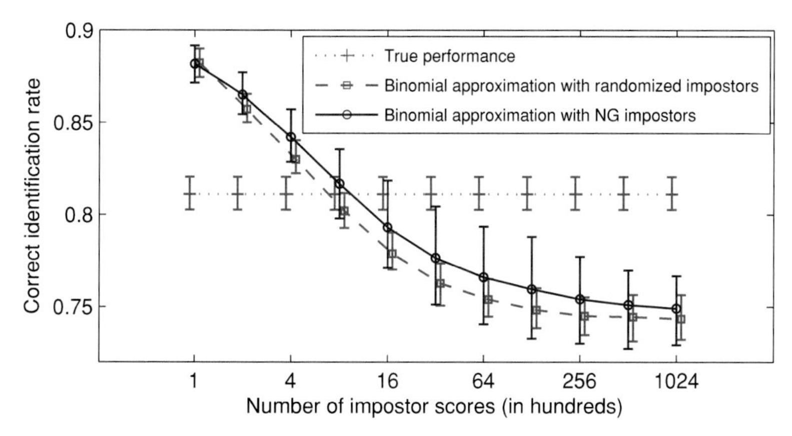


Figure 15.3. Dependence of predicted performance on the number of impostor scores used in binomial approximation for matcher "C" with randomized scores and for impostor scores chosen by the nearest genuine principle.

effect of binomial approximation that is dominant for larger number of bins and correspondingly smaller number of impostor scores used for approximations.

Here we repeat those experiments, but instead of splitting training identification trials into bins, for each training genuine sample $x$ we are using impostors from $K_n$ training identification trials with values of genuine scores closest to $x$. In this way, we are more precise in estimating $N_x(x)$ when the value of $x$ might have been near some bin's boundary.

Figure 15.3 contains the results of these experiments on set "C" (other sets have similar behavior). We called the method presented in this section "binomial approximation with NG (nearest genuine) impostors" and compared it with the binomial approximation method with randomized scores from previous section. For the same numbers of impostor scores used in binomial approximations ($K = 100K_n$), the selection of impostor scores using nearest genuine criteria has higher predicted performance than a random choice of impostors. This means that the influence of the score mixing effect is reduced, and the method does improve the prediction. On the other hand, the observed prediction improvements are not significant, and we can see that this method, similar to binomial approximation with randomized scores, is greatly influenced by the two previously described effects, score mixing and binomial approximation.

## 15.6 T-Normalization

Another technique, which was proposed in Grother and Phillips (2004) to account for score dependencies in identification trials, is to perform

T (test)-normalization of matching scores before applying binomial approximation prediction:

$$x_{ij} \to \frac{x_{ij} - \hat{\mu}_i}{\hat{\sigma}_i}, \tag{15.6}$$

where $x_{ij}$ is the $j$th score from the $i$th training identification trial, and $\hat{\mu}_i$ and $\hat{\sigma}_i$ are the sample mean and the sample variance of the scores in the $i$th training identification trial. Note that though Grother and Phillips (2004) use the term Z (zero)-normalization, it seems that they actually perform T-normalization by (15.6). (Z-normalization has a similar formula with $\mu$ and $\sigma$ derived using either all available scores or scores related to a particular enrolled template.)

Suppose we have some score density $p(x)$ with mean of 0 and variance of 1. Also, suppose that for each identification trial $i$ we are given two random parameters $\mu_i$ and $\sigma_i$, and the scores in the identification trial are independently sampled according to

$$p_i(x) = p_{\mu_i,\sigma_i}(x) = \frac{1}{\sigma_i} p\left(\frac{x - \mu_i}{\sigma_i}\right). \tag{15.7}$$

It is easy to show that in this case the mean of scores in the identification trial $i$ is $\mu_i$ and the variance is $\sigma_i$. By calculating sample mean and variance estimates, $\hat{\mu}_i$ and $\hat{\sigma}_i$, and by applying T-normalization (15.6) to the identification trial scores, the transformed scores will be approximately (because of approximations $\mu_i \approx \hat{\mu}_i$ and $\sigma_i \approx \hat{\sigma}_i$) distributed according to $p(x)$.

Equation (15.7) represents a possible model of how the dependencies between matching scores in identification trials originate. We can call it the *linear score dependency model*. Previously, Navratil and Ramaswamy (2003) described the T-normalization using the property of *local Gaussianity*, which assumes that function $p_i(x)$ is close to normal density with mean $\mu_i$ and variance $\sigma_i$. In our description we are not making any assumptions on the form of $p_i(x)$ except that it is generated for each identification trial by (15.7) using some common density $p$. There are also no assumptions on distributions of $\mu_i$ and $\sigma_i$ (which are randomly chosen for each identification trial).

According to the linear score dependency model the range of scores in each identification trial is shifted by $\mu_i$ and stretched by $\sigma_i$. Note that there are two types of scores in identification trials – genuine and impostors – and it is quite possible that they might have different dependence models. But the number of genuine scores in identification trials is limited (usually only one genuine score), and it is not possible to learn the dependency model for genuine scores. Therefore, we will assume that the same model is applied for both types of scores; the sample estimates $\hat{\mu}_i$ and $\hat{\sigma}_i$ can be computed using both genuine and impostor samples, but in this work we use only impostor score samples.

Table 15.2. *True Performances of Identification Systems ("True") and Prediction Using T-Normalized Scores and Binomial Approximation on a Full Set ("T-Norm and BA")*

| Matchers | True | T-Norm and BA |
|---|---|---|
| C | 0.811 | 0.818 |
| G | 0.774 | 0.602 |
| li | 0.823 | 0.838 |
| ri | 0.892 | 0.902 |

T-normalization is a linear transformation for each identification trial, and it does not change the order of matching scores. So, if the identification trial was successful, it will remain successful after T-normalization. Thus, instead of making performance prediction in an identification system with a linear score dependency model (15.7), we can make predictions in an identification system with T-normalized scores. More specifically, assuming that genuine and impostor scores in each identification trial are the result of a linear score dependency model and have distributions

$$m_i(x) = m_{\mu_i,\sigma_i}(x) = \frac{1}{\sigma_i} m\left(\frac{x-\mu_i}{\sigma_i}\right),$$
$$n_i(x) = n_{\mu_i,\sigma_i}(x) = \frac{1}{\sigma_i} n\left(\frac{x-\mu_i}{\sigma_i}\right) \quad (15.8)$$

after T-normalization genuine and impostor scores will be independently and identically distributed according to $m(x)$ and $n(x)$, and the closed set identification performance of the original system will be similar to the performance of the identification system with i.i.d. scores with densities $m(x)$ and $n(x)$.

Because the total number of impostor scores in our experimental setup is sufficient to make binomial approximation performance prediction of a closed set identification system with independent scores, we made such predictions on T-normalized scores for all four identification systems. Table 15.2 shows the results of this prediction.

The use of T-normalization seems to give almost perfect prediction results for three systems but failed for predicting the performance of identification system "G." This failure means that the linear score dependence model does not represent the set of matching scores in system "G," and we have to search for some other model of score dependence. Additionally, even if other systems do achieve a good performance prediction after T-normalization, it is not necessary that the linear score dependence model exactly describes the dependencies of scores in identification trials, and the actual dependencies might be more complex.

## 15.7 Resampling Methods

In this work we introduce the resampling method for predicting large-scale identification system performance. The method is rather simple: We simulate the work of the identification system by choosing the genuine and impostor scores from the training set. Specifically, for each training genuine sample, we choose $G - 1 = 2990$ training impostor samples. If the genuine score is the highest, then the identification trial is successful, and the performance of the simulated system is calculated as a proportion of successful identification trials.

It is clear that this method requires a larger number of training impostor scores than the number $G$ of enrolled persons in simulated system. But, because we analyzed that the number of impostor scores for binomial approximation should be at least 30 times more than $G$, we can expect that the approximation abilities of the resampling method will be on par with the abilities of the binomial approximation. To confirm the approximation abilities of the proposed method, we compared its performance with the binomial approximation method on an identification system with randomized scores (Section 15.3.2) using the full training set of $L = 2991$ genuine samples and $K = 2991 \times 100$ impostor scores. Whereas in binomial approximation method (15.4) for each genuine score we used all $K = 2991 \times 100$ impostors, in resampling method we were randomly choosing $G - 1 = 2990$ impostors for each genuine.

The results of these experiments are shown in Figure 15.4. Both methods show similar approximating performance. The spread of the error bars is also similar and slightly larger than the spread of error bars on test set. Note that evaluation on the test set ("True performance") works in essentially the same way as the resampling method. The only difference is that evaluation on the test set uses $2991 \times 2990$ test impostor scores with 2990 nonrepeating impostors for each genuine score, but the resampling method uses only $2991 \times 100$ impostors and has to repeatedly use impostors with each impostor used approximately 30 times. The reuse of training impostor samples explains the larger spread of error bars for a resampling method.

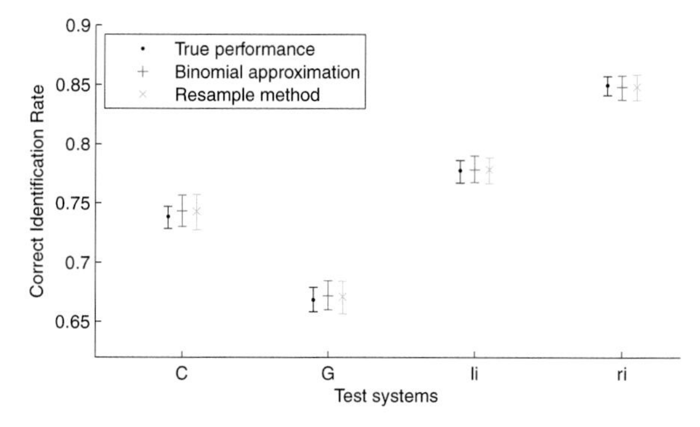


Figure 15.4. Performance prediction of identification system with randomized scores by binomial approximation and score resampling methods.

### 15.7.1 Resampling Using Genuine Score Neighbors

The key advantage of the resampling method and the reason for its use is that it allows us to more precisely control the score mixing effect when performing predictions. The binomial method requires mixing more than $30G$ impostors by formula (15.4) for each training genuine score, but the resampling method uses only $G - 1$ impostors for each genuine one. The binomial approximation effect did not allow us to correctly predict performance by approximating cumulative distribution functions $N_x(x)$ conditioned on genuine scores $x$ in Section 15.5. The resampling method is not susceptible to the binomial approximation effect and allows us to more precisely evaluate the benefits of utilizing genuine score conditioning.

In this section we modify the experiments of Section 15.5 using the resampling method. For each training genuine sample $x$ we are using $G - 1$ impostors from $K_n$ training identification trials with values of genuine scores closest to $x$. Since each training identification trial has 100 impostor scores, it is sufficient to use only $K_n = \lceil (G-1)/100 \rceil = 30$ closest training identification trials.

Figure 15.5 compares the performance of a resampling method utilizing the nearest genuine sampling method with the resampling method using random impostors and the true performance of our systems. Clearly, using a nearest genuine identification trial reduces the score mixing effect, but this reduction is still not sufficient for precise performance prediction. A similar reduction was observed for the binomial approximation method (Figure 15.3), but because of the binomial approximation effect we were not able to judge objectively the strength of using the nearest genuine principle.

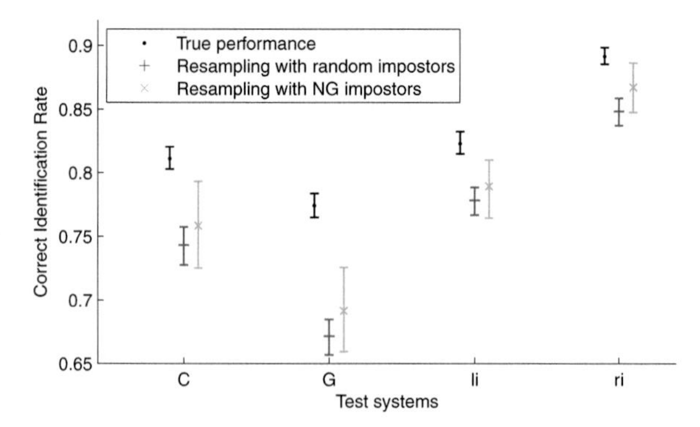


Figure 15.5. Performance prediction in original identification systems by score resampling methods with randomized sampling and nearest genuine sampling.

### 15.7.2 Score Resampling Using Identification Trial Statistics

To control the mixing effect in the resampling method we want to mix scores only from similar training identification trials. Selecting identification trials using the closest genuine scores of the previous section is just one possible way of specifying the similarity between identification trials. We expand this method by using statistics of identification trial score sets to determine the similarity between trials.

Let $T_i = \{x_{ij}\}_j$ denote the set of matching scores from the $i$th training identification trial and let $t(T_i)$ denote some statistic of this set. For example, $t(T_i)$ could be the sample mean $\hat{\mu}_i$ or the sample variance $\hat{\sigma}_i$ statistics used for T-normalization in Section 15.6. Define the distance between identification trials $T_i$ and $T_k$ with respect to statistic function $t$ as a distance between corresponding statistics of two sets:

$$dist_t(T_i, T_k) = |t(T_i) - t(T_k)|. \tag{15.9}$$

Denote $G_t$ as the number of impostor scores in training identification trials ($G_t = 100$ in our experiments). Then the resampling method with identification trial statistic $t$ for predicting identification system performance is formulated as follows:

1. For training identification trial $T_i$ and corresponding genuine score $x_i$, find $K_n = \lceil (G-1)/G_t \rceil$ training identification trials $T_k$ closest to $T_i$ with respect to distance $dist_t(T_i, T_k)$.
2. Choose random $G - 1$ impostors from selected identification trials; the simulated trial is successful if $x_i$ is bigger than all chosen impostors.

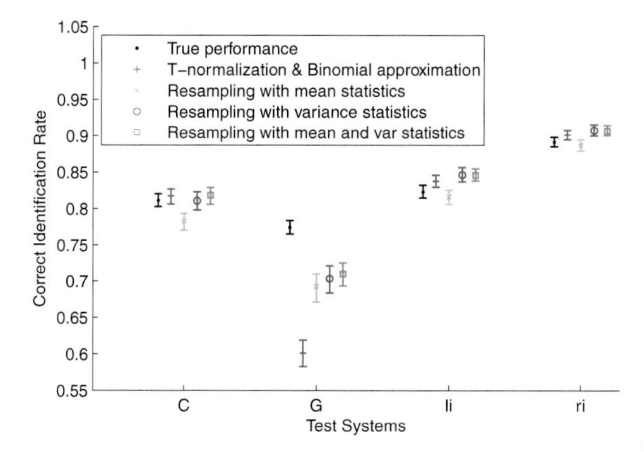


Figure 15.6. Performance prediction in original identification systems by T-normalization followed by binomial approximation and score resampling methods based on mean and mean-variance statistics.

3. Repeat 1–2 for all available training identification trials $T_i$ and calculate the predicted system performance as the proportion of successful simulated identification trials.

The proposed resampling algorithm is rather simple and does not require any parameter training. However, it does require proper selection of the used identification trial statistic $t$. In the rest of this section we will investigate the use of different statistics. Note that $K_n = \lceil (G-1)/G_t \rceil = 30$ in our experiments, so for each genuine score we are looking for 30 training identification trials out of a total 2991. Thus, the resampling method seems to be quite selective and might be able to significantly reduce the score mixing effect.

### 15.7.3 Resampling and T-Normalization

The performance prediction method based on T-normalization (eq. [15.6]) used two identification trial score statistics: sample mean $\hat{\mu}_i$ and sample variance $\hat{\sigma}_i$. We conducted experiments on using these statistics in resampling method and compared the results of prediction with T-normalization based prediction of section 15.6.

Figure 15.6 presents the results of these experiments. Note that when we use both mean and variance statistics, the statistics of identification trials are two-dimensional vectors $t(T_i) = (\hat{\mu}_i, \hat{\sigma}_i)$, and instead of simple absolute difference for calculating distance in (15.9) we use Euclidean distance.

The T-normalization method has quite good prediction performance for matchers "C," "li," and "ri," and the resampling method using mean and variance

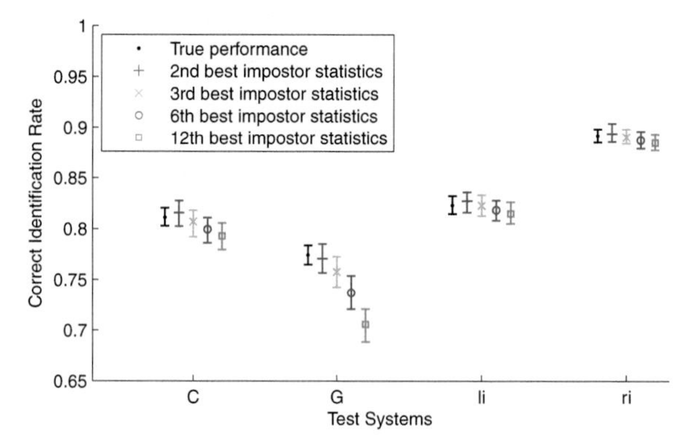


Figure 15.7. Performance prediction in original identification systems by resampling methods utilizing different $n$th-order statistics of identification trial score sets.

statistics is also close to the true system performance. The interesting feature here is that variance statistics apparently reduces the score mixing effect more than mean statistics. For matcher "G" on which the T-normalization method failed, we see better prediction results by resampling methods using either or both of these statistics, but the prediction is still far from true performance.

If we compare these results with the prediction results of Figure 15.5, we notice that any of the resampling methods with mean or variance statistics reduce the score mixing effect better than resampling using nearest genuine neighbors. Generally, we can view a genuine score from an identification trial as a statistic of the trial. But considering a single score as a statistic might not be a reliable way to model dependencies of scores in identification trials, and the poor prediction results of the nearest genuine score resampling method confirm this.

### 15.7.4 Resampling Using $n$th Order Statistics

The other type of frequently used statistics is the $n$th-order statistics

$$t_i^n = t^n(T_i) = \{\text{the value of } n\text{th highest element in } T_i\} \tag{15.10}$$

In our experiments we use a set of impostor scores in each identification trial $T_i$ to calculate $n$th order-statistics $t_i^n$ and use them in resampling method for prediction. Figure 15.7 shows the results of experiments.

Overall, using the second-order statistics or the second best impostor score gave the best prediction results. The prediction precision seems to decrease with the increased order of used statistics. Note that the last, 12th-order statistics correspond to $G_t/8$-th-order statistics. We also tried higher-order statistics, such as $G_t/4$ and $G_t/2$, but the prediction accuracy was consistently worse, and the predicted performance approached the system performance with randomized scores (Section 15.3.2).

There seems to be no theoretical proof of why the second best impostor statistic should allow making more precise predictions than any other statistic. We can reason that it simply better reflects behaviors of the high-score tails of impostor distributions in separate identification trials. If we needed to estimate other features of impostor distributions, we might have better results using other statistics.

### 15.7.5 Justification of Using Identification Trial Statistics

Consider the following identification trial score dependency model. Suppose that for each identification trial $T_i$ we are given a set of parameters $\boldsymbol{\theta}_i = \{\theta_i^1, \ldots, \theta_i^k\}$, and the scores in the identification trial are independently sampled according to

$$p_i(x) = p(x|\boldsymbol{\theta}_i). \tag{15.11}$$

As we already pointed out, all the matching scores in a single identification trial are generated using the same test biometric sample, and parameters $\theta_i$ could represent test sample quality, the amount of information contained in the test sample (e.g., number of minutia in test fingerprint), the closeness of other samples to the test sample, and similar characteristics of test sample.

For each identification trial $T_i$, we can extract a set of score set statistics $\boldsymbol{t}_i$. Thus, statistics are the random variables of parameters $\boldsymbol{\theta}_i$, $\boldsymbol{t}_i = t(T_i(\boldsymbol{\theta}_i))$, and if statistics are stable, then $\boldsymbol{t}_i \approx \phi(\boldsymbol{\theta}_i) = E(t(T_i(\boldsymbol{\theta}_i)))$. Assume that statistics $\boldsymbol{t}_i$ are chosen so that function $\phi(\boldsymbol{\theta}_i)$ is continuous and invertible. In this case we obtain that identification trials having close statistics $\boldsymbol{t}_i$ will have close parameters $\boldsymbol{\theta}_i$ and, as a consequence, close score densities $p_i(x) = p(x|\boldsymbol{\theta}_i)$. Therefore, we can simply use training identification trials with close statistics to estimate score densities $p_i(x)$ without explicit estimation of parameters $\boldsymbol{\theta}_i$.

In practice, because we have no knowledge of what parameters $\boldsymbol{\theta}_i$ might be, we cannot guarantee the good properties of function $\phi(\boldsymbol{\theta}_i)$. Intuitively, if we consider the statistics vector $\boldsymbol{t}_i$ to consist of many diverse statistics of the identification trial score set, then we are more sure that close statistics are the result of sampling close conditional densities $p_i(x)$.

### 15.7.6 Close Sampling Effect

Suppose that we are given a large number $L$ of training impostor trials, and we use a sufficiently large number of statistics in the resampling method. When we search for the closest training identification trials, we might find the identification trials very similar to the one we consider at the moment. Indeed, a sufficiently large number of available training trials will result in the existence of very similar trials, and if the chosen statistics reflects well the set of training identification trial scores, these very similar trials will have very similar statistics and will be found during a resampling method search.

In the extreme case, all found closest training trials will be exactly the same as the particular training trial whose genuine score we consider at the moment; the simulated trial will be successful if and only if that particular training identification trial was successful. The predicted performance for a larger system will be exactly the same as the performance of a smaller system, and the prediction algorithm will fail.

Though the extreme case seems to be improbable, some overestimation of predicted system performance might be observed in our experiments. For example, if we use the best impostor score instead of second- and other $n$th-order statistics in the resampling method, we will find that predicted performance will be almost the same as the performance in a smaller training system with $G_t = 100$ impostors. The reason for this is quite clear: The best impostor in the simulated trial will be among the best impostors in closest training trials, and all of them are close to the best impostor of currently considered training trial. We might call the effect of overestimating identification system performance due to too close neighboring trials as the *close sampling effect*. It seems that it is quite difficult to say whether the effect has an influence on particular prediction results. Still, we need to control the appearance of this effect by making sure that statistics used in the resampling method do not coincide with the property of the system we are trying to predict.

## 15.8 Discussion

### 15.8.1 Identifciation Models

Accounting for the dependencies between matching scores assigned to different classes during a single identification trial seems to be the key for correct prediction of identification system performance. The existence of this dependence has been mostly ignored in biometrics research so far. The problem lies in the difficulty of modeling this dependence and deriving any algorithms using it; therefore a simplifying assumption on score independence is usually made.

In Tulyakov and Govindaraju (2005a) we proposed using in addition to the currently considered score a best score from the identification trial besides the current (second best) score for making acceptance decisions in verification systems. In Tulyakov and Govindaraju (2006) we used the second best score in combinations of biometric matchers. To differentiate the models for score dependencies in identification trials from previously explored score dependencies in cohort and background models, we introduced the term *identification model*. We further formalized the notion of identification models utilizing identification trial score set statistics in Tulyakov et al. (2008).

Resampling methods utilizing identification trial statistics can be viewed as an extension of identification model research in the area of predicting the performance of identification systems. The usefulness of chosen statistics in the identification model is judged by the prediction precision, whereas in previous research the usefulness of statistics is determined by its ability to improve performance of either decision making or a combination algorithm. The current research complements well the previous studies – if some statistics is useful for prediction, it must contain information about score dependencies in identification trials and consequently can be successfully utilized in decision making or classifier combination.

Note that the *second best impostor* statistics used in experiments of this work is slightly different from the *second best score* statistics utilized in our previous research, where the *second best score* is calculated using all matching scores including the genuine one. The difference is that in current experiments we know precisely which scores are impostor and which score is genuine in the identification trials. Previous research modeled the situations where such knowledge is not available: For example, if we use some scores in an identification trial for a combination, we are not aware which score is genuine – the final goal of the combination algorithm is to find it. Nevertheless, both statistics are closely related, and current research confirms the use of second best score statistics advocated before.

### 15.8.2 Extreme Value Theory

The important part of identification system performance prediction research is modeling the distributions of scores in the tails, especially, he tail of an impostor distribution corresponding to high scores. Extreme value theory is a field of statistics investigating the behavior of distribution tails, and we can expect improvement in predictions if we use its techniques.

One of the results of extreme value theory states that the distribution of values of random variable $X$ satisfying the condition of being in the tail, $X > u$ for sufficiently large $u$, is close to the generalized Pareto distribution (GPD):

$$F_u(x) = P(X - u > x|X > u) \approx \begin{cases} 1 - (1 - kx/a)^{1/k} & k \neq 0 \\ 1 - \exp(-x/a) & k = 0. \end{cases} \tag{15.12}$$

The parameters $k$ and $a$ can be learned from training data by different methods (Hosking and Wallis 1987) for a particular choice of $u$. Equation (15.12) provides only an asymptotic approximation of the extreme value distribution of $X$ when $u$ approaches the supremum of all possible values of $X$. The derivation of sufficient conditions on the minimum number of samples of $X$, confidence intervals of $u$, $k$, and $a$, is a main topic for ongoing research in extreme value theory. Note that most existing research in extreme value theory is rather theoretical; the ability to predict the performance in identification systems might be used as an objective practical measure to evaluate the performance of extreme value theory methods.

The main assumption for the application of the extreme value theory is the independence and identical distribution of the samples $X$. Because there is a dependence between matching scores in identification trials, we expect that extreme value theory will have the same problem as the binomial approximation for performance prediction in identification systems – we would need to mix sets of scores from different identification trials to make good approximations and consequently will introduce score mixing effect into prediction.

One possible solution is to use identification trial score set statistics to select a close training identification trial. Though the results presented in Jarosz et al. (2005) seem to imply that extreme value theory provides better approximations than binomial model, it is not clear if using it along with score set statistics will deliver better prediction than resampling method. Another solution might be to try to parameterize the fitting of GPD to the tails of impostor distributions for different identification trials. Thus, instead of common parameters $u$, $k$, and $a$, we would need to find separate $u_i$, $k_i$, and $a_i$ for each training identification trial $T_i$. Statistics of identification trials $t_i$ can serve for such parameterization. Alternatively, we might consider joint density modeling of statistics and extreme values of $X$ by means of multivariate extreme value theory (Poon et al. 2004).

### 15.8.3 Performance Prediction in Open Set Identification Systems

Whereas the closed set identification problem assumes that the genuine user is enrolled and the match is performed against one genuine and $G - 1$ impostor templates, the open set identification problem assumes that a genuine user might not be enrolled, and the correct solution of the identification system will be to reject current identification attempt. Clearly, the analysis of an open set identification system should include the assumption of the prior probability of the user to be enrolled. It is not clear if proper analysis of open set identification systems has been presented before; recent works discussing open set identification (e.g. Grother and Phillips 2004) do not use such prior probability. In contrast to the traditional ROC curve used for evaluating verification systems and describing the trade-off between two types of errors, false accept and false reject, open set identification systems have three types of errors (Ariyaeeinia et al. 2006): the error of incorrectly choosing the first matching choice, the error of accepting the incorrect first choice, and the error of rejecting the correct first choice. The trade-off between three types of errors might be described by a two dimensional surface in the three-dimensional space, and we are not aware of any research using such performance measures.

Instead of considering the full system with three error types, we can consider the reduced open set identification problem assuming that the test user is always enrolled in the database, and the system has the ability to reject the first match choice. Such a system indeed will be quite useful because the first match choice might be an impostor, and rejecting such a choice is the correct decision. A similar approach is also taken explicitly in Ariyaeeinia et al. (2006) and in our work (Tulyakov and Govindaraju 2005a,b). In such a case we have two types of error – accepting the incorrect first choice and rejecting the correct first choice or identification.

A traditional decision to accept or reject the first choice in open identification systems is to compare the first matching score to some threshold $\theta$ (Grother and Phillips 2004). In Tulyakov and Govindaraju (2005a) we showed that such a decision is not optimal, and we get better results if instead of only a single first score $s^1$ we also use a second best score $s^2$ and base our decision on thresholding some learned function of these two scores: $f(s^1, s^2) > \theta$. We further explored this idea in Tulyakov and Govindaraju (2005b) and showed that the improvement is theoretically present even if scores in identification trials are independent (and impostor scores are identically distributed). The rate of improvement seems to decrease slightly with the increase of the number of impostors.

This discussion implies that the estimation of open set identification system performance is not an easy task. Although we can follow the traditional derivations (Wayman 1999; Grother and Phillips 2004; Jarosz et al. 2005) specifying that the false match rate in a system with $N$ impostors can be determined by the function of the false match rate of a verification system, $FMR_{1:N} = 1 - (1 - FMR_{1:1})^N$, and the false nonmatch rate stays the same, $FNMR_{1:N} = FNMR_{1:1}$, such measures are not adequate for proper performance description because of broad assumptions: (1) independence of matching scores in identification trials, (2) the decision based on thresholding a single top score, and (3) the whole system performance can be described by two numbers (note that open set identification systems have three types of error, so these false match and false nonmatch rates might not be sufficient). Therefore we restricted the topic of the current work to close set identification and left the investigation of open set identification systems for the future.

The results presented here suggest that the predictions of open set identification system performance might also have to deal with the score mixing effect, and we might have to use score set statistics for selecting close identification trials for testing. Note also that use of the second best score for making decisions is similar to using this score as the statistics of identification trials. Therefore, it is not clear how much benefit using identification set statistics might have on open set identification system already utilizing such scores for decisions.

## 15.9 Conclusion

In this paper we investigated the problem of predicting the performance of large-scale closed set identification systems. First, we showed the existing dependency in matching scores assigned to different classes during identification trials. This dependency has a major effect on the previously proposed algorithms for estimating system performance. Second, we showed that the binomial approximation prediction method introduces its own effect on performance prediction. Third, we discussed the T-normalization and its relationship to the prediction problem. Fourth, we proposed the new prediction method based on resampling available training scores using identification trial statistics. The utilization of identification trial statistics allows us to reduce the score mixing effect and delivers good prediction results. Finally, we discussed the results with respect to other research directions: identification models for decisions and matcher combinations, extreme value theory, and open set identification system performance prediction.

# References

*NIST Biometric Scores Set. http://www.nist.gov/biometricscores/.*

Ariyaeeinia, A. M., J. Fortuna, P. Sivakumaran, and A. Malegaonkar. 2006. Verification effectiveness in open-set speaker identification. *IEE Proceedings Vision, Image and Signal Processing*, **153**(5), 618–624.

Auckenthaler, Roland, Michael Carey, and Harvey Lloyd-Thomas. 2000. Score normalization for text-independent speaker verification systems. *Digital Signal Processing*, **10**(1–3), 42–54.

Bolle, R. M., J. H. Connell, S. Pankanti, N. K. Ratha, and A. W. Senior. 2005. The relation between the ROC curve and the CMC. Pages 15–20 of *Fourth IEEE Workshop on Automatic Identification Advanced Technologies, 2005.*

Bolle, Ruud M., Nalini K. Ratha, and Sharath Pankanti. 2004. Error analysis of pattern recognition systems–the subsets bootstrap. *Computer Vision and Image Understanding*, **93**(1), 1–33.

Doddington, George R., Mark A. Przybocki, Alvin F. Martin, and Douglas A. Reynolds. 2000. The NIST speaker recognition evaluation – overview, methodology, systems, results, perspective. *Speech Communication*, **31**(2–3), 225–254.

Grother, P., and P. J. Phillips. 2004. Models of large population recognition performance. Pages II–68–II–75, vol. 2 of *CVPR 2004. Proceedings of the 2004 IEEE Computer Society Conference on Computer Vision and Pattern Recognition, 2004.*

Hosking, J. R. M., and J. R. Wallis. 1987. Parameter and quantile estimation for the generalized Pareto distribution. *Technometrics*, **29**(3), 339–349.

Jarosz, Herve, Jean-Christophe Fondeur, and Xavier Dupre. 2005. Large-Scale Identification System Design. In: James Wayman, Anil Jain, Davide Maltoni, and Dario Maio (eds.), *Biometric Systems Technology, Design and Performance Evaluation*. Springer.

Johnson, A. Y., J. Sun, and A. F. Bobick. 2003. Using similarity scores from a small gallery to estimate recognition performance for larger galleries. Pages 100–103 in Sun, J. (ed), *Analysis and Modeling of Faces and Gestures, 2003. AMFG 2003. IEEE International Workshop on.*

Li, Weiliang, Xiang Gao, and T. E. Boult. 2005. Predicting biometric system failure. Pages 57–64 of Gao, Xiang (ed.), *CIHSPS 2005. Proceedings of the 2005 IEEE International Conference on Computational Intelligence for Homeland Security and Personal Safety, 2005.*

Marti, U.-V., and H. Bunke. 2001. On the influence of vocabulary size and language models in unconstrained handwritten text recognition. Pages 260–265 in Bunke, H. (ed.), *Proceedings. Sixth International Conference on Document Analysis and Recognition, 2001.*

Navratil, Jiri, and Ganesh N. Ramaswamy. 2003. The awe and mystery of T-norm. Pages 2009–2012 of *8th European Conference on Speech Communication and Technology (EUROSPEECH-2003).*

Poon, Ser-Huang, Michael Rockinger, and Jonathan Tawn. 2004. Extreme value dependence in financial markets: diagnostics, models, and financial implications. *Rev. Financ. Stud.*, **17**(2), 581–610.

Tulyakov, S., and V. Govindaraju. 2005a. Combining matching scores in identification model. In: *8th International Conference on Document Analysis and Recognition (ICDAR 2005)*.

Tulyakov, S., and V. Govindaraju. 2005b. Identification model with independent matching scores. In: *Biometrics Consortium Conference*.

Tulyakov, S., and V. Govindaraju. 2006. Identification model for classifier combinations. In: *Biometrics Consortium Conference*.

Tulyakov, Sergey, Zhi Zhang, and Venu Govindaraju. 2008. Comparison of combination methods utilizing T-normalization and second best score model. In: *CVPR 2008 Workshop on Biometrics*.

Wang, Rong, and Bir Bhanu. 2007. Predicting fingerprint biometrics performance from a small gallery. *Pattern Recognition Letters*, **28**(1), 40–48.

Wayman, J. L. 1999. Error rate equations for the general biometric system. *Robotics & Automation Magazine, IEEE*, **6**(1), 35–48.

Xue, Hanhong, and V. Govindaraju. 2002. On the dependence of handwritten word recognizers on lexicons. *IEEE Transactions on Pattern Analysis and Machine Intelligence*, **24**(12), 1553–1564.